The Routledge Dictionary of Turkish Cinema

D0075312

'Gönül Dönmez-Colin's *Dictionary of Turkish Cinema* is a scholarly tour de force from the doyenne of Turkish cinema studies, and a testament to her dedication that we must all be deeply grateful for. Carefully cross-referenced and extensive, it is written in a manner at once even-handed and discerning. Now that new Turkish cinema is in the global spotlight, the detailed and erudite entries in this remarkable and essential resource open the door onto a long and rich history that there is an urgent need to understand.'

Professor Chris Berry, *King's College London, UK*

'With each passing year it becomes ever clearer that Turkey has developed a major if still little known national cinema. Gönül Dönmez-Colin's rich, meticulously researched new book offers a profound insight into that cinema as well as gives us what will become the standard research text in that subject for years to come.'

Richard Peña, *Director Emeritus, New York Film Festival and professor of film Studies, Columbia University, USA*

The first critical and analytical dictionary of Turkish cinema, this book provides a comprehensive overview of Turkish cinema from its beginnings to the present day.

Addressing the lacuna in scholarly work on the topic, this dictionary provides immense detail on a wide range of aspects of Turkish cinema including: prominent filmmakers, films, actors, screenwriters, cinematographers, editors, producers, significant themes, genres, movements, theories, production modes, film journals, film schools and professional organizations.

Extensively researched, elaborately detailed and written in a remarkably readable style, the *Routledge Dictionary of Turkish Cinema* will be invaluable for film scholars and researchers as a reference book and as a guide to the dynamics of the cinema of Turkey.

Gönül Dönmez-Colin is a film scholar specializing in the cinemas of the Middle East and Central Asia. She is the author of *Turkish Cinema: Identity, Distance and Belonging*; *Cinemas of the Other: A Personal Journey with Filmmakers from the Middle East and Central Asia* and *Women, Islam and Cinema*, among other publications.

The Routledge Dictionary of Turkish Cinema

Gönül Dönmez-Colin

Routledge
Taylor & Francis Group

LONDON AND NEW YORK

First published 2014
by Routledge
2 Park Square, Milton Park, Abingdon, Oxon OX14 4RN

and by Routledge
711 Third Avenue, New York, NY 10017

Routledge is an imprint of the Taylor & Francis Group, an informa business

British Library Cataloguing in Publication Data
A catalogue record for this book is available from the British Library

Library of Congress Cataloging in Publication Data
Dönmez-Colin, Gönül.
The Routledge dictionary of Turkish cinema / Gönül Dönmez-Colin.
   pages cm
   Includes bibliographical references.
   1. Motion pictures–Turkey–Dictionaries. I. Title.
   PN1993.5.T8D66 2013
   791.4309561–dc23   2013021637
ISBN: 978-0-415-66626-8 (hbk)
ISBN: 978-1-315-85862-3 (ebk)

Typeset in Times New Roman
by HWA Text and Data Management, London

Printed and bound in the United States of America by Publishers Graphics,
LLC on sustainably sourced paper.

To my family

Figures

Acknowledgements

I would like to thank Joe Whiting for trusting me with this project and to all the staff of Taylor & Francis, for advice and assistance; Oliver Leaman for his continuous encouragement; International Istanbul Film Festival and Adana Golden Boll Film Festival for making it possible to view so many films and for providing the film stills; all film-makers who have been so generous with their time and my daughter Phyllis Katrapani and my husband André Colin for their moral support.

Introduction

Interest in Turkish cinema has never been stronger. The film industry is vibrant at home as well as on the international arena, receiving prestigious prizes at the Cannes, Berlin and Venice Film Festivals, participating in numerous panoramas and retrospectives worldwide, the comprehensive programme, 'The Space Between: A Panorama of Cinema in Turkey' at the Film Society of Lincoln Centre (April 27–May 10, 2012), a case in point. In 2012, local films represented 47 per cent of the total admission with 61 films, which is a long way from a decade ago when only nine Turkish films were released.

Studies of Turkish cinema and the preservation of film archives have been affected by indifference for many years. For lack of serious scholarship until the 2000s, even the existence of what is officially considered as the first film of Turkey, *Aya Stefanos'taki Rus Abidesinin Yıkılışı / The Demolition of the Russian Monument at St. Stephan* (Fuat Uzkınay, 1914) is open to debate. Several earlier films are lost, while a considerable number have decayed in the censorship vaults. As for writing about national cinemas, this is no longer a simple task of constructing a linear historical narrative describing the development of a cinema within a particular national boundary. We are no longer so certain about the coherence of the nation-state, and the idea of history is not so self-evident (Yoshimoto 2006: 24). 'Turkey is a country with several nations', Yılmaz Güney pointed out, 'for this reason, considering social contradictions and national differences, we must make films of "Turkey" and not "Turkish films".' This work does not equate 'Turkish' with the official definition of 'Turkishness', but espouses heterogeneity of ethnic identities. Furthermore, the dissolution of any stable connection between a film's place of production and/or setting and the nationality of its makers and performers has made it impossible to assign a fixed identity to much cinema (Ezra and Rowden 2006: 1) although this is not a new phenomenon. Cinema from its inception has been transnational, circulating more or less freely across borders. Turkish film production, from its origins, has been shaped as much by global or international pressures as by local or nationalist goals. Turkish cinema's historical positioning has been a triangular relationship with both the US and Europe, which has helped shape the essential global dynamics of local production. Cinema arrived as a Western invention and early Turkish cinema based itself on film, theatre or literature from the West.

The most prominent film-maker of the early years, Muhsin Ertuğrul, was foreign educated and worked in Germany and the USSR as an actor and director. German and French theatre and the Soviet revolutionary cinema were his inspirations. Until the founding of the republic, women's roles were played by Armenians, Greeks, or white Russians, when Muslim women were forbidden to act. When the film-makers after Muhsin Ertuğrul – Lütfi Ö. Akad, Osman Seden, Atıf Yılmaz (Batıbeki) – tried to develop a new film language, their role models were from the West. Even the commercial Yeşilçam cinema, often referred to as the truly 'national cinema', was 'truly national' only for the first ten years, according to the prominent film-maker, Halit Refiğ, when it was based on the traditional arts of entertainment, the *temaşa* arts, *orta oyunu* (improvised open air theatre) and *Karagöz and Hacivat* (shadow play), popularized in accordance with the political atmosphere of the period. Then it started to reach foreign markets, especially the neighbouring countries and exchange actors. Cüneyt Arkın made several films with Iranians before the Iran–Iraq War, while Hülya Koçyiğit was the favourite in Greece in the 1960s.

The arrival of cinema, a Western invention, in Ottoman Turkey is significant, but not surprising, as modernity had already entered the empire as a coveted mode of life. A year after the first screening in Paris in 1895, Alexandre Promio, the cinematographer of Auguste and Louis Lumière, visited Istanbul to shoot documentaries with the permission of Sultan Abdulhamit II. The following year, another Frenchman named Bertrand organized a private show at the court of the Sultan in Yıldız Palace in Istanbul, which was followed by public screenings at the fashionable Sponeck Restaurant in Pera (in the cosmopolitan European part of Istanbul) by Sigmund Weinberg, who opened the first movie theatre Cinema-Théatre Pathé Fréres in 1908. The district eventually changed its name to Beyoğlu but remained the centre of the film industry.

Western powers regulated the industry they introduced. French, American, German or Danish films were distributed by Western companies and shown to non-Muslims of Pera and eventually to upper class Muslims in cinema halls with French names: Ciné Oriental, Ciné Central, Ciné Magic, etc. Turkish names appearing ten years after the founding of the Republic. Publicity was printed in French, German, Armenian or Greek, but not in Turkish. Two Turkish men, Cevat Boyer and Murat Bey were the first Turks to screen films (1908) in the Şehzadebaşı neighbourhood in the old town, followed by Şakir and Kemal Seden, Ali Efendi and Fuat Uzkınay, who established the Ali Efendi Cinema in the Sirkeci neighbourhood (the European Central Station area) in 1914. Even with the Muslim–Turkish distributors, foreign films with utopic images of the West held the market. The Western identity of cinema was easily adopted with other technological inventions that represented modernity and progress, at least by the elite class.

The first official national film *The Demolition of the Russian Monument at St. Stephan* was made in 1914 by Fuat Uzkınay to record the demolition of a monument erected by the Russian army, although there is no evidence that this film was actually made. According to historian Burçak Evren, three other films were made previously within the borders of the Ottoman Empire: one was shot in 1905 inside the Yıldız Mosque by an unknown director; the second in 1911 by the Manaki Brothers, Yanaki and Milton from Macedonia, to document the visit of Sultan Mehmet Reşat V to Thessaloniki and Manastir, which is in the Macedonia Film Archives; and the third, in 1913, about the Hamidiye cruiser, also by an unknown director (Evren 1995).

Enver Pasha, a prominent *jeunes turc* and the main leader of the Ottoman Empire in both the Balkan Wars and World War I, ordered the establishment of a cinema institution following the German model to exploit cinema as a propaganda tool and Merkez Ordu Sinema Dairesi / MOSD (Central Army Office of Cinema) was founded in 1915, launching a solid relationship between the army and cinema. The output of the MOSD, however, was negligible for lack of infrastructure and qualified personnel. Weinberg began *Leblebici Horhor Ağa / Horhor Agha, The Chickpea Seller* (1916) with the army equipment, but the shooting was stopped when one of the leading actors died. The shooting of the first feature film, *Himmet Ağanın İzdivacı / The Marriage of Himmet Agha*, a free adaptation from Molière, was also suspended when most actors were recruited to the War of Dardanelles, and completed in 1918 by Uzkınay who replaced Romanian Weinberg who was deported (Özön 1970: 14–16) although other sources show Uzkınay as the cinematographer and Reşat Rıdvan as the director (Scognamillo 1990: 26).

In 1917, another military office, Müdafaa-i Milliye Cemiyeti (the Association for National Defence) was involved in cinema with Fuat Uzkınay at its head. A young journalist, Sedat Simavi made two films, *Pençe / The Claw* and *Casus / The Spy* (1917), which are the first complete films. A leading figure of theatre, Ahmet Fehim, drew controversy with *Mürebbiye / The Governess* (1919), an acerbic satire on the infatuation of the upper classes with the French culture through the adventures of a French seductress. The commandant of the occupying French forces found the film degrading the French women and banned its distribution in Anatolia.

The beginning of the cinema experience goes back to vaudeville, music hall and shadow play, *Karagöz and Hacivat*. Early Turkish cinema was particularly influenced by theatre under the monopoly of Muhsin Ertuğrul, credited for starting what came to be known as *The Period of Theatre Men* (1923–45), although these periods naturally overlap. *Ateşten Gömlek / The Shirt of Fire* aka *The Ordeal* aka *The Shirt of Flame* (1923) is considered as the first national film of the Republic of Turkey, screened on 23 April 1923, on the third anniversary of the founding of the Grand National Assembly in an Istanbul under occupation. Commensurate with the nationalistic content of the film, all roles were played by Muslim Turks including the women's roles as requested by the author of the story, Halide Edip Adıvar. During this period cinema borrowed from the theatre and did not seek a new language for the new medium.

As *The Period of Theatre Men* with the hegemony of Ertuğrul is comparable to the one-party system with its governing policy and perception of society, the period that follows, referred to as *The Transition Period* (1945–50) was a transition period for Turkish politics as well. With the change in municipality tax laws in 1948, a boost was given to the industry when the tax on national films was reduced to 25 per cent; film studios were established; organizations were formed and the first film festival was held; but exceptional works were rare. Cinema still continued to imitate the West and did not seek a new idiom, or a particular identity.

The new Republic implemented radical reforms in education, law and religion and culture and the arts gained importance; fine arts academies and conservatories were established but cinema was somewhat neglected despite praise from Atatürk who stressed its importance. The Ottoman past and the religious belief that forbids the image could be considered as a reason for this reticence. French cinema remained dominant at least until World War II, and even the Hollywood films were dubbed into French or shown with French and Turkish subtitles. Hollywood infiltrated the country by the 1930s. The national products were only poor imitations.

The crucial role of the classical Hollywood cinema in the formation of national cinemas is undeniable although it could never have complete control over how a particular national cinema is constructed. A national cinema as the culture industry exists in a complex web of economic, ideological and social relations and classical Hollywood constitutes only one aspect. Hollywood is dominant in the film market, which does not automatically mean it has been dominant trans-historically or trans-culturally (Yoshimoto 2006: 36). Yeşilçam cinema often found a way of appropriating the foreign into the national identity by creating 'Turkified' films with the local identity almost as defiance. Hollywood imitations have become the backbone of the commercial cinema today, whereas what is identified as art cinema carries a strong intertextuality with European masters of literature, particularly Russian, and cinema: Bergman, Godard, Antonioni, Angelopoulos and Tarkovsky.

The development of cinema is linked directly to the political and economic changes in Turkey. The populist Democrat Party (DP) elected in 1950 tried to reverse the historical, societal and cultural moves towards modernization. The concept of the West shifted from Europe to North America and the United States became the new model of modernity as an industrialized capitalist society. $1 billion of US aid was received between 1948–52 and Turkey joined NATO in 1952. The farmers were given easy loans and the prices of the crops were inflated. Imported tractors were sold to growers on credit. Highways and new roads were constructed as far as the remotest villages. The rural Anatolian capital was established enforcing its own culture. Yeşilçam, born during this period, reflects the tendencies towards populism in the governing policies. With the increased internal migration and a profitable market in Anatolia, scripts targeted the masses rather than an elite audience. Neither the producers nor the directors or actors questioned history, society or politics during a period when the Cold War experienced internationally had its repercussions in Turkey and laws were created to curb different expressions or tendencies, individual or collective. Despite the policies of a government that raged war against intellectuals, a number of exceptional film-makers such as Lütfi Ö. Akad, Atıf Yılmaz (Batıbeki), Metin Erksan and Memduh Ün entered the industry, starting a new era which came to be identified as *The Period of Cinema Men.*

The 1960s are considered as the Golden Years of Turkish cinema. Colour films began in 1963 and dominated the market by 1967. In 1966, with 241 films, Turkish cinema was the fourth in the feature film production worldwide. During this period, a new kind of cinema emerged influenced by the social and political atmosphere of the country after the *coup d'état* of 27 May 1960 and the establishment of a progressive constitution in 1961, which brought a more relaxed atmosphere that nourished arts. Translations of diverse ideologies, including Marxism–Leninism, became available. With the steady development of industrialization and the growing national awareness in the so-called Third World, of which Turkey was a part, a certain euphoria for the arrival of a socialist revolution was felt, which was reflected in the films of the 1960s–70s, with Yılmaz Güney in Turkey, Ousmane Sembene in Senegal and Fernando Solanes in Argentina, for example, as pioneers. The fervour of revolutionary change that heralded the 'new cinemas' had national and international dimensions, but the belief in the political function of cinema was fundamental. While the commercial films continued their dominance, engaged film-makers, encouraged by the new constitution gave some remarkable examples of social realism. *Karanlıkta Uyananlar / Those Awakening in the Dark* (Ertem Göreç, 1964) was the first to deal with the social consequences of the workers' strike; *Gurbet Kuşları / The Birds of Nostalgia* aka *Migrating Birds* aka *Birds of Exile* (Halit Refiğ, 1964) was the first to examine seriously the phenomenon of migration from rural areas to the urban centres; *Yılanların Öcü / The Revenge of the Serpents* (Metin Erksan, 1962), heavily censured for alleged communist propaganda, recounted one man's fight against the rural traditions; Erksan's *Susuz Yaz / A Dry Summer* (1963) received the Golden Bear at the Berlin Film Festival (1964); Yılmaz Güney drew attention with *At, Avrat, Silah / Horse, Woman, Gun* (1966) and Lütfi Ö. Akad's *Hudutların Kanunu / The Law of the Borders* (1966) was declared as the most important film up to its time. However, hopes for a censor-free cinema were shattered when the Constitution Court revived the censorship regulations established in 1939.

The period between 1960–80 is rather unique for Turkey in terms of social, economic and particularly cultural developments. Between 1960–70, the urban population increased by five million. The 1960s were marked by a rapid increase in urbanization and a relative relaxation when intellectual debate on politics, literature and cinema intensified. The role of the cinematheque (1965–80) as a social and cultural medium for dialogue is important in this context.

The political upheavals of the 1970s were not advantageous for cinema. The populist Yeşilçam film industry, which lacked the necessary infrastructure, was not prepared for the social, political and economic transformations, globally and locally. Although 298 feature films were made in 1972, some of these were shot in a few days with next to no budget; several were intended for the expatriate markets. Cinema began to lose its magic with the official arrival of television in 1968, which became the preferred mode of entertainment for the family, particularly during the bloody clashes on the streets. Under severe political censorship, pornography intended for the rural male migrant worker intensified. Several film-makers made engagé films to appear militant while others tried to bank-in on the success of the social-realist films in the West from developing countries, blending shallow realism with local colour and stereotyped exoticism with negligible aesthetic concerns.

Yılmaz Güney was a rare artist who could blend political messages with commercially successful populist films. His *Umut / The Hope* (1970), extolled by the intellectuals of the cinematheque, is considered a turning point in Turkish cinema. *Sürü / The Herd* (1978), scripted by Güney while in prison and directed by Zeki Ökten, foregrounding the tragic story of the disintegration of a nomad family, is one of the best films of Turkish cinema. *Yol / The Way* (Şerif Gören, 1982), also scripted by Güney, shared the Palme d'or with *Missing* (Costa Gavras) at the Cannes Film Festival, 1983. Süreyya Duru's village films, *Bedrana* (1974) and *Kara Çarşaflı Gelin / The Bride in Black Chadoor* (1975) were praised by the critics and successful at the box-office. Güney's young followers, Erden Kıral (*Hakkari'de Bir Mevsim / A Season in Hakkari*, 1983, winner of the Silver Bear at the Berlin Film Festival) and Ali Özgentürk (*Hazal*, 1979 and *At / The Horse*, 1982) started with engagé rural dramas, gradually moving to more personal films.

In the socio-economic atmosphere of the 1950s–60s that lionized capitalism, migration from Anatolia to the western metropolitan cities with industrial centres intensified. The DP's policy of modernizing agriculture did not benefit the landless peasants. The city was the utopia of the rural people with limited resources in terms of education, health care and entertainment. However, it soon became a dystopia for many, as the rate of migration was higher than the rate of industrialization, resulting in unemployment and housing shortages. The urban peasants began to work in unfamiliar jobs, as itinerant vegetable vendors or doormen in apartment buildings, while their spouses cleaned houses. They tried to safeguard the traditional rural lifestyles in makeshift abodes – *gecekondu* – they built on the outskirts.

Although migration stories always existed, serious studies about the reasons of migration, the trauma of displacement, the anxiety concerning the loss of identity and the conflicts between the rural migrants and the urban dwellers only began in the 1960s with *The Birds of Nostalgia* aka *Migrating Birds* aka *Birds of Exile* and *Bitmeyen Yol / The Unending Road* (Duygu Sağıroğlu, 1966), two classics that are the pioneers, and the Migration Trilogy of Lütfi Ö. Akad – *Gelin / The Bride* (1973), *Düğün / The Wedding* (1973) and *Diyet / The Blood Money* (1974), one of the most important works on migration.

The earlier films presented Istanbul as an attractive space with its historical and cultural identity, an identity at odds with the identity the migrants transported from rural Anatolia. This identity of the city as a traditional but also westernized space slowly transformed as the old neighbourhoods disappeared under the new construction schemes. In the migration films of the 1970s–80s, the Western cultural identity of the city is insignificant. In Ali Özgentürk's *The Horse*, the migrants live in city squares. The transformation of the city texture blurred the differences, but has not changed the stigmatization of the Anatolian peasant, often by those who were themselves stigmatized once (*Uzak / Distant*, Nuri Bilge Ceylan, 2002).

Migration to other countries, especially Germany, was intense between 1960–70, producing important cultural and economic changes. A vibrant transnational film-making industry exists today which has departed from the 'cinema of the affected' (Burns 2006: 133), or the 'cinema of duty' (Malik 1996: 202–15) (Tevfik Başer) to the 'cinema of double occupancy' (Elsaesser 2005: 118) (Fatih Akın).

Following the bloody *coup d'état* of 12 September 1980, parties and unions (including the union of cinema workers, Sine-Sen founded in 1978) were closed; both Gören and Özgentürk were imprisoned for one year without trial and tortured; books and films were burned and politics banned. In this period of systematic de-politization, a self-reflexive cinema emerged by a younger generation in an attempt to re-evaluate the past. Paris-educated Ömer Kavur (*Anayurt Oteli / Motherland Hotel*, 1987) established *auteur* cinema, which was not welcome for the general spectator weaned on Yeşilçam and Hollywood. While some local critics argued that the new approach was based on the point of view of European art cinema and presented Turkey as the 'impenetrable other', for some foreign critics a film like *Gizli Yüz / Secret Face* (Kavur, 1991) was pretentious. The West expected from the 'Third World', films with picturesque and exotic landscapes depicting harsh economic realities of daily life; the new urban angst stories were not exotic.

With the opening of film schools, the apprentice–master tradition of Yeşilçam slowly faded. Scripts with real characters, written by notable writers – Yaşar Kemal, Furüzan, Selim Ileri – terminated the typecasting of Yeşilçam. Spatio-temporality and narrative structure gained importance. With the belated arrival of feminism, focus shifted from men to women, with foreign soap operas featuring contemporary urban life-styles breaking some of the taboos of a society shaped by rural-traditional ideologies; sexuality began to be addressed although controversial points of view on sexual and religious identity have remained untouchable.

During the Turgut Özal years (prime minister and president, 1983–93) of liberal policies, Hollywood majors strengthened their hegemony and Warner Brothers in 1987, and United International Pictures (UIP), which distributed Universal, Paramount and Touchstone in 1989, entered the market, showing their films simultaneously with the rest of the world to curb piracy. They also began to distribute Turkish films. Opening multiplexes in shopping centres, they contributed to the consumerization of what was once considered culture and the closure of the small independent theatres. The video period ended and with the multiplication of channels, television became the major venue for mass entertainment. In the early 1990s, local film production was not more than ten films annually, with almost no distribution possibilities.

Film-makers such as Gören tried to follow the formulae of Hollywood to regain the audience. *Amerikalı / The American* (1993) was a box-office success and garnered the Public Jury Award of the Antalya Golden Orange Film Festival. Sinan Çetin had a remarkable box-office success with *Berlin in Berlin* (1992), a thriller about a Turkish family living in the Kreutzberg ethnic neighbourhood of Berlin. *Propaganda* (1999), a satire on border politics, was also successful at the box-office and won 11 international awards.

Creating an intertextuality with the Yeşilçam films of the 1960s and the popular Hollywood cinema, *Eşkıya / The Bandit* (Yavuz Turgul, 1997) combined commercially attractive elements (action, melodrama, romance, stars and technical superiority) with a solid script, professional acting and directing and technical perfection in the standards of the West (the result of co-production with European countries). Its national and international success was unprecedented. Western-style publicity (CD of the theme song, t-shirts, TV commercials, web sites and the eventual release of the VCD) played an important role in the interest garnered in the film. Another similar success story was *Istanbul Kanatlarımın Altında / Istanbul Beneath My Wings* (Mustafa Altıoklar, 1996). *Vizontele* (Yılmaz Erdoğan, Ömer Faruk Sorak, 2001) about the arrival of television to a remote town in the 1970s, starring the well-known comedian, Erdoğan himself, broke records with 3.6 million admissions. Its sequel, *Vizontele Tuuba* (Erdoğan, 2004), which takes place shortly before the 1980 *coup*, was also successful. The pseudo science fiction, *G.O.R.A.* (Cem Yılmaz, 2004), a parody of *Matrix*, *Fifth Element* and several other similar films, had record earnings of $30 million worldwide.

In the late 1990s, a new vitality was created by a new generation of film-makers who have grown during the years of modernization and have acquired a new set of values and approaches to life and cinema. Recognized in the West as well as nationally, these film-makers have tried to find a new language to mirror a society which has the privileged position of merging a rich tradition with the benefits of modernity. Nuri Bilge Ceylan is one of the pioneers of the New Turkish Cinema, who tells universal stories grounded in local culture and history. *Uzak / Distant* won the Grand Prix and the Best Male Actor award (shared by Mehmet Emin Toprak and Muzaffer Özdemir) at the Cannes Film Festival, 2003, which was the first time a Turkish film won an award at Cannes since *Yol*. *İklimler / Climates* garnered the Fipresci (Federation of International Film Critics) award in 2006; *Üç Maymun / Three Monkeys*, the Best Director in 2008 and *Bir Zamanlar Anadolu'da / Once Upon a Time in Anatolia*, the Grand Prix of the same festival in 2011. Equally talented others, Zeki Demirkubuz, Yeşim Ustaoğlu, Derviş Zaim, followed by Semih Kaplanoğlu, have been bringing home prestigious prizes from distinguished film festivals. They have created self-reflexive works often involving interior voyages, Demirkubuz examining the layers of Turkish society in dramas of entrapped individuals while Ustaoğlu taking a direct socio-political position. The collective guilt of the post-1980 *coup* trauma pervades most of these films. In *Once Upon a Time in Anatolia*, Ceylan underscores the guilt shared by everyone, from the prosecutor whose wife dies suddenly to the doctor who chooses to omit details in his report on the cadaver. The next generation, Özcan Alper, Emin Alper, Hüseyin Karabey, İnan Temelkuran, Seyfi Teoman et al., is committed to engagé cinema, deconstructing Turkish national identity to construct a larger identity incorporating the ethnic and cultural mosaic of Turkey. Economic pressures, unemployment, poverty, helplessness and male psychological impotence are at the core of their films, which are 'other centred' transcending nativist government policies.

Post-traumatic cinema regarding the military interventions has been generally equivocal from *Eylül Fırtınası / After the Fall* (Atıf Yılmaz, 2000) to *Babam ve*

Oğlum / My Father and Son (Çağan Irmak, 2005). The same applies to the civil war in the south-east, which has caused irremediable losses. Trauma is a debilitating kind of memory and, understandably, the event is not assimilated or experienced fully at the time, but only belatedly in its repeated possession of the one who experiences it (Caruth 1995: 4–5). In trauma theory, the impact of past crimes in a nation-state may evidence itself in the form of 'cultural symptoms' corresponding to those in individuals (Kaplan 2005: 68). The film-makers mentioned earlier are confrontational in their films in reflecting the lack of historical perspective, reconstruction of history, the paralysis, the disability, the numbing, the absence of narrative and the breakdown of language experienced in the post-traumatic society. The issue of masculinity in crisis is a recurring theme in Turkish cinema of the 2000s and 2010s, particularly within the current cultural context where the old fictions of masculinity are unravelling, underpinning the masquerade of masculinity and the fragility of its construction as a provisional and impossible ideal (Radstone 2001; Hammond, Humphrey, Randell and Thomas 2003). In some other films, male suffering is used as a metonym for the suffering of the nation. Unfortunately, such films do not reach large audiences. The box-office winners are the blockbusters, the big-budget films with television personalities and expensive special effects and most of these carry conservative narratives. The growth of corporate movie theatres has been narrowing the choices of audiences and blocking the chances of distribution for non-commercial films.

For the film industry, the 2000s have been the most productive. A small decrease was observed in the number of films theatrically released in 2012; 61 films of the total of 281 releases were local products, whereas in 2011, 70 films out of the 288 released were local. In the overall panorama of the decade, 2011 is the year with the highest number of local releases. Admission for the 70 films was 21,222,541 in 2011 and for the 61 films, 20,487,442 in 2012. However, the total admission has increased from 42,798,500 in 2011 to 43,935,763 in 2012. In 2011, Turkish films represented 50 per cent of the total admission and 47 per cent in 2012. Among the 288 new releases in 2011, *Eyvah Eyvah 2 / Alas Alas 2*, a sequel, was most extensively distributed, reaching the highest number of viewers (3,947,988 admissions with 356 copies). The top four films of 2011, as well as six of the top ten films, were Turkish films. A romantic drama *Aşk Tesadüfleri Sever / Love Likes Coincidences* (Ömer Faruk Sorak, 2011) reached 2,418,090 admissions as number two. *Kurtlar Vadisi Filistin / Valley of the Wolves: Palestine* (Zübeyr Şaşmaz, 2011) was number three with 2,028,057 admissions but the Turkish animation *Allah'ın Sadık Kulu: Barla / God's Faithful Servant: Barla* (2011), originally number four, surpassed *Valley of the Wolves: Palestine* with 2,186,696 admissions. While 2012 witnessed the highest number of admissions in the last 22 years, Turkey is still behind European countries in terms of admissions in proportion to the population of 75 million.

According to the Government of Turkey statistics of 2012, there are 567 cinema buildings, 2,093 screens and 268,072 cinema seats in Turkey. Unfortunately, several cities in Anatolia lack cinema halls. The films are classified under 11 categories: general public; 7+; 7A, under-sevens may watch with the family; 13+; 13A, under-13s may watch with the family; 15+; 15A, under-15s may watch with the family; 18+; includes elements of violence and horror; includes elements of sexuality; includes behaviour that may give a negative example. The average price per ticket in 2012 was 9.60 Turkish liras / 4.10 euros.

Since 2005, 267 films have received financial support from the government. Out of the 61 films released in 2012, 15 received the Ministry of Culture and Tourism's production and post-production funding, which is the only national support mechanism. The average support for feature films was 139,574 euros: for the first feature, 88,978 euros and for the post-production, 28,936 euros. Films that win international prizes or slots in A-class film festivals are not required to reimburse the loan. Besides supporting national productions, an amendment was made to the VAT law in 2009 to increase international productions and to subsidize co-productions. This has provided the legal framework to allow companies based abroad to rebate the VAT of their costs incurred in Turkey. The winner of the Oscar for Best Picture 2012, *Argo* (Ben Affleck), and the 23rd James Bond movie *Skyfall* (Sam Mendes) had scenes shot in Turkey.

Turkey annually partakes on average in four majority co-productions and two minority co-productions as a member of Eurimage, the Council of Europe Fund. Among the 70 films released in 2011, eight had European co-producers, including *Bir Zamanlar Anadolu'da / Once Upon a Time in Anatolia* (Ceylan), *Bizim Büyük Çaresizliğimiz / Our Grand Despair* (Seyfi Teoman) and *Saç / Hair* (Tayfun Pirselimoğlu). Five out of the 61 released in 2012 had European co-producers, including *Tepenin Ardı / Beyond the Hill* (Emin Alper), *Gözetleme Kulesi / The Watchtower* (Pelin Esmer) and *Araf / Somewhere in Between* (Yeşim Ustaoğlu). Most young film-makers come from advertising and continue in this medium to fund their films. A certain beer company has been sponsoring projects for 26 years, except overtly political ones. The average budget for a local production is 500,000 euros.

Free-market conditions apply to the film distribution industry, with no subsidies or incentives. Fourteen distribution companies were active in 2012, among which Özen Film, UIP, WB and Tiglon dominate 80 per cent of the market. Among the 281 releases in 2012, *Fetih 1453 / Conquest 1453*, a historical epic about the occupation of Istanbul by the Ottomans, with a $17,000,000 budget received the highest number of spectators in the last 25 years, with 6,565,850 admissions with 880 copies in 41 weeks and was sold to most European countries, the Middle East, Indonesia and Malaysia. The top three films of 2012 were Turkish films. Apart from *Conquest 1453* that appealed to nationalistic sensibilities, the romantic drama *Evim Sensin / You're My Home* reached 2,691,726 admissions and the comedy *Berlin Kaplanı / Berlin Tiger* reached 1,983,077 admissions. Seven out of 10 films that attained the highest attendance in 2012 were Turkish films, the total admission of these seven films representing 75 per cent of the total admission of the 61 releases (Şensöz 2013: 18–20).

Television productions and advertising films have been important venues for developing the technological and human capital for Turkish cinema since the deregulation of the monopoly of public broadcasting and the establishment of private television channels in 1990. The relationship between cinema and television is osmotic and not easy to reduce to a simple pattern. The number of directors and actors that straddle the two mediums is evidence of the fluidity and connectivity of the two mediums. The impact of television aesthetics on cinema is not negligible, which is perhaps why some film-makers try to homogenize popular cinema (Ostrowska and Roberts 2007: 145). Television networks do not commission films but there is a large market for television series. Turkish television series are sold to other Middle Eastern countries, North African and Balkan markets and interest has been growing.

The *Routledge Dictionary of Turkish Cinema* is an attempt to present Turkish cinema in a critical and analytical perspective. The entries include key films, directors, producers, actors, screenwriters, cinematographers, editors and other important contributors to the development of Turkish cinema as well as film journals and noteworthy genres and movements. Only narrative feature films are included, excluding documentary, short films and animation. The dictionary is not just a 'best of' in terms of award winners, although many such films are included. Rather than what each film is about, or what it means, the focus is on the kind of information the film produces and the readings it may invite, and not necessarily the reading we may impose. Subjectivity, critical judgement, or lack of space may result in omissions. An attempt has been made to include films that are the landmarks of Turkish cinema, that were significant at the time of their release and representative films from specific cycles. The film-makers and other film personalities are chosen for their important contribution to the cinema of Turkey, even with only one feature film as in the case of Fehmi Yaşar and Ahmet Uluçay.

Cross-cultural analysis is dangerous, as Kaplan points out, when we are obliged to read works produced by the Other (non-Western nations) 'through the constraints of our own framework/theories/ideologies', but can also be beneficial in terms of bringing different frameworks/theories/ideologies to the texts. Having originated in Turkey and not being dependent on the self/other dichotomy, my point of view would not be what Kaplan considers 'tentative' (Kaplan 1989: 40–50) although the language of film theory/criticism is Western and the West holds the power, the technical superiority and the right of judgement in the hierarchical binarism (Dennison and Song 2006: 175).

It is my wish that the present study will serve as a useful guide to explore a film industry that offers challenges in its diversity, originality and uniqueness.

4 May 2013, Lourmarin

Note

Words in **bold** that occur within an entry refer to other entries in the dictionary. RN refers to Real Name.

40 Quadratmeter Deutschland / Forty Square Meters of Germany (1986), a
German production by a Turkey-born film-maker, foregrounds the plight of an
Anatolian couple, alienated in a Western urban society in conflict with their
customs and traditions. 'Guest worker' Dursun (**Yaman Okay**) locks his young
bride Turna (Özay Fecht) in their small apartment to protect her from the 'evil
influences' of an alien world, which he considers corrupt. Resembling a frightened
bird, Turna ('crane' in Turkish) obeys her man as custom dictates, routinely
performing her homemaker duties, including copulation that resembles violation.
Cutting her hair silently is her only protest. The claustrophobic apartment in
Germany is delegated the same function as the decrepit bus parked at the centre
of Stockholm in ***Otobüs / The Bus*** (**Okan**, 1976), a sanctuary where traditional
values can be preserved. The walls that conventionally resolve the existential
tension between inside and outside by either drawing the exterior space inside,
or drawing the interior space outside (Thiis-Evensen 1987: 251) only intensify
Turna's confinement. The dialectic they express between openness and closure
– through the windows that often contribute to a building's sense of inside and
outside by announcing the mode of life within the building – is determined in
the narrative by the courtyard that briefly connects Turna to the exterior world
through a child, also framed inside her window. Yet, the images of a prostitute
at the street corner and the pot-smoking punks in the balcony above alienate her
further. Ironically, when she has the key to the door, she returns to her captivity
that perhaps offers her a false sense of security. Liberated by Dursun's sudden
death, she is at a loss over what to do with her freedom.

A pioneer in the 'cinema of the affected' (Burns 2006: 133) regarding Turks in
Germany, *Forty Square Meters of Germany* reconstructs the life of the couple in
the confines of a single space like a Greek tragedy while denouncing the patriarchal
ideology that victimizes women. A quarter of a century later, when second and third
generations play central roles in all sectors, including cinema (**Fatih Akın**) with
films that tell their stories – including the constraints of the immigrant experience
– no longer from the periphery, the victimized Turkish immigrant (particularly
the woman) motif has lost its cogency. Patriarchal ideology nonetheless is still a
menace to women's lives, both inside and outside Turkey.

The film received the Silver Leopard and the Prize of the Ecumenical Jury at the Locarno International Film Festival, 1986, Best Debut Film at the Rotterdam International Film Festival, 1987, among other national and international awards.

Director, Producer, Screenwriter: **Tevfik Başer**; Production: Tevfik Başer Film Production / Studio Hamburg Film Production; Cinematographer: İzzet Akay; Editor: Renate Merck; Music: Claus Bantzer; Sound: Bernhard Ebler; Art Director: Wolf Seesselberg; Cast: Özay Fecht, **Yaman Okay**, Demir Gökgöl, Mustafa Gölpınar.

A

Acı / Pain (1971) is the second part of the trilogy that began with *Ağıt / Elegy*, and was completed with *Umutsuzlar / The Hopeless Ones*, the same year. A milestone of Turkish cinema, the film shows a unity of style with its steady tempo and constant tension in the story of Anatolian men pushed to crime by customs and traditions. Ali (**Yılmaz Güney**) returns to his village after serving 15 years for killing Yasin. Visiting Yasin's grave, he asks forgiveness, offering himself to the bereaved family as a surrogate son. Rejected at first and attacked with a spade by Yasin's sister Zelha (**Fatma Girik**), he is accepted into the family gradually and romance is on the way, but evil forces of society will not leave him in peace. Blinded by Haceli Agha's (**Hayati Hamzaoğlu**) men, who kill Yasin's father, Ali

Figure 1 Yılmaz Güney and Fatma Girik in *Acı / Pain* (Yılmaz Güney, 1971) (Courtesy of International Istanbul Film Festival)

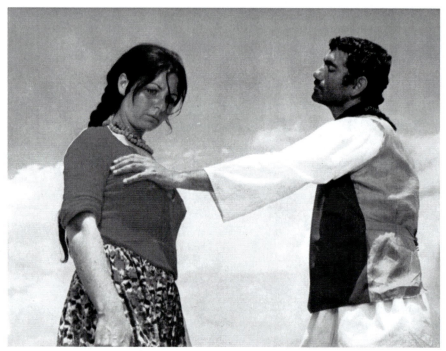

Figure 2   Acı / Pain (Yılmaz Güney, 1971) (Courtesy of International Istanbul Film Festival)

has no choice but to respond to violence with violence. An excellent marksman in his youth, he concocts an ingenious device for target practice using bells that Zelha places in different posts and manipulates with ropes. When the enemy arrives, Zelha rolls the bells in the direction of the attacker and Ali hits.

Made during the political turmoil and the economic crisis, the film demonstrates **Güney**'s remarkable circumlocution skill to avert the scrutiny of censorship while sending his message – be resourceful to combat oppression – to the audience, the bells serving as a pertinent trope for resistance. The samurai–spaghetti-western **genres** are revisited through the desolate landscape of Cappadocia; the character of **Güney** like a quiet and aloof Clint Eastwood (*A Fistful of Dollars*, Sergio Leone, 1964) and a samurai in white tunic and loose pants; the loyalty/disloyalty issue (the prison mate coveting his woman and denouncing him); the blood feud; the revenge; the romance; the fighting prowess; the relation of the hero to law / lawlessness; the violence; the decline of a traditional way of life and the demise of all principal characters in the finale. The gunplay that follows the confrontation between the lone gunman and the rogues is a fantastical sequence choreographed with precision. Relying on the gaze, the trademark of **Güney**, the dialogue is sparse, reinforcing the feeling of oppression and entrapment. The *mise en scène* contrasts the verticality of the 'fairy chimney' rock formations that shelter but also entrap and the horizontality of the sweeping landscape that promises freedom but not refuge. Haceli Agha, the emblem of masculinity defined by power and control is juxtaposed with Ali, the feminine element – the humble man seeking peace and expressing his feelings with flowers. **Güney** reiterates in the film the futility of individual salvation. Ali has transformed himself but the society has remained the same and violence is fatal for everyone.

Director, Screenwriter: **Yılmaz Güney**; Producer: Nami Dilbaz and Üveyiş Molu; Production: Başak Film and Özleyiş Film; Cinematographer: Gani Turanlı; Editor: **Şerif Gören**; Music: Metin Bükey; Cast: **Yılmaz Güney, Fatma Girik, Hayati Hamzaoğlu**, Mehmet Büyükgüngör, Oktay Yavuz

Acı Hayat / Bitter Life (1962), a 'black passion' film that is considered within the **social realist** movement focuses on housing shortages in the metropolis for the less advantaged, a staple theme in the cinema of a country that has experienced rapid industrialization and massive internal migration. Manicurist Nermin (**Türkan Şoray**) and welder Mehmet (**Ayhan Işık**) are in love, but lack the resources to establish a family. The hopes of the poor are built on lottery tickets, or a prosperous spouse, ambitions that often culminate in disappointment, or tragedy. As the city transforms itself, construction of concrete apartment blocks menace the poor neighbourhoods, the desolate modern landscape of new slums with the straight lines of the recent constructions, dead in their modernity evoking Italian neo-realist films, particularly Antonioni and Fellini. The rich are corrupt, their morals fluid, their women superfluous parasites in gauche costumes who kill time playing cards or having a pedicure while their irresponsible offspring party. Encouraged by her mother, Nermin, after a drinking binge, concedes to the advances of Ender (**Ekrem Bora**), the spoilt son of a prominent speculator, and Mehmet, who is now rich and merciless, sleeps with Ender's sister Filiz (Nebahat Çehre) for revenge, although open-minded Filiz gives herself willingly.

Both Nermin and Mehmet are the adventurer / *parvenu* (Bakhtin 1981: 125–6). As a manicurist, she eavesdrops on the intimate secrets of the rich but has no place among them; she remains lowly until the end. Mehmet is the real *parvenu*, the *nouveau riche* without social pedigree, the 'Great Gatsby' who finally arrives, but still cannot partake.

The living spaces establish the binaries of the rich and the poor according to **Yeşilçam** clichés; the poor in traditional wooden houses without water or electricity, but in neighbourhood atmosphere, the rich isolated in imposing villas in affluent suburbs. Nermin is seduced in an upscale holiday resort, deserted and uncanny, where Mehmet builds a modern villa, but admits that a house needs soul: 'Damn these cement graves!' Traditional Turkish music accompanies the images of the poor dwellings and Latin and North American popular music of the period, the extravagant mansions. Tight camera angles as Nermin and Mehmet dash down the decrepit staircase of an apartment they visit; the vertical tracking shot of two elevators – Nermin descending with her honour lost and Mehmet ascending as a social climber – and finally, the angle–reverse-angle shots of Nermin and Mehmet in the denouement confronting each other under the concealed gaze of Filiz are signature moments of **Erksan**'s work that also benefits from the black and white contrast. **Erksan**'s narrative nonetheless remains Eastern, embedded in local customs and androcentric religious traditions despite its modern film language and the frequent use of jazz music (Ornette Coleman). Women are peons, their 'honour' to be exploited at will, for passion or for revenge. Mehmet punishes Nermin for her greed by trashing her while she begs forgiveness. The fate of the woman who deviates is death: to cleanse her sin, Nermin walks to the sea on the beach where she was seduced.

Considered as one of the best love films ever made, *Bitter Life* was very successful commercially. The romance element was an inspiration to several other films, in addition to two television series that were made in the 2000s on the same subject. With *Bitter Life* **Türkan Şoray** received her first award during the first Antalya Golden Orange Film Festival.

Director, Screenwriter: **Metin Erksan**; Producer: Muzaffer Arslan; Production: Sine Film; Cinematographer: Ali Uğur; Editor: Özdemir Arıtan; Art Director: Semih Sezerli; Music: Fecri Ebcioğlu; Sound: Tuncer Aydınoğlu; Cast: **Türkan Şoray, Ayhan Işık, Ekrem Bora**, Nebahat Çehre

Açlık / Hunger (1974), a staunch indictment of the feudal system that oppresses men and women opens with the cries of babies and the image of a pregnant woman with six hungry children. Still a child, Meryem was sold to the landlord (Hüseyin Kutman) as a domestic servant and she has been sexually exploited. Hasan (Mehmet Keskinoğlu), unable to find a woman to share his poverty, marries the 'soiled' Meryem (**Türkan Şoray**), but leaves for the city when the draught destroys hopes. To feed her starving children, Meryem threatens the landlord with a knife demanding food in exchange for her once lost virginity. In a traumatic finale, Meryem is lynched by the desperate crowd for a piece of bread while the rain finally starts to pour.

Displaying filmic allegories of underdevelopment, *Hunger* is a precursor of **Bilge Olgaç**'s socio-politically oriented and gender-based films by exposing the retrograde customs of merchandizing little girls and childbearing unaided by pulling a rope. The use of a dissolve overlapping the image of the little girl washing the floor observed by the landlord, with her grown-up image is a well-designed transition, which skilfully avoids objectifying her body. The implication of the off-screen rape through the gaze of the village fool, who finds her half-naked on the cotton pile, is another example of **Olgaç**'s deliberate avoidance of voyeurism. Considered by doyen film critic Atilla Dorsay as the best film of **Olgaç** until its date (Dorsay 1989: 100), the weak point of *Hunger* is the one-dimensional presentation of the male characters: landless peasant Hasan is gentle and loving, whereas the landlord is immoral and despicable (a **Yeşilçam** cliché regardless of the political orientation).

Director, Screenwriter: **Bilge Olgaç**; Producer: Fethi Oğuz; Production: Funda Film; Cinematographer: Ali Uğur; Editor: İsmail Kalkan and Özdemir Arıtan; Music: Yalçın Tura; Sound: Necip Sarıcıoğlu and **Mevlut Koçak**; Cast: **Türkan Şoray**, Hüseyin Kutman, Mehmet Keskinoğlu

Figure 3 Cahide Sonku as Aysel in *Aysel, Bataklı Damın Kızı / The Girl From the Marshes* aka *Aysel, the Girl From the Swampy Roof* (Muhsin Ertuğrul, 1935) (Courtesy of International Istanbul Film Festival)

Adaptation of literary and theatrical works and popular forms like comic books has been prevalent throughout Turkish film history starting with the early years. ***Himmet Ağa'nın İzdivacı / Marriage of Himmet Agha*** (**Fuat Uzkınay** and **Sigmund Weinberg**, 1916–1918) from Molière's play, *Le Mariage Forcé / Forced Marriage* (1664); ***Aysel, Bataklı Damın Kızı / The Girl From the Marshes*** aka ***Aysel, the Girl From the Swampy Roof*** (**Muhsin Ertuğrul**, 1935) from Selma Lagerlöf's novella, *Tösen från Stormyrtorpet* (1908); *Şehvet Kurbanı / The Victim of Lust* (1939) from Joseph von Sternberg's film, *Der Blauer Engel / The Blue Angel* are some of the noteworthy examples. In the absence of legal procedures regarding copyright, **Yeşilçam** produced innumerable remakes of Hollywood, European and national films, 'borrowing' from filmic and non-filmic sources without acknowledging credit. According to veteran historian **Giovanni Scognamillo**, the main reasons for the adaptations and re-makes were: the number of productions exceeding the capacity of the film-workers – screenwriters were in demand particularly in the 1960s, when the annual production reached 200s; the inadequate production conditions and the possibility of commercial success by reaching wider audiences through popular works. Some of the foreign adaptations were loyal to the original, whereas others were Turkish versions, with alterations in characters, time and space, or adaptations to local lifestyles. The faithful adaptations of *Cinderella* or *Don Quixote*, or the authentic recreation of American or Italian superheroes, or cartoon characters were short lived and did not enrich Turkish cinema. The Turkish versions done in haste were not successful either, mainly because of the discrepancy between the narrative and the actual location (Scognamillo 1973a: 61–73). **Ertem Eğilmez**'s *Sürtük / The Tramp* (1965) (and its 1970 re-make) from Bernard Shaw's play *Pygmalion* (1913), a remake of Charles Vidor's *Love Me or Leave Me* (1955); **Metin Erksan**'s *Şeytan / The Exorcist* (1974) from *The Exorcist* (William Friedkin, 1973) and *İntikam Meleği* aka *Kadın Hamlet / The Angel of Vengeance* aka *Woman Hamlet* (1976) from Shakespeare; *Çirkin Dünya / Ugly World* (**Seden**, 1974) from *A Clockwork Orange* (Stanley Kubrick, 1971) are some of the well known **Yeşilçam** remakes in addition to Turkish versions of *Dracula*; *Tarzan*; *E.T.* (*Badi / Buddy*, Zafer Par, 1983); *Star Trek* (*Turist Ömer Uzay Yolunda / Ömer, the Tourist on Star Trek*, **Hulki Saner**, 1973); *Superman* (*Supermen Dönüyor / The Return of Superman*, Kunt Tulgar, 1979, remake of Richard Donner's 1978 classic); *Batman* (*Yarasa Adam – Bedmen / Batmen – Bedmen*, Günay Kosova, 1973); James Bond (*Altın Çocuk / Golden Boy*, **Memduh Ün**, 1966 and *Rambo* (*Korkusuz / Fearless*, **Çetin İnanç**, 1986). *Dünyayı Kurtaran Adam / The Man Who Saves The World* (**Çetin İnanç**, 1982) opens with the images of spaceships transposed from *Star Wars* and exploits footage from Soviet and American space programme newsreel clips. Most of the music is from *Raiders of the Lost Ark* with *Ben-Hur, Moonraker, Planet of the Apes* and *Battlestar Galactica* interspersed. The special effects and soundtracks from Hollywood movies were exploited mainly to reduce expenses. The plot of *The Man Who Saves the World* does not resemble *Star Wars*. Several of these films have become global cult classics over the years.

Texts alluding directly to each other as in 'remakes', if they are a specifically self-conscious form of intertextuality, may give the gratification of recognition to the audience and appeal to the pleasures of critical detachment rather than of emotional involvement (Chandler 1994). Inversely, Turkish remakes often appeared several years after the 'originals' and the audience for the national films was not the same as the audience for the foreign films, hence identification was unlikely. Whether the remakes were plagiarism is open to debate. Theoretician Nezih Erdoğan claims that as the technical and stylistic means of **Yeşilçam** were dissimilar to the cinema of the West, even the most faithful adaptations were distinct in their lighting, colour, dialogue, editing, or viewpoint. Financial limitations and mass production conditions led to the resumption of traditional visual forms – shadow plays, miniatures – and partiality to frontal shots, which created 'a hybrid cinema' that 'produced a cinematic discourse blending Hollywood-style realism with an unintentional Brechtian alienation effect' (Erdoğan 1998: 266). For film scholar Ahmet Gürata, 'The most significant element of the remake is the reinterpretation and negotiation of historical and social forces of modernism in Turkey'. While offering something like a homogenized picture of cultural and moral characteristics of urban Turkey, these films mobilized a resistance against some of the values depicted in original films. Asserting a localized version of modernity as opposed to the revolutionary and universalistic content of Westernization, the remakes can be best conceptualized in the framework of 'multiple or alternative modernities'.

Figure 4 Vurun Kahpeye / Strike the Whore (Lütfi Ö. Akad, 1949) (Courtesy of International Istanbul Film Festival)

A good example is the gender based moral codes – women must be attractive but chaste; pre-marital sex and adultery are taboos. The other is the importance of the family and the community (*mahalle*), threatened by the rise of individualism. In this sense, 'remade movies reflect the transmutation and negotiation of the dominant model of modernity' (Gürata 2006: 252).

The first literary adaptation from a national source was *Mürebbiye / The Governess* (1919) from the celebrated Turkish novelist, Hüseyin Rahmi Gürpınar's eponymous novel (1898). Out of the 15 literary adaptations between 1919–47, nine were by **Muhsin Ertuğrul**, including the controversial *Boğaziçi Esrarı* aka *Nur Baba / The Bosphorus Mystery* aka *Nur Baba* (1922) based on *Nur Baba* (Yakup Kadri Karaosmanoğlu, 1922) and *Ateşten Gömlek / The Shirt of Fire* aka *The Ordeal* aka *The Shirt of Flame* (1923), based on the renowned woman author Halide Edip Adıvar's 1922 novel. *Vurun Kahpeye / Strike the Whore* (1949), the first film of **Lütfi Ö. Akad** is another adaptation from Adıvar, which has had two remakes, by **Orhan Aksoy** (1964) and by **Halit Refiğ** (1973). In the 1950s, another woman, Kerime Nadir was the most popular novelist, with several of her **melodramas** adapted to screen (*Hıçkırık / The Sob*, **Atıf Yılmaz**, 1953 and **Orhan Aksoy**, 1965). In the 1960s, with the move towards a neo-realist cinema, adaptations of literary works on village life by established leftist authors (*Yılanların Öcü / The Revenge of the Serpents*, **Metin Erksan**, 1961–2 from Fakir Baykurt and *Susuz Yaz / A Dry Summer*, **Metin Erksan**, 1963 from Necati Cumalı) gained prominence. During the politically charged 1970s, Orhan Kemal, who began to contribute to Turkish cinema with scripts and dialogues in the 1950s, was one of the most adapted authors and **Erden Kıral**'s award-winning *Bereketli Topraklar Üzerinde / On Fertile Land*, 1979 is based on his eponymous novel of 1954. Ferit Edgü (*Hakkâri'de Bir Mevsim / A Season in Hakkari*, Kıral, 1983), Yaşar Kemal (*Ağrı Dağı Efsanesi / The Legend of Mount Ararat*, **Memduh Ün**, 1975 and *Yılanı Öldürseler / If They Could Kill the Serpent*, **Türkan Şoray**, 1981) and 'the most adapted author' **Osman Şahin** (*Ayna / The Mirror*, Kıral, 1984; *Derman / Remedy*, 1983 and *Firar / Escape*, **Şerif Gören**, 1984) have enhanced Turkish cinema. In the 1980s, with the belated feminist movement, the works of several women writers with a modernist point of view were adapted: Füruzan (*Ah, Güzel İstanbul / Oh, Beautiful Istanbul*, **Atıf Yılmaz**, 1966), Pınar Kür (*Asılacak Kadın / A Woman to be Hanged*, **Başar Sabuncu**, 1986) et al. The same period also saw the adaptations from religious texts such as Hekimoğlu İsmail's *Minyeli Abdullah / Abdullah of Minye* (**Yücel Çakmaklı**, 1989). With the emergence of *auteur* cinema, **Ömer Kavur** gave some of the best literary adaptations including his *chef-d'œuvre Anayurt Oteli / Motherland Hotel* (1986) from Yusuf Atılgan's eponymous novel, and *Gizli Yüz / The Secret Face* (1991) written by Orhan Pamuk, based on a theme in his novel, *The Black Book*.

Among the comic book adaptations, the most popular heroes of the 1960s identified as 'the Heroes with Swords', were Karaoğlan (swarthy boy) and Tarkan. Notorious for historical, cultural and political incorrectness, these films meant for adults, were interspersed with occasional erotic scenes. *Karaoğlan* (1965) adapted by Suat Yalaz from the cartoons he created in 1962 about a young Turkic hero fighting his archenemy, the leader of the Mongols, comprising seven films until 1972 and a mini television series in 2002 was so popular that a multi-million re-make was made in 2012 by **Kudret Sabancı**. *Tarkan* series started in 1967 (Sezgin Burak) were also very popular with six official adaptations – by **Tunç Başaran** (1969), Mehmet Arslan (1970, 1971, and three more in 1972) all featuring **Kartal Tibet**, legendary for his *Karaoğlan* renditions.

The literary adaptation in cinema, as pointed out by John Ellis (1982: 4) (cited in Sheen 2000: 14, cited in Grant 2002: 57) 'trades upon the memory of the novel, a memory that can drive from actual reading, or as is more likely with a classic literature, a generally circulated cultural memory'. The film audience is invited to *recall* the adapted work or the cultural memory of it. Conventional adaptations are expected to abide by the 'deontology of translating' their source (Cohen 1991: 131 cited in Grant 2002: 58) with the aim of reducing the difference and finding similarities whereas, 'free adaptations' are 'expected to *manifest* innovation and ingenuity with regard to interpreting (and not translating) the narrative systems of their 'sources' (Grant 2002: 57). In contemporary Turkish cinema, the adaptation takes a form of intertextuality (Kristeva 1980) and dialogism (Bakhtin 1981). While *Kıskanmak / Envy* (2009) of **Zeki Demirkubuz** is a classic adaptation from a literary work, *Yazgı / Fate* (2002) and *Yeraltı / Inside* (2011) are 'free' adaptations from Albert Camus's *The Stranger* and Fyodor Dostoevsky's *Notes from Underground*, respectively and *Masumiyet / Innocence* (1997) and *Kader / Destiny* (2006) are like a palimpsest of the Yeşilçam cinema. **Nuri Bilge Ceylan**'s *Kasaba / The Small Town* can be considered as a 'dialogic' work in Bakhtinian sense, carrying a dialogue with Anton Chekhov and particularly, his *The Cherry*

Orchard, whereas ***Bir Zamanlar Anadolu'da / Once Upon a Time in Anatolia*** (2011), from its very title to the clumsily buried corpse that a convoy searches all night to find, echoes (or 'refracts' according to Bakhtin) what Anatolia means with its rich (rocks resembling giant statues) but also dubious (the memories of the blood that was shed) past.

Adı Vasfiye / Her Name is Vasfiye (1985), based on five stories by Necati Cumalı foregrounds the identity search of a small-town woman through the perspectives of four men that traverse her life. Made in the aftermath of the 1980 *coup d'état*, the film reflects an apoliticized society where the chasm between the intellectual and the common man has widened. During an aimless stroll one morning, a creatively blocked young writer is encouraged by an elder to consider the cogency of the man on the street as the subject matter. Enticed by the captivating poster of a female singer, Sevim Tuna (**Müjde Ar**), he is drawn into her story: Her real name is Vasfiye; she was married to her childhood love, the driver Emin, but disillusioned by his womanizing, formed a liaison with nurse Rüstem, who was wounded on the leg by the jealous Emin who was jailed. Left alone, Vasfiye married Hamza, but divorced him when Emin was released. Disillusioned once again by the old habits of Emin, she formed a relationship with Doctor Fuat, but Emin never gave her up even though she became a 'fallen woman'.

Yılmaz reverses the gendered roles of the oppressor and the oppressed and inserts a few radical gender-benders into the narrative that questions the patriarchal traditions. Emin has a childhood phobia of guns; he chooses to study art (albeit does not succeed); blinded by love, he follows Vasfiye unconditionally and during their first night together, he is obliged to wear a woman's dress that comes out of her luggage. Vasfiye, on the other hand, is strong and determined; she arranges the elopement and the marriage. When cheated and beaten, she does not act like a victim. Married to older Hamza, she chooses physical pleasure over dull life, and elopes with Emin. She has no qualms about taking the lead when men excite her.

The film exposes a traditional society in transition towards modernity where morality is relative, but historically determined by men. Each man, who recounts his version of Vasfiye's story (all played by **Aytaç Arman**), is a personification of the Turkish machismo that considers women as property. There is also a fifth narrator, the diegetically invisible director. At the end, the young writer pleads with Vasfiye: 'Everyone has spoken about you. This is your life. Can't you tell it yourself, at least once?' Despite the critical point of view of the status quo in terms of gender politics, Vasfiye is not given a chance to speak in the film. Perhaps for a woman like Vasfiye, a chance to express herself in an androgenic society is utopic according to **Yılmaz**.

Director: **Atıf Yılmaz**; Producer: Cengiz Ergun; Production: Promete Film; Cinematographer: **Orhan Oğuz**; Screenwriter: **Barış Pirhasan** (based on five stories by Necati Cumalı in *Ay Büyürken Uyuyamam / I Can't Sleep During Full Moon*); Art Director: **Şahin Kaygun**; Music: Atilla Özdemiroğlu; Cast: **Müjde Ar**, **Aytaç Arman**, Yılmaz Zafer, **Macit Koper**, Levent Yılmaz, Erol Durak, Suna Tanrıverdi, Oktay Kutluğ

Ağıt / Elegy (1971), the poetic epic that is the best of the trilogy that includes *Acı / Pain* and *Umutsuzlar / The Hopeless Ones*, foregrounds the problematic of smuggling in the south-east border of Turkey, where choices are limited for landless peasants. The character of a lone bandit in search of truth despite persecution that **Yılmaz Güney** had developed in *Seyyit Han* aka *Toprağın Gelini / Seyyit Han* aka *The Bride of the Earth* (1968) is transferred to the smuggler, shunned by society for trying to earn his bread, while the benefiters of his transgressions receive respect. The legendary Çobanoğlu (**Güney**), an outlaw the villagers are eager to denounce to the gendarme for recompense, is a man with feelings, like the other smuggler, Hıdır, created and performed by **Güney** in *Hudutların Kanunu / The Law of the Borders* (**Akad**, 1966). His drama unfolds through the powerful images of the rocks falling incessantly over the ruins, barefoot children playing with garbage scraps and women in rags queuing to inoculate screaming children. His faith in communication lost, the smuggler observes silently, using language to concretize his misery in only one instance: 'the avalanches and the blood feuds have destroyed our villages. If they considered us human, would we hide in the mountains?', a subtle reference to the Kurds, called 'mountain people', also silenced by the ban on their language.

Güney had already experimented with epic realism in *Seyit Han*; *Elegy* interweaves the two **genres** with close-ups for the concrete details of the village life and extreme long shots for Çobanoğlu. The verticality of the landscape of Göreme with the pitiless landslides juxtaposes sharply with the horizontality of the parched steppe where the androgynous silhouette of the lone hero in white pants, holding a white umbrella, gradually becomes a dot on the horizon – more legend than real. The long shots that in Italian neo-realist films highlight the characters' interrelationship with their physical environment, accentuating their vulnerability and aloneness build a universal dimension to the drama of the underprivileged. The cinematography of Gani Turanlı gives the narrative a supernatural aura particularly during the cave scenes that he shot without artificial light but like a *camera obscura* used a hole in the rock as a lens and focused the light with a mirror on the opposite wall. The subsequent chiaroscuro evokes the traditional art of *Karagöz*, the shadow play that **Güney** also employed for the treasure hunt scenes of *Umut / The Hope* (1970).

Similar to *Seyyit Han*, *Elegy* plays with the Western **genre** that heroicizes the outlaw. Çobanoğlu is a rugged and resolute man who has made his home in the mountains, refusing to settle in the new village established after the landslides. There is a woman, the village doctor, who represents the notion of community (teaching other women to boil their water, inoculating their children). She brings the outlaw back to life by removing the bullet from the gendarme's rifle but fails to bring him back to the community. Like the lone cowboy of the Wild West, he is a restless individual, although one with deep feelings: he risks his life to thank the village doctor and visit the grave of his beloved. However, death is the unalterable destiny of the smuggler; censorship would not have it otherwise.

The village doctor is distinctive as the only independent woman in **Güney**'s cinema. She has a profession, and she is free to make moral decisions: she treats the wounded smuggler without informing the police, but does not protect him when he is cured (despite her warm feelings). The modern niece in *Arkadaş / The Friend* is also an independent woman, however, never having worked in her life, she is considered a parasite (Dönmez-Colin 2008: 124–5).

Director, Producer, Screenwriter: **Yılmaz Güney**; Production: Akün Film, Güney Film; Cinematographer: Gani Turanlı; Music: Arif Erkin; Cast: **Yılmaz Güney, Hayati Hamzaoğlu**, Bilal İnci; Atilla Olgaç, Yusuf Koç, Şahin Dilbaz, Şermin Hümeriç, Nizam Ergüden

Akad, Lütfi Ömer (b. Istanbul, 1916 – d. Istanbul, 2011) Director, screenwriter, editor, producer. The master of several distinguished film-makers, including **Yılmaz Güney**, Lütfi Ö. Akad deserves the honorific, the first true *auteur* of Turkish cinema. Akad's earlier education was mainly in French, whereas his higher education was completed at the School of Economy and Commerce. After a number of years as a bureaucrat, he entered the film world as an accountant, gaining his first directing experience while completing Seyfi Havaeri's *Damga / The Stigma* (1948). A failure in the eyes of the film-makers, the film was successful at the box-office, encouraging its producer Hürrem Erman and his partner **Sezer Sezin** (who later became Akad's favourite female lead) to trust Akad with *Vurun Kahpeye / Strike the Whore* (1949), his first film. In addition to its theme of the War of Independence, other factors that drew the crowds to *Strike the Whore* were

Figure 5 Türkan Şoray and İzzet Günay in *Vesikalı Yarim / My Licensed Love* (Akad, 1968) (Courtesy of International Istanbul Film Festival)

Akad's solid sense of cinema (mostly developed by watching foreign films and reading foreign film journals such as *Cahiers du Cinéma*) and **Sezin**'s rendition of the young woman of the new republic, ready to die for her ideals. With *Kanun Namına / In the Name of the Law* (1952), considered his *chef-d'œuvre*, Akad began to search for a personal film language. Taking the camera to the streets and shooting mostly clandestinely among the crowds, he presented a flesh-and-blood Istanbul, unlike the postcard images favoured by most film-makers. The critics identified in Akad's work the influence of the aesthetics of the American *film noir* (which Akad acknowledged) and the French poetic realism and the pessimism of Marcel Carné or Jean Renoir (which he contested). An important attempt toward realism, the film was a landmark for ending the monopoly of the theatre and establishing the language of cinema. In *Öldüren Şehir / The Murderous City* (1954), with **Kriton İlyadis** as cinematographer, Akad exploited the possibilities of light for dramatic effect using shallow focus in several scenes to manipulate the background for dramatic support. The camera is often static; the right, left or in-depth shots are created with the movements of the actors, which enables him, without cut, to acquire from the actors individual shot measures of different value, two- and three-shots and long shots that can transmit the tension of the context. He does not discard the traditional fade-to-black/fade-to-white altogether but after the fade-to-black, he proceeds with the next shot without a fade, creating 'a discreet flow like an undercurrent invisible on the surface' (Akad 2004: 203). His *Beyaz Mendil / The White Handkerchief* (1955) was heralded as the 'first realistic village film', but missed the opportunities to attend prestigious international festivals with the tightening of the control permits following the appearance and success of **Metin Erksan**'s banned *Susuz Yaz / A Dry Summer* (1963) at the Berlin Festival. *Yalnızlar Rıhtımı / The Quay of the Lonely Ones* (1959), adapted from *Quai des Brumes* (Marcel Carné, 1938) by the poet and novelist Atilla İlhan was according to Akad, 'a geometrical exploration of a certain *mise en scène*'. The film alienated the local audience with its structured dialogues, melancholic *chansons* and the veneer of French culture. The protagonist (Çolpan İlhan), the alcoholic diva of a nightclub, neither a virgin nor a prostitute, but an independent woman with choices is a precursor of other Akad women, notably, Sabiha of *Vesikalı Yarim / My Licensed Love* (1968).

According to historian Âlim Şerif Onaran, the first part of Akad's career ended with *Üç Tekerlekli Bisiklet / Tricycle* aka *The Three-Wheeled Bicycle* (1962) which he shot with **Memduh Ün**. After a period of silence, he returned with a documentary, *Tanrının Bağışı Orman / The Forest As the Gift of God* (1964), which carries resonances of *Cinema Novo* (Onaran 1994: 107). (He followed the theme of the preservation of the forests with seven other documentaries in 1973.) *Hudutların Kanunu / The Law of the Borders* (1966) was declared the most important film up to its time. Some critics of the period considered *Ana / The Mother* (1967), *Kızılırmak-Karakoyun* (1967) and *The Law of the Borders* carrying similar concerns about the plight of the peasants as a trilogy (Anatolian Trilogy). *Irmak / The River* (1972) can also be considered along these lines. *Licensed to Love*, *Kader Böyle İstedi / It Was Destiny* (1968) and *Seninle Ölmek*

İstiyorum / I Want to Die With You (1969) are referred to as his 'City Trilogy' or 'The Trilogy of Impossible Loves'.

The motif of the chased or trapped man is central to several of Akad's films, particularly *In the Name of the Law*, *Altı Ölü Var* aka *İpsala Cinayeti / Six Are Dead* aka *The Murder of İpsala* (1953), *Katil / The Killer* (1953), *The Murderous City*, *The White Handkerchief*, *Tricycle* aka *The Three-Wheeled Bicycle* and *The Law of the Borders*. The chase could be on village roads, or the city streets; **Ayhan Işık** jumps over rooftops and bridges and defeats several men single-handedly, a motif also exploited by **Osman Seden**, **Atıf Yılmaz** and **Orhan Elmas**.

The Migration Trilogy, *Gelin / The Bride* (1973), *Düğün / The Wedding* (1973) and *Diyet / The Blood Money* (1974) is about the repercussions of societal changes on the lives of the migrant families, especially women, during the unionization and politicization process that began in the 1960s and reached its peak in the 1970s. One of the most important works on migration, *The Bride* is a classic of Turkish cinema. Unlike **Halit Refiğ**'s *The Birds of Nostalgia*, which foregrounds the nostalgia of provincialism and conservative values, particularly with its ending, Akad's trilogy underscores the moveable nature of culture in the modern context, which can transform and liberate people. All three films are attempts at a realistic narrative with ethnographic accounts. At the centre is the woman as Mother, the backbone who takes action (played by **Hülya Koçyiğit** in all three films): Meryem of *The Bride* revolts against her father-in-law and enters the factory; Zelha of *The Wedding* shields her siblings; and Hacer of *Blood Money* is the first to achieve political awareness. For Akad, in the city, even in the shantytowns, the woman can break the chains of feudal oppression although liberation outside the home does not always equate with liberation behind the four walls, where patriarchy reigns. The essential point is the change, which may also be painful, acquiring a new identity often alienating the migrant from its past, which is further explored in the films of later generations, such as **Nuri Bilge Ceylan**'s *Uzak / Distant* (2002) (Dönmez-Colin 2008: 64).

Blacklisted as a communist following the trilogy, Akad was obliged to continue his profession under difficult circumstances, making short films and documentaries for the state television (TRT), such as the four-episode, *Dört Mevsim İstanbul / Four Seasons of Istanbul* (1990), a magic gift to his beloved city, shot with his regular cinematographer, Gani Turanlı. He was on the faculty of the Film and Television Department of the Mimar Sinan Fine Arts University for over two decades.

Akad's memoir, *Işıkla Karanlık Arasında / Between the Light and Darkness* (2004), at times an intimate, self-reflexive critique of a conscientious and modest artist, at times a valuable lesson, is an excellent chronicle of Turkish cinema, from the 1940s to the early 2000s, and an important document on the socio-economic climate of the country including its reflection on the artists.

Other noteworthy feature films of Akad are *Lüküs Hayat / Luxurious Life* (1950); *Tahir ile Zühre / Tahir and Zühre* (1951); *Arzu ile Kamber / Arzu and Kamber* (1951); *İngiliz Kemal Lavrens'e Karşı / English Kemal against Lawrence* (1952); *Görünmeyen Adam İstanbul'da / Invisible Man in Istanbul* (1955); *Gökçe Çiçek / Pretty Flower* (1973).

Figure 6 Tarık Akan in *Sürü / The Herd* with Melike Demirağ (Zeki Ökten, 1978) (Courtesy of International Istanbul Film Festival)

Akan, Tarık (b. Istanbul, 1948) Actor, screenwriter, producer; RN: Tarık Tahsin Üregül. One of the few actors in Turkish cinema who has merged stardom with professional acting, Tarık Akan has shared the lead with most women stars, remaining popular for four generations, due to his ability to renew himself. He entered the industry through a competition held by *Ses / Voice* magazine and played in insignificant movies as the handsome hero until the 1970s when the theatre director and critic Vasıf Öngören and film-maker **Ertem Eğimez** guided him with his technique. With *Maden / The Mine* (**Yavuz Özkan**, 1978) and *Kanal / The Channel* (**Erden Kıral**, 1978) he plunged into social and political cinema, creating memorable characters in *Sürü / The Herd* (1978) and *Pehlivan / The Wrestler* (1984) by **Zeki Ökten**; *Demiryol / The Railroad* (**Özkan**, 1979) and *Yol / The Way* (1982) and *Derman / Remedy* (1984) by **Şerif Gören**. Following the 1980 *coup d'état*, he was arrested for a speech he made in Germany. He wrote the accounts of this period in *Anne Kafamda Bir Bit Var / Mother, I Have Lice in My Head* (2002), which also includes anecdotes from the shooting of *Yol*. He has acted in more than 110 films and participated in several television series. In the 2010s, his political views on the indispensability of the Turkish army brought him severe criticism.

Akar, Serdar (b. Ankara, 1964) Director, screenwriter, producer, cinematographer. Infamous for directing *Kurtlar Vadisi İrak / Valley of the Wolves, Iraq* (2005), an ultra-nationalist film and TV series, Serdar Akar studied business management, but later graduated from the Film and Television Department of the Mimar Sinan Fine Arts University in Istanbul. He worked as assistant director in several noteworthy films of the 1990s before establishing the New Film-makers (Yeni Sinemacılar) Film Company with **Kudret Sabancı**. His first feature, the small-budget *Gemide / On Board* (1998) received several national awards and was invited to the Cannes Film Festival. He scripted *Laleli'de Bir Azize / A Madonna in Laleli*, interwoven with *On Board*, but directed by **Sabancı**, with the Romanian Ela Manea playing the female lead in both. *Dar Alanda Kısa Paslaşmalar / Offside* (2000), based on his youth in his natal village was chosen as the best Turkish film at the International Istanbul Film Festival 2001. However, the conventional style of *Maruf* (2001), a pastiche of literature, folklore, politics and psychology that builds a Shakespearean tragedy from the legends of the Anatolian Syriacs, did not garner interest. Having parted with New Film-makers after *Maruf*, Akar concentrated on television series until *Barda / In the Bar* (2006), an indictment of social and economical inequality and an accurate exposition of the unjust judiciary system, which provokes the citizens to take justice in their own hands. The aestheticized graphic violence in the film, especially against women, consumable rather than means to social critique, exceeded the violence in *On Board* or *A Madonna*. Unlike Tarantino's 'baddies' with a comic streak, the perpetrators of violence here were urban 'magandas' from the periphery, possibly from migrant families, the 'black Turks' disturbing the orderly lives of the 'white Turks' without apparent motivation (Göle, 2005). The good kids were drawn from a conservative point of view; remaining virgins while staying out all night at bars; in case of an unexpected pregnancy, marriage, rather than abortion, was the solution. *Gecenin Kanatları / The Wings of the Night* (2009), the story of a suicide-bomber, scripted by **Mahsun Kırmızıgül** (*Five Minarets in New York*) and Ahmet Küçükkayalı was an unbelievable love story with stock characters and mediocre acting. In 2011, he adapted one of his popular TV series, *Behzat Ç Seni Kalbime Gömdüm / Behzat Ç, I Buried You in My Heart* to wide screen, featuring an antihero (a policeman) who takes the law in his own hands, often with violence. He co-directed *Çanakkale Yolun Sonu / End of the Road* with Kemal Uzun and Ahmet Kahraman (2013).

Akay, Ezel (b. İnebolu, 1961) Actor, producer, scriptwriter and director. A graduate of the engineering department of the Bosphorus University, Ezel Akay studied theatre in the US. Co-founder of the production company, IFR (İstisnai Filmler ve Reklamlar / İstisnai Films and Commercials), he made over 500 commercials, co-produced **Derviş Zaim**'s *Tabutta Rövaşata / Somersault in a Coffin* (1997), **Yeşim Ustaoğlu**'s *Güneşe Yolculuk / Journey to the Sun* (1999) and *Karpuz Kabuğundan Gemiler Yapmak / Boats Out of Watermelon Rinds* (**Ahmet Uluçay**, 2004) among others and acted in **Zaim**'s *Filler ve Çimen / Elephants and Grass* (2001). He produced and directed his first feature, *Neredesin Firuze? / Where's Firuze* (2004), a musical social **comedy**/**fantasy** about the music industry, followed by *Hacivat Karagöz Neden Öldürüldü? / Killing the Shadow* (2006) and *7 Kocalı Hürmüz / 7 Husbands for Hürmüz* (2009), a re-make of the 1971 **Atıf Yılmaz** film, based on a popular 1960s stage play. He acted in all three. *Firuze* and *Hürmüz* parody the arabesque tradition whereas *The Shadow* is an attempt at pseudo-realism and a political satire on censorship of the artist.

Akay considers all his films political, but *The Shadow*, which draws attention to the execution of two legendary entertainers, Hacivat, a converted Muslim, and Karagöz, a regular blasphemer, by the oppressive state in the fourteenth century, is the most debated with obvious parallels to the censorship policies of the AKP (Adalet ve Kalkınma Partisi / Justice and Development Party) in power. Akay's exploitation of the western Orientalist paintings of the 1800s, including the Ottoman Osman Hamdi, has been ascribed to his Orientalist gaze. He maintains that the film explores Turkish identity while trying to reconcile with the vacuum that has existed since the founding of the republic between history and society, the latter Eastern in principle, Orientalist in essence, and the present political situation of the capitulation to religion by the nation state (Anonymous 2011).

Akın, Fatih (b. Hamburg, 1973) Director, screenwriter, producer, actor. Son of Turkish 'guest-workers', Fatih Akın studied Visual Communications at Hamburg's College of Fine Arts, but his real education is said to have been in his cousin's video-rental shop, where he discovered his mentor, Martin Scorcese. He showed promise with his first short *Sensin / Du bist es! Sensin / You're the One!* (1995), about a Turkish punk in Germany, who wants a girlfriend, compatriot but punk. His second short film, *Weed / Getuerkt* (1996) received several national and international prizes. His first feature, *Kurz und Schmerzlos / Short Sharp Shock* (1998) about three friends from the multi-ethnic Hamburg's criminal milieu – Gabriel, the tough Turk, recently released from prison, Costa, the somewhat inane Greek and Bobby, the handsome but dangerous Serb – won the Bronze Leopard at the Locarno Film Festival. Neither the plot nor the direction were original, the forceful music and striking visuals of the opening sequences slowly yielding to monotony, but the characters were well developed and well acted, the night shots of black and blue tones enhancing the claustrophobic atmosphere. *Im Juli / In July* (2000) was a romantic road movie with all the ingredients of the customary Western gaze and the Eastern object narratives – a young physics teacher with a mundane existence (the angst of affluent Western middle-class), a Turkish girl he falls in love with (the Orientalist imaginings of the West) and follows from Hamburg to Istanbul (the exotic vacation spot) and a German woman who loves him, who he'll stay with at the end (his German identity) after having been beaten, robbed, seduced and arrested for drugs during his wild odyssey through southeastern Europe (self-discovery of a Western man by the experience of the East). Both this film and *Solino* (2002), a tribute to all displaced people through the story of an Italian family who migrate to Germany, carry the elements of an artist in the making but lack the intimate passion of his 'Hamburg–Altona films'.

   Gegen die Wand / Duvara Karşı / Head On (2004), which won the Golden Bear at the Berlinale and ***Auf der Anderen Seite / Yaşamın Kıyısında / The Edge of Heaven*** (2007) which garnered the Best Screenplay award at the Cannes Film Festival, are the first two parts of a trilogy called *Liebe, Tod und Teufel / Love, Death and the Devil*. **Head On** is on love, ***The Edge of Heaven*** on death that brings loss, grief, revenge, recognition, guilt and forgiveness into life. *The Cut*, about the evil inherent in all human beings, will complete the trilogy. **Head On**

Figure 7 Auf der Anderen Seite / Yaşamın Kıyısında / The Edge of Heaven (Fatih Akın, 2007) (Courtesy of International Istanbul Film Festival)

and *The Edge of Heaven* foreground individual and collective identity, no longer reciprocally exclusive, within the context of two dissimilar urban environments – Hamburg and Istanbul. Akın's characters cross real or imaginary borders, defy them or surrender. Cognizant of the multiple and variable nature of identity, they negotiate territoriality. Akın considers *The Edge of Heaven* as the philosophical and political sequel to *Head On* and coming to terms with 9/11, the resulting Islam phobia and the perennial discussion on Turkey's joining the European Union. Just like *In July*, both films begin in Germany and involve a voyage to Turkey. Strong transitional tropes – borders, tunnels, seaports or airports, hotels and vehicles – underscore the spatio-temporality of this journey, which is a search for peace and tranquillity rather than a return to the roots.

One of the shining stars of new German cinema and the 'native son' awarded in national competitions in Turkey, Akın is an artist as 'intercultural' as his characters, moving 'between one culture and another, thus implying diachrony and the possibility of transformation' (Marks 2000: 6). In his work, the dominant culture is not posited as 'the invisible ground against which cultural minorities appear in relief', but rather 'a dynamic relationship between a dominant "host" culture and a minority culture' is implied. Unlike the transnational film-makers like Michel Khleifi and Trinh T. Minh-ha who would fit within Hamid Naficy's definition of transnational – the exile, the refugee, the émigré – intercultural film-makers Marks points out, 'though they identify with more than one cultural background, live in the country they were born' (Marks 2000: 6–7). From another perspective, he could be called a 'hyphenated national', or 'hyphenated at supra-state level' as a cosmopolitan elite, globally mobile and his cinema, a 'cinema of double occupancy' (Elsaesser 2005: 118). Turkey remains the locus of childhood vacations for Akın. The first image of Istanbul in *In July* is a painting on a restaurant wall, identically reproduced in authenticity when the protagonist reaches Turkey. The images that attract the camera are commercials advertising Turkey as the place of the sun, the sea and the cradle of civilization. *Crossing the Bridge – The Sound of Istanbul* (2005), a vibrant documentary on the multifaceted culture and music of the city is relayed through the gaze of a German musician, who begins his journey at the doorsteps of the legendary Grand Hôtel de Londres, somewhat anachronistic, even nostalgic with its *art nouveau* façade in the rapidly and haphazardly developing city. His nocturnal escapades into the backstreets of Beyoğlu, notorious for drugs, petty crime and gang activity (the site of violence in both *Head On* and *The Edge of Heaven*), show an alluring sub-culture with no threats.

Der Müll im Garten Eden / Polluting Paradise aka *Garbage in the Garden of Eden* (2012), a documentary about the consumer society's indifference to rubbish disposal, evidences Akın's evolution from a Germany-born Turk with a foreign gaze to more of an insider who identifies with the life-threatening issues of his parental country. Shot in the village of Akın's parents, where *The Edge of Heaven* ends, the film follows the struggles of the community, whose attempts to find a solution to the dumping site that destroys the tea plantations are faced with bureaucratic arrogance and political manoeuvring.

Akın's other films are the documentary, *Denk ich an Deutschland – Wir haben vergessen zurückzukehren / We Forgot To Go Back* (2001); the fiction, *Soul Kitchen* (2009) and the anthology film, *New York, I Love You* (2009). He is also the co-producer of successful first features by debut film-makers, *Takva / Takva – A Man's Fear of God* (**Özer Kızıltan**, 2006), *Chiko* (Özgür Yıldırım, 2008) and *Min Dit / Ben Gördüm / The Children of Diyarbakır* aka *Before Your Eyes* (**Miraz Bezar**, 2009) and screenwriter of *Kebab Connection* (Anno Saul, 2000).

Akın, Filiz (b. Ankara, 1943) Actor, singer; RN: Suna Akın. Filiz Akın, the first Western-looking elegant blonde star of Turkish cinema, renowned as 'the college girl', studied archaeology before starting her acting career with *Akasyalar Açarken / When the Acacias Bloom* (**Memduh Ün**, 1962) and played in over 120 films, mostly in the 1960s and 1970s. She was one of the top four stars (along with **Türkan Şoray**, **Hülya Koçyiğit** and **Fatma Girik**, referred to as *Kare-As / Square-Ace*) despite her blonde hair, customarily imaged as 'loose woman' in secondary roles. She played the lead opposite famous actors – **Tarık Akan**, **İzzet Günay**, **Kartal Tibet**, **Ediz Hun**, **Sadri Alışık**, **Ayhan Işık**, **Cüneyt Arkın**, **Kadir İnanır** – and the legendary singer Zeki Müren. In a period of crisis when **porno films** inundated the screens, she followed several of her colleagues and became a singer to earn her living. Her son İlker İnanoğlu, from her first marriage to director/producer **Türker İnanoğlu**, was a famous child star, particularly with the *Yumurcak / The Brat* series, playing opposite his mother. Two of Akın's distinguished films are *Gurbet Kuşları / Birds of Nostalgia* (**Refiğ**, 1964) and *Umutsuzlar / The Hopeless Ones* (**Güney**, 1971).

Akman, Nisan (b. Ankara, 1958) Director, producer, actor. One of the rare women directors of her epoch, Nisan Akman was introduced to cinema through her stepfather – actor and director, Tunca Yönder. She worked as assistant director and cameraman and shot commercials before her first film, the small-budget *Beyaz Bisiklet / The White Bicycle* (1986), which focused on the predicaments of women in androcentric societies. The schematic good/bad woman binaries, the untimely insertions of the motif of the white bicycle into the narrative and the claims of the critics that the script was plagiarized from Claude Goretta's *La Dentellière* (1977) (which Akman denied, maintaining it was inspired by the story of her manicurist), did not mar the film's success at the box-office. Akman made two more feature films, *Bir Kırık Bebek / A Broken Doll* (1987) and *Dünden Sonra, Yarından Önce / After Yesterday, Before Tomorrow* (1987). Despite the **Yeşilçam** clichés and the one-dimensional male characters – who drink, engage in extramarital affairs or desert the family – her films are noteworthy in foregrounding career achievement as part of female liberation and exposing the feudal mentality that thwarts it, unlike several films of the period by male film-makers that equate woman's liberation with sexual liberation. *A Broken Doll* is also significant for its message of peace and friendship in a period of attacks on Turkish diplomats by ASALA (Armenian Secret Army for the Liberation of Armenia): Artin is a close friend and when his wife dies, the Muslim family attend her funeral in the Armenian Church. The news of the assassinations on the radio hurts everyone. Akman unexpectedly stopped making films and settled in London, where she operated a restaurant, returning home 16 years later to work in television series.

Akpınar, Metin (b. Istanbul, 1941) Actor. Metin Akpınar co-founded Turkey's first cabaret theatre, Devekuşu (The Ostrich Cabaret Theatre) in 1967 along with **Zeki Alasya**, Haldun Taner and Ahmet Gülhan. He started his film career in 1972 as a comedian in **Ertem Eğilmez** films and his screen partnership with **Zeki Alasya** as the comic duo continued until the 1990s. He played opposite **Kemal Sunal** in the successful ***Propaganda*** (**Sinan Çetin**, 1999) and his *Papatyam / My Daisy* television series have been very popular, running the fourth season in 2011.

Akrebin Yolculuğu / Journey on the Clock Hour aka ***Journey on the Clock Hand*** (1997) is a love story that journeys through time. The deadly *ménage à trois* involving a young woman oppressed by an older man, the signature motif of screenwriter **Macit Koper**, blends with several key elements in **Kavur**'s previous work – the themes of alienation, isolation and lack of communication; an interior voyage toward an elusive but ultimate truth accompanying an actual one; a lone voyager who must search for the other and the spatio-temporal codes such as the clock tower (***Gizli Yüz / The Secret Face***, 1991); a small town hotel as the locus of the plot (***Anayurt Oteli / Motherland Hotel***, 1987) and a lake (***Göl / The Lake***, 1982).

Master Kerem (Mehmet Aslantuğ), an itinerant clock repairman, arrives in an Anatolian village where paradoxically time has ceased to exist. Even the clock tower that rises over the roofs of the wooden houses is no longer functional. Three life

Figure 8 Akrebin Yolculuğu / Journey on the Clock Hour aka *Journey on the Clock Hand*
(Ömer Kavur, 1997) (Courtesy of International Istanbul Film Festival)

stories are intertwined connecting the past with the present, or Kerem experiences
the same story at three different times. In his previous life, wearing his hand-woven
red scarf, he stayed in the same hotel, loved Esra (Şahika Tekand), tried to repair
the clock, was threatened by Esra's husband Agâh (**Tuncel Kurtiz**) and killed by
Esra, his childhood love, to prevent him from leaving. Before this life, he worked
in a shop on Tekerrrür (meaning repetition or return) Street; he was asked to repair
the clock and make a bell for the tower, for which he prepared the drawings, but
before he could retrieve the bell from the foundry, he was killed by Esra's husband
who discovered the illicit affair when Esra gave birth to a girl. These confusing life
circles slowly become coherent when the pieces of the puzzle are assembled – the
bell finally finds its place on the clock tower, the grave of the little girl and the grave
stone are revealed – and the essential question that **Kavur** poses regarding time,
life and death come to the foreground. Through the lake, which serves as a catalyst,
its still waters defying real time (the body that is never found) and its horizontality
offering a sharp contrast with the verticality of the clock tower, **Kavur** evokes time
and timelessness as in his previous work. Time is circular – the red scarf reappears
at the end and the medallion Esra throws into the lake resurfaces.

Another key motif of **Kavur**'s work is the relativity of the act of seeing. The
blind singers resembling the chorus in a Greek tragedy believe they can regain
their sight if they recover the bell they threw into the lake; to retreive the diary he
dropped in the same lake, Kerem is blindfolded, and mirrors reflect other mirrors.

Director, Producer: **Ömer Kavur**; Production: Alfa Film; Screenwriters: **Ömer Kavur**, **Macit Koper**; Cinematographer: Erdal Kahraman; Editor: **Mevlüt Koçak**; Music: Attila Özdemiroğlu; Cast: Mehmet Aslantuğ, Şahika Tekand, **Tuncel Kurtiz**, Nüvit Özdoğru, **Aytaç Arman**

Aksoy, Orhan (b. Bursa, 1930 – d. Istanbul, 2008) Director, screenwriter, actor and producer. The director of over 90 films, screenwriter of more than 50, actor of three and producer of one, in addition to several television films and series, Orhan Aksoy started his career as a projectionist in the now defunct Saray cinema in Istanbul. He worked as an editor for İpek Film Studios for nine years, making his first film *Şıpsevdi / Hasty Lover*, a **comedy** starring **Ayhan Işık** and Ajda Pekkan in 1963. A major film-maker of the most productive years of **Yeşilçam**, he built his fame with **melodramas** starring star-duos he created: **Hülya Koçyiğit** and **Ediz Hun** (*Kadın Asla Unutmaz / A Woman Never Forgets*, 1968; *Uykusuz Geceler / Sleepless Nights*, 1969; *Kezban Roma'da / Kezban is in Rome*, 1970), or **Hülya Koçyiğit** and **İzzet Günay** (*Kezban / Kezban*, 1968; *Kezban Paris'te / Kezban is in Paris*, 1971). He adapted several popular novels to screen such as *Hıçkırık / The Sob* (1965) and *Samanyolu / The Milkyway* (1967) by Kerime Nadir. He did the second re-make of *Vurun Kahpeye / Strike the Whore* (1964). *Dila Hanım / Mrs Dila* (1978) based on **Sefa Önal**'s script on blood feuds and starring **Türkan Şoray**, was a successful dark passion story. In the 1970s and 1980s when **melodrama** lost its popularity, Aksoy made musicals and romantic **comedies** with **arabesque** performers: **Orhan Gencebay** (*Sev Dedi Gözlerim /*

Figure 9 Hıçkırık / The Sob (Orhan Aksoy, 1965) (Courtesy of International Istanbul Film Festival)

My Eyes Said, Love Her, 1972; *Şöför / The Driver*; 1976), İbrahim Tatlıses (*Tövbe / Repentance*, 1981) and the transsexual singer Bülent Ersoy (*Yüz Karası – Şehvetin Sonu / Disgrace – The End of Fame*, 1981 about a male singer who wants to be a woman, a film ahead of its time). In the 1980s, he caught the spirit of the period with **Kemal Sunal** comedies carrying social messages (*Yakışıklı / The Handsome*, 1987; *Kiracı / The Tenant*, 1987). *Yumuşak Ten / The Soft Skin* (1994) was his last film. *The Director of Romantic Films: Orhan Aksoy* (Ersin Pertan, 2006) is a documentary on Aksoy.

Aksu, Yücel (b. 1966, Muğla) Director, actor, screenwriter, producer. Yücel Aksu made his mark with his debut film, *Dondurmam Gaymak / Ice Cream, I Scream* (2006), a mild social and political satire about life in an Aegean village (his natal place) during the years of President Süleyman Demirel (1993–2000) when traditional values, including religion and community solidarity, were debilitated with the new developments in tourism, technology, mass production and mass media. His second feature *Entelköy Efeköy'e Karşı / Ecotopia* (2011) used the same village to construct another mild socio-political satire about the clash between a group of ecologists dreaming of communal life and the villagers who would rather make money on the planned thermoelectric power plant. Employing the **meta-film** sub-**genre**, Aksu appears in the opening scenes explaining the plot to the villagers, who would rather see the screening. A graduate of the Nine September University in İzmir from the Faculty of Fine Arts, Cinema and Television Department (1993), Aksu is also the director of a documentary, *Anadolu'nun Son Göçerleri / Last Nomads in Anatolia* (2011) about a dying culture.

Alabora (Yücel), Derya (b. Istanbul, 1959) Actor. A talented character actor, Derya Alabora received accolades for her remarkable role as a free-spirited prostitute in *Masumiyet / Innocence* (**Demirkubuz**, 1997). A graduate of the theatre department of the conservatory of the Mimar Sinan University in 1982, she worked in theatre (state as well as private companies, including her own) before entering cinema in 1987 with a role in **Nisan Akman**'s *Bir Kırık Bebek / A Broken Doll* (1987). *Dönersen Islık Çal / Whistle If You Return* (**Orhan Oğuz**, 1993), *Salkım Hanımın Taneleri / Mrs Salkım's Diamonds* (**Tomris Giritlioğlu**, 1999), *İz / Traces* (1994) and *Pandora'nın Kutusu / Pandora's Box* (**Yeşim Ustaoğlu**), *Karanlıktakiler / In Darkness* (**Çağan Irmak**, 2009), *Siyah Beyaz / Black and White* (Ahmet Boyacıoğlu, 2010), *Die Fremde / When We Leave* (Feo Aladag, 2010) are some of the films with her noteworthy performances. She is popular for her role in the television series, *Şaşıfelek Çıkmazı / Cockeyed-Fate Dead-End.*

Alasya, Zeki (b. Istanbul, 1943) Actor, director, screenwriter. In a career that spans over half a century, Alasya has written scripts, directed films for theatrical release and for television and acted in more than 60 films, including television series. He studied at the Robert College in Istanbul, starting acting in 1959 as an amateur and joining several theatre troupes until co-founding Turkey's first cabaret theatre, Devekuşu (The Ostrich Cabaret Theatre) in 1967. After 1973, he concentrated on cinema, forming a comic duo with **Metin Akpınar** (*Köşe Kapmaca / Hide and Seek*, Alasya, 1979; *Davetsiz Misafir / Uninvited Guest*, Alasya, 1983; *Petrol Kıralları / Kings of Petrol*, Alasya, 1978). In 1998, he received the medal of the State Artist by the Ministry of Culture.

Algan, Ayla (b. Istanbul, 1937) Actor and singer. Distinguishing herself with her debut film **Karanlıkta Uyananlar / Those Awakening in the Dark** (**Ertem Göreç**, 1964), Ayla Algan studied acting at the Actor's Studio in New York after a childhood spent in France. Particularly remembered for her role in *Ah, Güzel İstanbul / Oh, Beautiful Istanbul* (**Atıf Yılmaz**, 1966), she has played in over 30 films, including television and mini series.

Alışık, Sadri (b. Istanbul, 1925 – d. Istanbul, 1995) Actor, singer, painter, writer. Interested in theatre since childhood, Alışık became a popular actor in cinema, reaching the zenith of his career during the socially demoralizing 1960s and 1970s as the honest optimist type who finds strength for love among the underprivileged. He started his acting career in 1944 with *Günahsızlar / The Innocent Ones* (**Faruk Kenç**); met his future wife, Çolpan İlhan on the set of *Yalnızlar Rıhtımı / The Quay of the Lonely Ones* (**Akad**, 1959) and gained audience appreciation with his roles in *Ah, Güzel İstanbul / Oh, Beautiful Istanbul* (**Atıf Yılmaz**, 1966) and *Küçük Hanımefendi / Little Missie* series (Nejat Saydam, 1961–62) with **Ayhan Işık** and **Belgin Doruk**. Alışık acted in over 200 films. His *Turist Ömer* series were very popular (*Turist Ömer Yamyamlar Arasında / Turist Ömer Among the Cannibals*, 1970 and *Turist Ömer Uzay Yolunda / Ömer, the Tourist on Star Trek*, 1973 by **Hulki Saner**). He was also the lead in the popular television series, *Kartallar Yüksek Uçar / Eagles Fly High* (Hüseyin Karakaş, 1983). He made albums, sang in nightclubs, painted and published a book of poems called *Bir Ömürlük İstanbul / Istanbul For a Lifetime*. Sadri Alışık Cinema and Theatre Awards are given annually in his honour at the Sadri Alışık Cultural Centre, established by his wife Çolpan İlhan.

Alper, Emin (b. Konya, 1974) Director, screenwriter, producer. A professor at the Humanities and Social Sciences department of Istanbul Technical University, Emin Alper made two short films, *Rıfat* and *The Letter* before his first feature, **Tepenin Ardı / Beyond the Hill** (2012), a family drama set in an Anatolian town. Through the microcosm of a disjointed family, **Beyond the Hill** narrates the history of a country reluctant to face its past, insecure about its present and uncertain about its future.

Alper, Özcan (b. Hopa, 1975) Director, screenwriter, editor. One of the leading representatives of the generation of film-makers with a political agenda that have appeared in the new millennium, Özcan Alper majored in history from the University of Istanbul. Starting in 1996, he attended film workshops at the Mesopotamia Cultural Centre (the present Nazım Hikmet Cultural Centre) and worked as assistant director including **Bulutları Beklerken / Waiting for the Clouds**

by **Yeşim Ustaoğlu**. His first work, the award-winning *Momi / Grandmother* (2000), dedicated to 'grandmothers, the language bearers', is a 25-minute film, shot on the plateau between Artvin and Ardahan in the almost-forgotten Armenian dialect Hemshin (his mother tongue), spoken by Armenians converted to Islam during the seventeenth century. The Court for State Security accused Alper of producing material intended to destroy the unity of the state, under article eight of the anti-terror law. The case was dropped when the law was repealed in 2003 after EU pressure. Focusing on the themes of search for identity and awakening to one's culture and language, *Sonbahar / Autumn* (2007), mostly in the Hemshin language, won over 30 national and international awards. *Gelecek Uzun Sürer / The Future Lasts Forever* (2011), mostly shot in Diyarbakır, is a reflection on collective memory and guilt, foregrounding the trauma of the three-decades-old civil war in the south-east of Turkey, which has claimed thousands of lives.

Altıoklar, Mustafa (b. Ordu, 1958) Director, screenwriter, producer, editor, actor. A medical doctor by training, Altıoklar made his first film *Denize Hançer Düştü / Balcony* about same-sex love in 1992, but drew attention with his second film, *Istanbul Kanatlarımın Altında / Istanbul Beneath My Wings* (1995), a landmark for starting western-style intertextual relay in Turkey. The story of attempts at flying during the Ottoman period, thwarted by censorship from the religious authorities, the film's depiction of the Ottoman sultan as homosexual stirred controversy, and the accuracy of the historical background drew polemic but the box-office success was unprecedented. *Ağır Roman / Cholera Street* (1997), a literary adaptation (Metin Kaçan) was the box-office champion of the year. He challenged the untouchable status of the army in *O Şimdi Asker / He is in the Army Now* (2002), the story of men of different ages and backgrounds who come together during paid military service and learn to deal with life and personal problems. Made with aid from the army, including lending of uniforms and some real soldiers acting as extras, the film criticized gently the rigidity of the military structure but presented the institution as the equalizer of discordant elements. It garnered 589,586 admissions in its first ten days. *Beyza'nın Kadınları / Shattered Soul* (2006) was an exploration of the **crime**-thriller **genre**, focusing on a woman serial killer in a country where serial killers do not exist. The fluctuating personalities of the protagonist – good housewife, sex maniac, selfless schoolteacher, religious fundamentalist – could have acquired a socio-political dimension as a reference to the issue of gendered identity in modern Turkey, but the script was not developed to motivate a coherent thought process. Altıoklar makes television series and continues his efforts to do quality cinema that can also be successful at the box-office. Some of his other fiction films are *Asansör / The Elevator* (1999) and *Banyo / The Bathroom* (2005).

Anayurt Oteli / Motherland Hotel (1987), one of the classics of Turkish cinema, is also the first character study. Based on Yusuf Atılgan's eponymous novel, written in 1973 in the aftermath of the 12 March 1971 '*coup* by memorandum' (but set in 1963), the narrative foregrounds a schizoid hotel manager in a provincial town, whose obsession with a mysterious passenger leads him to suicide. The atmosphere of the demoralized post-traumatic society of the 1980s, the actual period of the shooting of the film, is referenced through a sleepy provincial town where everything arrives with delay: the news, the music, the fashion, the politics and even the train from the capital, which brings the mysterious passenger. Inequalities, exploitation, social and political oppression, mistrust and bigotry prevail. Sexual starvation leads to aggression against the weaker, often the woman: Zebercet copulates with the insensate servant, the men's café is decorated with pictures of half-naked women and a groom kills his bride on the nuptial bed without apparent motivation ('she was a virgin'). A dead body on the street and an arrest in the restaurant are routine happenings.

The central trope is suffocation – the bride is strangled; Zebercet's uncle hangs himself; the scene from Kavur's *The Lake* viewed on television evokes strangling and Zebercet strangles the maid and hangs himself. The Republic Day parade, the collective prayer sessions in the marketplaces and the municipal loudspeakers connote the fear of engulfment. The rope used by the maid to hang the laundry, by the village men to threaten Zebercet and finally as the conduit for Zebercet's suicide is the key motif that drives the narrative.

Zebercet fantasizes about a woman, who appears late one evening and leaves the next morning. Turning her room into a temple, he fetishizes her towel, lipstick-marked tea glass and cigarette butts. When she does not return, he loses hope. The movies, the cockfights and copulation with the hypersomniac maid do not satisfy him anymore. After the disappearance of the old customer, now hunted by the police for strangling his daughter, he closes the hotel and severs all contact with the outside world. In the final episode, as he hangs from the ceiling, the door is ajar and sunlight fills the old mansion. Is he saved by death, or joined with the woman in the old photograph that resembles the mysterious passenger? Is she his mother lost when he was ten – after his circumcision, his attainment of manhood – from whom he was severed by his premature birth? Copulation with the maid, masturbation with the mysterious passenger's towel and the clumsy attempts at finding partners by stalking a disinterested young woman, accepting the advances of a 17-year-old boy but losing his nerve or trying to hire a reluctant prostitute could be codes for a desire to return to the womb through sex and orgasm (Freud 1922: 139; 1930: 24, 87). His suicide also evokes the same desire to end the pain, the struggle and awareness, or death can be erotically mollifying as a fantasy of sexual absorption by another (Rheingold 1967: 120–3), in this case, the mysterious passenger, or the mother, both lost to him in real life. (Paradoxically, **Kavur** claimed that the woman in the old picture was not the mother, but the woman for whom Zebercet's uncle hanged himself.) The fear of, or desire for, separation and individuation ('I am Zebercet', he repeats to the mirror and kills the maid who ignores him as a person during sex) to express feelings and ideas and act upon them despite anonymous conformity, particularly in the closed environment of a provincial town, can increase the annihilation anxiety. Even sexual pleasure can threaten one with guilt, punishment, psychotic fragmentation or death. Zebercet's identification in the courtroom with the groom who choked his bride as well as his identification with the uncle who had hanged himself for unattainable love

Figure 10 Anayurt Oteli / Motherland Hotel (Ömer Kavur, 1987) (Courtesy of International Istanbul Film Festival)

(as revealed during his conversation in the park with an elderly man) are part of his fantasy mechanism that uses transference as a defensive attempt to resist the present (Freud 1930: 81).

The principle locale, which has been frequently exploited in literature, carries a critique of modernism. The dates are significant. The old *konak* (mansion) was build in 1839, the year of the Tanzimat Decree (the Reforms) and converted into a hotel in 1923, the date of the Republic of Turkey, like other similar mansions, signifying the demise of the Ottoman Empire, the disintegration of conventional families and the search for identity in the new modernist age. Zebercet hangs himself on 10 November at 9.05, the date of Kemal Atatürk's death, coded as the disintegration of the republican identity. The hotel connects Zebercet to his ancestors, but it begins to engulf him, claiming time and devotion, limiting his freedom and weakening his ties with the outside. When his regression happens, he locks himself inside, which could be read as a trope for the womb as mentioned above, but the womb is also interchangeable with the country as the name of the hotel indicates (*Anayurt* means motherland).

The film is one of the best literary adaptations, however, unlike the explicit rendition of sexual desires and acts in the novel, **Kavur** concentrates on emotions. The past, elaborated in the book, is referenced only in two instances: through Zebercet as the intradiegetic-homodiegetic narrator (his mother died in 1960, the year of his circumcision and the year of the *coup d'état*; he got out of the army in 1971, the second *coup d'état*; he started to operate the hotel in 1980, the third *coup d'état*) and through the conversation in the park with an elderly man, where as the extradiegetic narrator, Zebercet identifies with Faruk Bey, his uncle and identifies the mysterious woman who visits his hotel as Semra Hanım, his uncle's infatuation.

The alienation of the individual in a modern society and the passage of time, a theme that **Kavur** developed in his later films, are at the centre of the narrative. Combined with his fascination with dreams, symbols and the hidden meanings of objects, *Motherland Hotel* stands as one of the masterpieces of Turkish cinema. The melancholy mood of the film is heightened with the shots of closed and phobic spaces – the hotel entrance with Zebercet's desk; the guest rooms; the restaurant where men eye each other with suspicion, or recount prison stories; the cinema showing karate films, the bloody cock-fight – and the filmic time itself, which is the night. The compositions accentuate verticality – the high ceilings of the old hotel, the corridors, the stairs and the facades – shifting to horizontal images – beds, prostration and murder, the protagonist, symbolically finding his identity through suicide by hanging (coming back to verticality).

The film received the Film Critics award at the 44th Venice International Film Festival, 1987; the Golden Montgolfiere at the 9th Nantes Three Continents Film Festival, 1987; the Bronze Prize at the 6th Valencia Mediterranean Film Festival, 1987 and several national prizes.

Director, Screenwriter: **Ömer Kavur** (based on a novel by Yusuf Atılgan); Producer: Cengiz Ergin; Production: Alfa Film; Cinematographer: **Orhan Oğuz**; Music: Atilla Özdemiroğlu; Art director: **Şahin Kaygun**; Cast: **Macit Koper**, Orhan Çağman, Şahika Tekand, Osman Alyanak, Yaşar Güner

Ar, Müjde (b. Istanbul, 1954) Actor, producer; RN: Kamile Suat Ebrem. Considered as the last star of Turkish cinema, Müjde Ar was the initiator of the image of the liberated young modern woman with sexuality in a period when established stars demurred at 'compromising' roles to protect their reputations. The child of Bulgarian immigrants, Ar studied German language and literature at the University of Istanbul, interrupting her studies at the age of 20 to work as a model, study theatre and marry. The audiences first met her through her role in **Halit Refiğ**'s film series, *Aşk-ı Memnu / Forbidden Love* broadcast on television. She entered cinema with *Babacan / Fatherly* (Natuk Baytan, 1975) opposite **Cüneyt Arkın** and until the early 1980s played in numerous **melodramas** and romantic **comedies**. Starting with *Ah, Güzel İstanbul / Oh, Beautiful Istanbul* (**Kavur**, 1981) (her first nude appearance), she began portraying real women with real issues – rebellious female characters addressing unequal gender politics – instrumental in returning the female audience to the theatres. ***Fahriye Abla / Sister Fahriye***

(**Yavuz Turgul**, 1984), reinforcing the new image of the independent woman was a breakthrough for Ar, which she continued with *Şalvar Davası / The Case of Baggy Pants* (**Kartal Tibet**, 1983), *Adı Vasfiye / Her Name is Vasfiye* (1985) and *Aaahh Belinda/ Oh, Belinda* of Atıf Yılmaz (1986). Among her other memorable roles is *Asılacak Kadın / A Woman to be Hanged* (**Başar Sabuncu**, 1987). As an activist, Ar is one of the founders of TÜRSAK (Turkish Foundation of Cinema and Audio-visual Culture), established in 1991 and is known for her efforts to develop film education in Turkey and ensure the government collaboration to improve Turkish cinema.

Arabesk / Arabesque in cinema is an extension of the traditional folk culture (literature/lifestyle) began as a music **genre** with Indian, Arabic and Anatolian flavour in the 1960s as migration from the countryside to the metropolises intensified. Fatalistic in outlook and masculinist in viewpoint, mostly sung by men, targeting the Anatolian migrant workers' malaise in modern metropolises, *arabesque* idealizes the rural home and through stories of unattainable love laments the impossibility of return, offering as an alternative the imposition of rural culture on modern urban life. Despite the ban on TV and the radio, arabesque music reached the public through the growing cassette industry and particularly on the collective minibuses driven by Anatolian youth servicing the shantytown settlements. In 1968, Orhan Gencebay started the arabesque film furore relying on his success in music. Soon the **genre** became very popular in **Yeşilçam** and remained so until the 1980s. İbrahim Tatlıses, who entered the music scene at a very early age as the provincial little İbo with an elegiac voice, was the hero of several of these films.

Despite opposition from both the secular and Islamist Turks and particularly the intelligentsia (**Yılmaz Güney** denounced the ideology as a decoy to divert people from the hardships of daily life), arabesque enjoyed unprecedented success, which could be attributed to its ability to provide a temporary (albeit artificial) relief for cultures in transition.

Arabesk / Arabesque (1988) is a satire that employs the clichés of the sub-**genre** – star-crossed lovers; dire misunderstandings; innocent maiden becoming 'fallen woman' (**Müjde Ar**) but gaining respectability via a kind-hearted man; penniless village boy (**Şener Şen**) with a golden voice getting discovered by the king of night clubs; losing sight/gaining sight and the happy ending. The film references Indian musicals with its song-and-dance numbers and parodies Hollywood – the gangster/king of the nightclubs imitates Marlon Brando's hoarse grunting in Francis Ford Coppola's *Godfather* (1972) – in an exploration of the structure and logic of arabesque that established itself in the cinema, the culture and the daily life of the country. The use of authentic arabesque songs is effectual in terms of satirizing the concept rather than the music itself and the song episode in the prison scene ensuing **Şen**'s original scuffle with the inmates is successful in terms of providing clues to the birth of arabesque as music, but also as an individual and social state of mind.

Director: **Ertem Eğilmez**; Producer: Nahit Ataman, **Türker İnanoğlu**; Screenwriter: Gani Müjde; Cinematographer: Aytekin Çakmakçı; Cast: **Müjde Ar**, **Şener Şen**, **Uğur Yücel**, Münir Özkul, Agah Hün

Araf / Somewhere in Between (2012), the fifth feature of the most prominent woman film-maker of Turkey presents a generation of young adults without a future. Trapped within the suffocating atmosphere of a provincial town of unemployment and external migration, the iron and steel factory that was a forerunner of modernity in the 1930s having lost its industrial prospect, they wait in a limbo between monotonous jobs and a miracle that would bring them closer to the coveted lives on television. Working in the restaurant of a complex on the busiest toll highway, the characters watch the vehicles pass while they go nowhere.

The opening scene of molten liquid metal pouring out of a huge ladle, not unlike the scorching fires of hell, forewarns the explosion of sexuality and desire, the loss of innocence and the ensuing pain. Eighteen-year-old Olgun (Barış Hacıhan) (ironically, meaning mature in Turkish) dreams of making money on a television show, by opening the right box to escape from his oppressive father and reconstructing a new family with his mother and Zehra (Neslihan Atagül), his co-worker. Zehra, on the threshold of adulthood like Olgun, neither a peasant nor city-bred, hopes to escape her spatio-temporal liminality through an affair with the older truck driver Mahur (Özcan Deniz), dreaming of distant lands as she stares at the Black Sea in the room where they make love. Mahur, weary of threading the roads pre-designed for him, seeks to escape his loneliness through sexual intercourse. Their fatal meeting and the ensuing dance of seduction, ironically during a wedding, when they abstract themselves from the surrounding traditional family atmosphere, is charged with sensuality although when their bodies physically unite behind closed doors, Ustaoğlu empties the love-making scene of any romanticism by moving the camera to the worn out feet of Mahur after the kiss.

Figure 11 Araf / Somewhere in Between (Yeşim Ustaoğlu, 2012) (Courtesy of Yeşim Ustaoğlu)

The realistic picture of provincial life caught between modernity and rural kitsch – Internet cafes, naively internalized television programmes, weddings where the exhilarated guests dance *kolbastı* (a popular dance of the Black Sea region), provincial discoes, claustrophobic homes, unhappy parents, women locked into dead-end marriages – merge with the images of snow and slush, heightening the atmosphere of darkness and doom for those in a limbo (*araf* in Turkish). As in Ustaoğlu's other films, the elliptic style reveals the resonances rather than the actual events (except the final episode, which does not spare details).

Unlike her previous work, in **Somewhere**, Ustaoğlu does not dwell on the reasons behind the situation, nor does she suggest an open door. A rather thinly developed parallel runs between the lack of pity towards unwanted animals (Olgun's father kills stray dogs) and humans (at the moment of crisis, Zehra is alone). The dynamism of the first part gradually yields to the clichés of **Yeşilçam melodramas** – the deceived and deserted maiden, an unwanted pregnancy and finally a loving man to restore order – while flirting with the **arabesque** culture. The language of the film is male dominant language with its limitations. The originality of the last episode – the youth shaped by game shows marrying live – does not eclipse the conservative nature of Zehra's choice. Frequent close-ups of Zehra while the others are depicted in mid-length shots steers the spectator's attention toward her plight, but in essence, just as in the majority of the films of the epoch, the issue is men whose character traits/circumstances determine the lives of women: Olgun's personality and pursuits counteract her relationship with Zehra; his father's alcoholism drives his mother out of the house; Derya's husband (an underdeveloped character) seems to be her main problem and Mahur is instrumental in Zehra's trauma. Homoerotic jokes, military service discussions, penis-size anxiety (as Olgun admits his inadequacy, the red truck of Mahur enters the frame like a potent phallic image) receive generous diegetic space whereas the issue of violence against women is nonchalantly circumvented.

Love between a young woman and a driver with a red truck, desertion and the eventual protection by another man recall the **Atıf Yılmaz** classic, **Selvi Boylum, Al Yazmalım / The Girl with the Red Scarf** (1977) (refuted by Ustaoğlu). Whereas **The Girl** presents a magnificent love story and in its finale, dares to ask the important question of the choice between love and labour to build a solid relationship, **Somewhere in Between** leaves the audience in the same limbo as the characters. Dissociated from the true nature of Zehra's feelings right at the outset, we remain so when the curtain falls.

Director, Producer, Screenwriter: **Yeşim Ustaoğlu**; Production: Ustaoğlu Film, CDP, The Match Factory, ZDF/arte, TRT; Cinematographer: Michael Hammon; Editor: Mathilde Muyard, Svetolik Mica Zajc, Naim Kanat; Art Director: Osman Özcan; Composer: Marc Marder; Sound Design: Sylvain Malbrant; Sound Engineer: Bruno Tarrière; Cast: Özcan Deniz, Neslihan Atagül, Barış Hacıhan, Ilgaz Kocatürk, Nihal Yalçın

Arakon, İlhan G. (b. Edirne, 1916 – d. Istanbul, 2006) Cinematographer, director, producer, screenwriter. One of the pioneers of Turkish cinema, İlhan G. Arakon got his first 16mm camera in 1937 and worked with different directors. In

1940, he opened the first photography exhibition of Turkey and in 1944 he started as a professional cameraman. One of the first to use zoom in Turkey, he is the cinematographer of 100 films and 400 shorts and documentaries, among which are his brother Aydın G. Arakon's *İstanbul'un Fethi / Conquest of Istanbul* (1951), which was screened at the first Berlin Film Festival; *Hıçkırık / The Sob* (**Orhan Aksoy**, 1965) and *Aşk-ı Memnu*, the television mini-series (**Halit Refiğ**, 1975).

Arkadaş / The Friend (1974), the last film **Yılmaz Güney** directed in Turkey, made following his release from prison during a general amnesty after having served 26 months, was very popular during a period of political strife, its theme song appropriated by the revolutionary youth. *The Friend* marks a second turning point in **Güney**'s career after *Umut / The Hope* (1970) and complements the earlier film. As a departure from the rural, unsophisticated heroes in conflict with nature and humankind, **Güney** casts himself as the charismatic Azem, a public worker visiting his childhood friend Cemil (Kerim Afşar) in a vacation village (what Foucault would call 'temporal heterotopia', linked to the transitory and precarious aspect of time, 1984: 46–9). Disillusioned with Cemil's decadent life that has distanced him from his humble roots, Azem disturbs Cemil's petit bourgeois wife, Necibe (Azra Balkan) with his judgemental eye although the young niece (Melike Demirağ) is more impressionable. The realization of the superficiality of his superfluous materialism destroys Cemil.

A strong criticism of the revolutionary youth that turn into apathetic bourgeois as middle-age approaches, the narrative unfolds through Azem's gaze, which can discern the futility of such existence while the vacationers are blinded by their identification with their life. The weak points of the film are the didacticism that produces caricaturized two-dimensional characters and the use of **Yeşilçam** clichés for the bourgeoisie – parties, bikinis, whisky and meaningless sex. **Güney** is at his best when he describes the lives of the disadvantaged in the natal village of Azem and Cemil.

Director, Scriptwriter, Producer: **Yılmaz Güney**, Production: Güney Film, Cinematographer: Çetin Tunca; Music: Şanar Yurdatapan, Atilla Özdemiroğlu; Cast: **Yılmaz Güney**, Melike Demirağ, Kerim Afşar, Azra Balkan, Nizam Ergüden, Ayşe Emel Mesçi, Kamran Usluer, Abdurrahman Palay

Arkın, Cüneyt (b. Eskişehir, 1937) Actor, director, screenwriter, producer; RN: Fahrettin Cüreklibatur. Trained as a medical doctor, Turkey's number one man of action and adventure famous for his trampoline jumps; reputedly coached in Italian and Kazakh circuses in acrobatics and horsemanship; the karate master, the pole-vaulter; the stuntman of his own roles despite several injuries; the Turkish Alain Delon, Clint Eastwood and John Wayne; with almost 300 films to his credit, started cinema with **Halit Refiğ**'s *Gurbet Kuşları / The Birds of Nostalgia* aka *Migrating Birds* aka *Birds of Exile* (1964). He changed his name to Cüneyt Arkın and became popular with **historical action films** – *Malkoçoğlu* series (1966–72) about the eponymous hero leading the Muslim armies against the Byzantines, *Battal Gazi* series and *Kara Murat*. Before the Lebanese civil war and the Iran–Iraq war, he made several films with Iranians when Turkish cinema was very popular in the Middle East. The Italians marketed his films in South America as George Arkin and the Chinese, Lee Arkin. In the 1970s, he appeared in politically engaged films (*Maden*, **Yavuz Özkan**, 1978; *The Adam Trilogy*, Remzi Aydın Jöntürk, 1970s). He owes his international fame to *Dünyayı Kurtaran Adam / The Man Who Saves the World* aka *Turkish Starwars* (**Çetin İnanç**, 1982), a plagiarized B-movie that has become a cult classic in the twenty-first century despite its reputation as the worst film ever made. Arkın also played in the remake, *Dünyayı Kurtaran Adamın Oğlu / Turks in Space* (**Kartal Tibet**, 2006).

Arman, Aytaç (b. Adana, 1948) Actor; RN: Veys el İnce. Interrupting his education in electrical engineering for economic reasons, Aytaç Arman entered cinema and built his career on exceptional films, starting with *Baba / The Father* (**Yılmaz Güney**, 1971). He excelled in *Bedrana* (1974) and *Kara Çarşaflı Gelin / The Bride in Black Chadoor* (1975) of **Süreyya Duru**; *Düşman / The Enemy* (**Zeki Ökten**, 1979); *Adı Vasfiye / Her Name is Vasfiye* (**Atıf Yılmaz**, 1985); *Gece Yolculuğu / Night Journey* (1987), *Melekler Evi / The House of Angels* (2000) and *Karşılaşma / Encounter* (2002) of **Ömer Kavur**; *Biri ve Diğerleri / One and the Others* (**Tunç Başaran**, 1987) and *Av Zamanı / Time for Hunting* (**Erden Kıral**, 1993). *Night Journey* garnered him the best male actor award of the 25th Antalya Golden Orange Film Festival.

Arslan, Thomas (b. Braunschweig, 1962) Director, screenwriter, producer, cinematographer, editor. Considered as one of the key figures of the 'Berlin School', Thomas Arslan has given remarkable examples of what may be defined as 'cinema of double occupancy' (Elsaesser 2005: 118). He spent four years of his elementary school education in Turkey, returning to Germany for high school, studying German language, literature and history and subsequently cinema at the German Film and Television Academy (DFFB) between 1986–92. His first film was *Kleines Fernsehspiel / Turn the Music Down* (1994). *Geschwister / Kardeşler / Brothers and Sisters* aka *Siblings* (1996/1997), the first part of the Berlin trilogy, focused on three siblings from Kreuzberg, a densely Turkish populated area of Berlin, living with their Turkish father and German mother. While the younger two try to alienate from their Turkish background, the eldest, Erol, lacking motivation in his life, chooses to remain a Turkish citizen and accepts the draft notice to serve in the army in Turkey. *The Dealer* (1999), which focuses on existential issues rather than social conflicts, carries an unusual story with minimal action through an inert protagonist whose Turkish origin is not stressed although he could be viewed as a continuation of Erol (played by the same actor, Tamer Yiğit). Berlin is depicted as an unidentifiable city with decrepit industrial spaces and decaying buildings with dark entrances that carry anonymity, although the narrative is not built on the spatial dichotomy between the periphery and the centre and the borders are not ethnic. *Der schöne Tag / One Fine Day* (2001), the last of the trilogy describes a long summer day in the life of Deniz, a 21-year-old

Berlin actress and dubbing artist. As a hyphenated film-maker in Germany, Arslan foregrounds cultural hybridity and not cultural clashes. The ethnically mixed backgrounds often lead his characters to a more cultivated form of identity, a timely shift from the 'cinema of duty' (Malik 1996: 203–4) that had characterized earlier films about Turks in Germany. *Aus der Ferne / From Far Away* (2005) is a documentary about going back to visit Turkey, whereas *Freinen / Vacation* (2007) is a domestic drama. *Im Schatten / In the Shadows* (2010), shot with a Red One digital camera and on a mini-budget, is a **genre** film, reminiscent of Jean-Pierre Melville, with an almost insignificant plot, with a focus on the mechanics of crime and the daily routine of a criminal. Space is limited but has its own presence, almost like a documentary.

Arslan, Yılmaz (b. Kazanlı, 1968) Director, screenwriter, producer, actor. The angry man of Germany's 'accented cinema', Yılmaz Arslan, of Kurdish origin, went to Germany in 1975 with his parents for medical reasons and spent a long period at a rehabilitation centre near Heidelberg for the physically handicapped where he founded the theatre group *Sommer–Winter / Summer–Winter.* In his first feature, *Langer Gang / Passages* (1992), handicapped youth play themselves in a fictionalized narrative that shows 'a microcosm of the "able" society outside, from the perspective of the disabled people…with the kind of point-of-view filming and camera positioning that encourages audience identification with the disabled' neither objectifying nor isolating them (Naficy 2001: 198). They are inside one of Germany's largest rehabilitation centres, built with the best intentions except concern for natural human needs such as love or privacy, resulting in aggravation of the existing problems of the physically handicapped.

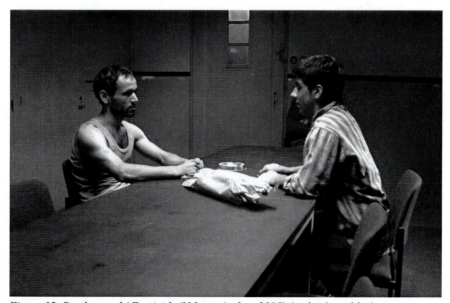

Figure 12 Brudermord / Fraticide (Yılmaz Arslan, 2005) (author's archive)

Arslan evacuates the building of its functions and concentrates on the inhabitants with neither sympathy nor compassion; the long corridors of the title become a metaphor for the position of the handicapped in a Foucauldian sense (Tremain 2005). His second film, *Yara / Seelenschmerz / The Wound* (1998), through the story of a Turkish woman forced by her parents to return to Turkey, exposes the emotional scars that haunt the lives of the young and the displaced, and his third film ***Brudermord / Fraticide*** (2005) focuses on misplaced youth through a story of ethnic hostility in Germany. The wound, sometimes physical and graphically displayed and other times so deep that it manifests itself in unexpected ways, is the principal motif of all of Arslan's films.

Arsoy, Göksel (b. Kayseri, 1936) Actor, producer, singer. The 'golden boy' of Turkish cinema, the blond star of innumerable films in a career that spans half a century, Göksel Arsoy was discovered by a producer while working at Istanbul's airport for a British airline and offered his first role in *Kara Günlerim / My Dark Days* (Sırrı Gültekin, 1957). He became a star with *Samanyolu / Milky Way* (Nevzat Pesen, 1959), forming the 'ideal couple' with **Belgin Doruk**. He played James Bond in the first Turkish Bond film, *Altın Çocuk / The Golden Boy* (**Memduh Ün**, 1966), plagiarized from *Thunderball* (Terence Young, 1965) and shot in London with the collaboration of British, French and Swedish television stars. Some of his unforgettable roles in the 1960s were in *Şehirdeki Yabancı / A Stranger in Town* (1962) and *Şafak Bekçileri / Guardians of Dawn* (1963) by **Halit Refiğ**. The latter was censored, among other reasons, for Arsoy's numerous kissing scenes while in uniform and crying at the grave of his martyred friend, acts not 'commensurate with the serious nature of the army'. During the sex furore in **Yeşilçam**, Arsoy tried a singing career with the aid of his uncle, the composer, Yesari Asım Arsoy and spent 14 years working in clubs. During the 1990s, he participated in several television series (Anonymous 2005).

Artemel, Talat (b. Istanbul, 1901 – d. Bolu, 1957) Actor, director, screenwriter. One of the rich cast of Turkey's first sound film, *İstanbul Sokaklarında / On the Streets of Istanbul* (**Ertuğrul**, 1931), Talat Artemel started working in theatre, moving on to cinema in 1928 as an actor in a short film, *Bir Sigara Yüzünden / Because of a Cigarette*. He acted in over 40 films, of which he directed seven and wrote the scripts of four. In 1944, he wrote and directed his first film, *Hürriyet Apartmanı / Hürriyet Apartman*. He was the first husband of **Cahide Sonku** with whom he acted in ***Aysel, Bataklı Damın Kızı / The Girl From the Marshes*** aka ***Aysel, the Girl From the Swampy Roof*** (1934–1935) and co-directed with **Sonku** and Sami Ayanoğlu, *Vatan ve Namık Kemal / Motherland and Namık Kemal* (1951).

Asılacak Kadın / A Woman to be Hanged (1986), one of the classics of Turkish cinema, adapted from a novel by a woman writer, Pınar Kür, who based it on a true story, shows woman's degradation in a gendered society. Both the book and the film were banned with charges of obscenity. **Müjde Ar** plays Melek (angel), the silent woman who does not act, but is acted upon. Her idyllic life in the village ends by the death of her protective grandfather and the move to Istanbul, where survival determines morality. Given by her stepfather to a modern upper class household as a maid, a common practice of child labour with the routine ritual of purging the lice by shaving the hair and burning the clothes, Melek gradually attracts the heir, an impotent voyeur (İsmet Ay), who procures her to the villagers for free. The arrival of the housekeeper's son on school leave is portentous, but his affection for Melek does not stop him from queuing with the other men although later he decides to save her by killing the landlord, unaware that the deceased had married Melek to avoid the monthly fee to her stepfather. At the court, Melek keeps silent except for her interior monologue, which shows her confusion as to why the young man admits his guilt when everyone is ready to punish her. The testimonies of the witnesses, the village men who raped her, conform to the androcentric ideology: she provoked them, resembling the women 'in those immoral magazines' and she did not resist. All the judges are male except one who seeks the truth, but her power is limited. Reluctantly, she also signs the death penalty.

All the major characters are women except the pervert heir and his character is somewhat underdeveloped. The housekeeper is the prototype of a village woman subservient to the boss for personal gain. She is merciless to Melek but sheds a tear when her tyrannical mistress dies. Her sense of honour and dignity is confined to her house. Meryem's violation in the master's house is only a passing joke at her husband's *rakı* (favorite alcohol of Turkish men) table.

Despite the hyperboles and the burlesque (Melek uttering obscenities in French to revive the memories of the pervert's now dead French mistress), the solid script, the economical narrative that foregrounds key moments, the critical transformations of the characters given in short takes rather than lengthy psychological investigations, the decaying *yalı* on the shore of the Bosphorus as a trope for the end of aristocracy and the inevitable transformation of grandeur to decadence are interwoven skilfully with a masterful *mise en scène*. The eradication of the gentry, through violence, by the emerging class, symbolized by the young and naive son of the housekeeper, is significant. Doyen film critic Atilla Dorsay considers the film 'perhaps the first example of bourgeois cinema in Turkey', suggesting that the theme of the demise of aristocracy evokes Visconti; the secret sins of the bourgeoisie Bunuel, particularly *Tristana* (1970) and *That Obscure Subject of Desire* (1977) and the perverse and fatal aspect of sexuality, Pasolini (Dorsay 1995: 319–20).

Director, Screenwriter: **Başar Sabuncu**; Producer: Ferit Turgut, Kadir Turgut; Production: Uzman Film; Cinematographer: Ertunç Şenkay; Music: Atilla Özdemiroğlu; Cast: **Müjde Ar**, Yalçın Dümer, İsmet Ay, Güler Ökten, Haldun Ergüvenç, Can Kolukısa, Gülsen Tuncer

Asiye Nasıl Kurtulur? / How Can Asiye Be Saved? (1986), focusing on prostitution, garnered interest at its time as a political film that reflects the demoralization of society in the 1980s in a period of high inflation during the transition to a market economy under the liberal policies of Turgut Özal who was prime minister between 1983–9. Based on a play by Vasıf Öngören, considered as one of the best examples of epic theatre in Turkey (staged during the 1960s when Brecht and political theatre were novelty), the film's episodic narrative pauses for comments and songs of the chorus, or the dance numbers, mixed with pantomime and mimicry. Its presentation of a narrator as the mouthpiece of the director, who defines the plot and characters, elicits comments and involves the audience; the interconnectedness of the episodes; the dominance of the mind over the senses; the absence of any possibility to identify with the characters; the open preparations of the decor that serve as distantiation effects and the transformation of Asiye from exploited to exploiter justify **Yılmaz**'s claim that it was the best example of epic cinema (Dönmez-Colin 2006: 145). The remarkable performance of **Müjde Ar** as Asiye is an important contribution to the film's success. (In the 1973 version by Nejat Saydam, a strictly commercial **melodrama**, Asiye was played by **Türkan Şoray**.)

Senniye Gümüşçü, the President of the Association to Combat Prostitution, and several members pay a visit to a brothel to respond to a complaint letter from a prostitute named Asiye about the inadequacy of the advice given in the booklets distributed by the association, but no one by that name exists there. The women propose to stage the absent Asiye's life for their visitors, asking questions to the guests at key moments to suggest solutions to Asiye's inevitable destiny – to become a prostitute just like her mother. When a rich client suddenly dies leaving behind a bag full of money, instead of giving the cash to the man's wife or to the police, she keeps it and continues her profession, exploiting the weaker ones. According to **Atıf Yılmaz**, in a capitalist system where everyone exploits each other and men exploit women, prostitutes cannot be saved unless they do to others what is done to them. In a rather provocative finale, Mrs Senniye and Asiye appear wearing the same clothes, blurring the line between the good and bad woman.

The film breaks **Yeşilçam** clichés about prostitutes by challenging the bourgeois notion of prostitution as a sickness to be cured, rejecting the classic 'fallen woman' notion by depicting the prostitutes as workers and questioning the double standards that morally judge the prostitute but not her customer. Illustrating the accountability of social and economical situations of an androgenic society for the perpetuation of prostitution, it emphasizes the futility of trying to eradicate prostitution as long as the conditions for women remain unchanged.

Director: **Atıf Yılmaz**; Producer: Cengiz Ergun: Production: Odak Film: Cinematographer: Kenan Davutoğlu; Screenwriter: **Barış Pirhasan**: Editor: **Mevlut Koçak**; Music: Sarper Özsan; Sound: Ertan Aktaş; Leading Players: **Müjde Ar**, Ali Poyrazoğlu, Hümeyra, Nuran Oktar, **Yaman Okay**, Güler Ökten, Füsun Demirel, Fatoş Sezer, Yavuzer Çetinkaya

Associations for the professionals of the audio-visual industry, although not up to Western standards, are an important part of the film industry. Some of the prominent guilds and trade unions are: SE-SAM – Professional Union of Film Producers, Importers and Cinema-Owners; FIYAP – Association of Film Producers; SODER – Cinema Actors' Association; FILM YÖN – Film Directors' Union; SINEKAM-

DER – Association of Cameramen, Set Workers, Technical Assistants and Studio Workers; BİROY – Professional Association of Cinema Actors; Istanbul Chamber of Commerce, Film Makers' Professional Committee of Film Producers, Importers, Cinema Owners and Video Distributors; Turkish Cinema Council; TURSAK – Turkish Foundation of Cinema and Audio-visual Culture and SİYAD – Turkish Film Critics Association. A new initiative is Yeni Sinema Hareketi / New Cinema Movement, founded in 2010 by about 30 young directors and producers who are successful in the international arena, with the aim of increasing co-operation, communication and solidarity between young film-makers and supporting the development of various production and distribution models.

Âşık Veysel'in Hayatı aka *Karanlık Dünya / The Life of Veysel, the Minstrel* aka *The Dark World* (1952–3) is the debut film of **Metin Erksan**, scripted by painter/ poet Bedri Rahmi Eyuboğlu with the camera work accomplished in the village of Âşık Veysel (1894–1973), a blind Alevi troubadour, and in Ürgüp. An attempt at an ethnographical rendition of village life through Veysel's story, the original title, *Karanlık Dünya* was changed to *Âşık Veysel'in Hayatı / The Life of Veysel, the Minstrel* by the censorship board, which censored the film for showing the Anatolian wheat fields infertile. It was released a year later with several cuts and insertions of pieces acquired from the American News Centre depicting brand new tractors and the lush fields of Iowa (Öztürk 1990: 2).

Director: **Metin Erksan**; Producer: Nazif Duru; Screenwriter: Bedri Rahmi Eyüboğlu; Cinematographer: Fethi Mürenler; Music: Orhan Barlas; Cast: Ayfer Feray, Ahmet Say, Kemal Bekir, Aşık Veysel Şatıroğlu, Hakkı Ruşen, Aclan Sayılgan, Kemal Öz

Aşk Filmlerinin Unutulmaz Yönetmeni / The Unforgettable Director of Love Movies (1990) is a **meta-film** that addresses the demise of **Yeşilçam** in the atmosphere of 1980s Turkey, parodying the cohorts of the new trend of political cinema. The nostalgia for the past is expressed through **Yeşilçam** films, which have lost their innocence. The life of Haşmet Asilkan (Grandeur Pure-blood) (**Şener Şen**), the director of countless romances of the golden years of **Yeşilçam**, loved by the crowds but ignored or shunned by the intelligentsia, is deteriorating. Divorced without custody over his children – one already supporting the headscarf – he decides to adapt his film-making to the changing times and shoot a film about a rich father and daughter and three terrorists. 'This will be a Haşmet Asılkan Film' will be stated in the generic, a notion **Turgul** is known to find pretentious. 'New lighting like in the commercials, new actors, everything new! The period of directors has started in cinema', Asılkan declares. But the subject is risky for the producers, who prefer films with and about popular singers. Haşmet is reproached for missing the opportunity to shoot sex films when it was the time. His over 100 films went unnoticed; he received no awards; the young are oblivious of his work. All he can gather is a half-blind cameraman (Yavuzer Çetinkaya) and an alcoholic recluse (Aytaç Yörükaslan). The star, **Müjde Ar** refuses to play the lead. Instead of sheep, he can only afford to sacrifice a rooster to consecrate the film as customary. In desperation, he wraps his negatives around his body to set himself on fire, but the match does not work. He keeps trying in tears while the phone rings. They want him to make a love story as before; he is the master. He unwraps the negatives. The turtle of the now dead alcoholic actor finally moves. The camera pans over the photos of the past stars while we hear dialogues from the films.

Allusions to the dark days of the military intervention of 12 September 1980, the house searches and the burning of 'subversive' books are subtly placed in the dialogues: 'You have so many books.' 'This is what is left after they took away the rest.' The open-market policies of Turgut Özal (prime minister and president 1983–93) and the rags-to-riches ambitions that have created an apolitical society that scorns intellectualism without material success, receive a sharp criticism. When Haşmet confesses to the young actor of his infatuation that he is a self-made man who has read thousands of books, always 'jealous of college graduates, diplomat's children, the painters, the writers, the sculptors. I was the son of a shoe-maker', the girl's response is: 'You're outside… It is awful not to succeed and to be outside as well'. The binaries of old and new are presented through Haşmet and the actor Nihat. While Nihat admits he prefers to live in the past, Haşmet stresses the necessity of change, but despite his efforts, he is left on the outside. The neighbour informs him that they will be shooting the Turkish *Rambo* next.

Director, Screenwriter: **Yavuz Turgul**; Producer: **Türker İnanoğlu**; Production: Erler Film; Cinematographer: **Orhan Oğuz**; Music: Atilla Özdemiroğlu; Editor: Mehmet Bozkuş; Art Director: Ziya Ülkenciler; Cast: **Şener Şen**, Pıtırcık Akerman, Aytaç Yörükaslan, Yavuzer Çetinkaya, Arif Akkaya, Şevket Altuğ, **Müjde Ar**, **Nubar Terziyan**, Cevat Kurtuluş, Nedim Doğan, Sami Hazinses

At / The Horse (1982), the second feature of **Ali Özgentürk**, a disciple of **Yılmaz Güney**, exposes oppression, unemployment, corruption, bureaucracy and social inequalities in the aftermath of the 1980 military intervention in the style of Italian neo-realism, evoking Vittorio de Sica's *Umberto D* and particularly, *Ladri di Biciclette / Bicycle Thieves* (1948). Prominent among the migration films of the 1980s, its focus is the new identity of the metropolis, no longer the utopia it was to the earlier migrants with its historical and cultural identity. The city's texture has been transformed, blurring the difference between the 'old Istanbulites' and the newcomers (non-diagetical **arabesque** music as a reminder of the degeneration of society and the erosion of cultural values), but the invasion by the periphery has not diminished the stigmatization of the poor Anatolian peasant, ironically, often by those who were stigmatized once. Even the shantytowns are inaccessible for the new migrants who find shelter in transitory spaces – cafés, roadhouses or construction sites. The aspirations of the migrants have also changed parallel to the socio-economical changes in society. Unlike the family in *Gurbet Kuşları / The Birds of Nostalgia* aka *Migrating Birds* aka *Birds of Exile* (**Halit Refiğ**, 1964), whose motivation is to educate their son for a better future, the peasant father Hüseyin (**Genco Erkal**), with his values adjusted to the open-market economy of the 1980s, equates education with social climbing. Reprimanded by a rich man for denting his Mercedes Benz with his vegetable cart, he does not fantasize that his son will defend him one day against the socially and economically powerful, but rather in the role of the rich man bullying a poor vegetable vendor (Akın 1983: 18). When he proudly asks his son to read the newspaper, he is not bothered with the content. The news item, 'A man who could not provide for his family committed suicide' is a forewarning he fails to comprehend. His issue is not with the system, but rather with his inability to be part of it. He is a genuine representative of the majority that have become apoliticized after three *coup d'états* in two decades. 'Try to save your own ship and don't get involved', his friend advises him. (Along with Cevher in *Endişe / The Anxiety* (**Şerif Gören**, 1974), Hüseyin is a rare protagonist that succeeds in moving the audience from anger to sympathy despite negative qualities.) The military has installed their fascistic ideology on the ordinary citizens; 'if they let me rule the country, I would start by hanging a few', one oppressed man laments (hanging political opponents was not unusual for the junta).

The film deconstructs the Anatolian's dream of Istanbul, paved with gold, with the images of the hopeful migrants arriving at the legendary Haydarpaşa Train Station (on the Eastern coast) encountering the gendarme asking for identity papers. **Özgentürk** returns to the identity issue with the birdman character who repeats: 'Tell me who you are! Neither the pasha, nor the slave! Neither the merchant, nor the tyro! Who? What are you good for? Whose side are you on? If you'll eat the bread, eat it together', warning the itinerant vendors about the futility of their hopes in a system where 'the bread is in the mouth of the lion'. The **Yeşilçam** cliché of the benevolent rich is overturned in the scene when Hüseyin, advised by the cynical cadaver trader, tries to give his son to an elderly childless couple (a tradition that results in the abuse of the poor children inside rich homes) to secure his education. Scrutinizing the boy with an acerbic expression from their high balcony, they ask his price.

The pitiable poet (İlhami Bekir Tez, playing himself) trying to sell his books like an itinerant vendor to the nonchalant boat passengers; Hüseyin desperately running after the municipal truck that has impounded his livelihood; the imprisoned minors; or the ageing blind prostitute servicing teenage boys – more like a mother than a sex-worker – are haunting images. The shooting of an **arabesque** music video that the father and son watch is significant in exposing the absurd inequalities of a system that idolizes the Anatolian **arabesque** singer but oppresses the Anatolian worker, the subject and commercial target of **arabesque**.

A woman with a red bag searches for her 'disappeared' son, her madness a trope for the psychopathological disorders of a post-traumatic society. A character out of a Greek tragedy, a soothsayer or harbinger, she is the mother of all children – victims of unemployment, economic inequalities, corruption, the bad educational system and totalitarian regimes – her red bag symbolizing the bloodshed, but her warning is heedless to those who 'don't see, don't hear', who 'pass in a hurry'. In the last episode, as the exultant cry of the crowds from the stadium shouting 'Goal!' overpowers her, she slowly turns her face to the audience, with an expression that can be perceived as a warning or reprimand.

Symbolizing the hopes of the father and the son, the horse appears in dreams, in the window of a shop, or as a portentous cadaver in the middle of busy traffic (an allusion to the dead horse of Cabbar in **Yılmaz Güney**'s *Umut / The Hope*, 1970). The system swallows its 'sons'. When the father is killed by another oppressed vendor, the son takes the coffin back to the village.

The Horse was completed by **Zeki Ökten** and other friends when **Özgentürk** was arrested by the junta during the post-production stage and kept for several months without trial. The film received several national and international awards, including the Ozu Prize (homage to Yasujiro Ozu) at the Tokyo Film Festival.

Director: **Ali Özgentürk**, Producers: **Ali Özgentürk** and **Kenan Ormanlar** Production: Asya Film, Kentel Film; Screenwriters: **Ali** and Işıl **Özgentürk** Cinematographer: **Kenan Ormanlar** Music: Okay Temiz; Editor: **Yılmaz Atadeniz**; Cast: **Genco Erkal**, Harun Yeşilyurt, Güler Ökten, Ayberk Çölok, **Yaman Okay**, **Macit Koper**, Selçuk Uluergüven

Atadeniz, Yılmaz (b. Istanbul, 1932) Director, screenwriter, producer, editor. Considered the pioneer of **fantasy films**, Yılmaz Atadeniz entered cinema in 1951 through his brother, Orhan Atadeniz (*Tarzan İstanbul'da / Tarzan in Istanbul*, 1952) as a technician, then editor. He made his first film, *Yüz Karası / Shameful* in 1963, becoming popular with *Yedi Kocalı Hürmüz / Hürmüz with Seven Husbands* (1964), establishing his production company in 1967, directing 102 features plus several documentaries and serials. He took his inspiration from foreign cartoons and *photo-romans* and adapted Hollywood serials, comic books and westerns, following the popular trends of the West. The *Kilink* movies (*Kilink İstanbul'da / Killing in Istanbul*, 1967 and *Kilink Uçan Adama Karşı / Killing Against the Flying Man*, 1967), which he shot simultaneously with the same costumes and sets, were inspired by the Italian *photo-roman*, *Killing* (first published in Italy by Ponzoni). *Çirkin Kıral / The Ugly King* (1966), a Mike Hammer plagiarization, gave **Yılmaz Güney** his screen identity during the first part of his career. Popular with the public, derided by the critics, the films of Atadeniz have now become cult classics; they circulate globally on the Internet and through DVD sales. A retrospective was held during the Festival Paris Cinéma 2009 under the title 'The Night of the Turkish Super-Heroes'. He is the president of SESAM (Association of Turkish Producers).

Ataman, Kutluğ (b. Istanbul, 1961) Director, screenwriter, producer. Social, political and sexual identity is the focus of Kutluğ Ataman's work, an engaged transnational multimedia artist and gay activist who crosses the borders between past and present and reality and fiction, but also cinema and the museum. Having experienced persecution and imprisonment after the 1980 military intervention, Ataman left Turkey for a period, studying theatre and cinema in the University of California in Los Angeles (UCLA). His first feature, *Karanlık Sular / The Serpent's Tale* (1994) was an experimental mystery thriller. His second, *Lola ve Bilidikid / Lola und Bilidikid / Lola and Bilidikid* (1998), a melange of **melodrama** and tragi-comedy, shot in Berlin, exposed the taboo of sexual identity and the oppression of the freedom of choice in patriarchal societies through parallel stories of doubly marginalized transvestites from the Turkish community,

Figure 13 Lola ve Bilidikid / Lola und Bilidikid / Lola and Bilidikid (Kutluğ Ataman, 1998) (Courtesy of Kutluğ Ataman)

homophobia and the coming of age of a 16-year-old youth of Turkish origin. *2 Genç Kız / 2 Girls* (2005), his third feature, focused on the choices of survival for young urban girls from different backgrounds – Handan, from uptown, the product of shopping malls and marketing and Behiye, from the outskirts, poor, angry and exploited. The images of free-spirited young women from a Muslim country surprised some foreigner viewers. But for Ataman there are as many centres as there are individuals (Dönmez-Colin 2012). Since 1997, Ataman has been exploring the boundaries between reality and fiction, through the medium of documentary as well as with his video installations with a focus on the construction of personal identities through stories that individuals narrate about themselves. In *Women Who Wear Wigs* (1997), composed of four videos, projected concurrently, four Turkish women who wear wigs (a political activist, a television personality with breast cancer, an anonymous Muslim student and a transsexual prostitute) justify their reasons. *Never My Soul!* (2001) (the title, referring to a **Yeşilçam** spoof, 'You can have my body, but never my soul!' is uttered by the virginal heroine) consists of two films shot and inter-cut to create one piece, which is

Figure 14 2 Genç Kız / 2 Girls (Kutluğ Ataman, 2005) (Courtesy of Kutluğ Ataman)

deliberately incoherent as a single narrative, what Ataman calls a 'parallax view' – a formal expression of the parallel situation of the protagonist as a transvestite.

Ataman's works have been exhibited worldwide and have won numerous prestigious prizes including the Carnegie Prize (2004) for his video installation *Kuba* about an alternative shantytown neighbourhood in Istanbul. Whereas some of his works such as *Turkish Delight* draw attention to the western Orientalist gaze and the prevailing cultural prejudice, other works such as *Testimony* touch upon political controversies including the Armenian genocide.

Ateşten Gömlek / The Shirt of Fire aka ***The Ordeal*** aka ***The Shirt of Flame*** (1923) based on a novel by Halide Edip Adıvar, made the year of the establishment of the Turkish Republic and screened in occupied Istanbul on 23 April 1923, the third anniversary of the founding of the Turkish Grand National Assembly, is considered as the first national film and the first film to deal with the War of Independence. Commensurate with the subject matter, all roles, including women's, were played by Turkish Muslims, which is another first for Turkish cinema.

Director, Screenwriter: **Muhsin Ertuğrul**: Producers: Kemal Seden, Şakir Seden; Production: Kemal Film; Cinematographer: Cezmi Ar; Cast: **Muhsin Ertuğrul**, Bedia Muvahhit, Neyyire Neyir (Ertuğrul), Behzat Butak, Refik Kemal Arduman, Vasfi Rıza Zobu

Auf Der Anderen Seite / The Edge of Heaven / Yaşamın Kıyısında (2007) problematizes the multiple, fragmented and fluid nature of identity. It is constructed through difference, relation to the Other, its *constitutive outside* (Derrida 1981; Laclau 1990; Butler 1993 in Hall 1996), based on excluding something and establishing a powerful hierarchy between the two poles (man/woman, etc.), every identity having at its 'margin', an excess and naming as its necessary that which it 'lacks' (Hall 1996). Lotte (Patrycia Ziolkowska), a blonde German student with a comfortable home in Bremen where etiquette forbids foul language, has just returned from soul searching in India. She meets Turkish activist Ayten (Nurgül Yeşilçay), a homeless brunette from the troubled East of political upheavals and human rights violations and merges into her identity. (The scene in an Istanbul apartment where she knocks on the door of a neighbour for the key to the terrace to pick up Ayten's gun is identical to an earlier scene with Ayten.) Lotte's mother Susanne (Hanna Schygulla), a bourgeois Bremen matron in her dead daughter's bed in Istanbul merges with her daughter through her diary as she discovers Lotte's sentiments about her mother's youth as a hippy in India. The aloof Nejat (Baki Davrak), the assimilated professor of German literature specialized in Goethe, who speaks broken Turkish and is critical of his guest-worker father Ali's (**Tuncel Kurtiz**) delight in physical pleasures, having climbed the social scale himself, makes the long journey to his father's natal village, waiting with humility on the edge of the beach for his return from the sea (to merge with the Other) as the credits roll.

The film deconstructs and reconstructs father/son and mother/daughter relationships with a strong reliance on chance happenings that transform lives, death appearing as the ultimate constant. **Akın**'s reliance on the preordained resonates Kryzsztof Kieślowski's *Trzy kolory: Niebieski, Bialy, Czerwony / Three Colours: Blue, White and Red* (1993–4) although his search for spiritual redemption is not divine. It rather resembles *Babel* (2006), the last of Alejandro González Iñárritu's *Death* trilogy, another transnational work that is built on a chronologically decentred narrative that relies on coincidences, death by a single shot appearing as a shared motif.

The film is divided into three chapters: 'Yeter's Death', 'Lotte's Death' and 'The Edge of Heaven'; and book-ended with a prologue and an epilogue (using the same sequence except the same song is sung by a male singer in the first and a female in the second) that show Nejat travelling from Istanbul to the Black Sea. Social and political possibilities of **melodrama** are explored, echoing the films of Rainer Werner Fassbinder (casting Fassbinder's fetish actor, Hanna Schygulla in a role counterpoising her 1970s image is like a seditious homage), although here the subversive angle of Fassbinder is replaced with overcharged emotion. The original German title and the French version both mean 'on the other side', whereas the

Figure 15 Auf der Anderen Seite / The Edge of Heaven / Yaşamın Kıyısında (Fatih Akın, 2007) (Courtesy of International Istanbul Film Festival)

Turkish title means 'on the edge of life'. Not only the characters but also the camera are often positioned on the edge, favouring through-the-glass shots or shots framed by windows or doors, underscoring the liminality of displaced characters in alien situations. Two deaths central to the narrative happen in foreign lands.

Production notes state that the relationship between Turkey and the European Union resembles a difficult love story and that the encounters between Ayten and Lotte; Ayten and Susanne; Nejat, Ali and Yeter (Nursel Köse), the prostitute Ali keeps/kills, could be parables for this unique bilateral relationship (Anonymous 2006: 32). However the introduction of large number of issues (state oppression, Turkish judiciary system, human rights, police brutality, Kurdish conflict, Islamist fundamentalism, same-sex love, generation gap, Europe's flower children becoming conservative matrons, German institutions excelling in efficiency but lacking in humanity), the exceedingly schematic design and characters that lack plausible justification of their motivations (such as Nejat's choice to leave his secure academic job to settle in Turkey) weaken the script. Ziolkowska's performance is outstanding, but Schygulla and Davrak are somewhat distant to the characters they represent. Yeşilçay is not plausible as a student activist although she shows her stamina in certain scenes such as the confrontation in Suzanne's kitchen (the intruding alien) when she answers her nonchalant comment, 'maybe things will be better when Turkey joins the EU' with a spontaneous, 'Fuck the European Union, yaa!' (voicing the sentiments of many Turkish citizens with the stalling of the negotiations).

Hamburg-born **Akın**'s films customarily begin in Germany and end in Turkey and the latter, not a *heimat*, but a third space constructed by characters unsettled in their present space, is often presented through a foreign gaze – quixotic backstreets of downtown Beyoğlu, the adjacent Cihangir district, inhabited by artists and film-makers and the Bosphorus – more fantasy than reality. What is important is the message of the film reminding the viewer of the interconnectedness of lives and the political optimism (albeit naive) that redemption and forgiveness can bring peace to the world. Spoken in three languages, German, Turkish and English, the film's inter-cultural and border-free stance is underlined with tongue-in-cheek humour in one of the earlier scenes during Ali's first visit to the prostitute, Yeter. 'Do you do French?' he asks her. She answers, 'French, Italian, Greek. I'll do it international for you'.

Director, Screenwriter: **Fatih Akın**; Producers: **Fatih Akın**, Klaus Maeck, Andreas Thiel, Jeanette Würl; Production: Corazón International, Anka Film, Dorje Film, NDR; Cinematographer: Rainer Klausmann; Editor: Andrew Bird; Music: Shantel; Cast: Nurgül Yeşilçay, Baki Davrak, **Tuncel Kurtiz**, Hanna Schygulla, Patrycia Ziolkowska, Nursel Köse

Aydın, Ali (b. Istanbul, 1981) Director, screenwriter. Recipient of the prestigious Lion of the Future award at the Venice Film Festival 2012 with his first feature, *Küf / Mold* (2012), Ali Aydın graduated in art management from the Yıldız Technical University and worked as assistant director in features and television series. Foregrounding a middle-aged railroad watchman's perseverance for news of his son who 'disappeared' 18 years earlier, the film underscores state oppression through an apolitical character (echoing the mother in **Tayfun Pirselimoğlu**'s *Hiçbiryerde / Innowhereland*, 2001, the average citizen who prefers not to see even when the tragedy hits home). The film carries the insignias of Turkish art house cinema of the last decade – minimal dialogue, long takes, fixed camera shots, beautifully lensed languid Anatolian landscape and Dostoevskian motifs (epilepsy, guilt). The script, however, wavers between the troubled relationship

Figure 16 Küf / Mold (Ali Aydın, 2012) (Courtesy of International Istanbul Film Festival)

of the protagonist with a younger colleague (a hyperactive, slimy and violent trouble-maker alluding to a lost generation) and a blasé police chief with a vein of humanity, developing the dramatic possibilities of neither. Nonetheless, the construction of charged scenes like the concluding episode that transmits to the viewer the heavy load of the protagonist in his journey through impersonal corridors of hospitals and morgues, returning home with the remains of his son in a wooden box, evidence a promising young talent.

Ayna / Der Spiegel / The Mirror (1984), shot in Greece, as a co-production between Germany and Britain during **Erden Kıral**'s years of self-exile in Germany, is based on **Osman Şahin**'s psychological drama, *Beyaz Öküz / The White Ox* about women and their repressed desires in patriarchal societies. The opening shots – the storm, the rain and the long silences – set the tone of a dark story of desire and death. The precarious life of a peasant couple is disturbed when the omnipotent landlord's whimsical brother (Hikmet Çelik) tries to seduce beautiful Zelihan (**Nur Sürer**) by throwing a flower into her pail. She throws the flower out with the water as if to cleanse her shame, but her face reflected in the mirror cannot hide the passion stirred. Her husband Necmettin (Suavi Eren) kills the man to restore his honour and they bury the corpse inside their home. Zelihan identifies the family ox with the dead man and begins to caress the animal.

Despite the theatricality of the dream sequences and the cow slaughter episode, the poetic drama created through the outstanding photography and the minimalist style in exposing the position of women as nonentities in a feudal system that devours the less advantaged brought the film several national and international awards.

Director, Screenwriter: **Erden Kıral**; Producer: Joachim von Vietinghoff; Production: Von Vietinghoff Fimproduktion, Zwites Deutsches Fernsehen (ZDF), Channel Four; Cinematographer: **Kenan Ormanlar**; Editor: Agape Dorstewitz; Sound: Luc Yersin; Music: Bryanmor Jones; Art Director: Nikos Perakis; Costume Designer: Heidrun Brandt; Cast: **Nur Sürer**, Suavi Eren, Hikmet Çelik, Vassilis Tsanglos, Vera Delud, Nikos Skiadis

Aysel, Bataklı Damın Kızı / The Girl From the Marshes aka *Aysel, the Girl From the Swampy Roof* (1934–5), a **melodrama** with overt influences of Soviet cinema is considered as the first **rural film**. An adaptation from Selma Lagerlöf's novella, *Tösen från Stormyrtorpet* (1908) and Swedish director Victor Sjöström's eponymous film of 1917, the film set the precedence for rape, pregnancy and abandonment stories. An 18-year-old maid, Aysel is raped by the feudal landlord and she delivers a child. As a young woman with sound judgement, she files a paternity suit and demands alimony, but withdraws her claim to save the father of her child from the embarrassment of lying at court. Despite its pretentious approach to rural life, the film was very popular, which could be attributed, along with **Ertuğrul**'s meticulous attempt at realism, the mastery in framing, lighting and imaging, to the employment of skilful voyeurism. The 'fountain eroticism', depiction of young women discussing men freely or flirting with them while fetching water and the ritual of the woman washing the feet of the man coming from the field soon became staple motifs, although the latter has remained controversial as a possible interpretation of the slave status of women (Dönmez-Colin 2004: 32). The most remarkable aspect of the film is the performance of **Cahide Sonku**, a former theatre actress. The film launched **Sonku** as the first star of Turkish cinema. The scarf she wore as Aysel is said to have started a folkloric fashion. A remake was made in 1969 by Zafer Davutoğlu from a script of **Osman F. Seden**.

Director: **Muhsin Ertuğrul**; Producer: **Muhsin Ertuğrul**, Kâni İpekçi, **İhsan İpekçi**, Production; İpek Film; Screenwriter: Nazım Hikmet Ran (under the pen-name of Mümtaz Osman); Cinematographers: Cezmi Ar and Remzi Ar; Music: Cemal Reşit Rey; Decor: Nicola Peroff; Cast: **Cahide Sonku, Talat Artemel**, Feriha Tevfik Negüz, Sait Köknar, Mahmut Morali, Behzat Butak, İ. Galip Arcan, Sami Ayanoğlu, Hazım Körmükçü

B

Baba / The Father (1971), a revenge **melodrama** foregrounding the plight of the economically disadvantaged during the process of modernization, focuses on a family man who serves a long prison sentence for a crime committed by a wealthy man's son. During his incarceration, the culprit seduces his wife; initiates his son to the mafia and pushes his daughter to prostitution. Vowing to take revenge, he is shot by his son who does not recognize him.

Iron bars, seagulls flying over waves, the sounds of steamboats, a crying baby, a lullaby-singing granny, two schoolchildren and the sad face of a poor man (**Güney**) dominate the preliminary images. In a tight frame that traverses the glass, the discreet camera observes a family eating on the floor, the signature angle–reverse-angle shots of **Yılmaz** replacing dialogue. Cemal Akyol (the family name meaning pure path), preparing for the medical examination required from candidate immigrants to Germany, observes his face and its reflection in the mirror, projected simultaneously as if to separate the character from his self-reflection. The desperate underdeveloped are ready to change their identity, even to shave their moustache, the insignia of Turkish masculinity that reversely stigmatizes them as a visible 'other'. Coupled with the image of adult men in a row with their mouths open for inspection by the German medical authority, these powerful tropes not only draw attention to Turkey's aspirations to join the European Union, but also serve as precursors of the contemporary debates of 'integration' or 'assimilation'.

The problematic of change in the new order is approached from the aspect of architecture through the transformation of the traditional *yalı*, a family mansion on the shore of the Bosphorus where Cemal had served a protective patriarch, to a modern dwelling during ten years of incarceration. The loss of moral values in the process is underscored through the social positions of Cemal's children: a son proud to serve the mafia and a daughter in the brothel. Unaware that the customer is her father, she tells her story: 'I used to have a nose like you but got it fixed. I've lost my nose and my identity here'. The intimacy, the tempo and the charged moments that pass between them recall a similar episode in Wim Wenders' *Paris, Texas* (1984).

The Father coalesces the two filmic personæ of **Güney**, the socially and politically committed artist and the populist man of cinema. The focus on the

Figure 17 Baba / The Father (Yılmaz Güney, 1971) (Courtesy of International Istanbul Film Festival)

socio-economic aspects of the systems of prison and prostitution and the composition of the victim/villain confrontation are his insignia as an engagé artist although the emotional aspect of the personal tragedy is what builds the audience identification. The second part, which resonates **Güney**'s earlier 'ugly king' period of action/adventure **genre** with a focus on revenge with violence, was dictated by his producer, İrfan Ünal, according to **Güney**. A compromise was made to release the film in the uptown cinemas of Beyoğlu (Coş and Ayça 1975a: 3–17).

The Father won the Best Film and Best Actor awards at the Adana Golden Boll Film Festival (1974) while **Güney** was in prison. With pressure from the mayor, the jury changed their decision and gave the Best Film award to **Yılmaz Duru**'s *Kara Doğan / Black Falcon* (1972) and Best Actor award to **Cüneyt Arkın**.

Director and Screenwriter: **Yılmaz Güney**; Producer: İrfan Ünal; Production: Akün Film, Cinematographer: Gani Turanlı; Editor: **Şerif Gören**; Music: Metin Bükey, Yalçın Tura; Sound: Necip Sarıcıoğlu; Cast: **Yılmaz Güney**, Müşerref Tezcan, **Aytaç Arman**, Ferudun Çölgeçen, Nedred Güvenç, Nimet Tezel, Mehmet Büyükgüngör, Yeşim Tan

Babamın Sesi / Dengê Bavê Min / The Voice of My Father (2012), shot in a pseudo-documentary style, interrogates modes of preserving memory – from photographs and diaries to film footages. The film is based on a true story and co-director **Zeynel Doğan** (as Mehmet) and his mother as Basê play themselves. Ageing Basê lives alone in Elbistan in southern Turkey, waiting for her older son, Hasan who has joined the guerrillas to come and settle. She attributes the silent calls she receives to Hasan. When her younger son Mehmet who lives in Diyarbakır comes across an audiotape of his mother and himself as a boy, meant for his father abroad, he visits his mother to find the tapes from his father and to convince her to come and live in the city. Basê is focused only on Hasan, but Mehmet tries to hang around the house to learn more about the past. The film breaks the conventional narrative, merging the past with the present through the voices on the tapes, particularly that of the father Mustafa that brings another aspect to the scattered Kurdish nation, that of the refugee or exile, at the same time forcing the collective memory to remember events like the massacre of the Alevi population in Maraş (1978). In that sense the empty rooms of the house serve as a trope for the past long buried.

Director: **Orhan Eskiköy**, **Zeynel Doğan**; Producer: Özgür Doğan; Production: Perişan Film; Screenwriter: **Orhan Eskiköy**; Cinematographer: Emre Erkmen; Editor: **Orhan Eskiköy**, Çiçek Kahraman; Art Director: Yunus Emre Yurtseven, Meral Efe; Cast: Asiye Doğan, **Zeynel Doğan**, Gülizar Doğan

Bal / Honey (2010), the third and final segment of the *Yusuf Trilogy*, is a poetic dialogue with nature with a focus on tempo-spatiality and memory. Yusuf, who is adult in ***Yumurta / Egg*** (2007) and adolescent in ***Süt / Milk*** (2008), is a sensitive child of school age who lives in a secluded area in the Anzer valley in the eastern Black Sea region, famous for its honey with therapeutic powers. He idolizes his beekeeper father, Yakub, their strong bond often excluding the mother. When the father does not return from one of his trips to the interior, the son and the mother, both cognizant of his death, hide the tragedy from each other. At the end, the boy spends a night in the forest under a giant tree similar to the one adult Yusuf sleeps under in *Egg* after the funeral of his mother, becoming one with nature, transcending the material world through the experience of life and death and this is where the seeds of Yusuf as a poet are sown.

Yusuf's world is one of magic encompassing the mysterious forest, the foggy mountains, the swaying moon in the water pail, within reach yet elusive, and the enigmatic rites and rituals at the grandmother's. His beekeeper father is the spiritual element in his life, who initiates him to the first step of social acceptance by teaching him to read. (The first word uttered in the film is 'Read!' spoken by the diagetically absent father.) He connects him with nature during their trips to the forest with the donkey and the hawk and listens to his dreams, whereas his mother is the worldly element, who wants Yusuf to drink his milk and worries about his future. Together they represent the existential duality of his nature.

The story carries religious resonances: Yusuf, as the Islamic version of Prophet Joseph and Yakub as the Prophet Jacob (Book of Genesis). Yusuf's dreams, which

Figure 18 Bal / Honey (Semih Kaplanoğlu, 2010) (Courtesy of Semih Kaplanoğlu)

he only shares with his father, are as significant as the dreams of Prophet Joseph, who was ordained by god to interpret dreams. Through his dreams, Yusuf, who, as we already know from the earlier two films, will become a poet, is also able to foreshadow (the image of the father suspended in mid-air in the forest in the opening episode) and hence, refract the binaries of cause/effect and dream/reality. A poor performer in school, he reads the *hadiths* (sayings ascribed to Prophet Mohammed) to his father. At his grandmother's on the Night of Mir'aj (Ascension), he hears the story of Prophet Mohammad, who, with Gabriel travelled from Kaaba in Mecca to Aqsa mosque in Jerusalem on a night journey and climbed the Mir'aj (the ladder) to the seven skies, visiting different levels of heaven and hell and meeting angels and prophets including Abraham, Moses and Jesus and finally Allah. Reaching the sky, he was offered wine, milk and honey, of which he chose milk, the title of the previous film in the trilogy. Milk plays an important role in this film, as a sign of father–son conspiracy when the father drinks the milk Yusuf refuses and to display Yusuf's mischievous nature when he puts a piece of hair to his glass (which links with his switching of notebooks with a friend when the teacher inspects the homework) and finally indicating his feelings for his grieving mother when he swallows the whole glass. Yusuf's attempt to catch the reflection of the moon in a pail and immersing his face in the water on the Night of the Mir'aj is significant. The Mir'aj is celebrated according to the lunar calendar – the sighting of the Rajab moon – but the moon also links with the second dream of Prophet Joseph (Qur'an, sur'ah 12 –Yusuf – ayah 4), the sun as the father and the moon as the mother, hence prevising the strong bond he will develop with his mother. In the last episode, Yusuf uniting in spirit with his dead father Yakup in the darkness of the forest alludes to Prophet Joseph's experience in the well, its darkness leading to an actual raising of spiritual status and illuminating Joseph with inspiration and in the case of Yusuf, preparing the formation of a poet. The leitmotif of the well appears regularly in *Egg*.

The eco-sensitive script of *Honey* is like an experiment in 'eco-poetics', which Bate, drawing on Heideggerian philosophy of 'dwelling' (Heidegger 1962, 1971) defines as 'poems as imaginary parks to breathe non-toxic air' (Bate 2000: 64). It focuses on issues like the aesthetic representation of nature and art as mediated by human-centric values, culture and landscape, particularly in poetry. However, nature here is in a complex dialogue with the human inhabitants and the relationship between the two is not always harmonious. The ecological concern, the dying of the Anzer honey culture and the difficulties of obtaining it leading to Yakub's death, integrate romanticism with realistic elements. Following a Heideggerian line of thought, one may establish poetry as the primary **genre** which embodies in its form the ecstasies and agonies of nature. (Adult Yusuf publishes a poetry book entitled *Bal / Honey*, which connects him with his father.)

Director and Producer: **Semih Kaplanoğlu**; Production: Kaplanfilm, Heimatfilm, ZDF/ Arte; Screenwriters: **Semih Kaplanoğlu** and Orçun Köksal; Cinematographer: Barış Özbiçer; Editors: Ayhan Ergürsel, **Semih Kaplanoğlu**, Suzan Hande Güneri; Art Director: Naz Erayda; Sound: Matthias Haeb; Cast: Bora Altaş, Erdal Beşikçioğlu, Tülin Özen

Başaran, Tunç (b. Istanbul, 1938) Director, screenwriter, producer, actor, editor. One of the prominent film-makers of Turkish cinema, Tunç Başaran left his university studies in literature to script dialogues for **Memduh Ün** and worked as assistant to **Lütfi Ö. Akad**, **Halit Refiğ**, **Atıf Yılmaz** and **Ertem Göreç** as well as **Ün**. For his first feature *Hayat Kavgası / Survival* (1964), he collaborated with the author and screenwriter, Orhan Kemal. Before switching to the advertisement sector in 1972, he directed about 40 commercial films, among which *Murtaza* (1965), an adaptation from Kemal's eponymous novel of 1952, foregrounding the tragic dimensions of loyalty to discipline, acted with conviction by **Müşfik Kenter**, drew attention. He returned to cinema in 1986 with an existential angst film *Biri ve Diğerleri / One and the Others* that reflected the trend of the times for personal films. *Uçurtmayı Vurmasınlar / Don't Let Them Shoot the Kite* (1989), a prison story told from a child's point of view, had national and international success and has become one of the classics of Turkish cinema. *Piano Piano Bacaksız / Piano Piano Kid* (1991), also told from the point of view of a child, was not very successful. *Uzun İnce Bir Yol / A Long, Narrow Road* (1993), an experiment in the **fantasy-horror genre** foregrounding the encounters of a man and his foreign wife with the angel of death on their way home from Europe, lacked the emotional intensity of the previous two films. *Sen de Gitme Triandafilis / Please Don't Go* (1996), a sentimental story about the passion of the mentally retarded daughter of an affluent Greek family for a French soldier, was set in Antakya in the 1930s when the Turks, the Arabs, the Greeks, the Jews and the Armenians lived together. Similar to *One and the Others* and *The Kite*, the film's main motif was confinement and entrapment. *Kaçıklık Diploması / Graduate of Insanity* (1998), an offbeat film about manic depression, included references to Kemal Atatürk. *Abuzer Kadayıf / Abuzer Baklava* (2000), a black **comedy** on the degeneration of Turkish society featuring a protagonist inspired by the arabesque singer İbrahim Tatlıses, was the most uninspiring film of Başaran. He completed *Sinema Bir Mucizedir / Cinema is a Miracle* (2005) about provincial life, children and cinema, started by his master **Memduh Ün**. *Vesaire Vesaire / Etc Etc* (2008) was a failure lacking a sound script and credible acting despite impressive cinematography. Başaran has also made films for television and has contributed to television series.

Başer, Tevfik (b. Çankırı, 1951) Director, screenwriter, producer. Known for his debut feature, ***40 Quadratmeter Deutschland / Forty Square metres of Germany*** (1986), in the 1970s, Başer was trained in London as a photographer and graphic designer. He settled in Germany in 1980 to study at the Academy of Fine Arts in Hamburg and began to work as cameraman, director, screenwriter and producer. Following the international success of his first feature, he concentrated on the lives of the Turkish 'guest workers' caught between the relatively favourable possibilities of assimilation to the host society and loyalty to their own values. His second film, *Abschied vom Falschen Paradies / Farewell to False Paradise / Yanlış Cennete Elveda* (1988) was about a Turkish woman imprisoned for killing her abusive husband. Finding the freedom denied to her all her life, paradoxically within the walls of the prison, only the news of her release and deportation to Turkey to face the impending death sentence would lead her to desperation. The film underscores the self-development of the protagonist in a German prison – western garments replacing traditional clothes, German lessons from compassionate inmates and the possibility of a romance – rather than the actual mariticide, and schematizes the binaries of the matriarchal prison environment and the patriarchal tyranny in her life outside. It was criticized for its alleged endorsement of assimilation of western values as an asset for integration into the German society and for liberation, a point of view favoured by German politics but not necessarily by the Turkish diaspora. Both films have raised concerns in terms of underpinning negative images and prejudices and hence provoking othering of the minorities in the West and although a work of art should stand on its own, Başer found it difficult to raise funds in Germany when he tried to ensue other subjects. *Lebewohl, Fremde / Farewell, Stranger* (1991), about a Turkish poet seeking asylum and a woman who shares his pain despite the absence of a common language, did not receive much attention despite the relevance of the subject, the subtle camera work and the lingering images of nature that skilfully reflect the mind-frame of the stranger who waits in uncertainty. Başer is on the faculty of the Kadir Has University in Istanbul.

Batıbeki, Atıf Yılmaz (Atıf Yılmaz) (b. Mersin, 1926 – d. Istanbul, 2006) Director, screenwriter, producer. Born to a middle class bureaucrat family, Atıf Yılmaz showed interest in cinema from a very early age. Failing to enter the fine arts, he studied law but followed fine arts classes clandestinely until caught. He reviewed films, participated in exhibitions as part of the Attic Painters, designed posters, wrote scripts and worked as assistant director before making his first feature, *Kanlı Feryat / The Bloody Cry* (1951), a **melodrama**. *Gelinin Muradı / The Dream of the Bride* (1957) is considered as his first non-commercial feature.

Yılmaz's systematic focus on women has gained him the reputation of 'the director of women's films'. A chronological chart of his work would trace Turkish cinema's evolution regarding women's issues. In the 1960s and 1970s, the resolution of social or economical problems was regarded as a panacea for solving the problems of women: *Ah Güzel Istanbul / Oh, Beautiful Istanbul* (1966), *Kuma / The Second Wife* (1974) and ***Selvi Boylum Al Yazmalım / The Girl With the Red Scarf*** (1977) are based on this premise. In the 1980s, with the delayed arrival of feminism, women's issues began to be perceived as having intrinsic significance independent of other elements: ***Mine*** (1983), *Bir Yudum Sevgi / A Taste Of Love* aka *A Sip of Love* (1984), *Dul Bir Kadın / A Widow* (1985), ***Asiye Nasıl Kurtulur? / How Can Asiye Be Saved?*** (1986) and ***Adı Vasfiye / Her Name is Vasfiye*** (1986) are manifestations of this trend. The independent woman motif surfaced during the transition to open-market economy as women began to join the workforce: *Aaahh Belinda / Oh, Belinda* (1986) presented a spoiled career woman working for a shampoo commercial who suddenly transforms into a bank employee running home after work to perform homemaker duties. Despite their dissimilar backgrounds, both women are in a constant struggle for self-assertion in a machistic society. *Hayallerim, Aşkım ve Sen / My Dreams, My Love and You* (1987), a critique of the studio and star system with **Türkan Şoray** playing herself, chronicled three stages in the life of a **Yeşilçam** star: as a character in **melodramas**, as a sex object and as a reborn hero. Beginning with the 1990s, sexual choices and marginality surfaced when predominantly urban women attempted to rebel against dogmatic traditions and religion: *Düş Gezginleri / Walking After Midnight* (1992) on lesbianism and *Gece, Melek ve Bizim Çocuklar / The Night, the Angel and Our Gang* (1994) about transvestites and male prostitutes, are the best examples of this period. His last film, *Eğreti Gelin / The Borrowed Bride* (2005) about an Ottoman tradition of hiring professional women to prepare boys for marriage, celebrated free love despite its tragic story.

In a career spanning over 50 years and involving more than 100 films, Yılmaz gave Turkish cinema landmark films that have influenced generations, such as *Adak / The Sacrifice* (1979) and ***Selvi Boylum, Al Yazmalım / The Girl With the Red Scarf*** (1977). He was the master of many including **Yılmaz Güney**; his films received accolades at film festivals although critics have disparaged his attention to the trends of the moment – feminism, lesbianism, homosexuality – pointing at commercially motivated patterns (at least one love-making scene in each film). Yılmaz considered cinema an art for the masses, made according to the demands of the viewers.

At the time of his death, Atıf Yılmaz was working on a new film, *Ada / The Island.* Some of his other noteworthy films are *Bir Şöförün Gizli Defteri / The Secret Diary of a Driver* (1958); *Alageyik / The Hind* (1959); *Suçlu / The Guilty* (1960); *Erkek Ali / Ali, the Man* and *Keşanlı Ali Destanı / The Legend of Ali*

Figure 19 Gece, Melek ve Bizim Çocuklar / The Night, the Angel and Our Gang (Atıf Yılmaz, 1994) (Courtesy of International Istanbul Film Festival)

Figure 20 Eğreti Gelin / The Borrowed Bride (Atıf Yılmaz, 2005) (Courtesy of International Istanbul Film Festival)

Figure 21 Atıf Yılmaz with the portrait of star, Türkan Şoray, made by Gülsün Karamustafa (Istanbul 2003) (Photo: Gönül Dönmez-Colin)

from Keşan (1964); *Yedi Kocalı Hürmüz / Hürmüz with Seven Husbands* (1971); *Dağınık Yatak / Untidy Bed* (1985); *Kadının Adı Yok / The Woman Has No Name* (1987); *Dul Bir Kadın / A Widow*; *Arkadaşım Şeytan / My Friend, The Devil* (1988); *Berdel / Bride Barter* (1990); *Bekle Dedim Gölgeye / Distant Shadows* (1991); *Nihavent Mucize / Miracle Ma Non Troppo* (1997); and *Eylül Fırtınası / After the Fall* (1999). He collected some of his memoirs and thoughts on cinema in *Söylemek Güzeldir / It is Good To Tell.*

Bedrana (1974) is an indictment of the feudalist system, the archaic customs and traditions and the underdevelopment through a legendary love story between the shepherd Davut (**Aytaç Arman**) and the beautiful Bedrana (**Perihan Savaş**). Davut and Bedrana elope and take shelter with the landlord (Tuncer Necmioğlu), whose shepherd Hamza (İhsan Yüce) kidnaps Bedrana while Davut is dispatched on a smuggling job. Wounded while resisting rape, Bedrana is taken to hospital. Unable to 'cleanse his honour' himself, Davut pleads with the doctor not to save her despite his belief in her innocence. According to customs, she is considered 'soiled'. When she is cured, he tries to convince her to commit suicide. Under pressure, Bedrana hangs herself. Film critic Atilla Dorsay questions the meaning of love within the context of the characters in the film, underlining the economic and moral dimension. 'Davut does not kill Bedrana himself, not because he is incapable of killing the one he loves, but because he knows the punishment for such a crime' (Dorsay 1989: 83).

The film has retained its contemporaneity considering the immediacy of crimes of honour even decades later and the increase in the films about honour killings. Successful at the box-office and praised by the critics as a 'triumph of realism', the film, nonetheless, received some criticism regarding the ending that shows the husband firing at the corpse (as a trope for firing at the customs, traditions and the society) conflicting with the overall message.

Despite **censorship**, *Bedrana* won numerous awards at film festivals including Cidalc at the Karlovy Vary Film Festival.

Director, Producer: **Süreyya Duru**; Production: Murat Film; Screenwriters: İhsan Yüce and **Vedat Türkali** based on two stories, *Bedrana* and *Hamus* by Bekir Yıldız; Cinematographer: Ali Uğur; Music: Mevlut Canaydın; Cast: **Perihan Savaş**, **Aytaç Arman**, İhsan Yüce, Tuncer Necmioğlu, Talat Özbak, Sırrı Elitaş

Bereketli Topraklar Üzerinde / On Fertile Lands (1979) is based on Orhan Kemal's eponymous **social realist** novel (1954) about the plight of poor peasants in the late 1940s in post-World War II Turkey that has experienced neither the industrial revolution nor the land reforms. Supporting the Marxist dialectic, the film focuses on Ali (**Yaman Okay**), Yusuf and Hasan (echoing Tom, Jim and Muley of *Grapes of Wrath*, Ford, 1940 that had left a strong impression on Kıral), three friends who wish to improve their social and economic status by working in the city (which they desire and fear), but find themselves defenceless against hunger, oppression, exploitation and unemployment.

Just like *Kanal / The Channel* (1977), the opening sequences, using head-on camera angles, show desperate seasonal labourers, men with a few teeth and impoverished children, the invisible people, staring directly at the camera evoking the sharecropper images of Walker Evans (1903–75) that expose the rural poverty in South Alabama during the Great Depression (Agee and Evans, 1939). The camera pans over the tattered tents, but discreetly stays outside as the narrator informs us that Çukurova's land is fertile and its people are patient. Even if they die, there is always the other world. One must always compare with the one below and not the one above and be grateful, as the prophets have said. The same comments and the accompanying images book-end the film. In between is the naked truth, presented like an objective reportage without losing the literary complexity and the poetic beauty of Kemal's text. Aware of the improbability of narrating so much poverty with traditional forms and feeling the agony of the intruder, **Kıral** searches for a new film language that would raise consciousness while preserving the dignity of the workers, denied to them by the system. The scene of the dying man helped to the toilet by a criminal, handled so discreetly not to multiply the shame, is one of the moments to be remembered along with the scene of helpless Yusuf burying his face in the 'fertile' mud of Çukurova when his friend Ali bleeds to death.

Kıral's artistic merits carry the film beyond political treatise by creating three-dimensional and complex characters with basic needs – food, sleep, sex and even love. Human life is reduced to physical survival, but Ali is able to think of the warmth of Fatma despite reprimands that in their condition to dream is a luxury and Hasan on his deathbed remembers the hairpin he had promised to her little girl. On the other hand, a man who offers quinine to a young woman suffering from malarial paroxysms, subsequently rapes her. The tyrant foreman who abuses the workers is helpless when his daughters enter the brothel. The young boss refuses to take the wounded man to the hospital so as not to dirty his car.

The socially awakened, lumpen-proletariat, the stool pigeon, the anarchist, the unionist and the opportunist all find their way into this human landscape at the brink of industrialization but not ready for solidarity, although 'I am a labourer, not a slave' has begun to be heard among the crowd. The cross-cutting of countless men sleeping in a row and the deafening clamour of the machines also lined up in a row suggests a move beyond individual destinies to the plight of poor labourers anywhere, anytime. The mechanization of human beings brought by the capitalistic system is underscored in a powerful scene when the boss and the foreman force the labourers to work at maximum speed, the camera depersonalizing them by focusing on their moving lips only until the horrific climax, when the haymaker – the symbol of capitalism and inequality – devours the labourer (Ali loses his arm).

A period film that has retained its contemporaneity after decades, *On Fertile Lands* received the Best Film award at the Antalya Golden Orange Film Festival in 1981, but the award was retracted with pressure from the military government and **Kıral** was compensated with the Best Director award, which he refused. The film was banned and the negatives lost. Discovered 28 years later in a warehouse in Switzerland, it was restored by the Groupama Film Foundation in France and shown in Turkey during the Istanbul International Film Festival, 2008.

Director: **Erden Kıral**; Producer: **Tuncel Kurtiz**, Nuri Sezer; Production: Irmak Film, Doga Film, Polar Film; Screenwriters: **Erden Kıral, Tuncel Kurtiz**, Mahmut Tali Öngören; Cinematographer: **Salih Dikişçi**; Editor: Mehmet Özdemir; Music: Sarper Özsan; Cast: **Tuncel Kurtiz**, Erkan Yücel, **Nur Sürer**, Osman Alyanak, **Yaman Okay**, Özcan Özgür, Bülent Kayabaş, **Menderes Samancılar**

Beş Vakit / Times and Winds (2006) focuses on three adolescents whose lives are regulated by the movements of the sun and the moon and the prayers resounding five times a day from the minarets. The villagers struggle with the harsh conditions of nature and the insularity of the village. Despite displays of solidarity among the neighbours and gratitude to the young woman teacher – sharing their bread and milk – affection and tenderness seem to be forgotten in the daily struggle. The patriarchal system has normalized the physical abuse of women and children. Even the young schoolteacher perpetuates the dominant system by keeping silent. Methods of raising children have not changed for generations; emotions are withheld and physical punishment is the method of reprimand.

The film begins with a night scene, dotted with village lights in the distance and the moon, which would later appear in several key moments in different shapes, passing through the clouds. It ends in daybreak. In between these two scenes,

Figure 22 Beş Vakit / Times and Winds (Reha Erdem, 2006) (Courtesy of Reha Erdem)

teenagers Ömer, Yakup and Yıldız experience the pains of the liminality of their age, manifested through rage, shame, sexual desire and love. The son of the *imam*, Ömer is the black sheep for his father, who favours the younger brother, a maths wizard who can also recite from the Qu'ran. Yakup, in love with his teacher is enraged to witness his father watching her and Yıldız (Elit İşcan) is disturbed to discover her beloved father making love to the mother she resents. The children try to stop time's flow by prostrating themselves among the dead leaves, to avoid entry to the cruel adult world. Nature offers peace to children, vacillating between its circular rhythm and the rhythm of time socially organized by five prayers, although **Reha Erdem** does not romanticize nature.

Figure 23 Beş Vakit / Times and Winds (Reha Erdem, 2006) (Courtesy of Reha Erdem)

Figure 24 Beş Vakit / Times and Winds (Reha Erdem, 2006) (Courtesy of Reha Erdem)

The sound and the image, taking turns to precede each other and often counteracting, induce audience imagination. Sound also defines characters; the neighing of the horse accompanies the wimpish Zekeriya (Taner Birsel) and the seagulls cry when he is in trouble. The background music of Arvo Pärt intensifies the spiritual dimension of the rituals (the repeated prayers, the sacrifice), but becomes histrionic during Ömer's patricide contemplations as it accompanies the moon in mock *film noir* style. The same tongue-in-cheek humour teases the audience when the camera suddenly jolts towards the sky as Ömer is about to push his father over the cliff, but lands on *imam*'s neatly folded clothes as a sad prayer is heard. On the other hand, the theme melody, *Orient and Occident* transcends the binaries of children/parents, obedience/rebellion and life/death that are the key elements in the film to an apprehension of tradition/ modernity and hence East/West that from the microcosm of the little village extends to the rest of the country and its pains of liminality in the long process of transition to modernity. The final episode, with the image of Ömer, who had tampered with his sick father's medicine, now repentant and praying for his recovery, suggests a final reconciliation of discordant elements.

Director, Screenwriter, Editor: **Reha Erdem**; Production: Atlantik Film; Producer and Art Director: Ömer Atay; Cinematographer: Florent Herry; Music Arvo Pärt; Cast: Özkan Özen, Ali Bey Kayalı, Elit İşcan, Utku Barış, Bülent Yarar, Taner Birsel, Yiğit Özsener, Selma Ergeç, Tarık Sönmez

Bezar, Miraz (b. Ankara, 1971) Director, producer, actor, screenwriter, editor. Germany-based Kurdish film-maker, Miraz Bezar comes from a political family that immigrated to Germany when he was nine years old. He studied at the Film and Television Academy in Berlin (DFFB) and made several shorts that travelled to international film festivals. A visit to Diyarbakır to have a first-hand account of the conflict, gave rise to the film, *Min Dît / Ben Gördüm / The Children of*

Figure 25 Min Dît / Ben Gördüm / The Children of Diyarbakır (Miraz Bezar, 2009) (Courtesy of International Istanbul Film Festival)

Diyarbakır (2009), co-produced by **Fatih Akın**. The first film in Kurdish to compete at the Antalya Golden Orange Film Festival winning the Jury Special Prize, *The Children of Diyarbakır*'s focus is the traumas of the 1990s shot through the eyes of children. Foregrounding absence and memory, the film is structured around the tapes left behind by a mother, which give comfort to all children, including her own, underscoring the enrichment of the local oral culture despite strict **censorship** of the language. Its use of the word Kurdistan in the lyrics of a song titled *Ka Welate Min Kurdistan?* (*I cry out and wail. Where is my country Kurdistan?*), interrupted by the police diegetically, and the mention of JİTEM, an acronym for Jandarma Istihbarat ve Terörle Mücadele (Gendarmerie, Intelligence and Counter-Terror) created controversy in Turkey.

Bir Zamanlar Anadolu'da / Once Upon a Time in Anatolia (2011), through the mundane story of a corpse that cannot be found, skilful chiaroscuro and the powerful language of the gaze laden with untold (hi)stories, interrogates collective memory's tendency to shroud the crimes of the past. Serving as one of the principal metaphors, the window in the opening sequence reveals through its foggy glass three men drinking inside a car repair shop. At the end, the gaze of the spectator, through the gaze of the doctor, is directed toward the window in a mortuary framing a woman and a boy walking near the schoolyard. As the camera lingers on the knob, the possibility of connecting the inside with the outside is suggested perfunctorily, but it does not materialize.

A corpse is buried in haste and the accused cannot remember where. One fountain looks like another in the darkness. Bureaucrats of diverse echelons simulate professional concern. In a car that carries the accuser and the accused, conversation is regulated through power hierarchy, be it an absurd discussion about buffalo yogurt. Characters are driven to subservient situations by their

Figure 26 Bir Zamanlar Anadolu'da / Once Upon a Time in Anatolia (Nuri Bilge Ceylan, 2011) (Courtesy of NBC Film and Zeynep Özbatur Atakan-Zeyno film/Yapımlab)

motivations: Commissar Naci (**Yılmaz Erdoğan**) needs a prescription for his son; the *mukhtar* (Ercan Kesal) needs a morgue to preserve the corpses for the arrival of relatives from abroad (reference to migration and the aged population in the villages) and the autopsy technician needs to modernize his workplace. Of those out of the bureaucratic echelon, the murder suspects Kenan (Fırat Taniş) and Ramazan, the beautiful young daughter of the mukhtar; Gülnaz, the wife of the victim and her son Adem and even the victim, Yaşar remain silent.

As the plot develops, personal corpses that torment the lead characters appear as unexpected ghosts. Nusret (Taner Birsel), the cocky prosecutor is haunted by the mysterious death of his wife after childbirth, but he does not want to consider suicide that might be connected with his infidelity; Doctor Cemal (Muhammed Uzuner) suffers from ambiguous feelings toward his ex-wife, her presence confined to a few pictures in a drawer; the commissar is burdened with the feeling of guilt about his disabled child and the murder suspect, touched by the radiant beauty of a peasant girl, sheds tears for the boy he has orphaned (supposed to be his own).

Adultery is a familiar theme in **Ceylan**'s work, so is dishonesty. The doctor as an outsider tries to keep his distance by maintaining the outsider's gaze, but significantly, a drop of blood jumps to his face during the autopsy. He signs the papers without further interrogating the presence of dust in the victim's lungs, hence joining the majority who live in blissful ignorance, the central theme of **Ceylan**'s previous work, *Üç Maymun / Three Monkeys* (2008) – see no evil, hear no evil, speak no evil.

The intertextuality (Kristeva) of **Ceylan**'s work, both horizontal and vertical (Fiske 1987: 108, 117) – and whether by deliberate choice or not – can be coded at different levels by different spectators. The best buffalo yogurt discussion, between the commissar and his inferior while searching for a cadaver, echoes the best hamburger discussion before a massacre in Quentin Tarantino's *The Pulp Fiction* (1994); the rolling of the apple conjures Parajanov's *Sayat Nova / The Colour of Pomegranates* (1968) and the aerial shot of the roof-tops divided by

Figure 27 Bir Zamanlar Anadolu'da / Once Upon a Time in Anatolia (Nuri Bilge Ceylan, 2011) (Courtesy of NBC Film and Zeynep Özbatur Atakan-Zeyno film/Yapımlab)

the straight line of a street evokes the courtyard shots of Zhang Yimou's *Da hong deng long gao gao gua / Raise the Red Lantern* (1991), whereas the title is an overt homage to Sergio Leone (*C'era una volta il West / Once Upon a Time in the West*, 1968; *C'era una Volta in America / Once Upon a Time in America*, 1984). The quest on the hillside, with profound philosophical allusions and repetitions with minor alterations, recalls Abbas Kiarostami's *Ta'm-e Gilas / Taste of Cherry* (1996) although Kiarostami's style is minimalist pseudo-documentary. The motif of the distant gaze of the urban intellectual alien to the Anatolian landscape has had its precedent in Turkish cinema in the works of **Ömer Kavur**, **Erden Kıral**, **Yılmaz Güney** et al. and the disposition of the intellectual regarding the city and the country are strong motives in **Ceylan**'s *Mayıs Sıkıntısı / Clouds of May* (1999) and *Uzak / Distant* (2002). The monotony of the provinces – same fountains, same hills, same steppes – is in all his films starting with *Koza / Cacoon* (1995). As a minor detail, the theme song of *Love Story* on the commissar's cell-phone connects with the ring on Hacer's cell-phone in *Three Monkeys*, another melodramatic love song.

The crime and the punishment as well as the innocence and the conscience are essential Dostoyevsky themes that constantly appear in **Ceylan**'s films, whereas the reliance on characters rather than plot development reflects his passion for Chekhov. Portraits of characters from the soil of Anatolia as metonyms for the country evoke the exiled poet Nazım Hikmet's epic in verse, *Memleketimden İnsan Manzaraları / Human Landscapes from My Country* (1939). The darkness that surrounds the first part of the film – an apt trope for the collective darkness that covers the crimes of centuries committed on this land – and the sense of collective guilt that pervades the narrative and the imagery evoke the celebrated author Yaşar Kemal's *Fırat Suyu Kan Akıyor Baksana / Look, the Euphrates is Flowing with Blood* (1997) that underscores the mass graves of the disappeared, the ethnic cleansings and the genocide of the Armenians. Their ghosts appear unexpectedly like the human figure on the illuminated rock although Ceylan does not profess to be a political film-maker.

Another key concept in the film is the element of chauvinism that defines a society where lying, cheating, swearing and bullying men dominate: a pompous prosecutor, imagining he resembles Clark Gable and disregarding his adultery, almost blaming his wife for her suicide, 'people do it to punish the other' as he claims; a detached doctor who can love a woman only from distance, recalling Mahmut's nostalgic love for his ex-wife in *Distant*. Women are invisible – dead, estranged, an unheard voice on the telephone or simply silent. Nonetheless, they are trouble for men from the prosecutor's dead wife to the commissar's nagging wife. The dead man's wife, Gülnaz, wears her red scarf like Hester's embroidered 'A' for adultery in the American classic, *The Scarlet Letter* (Hawthorne, 1850), a close-up shot revealing the high-heeled shoes she wears to the morgue, like Hacer (*Three Monkeys*) who will not admit guilt. The daughter of the mukhtar mesmerizes all men; she is the light that briefly illuminates the darkness, a mirage in a desert, serving tea to quenched men; the ideal woman – young, pure, beautiful and 'silent'.

Director: **Nuri Bilge Ceylan**; Producers: **Zeynep Özbatur Atakan**, Mirsad Purivatra, Eda Arıkan, İbrahim Şahin, Müge Kolat, Murat Akdilek, **Nuri Bilge Ceylan**; Screenwriters: **Nuri Bilge Ceylan**, Ebru Ceylan, Ercan Kesal; Cinematographer: **Gökhan Tiryaki**; Editors: **Nuri Bilge Ceylan** and Bora Gökşingöl; Art Director: Dilek Yapkuöz Ayaztuna; Sound Editor: Thomas Robert; Cast: Muhammed Uzuner, **Yılmaz Erdoğan**, Taner Birsel, Ahmet Mümtaz Taylan, Fırat Taniş, Ercan Kesal, Erol Eraslan

Bizim Büyük Çaresizliğimiz / Our Grand Despair (2011) is based on Ankara author Barış Bıçakçı's 2004 novel. The narrative follows the uneven relationship between two male childhood friends and a young woman they both love. Nihal (Güneş Sayın), unexpectedly orphaned due to a car accident, appears like a mirage in the humdrum lives of the unusual couple, platonically attached to each other, and opens new channels of affection and sensuality although the issue in the film is not her trials to overcome the tragedy or the generosity of her youth, but rather the crisis experienced by two men approaching middle age: 'our grand despair is

Figure 28 Bizim Büyük Çaresizliğimiz / Our Grand Despair (Seyfi Teoman, 2011) (Courtesy of Bulut Film – Yamaç Okur and Nadir Öperli)

our voices are no longer among the voices of children', is the lament. In a story that takes place in the capital Ankara where the state hovers over the ordinary man like a big brother with the imposing architecture of the government buildings and the excessive visibility of dark suits, men reluctant to mature stands as an apt metaphor for the position of the citizens. However, this is not the concern of **Teoman**, whose focus is male bondage and the repercussions of female intrusion. Family is the central motif and food often serves as a metonym for the family. Scenes centred around the kitchen, the nucleus of the family and related activities – food shopping, cooking and eating – establish the two males as a couple, the burly Çetin (Fatih Al) who works outside pushing the cart in the supermarket while the self-reflexive Ender (İlker Aksum), the home-maker, gently touches the handle. Despite all coding to the contrary, throughout the film **Teoman** tries to convince the audience that the boys conform to the norms of the state: they are heterosexual; they just prefer each other to any woman that may have come their way. The appearance of Nihal seems to disturb the equilibrium. She is the ideal woman – beautiful, childlike and innocent, but not bashful to test her charms such as asking Ender to write a poem for her, or telling each one (separately) that she missed him when she was away. During a bucolic scene, the child-woman, the virgin in her angelic white robe, almost slides in the air, nonchalant to the gaze of the two adoring men. The unapproachable nature of the object of desire heightens the yearning and rivalry gnaws at the male bonding. To satisfy the ego, each wants to be more liked by the woman. Comparison of down-to-earth Çetin with mentally retarded Lennie in Steinbeck's *Of Mice and Men* by bookish Ender is not fair, but it is not unusual for men to acquire a competitive streak when the issue is woman. In fact, **Teoman** is quite successful in exposing the psyche of the male in traditional conservative societies, where a woman is adored from distance and her charm melts when she becomes flesh and blood (having a boyfriend, having an abortion). No longer a mirage, she is to be tolerated, protected if necessary, by the bonded males, who speak the same language despite their differences. In fact, Çetin is not so much upset with Nihal's abortion as with losing his chance to prove

Figure 29 Bizim Büyük Çaresizliğimiz / Our Grand Despair (Seyfi Teoman, 2011) (Courtesy of Bulut Film – Yamaç Okur and Nadir Öperli)

his protective male power when her boyfriend accompanies her and takes her to his home after the incident. The unanimous decision is to send her away.

The film's strong points are the beautiful outdoor images captured by the camera of Birgit Gudjonsdottir, such as the fairground after the rain when water glistens on the asphalt, and also its tempo in balancing electric moments with silences that allow the spectator moments of reflection. The insistent return of the camera to Nihal's chair after she is gone is a remarkable rendition of the agonies of absence. However, Nihal's evolution from a mirage to a real woman is somewhat sudden for the audience as her character is the least developed of the trio; the first clues must be when she stops calling them 'elder brother' and declares, 'We are not butterflies. We are just like you. You render mysterious what you don't understand' (echoing standard feminist clichés). Essentially, she is presented as a male fantasy object, with emphasis on her beauty and radiance. The two male leads, acted by professionals, are more convincing. In summary, **Teoman**'s film is a well-constructed work that carries the trend of 'masculinity in crisis' films that have marked the cinema of Turkey in the new millennium.

Director: **Seyfi Teoman**; Producer: Yamaç Okur, Nadir Öperli; Production: Bulut Film, Unafilm, Circe Films; Screenwriters: **Seyfi Teoman**, Barış Bıçakçı; Cinematographer: Birgit Gudjonsdottir; Editor: Çiçek Kahraman, Art Director: Nadide Argun; Music: Sakin (Cenker Kökten); Cast: İlker Aksum, Fatih Al, Güneş Sayın, Taner Birsel, Baki Davrak, Mehmet Ali Nuroğlu, Beril Boz, Damla Kabakçı

Bora, Ekrem (b. Ankara, 1932 – d. Istanbul, 2012) Actor, RN: Ekrem Şerif Uçak. One of the top stars of **Yeşilçam**, Ekrem Bora entered cinema after winning a magazine competition. He started acting in 1955, but *Acı Hayat / Bitter Life* (**Metin Erksan**, 1962) is considered his first remarkable appearance. During a career that spanned over half a century, he played different characters in innumerable films, but his reputation rests on his 'bad guy' typology, which could gather audience sympathy through nuanced acting that could reflect the duality of the human nature. Recipient of the Best Male Actor Award at the Antalya Golden Orange Film Festival twice, with *Sürtük / The Tramp* (**Ertem Eğilmez**, 1965) in 1966 and *Soğuktu ve Yağmur Çiseliyordu / It Was Cold and Raining* (**Engin Ayça**, 1990) in 1991, he is memorable for his roles in *Suçlular Aramızda* (**Erksan**, 1964), *Bozuk Düzen / The Corrupt Order* (Haldun Dormen, 1965), *Dikkat Kan Aranıyor / Attention! Blood is Wanted* (Temel Gürsu, 1970) and *Mazi Kalbimde Yaradır / The Past is a Wound in My Heart* (**Osman F. Seden**, 1970). (The English titles of the last two films are literary translations.)

Bornova / Bornova (2009) is a film that overturns the classical male-bondage etiquette and the traditional codes of honour in depicting liminal characters searching for their place in a society of survival of the fittest. It also questions the given and acquired identities. The camera is set in front of a grocery store and the events progress in its vicinity. The protagonist Hakan (Öner Erkan), an optimist back from military service, lives on the laurels of his football player days, hanging around while waiting for a job to drive a taxi and dreaming of

Figure 30 Bornova / Bornova (İnan Temelkuran, 2009) (Courtesy of İnan Temelkuran)

forming a decent family with his secret love, Özlem (Damla Sönmez). Salih (Kadir Çermik) is the bad boy, the son of a respectable schoolteacher mother and a once esteemed now disgraced civil servant father, who lost his job during the 1980 *coup d'état*. He sells drugs to teenagers, including Özlem, and lusts after her. Murat (Erkan Bektaş) is a wasted activist; a perennial philosophy student, he earns his living writing erotic fantasies. At the end, Salih is dead, Hakan is the murderer and Murat is the witness. The two citations in the opening sequences are from General Kenan Evren, who masterminded the 1980 *coup* resulting in deaths, disappearances, torture and brutal **censorship**, and from a pop star, Demet Akalın. What they have in common is the passion for fast money and fame, the neo-liberal policies that have resulted in the deterioration of the middle and lower middle class and the widening of the gap between the rich and the poor. For the generations born thereafter, the only politics left is nationalist, bellicose and masculinist based on given identities – man, Turk or Kurd – none of which are earned, yet the characters try to use them for their profit.

   Temelkuran overturns the clichés of **Yeşilçam** by exposing an uncanny neighbourhood where the local boys are no longer the guardians of the honour of the neighbourhood girls but rather the perpetrators of its loss. Salih rapes Özlem and worse, he talks about it to Murat (it could also be his fantasy) who turns it into a story to sell. What remains constant is the reliance of women on men for salvation, a time-honoured notion in masculinist societies (and their cinema). Özlem, the femme-fatale, despite her tough looks and rough acts, waits for a man to save her and she is successful. In the last episode, the couple sitting in the tea gardens look like any ordinary couple. In contrast to the opening scene depicting Hakan returning from a funeral, we notice Özlem, now his wife, with a swollen belly. The sun is shining and the birds are chirping, but death is omnipresent. To cover one murder they have committed, they discuss another, calmly and serenely, but still with the nervous ticks of being squeezed in a corner.

The strength of the film is the way **Temelkuran** builds his narrative with a larger vision than the local and places the quandaries of the depoliticized young within a more global context. Through skilful editing, he creates a distantiation effect. Small windows open to the past, the terror of the past merging with the present and the characters experience both simultaneously. The ambiguity of the final scene allows the viewer the possibility to reflect on the plight of the characters and society itself.

Director, Producer, Screenwriter: **İnan Temelkuran**, Production: Temelkuran Film and Music; Cinematography: Enrique Santiago Silguero; Editor: Erkan Telemen: Music: Harun İyicil, Ferid Özgüner; Sound: Kerem Aktaş; Art Director: Natali Yeres; Cast: Öner Erkan, Kadir Çermik, Damla Sönmez, Erkan Bektaş, Öner Ateş, Murat Kılıç

Brudermord / Fraticide (2005) focuses on the hyphenated identities at 'sub-nation level' (Elsaesser 2005: 118) of Anatolians who had gone to Germany as guest workers in the 1950s. The voiceover in the opening sequence, belonging to Ibo, the only survivor of the bloodbath that the film exposes graphically, warns the viewer of the fate of the 'money dreamers', who lose their souls; a familiar theme of the migration films of the 1960s to 1980s, from **Birds of Nostalgia** to **Akad**'s *Anatolia Trilogy*. The film begins with a car speeding through arid land, with an out-of-frame driver, stopping periodically to ask directions to the Karaman family. His mission is to take his younger brother Azad to Germany despite the unwillingness of the boy, who is suspicious about the source of the dollars Semo has been sending. In another space, an old grandfather sacrifices a lamb and with its blood instructs his 11-year-old grandson, Ibo, orphaned by the Turkish army, to be a man and to take destiny in his own hands. The two meet in a hostel for Kurds without papers. To supplement the German government's meagre assistance, Azad works as a barber in the toilet of a *döner kebab* stand and little Ibo helps by holding the mirror. Accosted by two Turkish punks with a bulldog one night, they barely escape but the sign Azad makes with his fist determines his fate. He is recognized by one of the punks while arguing with Semo for procuring East European women and during the scuffle, Semo knifes one of the punks and the blood feud results in the death of everyone except little Ibo.

Strong scenes like the violent rape of young Ibo by the Turks may be perceived as promoting hatred against Turks. Yet, the parents of the punks are presented as peaceful Anatolian peasants who are hurt by the behaviour of their sons – two unemployed youths, alienated both from the nation of their parents and the social fabric of their society, whose frustration manifests itself in crime. **Arslan**'s protagonists, when they lose their cultural identity, either go mad (*Yara / The Wound*), or resort to violence (*Fraticide*). By challenging simplistic judgements regarding the concept of 'homeland', particularly for the Kurds, the film also sends a message to the Kurdish community in exile to aid the refugees instead of promoting otherness by stressing their victimization.

The film succeeds in keeping the audience in a limbo, between the cruel reality of street violence and the fantasy interspersed through the narrative, either like a Greek tragedy with the chorus of old women evoking the legend of the Kurds, or animation sequences attached to the character of young Ibo, to give a magical atmosphere to his lost childhood.

Director, Screenwriter: **Yılmaz Arslan**; Producers: **Yılmaz Arslan**, Eric Tavitian, Eddy Geradon-Luyckx, Donato Rotunno; Production: Tarantula, Yılmaz Arslan Film; Cinematographer: Jean François Hensgens; Editor: André Nendocchi-Alves; Sound: Laurent Benaim; Music: Evgueni Galperine; Cast: Xewat Geçtan, Erdal Çelik, Nurettin Çelik, Bülent Büyükaşık, Xhiljona Ndoja, Oral Uyan

Bulutları Beklerken / Waiting for the Clouds (2004) challenges the official history of the deportation of the Pontus Greeks of the Black Sea during the harsh winter of 1916 when the Ottoman army evacuated the villages west of Russian-occupied Trabzon sending an estimated 350,000 to 500,000 people to death from cold, hunger and sickness. In 1924, repatriation of the ethnic Greeks and Turks took place according to the agreement between the rulers of Greece and Turkey. Those who remained converted to Islam for survival and kept their identity secret.

Told from an 8-year-old male child's point of view, the diegetic time is 1975, a turbulent period of ultra-nationalism united against the leftist movement fermenting in the universities and unions. The first part is in Trebolu, the natal village of Eleni/Ayşe in Turkey, and the second in the Kalamaria region of Thessaloniki in Greece, home to exiled Pontus Greeks. During the deportation, Eleni and her brother Niko were saved by a Turkish family after their father was shot and their mother died of starvation. While Niko was transported to Greece with the other orphans, Eleni, striving for security, remained with the family,

Figure 31 Bulutları Beklerken / Waiting for the Clouds (Yeşim Ustaoğlu, 2004) (Courtesy of Yeşim Ustaoğlu)

becoming Ayşe and concealing her identity for 50 years, living with the guilt of abandoning her brother. After the death of her Turkish sister Selma, the memories of her hidden past haunt her and she tries to regain her identity through language, uttering garbled words in Greek. Mehmet, a precocious child is the first one to notice the change and connect her mumblings with the accent of the visitor Thanasis, another orphan, once transported to Greece, who joined the partisans during the war and was forced into exile in the Soviet Union. Meeting Thanasis is a catharsis for Ayşe/Eleni, who externalizes her feelings of guilt and takes the journey to Greece to join her brother, but memory is selective and Niko has made a decision to erase her from his past; she is not in his family photos – until Eleni shows him the faded photo she has kept all these years.

Along with its visual beauty, the unobtrusive directing of **Ustaoğlu**, her skilful balance of motion and 'un-motion' and her elliptic editing play a major role in enhancing the intensity of the spatio-temporality of the characters, the interrogation of collective memory, the role of language in defining identity and the meaning of home, homeland and foreigner.

Director: **Yeşim Ustaoğlu**: Producer: **Yeşim Ustaoğlu**, Behrooz Hashemian; Production: Ustaoğlu Film; Screenwriters: **Yeşim Ustaoğlu**, Petros Markaris based on *Tamama* by George Andreadis; Cinematographer: Jacek Petrycki; Editors: Timo Linasolle, Nicolas Gaster; Music: Michael Galasso; Cast: Rüçhan Çalışkur, Rıdvan Yağcı, İsmail Baysan, Dimitris Kamberides, Suna Selen, Feride Karaman, Jannis Georgiadis

Büyük Adam, Küçük Aşk aka ***Hejar / Big Man, Small Love*** (2001), foregrounding an unusual friendship between a retired republican judge and a five-year-old Kurdish orphan, is the first feature to deal with the restriction of the Kurdish language. Little Hejar is brought to the metropolis by a relative after losing her family during an attack on her village. There she survives a bloody raid by the police and is sheltered by an elderly next-door neighbour, a retired judge devoted to Kemalist ideology. The housekeeper Sakine, 'an assimilated Kurd', serves as a bridge between the two as the mutual mistrust is very strong. The judge forbids Kurdish to be spoken in the house; citizens of Turkey must speak Turkish. The transformation comes when he is ready to utter the Kurdish word 'Negri!' (don't cry) to little Hejar, who misses her dead mother.

Despite its melodramatic mood, politically correct stand, mainstream attractions (the shopping spree of the reconciled duo at Benetton) and sub-plots that do not blend with the narrative, *Hejar* is important in exposing the deficiencies of the nationalist model of socio-cultural Westernization and the gap between the 'white Turks' and the 'black Turks' (Göle 2005). The judge is astounded to see Eastern Anatolia, with all its poverty, ignorance, feudalism and patriarchy, transplanted to the outskirts of modern Istanbul.

Despite its positive intentions and international accolades, *Hejar* was received with scepticism by Turks questioning **İpekçi**'s motives for choosing a subject that assumedly attracts Western funding organizations, while the Kurds remarked: 'Does one have to be cute like Hejar or "assimilated" like Sakine to be accepted by

Figure 32 Büyük Adam, Küçük Aşk aka Hejar / Big Man, Small Love aka *Hejar* (Handan İpekçi, 2001) (Courtesy of International Istanbul Film Festival)

the Turks?' Auto-censorship often plays a crucial role for the ambiguous political stance. Even then, the Ministry of Culture, which partially funded the film, tried to censor it after prestigious awards at the national film festival in Antalya and nomination as Turkey's entry to the Oscars in a foreign language, accusing the film of highlighting Kurdish nationalism and portraying the Turkish police negatively. Although the film had already passed the scrutiny of the **censorship** board and was released in October 2001, it was withdrawn from cinemas on 2 March 2002 by the Supervisory Council of Cinema, Video and Music Productions of the Ministry of Culture for violating the principle of the indivisible integrity of the state. **İpekçi** was brought to trial but the charge was eventually dropped as 'no element of crime' was found.

Director, Producer, Screenwriter: **Handan İpekçi**; Production: Yeni Yapım Ltd., Hyperion S.A., Focus Film; Cinematographer: Erdal Kahraman; Editor: Nikos Kanakis; Music: Serdar Yalçın, Mazlum Çimen; Cast: Şükran Güngör, Dilan Erçetin, Füsun Demirel, **Yıldız Kenter**, İsmail Hakkı Şen

C

Camdan Kalp / A Heart of Glass (1990) focuses on the divide between the urban intellectual male–master and the rural migrant female–servant through the tragedy of a disillusioned film-maker who tries to solve his personal problems by solving the problems of others. Kirpi (meaning porcupine) (**Genco Erkal**) is out of tune with the changing times and at an impasse with his marriage to dubbing artist Naciye. When the cleaning woman Kiraz (**Şerif Sezer**) solicits his help regarding her abusive husband's plans to have a second wife (Füsun Demirel), as a good-natured tolerant benefactor, he cannot refuse. This involvement takes him to Kiraz's natal village in feudal Anatolia as well as the replica of Anatolia in Istanbul, the slums in the periphery of the metropolis.

Anatolian women have been working in middle-class homes as domestic workers for decades, referred to as 'woman', accepting without recourse, low wages, abuse and assault (often sexual). Rural migrants are indispensible to middle-class existence, the middle class defining itself 'in contradistinction to the peasants', the contact between the two giving rise to 'intensified forms of boundary-defining activity' (Özyeğin 2002: 47). The tolerance of the liberal vision can be very repressive, as a substitute for recognizing the Other, whose minoritarian identity is often tolerated as deviant, of lesser worth and acceptable only behind the closed doors of private life and unacceptable in the public sphere. The Anatolian cleaning woman arrives at the bourgeois home, changes her clothes beside the door and renders her identity invisible to be tolerated by the bourgeois employer, a tolerance which aims at managing 'the demands of marginal groups in ways that incorporate them without disturbing the hegemony of the norms that marginalize them' (Brown 2006: 36) which is 'a mode of incorporating and regulating the presence of the threatening Other within' (Brown 2006: 27) (see also *Çoğunluk / Majority*). In this sense, **Yaşar**'s film is significant in exposing the conflict between the acquired knowledge about the other and the reality when the other becomes visible. Kirpi's journey reveals the cultural and moral dilemmas of Turkey as he experiences a world of poverty, underdevelopment and tradition alien to him. While he risks his life to protect Kiraz, she has already accepted the second wife to avoid beatings and to improve her standard of living (the other woman has a television set). Kirpi is killed by Kiraz's brothers, who mistake him for her lover.

Yaşar resorts to humour and supernatural details while exposing Kirpi's culture shock. References to cinema are numerous: the anti-hero Kirpi is a revival of Haşmet Asilkan in *Aşk Filmlerinin Unutulmaz Yönetmeni / The Unforgettable Director of Love Movies* (**Yavuz Turgul**, 1990); an urban intellectual amidst Anatolians alien to him recalls **Erden Kıral**'s *Hakkari'de Bir Mevsim / A Season in Hakkari* (1983) that also features **Genco Erkal** in the lead and **Şerif Sezer** as the woman disturbed by the arrival of a second wife asking his help. In fact, in one scene, Kirpi reads Ferit Edgü's *O / Him* – the base of the script of *A Season*. Among other allusions to cinema is the scene at the police station when Kirpi, the urban intellectual, wants to make an inside joke by telling the rural commissar the name of his German friend is 'Fritz'. 'Surname?' demands the commissar. 'Lang', answers Kirpi. The commissar retorts, 'You mean the one who made *Metropolis*?'

Yaşar uses magic realism particularly in the Anatolian episodes such as the Germans arriving to purchase a virgin bride, or the scene when the young woman transforms into a tea table to hide from her pursuers.

Director, Producer, Screenwriter: **Fehmi Yaşar**; Cinematographer: Erdal Kahraman; Music: Okay Temiz; Cast: **Genco Erkal**, Deniz Gökçer, **Şerif Sezer**, Füsun Demirel, Aytekin Özen, Macit Sonkan, Cemal San, Ersen Ersoy

Cenneti Beklerken / Waiting for Heaven (2006) is a historical costume drama that uses the past as a conduit to understand the present and the question of identity in a modern context by extrapolating the dichotomy of Eastern art versus Western. The themes of individual and collective memory, the emotional distance created by its loss and the search for identity when values are transitory are also prominent in the film. In the seventeenth century in Istanbul, the capital of the Ottoman Empire, Eflatun (Serhat Tutumluer), a miniaturist draws the face of his dead son in the Western tradition to preserve a realistic image, but this act distances him from the style of painting taught by his masters. Instead of punishment, the *vizier* sends him on a mission to draw a Western-style portrait of Danyal, the pretender to the throne, as proof of his decapitation. His apprentice Gazal held as hostage to ensure his return, Eflatun commences an arduous journey to the heart of Anatolia torn by mutinies and rebellions, accompanied by the palace guards. His dramatic encounter with a painting similar to *Las Meninas / The Maids of Honour* (1656), the magnum opus of Diego Velázquez, is a turning point for Eflatun.

The film aesthetically integrates the Ottoman art of miniature, which takes its essence from Islam, into the Western art of cinema. The miniaturist is not concerned with the sense of perspective or the optical illusion of three-dimensions. Figures or objects neither overlap nor conceal each other. Time and space are fluid. A place depicted in one miniature is redrawn in the next in a different colour and/or form. Events known to have occurred at different times or in different places may be drawn together. Before Eflatun's journey, the overriding colours are those of the miniature art; through the journey, the Western style of lighting is employed and at the end, we return to the pure reds of the miniature. Space and time are opaque. Initially, as the convoy rides towards a rock, the camera descends to reveal the caves, each one with a different space and narrative. In a

Figure 33 Cenneti Beklerken / Waiting for Heaven (Derviş Zaim, 2006) (Courtesy of Derviş Zaim)

dream sequence, Eflatun's childhood hut enters the frame. His image in the mirror is replaced by the image of Prince Yakub from the desert, now dead. On the return journey, Istanbul first appears in the caravanserai frames, then it enters the actual frame. The shadow, the cave and the mirror are allusions to Plato and the name of the protagonist is the Turkish translation of the philosopher's name.

Facing the Western painting, which resembles *Las Meninas*, Eflatun notices the opaqueness of time and space and the disparity between the time and space reflected in the mirror and that depicted in the painting itself. Encountering this feature of Western art leads Eflatun to re-evaluate his earlier beliefs about cultural differences and meeting points, his revelation serving as a trope for Turkey's geopolitically and socially unique advantage to unite two diverse and at times oppositional cultures (Dönmez-Colin 2008: 187–9).

Director, Screenwriter: **Derviş Zaim**; Producers: **Derviş Zaim**, Baran Seyhan, Elif Dağdeviren Güven, Bülent Helvacı; Production: Marathon Filmcilik, Sarmaşık Sanatlar, Hermes Films, Tivoli Film; Cinematographer: Mustafa Kuşçu; Editor: Ulaş Cihan Şimşek;

Music: Rahman Altın; Art Directors: Serdar Yılmaz, Elif Taşçıoğlu; Cast: Serhat Tutumluer, Melisa Sözen, Mesut Akusta, Nihat İleri, Mehmet Ali Nuroğlu, Numan Acar

Censorship, which officially lasted about six decades, was instrumental in moulding the identity of Turkish cinema, particularly during the **Yeşilçam** years when life was shown through tinted glasses. **Ahmet Fehim**'s *Mürebbiye / The Governess* (1919), an indictment of the upper-class infatuation with French culture through the adventures of a French seductress, is considered the first film to be censored (for lack of serious study of censorship preceding this date). Although **Fehim** defended his work as the peaceful protest of an artist against the occupation, the commandant of the occupying French forces banned the distribution of the film in Anatolia for degrading the French woman (Özön 1962: 48).

Regulation on the Control of Films and Film Scripts, based on the antidemocratic *Law on the Duty and Authority of the Police* (14 July 1934) and *Law on the Organization of the General Management of the Press and Its Duties* (26 May 1934), was established on 19 July 1939 during the tense atmosphere of the anticipated world war. A censorship board, the Central Control Commission, connected to the Ministry of Interior was created. The regulation is said to have been inspired by Mussolini's *Codice di Censura* although censorship of the press, literature and theatre had its antecedent in 1880 with the establishment of the Investigation and Inspection Commission during the reign of Sultan Abdülhamit (Özön 1995: 297). Minor changes were made in the statutes in 1948 and 1958. A commission constituting members from state departments, including the police, the military and representatives of the Ministry of Education inspected the script as well as the final product, in some cases sending those who did not comply into exile. The Ministry of Interior had the power to observe the shooting process. Permission was mandatory for sending the negatives abroad for post-production, distribution or festival participation. Scripts that 1) made political propaganda of another state; 2) defamed a certain race or nation; 3) offended the feelings of friendly states and nations; 4) made religious propaganda; 5) made political, economic and social propaganda of ideology against the regime; 6) were found harmful to public decency, morality and national feelings; 7) made propaganda against the military profession and offended the military's honour and esteem; 8) were harmful to the order and security of the country; 9) incited crime; 10) included scenes that were vehicles to propaganda against Turkey, were not accepted. Doctors, lawyers and especially the police force could never be depicted in a negative light. After the script was accepted and the distribution permission granted, the film could still be banned, if found objectionable by a governor or a bureaucrat. The presence of two members from the Security General Directorate in the commission, one as the president, but the absence of representatives from the film sector; the unctuous nature of the regulations open to various interpretations and the lack of proper recourse were the major drawbacks to the development of a healthy film industry (Özön 1995: 249–57, 266).

The board's priority was the presentation of an ideal image of the state and the nation although their concerns varied with time. In the 1950s, apprehension over the exposure of underdevelopment resulted in the banning of **Metin Erksan**'s *Aşık Veysel'in Hayatı* aka *Karanlık Dünya / The Life of Veysel, the Minstrel* aka *The Dark World* (1952) and the refusal to grant official permission to his *Susuz Yaz / A Dry Summer* (1963) to participate at the Berlin Film Festival. His *Yılanların Öcü / Revenge of the Serpents* (1962) was released only after President Cemal Gürsel, the general responsible for the 1960 *coup*, impressed by the film, cancelled the ban. During the political turmoil of the 1970s, when sexploitation films had free reign, **Yılmaz Güney**'s *Umut / The Hope* (1970) was banned for exposing poverty and class exploitation. **Halit Refiğ**'s *Yorgun Savaşçı / The Tired Warrior* (1980), made for TRT (Turkish Radio and Television) was deemed against Atatürk and the War of Independence and burned by the junta. **Erden Kıral**'s *Hakkari'de Bir Mevsim / A Season in Hakkari* (1983) was deemed subversive and damaging to the integrity of the state and the nation.

Güney resorted to narrative circumlocution to thwart the state censorship: a facial expression, a particular glance, or the missing part of a dialogue could convey his message to the masses. Unfortunately, many of his colleagues were not so resourceful. **Yeşilçam** contributed to the establishment of an escapist cinema removed from the social, political and economic realities of Turkey.

Imported films were customarily scrutinized by the City Censorship Committees in Istanbul or Ankara. Some of the banned films were Otto Preminger's *Man With the Golden Arm* for dealing with the subject of narcotics, Jules Dassin's *Jamais le Dimanches / Never On Sunday* for glorifying prostitution, David Lean's *Lawrence of Arabia* and Elia Kazan's *America America* for anti-Turkey sentiments, Antony Mann's *El Cid* for anti-Muslim sentiments, Sam Wood's *For Whom the Bells Toll*, an adaptation of the Hemingway novel, for repeating the word 'communists' (which was changed to 'enemies' during the dubbing for release permit) (Dorsay 1965: 2).

In 1986, the censorship board was removed from the Ministry of Interior and connected to the Ministry of Culture and Tourism and the pre-scrutiny of scripts from the centre was abolished in practicality but the authority of the local administrations to ban films was retained. **Ali Özgentürk**'s *Su da Yanar / Water Also Burns* (1987) was banned in more than 50 provinces, obliging the director to appear in each province to defend his case.

Officially abolished in 1998, censorship still plays a crucial role in Turkish cinema's stand on controversial issues through subtler forms of control and financial pressures (difficulties in obtaining funds and/or entering the distribution/ exhibition network), which often lead to self-censorship. Explicit sexual scenes are rare, but some of the previously taboo subjects have begun to receive realistic treatments. Incest is the focus of *Meleğin Düşüşü / Angel's Fall*, **Semih Kaplanoğlu**, 2004; *Atlı Karınca / Merry-Go-Round*, İlksen Başarır, 2010 and *Derin Düşün-ce / When Derin Falls*, Çağatay Tosun, 2012 and films like *Zenne* (M. Caner Alper and Mehmet Binay, 2011) depict homosexuality, traditionally fodder for comedy, through real characters. Despite the on-going civil war in south-east Turkey, Kurdish film-makers have been able to express their concerns through films, most of which are funded by the government (***Gitmek / My Barlon and Brando*, Hüseyin Karabey**, 2008; *Bahoz / Fırtına / The Storm*, **Kazım Öz**, 2008; *İki Dil, Bir Bavul / On The Way to School*, 2009 by Özgür Doğan, **Orhan Eskiköy** and ***Babamın Sesi / Dengê Bavê Min / The Voice of My Father*** by **Zeynel Doğan, Orhan Eskiköy**; *Min Dît / Ben Gördüm / The Children of Diyarbakır*, **Miraz Bezar**, 2009; *Ana Dilim Nerede / Zone Ma Koti Yo / Where is My Mother Tongue*, Veli Kahraman, 2012). However, such films are not shown on television. Films shown on television may have episodes removed without permission from the copyright holders. Masking the smoking scenes on television screenings has become standard with the ruling Justice and Development Party – AKP. In the restored DVD of **Akad**'s Migration Trilogy, released in 2011, the smoking scenes are masked. A prime time soap opera on the life of the Ottoman emperor, Suleiman The Magnificent, *Muhteşem Yüzyıl / The Magnificent Century* (**Yağmur Taylan** and **Durul Taylan**) was condemned by Prime Minister Tayyip Erdoğan and Islamist groups for defaming the famed sultan by showing him as a hedonist, but still continues to be aired with unprecedented success in Turkey and the rest of the Middle East and the Balkans.

The question remains why an authentic documentary on Kemal Atatürk, the founder of the Turkish Republic, has never been made. Certain subjects are still untouchable and hence the mediocre Atatürk films that are either **melodramas** or like school books: **Zülfü Livaneli**'s *Veda / Farewell* and Turgut Özakman's *Dersimiz Atatürk / Today's Lesson is Atatürk* are two examples. Renowned documentarian and biographer Can Dündar's account of the leader's life, *Mustafa*, divided the nation. As the first name in the title indicates, it was an attempt at an intimate portrait of the leader who led a lonely life with no one to share his sentiments about the history being built. Showing him as a human being who could flirt, dance, drink, break his heart, miss his mother and err, broke the taboos. How could he be lonely with the whole nation behind him? Discussions also revolved around the reasons behind showing him chain-smoking, whether he really mentioned an autonomous land for Kurds and whether he really was a dictator.

The government subventions have been instrumental in the new vitality observed in Turkish cinema in recent years. However, in 2012, the Ministry of Culture and Tourism declared its intentions to support films successful at the box-office and films 'for the family' as a priority, which received a strong reaction from the prominent voices of quality cinema, labelling this decision as a form of censorship. Their films, although praised at international film festivals, are limited in terms of box-office figures.

Ceylan, Nuri Bilge (b. Istanbul, 1959) Director, producer, screenwriter, cinematographer, editor, actor, photographer. The most celebrated contemporary Turkish film-maker internationally, Nuri Bilge Ceylan has distinguished himself with personal self-reflexive films that have won awards at prestigious films festivals, including the Grand Prix twice (2003 and 2011) and the Best Director

Figure 34 Nuri Bilge Ceylan from *İklimler / Climates* (2006) (Courtesy of International Istanbul Film Festival)

(2008) at the Cannes Film Festival. Ceylan graduated in electrical engineering from the Bosphorus University in Istanbul, where he pursued his interests in visual arts and music through elective courses and film clubs, gradually focusing on photography. Following voyages from London to Katmandu, he decided to do his military service, which offered him the opportunity to reflect on his future. Deciding on cinema, he entered the Mimar Sinan University, but left after two years. He made his directorial debut with the 20-minute black-and-white *Koza / Cocoon* (1995) about an estranged elderly couple, enacted by his parents, which competed at the 48th Cannes Film Festival. His first feature **Kasaba / The Small Town** (1997), the second, **Mayıs Sıkıntısı / Clouds of May** (1999) and the third, **Uzak / Distant** (2002) star his family and friends and almost all technical credits belong to Ceylan. **The Small Town** evokes his childhood, spent in his father's birthplace, Yenice, an in-between space that defines the identity of its inhabitants. **Clouds of May** is a claustrophobic picture of a small town with its conformism, normalcy and family-centred insularity and complacency that drive its young to seek a better life in the city. **Distant** presents a disillusioned urban intellectual 'distant' to his provincial roots, his family, women and himself. **İklimler / Climates** (2006) on the disintegration of a relationship affected mostly by the 'distant' personality of the male partner, can be considered a prequel to **Distant**. These four films can be considered a tetralogy according to this author, A Portrait of the Provincial Artist as an Urban Intellectual. With **Climates**, Ceylan widens the narrative from the individual to the couple although the focus is still on the male protagonist, whereas *Üç Maymun / Three Monkeys* (2008), which is on deceit in several forms and levels, focuses on a family. **Bir Zamanlar Anadolu'da / Once Upon a Time in Anatolia** (2011), widening the screen to cinemascope, also widens its scope to encompass the country and its historical and socio-political landscape through a murder story without suspense.

Deceit and dishonesty is one of the most prominent motifs in his work, perhaps as a trope for the art (and artifice) of cinema itself: in *Clouds*, the director/ protagonist conceals from his parents that he is recording their personal life and uses his cousin Saffet with a false promise of offering aid in finding him a job in the city. Little Ali, promised to receive a musical watch if he carries an egg in his pocket for 40 days intact, resorts to stealing to replace the broken egg. In *Distant*, Mahmut intimidates his cousin Yusuf with a Tarkovsky film, but switches to porno when he leaves. Yusuf phones his mother long distance without asking Mahmut's permission and tells her he is whispering not to wake him. Mahmut accuses Yusuf of stealing an old watch and does not inform him when he finds it in a drawer. In *Three Monkeys*, justice is thwarted when an innocent man assumes the crime he does not commit and a chain of deceitful events follow. In *Anatolia*, the doctor wilfully omits an important detail in his report about the cadaver. Adultery appears regularly: in *Distant*, Mahmut's mistress seems to have another partner; in *Climates*, İsa cheats on his partner and lies to her; in *Three Monkeys*, Hacer sleeps with her husband's boss; in *Anatolia*, both the victim's wife and the prosecutor are adulterers.

Ceylan presents a society at the threshold of modernity suffering from the erosion of traditional cultural values. Unemployment (the closing of the factories) and migration to the metropolises for social and economic advancement are recurring themes, as well as the divide between the urban and the rural and the intellectual/artist and the ordinary citizen. Most of his films critique the bureaucrats that he had observed as a youth through his father's occupation, but *Once Upon a Time in Anatolia* is a forceful satire on bureaucracy and the absurd and infantile echelons of hierarchy.

Ceylan's earlier work displays influences of Andrei Tarkovsky (Deleuzian *time-image* and recollection-images of Bergson) and Abbas Kiarostami (particularly the repetitions that are in the Deleuzian sense, not the reoccurrence of the same thing, but the beginning of a new one and a refusal to remain the same). The spatial composition, the ellipses in the narrative, the 'intermediate spaces' and 'still lives' highlighting the paradox of humanity's presence by its absence evoke Ozu, although Ceylan maintains that for him Chekhov is the main influence (Eleftheriotis and Needham 2006: 20–1).

Revered in art film circles, particularly in France, Ceylan's cinema is 'distant' to general spectators in Turkey; his followers are limited to cinephiles and film students. *Distant* was seen by 63,845 in 21 weeks; *Climates* by 35,345 during the same time period and *Three Monkeys* had 127,668 viewers in 15 weeks of release, partly owing to its melodramatic content. *Anatolia*, considered more accessible with its murder-mystery narrative, but disadvantaged by its extremely slow first 90 minutes that happen in the dark, had 18,573 viewers in 78 cinemas on its first weekend.

Since 2003, Ceylan has been devoting his time to both cinema and photography. In 2013, he started a new project, *Kış Uykusu / Winter Sleep*, with considerable support from **Eurimage** and produced by **Zeynep Özbatur Atakan**.

Children's film designates films that concentrate on the lives of children and are targeted at young audiences. The **genre** often crosses over to **comedy** and **fantasy films**. The innocence ascribed to children, like animals, often makes them an object, if not the subject, of trauma films, such as war, to provoke emotion and moral satisfaction. Our response to children on screen, according to André Bazin, is a form of 'anthropomorphism' (Bazin 1997: 121), implying that in many **war films** adults use children as a blank on screen to project their adult emotions and fears, the same way they ascribe human qualities to animals (Lury 2010: 106). **Yeşilçam** exploited the melodramatic potential of children on screen and films featuring child actors were very popular. In the 1960s, Ayşecik (little Ayşe), enacted by Zeynep Değirmencioğlu, rich or poor, urban or rural, an orphan or an important heiress, was always a precocious child who was the mediator, reconciling adults lacking judgement; she could also be the breadwinner, or mother to her siblings. Close to 40 *Ayşecik* films were made, many of which were un-credited adaptations from world classics, *Snow White and the Seven Dwarfs*, *Cinderella*, *Pollyanna* and *Wizard of Oz* (*Ayşecik ve Sihirli Cüceler Rüyalar Ülkesinde / Ayşecik and the Magical Dwarfs in the Land of Dreams*, **Tunç Başaran**, 1971). Ayşecik was followed by her real-life cousin, Ömer Dönmez as Ömercik (little Ömer). Yumurcak (little devil), Afacan (little mischief-maker) or Sezercik (little Sezer) were children of popular film-makers or actors. *Afacan Küçük Serseri / Afacan, the Little Tramp* (Ülkü Erakalın, 1971) won the first prize at a children's film festival in Milan, Italy. The furore ended with the gradual demise of **Yeşilçam**.

Figure 35 Kız Kardeşim – Mommo / Mommo – The Bogeyman (Atalay Taşdiken, 2009) (Courtesy of International Istanbul Film Festival)

Children have begun to appear in realistic roles and often as a metonym for wider suffering in political films such as *Uçurtmayı Vurmasınlar / Don't Let Them Shoot the Kite* (**Tunç Başaran**, 1989), *Büyük Adam, Küçük Aşk* aka *Hejar / Big Man, Small Love* (**Handan İpekçi**, 2001), *Kız Kardeşim – Mommo / Mommo – The Bogeyman* (**Atalay Taşdiken**, 2009) and *Min Dit / The Children of Diyarbakır* (**Miraz Bezar**, 2009). *Bal / Honey* (**Semih Kaplanoğlu**, 2010) and *Can* (**Raşit Çelikezer**, 2012) carry stories involving children or are told from their point of view. *Karpuz Kabuğundan Gemiler Yapmak / Boats Out of Watermelon Rinds* (**Ahmet Uluçay**, 2004), *Beş Vakit / Times and Winds* (**Reha Erdem**, 2006) and *Hayat Var / My Only Sunshine* (**Reha Erdem**, 2008) focus on adolescents without necessarily addressing the adolescent audience. Commercial cinema has shown a strong tendency to reprise the success formula of **Yeşilçam** with child actors regularly occupying the screens: *Mevsim Çiçek Açtı / Spring Blossoms* (Levent Üngör, 2012); *El Yazısı / One Day or Another* (Ali Vatansever, 2012).

Cinematheque was founded in 1965 with help from Henri Langlois, the French film archivist and cinephile (born in Ottoman İzmir) by intellectuals who gathered around the film journal, *Yeni Sinema / New Cinema*. The 15 founding members were **Muhsin Ertuğrul**, Sabahattin Eyuboğlu, Aziz Albek, **Nijat Özön**, Semih Tuğrul, **Onat Kutlar**, Tuncan Okan, Hüseyin Hacıbaşoğlu (President), Tunç Yalman, Cevat Çapan, Adnan Çoker, Adnan Benk, Mahzar Şevket İpşiroğlu, Macit Gökberk and Şakir Eczacıbaşı. Publishing interviews with celebrated film-makers such as Godard and Antonioni; screening masterpieces of European cinema, particularly the Soviet Revolutionary Cinema and organizing discussions on the French *nouvelle vague*, Italian neo-realism and Brazilian *Cinema Novo,* the group aimed at establishing resistance against **Yeşilçam** similar to the resistance of European art cinema against Hollywood. They also criticized the new **social realist** movement for lacking theoretical basis and artistic maturity comparable to the standards of the West (with the exception of **Yılmaz Güney**). After reaching its peak during the mid-1970s, the **cinematheque** was closed in 1980 by the military regime and never re-opened.

Comedy is considered to have begun in Turkish cinema with the first feature film, *Himmet Ağanın İzdivacı / The Marriage of Himmet Agha* (**Weinberg/ Uzkınay**, 1916–18). Şadi Fikret Karagözlü, a theatre actor popular with the role of 'Bican Efendi' fashioned after Charlie Chaplin, initiated the transfer of the comic character to cinema culminating in a 22-minute feature, *Bican Efendi Vekilharç* (1921), with a number of sequels, with **Fuat Uzkınay** behind the camera (Scognamillo 1987: 32; Özön 1995: 19–20).

Comedy gained a new dimension in the 1960s with the emergence of talented comedians, and most film-makers tried the **genre**: *Fıstık Gibi Maşallah / Like a Peach, May God Protect Her* (Hulki Saner, 1964, an adaptation of Billy Wilder's *Some Like It Hot*, 1959), **Türkan Şoray** replacing Marilyn Monroe and İzzet Günay and **Sadri Alışık** as the involuntary transvestites; **Atıf Yılmaz's** *Ah, Güzel İstanbul / Oh, Beautiful Istanbul* (1966) and **Halit Refiğ**'s satire on Hollywood comedies, *Kızın Var mı Derdin Var / If You've Got a Daughter, You've Got a Problem* (unofficial English translation) (1973), inspired by Vincente Minelli's *Father of the Bride* (1950), are some of the prominent examples. **Öztürk Serengil** created 'Adana'lı Tayfur' (Tayfur from Adana), a character who distorted words and used foul language and **Sadri Alışık** followed with the 'Tourist Ömer'. Both represented *lumpen* marginal characters. None of these films contributed significantly to the comedy **genre**. In the 1970s with the contributions of distinguished comedy writers such as Aziz Nesin, real comedians – **Kemal Sunal, Zeki Alasya, Metin Akpınar** – emerged bringing their stage talent to cinema. **Ertem Eğilmez**, inspired by Frank Capra's comedies about small people standing against the powerful, made films that showed good people of old neighbourhoods fighting against the system, the rich and the mighty and winning the battle in a naïve way. **Atıf Yılmaz, Zeki Ökten** and **Kartal Tibet** also made comedy films. **Sunal**'s 'Şaban' character, which mostly relies on mimicry for humour, has never lost its popularity although **Şener Şen, İlyas Salman, Alasya** and **Akpınar** also contributed immensely to the development of the **genre** which began to underscore social issues in the 1980s, although most comedies were slapstick (Onaran 1994: 188). By the 1990s, the industry practically collapsed with the economic crises. Starting with the 2000s, with the increase in the quantity of the films made (but not necessarily the quality), comedy films have displayed two major trends in terms of content/theme, structure/topic/ cinematography: films with a good script, good direction and acting and quality visual and technical features (***Vizontele***, Yılmaz Erdoğan, Ömer Faruk Sorak, 2001; *Vizontele Tuuba*, **Erdoğan**, 2004; *Beynelmilel / International*, Muharrem Gülmez, **Sırrı Süreyya Önder**, 2007; *Hokkabaz / The Magician*, Taner Baltacı, **Cem Yılmaz**, 2006; *O Şimdi Asker / He's in the Army Now*, **Mustafa Altıoklar**, 2002) and the mainstream Hollywood copies, based on shallow and banal stories, forced gags and derogatory points of view of the 'other', particularly the woman. The second can be named as 'kitsch comedies', for example *G.O.R.A.* (**Sorak**, 2004), *A.R.O.G.* (**Cem Yılmaz**, 2008) or *Recep İvedik* (Togan Gökbakar, 2008). Some other comedy films are experiments that do not belong in either category, and often do not find distribution possibilities, or do poorly at the box-office (*Fasulye / Bean*, Bora Tekay, 2000; *Güle Güle / Raindrop*, **Zeki Ökten**, 2000; *İnşaat / Under Construction*, **Ömer Vargı**, 2003; *Korkuyorum Anne* aka *İnsan Nedir ki? / I'm Scared* aka *What's Human Anyway*, **Reha Erdem**, 2004; *Dondurmam Gaymak/ Ice Cream, I Scream*, **Yüksel Aksu**, 2006; *Hacivat Karagöz Neden Öldürüldü? / Killing the Shadow*, **Ezel Akay**, 2006) (Karakaya 2011: 53).

Coşkun, Mahmut Fazıl (b. 1973) Director, screenwriter. A graduate of the Istanbul Technical University in Electrical Engineering in 1995, Mahmut Fazıl Coşkun studied television and digital media at UCLA and made three shorts in the US before returning to Turkey where he directed three documentaries and won awards. His first feature, ***Uzak İhtimal / Wrong Rosary*** (2008), about a naive muezzin's love for a Catholic candidate for a nun, brought him the VPRO Tiger Award of the Rotterdam Film Festival 2009, a first for Turkish cinema. His second film *Yozgat Blues* (2013) is about the loneliness of three people, a

Figure 36 Yozgat Blues (Mahmut Fazıl Coşkun, 2013) (Courtesy of International Istanbul Film Festival)

disillusioned singer of once-popular French songs (or rather one song) who goes to the provincial town of Yozgat for a few gigs, a young woman with no prospects who accompanies him to make a duo and the local barber who is trying to find a partner. The provincial town is more alive than in the films of **Demirkubuz** with no one hanging around hotel lobbies watching old movies, but rather following enterprising schemes. **Arabesque** is still fashionable. Girls go on blind dates and poetry sessions garner interest.

Crime films began in the 1940s (*Yılmaz Ali*, **Faruk Kenç**, 1940) and soon became very popular, *Kanun Namına* (**Akad**, 1952) as the most accomplished one. By the 1970s and 1980s, the popularity of the crime **genre** including gangster films, mafia films and 'whodunit' films exceeded that of adventure films in connection with the social and political atmosphere when citizens needed to feel secure, thinking the police force would protect them from violence and solve unsolved crimes.

    Yavuz Turgul is perhaps unique in bringing a local language to the **genre**. He had unprecedented success with *Eşkıya / The Bandit* (1996), which combines the crime **genre** with **melodrama**; *Gönül Yarası / Lovelorn* (2005) and *Kabadayı* (2007) carry elements of the crime **genre** and *Av Mevsimi / Hunting Season* (2010) is an important example of the **genre** with its sound character development, narrative, editing and the weaving of the victim–murderer–detective triangle within the conventions of the **genre** while developing for the audience the suspense aspect as to the identity of the murderer.

Turgul's most important contribution is the way he deals with the characters from a **social realist** perspective, delving into the sociological depths of the crime within a structure that blends the stereotypes of the **genre** with local motifs. Through the relationship between the victim and the perpetrator, he underscores the importance of social criticism, including within the **genre** the transformation of the balance of power in society with migration from the country to the city and the struggles perpetuated by class differences. He identifies the victim from a **social realist** approach and places the concept of customs within the cause/effect relationship as a local agent. In that sense, the closing remarks in *Hunting Season* are significant: 'we looked for the reason behind Pamuk's death in the triangle of love, betrayal, honour. It's like this in Turkey. Our murders are not very creative… victim of customs, honour killings or a jealous lover…We changed our point of view and we saw' (Aytaş, Tüysüz and Ulutaş 2011: 51).

Some of the other films in the crime **genre** that drew attention in the 2000s were *Polis / Police* (**Onur Ünlü**, 2007), *Pars Kiraz Operasyonu / Pars: Operation Cherry* (**Osman Sınav**, 2007), *Sis ve Gece / The Night and the Fog* (Turgut Yasalar, 2007) and *Başka Semtin Çocukları / Children of the Other Side* (Aydın Bulut, 2008). In a country where serial killers do not exist, cinema created films like *Melek Yüzlü Cani* aka *Nefret / The Butcher with the Face of an Angel* aka *Hate* (unofficial English title) (Aram Gülyüz, 1986) about a pervert who kills prostitutes, *Beyza'nın Kadınları / Shattered Soul* (**Mustafa Altıoklar**, 2006) about a woman butcher with personality disorders and *Ejder Kapanı / Dragon Trap* (**Uğur Yücel**, 2010) about a man who kills paedophiles – a film that uses classic Hollywood clichés to tell a story imbued in local colour.

Ç

Çakmaklı, Yücel (b. Afyonkarahisar, 1937 – d. Istanbul, 2009) Director, screenwriter, producer. The initiator of *milli* cinema (**national cinema** with a religious base) within the structure of **Yeşilçam**, Yücel Çakmaklı began as a film critic, worked as assistant director to **Osman Seden** and **Orhan Aksoy**, formed Elif Film in 1969 and made films for the state television, TRT, between 1975–90. His first feature, *Birleşen Yollar / Crossing Roads* aka *Merging Paths* (1970), released during political upheavals and the reign of soft porno, became the prototype for Islamic films that use the formula of a love interest between an innocent traditional person (**İzzet Günay**) and a degenerate modern one (**Türkan Şoray**). *Oğlum Osman / My Son, Osman* (1973), exalting religious feelings with inserted documentary footage, and *Kızım Ayşe / My Daughter, Ayşe* (1974), recounting the evils of modernity, were very popular. *Memleketim / My Homeland* (1975), through a non-consummated romance between a medical student with nationalist ideals (**Tarık Akan**) and his love object (**Filiz Akın**) fascinated by western values, attributed the unhappiness of the couple to the east/west divide in Turkish culture. *Minyeli Abdullah / Abdullah of Minye* (1989), narrating the sufferings of a man dedicated to Islam, received unprecedented box-office success (530,000 viewers) that led the way for an upsurge of religious films and a trend that came to be know as 'white cinema'. A sequel was made the following year. Among Çakmaklı's other popular films are *Zehra* (1972) and *Sahibini Arayan Madalya / A Medal Searching for its Owner* (1989).

Çelik, Reis (b. Ardahan, 1961) Director, screenwriter, producer, cinematographer, composer, editor. A socio-politically oriented film-maker, Reis Çelik studied economics at the University of Istanbul and music and drama at the Istanbul Municipal Conservatory and worked for national newspapers as a correspondent in political and economic affairs. He was instrumental in establishing the Centre for Video-Television in 1983, the base for the first private channel of Turkey (ATV). In the absence of legal permission, video-newspapers were organized and sold on news-stands. Çelik also shot around 600 commercials, made political campaign films and held exhibitions of his photography from travels in the Middle East, Asia, Europe and Australia. His first feature, *Işıklar Sönmesin / Let There Be Light* (1996) was a humanist story that brought face to face, a Kurdish rebel representing PKK (the outlawed Kurdistan Workers' Party) and a member of the Turkish Armed Forces. Despite its schematic structure and the didactic ending, the film is noteworthy, not only for the spectacular winter images of the mountainous southeast Turkey but more importantly, for addressing a previously taboo subject at the height of the civil war. However trying to tread a neutral ground while circumventing state censorship brought him strong criticism. With his second feature, Çelik tackled another taboo subject, the execution of Deniz Gezmiş, the charismatic leader of the Marxist–Leninist student movement by the military regime. *Hoşçakal Yarın / Good-bye Tomorrow* (1998) was based on the court records and the memoirs of the lawyer who defended the legendary hero and his friends who were hanged in 1972 on charges of terrorism and undermining the democratic regime. The film questions the fairness of the execution of young men who have not committed a serious crime, but does not dwell on the ideology of the movement. *İnat Hikayeleri / Tales of Intransigence* (2004) with remarkable cinematography of winter scenes, shot on a frozen lake under a heavy blizzard and below –35 degrees, relies on improvisation, echoing early forms of story-telling. *Mülteci / Azül / Refugee* (2007) foregrounds the plight of political refugees in Europe through the story of an apolitical youth from south eastern Anatolia, caught between the police and the insurgents by being in the wrong place at the wrong time. Entering Germany illegally, he is placed in an inhumanly efficient refugee camp to wait for the decision of the authorities, which results in him losing his mind. *Lal Gece / The Night of Silence* (2012), the fifth film of Çelik, on the burning issue of child brides, was awarded the Crystal Bear at the Berlin Film Festival 2012.

Çelikezer, Raşit (b. İzmir, 1969) Director, producer, screenwriter, playwright. A graduate from the Faculty of Fine Arts Cinema – TV section of the Nine September University in İzmir, Çelikezer has made short films and shot over 300 episodes for television series. His first film, *Gökten Üç Elma Düştü / Three Apples Fell From the Sky* (2008) was more suitable for television than for the wide screen. With *Can* (2011), a **melodrama** about the disintegration of the marriage of a childless couple after adopting a baby, he tried to break the linear narrative with flash-forwards, which was not very successful. The film's premise of approaching adoption from the point of view of the woman was original but the underdeveloped characters whose actions were not justified and the conservative message of motherhood were the drawbacks. *Can* received the World Cinema Dramatic Jury Special Prize for Artistic Vision at the Sundance Film Festival 2012, and subsequently travelled to a number of festivals.

Çetin, Sinan (b. Kars, 1953) Director, screenwriter, producer, actor, cinematographer, publisher. Known for his provocations, particularly derogatory remarks about art cinema, which he believes survives on alms from the state, shunned by leftist intellectuals for his political change of heart, Sinan Çetin studied art history at the University of Ankara, starting his film career in 1975 as assistant director to **Zeki Ökten** in *Hanzo*. His first feature, *Bir Günün Hikayesi / The Story of a Day* (1980) was severely cut by the censors. *14 Numara / Number*

14 (1985) about the harrowing life of prostitutes in the now defunct Abanoz Street (the red light district where state-endorsed prostitution was supervised through identity cards; opened in 1884 during the Crimean War, closed briefly after the establishment of the Republic, the operation was terminated in the late 1970s) was a pioneer in underscoring the legal–illegal position of the prostitutes. Despite its sketchy characters and underdeveloped script, the film captured the audience with its realistic images and along with the earlier *Çiçek Abbas / Abbas in Flower* (1981) (written by **Yavuz Turgul**) and *Çirkinler de Sever / The Ugly Also Love* (1982), both featuring **İlyas Salman**, it belongs to the so-called 'leftist period' of the film-maker. His *Prenses / The Princess* (1986) was criticized for advocating that readiness to sacrifice oneself to a cause – Marxism, Fascism, Christianity, Islam – could only lead to terrorism. *Berlin in Berlin* (1992), inspired by an Eastern custom that forbids killing the enemy while he is a guest in the house, was very successful. *Bay E / Mr E* (1995), Çetin's favourite, about an intellectual lost in Anatolia was a failure. *Propaganda* (1998), inspired by his childhood experiences as the son of a customs officer, was criticized by the local press but did well at the box-office, mainly due to the presence of the two popular comedians, ***Kemal Sunal*** and ***Metin Akpınar***, and it won awards at national and international film festivals. *Komiser Şekspir / Commissar Shakespeare* (2000) and *Kağıt / The Paper* (2010) are some of the other films of Çetin whose work has shown a decline in artistic terms, particularly with *Banka / The Bank* (2002), *Romantik / The Romantic* (2007) and *Çanakkale Çocukları / The Children of Gallipoli* (2012). He is the founder of Plato Film Production (1986) one of the most successful production companies in Turkey, which also offers academic programmes.

Çıplak Vatandaş / The Naked Citizen (1985), the first film of **Başar Sabuncu**, is a good example of the satirical approach of conscientious cinema to the social-climbing ambitions that peaked during the Turgut Özal years (prime minister and president 1983–93) with the introduction of open-market economy when quick riches schemes attracted citizens suffering high inflation. Whereas commercial cinema has produced schematic fantasies – the protagonist suddenly becoming a famous singer, marrying a rich person or winning the lottery – serious cinema tried to depict the dramas of the individuals realistically, often using the **genre** of **comedy** for social criticism.

Unable to provide for his large family with the meagre salary of a functionary, İbrahim, a kind-hearted family man, starts moon-lighting which leaves him exhausted. Running naked to the street in a mad frenzy, he catches the attention of a journalist and a newspaper begins to exploit his story, leading to his appearance in television commercials as literally the 'naked' citizen. The film's message is that in an irrational society upward mobility is possible only through madness.

The malaise of a society in transition – the plight of the workers unable to strike, the unemployed with no prospects, the retired with inadequate pensions, the street vendors menaced by the police and ridiculed by society and the tenants evicted without recourse – are exposed with gentle humour with a remarkable performance from the celebrated comedy actor, **Şener Şen**. The fact that naked protestors continue to appear in real life is evidence of the contemporaneity of the concerns in the film.

Director, Screenwriter: **Başar Sabuncu**; Producer: Ferit Turgut, Kadir Turgut; Production: Uzman Filmcilik; Cinematography: Ertunç Şenkay; Editor: **Mevlut Koçak**; Music: Melih Kibar; Sound: Ertem Esenboğa; Cast: **Şener Şen**, Salih Kalyon, Burçin Terzioğlu, Nilgün Akçaoğlu, Tuncay Akça, Renan Fosforoğlu, Kamran Usluer, Bilge Zobu, Pekcan Koşar, Zihni Küçümen, Candan Sabuncu, Ayşe Kökçü

Çoğunluk / Majority (**Seren Yüce**, 2010) exposes the masculinist structure of Turkish society using the classic narrative structure of **Yeşilçam** by orienting the dramatic structure around the family. Crucial matters – money, women, nation, army – are discussed around the dinner table, or rather propounded by the patriarch and ratified by the others who continue eating with one eye on the television screen. As a subversive detail, the protagonist Mertkan (Bartu Küçükçağlayan) chooses such moments to masturbate in his room.

Mertkan's father is in the construction business, the traditional metier of the corrupt nouveau rich of **Yeşilçam**, which has not lost its relevance in contemporary society with continuous migration from the countryside requiring more dwellings and the countless illegal schemes that are the nightmares of urban planning. The living space of the family and the cars they drive show their ostentatious taste. The father expects his sons to be like him, marry a suitable girl, take over the family business and bully the lesser advantaged; the status quo has to be maintained. Masculinist traits are reproduced generation after generation. A chubby boy unable to keep pace with his father continues to run to please him; at home he is cruel to the cleaning woman; he hangs around shopping malls with his friends, jeering at skaters (gendering the sport as feminine) and mocking those who fall on the ice (men don't fall). The father and son visit the sauna where men discuss business. The military service is perceived as an institution that makes men out of boys. Mertkan boasts of his sexual prowess in male company, demeaning the woman he loves, and abandons his love interest without protest on orders from his father – unlike Bekir in a similar family situation in **Demirkubuz**'s 2006 feature *Kader / Destiny*, who surrenders himself to love. Incidentally, in both films, the father is played by the same actor, Settar Tanrıöğen, who is rather typecast.

Having never taken the collective minibus in a city where this is the most functional way of transportation, Mertkan's encounter with the 'other' is confined to the cleaning woman, 'the outsider within' (Özyeğin 2002: 45), whose minoritarian identity (Brown 2006: 36) is tolerated for convenience ('She smells bad,' complains Mertkan. 'Do you expect a peasant woman to smell of perfume?' retorts his mother); then Gül, who tries to awaken sensibilities in him but fails and the taxi-driver (Erkan Can), whose taxi he damages and then escapes responsibility. Although he shows a minor reckoning with his conscience in each case, it does not last. At the end, when he bullies the construction workers, his only concern is his security. He has become the man his father wanted him to become. Soon, he will be the grandfather in *Tepenin Ardı / Beyond the Hill* (**Emin Alper**, 2012), living in paranoia of the other.

Figure 37 Çoğunluk / Majority (Seren Yüce, 2010) (Courtesy of International Istanbul Film Festival)

The patriarchal family structure; the gendered division of family management – father as the provider and mother as the home-maker; the victimization of women who perpetuate their victimization by self-identifying as victims (the mother complains and cries but instead of taking action, drowns her misery in soap operas) and male sexual intercourse as endorsement of power (after sleeping with

Figure 38 Çoğunluk / Majority (Seren Yüce, 2010) (Courtesy of International Istanbul Film Festival)

Gül, Mertkan smiles at himself in the mirror with newly acquired confidence) are the general tendencies of the Muslim/Turkish society that are rendered with precision in the film. The importance of money-making, even shady, if the end justifies the means, versus education/culture; the social and political conservatism that includes nationalism (Mertkan means 'brave blood'); the self-identification as 'Muslim (sunni) and Turk' and the exclusion of those who are not 'us', are attributes that define the middle class that evolved during the liberal politics of the 1980s and has been established permanently. The family in the film is a metonym for the nation, and apoliticized Mertkan is the ordinary citizen, trained to obey without questioning the authority of the father figure, be it the patriarch at home, the state, the army or the religion. In that sense, the ending of the film, with 'majority' written on a blackboard like in an elementary school, is significant.

Yüce gives importance to details in defining the space of each character. Both Mertkan and Gül live in the periphery, habitations constructed with the population boom, the concrete cement blocks that have created inhuman landscapes. Gül is identified with smaller spaces – the stairs leading to her apartment are narrower than Mertkan's; slippers are placed beside the door and not inside the cupboard, but both dwellings are dark and uncanny. Mertkan always arrives in the dark, whether to his home or Gül's, and seems to lack space to manoeuvre – inside his room, he is confined to a corner, at dinner table, he tries to be invisible. When outside, he is either cruising with friends in a car or getting drunk in discotheques, both dark places. He notices the beauty of the Bosphorus for the first time when Gül takes him on a ferryboat.

The fundamental role of television in people's lives, which nurtures 'watching' rather than 'acting' is well positioned in the film. The television is on while the family eats, regular glances at the screen serve as escape routes from confrontation; Mertkan turns the television on after having sex with Gül, shielding himself against real intimacy; his mother informs him about the accidental death of the housemaid while her eyes are on the television, which reveals another tragedy. She cries the way people cry watching soap operas.

The definition of a young Kurdish woman is problematic. A sociology student who waitresses to support her studies while risking reprisals from her family is charmed by an ignorant and immature boy who has never read a book and her dream is to marry a handsome man! In her neighbourhood, burglaries happen; her family follow the typical honour codes and take her back by force. The film follows the tradition of **Yeşilçam** by refraining from identifying Gül as a Kurd. Her natal place, the father's advice to Mertkan to avoid those who want to 'divide the country' are clues for the local audience, but foreign viewers unfamiliar with Turkish geography often think she is a gypsy. Perhaps, her 'other-ness' is the important issue and as Mertkan's friend says, 'Gypsy, Kurd, communist…all the same'.

The film is made from the point of view of the majority and therefore, the realistically developed characters belong to the so-called majority. The rest are presented as figures that appear as handicaps in the development of Mertkan's character into a bona fide fascist (or they are the doors that open, offering him the possibility of creating himself from zero rather than perpetuating the vicious circle, but he cannot see).

The question remains: are they the majority, or are the majority those like the taxi driver, the construction workers, the cleaning woman, the sociology student waitressing to support her studies, or the ordinary citizen who takes the collective minibus to work from the settlements in the outskirts?

Director, Screenwriter: **Seren Yüce**; Producers: Sevil Demirci, Önder Çakar; Production: Yeni Sinemacılık; Cinematographer: Barış Özbiçer; Editor: Mary Stephen; Art Director: Meral Efe; Sound: Mustafa Bölükbaşı; Cast: Bartu Küçükçağlayan, Settar Tanrıöğen, Nihal Kolda, Esme Madra, Erkan Can

Çölgeçen, Nesli (b. Manisa, 1955) Director, screenwriter, producer, cinematographer. A graduate in journalism from the Faculty of Political Sciences of Ankara University, Nesli Çölgeçen began to direct short films and documentaries in 1979. His first feature was *Kardeşim Benim / My Brother* (1983). ***Züğürt Ağa / The Broke Landlord*** (1985) and *Selamsızlar Bandosu / The Band* (1987) participated in several national and international festivals and won awards. *İmdat ile Zarife / Zarife, the Dancing Bear* (1991), exposing the cruel treatment of bears as a spectacle in the cities was not successful nationally but won the Grand Prize at the Canary Islands International Environment Nature Films Festival (1991). After a long period that he spent making documentaries and commercial films, he made the thriller, *Oyunbozan / Unfair Game* (2000). *Son Buluşma / The Last Meeting* (2008), a docu-drama, was about the three remaining veterans of the War of Independence. *Denizden Gelen / Brought By the Sea* (2009), a Turkish version of *Welcome* (Philippe Lioret, 2009) was about a policeman who impulsively becomes mentor to an illegal black child from Ghana and risks prison to help him. Unlike *Welcome*, here the hero (or anti-hero) dies and the refugee is alive. A number of films about Turkish illegals exist in the west, but it is rare for cinema to focus on illegal immigrants in Turkey, the number of which rises rapidly. Çölgeçen continues to work on various audio-visual art forms while lecturing at Bilgi University in Istanbul.

D

Dal, Behlül (b. Istanbul, 1922 – d. Antalya, 2002) Director, screenwriter, producer. A pioneer of short film and documentary and founder of the Antalya Golden Orange Film Festival, Behlül Dal attended the Faculty of Law of Ankara University, leaving his studies for military service, after which he began to direct plays in Antalya. In addition to numerous national and international awards, he broke records winning the short film award eight times at the Golden Orange. Having made almost 300 short films, most of which are about Antalya, he also shot three feature-length dramas, *İnsanlık İçin* aka *Kuduz / For Humanity* aka *Raby* (1958) (with Asaf Tengiz), *Kıbrıs Şehitleri / The Martyrs of Cyprus* (1959) and *Istırap Çocuğu / The Child of Sorrow* (1960), all black and white. Golden Orange gives a Special Jury Award annually to his name.

Dar Alanda Kısa Paslaşmalar / Offside (2000) is a narrative-driven film that depicts the macho world of men similar to ***Gemide / On Board*** (1998), the director's debut feature, except for the graphic violence. The concept of neighbourhood as the nucleus of ordinary lives, which had served **Yeşilçam** for decades, is revisited through adventures of an amateur football team in provincial Bursa in the early 1980s. Suat, in his thirties, who still lives with his family and works at his father's shop, practises as the goalkeeper for Esnaf Spor (Tradesmen's Sport) and dreams of becoming professional. He is in love with the neighbourhood beauty, Nurten. The community's only wish is to be the champion to achieve professional status, which interests Cem, the young and ambitious president of Ülkü Spor (Ideal Sport). While the new transfer, the good-looking Serkan, captures the hearts of the young women, Suat drowns his sorrow in the arms of the prostitute Aynur (rumoured to be Armenian, a **Yeşilçam** cliché of giving non-Muslim identity to prostitutes), ignorant of her history with his coach Hacı. Key remarks, 'The ship is like the country' find their equivalent in 'Life is like football. People play it together. If you're not competent, you lose… It is a game played with a team. If the team is not good, you can't win.' The confinement and claustrophobia of the ship and the aggressiveness of the captain and crew are replaced with the suffocating atmosphere of a seemingly friendly neighbourhood on the way to extinction that offers temporary false security before the explosion. Tradition's loss to modernity is underscored with the demolishing of the old neighbourhoods and the demise of the elderly, some leaving surprises behind, such as the Armenian who is taken to the Muslim cemetery by mistake (reference to an actual event in **Yeşilçam**), an allusion to the days before 'othering' when all lived together peacefully, at least on the surface.

Director: **Serdar Akar**; Producers: Üstün Karabol, Nida Karabol; Production: Umut Sanat Filmcilik; Screenwriters: **Serdar Akar**, Önder Çakar; Cinematographer: Mehmet Aksın; Editors: Hakan Akol, Onur Tan; Music: Fahir Atakoğlu; Cast: Fatih Akyol, **Müjde Ar**, Savaş Dinçel, Rafet El Roman, Erkan Can, Şahnaz Çakıralp, Uğur Polat, İamail İncekara, Sezai Aydın, Kemal Kocatürk

Demirkubuz, Zeki (b. Isparta, 1964) Director, producer, screenwriter, cinematographer, editor, actor. A truly independent film-maker who finances his small-budget films himself, Demirkubuz delves into the dark corners of his characters' inner worlds without losing sight of the external circumstances that produce such characters. His self-reflexive cinema is imbued in local colours (from strong beliefs in destiny to intricately crafted minute details of the Turkish psyche, the mannerism, the oddities and the manner of living). One may define his cinema as truly national without being nationalistic. At the same time, the underlying historical, social and political circumstances of his characters are entirely universal.

Demirkubuz served a three-year prison sentence for Marxist and Maoist beliefs when he was only 17, earned his living pushing a cart in Istanbul as a fruit vendor, worked for eight years as assistant to notable film-makers including **Zeki Ökten** (***Sürü / The Herd***, 1986) and studied at the Department of Communications of the University of Istanbul.

Figure 39 Zeki Demirkubuz in *Bekleme Odası / The Waiting Room* (Demirkubuz, 2003) (Courtesy of International Istanbul Film Festival)

Figure 40 Yeraltı / Inside (Zeki Demirkubuz, 2011) (Courtesy of International Istanbul Film Festival)

Prison as a panopticon in the Foucaultian sense (Foucault 1995: 216) is a strong motif in his films. *C Blok / Block C* (1994), his first film, explores the interrelation between urban lives and post-modern architecture. Not only does the title refer to his cell number, but as Chris Berry points out scenes of urgent sexual passion between the maid and the janitor's son combined with scenes in which the latter watches the protagonist resemble the fusion of fantasies and real experiences of persecution and lust typical of prison dramas (Berry 2006: 21). *Innocence / Masumiyet* (1997), which brought him international recognition and accolades, starts inside a prison, in the room of the head warden, with a door that will not close (a Bressonian obsession that is repeated in his other films), where we hear the plea of the protagonist to continue his incarceration. In the thriller *Üçüncü Sayfa / The Third Page* (1999), several locales resemble prison cells, from dingy basement flats to murky corridors. *Yazgı / Fate* (2002), inspired by Albert Camus's *The Stranger*, foregrounds a protagonist indifferent to life. *Itiraf / Confession* (2001) is a mystery drama on guilt, fidelity and conscience. *Bekleme Odası / The Waiting Room* (2003) is about personal and professional integrity through a successful film-maker (Demirkubuz himself) suffering from inertia as he prepares to adapt Dostoyevsky's *Crime and Punishment* to screen. They complete the trilogy of explorations of the feeling of guilt, which Demirkubuz calls *Karanlık Üstüne Öyküler / Tales About Darkness*. (*Fate* and *Confession* were screened simultaneously in the *Un Certain Regard* section of the Cannes Film Festival, a rarity in that festival's history.) *Innocence* was re-visited in 2005 with **Kader / Destiny** (2005), another **melodrama** of black passion that gave a past to the characters of the earlier film.

While *C Blok* interrogates the impact of modernity on middle-class urban lifestyles, ***Innocence, The Third Page*** and ***Destiny*** shift to the disadvantaged 'others'. *Kıskanmak / Envy* (2009) explores the dark side of human nature through a *Madame Bovary* story with layered allusions to Fyodor Dostoevsky's *Crime and Punishment*. *Yeraltı / Inside* (2011), a 'free adaptation' like *Fate*, this time from Dostoevsky's *Notes from Underground*, is built on the question of personal honesty and integrity, the principal theme of Demirkubuz's œuvre.

An important representative of the generation that launched what came to be known as the **New Turkish Cinema**, the style of Demirkubuz is distinct from the cerebral aesthetics of **Derviş Zaim** or the visual self-reflexivity of **Nuri Bilge Ceylan**. The cinemas of **Ceylan** and Demirkubuz are both self-referential, but Demirkubuz draws his inspiration from **Yeşilçam** which he experienced first hand during his long years as assistant director, narrating personal and political stories within this tradition. His characters, whether rebounded from one city to the other as in *Innocence* and *Destiny*, from one socio-economic class to the other as in *C-Block*, *The Third Page* and *Confession* or in and out of jail, as in *Innocence, Fate* and *Destiny* are always marginal. The cities are acoustically visible though barely identifiable (except Ankara in *Yeraltı / Inside*, 2011), the camera favouring indoor shots, or unlit streets.

Bleak interiors, soulless hotel rooms, dim corridors and gloomy, basement apartments intensify the feeling of entrapment that swallows the transient who move in vicious circles as strangers to their prescribed identities. Several crucial action scenes, most of them violent, take place on the thresholds. In *The Third Page*, İsa is harassed on the threshold before Meryem comes to his aid. In *Fate*, Musa and his neighbour meet each other between the two doors when the latter is wounded and bleeding; the violence of the neighbour against his girlfriend and his subsequent arrest are heard/seen through the door. Musa watches the adultery of his wife without entering the flat by catching an image of her naked back on the bed and noticing a pair of men's sneakers beside the door. Returning home after his release from prison, he witnesses the domestic life of his neighbour across the corridor when the woman rings the doorbell to ask for some eggs.

Confession scenes are the trademark of **Demirkubuz**. In *Innocence*, Bekir tells his story in the park to Yusuf as the camera shifts from his face to the little girl in the distance, the audience reflecting on her future. In *Confession* while the wife will never admit adultery, confession of a different kind emerges.

An important narrative principle for Demirkubuz is the Ozu-style ellipses; the omission of plot material – the moments of intense emotion that are the backbone of Hollywood – or even an event: the 'minor ellipses' in which certain plot points are dropped, the 'surprise ellipses' where plot points prepared for by dialogue as action are omitted and the 'dramatic ellipses' whereby something occurs off-screen (particularly in *The Third Page*, *Fate*, *Confession* and *Inside*). Silences and spaces between things stress the crisis of communication. The de-emphasis on drama and the emphasis on mood and tone impose active viewer participation to reintegrate constantly into the action and reorient within filmic time and space. Demirkubuz also pays attention to transitional spaces between actions often devoid of human figures, which help the viewer understand the scene change or locale and prepare them for the retrospective activity of reorienting themselves in the next scene, as the narrative information is postponed, but just like in Ozu, it is not always clear where the next locale is going to be and how much time has passed (Eleftheriotis and Needham 2006: 20–1).

Demirkubuz's films are deeply political, from the upstairs–downstairs interaction in *Block-C* displaying mercilessly the middle class created after the 1980 *coup d'état* that apoliticized the society, to the problem of unemployment (so many adult men spend their time in front of the television set in hotel lobbies in *Innocence* and *Destiny*). The drab existence of the **Yeşilçam** workers without job security is underscored through İsa in *The Third Page*, who acts in small roles. In *Innocence* the characters try to escape from their *huis-clos* lives through their passion (Uğur is infatuated with Zagor, Bekir and Yusuf with Uğur) but references to socio-economic circumstances are subtle, whereas *Destiny* holds a mirror to the underdogs. *Envy* is a portrait of new Turkey after Independence as envisioned by Kemal Atatürk with women, rid of the veil, attending Western-style parties in smart outfits even in the provinces, a perfect facade. What has really changed for women behind the closed doors, Demirkubuz seems to ask. Family is sacred, passion is sin and deviations from the norms must be punished severely. *Inside* is a strong indictment of the intellectuals who have sold their ideals.

Demirkubuz is also the director of a documentary called, *Barış Expresi / Peace Express* (1996).

Dikişçi, Salih (b. Malatya, 1940 – d. Istanbul, 2009) Cinematographer, director, screenwriter, producer, actor. Having worked as cinematographer in over 230 films and television series, Salih Dikişçi is the four-time recipient of the Best Director of Photography award at the Antalya Golden Orange Film Festival. He is particularly remembered for his exceptional work in *Bereketli Topraklar Üzerinde / On Fertile Lands* (**Kıral**, 1979), *Kızılırmak Karakoyun* (**Akad**, 1967) and *Kırık Bir Aşk Hikayesi / A Broken Love Story* (**Kavur**, 1982).

Diyet / The Blood Money (1974) is the third part of the Migration Trilogy of **Lütfi Ö. Akad**, which somewhat begins where *Gelin / The Bride* (1973) ends. Meryem/Hacer (**Hülya Koçyiğit**) is now a factory worker living with her father, Yunus Dede and her two children. When a worker named Mustafa has an accident, the foreman gives his job to his countryman, Hasan (Hakan Balamir). Hacer eventually marries Hasan, and they both work overtime with minimum wage, but Hacer begins to ask questions.

The predicaments of the Anatolian migrants are presented from two points of view: the young worker happy to leave the backward conditions of the village sees a future where his sweat will be rewarded, and the elderly Yunus Dede, who cannot adapt to city life, misses the insularity of the village where people know and respect each other. He tells his friend: 'If you pull a tree from its earth, no matter what you do, it does not work…We thought human kind would survive without the roots.' His friend responds: 'The problem is not that. We peasants are used to till the land and leave the rest to God… It is not like that here.' To contribute to the family income, Yunus is obliged to sell balloons on the street, until death relieves him.

Earlier in the film, the main conflict is between man and technology, which destroys human values and alienates man. Soon attention is drawn to the power machinery. A remnant of feudalism, the boss employs those who accept low rates without union protection. His son, more modern and more human in appearance, is no different and the foreman turns against his people for personal benefit.

Akad chooses characters from different echelons of political awareness for the message of organized combat to achieve freedom and rights. Initially, few have confidence in the union. Hacer is unaware of the possibilities to rise against exploitation, but has an intuitive sense, whereas Hasan informs on the others to ingratiate himself with the bosses. In the dramatic finale, when the boss divides the unionized from the non-unionized, Hasan stays with the non-unionized but Hacer, after a moment of hesitation, joins the unionized, holding on to the wheelchair of Mustafa. Blood money is paid when Hasan loses his arm to a machine. Hacer attacks the machines but soon realizes that the real culprits are those without political consciousness. By showing the evolution of characters to political awareness, **Akad** sends a stronger message than he would have by sermons, through those who have already acquired this awareness (Dönmez-Colin 2008: 63).

Director, Scriptwriter: **Lütfi Ö. Akad**; Producer: Hürrem Erman; Production: Erman Film; Cinematographer: Gani Turanlı; Cast: **Hülya Koçyiğit**, Hakan Balamir, **Erol Taş**, Erol Günaydın, Güner Sümer, Turgut Savaş, Yaşar Şener, Atıf Kaptan

Doğan, Zeynel (b. Kahramanmaraş, 1979) Director. Graduating in Communications from the Anadolu University, Zeynel Doğan began working at the Cinema Workshop of the Diyarbakır municipality, where he presently is the director. With **Orhan Eskiköy**, he directed fiction feature, *Babamın Sesi / Dengê Bavê Min / The Voice of My Father* (2012), which has received acclaim.

Doruk, Belgin (b. Ankara, 1936 – d. Istanbul, 1995) Actor. One of the most loved and the most productive actors for a long period, Belgin Doruk played in numerous **melodramas** and sentimental comedies – from a romantic young girl to an urban doll with furs, cars and maids in a superficial world of false dreams – in films that endorsed conservative bourgeois values. Sexuality was never evident. The *Küçük Hanım / Little Miss* series (1960s–70s), in which she appeared as the spoiled young heiress opposite one of the most coveted *jeune premier* of the period, **Ayhan Işık**, were very popular.

Duru, Süreyya (b. Samsun, 1930 – d. Istanbul, 1988) Director, producer, screenwriter, actor. One of the prominent film-makers of **Yeşilçam** directing about 50 films and producing a dozen, Süreyya Duru left his studies in law in 1954 to work at his father Naci Duru's company, Duru Film. He was the production chief in **Lütfi Ö. Akad**'s *Beyaz Mendil / The White Handkerchief* (1955), directing his first feature, *İstanbul'da Aşk Başkadır / Love is Different in Istanbul*, a love story between a journalist and a foreign woman in 1961. Before forming his company, Murat Film in 1970, he tried his hand in all **genres** of **Yeşilçam**, from local and foreign literary adaptations, historical adventure films to the very popular action, adventure and **fantasy** yarns – the *Malkoçoğlu* series starring **Cüneyt Arkın** and the box-office champion, *Keloğlan* (1970). 1974 was a turning point in his career when he chose to focus on social issues with three films that can be considered a trilogy (Dorsay 1995: 123). *Bedrana* (1974) and *Kara Çarşaflı Gelin / The Bride in Black Chadoor* (1975) were praised by the critics and successful at the box-office although the latter suffered severely in the hands of censors. His urban film, *Güneşli Bataklık / The Sunny Marsh* (1977), considered as the first engagé **melodrama** of Turkish cinema was rejected on the grounds that it promoted separatism, endorsed murder and anarchism and insulted the police. (The decision was reversed after two years, but by then the political context had lost its contemporaneity.) Despite his original approach to film-making, due to box-office concerns, Duru made a religious film, *Rabia: İlk Kadın Evliya / Rabia: The First Woman Saint* (1973) and a number of soft porn films (*Çılgın Arzular / Wild Desires* (1974); *Azgın Bakireler / Desperate Virgins*, 1975). During a period when Turkish cinema was on the decline, he drew attention with *Fatma Gül'ün Suçu Ne? / What's the Crime of Fatma Gül?* (1986), once again indicting customs and traditions that oppress women, a rare work for an androcentric cinema. At the time of his death, Duru was working on *Ada / The Island* about the last attempt of an estranged couple for reconciliation (completed by his daughter Dilek Günaltay and cousin Metin Duru). In addition to numerous national awards, Duru was honoured twice at the Karlovy Vary Film Festival with the Cidalc award for *Bedrana* in 1974 and the Special Prize of the Unions for *The Sunny Marsh* in 1978.

Duru, Yılmaz (b. Adana, 1933 – d. Istanbul, 2010) Director, producer, screenwriter, composer, actor, dancer. Director of about 35 films, producer of 16, actor in almost 70, Yılmaz Duru started as a dancer, moving on to acting in 1954. After studying cinema and television in the United States, he returned to Turkey to found his company, Tura Film (1964) and began directing and producing. In 1979, he realized the first co-production with the USSR, *Ferhat ile Şirin, Bir Aşk Masalı / My Love, My Sorrow* (1978), in which he also acted. He is the recipient of several national awards including the Golden Orange for *İnce Cumali* (1968) starring **Yılmaz Güney** in the titular role and the lifetime achievement award of the same festival in 1997.

Duvar / Le Mur / The Wall (1983) is the last film of **Yılmaz Güney**, made in France during his exile and funded partly by the French Ministry of Culture. Based on the 1974 riot in a children's ward in Ankara, which **Güney** witnessed and later turned into a novel called, *Soba, Pencere Camı ve İki Ekmek İstiyoruz / We Want a Stove, a Window Glass and Two Loaves of Bread*, the film was shot in an old abbey outside Paris. Except for **Tuncel Kurtiz** and Ayşe Emel Mesci, all players were non-professional. The narrative is placed entirely inside a prison, which is divided into men's, women's, boys' and anarchists' cells. The trope of prison serves a triple function in **Güney**'s films: to represent the concrete one he knew well, the imprisonment of society *en masse* and the prison of our minds. For *The Wall*, he chose the prison motif particularly to expose the political situation in Turkey following the 1980 military intervention. According to **Güney**, the film presented the outsider's point of view in narrating the desperate hopes of the prisoners such as the children praying to be transferred to a better jail rather than demanding their freedom. For **Güney**, change could not happen by escaping from reality with empty dreams, but within realities. 'Good prison' did not exist.

For an artist like **Güney** who received his energy from his audience, exile was counterproductive. He had the freedom but not the 'ammunition' to create and *The Wall* could not compete with the films he had made in Turkey. It is a harsh and vengeful film carrying the bitterness of an exceptionally talented artist condemned to spend the best years of his life behind bars and to die in exile.

The Wall was banned in Turkey for almost 17 years.

Director, Screenwriter: **Yılmaz Güney**; Producer: Marin Karmitz; Production: Güney Film, MH2 Productions, Ministery of Culture of the French Republic, TF1 Films; Cinematographer: İzzet Akay; Editor: Sabine Mamou; Music: Setrak Bakirel, Ozan Garip Şahin; Cast: **Tuncel Kurtiz**, Ayşe Emel Mesci, Malik Berrichi, Nicolas Hussein, Isabelle Tissandier, Ahmet Zirek, Ali Berktay, Selahattin Kuzmoğlu, Jean-Pierre Colin, Jacques Dimanche

Düğün / The Wedding (1973), the second part of the Migration Trilogy of **Lütfi Ö. Akad**, which chronologically precedes the first part, *Gelin / The Bride* (1973), foregrounds a migrant family arriving in Istanbul to make a living with the help of an uncle. The customary pattern of job hunt is through a relative; to a lesser extent, searching door to door; applying to the Unemployment Office is hardly an option. (In *Uzak / Distant*, **Nuri Bilge Ceylan**, 2002, Yusuf follows the same pattern.)

The documentary-style establishing shots – a rarity in the 1970s, except perhaps for *Umut / The Hope* (**Yılmaz Güney**, 1970) – show the southern town of Urfa with shops without customers, idle men sitting around and vendors selling nothing. Suddenly the camera shifts to a bustling square in Istanbul, accentuating the energy that emanates from the crowds; the street vendors sell anything from bagels to brooms and the shoe-shiners and the porters ply their trade, a vibrant action of buying and selling that makes the city very appealing to the newcomers.

Determined not to return to Urfa, Halil (Kâmuran Usluer) and his siblings (Zelha, İbrahim, Cemile, Habibe and Yusuf) settle in the shantytowns of Istanbul. (Just like *The Bride*, imbued with religious motifs, the names of the brothers are significant, Yusuf as Prophet Joseph, thrown into a well by his brothers and İbrahim as Abraham.)

As the eldest, Halil assumes the responsibility for the family doing marginal transitory jobs, such as selling old clothes on the street to earn the capital for a small business – the dream of most migrants, who are cautious about working for someone else, but his obsession only leads to the disintegration of the family ties. He marries Cemile to the kebab seller for money and she is forced to work as a cleaning woman to reimburse her husband; Habibe, the second sister, in love with someone else, is coerced into marrying a rich widower. During a street fight among the vendors, İbrahim wounds a man, but the youngest, Yusuf, assumes the crime as a practical solution to keep the breadwinner from jail. Just as he is indifferent to his sisters' unhappiness, Halil does not reflect about the lost dreams of the boy who wants to be educated. Only one sister shows reaction to his materialistic practicality

– the oldest Zelha (**Hülya Koçyiğit**), who has already made sacrifices for her siblings, including leaving behind the man she loved. In an hyperbolical scene, which lacks credibility considering the position of women in patriarchal societies, she appears like a mystic saviour, interrupting the wedding to claim Habibe while İbrahim announces that he will surrender to the police and save Yusuf.

Akad's point of view is not pessimistic as Zelha's boyfriend Ferhat from Urfa is already in Istanbul and he may find work in a factory although whether the two will unite is left open. What is important is the change, even though change begets sacrifices. In fact the motif of sacrifice is as essential to *The Wedding* as to *The Bride*. Unfortunately, *The Wedding* lacks the forceful energy of *The Bride*.

Director, Scriptwriter: **Lütfi Ö. Akad**; Producer: Hürrem Erman; Production: Erman Film; Cinematographer: Gani Turanlı; Music: Metin Bükey, Cast: **Hülya Koçyiğit**, Kâmuran Usluer, Erol Günaydın, Turgut Boralı, Ahmet Mekin, Hülya Şengül, İlknur Yağız, Altan Günbay

Düşman / The Enemy (1979), a collaboration between **Zeki Ökten** and **Yılmaz Güney** is about unemployment and the problems facing workers. İsmail (**Aytaç Arman**), an over-qualified worker unable to find employment, accepts the humiliating job of poisoning dogs and asks his father for money, resulting in the break-up of his marriage to a woman who dreams of a better life.

Condemning prostitution as a social evil created by the capitalist order that considers women as merchandise, the film draws a parallel between the workers, who queue to attract employers, and prostitutes. The scenes showing hungry and hopeless workers pushing each other to climb on a truck to grab a scarce job are very powerful. In the struggle for survival, human values are lost. No one pays attention when a man falls and is injured. A corpse draws attention when the tabloid covering it displays scantily clad women. Man's cruelty to man is displayed in another episode when a desperate prostitute tries to jump over the railing of a balcony and the sex-starved men of all ages gaze at her nudity, oblivious of her misery.

According to **Güney**, the film holds a mirror to real life. 'The enemy does not only live outside us and attack from outside. It also lives insidiously in our thoughts, relations, habits, impressions and behaviour because the dominant class controls the oppressed dependent, not only in economic issues but social life, culture, ways of living and habits as well', says **Güney** in the manifesto he scripted for the release of the film in Germany in 1982 (**Güney** 1982: 208–12).

The winner of international awards, *The Enemy* was refused for competition by the Antalya Golden Orange Film Festival administration in 1981 along with *Sürü / The Herd* (1978), both directed by **Zeki Ökten** and scripted by **Yılmaz Güney** and now considered as classics of Turkish cinema. The belated awards to *The Enemy* – Best Director (posthumously), Best Actor, Best Actress – were given in Antalya in 2011.

Director, Editor: **Zeki Ökten**; Producer, Screenwriter: **Yılmaz Güney**; Production: Güney Film; Cinematographer: Çetin Tunca; Music: Arif Sağ, Yavuz Top; Sound: Tuncer Aydınoğlu, Necip Sarıcıoğlu; Cast: **Aytaç Arman**, Güngör Bayrak, **Macit Koper**, Şevket Altuğ

E

The Edge of Heaven / Yaşamın Kıyısında (see *Auf Der Anderen Seite*)

Eğilmez, Ertem (b. Trabzon, 1929 – d. Istanbul, 1989) Director, producer, screenwriter, publisher. A master of popular comedies with a social message, Ertem Eğilmez graduated in economics from the University of Istanbul, following it with a career in publishing of popular pocket books, calendars featuring scantily-clad models and a comics magazine. Soon he established Efe Film (1961), which collapsed, and then Arzu Film (1964), producing and directing mostly comedies, usually with the same team. What came to be known as 'Arzu Film Comedies' often carried a social message. He broke records with *Sürtük / The Tramp* (1965), a re-make of Bernard Shaw's *Pygmalion*, which, just like most re-makes of **Yeşilçam**, re-imagines the original narrative in the confrontation between the East and the West, trying to find a middle way between the rural/East and the urban/West. After several **melodramas** with the stars of **Yeşilçam**, he began to focus on comedies mirroring the daily lives of ordinary citizens such as *Hababam Sınıfı / The Rascal Class* aka *The Chaos Class* aka *Outrageous Class* (1975), directing its five sequels (a few more were made by different film-makers). *Canım Kardeşim / My Dear Brother* (1973) was praised by the critics ('echoing Sica–Zavattini duo, the Italian comedies, British comedies of the 1950s and a bit of Hollywood, but using our characters, our subjects and our locale, with a remarkable use of Istanbul', Dorsay 1989: 107), receiving four awards at the Golden Orange Film Festival, but failing at the box-office. *Banker Bilo* (1980), slating quick riches schemes through an innocent rural migrant's degeneration in the city and *Namuslu / The Honest* (1984), adapted by **Başar Sabuncu** from his play about a trustworthy paymaster, who is respected when he is mistaken for a thief, are two successful comedies with acerbic social criticism. Master of famous actors – **Tarık Akan**, **Kemal Sunal**, **İlyas Salman** – and film-makers – **Yavuz Turgul**, **Sinan Çetin** – he directed over 40 films, producing around 100. He is best remembered for *Arabesk / Arabesque* (1988), his last film, a mild satire on the **arabesque** culture that reached its peak in the 1980s, engulfing the film and music industries as well as life-styles.

Elçi, Ümit (b. Silifke, 1948) Director, screenwriter, producer. Best known for *Mem û Zin / Mem and Zin* (1991), based on Kurdish poet Ehmedê Xanî's classic love story from the seventeenth century, Ümit Elçi is a graduate in English Language and Literature from the Bosphorus University in Istanbul, receiving his masters from the London Film School. Following a few years in the advertisement sector, he scripted and directed his first film, *Kurşun Ata Ata Biter / Hero's Way* (1985), a literary adaptation that foregrounds **gender** inequalities in feudalistic systems, followed by *Bir Avuç Gökyüzü / A Handful of Sky* (1987) and a four-part musical series for television, *Fosforlu Cevriye / Glittering Cevriye* (1989). *Mem and Zin*, shot at the height of civil war, recounts the story of two lovers who meet during *Newroz* (New Year) celebrations, exchange rings and separate, a forceful trope for the dispersion of Kurds over several countries. He wrote and directed the award-winning *Böcek / Insect* (1995), a literary adaptation about a police chief with an aversion to women and intellectuals, who perceives those around him as cockroaches and plans to purify the society by destroying them; after his dismissal from the police force, he begins to vanish himself. The film draws attention to the role terrorism and violence play in creating pathetic characters. In addition to *Hoşgeldin Hayat / Welcome Life* (2004), he has made a documentary about the 1996 hunger strikes against the use of isolation cells in prisons, which resulted in deaths and permanent disabilities, *Su Damlasına Sığdırılan Yaşam / Life in a Drop of Water* (2002), which takes its name from a water pipe that was used to moisten the strikers' lips.

Elmas, Orhan (b. Istanbul, 1927 – d. Istanbul, 2002) Director, screenwriter, actor, author. One of the important names of **Yeşilçam**, who directed about 120 films and a number of television series, Orhan Elmas began as a journalist, moving on to acting with **Muhsin Ertuğrul**'s *Yayla Kartalı / The Eagle of the Plateau* (1945) and appeared on stage in several Istanbul theatres. He moved behind the camera in 1953, drawing attention with *Kanlı Firar / Bloody Escape* (1960) from a story by **Metin Erksan** starring **Ayhan Işık** and **Belgin Doruk** (one of the most popular duos) and *Duvarların Ötesi / Beyond the Walls* (1964), a film with leftist overtones, about seven escapees cornered inside a depot (scripted by Elmas, **Vedat Türkali** and Turgut Özakman). *Ezo Gelin Alevden Gömlek / Ezo Bride, Shirt of Fire* (1956) based on a story by acclaimed poet Behçat Kemal Çağlar, scripted by Elmas and Çağlar and starring Hümaşah Hican as the legendary Ezo was very successful (although the story had very little to do with the actual character and events). Elmas made a second version of this love tragedy, *Ezo Gelin / Ezo, The Bride* (1968), produced by **Memduh Ün** with **Fatma Girik** playing Ezo, which won the Second Best Film and Best Woman Performer (**Girik**) awards at the Adana Golden Boll Film Festival, 1969. The film touched the hearts of the audiences with its realistic depiction of the tragedies of rural people suffering under the yoke of archaic traditions, but also the utilization of elegiac *ghazals* that allow the characters express their sorrow in poetry while lamenting the unfairness of the causes. **Girik** received the same award the following year in Adana with her role in Elmas's *Boş Beşik / The Empty Cradle* (1969), considered among the classics of **Yeşilçam**. (The third, coloured version of *Ezo*, scripted by Elmas and directed by **Feyzi Tuna**, with **Fatma Girik** again as Ezo, was the least successful. Critics found it pretentious, superfluous and amateurish with false folkloric elements.)

Endişe / The Anxiety (1974), focuses on the plight of agriculture workers (customarily presented in cinema as extras) and the oppression of women in a liminal society still under the yoke of feudalism. The opening shots establish the conditions of cotton pickers in a *cinéma vérité* style; they arrive from the plains in truckloads (**Güney** is seen among them) and live in ramshackle tents. The camera picks out a crying child, a desperate man selling his gun (as Cabbar does in *Umut/ The Hope*, **Güney**, 1970), then pans over factories and industrial sites. The radio announces the closure of enterprises, the rate of inflation, the price of coal, the increase in house rentals, a general attending a NATO meeting in Germany (Turkey has been a member since 1952), and the taking of Famagusta (Cyprus) by the Turkish army; then switches to chants from the Qur'an to announce *iftar*, the end of fasting in *Ramazan*. With a small homage to cinema, the film displays children excited about the arrival of a 16mm machine; they watch *Tarzan*, *Laurel and Hardy* and *Gone with the Wind* from a hole.

Cevher (Erkan Yücel) works in the cotton fields with his wife, daughter, son, sister and brother-in-law. Earning a living from picking cotton has become harder with the arrival of mechanization. Some workers try to unionize against the exploitative landlords who are opaque about the fees; work has stopped. Anxiety increases when the government delays the announcement of the base price of cotton. Harassed for money concerning a blood feud, Cevher breaks the strike under the bitter gaze of the other workers. His daughter, who he wants to give to the middle-aged and already married foreman to pay his debts, elopes with her lover when he falls asleep in the fields. He has neither the money to pay for the blood feud, nor his daughter to offer to the head farmer. There is no escape from the approaching enemies.

The alienation of Cevher is similar to Cabbar's in *The Hope*; both men search for personal short-term solutions to their problems, not having gained political consciousness, although the surrealistic quality of the later episodes in both films suggests a certain cynicism about the validity of labour movements in repressive feudal societies.

Reviewing the film at its time, local critic Nezih Coş underlines the diversion from the theme of exploitation of the workers that the emphasis on the price of cotton creates and circumvents the real issue of underdevelopment. The export price of cotton is dependent on the US and European markets as well as the local market, and the exploitative landlord is also exploited by the rich merchants. The envy of Cevher's friend Remo for the cement factory workers suggests a fundamental difference between the agricultural and industrial workers, an erroneous point of view that disregards the exploitation of all workers by the capitalist system. The agriculture workers are doubly handicapped as seasonal workers. For Coş, the film follows the concept of materialist cinema in presenting the cotton issue from the class perspective; trying to find a solution to benefit the workers; rejecting the 'powerful heroes' of the idealist cinema and defending the masses; attempting to break the templates of narrative cinema that relies on dramatic expression (although the blood feud and the elopement of the daughter are narrative cinema) and relying heavily on alienation rather than identification. Yet, it fails to offer effective alternatives. The main consciousness-raising is determined as unified action, but the target audience is the urban intellectual. Produced within **Yeşilçam**, it is unlikely to reach the cotton workers whose only chance to watch a movie is through an eyehole in a portable machine (Coş 1975).

Güney was arrested (13 September 1974) while shooting *Anxiety* for allegedly killing a judge during a dispute at a restaurant. **Şerif Gören** assumed the shooting of the film, which was scripted by **Güney** during his previous jail sentence. The opening shots belong to **Güney**. The film received several awards, including Best Film, Best Director (**Şerif Gören**), Best Screenwriter (**Yılmaz Güney**), Best Director of Photography (**Kenan Ormanlar**), Best Actor (Erkan Yücel) at the 12th Antalya Golden Orange Film Festival (1975) and Best Actor (Erkan Yücel) at the San Remo Art Films Festival.

Director: **Şerif Gören**; Production: Güney Film; Producer, Scriptwriter: **Yılmaz Güney** with **Ali Özgentürk** as the script assistant; Director of Photography: **Kenan Ormanlar**; Music: Şanar Yurdatapan, Attila Özdemiroğlu; Cast: Erkan Yücel, Kamuran Usluer, Ayşe Emel Mesçi

Erdem, Reha (b. Istanbul, 1960) Director, screenwriter, editor. One of the most original representatives of the Turkish cinema that has achieved international praise in the new millennium, Reha Erdem has built his work on a continuous dialogue between reality and the imaginary, urging the audience to search for a new perspective towards life. The topic and the **genre** vary considerably in his films but the difficulty of preserving one's humanity and dignity in a rapidly changing world and the impossibility of communication where love has ceased to exist are the main motifs. Spatio-temporality is the decisive element. Characters condemned to in-between stages and to liminal spaces suffer; children on the threshold of adulthood suffer the most, the William Blake poem, *Infant Sorrow* that young Yekta regurgitates in his debut feature, *A ay / Oh, Moon* (1989) setting the tone. The locus of *Beş Vakit / Times and Winds* (2006) is a claustrophobic village between the mountain and the sea where children find peace prostrating themselves among dead leaves. *Oh, Moon* occurs in one mansion of past grandeur on an upper-class residential island and another on the shores of the Bosphorus, 'crisis heterotopias' (Foucault 1984: 46–9), where an adolescent shifts between two eccentric aunts, finding solace in her trips to the hilltops, closer to nature. In *Hayat Var / My Only Sunshine* (2008), Hayat lives with her suffocating grandfather and marginal father in a makeshift hut along the Bosphorus, stuck between the land and the sea, a 'heterotopia of deviation' (Foucault 1984: 46–9). Abused by the grown-ups, she hides inside nature, often perching on tree branches like an animal. In *Cosmos*, two youngsters in a border town marking two unfriendly countries develop an animal-like language to communicate during their private moments outside the village boundaries, usually beside a river.

Revolt against parents, particularly the patriarchy, is the central motif. The male is the breadwinner, with the power to make vital decisions but lacking in love and tenderness and often sick. The mother is absent in *Oh, Moon, Korkuyorum Anne* aka *İnsan Nedir ki? / I'm Scared* aka *What's Human Anyway* (2004), *My Only Sunshine* and *Kosmos* (2009) and is identified with the water in *Oh, Moon* and *I'm Scared* aka *What's Human Anyway.* In **My Only Sunshine**, the protagonist finds freedom and love as the boat cuts across the waves of the Bosphorus towards the horizon. The water as the third space (Bhabha, Foucault – heterotopia) to escape the liminality of the city in the process of transformation to modernity is evident in **Kaç Para Kaç / Run for Money** (1999) and **Kosmos** as well.

With discernible influences of the new South-east Asian cinema, particularly the two masters, Tsai Ming Liang and Apichatpong Weerasethakul, Erdem's cinema is not narrative driven; instead, editing drives the narrative and determines the emotion and rhythm of the film. Deliberately avoiding naturalism, he controls the emotion to elicit from the spectator through the choice of diegetic space, costumes, colours, light and filter (aided by his regular cinematographer, Florent Herry). His use of music counteracts clichés, be it Vivaldi in *Oh, Moon*, heart-breaking violins in *Mommy, I'm Scared* aka *What's Human Anyway?*, Arvo Pärt in **Times and Winds**, or **arabesque** in **My Only Sunshine**, the only film that uses lyrics. Music frequently becomes part of the dramatic action and even determines editing, the assumed diegetic sound unexpectedly becoming non-diegetic or intra-diegetic. In **Times and Winds**, the Orthodox church music that accompanies life in a Muslim village serves as a distantiation device.

Erdem left his studies in history to go to Paris (1983) where he received his master's degree in Plastic Arts from the Paris VIII University. While in France, he made three short films, worked as a cameraman and acquired experience in sound engineering. His first feature, the innovative black-and-white *Oh, Moon*, a French–Turkish co-production, was screened at international festivals, winning awards. He directed television commercials before his second feature, **Kaç Para Kaç / Run for Money** (1999), a conventional narrative, which used Istanbul as a functional background to a satire on bourgeois morality. *Mommy, I'm Scared* aka *What's Human Anyway* involved the spectator in its rhythm emotionally through jump-cuts and extra-diegetic music that stressed the similarities between people – 'made of flesh, bone, fat and nerve' – who share the same fears, loves and hates. A story with local colour, the film was awarded in all the national film festivals it attended, but also travelled to many international ones. With **Times and Winds**, his first digital film, Erdem explored the precarious world of adolescence in the hermetically sealed rural milieu. He followed it with **My Only Sunshine**, returning to the city but only the periphery. **Kosmos**, which takes place in a remote provincial town, restates the dominant theme of Erdem's work: love as the only remedy to survive in a loveless society. With **Jîn** (2013), about a young Kurdish guerrilla's *impasse*, Erdem continues the motif of the destruction of nature by human folly that he underscored with **Cosmos**.

He has written the scripts of all of his films except *Mommy, I'm Scared* aka *What's Human Anyway?* which he co-scripted with Nilüfer Güngörmüş. With Ömer Atay, he is the co-founder of Atlantik Film, founded in 1994.

Erdoğan, Yılmaz (b. Hakkari, 1967) Director, actor, screenwriter, producer. Very popular as a comedy actor, Yılmaz Erdoğan started in theatre as a writer and actor, founding the Beşiktaş Cultural Centre and BKM Players in 1994 with

Necati Akpınar. He wrote the scripts for several television films and acted in them while publishing poems, stories and essays. He wrote *Vizontele* (2001) about the arrival of television in his native town, directed it with **Ömer Faruk Sorak** and acted in it. The film broke box-office records, reaching 3.5 million spectators. *Vizontele Tuuba* (2004), its sequel; *Organize İşler* (2005) about a gang of car thieves in Istanbul and *Neşeli Hayat / Jolly Life* (2009) about the first Santa Claus in a Muslim neighbourhood, were also box-office hits. *Kelebeğin Rüyası / The Dream of the Butterfly* (2013) is a **melodrama** about two young poets suffering from tuberculosis in the mining town of Zonguldak in 1971. Erdoğan acted in all his films as well as playing the police chief in **Nuri Bilge Ceylan**'s *Bir Zamanlar Anadolu'da / Once Upon a Time in Anatolia* (2011). He also acted in Bahman Ghobadi's *Rhino Season* (2012).

Ergun, Mahinur (b. Bursa, 1956) Director, screenwriter. One of the major women film-makers of a period when women refrained from going behind the camera, Mahinur Ergun graduated from the Cinema and Television department of the Ankara Journalism and Broadcasting Academy in 1978. She directed her first feature, *Gece Dansı Tutsakları / Prisoners of a Night Dance* in 1988. After *Med Cezir Manzaraları / Tidal Waves* (1990), she made *Ay Vakti / Moon Time* (1993), about a middle-aged man, his mistress and her daughter, a film that places the binaries of good woman/bad woman, housewife/free woman in their traditional context. The protagonist (**Zühal Olcay**), the young and 'liberated' mistress, is an irresponsible, ill-mannered and manipulating parasite, who runs in circles. The legal wife (Füsun Demirağ) is homey, focused and in control, using her housewifely skills (preparing her husband's favourite dishes, appearing commiserating) to regain her man. Her character is developed to evoke audience sympathy. Ergun, who has been concentrating on television series, was instrumental in the training of the popular film-maker, **Çağan Irmak**.

Erkal, Genco (b. Istanbul, 1938) Actor. A distinguished actor on stage and in cinema, Genco Erkal has given some of his memorable performances in *At / The Horse* (**Ali Özgentürk**, 1981), *Faize Hücum / The Rush on Interest* (**Zeki Ökten**, 1983), *Hakkari'de Bir Mevsim / A Season in Hakkari* (**Erden Kıral**, 1983), *Camdan Kalp / A Heart of Glass* (**Fehmi Yaşar**, 1990) and *Pazar-Bir Ticaret Masalı / The Market – A Tale of Trade* (Ben Hopkins, 2008). He received the Best Actor award twice at the Antalya Golden Orange Film Festival, with *The Horse* in 1982 and *The Rush on Interest* in 1983.

Having graduated from Robert College in Istanbul where he began amateur acting, he studied psychology at Istanbul University, and established the Dostlar Theatre in 1969 of which he is presently the art director.

Erksan, Metin (b. Çanakkale, 1929 – d. Istanbul, 2012) Director, screenwriter, producer; RN: İsmail Metin Karamanbey. Graduating from the Faculty of Arts of Istanbul University in Art History–Aesthetics in 1952, **Metin Erksan** is considered as the first *auteur* of Turkish cinema and an important representative of the **social realist** period, which flourished following the 1960 *coup d'état*. *Gecelerin Ötesi / Beyond the Nights* (1960) is regarded as the first **social realist** film of Turkish cinema (Özgüç 2003: 75). Foregrounding the victims of a political system that targets to raise a millionaire in every neighbourhood, the film is a harsh indictment (within the limits of censorship) of the social and economic condition. *Susuz Yaz / A Dry Summer* (1963) is the first Turkish feature to receive the Golden Bear at the Berlin Film Festival (1964). A politically engaged film-maker, Erksan was the founder of Sine-İş (the Union of Turkish Cinema Workers) and the Labour Party's candidate from Istanbul in the general elections of 1965.

Erksan's cinema is often referred to as the 'cinema of resistance.' The protagonists rebel against the societal norms, risking alienation. Black passion and obsessive rapacity for possession reach psychopathological dimensions in his films. *Aşık Veysel'in Hayatı* aka **Karanlık Dünya / The Life of Veysel, the Minstrel** aka **The Dark World** (1952–3), his first film along with *Yılanların Öcü / The Revenge of the Serpents* (1962) and *A Dry Summer* comprise the 'village trilogy'. Osman's greed to possess – the water and the young wife of his brother – in *A Dry Summer*, continues in **Kuyu / The Well** (1968), where Osman ties a rope around Fatma and drags her through the arid landscape to coerce her to marry him despite constant rejection and humiliation. **Suçlular Aramızda / The Culprits Are Among Us** (1964) holds a mirror to the social and cultural structure of the country through an ordinary story about a fake necklace.

The focus on the relationship between the individual and society remains constant in Erksan's films, manifested through housing problems in the rural milieu (*Yılanların Öcü / Revenge of the Serpents*, 1962) and in the city (*Acı Hayat / Bitter Life*, 1962) and the apathy and egotism of the rich systematically disadvantaging the poor (*The Culprit Are Among Us* and *Bitter Life*). These films caricaturize the rich and exalt the poor, and send a warning message to social climbers.

In *Sevmek Zamanı / The Time to Love* (1965) and *Kadın Hamlet-İntikam Meleği / Woman Hamlet – Angel of Vengeance* (1976), the fantastic narrative determines the form. A Turkified rendition of Shakespeare's classic play, using a **gender** twist that offers a pleasurable identification for the female spectator, *Woman Hamlet – Angel of Vengeance* uses the fisheye lens to create an eerie effect. The Roman costumes, a bedroom behind a door constructed on an empty field, instruments tied to a scarecrow and an imaginary orchestra playing Dimitri Shostakovich's Hamlet suite from a tape-recorder, create a supernatural atmosphere that the final scene recapitulates: with blood splattered over her white suit, Hamlet claims revenge until her last breath. The scene when she destroys the targets in the shooting gallery is meaningless within the context of the narrative but remarkable visually.

With the transition from black and white to colour, Erksan's films began to manifest **arabesque** tendencies and commercial concerns although *Şeytan / The Exorcist* (1974), plagiarized from its Hollywood version and *Woman Hamlet – Angel of Vengeance* are considered as cult films or 'surrealist' **melodramas** despite the farcical theatricality of acting and the use of hyperbole. The inclusion of the song, *Bu Düzen Böyle mi Gidecek? / Is this System Gonna Last Forever?*

(Timur Selçuk) in *Hamlet* was courageous considering the film was made in the precarious period between the two military interventions. The use of the traditional Anatolian *ney* music during the funeral of Hamlet's father is a reminder of Erksan's *ulusal* cinema period (see **national cinema**) and a sharp contrast to his preference for jazz in the urban films of his **social realist** period, such as *The Culprits Are Among Us*.

Erksan, who remained a controversial figure in Turkish cinema, known for his oppositional intellectual identity, maintained that 'Art narrates the person, not the problem. It narrates the person having the problem' (Anonymous 1966: 15 quoted by Altınay 1990: 12). His cinema is an amalgam of modernist themes: the existential aloneness of the individual, metaphysics (the clash of good vs. evil) and Marxism; although later he changed his Marxist views, declaring there were no social classes in Turkey. He always advocated that the state should stay away from cinema. His **social realist** period was praised, but in the period when he advocated *ulusal* cinema he was severely criticized and several of his films were met with disinterest. After a number of commercial films and series for the TRT (Turkish Radio and Television), Erksan abandoned filmmaking in 1983 and started to teach at the Mimar Sinan University. From 2007 until his death, he was on the faculty of Işık University, where he bequeathed his comprehensive library and archives.

Metin Erksan'ın Tutkusu / The Passion of Metin Erksan (Sadık Battal, 2010) is a documentary on the director.

Ertuğrul, Muhsin (b. Istanbul, 1892 – d. Istanbul, 1979) Director, actor, screenwriter, producer, editor, art director, general manager of the state theatre. The man who introduced **melodrama** to Turkish cinema with his first feature *Istanbul'da Bir Facia-i Aşk / A Love Tragedy in Istanbul* (1922) and sound with *İstanbul Sokaklarında / On the Streets of Istanbul* (1931); directed *Ateşten Gömlek / The Shirt of Fire* aka *The Ordeal* aka *The Shirt of Flame* (1923), considered as the first national film; brought home the first international award, an honorary mention from the second Venice Film Festival (1934) with *Leblebici Horhor Ağa / Horhor Agha, The Chickpea Seller* (1934) and initiated the category of **village films** with *Aysel, Bataklı Damın Kızı / The Girl From the Marshes* aka *Aysel, the Girl From the Swampy Roof* (1935), Muhsin Ertuğrul is the most prominent film-maker of the early years of Turkish cinema. Foreign educated, Ertuğrul worked in the USSR and Germany as an actor and director, forming his company, Istanbul Film in Berlin. Returning from Germany in 1922, he started a new era with his background in German and French theatre and Soviet revolutionary cinema. The period eventually came to be known as *The Period of Theatre Men* (1923–40).

A Love Tragedy in Istanbul, based on the life of a notorious seductress, murdered by one of her desperate lovers, was the forerunner of 'bad woman' films, a warning to the urban *petit bourgeois* males about the consequences of following blind passion. The popularity of formula films often including murders, false accusations and loss of memory but culminating in a happy end with a twist of the plot, extended to the next four decades. Ertuğrul established the 'heroic Turkish soldier' motif with the famous epic *Bir Millet Uyanıyor / A Nation is Awakening*

(1932) and again other film-makers followed at his footsteps, but except for **Lütfi Ö. Akad**'s *Vurun Kahpeye / Strike the Whore* (1949), considered among the classics of national cinema, several of these films passed unnoticed.

On the Streets of Istanbul surpassed *A Love Tragedy in Istanbul* as a **melodrama**. Shot in Egypt, Greece and Bursa in Turkey with the sound effects done in Paris, foregrounding two brothers who play the accordion on the streets and sing, the film was far removed from the realities of Turkish life (busker culture did not exist) but contributed to the forming of the major studio of the country, İpek Film.

Şehvet Kurbanı / The Victim of Lust (1939), inspired by *Der Blauer Engel / The Blue Angel* announced the Turkish Marlene Dietrich in the sensual **Cahide Sonku**, the first woman to introduce eroticism to Turkish cinema, who was very successful in her role as a mysterious temptress, although her blonde hair and European appearance appealed mostly to the urban middle class.

In almost all Ertuğrul films, *Darülbedayi* (Municipal Theatre) actors played; cinema actors appeared only after 1950.

A recipient of the Goethe medallion from Germany for his contribution to cinema, Ertuğrul was derided by the critics for emulating the West rather than contributing to the emergence of a national cinema inspired by local culture, although his viewpoint was entirely in accordance with the Westernization policies of the state.

Eskiköy, Orhan (b. Istanbul, 1980) Director. A graduate of public relations from the Faculty of Communications, Ankara University, Orhan Eskiköy drew attention with his student films, while working as an assistant and cameraman on various projects. The documentary he made with Özgür Doğan, *İki Dil, Bir Bavul / On*

Figure 41 İki Dil, Bir Bavul / On the Way to School (Orhan Eskiköy and Özgür Doğan, 2009) (Courtesy of Orhan Eskiköy)

the Way to School (2009) about a young Turkish teacher's tribulations in trying to teach elementary school in a remote Kurdish area, received international acclaim. His first feature, **Babamın Sesi / Dengê Bavê Min / The Voice of My Father** (2012), which was made with **Zeynel Doğan**, received several national awards. In 2011, he was chosen by the Sundance Institute along with **Aslı Özge**, Nesimi Yetik, and Melisa Önel for a Sundance Lab project in Turkey.

Esmer, Pelin (b. Istanbul, 1972) Director, screenwriter, producer, cinematographer, editor. A graduate in sociology from the Bosphorus University in Istanbul, Pelin Esmer attended film workshops of **Yavuz Özkan** and worked as an assistant in documentaries, features and commercials before her documentary, *Koleksiyoncu / The Collector* (2002), which was invited to several film festivals and won awards. The same year she made an experimental short film, *Kar / Snow.* In 2005, she created the film company, Sinefilm. When she came across an article about village women doing theatre, she decided to shoot *Oyun / The Play* (2005). Screened in over 50 festivals, the docu-drama that obscures the line between fiction and documentary has won 14 awards including the Best Documentary Film-maker at the Tribeca Film Festival. *11'e 10 Kala / 10 to 11* (2009), a fictionalized version of *The Collector*, featuring her uncle, a compulsive collector, as a trope for the memory of the city that is rapidly changing and **Gözetleme Kulesi / The Watch Tower** (2012) on vulnerability of women in androcentric societies are her two fiction films that have won several prestigious awards.

Eşkıya / The Bandit (1996) is a landmark for Turkish cinema, returning the audience alienated by adventure yarns, **porno films** and existential angst films with *auteur* pretentions in large numbers to the cinema halls. Mirroring the times of wild capitalism encouraged by the 'a millionaire in every neighbourhood' policy of Turgut Özal, prime minister and president between 1983–93, the film arrived at an appropriate time when, next to inflation, corruption was the most discussed subject. Box-office figures surpassed the most popular Hollywood films, with attendance figures over 2.5 million. Cities without cinema halls such as Urfa – where some episodes were shot – cleared the dust from the abandoned halls to show *The Bandit.* International accolades and foreign commercial release followed. An entirely Western-style marketing campaign contributed considerably to the film's success, but the main factor was that people saw themselves in it; finally a film about their lives. The response from different ideological poles was unanimously positive.

A star falls from the sky when a bandit dies, according to an old south-east Anatolian legend. Baran (**Şener Şen**), who once took to the Cudi Mountains to revenge his father, pushed to the mine fields by the chief of the clan, is transplanted in the middle of the slums of Istanbul. Having served 35 years in prison, he is in pursuit of the man who betrayed him – his best friend Berfo (Kamuran Usluer), who escaped to the big city with his gold and his woman, Keje (Sermin Şen). Baran's adventures in the back streets of Istanbul, the city that smells 'like an animal corpse', expose a world of ageing prostitutes, merciless pimps, forsaken actors, girls with Cinderella dreams and youths with ambitions of becoming millionaires overnight. Young Cumali (**Uğur Yücel**), a minor crook, declares, 'My father's biggest mistake was to settle for a job as a waiter when he arrived in Istanbul. That's when he lost the game.' His gang asks the mafia boss to take them on; mafia connotes respect. In a corrupt society where the motto is 'survival of the fittest', a tragic hero like Baran who lives for love and according to the old-fashioned codes of ethics will always be betrayed. The only winners are traitors like Berfo, who has become a multi-millionaire. In a scene reminiscent of the westerns, the bandit decides to take the law in his hands and a massacre follows. Chased by police bullets over the rooftops of Istanbul, Baran flies into empty space. A star falls from the sky that moment to be seen only by his beloved.

The bandit arriving at his flood-devastated village in the opening sequences and meeting a mad woman like the prophesying witches of *Macbeth* who advises him against leaving, and plunging into the sky amidst the fireworks in the *grand finale*, recall the novels of Yaşar Kemal that underscore the legendary aspect of reality rather than questioning credibility. Life in the serpentine alleys of the Tarlabaşı slums, on the other hand, is very real. **Turgul** exposes with precision the degeneration of society, the economic crisis, the mismanagement, the corruption and the lack of education demoralizing citizens with nothing left to lose. The modern bandits are like Baran's old friend – the industrialist, the loan shark and alleged narcotics dealer Mahmut Bey (alias Berfo) – the 'respectable' who sit on high thrones. 'No bandits are left on the mountains' the mafia boss declares, 'now they are all in the city.'

Curiously, although Baran, Berfo and Keje are Kurdish names and the village under water refers to the building of the dam that caused the relocation of many

Figure 42 Eşkıya / The Bandit (Yavuz Turgul, 1996) (Courtesy of International Istanbul Film Festival)

Figure 43 Eşkıya / The Bandit (Yavuz Turgul, 1996) (Courtesy of International Istanbul Film Festival)

Kurdish villages, the word 'Kurd' is never mentioned in the film. The bandit wears a black *shalvar* and supports a *poshu* (the traditional scarf that has also become a symbol of liberation), but his Kurdish identity is irrelevant to the narrative. According to **Turgul**, Baran's tragedy arises not from his oppressed existence as a Kurd, but from his inability to progress with modernity, which has turned the traditional man into a fossil, a phenomenon that affects Kurds and Turks alike (Dönmez-Colin 2008: 93).

Director, Screenwriter: **Yavuz Turgul**; Producer: Mine Vargı; Production: Filma-Cass, Artcam, Geopoly; Cinematographer: Uğur İçbak; Editors: Hakan Akol, Onur Tan; Art Director: Ziya Ülkenciler; Music: Aşkın Arsunan, Erkan Oğur; Cast: **Şener Şen**, **Uğur Yücel**, Sermin Hümeriç, Yeşim Salkım, Kamran Usluer, Ülkü Duru, Özkan Uğur, Melih Çardak

Eurimage is the Council of Europe Fund, located in Strasbourg, France, for the co-production, distribution, exhibition and digitization of European films, with the aim to promote the European film industry. It was created in 1988 and currently has 36 member states. Turkey has been a member since 1990. Almost 90 per cent of the fund's resources originate from member state contributions. In 2012, the total amount for co-production was 21,160,000 euros, 94 per cent of the total budget, for 68 European productions. In 2013, the total amount awarded for co-production was established as 500,000 euros. The films awarded are expected to meet the criteria of 'European' film. Originally, Turkey had a tendency to engage in co-productions with the Central European and Balkan countries for pragmatic reasons – geographical proximity, the relative reduction of the waiting period and spending restrictions as a certain portion of the funding expected from the partner European nation must be spent in that country or region. However, Germany and France are the preferred countries in the 2000s in addition to Greece for the majority-co-productions. Eurimage has played an important role in the improvement of the technical quality of Turkish films and has given Turkish cinema the visibility it lacked outside its borders. It has also been instrumental in the realization of certain projects that would have difficulties raising funds locally, due to style or content. However, Eurimage and similar European funds have a tendency to become 'Euro-pudding' when concern for obtaining the fund overcomes the artistic choices of the film-maker; a role/location designed for including an actor/locale of the partner country may be inserted in the narrative without other justification. Another concern is the repercussions of such funding. Sceptics argue that a certain self-Orientalization has been manifest in recent productions that foreground issues of human rights, predicaments of women and the exclusion of minorities, subjects that are the priorities of Eurimage. How far does the possibility of European finance affects the choice of subject matter? Leading film-makers **Yeşim Ustaoğlu** and **Nuri Bilge Ceylan** do not support the contention that Eurimage funds only political or controversial projects. **Ceylan** agrees that the West expects certain types of films from Turkey, but content is not the only crucial issue; originality, rather than exoticism is the deciding factor (**Derviş Zaim** 2008: 86–108).

F

Fahriye Abla / Sister Fahriye (1984), the debut feature of **Yavuz Turgul**, is a love story that focuses on characters who evolve with experiences without alterations in principle elements of their characters, a key element that has become **Turgul**'s principle trait. Inspired by the renowned bard Ahmet Muhip Dıranas's poem, the film features young Fahriye (**Müjde Ar**), suffocating in her mundane environment. She escapes to the dream world of love as the non-diegetic song repeats 'always the same, always the same'. Imprisoned for wounding her unfaithful lover Mustafa, she gains consciousness through Sevgi, a political prisoner and finds a job after release but just when she is about to love foreman Cemal, Mustafa comes to claim her. The film establishes the gendered binaries that have become staple archetypes in Turgul's later films, monitoring the structure, the narrative and the prevalent themes. A passionate young woman, whose sexuality is a potential danger to men (Fahriye) and an older sage woman, often a prisoner (Sevgi), asexual but compassionate; a restless young man, rash and irresponsible (Mustafa) and an older dependable wise man (Cemal); one man desires the young woman while the other one respects her. Another staple **Turgul** motif, the clash of modernity and tradition in a society in transition also has its roots in this film. **Turgul** presents a closed society on the threshold to free-market economy when gender issues also surface parallel to the belated development of feminism. Arranged marriages are still the norm; Fahriye is scrutinized in the women's *hamam* (public bath) according to tradition and recommended to a jeweller from the provinces while Mustafa is forced to marry a wealthy girl. Premarital sex is clandestine and virginity is still a commodity. Fahriye is returned home as 'damaged merchandise'. Yet women are willing to change the androcentric order: 'divorce is the fashion these days' one comments. When Fahriye's mother is reminded by her husband to know her place ('you're a woman'), she responds 'that was before'. Fahriye reprimands Mustafa, who beats Cemal to protect her honour. 'Who are you to be the guardian of my honour?' She has begun to question the peripheral role of passive victim imposed by the patriarchal cultural universe, which negates the expansion of the Habermasian public sphere. Mustafa also evolves. Subordinated to his domineering father, he finally recognizes the patriarch as his utmost fear: 'Because of fear, I am full of shit. The worse is loveless-ness.' He decides to find a job in the factory like Fahriye to gain economic freedom to escape the clutches of the family that regulates the lives of the children as long as they are dependent (unlike the apathetic Mertkan in *Çoğunluk / Majority*, **Seran Yüce**, 2010 who continues in his father's footsteps).

The film opposes the hegemonic imperatives of the patriarchy by emphasizing the need for women (and other subordinated cultural groups) to challenge the limitations posed by the largely chauvinistic public–private dichotomy. It subverts the phallocentric view of women as inferior and apolitical and interrogates anti-public-sphere form of authority by pillorying the despotic fathers of Mustafa and Fahriye, hence serving as a 'discursive arena where the members of subordinated social groups invent and articulate counter-discourses to formulate oppositional interpretations of their identities, interests, and needs' (Fraser 1990: 67).

Director, Screenwriter: **Yavuz Turgul**; Producer: Engin Karabağ; Production: Kök Film; Music: Atilla Özdemiroğlu; Cinematographer: Çetin Tunca; Cast: **Müjde Ar**, Tarık Tarcan, İhsan Yüce, Kadir Savun, Ayşe Demirel, Haldun Ergüvenç

Fantasy films and their subgroups – science-fiction, horror, adventure stories, romantic fairy tales, or fairy tales that offer an escape to magical kingdoms – create a world where the normal laws of physics and biology are suspended. If successful, they may offer a new form of reality and even serve as a social commentary.

The **fantasy-horror** films in Turkish cinema, mostly adaptations from the West that are fashioned after the Hollywood model, generally employ Western/Christian cultural codes, which are alien to the Eastern/Muslim Turkish culture. *Dracula İstanbul'da* (Mehmet Muhtar, 1953) is a Turkified version of Bram Stoker's novel *Dracula* (1897), which takes place in Istanbul. The cross is replaced by garlic and the lawyer ignores all warnings against entering the chateau, counting on his faith in Allah, but the vampire is alien to Turkish culture. Nonetheless, the film avoids saturation with Islamic elements to sustain certain credibility when presenting Turkish realities. The overall serious atmosphere is interrupted occasionally with gems of local humour such as in the last episode, when the husband discards all garlic in the house, his wife saying, 'But I was supposed to cook *imam bayıldı*', a Turkish eggplant speciality. The woman suffering from the bite by Dracula is advised it will pass once she is married. In the absence of digital effects or even the financial means to stage sets, 30–40 people were brought in to smoke together to create the fog scene.

Metin Erksan's *Şeytan / The Exorcist* (1974) is freely adapted from William Friedkin's titular Hollywood version (1973) and Turkified, replacing Christian rituals with Muslim ones, such as the ritual of exorcism performed while reading the Qur'an, which is not compatible with Islam. *Karanlık Sular / The Serpent's Tale* (**Kutluğ Ataman**, 1994) is an experiment with **fantasy-horror** with political overtones. **Atıf Yılmaz**, inventing a sub-group, 'Fantastic Film with Social Content' made several comedies with metaphysical elements often to circumvent censorship, but did not use supernatural characters and did not experiment with horror. The fantastic elements surfaced through themes related to the characters' lives and nourished by their problems. *Adı Vasfiye / Her Name is Vasfiye* (1985),

Aaahh Belinda / Oh, Belinda (1986), *Hayallerim, Aşkım ve Sen / My Dreams, My Love and You* (1987) and *Arkadaşım Şeytan / My Friend, the Devil* (1988) (from **Ümit Ünal**'s script) can be classified as **fantasy** films. (He returned to the **genre** in 1997 with *Nihavent Mucize / Miracle Ma Non Troppo*, which was a failure.) *My Friend, the Devil*, about a man who sells his soul to the devil, is a good example of his style of merging **comedy**, musical and social satire with fantastic elements. A musician talks to dummies in a shop window and they come alive, performing a song-and-dance in **arabesque** style (a reference to the fashion of importing Egyptian films) while he plays the guitar. His soul is the prisoner of the egg the devil holds, but no one needs the soul anymore when everything is money and humans are more evil than the devil. 'Who is ruling you now', he asks the devil, 'can't be the god?' referring to the machines, the robots, the holdings and the multi-nationals. **Yılmaz**'s identification of the devil through Christian codes is interesting; in the Muslim religion the devil belongs to the other world and there can be no question of it possessing a human soul.

Durul and **Yağmur Taylan**'s horror **comedy**, *Okul / School* (2004), fashioned after Hollywood foregrounding the misadventures of youngsters on the anniversary of their love-struck friend's suicide, and *Küçük Kıyamet / Little Apocalypse* (2006), an attempt at an exploration of the psychology of earthquake trauma, garnered interest. **Ümit Ünal**'s horror/thriller *Ses / The Voice* (2010) was also successful with its solid dramatic structure although his **fantasy** suspense/thriller *Nar / Pomegranate* (2011) on the uniqueness of personal identity, which can be as different as the seeds of a pomegranate, was spread rather thin, addressing topics from class differences to lesbianism.

In the 2000s, several horror film attempts have exploited the Muslim religion while adhering to Western/Christian cultural codes in narration. Hasan Karacadağ who believes he has formulated the 'Islamic horror film **genre**' made *Dabbe I* (2005) and *Dabbe II* (2009), inspired by the Qur'anic verses about the apocalypse, claiming the Internet is the end of the world prophesied in the Qur'an. Karacadağ is motivated by the *semum* creatures (including the devil, created from fire, jealous of humans and harmful to them) mentioned in the *Hicr sur'a*, verses 26–27 of the Qur'an; his *Semum* (2008), about a woman who loses control of her body and harms others, combines animation and digital effects. In *Musallat* (Alper Mestçi, 2007), a djin enters the body of a person and makes him suffer (*djin sur'a* 72, verse 6). *Büyü / Spell* (**Orhan Oğuz**, 2004) about an ancient black magic that creates terror when triggered by a group of archaeologists, uses Qur'anic verses on the poster (*Bakara sur'a*, verse 102). *Araf / Purgatory* (Biray Dalkıran, 2006) about a dance student suffering the emotional consequences of abortion, converts the Christian religious motifs of guilt and repentance to an Islamicized version inspired by the Qur'anic verses, replacing the fairies with genies and demons and adopting the traditions of Far East cinemas. *Cehennem 3-D / Hell-3D* (2010) of Dalkıran is the first 3D film in the horror film sub-**genre**. Shunned by religious authorities, such films do well at the box-office.

Science fiction by itself does not exist in Turkish cinema. Underdevelopment in science and technology could be one of the reasons, which also manifests itself in literature – not more than 90 original science-fiction books have been published in Turkey since the 1940s, science-fiction magazines starting only in the 1970s. Science-fiction elements are interspersed in adventure and **comedy** films and parodies without proper context and continuity to create dramatic effect. In essence, these are very low budget escapist B-movies shot in a few days, lacking technical qualities and artistic merit, although some of them have become cult films in the twenty-first century. *Görünmeyen Adam İstanbul'da / Invisible Man in Istanbul* (**Osman Seden**, 1955), *Uçan Daireler İstanbul'da / UFOs in Istanbul* (Orhan Erçin, 1955), *Kilink Uçan Adama Karşı / Kiling vs. Flying Man* (**Yılmaz Atadeniz**, 1967), *Dünyayı Kurtaran Adam / The Man Who Saves the World* (**Çetin İnanç**, 1982) are some examples. More recent films, *G.O.R.A.* (**Ömer Faruk Sorak**, 2004) or *A.R.O.G.* (Ali Taner Baltacı, **Cem Yılmaz**, 2008) have acquired certain standards in visual effects, but they are insubstantial comedies made for the box-office and they succeed in what they try to accomplish. On the other hand, short films by a number of newcomers have shown promise with thematic diversity (Akşit 2011: 66–8).

Fehim, Ahmet (b. Istanbul, 1856 – d. Istanbul, 1930) Director, actor. A leading figure of theatre, Ahmet Fehim decided to go behind the camera when he was 62 with a script he knew well from his days in theatre, the controversial *Mürebbiye / The Governess* (1919). A sex-vaudeville about a French seductress called Angelique, adapted from the 1898 novel of the renowned author Hüseyin Rahmi Gürpınar and produced by the War Veterans' Association with **Fuat Uzkınay** as the cinematographer, *The Governess* is the first literary adaptation. The commandant of the occupying French army found it degrading to French women and banned its distribution in Anatolia despite Fehim's argument that his work was a silent protest of the artist against the occupation (Özön 1962: 48). Notwithstanding its shortcomings in terms of *mise en scène*, the film drew attention as a local work addressing current issues, particularly the infatuation of some circles with Western lifestyles (which was the main thrust of Gürpınar's novel) (Scognamillo 1987: 28–9). He followed it with *Binnaz* (1919), which he shot with Fazlı Necip from a work by Yusuf Ziya Ortaç, another renowned author. **Uzkınay** was again responsible for the cinematography. Considered as Turkey's first historical film, *Binnaz* was shot inside the Topkapı Palace, the narrative placed in the decadent Tulip Era of the Ottoman Empire, featuring the titular heroine as a beautiful seductress. A minor work in comparison to *The Governess*, the film suffered from the influences of theatre, just like the previous work, but became the first commercial film, rumoured to have been sold to England for £5,000 (Onaran 1994: 16). Fehim's memoirs that were serialized in a newspaper in 1926 were published as a book in 1977.

Filler ve Çimen / Elephants and Grass (2001) is loosely based on a scandal in 1996, (Susurluk) when an ordinary traffic accident exposed the involvement of the government and the police with the mafia and other illegal, subversive elements. A former deputy chief of the Istanbul police, the leader of the ultra-nationalist organization Grey Wolves, a convicted fugitive wanted for drug trafficking and murder and a beauty queen turned mafia hit-woman died in the incident, whereas a member of the parliament who was also at the head of a large group of village guards in the south-east was injured. The Interior Minister resigned and the police chief of Istanbul was suspended but 'deep state' has remained a burning issue.

The title of the film refers to an old saying 'when the elephant stomps, grass suffers'. Havva Adem (Eve Adam, 'everyman') is an athlete needing sponsorship for the upcoming marathon. If she wins, she will use the prize money for an operation for her brother, veteran of the civil war in the south-east, who is confined to a wheelchair. **Zaim** uses *ebru*, the Ottoman art of marbling (transferring paint that floats on water onto paper without the possibility of repeating the same design) that Havva Adem practises as a trope for the unique lifespan of each individual and the question of free will and destiny. As an apolitical ordinary citizen, Havva's life is like the drops in the marbling pot, at times guided by her own initiative, but other times directed by powers bigger than her. At the end, she tries the impossible by practising *ebru* under the snow in the pool and almost succeeds in a fantastic way. A minor trope is the box of erasers that she gives to children, an object that provides the capacity to obliterate mistakes, but also the incentive to repeat them, which is significant as a reference to the tendency of Turkish collective memory to obliterate the undesirable.

A weaker point in the film is the saturation of sub-plots that at times undermine the main plot, such as the mafia, the Kurdish guerrillas, the suicide bombers, the drug-trafficking Colombians, the secret service and the Alevi minority.

Director, Screenwriter: **Derviş Zaim**; Producer: Ali Akdeniz; Production: Pan Film; Cinematographer: Ertunç Şenkay; Editor: **Mustafa Presheva**; Music: Serdar Ateşer; Cast: Haluk Bilginer, Senem Çelik, Ali Sürmeli, Bülent Kayabaş, Uğur Polat, Taner Barlas, Taner Birsel

Film festivals in Turkey, where the number of cities without movie theatres is very high, assume the role of nourishing film culture in addition to displaying the latest national and international products. Lack of sufficient funds and exhibition halls, overt or covert forms of censorship, political manoeuvring, rivalries among producers, distributors and other festivals, as well as religion- or tradition-based animosities are often detrimental to the smooth operation of a film festival.

The International Istanbul Film Festival (IIFF), the most prestigious film event of the country, was founded in 1982 as a small, week-long programme by a handful of cinephiles in response to the closure of the **cinematheque** after the 12 September 1980 *coup d'état*. The event progressed into a full-fledged festival in 1988 with the goals of introducing quality foreign films to Istanbul audiences and showcasing quality Turkish films to the international guests under the umbrella of the İstanbul Kültür Sanat Vakfı / Istanbul Culture and Art Foundation (IKSV), a non-profit, non-governmental organization founded in 1973. The festival has suffered from lack of exhibition space after the closure of the independent cinema halls, either unable to compete with the multiplexes, or torn down to be replaced by shopping malls as in the case of the historical Emek Theatre. Yearly admission of around 150,000 is not a large number for a city of 15 million.

Organized by the Antalya Foundation for Culture and Arts with the support of the Antalya Metropolitan Municipality, the Antalya Golden Orange Film Festival, the oldest in Turkey, owes its beginnings to the establishment of the commercial Turkish cinema, **Yeşilçam**. Started in 1956 as part of the Antalya Art Festival, with the Film Competition initiated in 1964, the Golden Orange has served the industry as a national festival with prestigious awards, but suffered enormously under the heavy censorship of military regimes and was cancelled twice (1979 and 1980).

The Festival on Wheels, originating in the capital Ankara, began in 1995 with the mission to present outstanding examples of European and Turkish cinema to film enthusiasts living outside the country's cultural centres and continues to do so successfully. Ankara's Flying Broom International Women's Film Festival, founded in 1998, screens features, shorts, documentaries and animation by women from Turkey and abroad. Since 2004, Fipresci (the Federation of International Film Critics) has been authorized to give a Best Film award and the festival promotes itself as the only women's film festival in the world to give this prize.

In tune with the traditional atmosphere of Adana – the cotton-growing southern city, which gave the film world **Yılmaz Güney** and several other distinguished film-makers – the International Adana Golden Boll Film Festival screens feature films along with nationally produced shorts and student films. Beginning in 2008, its municipal organizers decided to broaden its scope to include the Mediterranean countries. The festival was held for the first time in 1969, but was cancelled between 1973 and 1992 for political reasons; in 1997 and 1999, because of an earthquake and in 2010, because of the Israeli attack on a Turkish ship carrying humanitarian aid to Gaza, which resulted in the murder of several Turks.

Two festivals in Istanbul focus on documentaries: Documentarist (Istanbul Documentary Days) founded in 2008 to support creative documentary filmmaking and to showcase the most recent films around the world and the International 1001 Documentary Film Festival, started in 1997 by the Association of Documentary Filmmakers in Turkey to encourage quality documentary production. National short films have been exhibited at the Golden Orange Film Festival since its inception. The first short film screening and competition in Istanbul was held in June 1967, organized by the film club of Robert College, a private American secondary school, and called the Hisar Short Film Competition. The most mature short film festival of today, the Istanbul Photography and Cinema Amateurs Club Short Film Days, was started in the 1980s and was instrumental in changing the general attitude toward short films by showing good examples of the form from the West; soon afterward, short film competitions were begun within established film festivals or as separate events.

In the last decade, along with specialized film festivals in metropolises (!f Istanbul AFM International Independent Film Festival), several international festivals have started in various provincial towns, commensurate with the surging interest in film studies and the unprecedented success of Turkish films at international festivals. None of these festivals features a market.

Film journals is a subject neglected by film scholars in Turkey. According to archivist Burçak Evren, the first Turkish film magazine, *Ferah* was published in 1914, the same year as *Aya Stefanos'taki Rus Abidesinin Yıkılışı / The Demolition of the Russian Monument at St. Stephan*, considered the first national film. During World War I, a number of magazines focusing on art and literature such as *Temaşa* (1918–20), *Yarın* and *Dergah* (1921–2) devoted space to cinema. Before changing to the Latin alphabet in 1923, weekly magazines were published in Ottoman and French – *Le Courrier du Cinema*, *Opera-Ciné*, *Le Film*, *Artistic-Cine* – but they did not last more than a year, except *Le Film* which continued for about three years. After 1923, cinema magazines and cinema sections of political newspapers featured mostly gossip about Hollywood and European film industries. With the increase in the number of national films made and the cinema halls in operation, the number of magazines increased in the mid-1930s, spreading to Ankara and İzmir, the most prominent one being *Yıldız / Star* (1938–54), which gave importance to national cinema, particularly in the 1950s, publishing critiques of newly released films. In the same period, cinema owners began to publish promotion magazines. In the 1940s, *photo-roman* style special editions and annuals displaying pictures of popular artists (often exploiting eroticism) were popular. In the 1950s, some newspapers began to approach cinema seriously but magazines did not follow suit, except **Nijat Özön**'s *Sinema* (1956), considered the first serious film journal. In the 1960s, with the founding of the **cinematheque**, a medium was created for serious cinema, giving birth to dedicated journals. The most prominent one, the monthly *Yeni Sinema / New Cinema*, which survived 30 editions (1966–70), was like a textbook for cinephiles. Ten years later, an attempt was made to revive it but it lasted for only two editions. *Özgür / Independent* (which was later changed to *Ulusal / National*) published by the Turkish Film Archive as an alternative to *New Cinema*, concentrated on local films, supporting the film-makers excluded by the **cinematheque** group. In the same period, *Ses / Voice* and *Artist* were founded, two long-lasting magazines that gave to Turkish cinema some of its best actors through the contests they organized. During the stagnant 1970s, an important journal with left politics, *Yedinci Sanat / The 7th Art* was born. With the advancement in publishing technology, attempts were made in the 1980s at glossy magazines, most of which promoted their own market and were short lived. *Antrakt / Entr'acte*, with modern standards and foreign cinema concentration, made its mark in the 1990s (Evren 1993: 13–22). From the 2000s to the present, the most successful independent film journal appearing regularly each month is *Altyazı / Subtitle*, a publication of the Mithat Alam Film Centre at the Bosphorus University, originally founded in 2001 by a group of students.

Film museums are rare in Turkey. In Istanbul, Türvak Sinema-Tiyatro Müzesi / Turvak Cinema and Theatre Museum, a private enterprise, was founded in 2001 by **Türker İnanoğlu**, establishing its permanent location in the Beyoğlu district in 2011. The museum houses over 1,000 cinema and television devices, 4,200 copies of various Turkish films, over 6,000 Turkish film posters, over 10,000 cinema–theatre stage photographs and over 12,000 hours of television programmes and

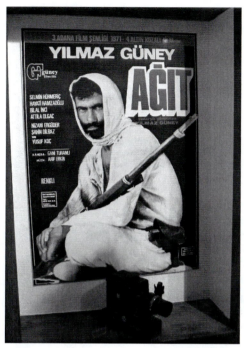

Figure 44 Adana Cinema Museum: poster of *Ağıt / Elegy* (Yılmaz Güney, 1971) with Güney. Photo: Gönül Dönmez-Colin

Figure 45 Adana Cinema Museum: from *Ben Öldükçe Yaşarım / I Live as Long as I Die* (Duygu Sağıroğlu 1965) with Güney. Photo: Gönül Dönmez-Colin

Figure 46 Adana Cinema Museum: *Seyyit Han* aka *Toprağın Gelini / Seyyit Han* aka *The Bride of the Earth* (Güney, 1968). Photo: Gönül Dönmez-Colin

series in its archive in addition to a collection of 60,000 books and periodicals. In the provincial town of Adana, the birthplace of **Yılmaz Güney** and other distinguished personalities of cinema, plastic arts and literature and the pulse of the industry during its prime with 250 open-air cinemas, the Adana Cinema Museum was inaugurated in 2011 with the joint efforts of the municipality, the prefecture and the International Golden Boll Film Festival. It includes film posters and stills, pictures of film-makers from Adana, their cameras, costumes, scripts and other related objects, as well as a wax figure of **Güney** and the originals of the letters he wrote from jail to his wife and friends. A large collection of publications dating back to 1891 complements the exhibitions.

Film schools began to be established in the 1990s with the new vitality observed in cinema through the movement of **New Turkish Cinema**. Around 15 universities provide film and television studies and the numbers are growing. Some of the most prominent ones are within the structure of the Mimar Sinan Fine Arts University, Marmara University, Bahçeşehir University, Bilgi University, Yedi Tepe University, Maltepe University, Bosphorous University, and TÜRVAK Film and Cinema School in Istanbul; Anadolu University in Eskişehir; Nine September University in İzmir and Ankara University.

Fotoğraf / The Photograph (2001), reminiscent of Thomas Hardy's often quoted poem, 'The Man He Killed', narrates the story of two young men, a Turk and a Kurd, who become friends during a long bus journey from Istanbul to Diyarbakır at the height of the civil war. The atmosphere of oppression is heightened with the frequency of checkpoints as they near their destination, where they are to separate, one to the army for his military service and the other to join the guerrilla operations. Next time they meet will be on the battlefield.

In the opening sequences, the camera turns around the Statue of Victory while the 10th Anniversary March of the Turkish Republic, with a clearly nationalistic refrain of 'We are Turks, the head of all heads; we were there before history and we will be after' is heard. This is subtitled into Kurdish as if to defy and mock the official one-language policy. The film is shot mostly in Kurdish (subtitled into Turkish/Kurdish) during a period when speaking Kurdish was forbidden. The narrative relies on the gaze and the silence, practising circumlocution, the trademark of **Yılmaz Güney** and most Third Cinema film-makers. The message of oppression is transmitted through small details – the changing of the music cassette from Kurdish to Turkish when the minibus nears the checkpoints; the expressionless faces of the passengers as they watch the news footage of a bloody conflict and the graffiti in a toilet, 'The soldier will come back in a coffin'.

Despite the schematic narrative and the underdeveloped script that disadvantage the dramatic structure, particularly a handicap during the journey when the dialogue meanders, as the first Kurdish production within Turkey, made by a Kurdish film-maker with limited resources, the film is significant as a pioneer. It was realized with the support of the Mesopotamian Cinema Collective, contributions from students, tradesmen, workers, engineers and businessmen and revenues from organized concerts, the film crew agreeing to work as volunteers. Due to the sensitive subject matter, the distribution had to proceed through alternative channels as well. Nonetheless, it was shown in several major cities, reaching 25,000 spectators. Festival reception was positive with a number of national and international awards.

Director, Screenwriter: **Kazım Öz**; Producer, Art Director: Özkan Küçük; Production: Mezopotamia Cultural Centre; Cinematographer: Ercan Özkan; Music: Mustafa Biber; Cast: Feyyaz Duman, Nazmî Kırık, Mizgin Kapazan, Muhlis Asan, Zülfiye Dolu

G

Gegen die Wand / Duvara Karşı / Head-on (2004), a Golden Bear winner at the Berlin Film Festival as a German production, focuses on two misplaced Turkish–German characters and their quest for visibility in forming personal identities in an environment where identities are imposed by situations exterior to the characters. Cahit (Birol Ünel) and Sibel (Sibel Kekilli) feel more at home among other marginal characters like themselves – Germans or other Europeans – than among Turks; a Turkish bus driver throws them out for 'bad behaviour' and Cahit is uncomfortable in the company of Sibel's chauvinist brothers. The free-spirited Sibel had her antecedent in Ceyda (İdil Üner), the sister of Gabriel in *Kurz und Schmerzlos / Short Sharp Shock* (1998). Her family is not the typical conservative Muslim family, but patriarchal tradition reigns – her nose is broken by her brother for being with a boy. She is in the habit of suicide attempts as silent screams. Cahit is also self-destructive; the reasons are not disclosed. **Akın** underscores the disorder in Cahit's life through his living space – empty beer bottles and litter – trash images that are often filmic codes of a crisis, garbage often intertwined with attitudes about race, nation and ethnicity, but counteracts the trope by showing Cahit at home in this chaos. He is disturbed when Sibel tidies the place like a proper Turkish homemaker, the guardian of the interior space – another imposed identity that contradicts her rebellious nature, but serves as a premonition. At the end, Cahit, released from prison where he served a sentence for a crime of passion *a la turca*, arrives in his country of origin, clean-shaven, looking for Sibel, who has surrendered the fight and accepted the imposed identities of society by becoming a middle-class homemaker, her short hair coding an orderly life, at least in appearance. The majority has won. (Anything connected with their life together is now confined to impersonal and transitory spaces – airports, bus stations and hotel rooms.)

Head-on carries the usual elements of Turkish **melodrama** from *kara sevda* (dark passion) and rape to honour, but results in a work as hybrid as its characters. The chaos surrounding the couple in their life in Germany, particularly the cafe scenes at night and the living space of Cahit mentioned above, shown in soft lights, have a Fassbinderian quality that renders them appealing. The musical interludes, *fasıl* on the shores of the Bosphorus, a Brechtian intervention as **Akın** admits, book-end the chapters, but also reveal a postcard kitsch quality

Figure 47 Gegen die Wand / Duvara Karşı / Head-on (Fatih Akın, 2004) (Courtesy of International Istanbul Film Festival)

presenting Turkey as a vacation dream. (The intertextual relay of the film on the poster is noteworthy: naked lovers in embrace positioned on the right corner while the image of a prominent mosque, one of the tourist attractions, towers in the background, which is a non-diegetic image.) After both hitting the bottom, the reunion of the protagonists happens in Turkey. Does **Akın** suggest return to roots as a solution? He maintains the insignificance of the geographical location when 'an imaginary space' to escape is the issue for the protagonists. Although that 'imaginary space' is Turkey, the homeland of their parents (a motif that re-appears in **Akın**'s films), alienation is not defined in cultural terms. Intercultural cinema (Marks 2000: 7) is less 'loaded' than 'hybrid', not the property of any single culture but mediates at least in two directions.

Director, Screenwriter: **Fatih Akın**; Producers: **Fatih Akın**, Mehmet Kurtuluş, Stefan Schubert, Ralph Schwingel, Andreas Schreitmüller; Production: Bavaria Film International, Arte; Cinematography: Rainer Klausmann; Editor: Andrew Bird; Art Directors: Sima Bradley, Nergis Çalişkan; Music: Alexander Hacke, Maceo Parker; Cast: Birol Ünel, Sibel Kekilli, Catrin Striebeck, Meltem Cümbül, Stefan Gebelhoff, Francesco Fiannaca, Güven Kıraç

Gelecek Uzun Sürer / The Future Lasts Forever (2011) interrogates personal, historical and collective memory. The film begins with the sound of airplanes. A galloping horse, a distinct metaphor for freedom for the Kurds who live in the lands evacuated by the Armenians, the first tamers, survives the first shot, is wounded with the second and dead with the third. The narrative develops through an outsider, a young ethno-musicologist, Sumru (Gaye Gürsel) who records

Figure 48 Gelecek Uzun Sürer / The Future Lasts Forever (Özcan Alper, 2011) (Courtesy of Özcan Alper)

elegies, testimonials of the Kurdish survivors of atrocities, eloquently delivered, mostly by women, before a wall of thousands of identity photos. The witnesses face the camera and recount their trauma while the blue-tinged documentaries merge with fiction to expose police brutalities, unsolved murders and the burning of villages. Sumru's involvement in the project is linked to her personal loss: three years earlier, her boyfriend Harun joined the guerrillas. In flashbacks, she is shown singing *Vinceremos* (we shall be victorious) with him on a bus of Kurdish students, then sitting on a train, the sign of the crescent and the star on the window (emblem of the Turkish flag) entering between them, then alone reading Harun's letter. At the train station, Diyarbakır is established as a multi-ethnic centre joining different sections of the country. It is also a city with history, with black basalt walls, Roman ruins and dilapidated churches, trying to contest the present amnesia. Antranig, the custodian of the decrepit Armenian church Sourp Giragos, is afraid history will be buried if he leaves to join his daughters in Switzerland. (His name has several semantic references in Armenian, most importantly meaning 'the first-born', but also the name of the famous guerrilla commander fighting for survival.) He asks Sumru, in Armenian, if she speaks the language and she answers that she is a *Hamshentsi* (descendant of the Armenians from Hamshen who converted to Islam in the seventeenth century). Sumru asks to listen to the elegy sung by Antranig's mother. On her third visit, as the rain falls heavily on the porch, Antranig explains that his mother was a victim of the 1915 *chart* and leaves Sumru to listen alone on the porch. The crimes against the Kurds are superimposed on the crimes against Armenians.

The film alludes to literature and cinema. The title is taken from Louis Pierre Althusser's (1918–90) autobiography, *L'avenir dure Longtemps / The Future*

Lasts Forever (1985); the opening quote is from the Italian writer and poet Cesare Pavese: 'When the war ends one day, we have to ask ourselves this: What are we to do with the dead? Why did they die?' For **Alper**, the quote précises Turkey's last 30 years, the dead soldiers and guerrillas and the unsolved murders and perhaps precipitates an interrogation of our memory, understanding through empathy and dialogue to find a solution to chronic political issues and to war using the language of politics, not ammunition. *Oza* (Voznesensky, 1964), a poem about love and separation, also appears as a motif.

The character whose path crosses Sumru's is Ahmet (Durukan Ordu), the disillusioned Kurdish man who has interrupted his education to return to Diyarbakır. He sells pirated DVDs, very common in Anatolian cities that lack cinema halls, and operates a self-styled cinemateque, 'Cinamed', forcing his simple-minded friend to watch the languid river journey of Lenin's gigantic statue (*Ulysses' Gaze*, Theo Angelopoulos, 1995) on a blue-tinged television screen. His room is decorated with posters of *Yol / The Way* (**Şerif Gören**, 1982), *Xala* (Ousmane Sèmbene, 1995) and others, films that correspond to **Alper**'s concept of Third Cinema. Graffiti from Franz Fanon's *The Wretched of the Earth* (1961) also appear. He is Sumru's confidante and soon becomes attracted to her, knowing tragedies (including the death of Sumru's boyfriend) have destroyed the potential for love. The conversation between them about the future happens in the dark orange moonlight, during a scene reminding one of Rembrandt paintings or black-and-white German expressionist films; he dreams of Socialist compassion, rights for the workers and a world without borders.

A wild black horse wanders aimlessly on white snow at the end (linking with the testimony of one of the survivors describing the mass shooting of animals by the soldiers, while one horse escapes; 'as if our hopes escaped the tyranny and reached freedom', the peasant woman comments). A beautiful Armenian lullaby, accompanied by *saz* (recorded by Ludvig Durian, music by Khatchatur Avestissian), orchestrated with a haunting *melisma* (sung by the Chamber Music Choir of Radio Yerevan), concludes the film.

The immediacy of the subject chosen and the expert cinematography, contrasting the breath-taking beauty of nature with the human tragedy while following the routine of daily life in crowded alleys and at the dynamic train station, are commendable in the film. The weaker points are the somewhat forced merging of the otherwise exceptionally powerful documentary and documentary-style footage with the narrative; the lack of sufficient distance on the part of **Alper**, gravitating the film toward 'cinema of duty' and the underdevelopment of the characters, except for Ahmet. As a sensitive and somewhat timid Anatolian youth, a film buff impressed by an educated city woman (the scene in front of the mirror is memorable), cautious about the outcome of attachment to someone mourning the absence of a lover, he is more flesh and blood.

Among the awards the film received are Fipresci (Federation of International Film Critics) Best Film at the 16th Kerala International Film Festival, 2011 and Best Turkish Film at the 18th Adana Golden Boll International Film Festival, 2011.

Director, Screenwriter: **Özcan Alper**; Producers: Soner Alper, Ersin Çelik; Production: Nar Film; Cinematographer: Feza Çaldıran; Editor: Ayhan Ergürsel, Thomas Barkenhol, Özcan Alper, Umut Sakallıoğlu; Sound: Mohammed Mokhtary; Music: Mustafa Biber; Art Director: Tolunay Türköz; Cast: Gaye Gürsel, Durukan Ordu, Selman Ünlüsoy, Sarkis Seropyan, Osman Karakoç

Gelin / The Bride (1973), one of the most outstanding works on migration, is the first part of the Migration Trilogy that includes *Düğün / The Wedding* (1974) and *Diyet / Blood Money* (1975). Unlike the majority of migration films, the uprooted family is not poor, but their mentality is feudal and patriarchal. Their aim is to build roots in the city through economic advancement and the women are expected to obey the men unconditionally.

The title is significant. The word *gelin* has a dual meaning in Turkish: the bride and the daughter-in-law. Within the feudal system, she is the most exploited without recourse to rebellion, but **Akad**'s focus is not her position as a victim, but rather her role as the representative of the new rural woman that migration has created; a binding force for the family with her maternal instincts and an active participant in her fate. To stress the pivotal position of the protagonist Meryem (**Hülya Koçyiğit**) in the narrative, the camera persistently follows her; in the crowd scenes, the attention is always drawn to her.

The film uses her interstitiality between her parents' home in the village and her in-laws' home in the city as a trope for the liminal position of displaced migrants in a society experiencing an unhealthy progress. The exodus to the metropolises of the west, triggered by economic deadlock in the villages, carries dreams of social climbing and quick riches. The head of the family, Hacı İlyas (Ali Şen) represents the pains of transition from feudal underdevelopment to capitalism that Turkey experienced after the 1950s. The décor inside their house illustrates the in-between status of the family, mixing the traditional – the wall-carpet, the coffer, the dining table on the floor, the Qur'an – with the modern – the radio, the alarm clock. The family continues to preserve the tradition of respecting the elders and celebrating religious holidays, but such values seem to have lost their essence. Degeneration as the outcome of the trauma of alienation, the loss of identity and the insecurity are felt at different levels: Meryem's sick son is not taken to a doctor to save the money to open a better shop uptown; the older daughter-in-law, the mother of two healthy children, patronizes Meryem. Symbolically, the boy dies on the day of the *Kurban Bayramı*, the religious holiday when a sheep is sacrificed, his death as a trope for all the sacrifices Turkey has made – the human values, the love, the respect – in the efforts to embrace capitalism.

The husband's position is also in-between. He feels the pain of the injustices toward his wife, but, within the feudal structure, he bows down to his elders. (Just like Şivan in *Sürü / The Herd*, **Zeki Ökten**, 1978, who is helpless when his father insults his wife, Berivan.) Only after the tragedy will he be able to take a stand. When Meryem disrupts the patriarchal order by leaving the family to work in the factory, he does not kill her as his father demands, but joins her to start a new life (Dönmez-Colin 2008: 59–61).

Director, Screenwriter: **Lütfi Ö. Akad**; Producer: Hürrem Erman; Production: Erman Film; Cinematographer: Gani Turanlı; Music: Yalçın Tura; Cast: **Hülya Koçyiğit**, Kerem Yılmazer, Kahraman Kıral, Ali Şen, **Aliye Rona**, Kâmuran Usluer, Nazan Adalı, Seden Kızıltunç

Gemide / On Board (1998), shot simultaneously with ***Laleli'de Bir Azize / A Madonna in Laleli*** by **Kudret Sabancı** using the same crew, is an attempt at a new cinema language. An anchored ship responsible for loading sand is the home to four lumpen characters, Captain İdris (Erkan Can) and his men, Kamil, Boxer and Ali, anti-heroes who smoke hashish, eat, drink and drown in guilt and paranoia in a ship that never sails. Rape or murder does not disturb their conscience, but the possibility of being caught does. When Boxer is robbed on shore, they go to Istanbul for revenge, wound the gang leader and return with the booty – a young foreign woman, a 'virgin prostitute', whose silent presence brings more disorder. The interior monologue of the captain in the opening scene, 'the ship is like the control. Everything has to be orderly and under control. The regulations, the laws, the order must be respected... I am like the prime minister... You are the citizen' states the obvious metaphor of the ship as the country. The economic crises and the lack of trust in the judicial system have created citizens ready to take justice in their own hands; in the absence of a dependable democratic system, a new citizen with a 'the end justifies the means' mentality has been created, normalizing wrong-doings. No one trusts each other and women are silenced, raped and murdered regularly. In that sense, the rape of the silent woman on the ship becomes a metonym for the citizens.

Although rape is shown as sexual aggression and without any voyeuristic display of sexual organs, the physical and verbal violence directed against the interminably silent women is emotionally violent; the tragi-comic tempo often loses momentum and scenes such as the woman falling on the knife – *bête noir* for some audiences – are contrived. On the other hand, the film is representative of the post-1980 *coup d'état* Turkish cinema that underscores the theme of 'masculinity in crisis', the outcome of the feeling of guilt for remaining silent, which has created a sadomasochistic cultural medium.

Director: **Serdar Akar**; Producers: Önder Çakar, Sevil Çakar; Production: Yeni Sinemacılar; Screenwriters: **Serdar Akar**, Önder Çakar; Cinematographer: Mehmet Aksın; Editor: Nevzat Dişiaçık; Music: **Uğur Yücel**; Cast: Erkan Can, Naci Taşdöğen, Yıldıray Şahinler, Haldun Boysan, Ella Manea

Gender politics carry a masculinist bias in the historically gendered Turkish cinema. The representations of women can be mystificatory, manipulative, objectifying and disempowering in accordance with the trends of the period: fodder for comedy as nymphomaniacs when discourse on actual relationships is taboo (***Pençe / The Claw,*** 1917; *Mürebbiye / The Governess*, 1919; *İstanbul'da Bir Facia-i Aşk / A Love Tragedy in Istanbul*, 1922; *Şehvet Kurbanı / The Victim of Lust*, 1939); metonyms for the republic during the nation building (**Muhsin Ertuğrul**'s characters, liberated and equal to men in love and life, echoing the social reforms envisioned by Atatürk or **Akad**'s idealist teacher Aliye in *Vurun Kahpeye / Strike the Whore*, 1949); obedient daughters/housewives or marginal outcasts (prostitutes) when family values are imperative (**Yeşilçam melodramas**); torchbearers of modernity during the transition to Occidental capitalism (Migration Trilogy of **Akad**, 1973/1975) and mute characters silenced by an act of violence, physical or mental (*Sürü / The Herd*, **Zeki Ökten**, 1978; *Eşkıya / The Bandit*, **Yavuz Turgul**, 1996; *9*, **Ümit Ünal**, 2002; *Masumiyet / Innocence*, **Zeki Demirkubuz**, 1997); a mirage, a fantasy, or simply invisible in the traumatic years from the three *coup d'état*s to the present (most films of **Nuri Bilge Ceylan**). Such traits are overlapping and interchangeable from one period to the other, but the masculinist nature of cinema remains constant. An industry dominated by men has presented woman 'as what she represents for man, not in terms of what she *actually* signifies. Her *discourse* (her meanings, as she might produce them) is suppressed in favour of a discourse structured by patriarchy in which her real signification has been replaced by connotations that serve patriarchy's needs' (Kaplan 1983: 18).

Culture expects women to show greater acceptance or commitment to the value system than men, and such expectations form women's identities and their role in society (Anzaldúa 2010: 1019). Men have traditionally been presented as adventurers, warriors, charmers, seducers, rich heirs, family heads, doctors, lawyers, soldiers, policemen, employers or business executives. Women could only *serve* the society as teachers, nurses, bank clerks, secretaries or housemaids; they could not be shown in administrative positions. Work outside the home was acceptable only under economic shortage; money earned had to be delivered to male members. The fact that all aspects of the industry except the acting was in the hands of men, naturally affected the output. It took a long time before cinema stopped showing career woman as an anomaly that had to be resolved by domestication before the end of the film. Some films that initially focused on the emancipation of working women steered towards the process of re-gaining the femininity lost by the desire for emancipation. In the portrayal of sexuality and its consequences, double standards prevailed: women in general enjoyed sex only within the monogamous marriage, while men were allowed extramarital sex. Women who violated this rule of limited sexuality were considered loose and they often got what they deserved. **Gören** contravened the status quo by presenting independent women in *Derman / Remedy* (1984), *Kurbağalar / The Frogs* (1985) and *Firar / The Escape* (1984), but he also made *Güneşin Tutulduğu Gün / The Day of the Eclipse of the Sun* (1983) where a young woman from the periphery chooses prostitution for social climbing but ends on a pile of garbage, raped by the neighbourhood kids – a warning to those who may think of deviating from the norm.

Rural melodramas structured the narrative around the highest-ranking male member of the family, usually the father who maintained the patriarchal ideology although *Sürü / The Herd* (**Zeki Ökten**, 1978) and *Yol / The Road* (**Şerif Gören**, 1982) show the collapse of such a system. In the post-junta films, men have become anti-heroes in the urban environment, struggling with their masculinity which seems to be in crisis, caught between the competing and complementary aspects of two patriarchal forces, the military and the Islamic tradition (*Gemide / On Board*, **Akar**, 1998; ***Bornova Bornova***, **İnan Temelkuran**, 2009). The possibility of return to the roots – the natal village in the countryside, the idealized mother as 'the keeper of Islam/order', representing the womb – is presented as a relief, even temporary (*Yumurta / Egg*, **Semih Kaplanoğlu**, 2007).

Turkish cinema's tropes have been systematically gendered: Istanbul is often referred to as a 'whore' – *Gurbet Kuşları / The Birds of Nostalgia* aka *Migrating Birds* aka *Birds of Exile* (**Halit Refiğ**, 1964); *Anlat İstanbul / Istanbul Tales* (Ömür Atay, Selim Demirdelen, **Kudret Sabancı**, Yücel Yolcu, **Ümit Ünal**, 2005) – or inversely, the prostitute is a metaphor for Istanbul – *Ah, Güzel Istanbul* (**Atıf Yılmaz**, 1966 and **Ömer Kavur**, 1981).

Islamic religious discourse is generally carried over the female body (the headscarf, the covering of the body, the preservation of virginity until marriage) not unlike the early bourgeois sense of the body in Western culture 'as a hermetically sealed container impermeable to outside influence' (Ferguson 1997: 1–32). Turkish cinema from its beginnings endorsed conservative bourgeois values avoiding sexuality. Films validated the sacrosanctity of marriage not to offend the family women, the largest part of the audience. The deceived and deserted village maidens and the *vamp* and the *femme fatale* who paid for their 'sins' with their lives were motifs close to the Muslim society where patriarchal control was sustained through the (idealized) family, the identity of the woman split into *aile kadını* (the family woman), the organizer of the inner/private space and *hayat kadını* (literally *life woman*, a euphemism for the prostitute), the woman who disrupts the order by crossing over to the public space, the domain of men. As a wife and mother, the woman was the 'keeper of Islam' (Saktanber 2002: 55) but she could also be the source of disorder. In *Yol*, all five prisoners are in a quandary regarding women. 'Whenever there is trouble, there is a woman behind it', the commissar declares in **Ceylan**'s *Once Upon a Time in Anatolia*. Woman's sexuality is a potential threat to men's dignity and hence, the destruction of the social stability, which it is man's duty to safeguard. The woman's responsibility is to protect the private space against external pollution.

With migration to the cities and the issue of the rural man seeking a new identity in a liminal space, cinema invented a new identity for women – submissive characters that accepted suffering and humiliation arising from customs and traditions, although in **melodramas** between 1965 and 1975, one may find strong female characters created under the influence of socialist ideologies, who would challenge the status quo and find individual voices.

One of the contradictions of commercial cinema in the representation of women was the 'lumpen woman' exhibiting macho muscle power, vulgar jests, mimicry and laughter, foul language and the dress code of the male sub-culture, against the social, cultural and religious structure of the Muslim family. Such films were very popular in the 1960s (as long as the woman could act like a woman at home, obeyed her man and begat progeny). The unprecedented success of *Şöför Nebahat / Nebahat, The Driver* (**Metin Erksan**, 1959/60) resulted in sequels. In a social structure of gender gap, 'such films distorted the predicaments of women by creating schizophrenic characters and/or false images. They also confirmed the ingrained attitude that women could only be heroes if they acted like men' (Dönmez-Colin 2004: 35).

During the golden age of **Yeşilçam**, the four top stars were typecast according to alleged audience expectations: **Türkan Şoray**, the oppressed sexual woman; **Hülya Koçyiğit**, the oppressed asexual woman; **Filiz Akın**, the petit bourgeois woman; and **Fatma Girik**, *erkek Fatma* (male Fatma), not masculine, but brave, honest and straightforward like a man (Dönmez-Colin 2004: 36). Stars refused risqué roles to protect their reputation.

In the 1980s, with the transition to an open-market economy, more women began to join the workforce, which had repercussions in the family structure. The widening of education opportunities and the late arrival of feminism led to a re-evaluation of woman's identity. With **Atıf Yılmaz** leading the way, several others – **Ömer Kavur**, **Şerif Gören** – focused on the 'new woman' (neither a virgin, nor a prostitute) with **Müjde Ar** as the new star personifying the intelligent independent modern woman with sexuality. **Yılmaz** either ignored the family, the backbone of **Yeşilçam**, or showed its disintegration. Small-town women (*Mine*) or slum-dwellers (*A Taste of Love*), his women took bold steps as individuals and were often rewarded positively, although liberation was generally equated with sexual liberation.

Internationally celebrated, **Yılmaz Güney**'s cinema has remained problematic, defined as 'macho' cinema that depicts woman as subservient to man. **Güney** maintained that when he showed the oppression of women, he also showed the humiliation of men (**Güney** 1994b: 242–2), which corresponds to Pierre Bourdieu's observations about manliness and honour in Muslim Mediterranean societies, 'Male privilege is also a trap, and it has its negative side in the permanent tension and contention, sometimes verging on the absurd, imposed on everyman by the duty to assert his manliness in all circumstances…*Manliness,* understood as sexual or social reproductive capacity, but also as the capacity to fight and to exercise violence (especially in acts of revenge) is first and foremost a *duty*' (Bourdieu 2001: 50–51).

The portrayal of women as the cause and the recipient of male anger and frustration, and the linking of violence and sex are not new to cinema. Some films use violence against women as a metaphor, but often the woman is the victim. In some films, the violence appears as an indirect manifestation of the political oppression of men, linked through an unequal power relationship with the rapist. In others, the woman is used as a scapegoat in a revenge situation between rival groups. Sexual violence against women at times serves as a symbol for the political and sexual impotence of men in a system that systematically strips them of power: they do to women what the state does to them (Dönmez-Colin 2004: 80). *İki Kadın / Two Women* (1992) by **Yavuz Özkan** about the relationship between a call-girl and the wife of a politician who rapes her, uses the two women as a trope for a nation raped by bad politicians, but ignores the issues of women, identifying them through relationships and associations with men (Eyüboğlu 2001: 37–45).

The increase in male macho **melodramas** since the late 1990s displaying violence, anger and hate towards women who are silent characters, is attributed to the guilt of unaccounted long-lasting military interventions, poverty and unemployment and the lack of social consciousness or political criticism, which play a role in turning the compressed anger of the tarnished egos towards the nearest 'other', the woman (Süalp, 2009). Stereotypical and sexually biased films of **Yeşilçam** are re-visited not only in commercial cinema (*Recep İvedik*, Togan Gökbakar, 2008), but also in so-called 'art house'; in *On Board*, *Laleli'de Bir Azize / A Madonna in Laleli* (**Sabancı**, 1998) and *Barda / In the Bar* (**Akar**, 2006), women are 'silenced' characters, 'foreigners' or inanimate objects who will not show reaction even when raped. Mehmet Güleri's visually dramatic *film noir*, *Gölge / Shadow* (2008) revives the *vamp* and *femme fatale* sub-**genre**s including a nymphomaniac with psychopathological disorders. Other clichés persist in the portrayal of women. In *Hiçbiryerde / Innowhereland* (**Tayfun Pirselimoğlu**, 2002), the protagonist Şükran works at the ticket office of the central station at the heart of Istanbul, but she is presented like a submissive housewife who never leaves home; the young activist, unattractive and very masculine, appears in army fatigues. In **Çağan Irmak**'s *Karanlıktakiler / In Darkness* (2009) apart from its 'othering' of Anatolians and particularly an ethnic minority (the Kurds), the depiction of women is also problematic. The mother has brought shame to her family as a young girl by being raped and impregnated and giving birth to an 'abnormal' child, whose umbilical cord she has not yet severed. The aunt is a shrew, the receptionist is moody and simple-minded and the boss, an attractive and successful woman, cries at work over a hopeless love affair (similar attributes to a successful career woman are to be found in **Yeşim Ustaoğlu**'s **Pandoranın Kutusu / Pandora's Box**, 2008).

Nuri Bilge Ceylan, modern Turkey's internationally most accomplished film-maker, often casts women in traditional roles – wives, mistresses, mothers and sisters (***Uzak / Distant***, 2002). In *İklimler / Climates* (2006), Bahar (meaning spring), the partner of an older philanderer, expresses her sadness through her silences and tears just like the silent women of the **Yeşilçam melodramas**. Hacer in ***Üç Maymun / Three Monkeys*** (2008) and Gülnaz, the wife of the victim in ***Bir Zamanlar Anadolu'da / Once Upon a Time in Anatolia*** (2011) disrupt the male order by committing adultery but do not repent. (For further discussion on **Ceylan**'s films, please refer to individual entries.)

Zeki Demirkubuz, within the framework of male **melodramas**, succeeds in portraying multiple identities of the modern Turkish woman often by reversing traditional moral values. In *Masumiyet / Innocence* (1997) and *Kader / Destiny* (2006), the 'fallen woman' merits respect with her individuality and free will. In *C Blok / Block C* (1994), *Innocence*; *Üçüncü Sayfa / The Third Page* (1999) and *İtiraf / Confession* (2001), the patriarchal backbone, the male authority and its forte, the 'honour' are dismantled when the man forces the woman to confess (about sex) and she does not – she either remains silent, screams in anger, or finds means of silencing the man. Even when the man points a gun, the 'phallic symbol', it does not create fear. (In *Innocence*, Uğur: 'Shoot if you're a man!' and in *The Third Page*, Meryem: 'If you gonna shoot, shoot, otherwise get lost, my husband will be arriving soon'!) (Koç 2004: 185–94).

The treatment of gender in the films of **Reha Erdem** and his generation tends to be more individual and urban than the more collective and rural depictions of **Yeşilçam**. **Erdem** disrupts the gender myth in *Beş Vakit / Times and Winds* (2006), presenting male characters sick in old age, subservient to father authority during adulthood and fantasizing patricide during adolescence. In *Korkuyorum Anne aka İnsan Nedir ki? / I'm Scared aka What's Human Anyway* (2004), characters are scared of events associated with becoming a man – circumcision, military service and leaving home. In *Hayat Var / My Only Sunshine* (2008), Hayat is silent but rebellious, the only winner – despite constantly being victimized – in an environment where males are incapacitated (sick old man dependent on oxygen tubes, marginal adult wavering between identities and unable to take care of his daughter, drunken men seeking prostitutes or drugs). In *Kosmos*, the protagonist is out of place in the men's café where he shouts he wants love, considered a feminine trait.

What is noteworthy in *My Only Sunshine* and **Semih Kaplanoğlu**'s *Meleğin Düşüşü / Angel's Fall* (2004) is when all systems fail, women take action; young Hayat chooses the utmost rebellion – she opens the door and leaves and Zeynep in *Angel* does not wait tied to the rock like Andromeda until Perseus slays the monster and saves her, but takes destiny into her own hands.

In the 2000s conservatism and regressiveness has shown marked increase in Turkish society in terms of women's freedom and equality (honour killings, child marriages, forced suicides) under the rule of the AKP (Justice and Development Party), which operates on the basis of exceedingly traditional and retrograde concepts of gender and sexuality. An ostentatious fairy tale *Ya Sonra? / And Then What?* (Özcan Deniz, 2010), considered by a large number of spectators as a sweet love story, condones the idea that for the husbands of women who work outside the home, it is normal to worry that they may become prostitutes. The couple reunites in the film, not because the husband learns a lesson and comes to terms with his wife's career but when he claims 'his woman' by brute force. Two films made by distinguished women film-makers from different generations, *Araf* (**Yeşim Ustaoğlu**, 2012) and *Gözetleme Kulesi / The Watch Tower* (**Pelin Esmer**, 2012), foreground unwanted pregnancy and challenge the fallacious 'motherhood instinct' although both films resolve the security/survival issue through the protection of a benevolent man, which is the solution **Fatih Akın** also sees fit for his rebellious protagonist Sibel in *Gegen die Wand / Duvara Karşı / Head-on* (2004). Abdullah Oğuz in *Mutluluk / Bliss* (2007) has changed the ending of **Zülfü Livaneli**'s eponymous novel that allows the rape victim protagonist to build her life on her own and created a happy end with the man who was in charge of killing her. It seems that Turkish cinema has not come far from **Yeşilçam melodramas** with the maidens in distress saved by benevolent men, one of the best examples of which is *Selvi Boylum, Al Yazmalım / The Girl with the Red Scarf* (Atıf Yılmaz, 1977).

Genre is a product of a three-way negotiation between audiences, film-makers and film producers. Genres are dynamic; they continually change, modulate and define themselves (Turner 2008: 56). Historically, the Turkish film industry has been indifferent to experimenting with genre, preferring reliable **melodramas** and **comedies**, which serve as a catharsis, particularly in times of crisis, although different genres and sub-genres have always existed. Early cinema followed the latest trends in the West, adapting these to local circumstances. As spectator expectation is an important aspect of genre, when the family was the principal spectator, **war films** and **historical films**, which intersected with the **melodrama** genre, were popular. In the 1970s–80s, the sub-genres of **children**'s **films** and **crime films** gained popularity although musicals, film noir and horror movies (see **fantasy films**) did not garner much attention. The adventure genre generally overlapped with **crime** and **historical films** and its popularity was limited to male spectators; **Cüneyt Arkın**, Serdar Gökhan and Mahmut Cevher were very popular as the undefeatable heroes that overcame all obstacles to save and protect their love interest. They fought with fascistic chauvinism, justifying violence initiated by the enemy, not unlike the Polat Alemdar character of the controversial *Kurtlar Vadisi Irak / Valley of the Wolves, Iraq* (**Akar**, 2005). In modern Turkey, where nationalism has been on the rise, particularly manifest in soccer games, celebrations of national holidays and 'going to the army' festivities, 'historical fantasies' have become cult films, predominantly favoured by guideless adolescents who identify with the characters. *Valley of the Wolves: Terror* (2007) was taken off the air for inciting the young to violence after several incidents when the perpetrators admitted they were inspired by the actions of Alemdar.

Porno films gained popularity in the 1970s among the single Anatolian male audience during a period of intensified migration of men from the countryside. Censorship was severe on engagé films, but ignored this furore, which lasted until the 1980 *coup*.

Social films with a sub-genre of political cinema started in the 1960s about urban and rural life, blood feuds, bride-price, feudalism, problems of workers, migrants in large cities, economic problems, education, social and political consciousness (see **social realist** movement). The decade 1970–80 gave some of the best examples of political films, which came to an end with the 1980 military intervention.

The category of **meta-films** (*matruşka* films), focusing on the insider issues of the film industry, gave some of the best examples of the sub-genre in the 1980s and continues sporadically today; **Nuri Bilge Ceylan**'s *Mayıs Sıkıntısı / Clouds of May* (1999) is one of the remarkable examples.

Gerede, Canan (b. New York, 1948) Director, screenwriter. Spending most of her childhood and youth outside Turkey due to her father's ambassadorial duties, Gerede studied theatre improvisation in Caracas and New York (Academy of Dramatic Arts). Between 1978–82, she worked as assistant to **Atıf Yılmaz** and **Yılmaz Güney**. After a short video, *The Other Side* (1987) and a number of video documentaries including *Abidin, Sen Mutluluğun Resmini Yapabilir misin? / Abidin, Can You Paint Happiness?* (1988), a portrait of the Turkish artist exiled in Paris, she made her first fiction feature, *Robert'in Filmi / Robert's Movie* (1991), a road movie with remarkable photography about the tumultuous relationship between a middle-aged American war photographer and a young androgynous Turkish singer with issues of sexual, social and political identity. The film provoked the religious sensitivities of Turkish society by showing a love scene while *ezan* (the call from the minaret for prayer) is heard non-diegetically. Her next two films, which feature her daughter Bennu Gerede in the lead, foregrounded domestic violence directed at women. *Aşk Ölümden Soğuktur / L'amour est plus froid que la mort / Love is Colder Than Death* (1995) is a **melodrama** (homage to Fassbinder), based on the tragic true story of a gypsy **arabesque** singer, victimized by the androcentric society. *Parçalanma / Split* (1999), produced by Icelandic film-maker Fridrik Fridriksson, based on a true story of an Icelandic woman's fight for the custody of her daughters taken to Turkey and Islamicized by her estranged husband, confronted the rise of fundamentalism in Turkey and the flaws in the judiciary system. However, its partial and clichéd point of view, manifested through the bias of the heroine towards a country and a nation, evoked sensationalist Hollywood movies about the Orient and could not be distributed in Turkey. Dialogues referring to religion were censored when shown on television.

German–Turkish / Turkish–German cinema has emerged in the last two decades as an integral part of post-unification German cinema and transnational European cinema. Film-makers have moved beyond the early focus on guest workers and victim narratives, the 'cinema of the affected' (Burns 2006: 133), or the 'cinema of duty' (Malik 1996: 202–15) and scholars have begun exploring the hybrid identities involved in what has become the 'cinema of double occupancy' (Elsaesser 2005: 118).

Cultural theorists such as Edward Said consider displacement from the 'third' to the 'first' worlds, born of economic necessities, as the effect of a newly developed relationship between the West and the non-West, asserting the need for an active politics of self-location in situations where cultural and national affiliations are hybrid but slanted towards the West (Said 1994). Displacement in the post-colonial or third world always has a material base. After World War II, when Germany was short of labour, workers from underdeveloped countries were invited as *gastarbeiter* (guest workers). Some of them settled in Germany, visiting home during religious holidays and building a house for the return one day, an option that is a survival skill, 'homeland' as a space of resistance to subordination, in the struggle for identity, as Germans to Turks in Turkey and as Turks to Germans in Germany, even though that journey back home may never materialize (*Denk ich an Deutschland – Wir haben vergessen zurückzukehren / We forgot to go back*, **Akın**, 2001). Today, many Turks are active in the German economy, culture and politics as 'hyphenated nationals', their identity coming from a 'double occupancy' that functions as a divided allegiance: to the nation-state into which they were born and to the homeland from which (one or both of) their parents came, and 'cinema seems to have become the most prominent medium of self-representation and symbolic action that the hyphenated citizens of Europe's nation states have made their own' (Elsaesser 2005: 118), Turkish–German film-makers being one of the most prominent groups.

In the early years of Turkish migration, a socially critical sub-**genre** of film and literature surfaced in Germany, focusing on the oppressive working and living conditions of the male guest-worker: Rainer Werner Fassbinder's *Angst essen Seele auf / Fear Eats the Soul* (1973) and Jörg Gförer's *Ganz unten / At the Bottom of the Heap* (1986) are prominent examples of this 'sub-state cinema' within the New German Cinema of the 1970s. Toward the end of the 1980s, the cinematic gaze shifted to cultural differences and the plight of Turkish wives and daughters who eventually followed these men to Germany. The young woman, deprived of her freedom and rights by her traditional family, such as in Hark Bohm's *Yasemin* (1988), became the main motif of narratives focusing on Turkish immigrants. (In a sense, **Akın**'s *Head On* resuscitates this motif.) The dominant theme was the clash of cultures.

The first wave of films made by Turkish film-makers such as **Tunç Okan** (*Otobüs / The Bus*, 1974) and **Tevfik Başer** (*40 Quadratmeter Deutschland / Forty Square Meters of Germany*, 1986), were the continuation of the *gastarbeiterkino* (guest-worker cinema) of the New German Cinema, reflecting the culture shock, isolation, racism and dilemmas of identity. A new realism is observed in the cinemas of 'hyphenated nationals' such as **Fatih Akın** in the way they focalize ordinary concerns such as the generation gap, the sexual freedom of women or societal problems such as drug abuse. Aware of the issues of the dichotomy of living in between two cultures and two languages, they also have new concerns that reflect their circumstances and relationships to the space they occupy. In addition to **Fatih Akın**, **Thomas Arslan**, **Yılmaz Arslan**, **Yüksel Yavuz**, **Aslı Özge**, **Kadir Sözer**, Zuli Aladağ, Sülbiye Günar and **Ayşe Polat** are some of the other distinguished names whose works are enriched by their status as 'double-occupants'.

Girik, Fatma (b. Istanbul, 1942) Actor, producer, politician. During the period of the star system, as 'male Fatma', the *lumpen* woman, Girik was the antidote to the empty-headed bourgeois doll represented by **Belgin Doruk**. Her first leading role was in Seyfi Havaeri's *Leke / Stain* (1957). *Ölüm Peşimizde / Death is Chasing Us* (**Memduh Ün**, 1960) made her a star. She received the Best Actress award of the Antalya Golden Orange and Adana Golden Boll Film Festivals several times with her memorable roles. She acted in over 180 films (many of which were directed by her partner, **Memduh Ün**) and television series. She was the mayor of an affluent district in Istanbul between 1989–94.

Giritlioğlu, Tomris (b. Konya, 1957) Director, producer, screenwriter. A film-maker renowned for her commitment to the plight of ethnic minorities, Tomris Giritlioğlu studied English language and literature at the Hacettepe University, Ankara before starting in 1981 as assistant producer for the children's programmes of the state television (TRT), moving on to directing docu-dramas. Her first feature, *Kantodan Tangoya / From Canto to Tango* (1988) was about the self-reckoning of a republican intellectual. She started a trilogy on the infamies of recent Turkish history regarding the non-Muslims with *Suyun Öte Yanı / The Other Side of the*

Water (1991), a film that merges the diegetic time of 1983 with the past and the present, the time and the space and dreams/remembrances and reality through parallel stories of the victims of the 1920s population exchange between Greece and Turkey and the 1980 *coup d'état*. After shooting *Yaz Yağmuru / Summer Rain* (1994), which she considers her most personal film, and the big-budget *80. Adım / The 80th Step* (1996), about a charming activist jailed during the military regime of 1980 coming to terms with the past and adjusting to the present (shot in Bangkok and Istanbul), Giritlioğlu returned to the trilogy project with *Salkım Hanımın Taneleri / Miss Salkım's Diamonds* (1999) about the infamous property tax that destroyed many non-Muslim families in 1942. The film triggered a witch-hunt, with strong reactions particularly coming from nationalist circles, including members of parliament, but did very well at the box-office with 900,000 viewers. *Güz Sancısı / Autumn Pain* (2008) focused on the 6–7 September events that in 1955 resulted in the vandalization of non-Muslim property, the Greek population of Beyoğlu suffering the most. Since 2002, Giritlioğlu has been directing films and television dramas independently.

Gitmek / My Marlon and Brando (2008) is a film that provokes preconceived notions about **gender**, identity, the other and cinema itself. In the style of a road movie that progresses from the west to the east rather than the customary exodus from the east to the west, and transporting an urban woman to assumedly threatening areas where she is the other, **Hüseyin Karabey** builds a strong trope for the uprooted Kurdish people denied their language and 'othered' amidst the 'white Turks'. Theatre performer Ayça (Ayça Damgacı) plays herself in a fiction film inspired by her actual love story with an Iraqi actor, Hama Ali (Hama Ali Khan) who she met during the shooting of *Sarı Gelin / Yellow Bride* (Ravin Asaf, 2001). In Istanbul, she struggles to survive with paranoid neighbours; the constant

Figure 49 Gitmek / My Marlon and Brando (Hüseyin Karabey, 2008) (Courtesy of Hüseyin Karabey)

male gaze that scrutinizes every movement of a single woman; a superfluous work-mate; a perfectionist boss and the urban loneliness. Impatient with her lover's delay in joining her, she takes the initiative to join him in Iraq, but she chooses the wrong time as US President Bush has just declared war.

A woman's point of view has become rare in contemporary Turkish cinema, which has produced silent/invisible characters, exploited as decorative objects. Ayça is an overweight woman of no particular charm, who thrives on visibility – she is a performer who is not intimidated about dancing alone in discotheques or shouting louder than the neighbours when they object to her loud music. She is neither invisible, not silent. Walking to the public phone to call her lover at night is normal for her, being harassed by men is not, even in a closed country like Iran. She is not passive; she is assertive, at times rather self-centred and lacking in empathy. Her narrative is not always privileged and her physical appearance does not induce identification, which gives the spectator the possibility to become an active participant and view the possibilities of multiple positions with which to identify.

In an age when truth is defined by what the media constantly transmits on the television screen, **Karabey** tries to tell another truth by using the same medium. Hama Ali appears on the screen through the videos he sends; he may be an illusion.

Figure 50 Gitmek / My Marlon and Brando (Hüseyin Karabey, 2008) (Courtesy of Hüseyin Karabey)

What is important is the journey: 'wealthy with what you have gained on the way, not expecting Ithaca to make you rich' (Cavafy 1992). Ayça's meeting with Hama Ali does not materialize but having experienced the other, she is a richer person, so is **Karabey**, born in Istanbul without the privilege of speaking Kurdish. Just like the wedding that unexpectedly appears in the middle of the road where army trucks ply from one operation to the next, or the actor who plays the taxi driver stopping to water the grave of his loved one(s) in an abandoned village, the script often follows its own path, leading him to his own roots.

The border, not as a simple divide between two nations, but as a psychic, cultural and social terrain that we inhabit and that inhabits all of us, is a strong motif in the film. **Karabey** uses the linguistic border crossing as an important conduit against the hegemonic structures that limit individual expression, or impose stereotypes based on race, **gender** or nationality (Anzaldúa 1987). In a country where the Kurdish language was banned for decades and is still shunned, Ayça's frustrations in trying to learn Kurdish or feeling handicapped as a unilingual person is the reversal of the experiences of the Kurds in the rest of Turkey.

My Marlon and Brando is a testament to **Karabey**'s commitment to using his cinema as a vehicle for political activism while maintaining artistic standards, a legacy of his mentor, **Yılmaz Güney**.

Director: **Hüseyin Karabey**; Producers: Sophie Lorant, Lucinda Englehart, **Hüseyin Karabey**; Production: Asi Film; Screenwriters: **Hüseyin Karabey**, Ayça Damgacı; Cinematographer: Emre Tanyıldız; Editor: Mary Stephen; Art Director: Alper Yanar; Music: Kemal Sahir Gürel, Hüseyin Yıldız, Erdal Güney; Cast: Ayça Damgacı, Hama Ali Khan, Mahir Günşıray, Nesrin Cavadzade, Cengiz Bozkurt, Ani İpekkaya, Volga Sorgu

Gizli Yüz / The Secret Face (1991) is a modern fairy tale with *sufi* overtones. A young mild-mannered provincial man is hired by a beautiful mysterious woman to photograph men's faces in nightclubs. She finds an enigmatic face, the object of her search, in the photograph of a watchmaker and disappears with him. Infatuated by her memory, the young man embarks on a journey through his natal village to the inner depths of Anatolia. An innocent and humble Parsifal, searching for the Holy Grail, he meets his mother, the dark widow (Herzeleide or Heartsorrow) mourning for a husband who loved another. He experiences an inner mystical truth, a first touch of consciousness, when he is not ready for it. His feeling for the mysterious woman, the carrier of his inspiration (White Flower) is asexual; there is no seduction. His quest, which takes him to the mysterious land of the subconscious (spending the night inside a clock tower, the only place in town where the tower cannot be seen) is the quest for personal identity as in the timeless allegory of the myth of Parsifal, which in Jungian terms describes the passage from boyhood to manhood, the trials in the quest for the Grail (the feminine aspect of beauty that contains and transforms), an insight into the behaviour of man in relating to feminine elements and the difficulties of reconciling masculinity with *anima*, the unconscious feminine element *within* (Johnson 1989).

At the end, when the image of the photographer merges with the image of the mysterious woman, the merging of the masculine and feminine elements is also

Figure 51 Gizli Yüz / The Secret Face (Ömer Kavur, 1991) (Courtesy of International Istanbul Film Festival)

a merger of the East and the West as the journey of the young man also evokes the dervish philosophy of following the road and searching for letters in faces to decipher character stories, the starting point of the film, which is thematically based on Persian philosophy as **Kavur** explained during a press conference on 17 April 1991, the dominance of the colour blue (the car, her coat, a blue ribbon) also being connected to Sufi mysticism.

The film is divided into four spatial segments, The City of Cities, The City of the Dead, The City of the Forlorn and The City of Hearts, but only the first is

Figure 52 Gizli Yüz / The Secret Face (Ömer Kavur, 1991) (Courtesy of International Istanbul Film Festival)

identifiable (Istanbul, with its monuments and back streets with naked poverty). Reality is often blurred with fantasy in a mystical atmosphere where spatio-temporality is vague although the film never loses contact with the tangible. In the City of the Forlorn, the bureaucrat in charge of water is paid a salary for four years for a project that was started with a show of politicians and engineers, but has since been forgotten. The shots of ruins, poor neighbourhoods, idle men in cafes, and the illegal butchering of old horses reflect the socio-economic atmosphere of a country after three military interventions. The juxtaposition of the verticality of the barren trees (with roots that prevent them from reaching the sky) and the horizontality of the barren landscape of endless asphalts, bridges, and night trains is foreboding. In The City of Hearts, where townspeople arrive with their clocks to open their hearts, one man laments he cannot express himself in his mother tongue (alluding to the ban on the Kurdish language).

The small town with its restrictive mentality, its boredom and suffocation, a crucial leitmotif in *Anayurt Oteli / Motherland Hotel* (and an important locus in the films of **Nuri Bilge Ceylan**) is a determining element in *The Secret Face* as well. 'Does one get used to it?' 'No, one wants to get used to it until one dies.'

Kavur uses a circular narrative. Spaces evoke a sense of *déjà vu*; the street with the clock-repairer's shop is identical in The City of Cities and The City of Hearts. Through the gaze of a young man, the camera directs the viewer to an identical poster; to the same lopsided street sign; the same balloons on the grocer's door; the same child playing hopscotch and the same ragman hollering for old clothes. The lamp, the mirror and the iron left behind in the woman's house in The City of Cities, objects of her dreams, emerge at the end, again as dreams, out of the ragman's bag.

The Secret Face is based on a script by Nobel laureate Orhan Pamuk, inspired by an episode in the 'Love Stories on a Snowy Evening' chapter of Pamuk's *The Black Book.* **Kavur** maintains that in the film 'the evolution of time, the conflux of two different worlds, two different cultures and the impact of one on the other are told in an oblique parallel to a story of a passion'. They are connected to the central theme of the erosion of local traditions, cultures and handicrafts, among which is the repairing of the clocks. 'In a changing world, the traditional occupations of the East give way to Western inventions – batteries, electronic devices – and these life-styles are imposed with a different marketing. This is the impasse of the East–West dilemma' (Tan 1991: 57).

The film received several awards, among which are the Best Film, Best Script (Orhan Pamuk), Best Actor (Fikret Kuşkan), Best Music (Cahit Berkay) and Best Editing (**Mevlüt Koçak**) awards at the 28th Antalya Golden Orange Film Festival; the Best Film award at the 20th Montreal New Cinema Film Festival and the Critics award at the Bastia Mediterranean Film Festival.

Director: **Ömer Kavur**; Producer: Sadık Deveci; Production: Alfa Film; Screenwriter: Orhan Pamuk; Cinematographer: Erdal Kahraman; Editor: **Mevlut Koçak**; Music: Cahit Berkay; Cast: **Zuhal Olcay**, Fikret Kuşkan, Savaş Yurttaş, Sevda Ferdağ

Gök, Şahin (b. Siirt, 1952 – d. Istanbul, 2013) Director, screenwriter. A graduate of journalism and communications, Şahin Gök started working on sets in 1969 and shortly moved on to assistantship. His first feature was *Kurban Olduğum / I Sacrifice Myself For You* (1980). He broke the moulds of mainstream cinema with *Potente Feneri / The Potente Lighthouse* (1988) (literal translation), and tried to continue along these lines with *Eskici ve Oğulları / Ragman and His Sons* (1990) and *Kızılırmak Karakoyun / Red River Black Sheep* (1993) (Özgüç 1994b: 64). He also made videos and television series. *Siyabend u Xece / Siyabend and Xece* (1993), based on the eponymous Kurdish legend about young lovers, was interrupted during the shooting by the arrest of the producer; the negatives were smuggled out of Turkey by the two foreigners on the team. Originally shot in Turkish, the film was later dubbed into Kurdish in Europe where editing and sound were done without the director. (**Yılmaz Erdoğan** appears in his first film role as Xece's brother.)

Göreç, Ertem (b. Bursa, 1931) Director, screenwriter, editor, actor. Launching his career in cinema in 1949 as editor and assistant director to prominent film-makers, while playing basketball for the national team, Göreç wrote the script for **Memduh Ün**'s *Üç Arkadaş / Three Friends* (1958), one of the classics of Turkish cinema. His first feature, *Kanlı Sevda / Bloody Love* was made in 1959, but his breakthrough came with the **social realist** *Otobüs Yolcuları / The Bus Passengers* (1961). *Karanlıkta Uyananlar / Those Awakening in the Dark* (1964) is the first Turkish film to deal with strike and unionization. He started a new era of fairy tales with *Pamuk Prenses ve Yedi Cüceler / Snow White and the Seven Dwarfs* (1970), which stands among his other films for children, *Ayşecik Fakir Prenses / Little Ayşe, the Poor Princess* (1963) and *Sezercik, Küçük Mücahit / Little Sezer, the Freedom Fighter* (1974). In addition to short documentaries, educational films and newsreels, he directed over 70 features. Since the 1990s, he has been continuing his career organizing workshops, special screenings and television programmes, particularly foregrounding **Yeşilçam**.

Gören, Şerif (b. Xanthi, Greece, 1944) Director, screenwriter, producer, editor, actor. The director of *Yol / The Way* (1982), Turkey's only Palme d'or winner to present at the Cannes Film Festival 1982, received ex æquo with Costa-Gavras's *Missing*, Şerif Gören started his film career as editor and assistant director, particularly to **Yılmaz Güney**. In 1974, he had his first directorial experience completing *Endişe / Anxiety*, interrupted by the imprisonment of **Güney** and won the Best Director award at the Golden Orange Film Festival in Antalya. With more than 40 features, he tried several **genres** from **comedy** to **melodramas** with a dose of eroticism, always maintaining a critical view on societal issues. *Köprü / The Bridge* (1975) foregrounds the tradition's resistance against modernity in the story of an idealist engineer's endeavours to build a bridge over the Euphrates despite opposition from his people; *Derman / Remedy* (1984) also focuses on the clash of modernity and tradition; *Katırcılar / The Muleteers* (1987) exposes the cruelty of nature to those who are already disadvantaged. *Almanya Acı Vatan /*

Deutschland Tragischer Lebensraum / Germany Bitter Home (1979), on the moral and economic alienation of a woman guest-worker, and *Polizei* (1988), a **Kemal Sunal comedy** that underscores the social exclusion of the immigrant, were made in Germany. *Remedy, Kurbağalar / The Frogs* (1985) and *Firar / The Escape* (1986) are noteworthy examples of the realistic depiction of the new independent woman of the 1980s. He made *Amerikalı / The American* (1993) with the intention of rivalling Hollywood at the box-office, achieving his aim. Gören returned to feature film making after 18 years with the rather unsuccessful *Ay Büyürken Uyuyamam / I Can't Sleep When the Moon is Full* (2011) based on four stories by renowned author, Necati Cumalı.

Gözetleme Kulesi / The Watch Tower (2012) is a social commentary on crime and punishment that questions the oxymoron of the society-imposed motherhood instinct, the combat with one's conscience and the single woman's fragile existence in patriarchal Turkish society where a family home can be as uncanny as a dark street corner (girls are regularly raped by family members). The first part of the film introduces two unlikely characters, Seher (Nilay Erdönmez), a young university student working as a hostess on the intercity buses and sleeping at the roadside café, and Nihat (Olgun Şimşek), a taciturn watchman assigned to the forest tower to detect fires and inform other men that the situation is normal, a refrain heard regularly. Seher's job 'in transit' serves as a trope for her liminal state, the conditions of which are not yet revealed to the spectator although a premonition is felt by her edginess. The second part, with scenes inside the watchtower in the deep forest, the heart of darkness, is about the interior world of the characters, when they face the circumstances that have brought them there. The cafe is central to the film, the liminal space between the public and the private, where the two meet and where private becomes public when Nihat discovers Seher's secret.

The character of Nihat as the man in charge of the gaze is 'situation normal' in a society that traditionally operates on constantly watching and scrutinizing the other and judging, from micro to macro level, and not surprisingly all watchmen are male. Alternatively, the man with the lens is perhaps a metaphor for cinema. Nihat's job is to say 'situation normal' (Shoot!); his script about the repentant protagonist of an accidental crime (losing his family in a car crush) is ready to go, but he cannot help getting involved in the unexpected new scenario (a young woman giving birth alone in a dingy basement and abandoning the baby) for which he is not ready. The improvisation will rely on learned (human and parental) instincts. Judgemental as the outsider with the lens – the eye of society – and as a man who represents the masculinist mechanism of that society (the watch tower, a phallic image?), he wants to bring her situation to 'normal' and achieve his own redemption.

With a revived interest in Turkish cinema about the predicaments of women, particularly regarding pregnancy (**Yeşim Ustaoğlu**'s *Araf / In Between* appeared at the same time), one wonders about the conventional solution that both of these films by women film-makers offer. The protagonists, after having been through hell, decide to form a family with a man they do not love. In a society that does not give the right to women to stand on their own, perhaps, it is expected that women depend on men for their security/survival.

The Watchtower garnered five awards at the Adana Golden Boll Film Festival, including the Best Director and Best Actress.

Director, Screenwriter: **Pelin Esmer**; Producers: Nida Karabol Akdeniz, **Pelin Esmer**, Tolga Esmer; Production: Sinefilm, Arizona Film, Bredok Film; Cinematographer: Özgür Eken; Editor: Ayhan Ergürsel, **Pelin Esmer**; Sound: Kasper Munck-Hansen; Art Director: Osman Özcan; Cast: Olgun Şimşek, Nilay Erdönmez, Laçin Ceylan, **Menderes Samancılar**, Rıza Akın

Gramofon Avrat / Gramophone (1987) is the first **Yeşilçam** film of **Yusuf Kurçenli** who customarily had funded his films independently. The main attraction is **Türkan Şoray** as Cemile, nicknamed 'Gramofon' for her beautiful voice. In the 1930s, in a provincial town on the threshold of modernization, she becomes very popular with her erotic dance during the *oturak alemi*, a clandestinely arranged private banquet with musicians, conducted for the pleasure of the elite males according to conventions that permit the dancer to feed the men and offer *rakı*, but forbid actual contact. Gramofon dreams of settling in a big town with the aged dancer Azime (Güzin Özipek) who exploits her while her secret admirer, the phaeton driver Murat (Emin And), ferries her to various meetings. When Murat is jailed for murdering her aggressor and Azime dies suddenly, she chooses to join the brothel to support Murat rather than become the mistress of a rich but possessive textile merchant.

The film is open to a number of readings: as the story of an independent woman in control of her destiny despite societal limitations and as an anthropological study of an androcentric culture where the place of the woman remains constant despite revolutions. The Westernization reforms, imposed from above, are often at odds with local customs and traditions, one of the manifestations of which is the reaction to the Outward Appearance Law (1934). The centre of transformation has shifted from Istanbul to the capital Ankara and to the provinces and men have adopted the fedora hat, but the pressure–resistance dialectic between women and the state that has its contemporary counterpart in the headscarf issue has already started. Most women (particularly lower uneducated class) hide their fashionable dresses tailored by modern seamstresses like Münevver (Gülsen Tuncer) under the black chador. In a society in transition to modernity, old customs, such as the *oturak alemi*, traditionally conducted in discretion, not allowing even a gaze from the male participant, are gradually becoming sex parties. Although **Kurçenli** foregrounds the human aspect rather than highlighting the tense socio-political atmosphere of the period, the satirical representation of the urban intellectual removed from Anatolian realities is very precise. The teacher comments: 'Gramofon! Even this name is enough to endorse the genius of our people' and 'Turkish ballet will be born from this dance.' The tongue-in-cheek humour is extended to the school play where children wear wings to represent 'angels of civilization' (one with a broken wing) and a blond teacher in a toga appears as the 'civilization'. An enigmatic aspect of the seamstress character, a trope for modernity, is her subtle depiction as a lesbian. Her eyes linger on Cemile on several occasions; she makes a symbolic gesture of caressing Cemile's foot when she gives her a pair of elegant shoes and Cemile spends a night with her in the same bed although the camera does not reveal any further action other than Cemile's arm accidently dropping over Münevver's. The transformation of Gramofon from a carefree blithe beauty to a selfless woman with maturity (an old **Yeşilçam** cliché) lacks credibility although her independent spirit is a novelty.

Director: **Yusuf Kurçenli**; Producers: Lokman Kondakçı, Tufan Güner; Production: Varlık Film; Screenwriters: **Kurçenli**, Ayşe Şasa from a story by Sabahattin Ali; Cinematography: Kenan Davutoğlu; Music: Arif Erkin Güzelbeyoğlu; Cast: **Türkan Şoray**, Hakan Balamir, Emin And, **Menderes Samancılar**, Güzin Özipek, Ferda Ferdağ, Gülsen Tuncer.

Gurbet Kuşları / The Birds of Nostalgia aka ***Migrating Birds*** aka ***Birds of Exile*** (1964) is the first serious examination of the phenomenon of migration from rural areas to the urban centres and along with *Bitmeyen Yol / The Never Ending Road* (**Duygu Sağıroğlu**, 1965) is the best work on migration produced in the 1960s. When their small business collapses, a family from Maraş in the south sells the ancestral home and the shop to seek their fortune in Istanbul. The university education of their son is the second reason for the decision to migrate. The film begins at the Haydarpaşa train station, on the Asian side, metaphorized in several migration films as the threshold where Anatolian migrants have their first glimpse of Istanbul. The family embarks on the ferry with others carrying the same fate expressing amazement at the magnificent Topkapı palace, the mosques, the Galata tower and the modern buildings. 'Whore Istanbul! I am coming to conquer you,'

Figure 53 Gurbet Kuşları / The Birds of Nostalgia aka *Migrating Birds* aka *Birds of Exile* (Halit Refiğ, 1964) (Courtesy of International Istanbul Film Festival)

one character shouts, 'I'll be your king!' But for some, the river to be crossed is Acheron, the river of sadness. The film ends in the same location when the family return home the way they came, except for some missing members – chased by her brother who caught her prostituting, the daughter threw herself off the roof-top and the youngest son remained behind to marry a city girl. As they leave, a new family arrives, with the same actors repeating the same dialogue. Migration continues. As Sophocles claims 'the gloomy Hades' keeps enriching himself with their 'sighs and tears'.

The family's misadventures are not exceptional. The boys become involved with women and waste the family income – the driver Murat (Tanju Gürsu) with a bar girl; the garage mechanic Selim (**Cüneyt Arkın**) with his boss's wife, the Greek Despina and Kemal, the university student with a rich classmate, Ayla (**Filiz Akın**), concealing his background from her. Fatma (Pervin Par) is led astray by a 'bad' neighbour.

Unlike the migration films of the 1970s–80s that display a city whose texture has transformed with the invasion of its periphery, the city here carries both its traditional and Westernized identity. Different social classes live side by side without forming a whole, although to make the adaptation smoother, the Maraş family chooses the traditional section with neighbours leading similar lives. The shanty towns have not yet become part of the narrative. They appear once in a long shot from the vantage point of Kemal and Ayla as a distant image.

Refiğ employs a universal film language with skilful depth of field and triangular spatial arrangements, but instead of examining the social inequalities within the context of class relationships, he looks for private reasons behind the

Figure 54 Gurbet Kuşları / The Birds of Nostalgia aka *Migrating Birds* aka *Birds of Exile* (Halit Refiğ, 1964) (Courtesy of International Istanbul Film Festival)

social and economic failure of the family. Promoting hard work and patience, he shows the beggar that the family had met earlier as an example of a man who knows how to succeed in the big city, which reflects his involvement with the *Yön* movement after the 1960 *coup*, a movement that sought a socialist method of development with emphasis on nationalism and work ethic. His anti-migration and anti-Western stand is commensurate with the theories he developed later about *ulusal* cinema (**national cinema**). At the end, Kemal refuses to emigrate to the United States, choosing social and national duty to his country, and the family return to Maraş to improve the conditions in their town (Daldal 2003: 188).

The film has been compared to Luchino Visconti's *Rocco e i suoi fratelli / Rocco and His Brothers* (1960); both start at a major train station with a family arriving from the provinces, but for **Refiğ**, there are major differences. Visconti's epic foregrounds the class struggle in an industrialized society, whereas his film draws attention to such struggles in a society that has not yet been industrialized. Furthermore, the migrants arrive in Istanbul with a conqueror mentality. Visconti's modest family does not have such aspirations (Türk 2001: 152).

Director: **Halit Refiğ**; Producer: Recep Ekicigil; Production: Artist Film; Screenwriters: **Halit Refiğ**, Orhan Kemal, Turgut Özakman; Cinematographer: Çetin Gürtop; Editor: Mehmet Bozkuş; Cast: Pervin Par, **Filiz Akın**, Tanju Gürsu, Sevda Ferda, **Cüneyt Arkın**, Özden Çelik, Önder Somer, Mümtaz Ener, Gülbin Eray

Gülüşan (1985) is an unusual love story that blends the elements of fantasy and myth within a realistic premise, exposing rural lives locked inside customs and traditions. Four characters, one of them blind, live within the confined space of a village house with a small garden that includes a foreboding well. Mestan (Halil Ergun), who has two supposedly barren wives, blindfolds and kidnaps a woman who he thinks was gazing at him. Suffering from remorse when he discovers her blindness ('rotten merchandize'), he tries to return her but to protect the family honour, her father refuses to accept her. She becomes the third wife, which results in tragedy.

The film's initial premise is male child fanaticism but **Olgaç** elaborates on the suppressed sexuality of rural people (a lesbian relationship between the first two wives is hinted). Macho Mestan can transform into a sensitive and generous human being through the sensual touch of Gülüşan, but he can only externalize his sensuality in the comfort of blindness, which eliminates shame. As a product of his culture, he still beats the other two wives, lecturing, 'No matter how many women in a house, the word belongs to men. Don't forget, you eat my bread.' He could change if his environment could change. The women, also products of a feudal system, conspire to crush the weaker rather than unite to fight the oppressor. The portentous black well at the centre of the idyllic garden stands as a conspicuous trope for customs, traditions and the patriarchal bias of religion that must devour in its darkness those who deviate from the norm.

Director, Screenwriter: **Bilge Olgaç** (based on a story by **Osman Şahin**); Producer: Şeref Gür; Cinematographer: Hüseyin Özşahin; Music: Timur Selçuk; Cast: Halil Ergün, Yaprak Özdemiroğlu, Meral Orhonsay, Güler Ökten, Tilbe Saran, **Müşfik Kenter**, Bedia Ener

Günay, İzzet (b. Istanbul, 1934) Actor. Memorable for his role opposite **Türkan Şoray** in **Akad**'s *Vesikalı Yarim / My Licensed Love* (1968), İzzet Günay's film career includes over 120 films. He started as a stage actor, moving to cinema with a small role in 1958 in *Kırık Plak / Broken Record* (unofficial English title), leaving during the 1970s crisis to work as a soloist in Turkish classical music for seven years. He also operated an antique shop for 14 years. He has been selective in the roles he has chosen for cinema and television.

Güneş, İsmail (b. Samsun, 1961) Director, screenwriter, actor. Starting his film career in 1978 as assistant director, İsmail Güneş made his first feature, *Gün Doğmadan / Before the Sun Rises* in 1986. *Çizme / The Boot* (1991), *Beşinci Boyut / Fifth Dimension* (1993), *Gülün Bittiği Yer / Where the Rose Wilted* (1999), *Sözün Bittiği Yer / Where the Word Ends* (2007), *İmam / The Imam* (2005) are the films of this director who began within the Islamic cinema but gradually moved to films with social and political concerns. *Ateşin Düştüğü Yer / Where the Fire Burns* (2012) about honour killings won the Grand Prix and the Fipresci awards at the Montreal World Film Festival and also represented Turkey at the foreign Oscars, 2012.

Güneşe Yolculuk / Journey to the Sun (1999), made at the height of the civil war in the south-east of Turkey by a young woman, exposes the inequalities and injustices of a political system that is based on the One Nation policy. Carrying the humanistic message of the possibility of friendship between opposing factions, the script was inspired by newspaper articles on Kurdish villages that have been

Figure 55 Güneşe Yolculuk / Journey to the Sun (Yeşim Ustaoğlu, 1999) (Courtesy of Yeşim Ustaoğlu)

Figure 56 Güneşe Yolculuk / Journey to the Sun (Yeşim Ustaoğlu, 1999) (Courtesy of Yeşim Ustaoğlu)

marked, burned and evacuated. Two young migrants, the apolitical Turkish Mehmet (Nevruz Baz) from an Aegean town and the Kurdish activist Berzan (Nazmi Kırık) from an Iraqi border village, meet during an uproar following a soccer match in a moment of heightened ultra-nationalistic sentiments. Mehmet, who detects leaks for the municipality in the underground water pipes with a long brass rod he calls 'the flute' while ironically remaining ignorant of the real rumble on the ground, is protected from the hooligans by Berzan. A friendship develops between the two uprooted men whose hopes for the future are built around love; the free-spirited Arzu (Mizgin Kapazan) for Mehmet and the beautiful Şirvan left in the village for Berzan. Drawing the attention of the police with his dark complexion, Mehmet is arrested as a terrorist suspect when an abandoned gun is found next to him on the minibus and his carrying a cassette of Kurdish music (a gift from Berzan who sells them under the Galata bridge) complicates matters. Tortured in police custody, rejected by his roommates and fired from his job, he is sheltered by Berzan, who, Mehmet – and the audience – eventually understand through an image on the television screen showing him among the relatives of the prisoners on hunger strike, is a sympathizer of the PKK, the outlawed *Partiya Karkêren Kurdistan / Kurdistan Workers' Party*, equated with terrorism. His death in police custody is also revealed through the same medium. Mehmet, who had lived incognizant of the other Turkey, starts a long journey to the east, a symbolic migration in reverse, carrying Berzan's coffin. He discovers a new world of abandoned villages with houses marked by red crosses, intimidating army tanks in village squares (documentary footage **Ustaoğlu** obtained from the police using alternative means), banned newspapers distributed via children and people who do not speak the official language. (Close to 9,000 settlements are said to have been destroyed and three million displaced; Bozarslan 2001: 45.)

When Mehmet, whose family name is Kara (black in Turkish), feels 'othered' by the dominant system for his swarthy appearance, he sprays yellow paint on his hair. At the end of his journey, through makeshift adobes in the outskirts, garbage piles that are the livelihood of many, the police brutality, the terror of marked doors and the ecologically ravaged and war-torn south-east, he is able to put himself in the place of the other and feel the other's pain and when asked his hometown, is able to say, 'Zorguç'. Ironically, the inquirer, a commando returning from military service, is from Tire, Mehmet's native town; hence begins a new circle.

Ustaoğlu's style is close to Italian neo-realism in narrating ordinary episodes from daily life. When the camera focuses on one of the busiest squares of Istanbul preparing for the day's activities, it gives the illusion of catching the action by chance. The two characters are part of the crowd and their story is the story of the ordinary citizens. The radio announcements and the news on the television create an atmosphere of common life and common involvement. The repeated announcement of the truck selling *Ay Gaz* (tube gas), a familiar sound of the cityscape, serves no narrative purpose but is indicative of the city and the atmosphere surrounding the characters. The plot unfolds through images that flow like water, a crucial element, laden with spiritual connotations embedded in the regional culture and as a trope for life. Mehmet detects leaks in the water pipes; Arzu works in a laundromat and Berzan makes his last journey (in a coffin) on the water. The long opening shot is the reflection of Mehmet in the water carrying Berzan's coffin and the closing shot shows Berzan's coffin floating on the water while Mehmet counts the seagulls and the electric pylons in front of the setting sun as an army post with barbed wire enters the frame.

The recipient of the AGICOA Prize Blue Angel and the Peace Film Prize at the Berlin Film Festival, 1999 (its screening coinciding with the arrest of Abdullah Öcalan, the leader of the PKK), the film was hailed by several local journalists as 'the best Turkish film of the last ten years' and a realistic picture of the civil war and the resulting migration that transformed urban life, and **Ustaoğlu** was embraced as the new **Yılmaz Güney** and the Ken Loach of Turkey amidst reprovals of exaggerating the problems of the country for financial support from Europe (particularly organizations concerned with human rights issues). State censorship was not the issue, but distributors were reluctant to take a chance with a 'risky' film (and one with Kurdish dialogue, forbidden at the time) and *Journey to the Sun* was shown in Turkey a year after its international success.

Some of the other noteworthy awards that the film received are Valladoid International Film Festival, Special Jury Prize, 1999 and International Istanbul Film Festival, Best Turkish Director, Best Turkish Film, Fipresci (Federation of International Film Critics) and People's Choice.

Director, Screenwriter: **Yeşim Ustaoğlu**; Producer: Behrooz Hashemian; Production: IFR, The Film Company Amsterdam, Medias Res Berlin, Fabrica, Arte / ZDF; Cinematographer: Jacek Petrycki; Editor: Nicolas Goster; Music: Vlato Stefanovski; Cast: Nevruz Baz, Nazmi Kırık, Mizgin Kapazan, Nigar Aktar, İskender Bağcılar, Ara Güler

Güney, Yılmaz (see **Pütün**)

Gürses, Muharrem (b. Amasya/Merzifon, 1915 – d. Istanbul, 1999) Actor, scriptwriter, director, producer, novelist. Originally starting in theatre, Muharrem Gürses played an important role in the establishment of the village **melodrama**, adapting several of his serialized novels in the 1950s and 1960s onto the wide screen, *Yedi Köyün Zeynebi / Zeyneb of Seven Villages* (1956) being one of the most popular. Known as Gürses **melodramas**, these mostly inflated love stories juxtaposed good/bad, rich/poor, pretty/ugly binaries resulting in the triumph of positive values culminating in a happy end. He switched to a series of 'saint' films – Saint Joseph, Saint Suleiman – for a period and played the lead in several historical films produced by his two companies.

He is said to have discovered **Muhterem Nur**, the star of 'emotional drainage' films. Together they made the most sentimental **melodramas**, most of which display the pains of the oppressed Eastern man whose life is dependent on fate. Relying on the traditional *tuluat* (improvisation) and *meddah* (public story teller) theatre in terms of narrative development and a rough elementary style, Gürses focused on the realities of the urban or rural underdeveloped masses, which the intellectual urban audience failed to see. According to some sources, he broke the world record as the man who made the largest number of films – three to four films a week and up to seven films from the same script. Shunned by intellectuals, he aimed at the Anatolian audience, whom he knew well. A large number of his films were destroyed in the National Film Archives fire.

H

Hakan, Fikret (b. Balıkesir, 1934) Actor, director, producer, screenwriter; RN: Bumin Gaffar Çitanak. Honoured as the Artist of the State in 1998, Fikret Hakan started as a stage actor while publishing poems and short stories under his real name. His breakthrough on screen came with **Akad**'s *Beyaz Mendil / The White Handkerchief* (1955). He was the most productive in the 1960s–70s, working with distinguished film-makers as the lead in several landmark films: *Yılanların Öcü / Revenge of the Serpents* (**Metin Erksan**, 1962), ***Karanlıkta Uyananlar / Those Awakening in the Dark*** (**Ertem Göreç**, 1964), *Bitmeyen Yol / The Never Ending Road* (**Duygu Sağıroğlu**, 1965). Hakan's career in cinema encompasses acting in almost 170 feature films, television dramas and series, including a stint with Hollywood, playing the local colonel in Peter Collinson's *You Can't Win 'em All* (1970) starring Tony Curtis and Charles Bronson, and directing five films. In 2013, he published a book, *The History of Turkish Cinema.*

Hakkari'de Bir Mevsim / A Season in Hakkari (1983) is the first film of what may be considered as the 'intellectual in exile' tetralogy of **Erden Kıral**, with ***Mavi Sürgün / The Blue Exile*** (1993), *Av Zamanı / Time for Hunting* (1988) and *Yolda / On the Way* (2005) to follow. An urban intellectual (wearing a duffel coat, carrying the French newspaper *le Monde*) arrives in a village buried in snow and becomes part of the lives of its inhabitants. The film opens with a long shot of the hillside, a dark silhouette approaching with difficulty in the snow. The spectator's gaze is that of the unseen villagers, whose presence is felt through sounds, the most prominent being the poundings of pestle in synchrony with the heartbeats of the climber. Then the camera shifts to the viewpoint of the stranger; his first impression is a village perched on a hill as if it has grown there. Entering the village, surrounded by the dogs that announce his intrusion, he is met with the stare of the children, of women peeking behind closed windows, of men on the rooftops. In the land of the rural, shunned in the city as 'dirty, illiterate, smelly', he is the outsider. The first real awareness of his otherness comes when he is unable to drink tea, cracking the sugar in his mouth. The villagers are tolerant; they laugh but not condescendingly. Sparse information is given to the spectator about his background and only through interior monologues ('me, who does not remember where he comes from, or does not want to remember, will one day find the other while searching for oneself');

the unsent letters to his wife ('You want me to take a picture. I could take pictures of the children with naked feet with this modern contraption. Photography is civilization, we can compile them in a book, or civilized people could hang them on their walls to be grateful for what they have'); a letter from her ('I would find you if they gave me permission') and his musings in front of the typewriter ('How do you describe the sea to someone who's never seen it?'). He teaches the children about the sun and the world that turns around it and about the sea while hearing conflicting stories about the inhabitants, from the *mukhtar*, the official authority, and his diabolical double, his brother-in-law, the restless outlaw Halit, both of them staunch believers in bigamy. As an educated city man, he is revered in the village and expected to solve problems such as the epidemic that kills the children. The scene when the *mukhtar*'s wife Zazi approaches him to mediate in the conflict regarding her husband's plans to take a second wife is particularly powerful. Her head is modestly turned to the side as she expresses herself through her son, except at the end when she loses patience.

Anecdotal in structure, indeterminate in time, the narrative flows through the stranger's subjective viewpoint, recording village life anthropologically. As his character transforms, he learns to understand simple people by observing them and to speak with the gaze, not the words. Then, the camera drops him to follow Zazi – examining herself in front of the mirror, wondering about the motivation of her husband to take another woman; shopping with the *mukhtar* for the wedding; preparing the nuptial bed, causing a break in audience identification with the protagonist, and yet not dwelling enough on Zazi to enter her psyche. When it returns to the protagonist, the continuity is somewhat lost.

The geographical location as stated in the title and the *poshu* on men's head identify the village as Kurdish, but it could be any other. The village is out of politics, out of history and even out of religion – there is hardly a minaret in existence. People accept their destiny without question, rather rare for a Kurdish village. The classroom episodes recall the docu-drama, *İki Dil Bir Bavul / On the Way to School* (**Orhan Eskiköy**, Özgür Doğan, 2008), which is a more realistic picture of a Kurdish village, where hardly anyone speaks Turkish and the Turkish teacher is respected but with a distance. Considering the period in which *Hakkari* was shot, **Kıral**'s possibilities of realism were naturally limited. Even then, the film was censored for five years, mainly for 'exposing underdevelopment', and **Kıral** was arrested at the airport on his return from the Berlin Film Festival (1983), where he received four awards, including the Silver Bear and Fipresci (Federation of International Film Critics).

Critics underscore the resemblance between the film and Francesco Rosi's *Cristo si è fermato a Eboli / Christ Stopped in Eboli* (1979), based on the anti-fascist Carlo Levi's autobiographical eponymous novel, although *Hakkari* is based on writer Ferid Edgü's work, *O / He* (1977), which is also autobiographical.

Director: **Erden Kıral**; Producer, Cinematographer: **Kenan Ormanlar**; Production: Data Inc., Kentel Film; Screenwriter: **Onat Kutlar**; Editor: **Yılmaz Atadeniz**; Sound: Cemal Kıvanç; Music: Timur Selçuk; Cast: **Genco Erkal**, Erkan Yücel, **Şerif Sezer**, Rana Cabbar, Erol Demiröz, Berrin Koper, **Macit Koper** and the children of Yoncalı village

Hamzaoğlu, Hayati (b. Trabzon, 1933 – d. Antalya, 2000) Actor, producer. The villain of **Yeşilçam**, Hayati Hamzaoğlu played in over 200 films between the 1950s and 1990s, some by notable film-makers: **Atıf Yılmaz** (*Keşanlı Ali Destanı / Keşanlı Ali's Epic*, 1964); **Metin Erksan** (*Kuyu / The Well*, 1968); **Yılmaz Güney** (*Seyyit Han*, 1968; *Bir Çirkin Adam / An Ugly Man*, 1969; *Aç Kurtlar / Hungry Wolves*, 1969; *Ağıt / Elegy*, 1971; *Acı / Pain*, 1971; *Umutsuzlar / The Hopeless Ones*, 1971) and **Osman F. Seden** (*Damga / Stigma*, 1984). He won several national awards including Best Supporting Actor in **Metin Erksan**'s *The Well* (at the Adana Golden Boll Film Festival, 1969). In a system that lacks an infrastructure to protect artists, he died poor and alone.

Haremde Dört Kadın / Four Women in a Harem (1965) is a period film set in the last days of the nineteenth century, just before the collapse of the Ottoman Empire. Through the intrigues in a harem, the film exposes the transition period with a critical eye.

Most characters are tropes for certain elements of the period. The principal one is the Ottoman *pasha* named Sadık (meaning faithful, obviously to the sultan) (Sami Ayanoğlu), a metonymy for the Ottoman Empire as the father figure for its subjects. The film takes place inside his palace, except for the final scenes. He is depicted as an infertile corrupt lecher preparing to have a fourth wife at his advanced age, who receives bribes from the foreigners. He has two nephews: Doctor Cemal (**Cüneyt Arkın**), the *jeune turc* (member of the revolutionary party in the Ottoman Empire, which deposed Sultan Abdulhamid II in 1908) who is seriously in love with the *pasha*'s future wife and dreaming of eloping to Paris with her, and the self-centred soldier/philanderer Rüştü (Tanju Gürsu), who has his eye on the status of the *pasha* and is ready to betray him.

The East/West dichotomy of the period is presented through the French dressmaker, Annet (wearing a cross around her neck), who is 'caricaturized and grotesque' as **Refiğ** admits, 'very similar to the character in *Mürebbiye / The Governess* (**Ahmet Fehim**, 1919)' (Türk 2001: 197). Unimpressed with her demonstration of Western dancing on New Year's Eve, which, according to him is the '*gavur çiftetelli*' (non-Muslim version of the popular Turkish folk dance), the *pasha* takes the floor, 'who ever loves me, comes after me. Ottoman is not dead'. As to her inquiry about the *jeune turcs* asking for freedom from Paris, 'they are *gavur* and not Ottoman', he responds.

One of the issues underscored in the film is the status of women, which **Refiğ** approaches through the *harem*, the structure that separated the men from the women, investigating the factors that led to its demise. When Cemal informs the wives that the struggle is for their freedom as well, they do not agree. Their opinions on freedom, democracy and women's rights conflict with the opinions of the *jeunes turcs*. The women prefer things as they are because the *pasha* takes care of them. In fact, when finally free, they are scattered around, thrown from the riches of captivity to the rags of freedom, in a society not prepared to take care of itself.

Coupled with the depiction of a lesbian relationship between the first two wives – a frequent occurrence in the harem that is generally veiled – the political satire in the film raised the ire of certain factions that tried to prevent its screening at the Antalya Golden Orange Film Festival in 1966 by destroying the reels and reducing its chance at the box-office despite positive reviews. Its broadcast on the state television (TRT) in 1974 created a scandal. Years later, it would be identified as a classic and shown on several private channels without negative reaction (Türk 2001: 199).

Director: **Halit Refiğ**; Producer: Nüzhet Birsel, Özdemir Birsel; Production: Birsel Film; Screenwriters: **Halit Refiğ, Kemal Tahir**; Cinematographer: Memduh Yükman, Mark Rafaelyan; Music: Metin Birkay; Art director: Stavro Yuanidis; Cast: **Cüneyt Arkın**, Ayfer Feray, Tanju Gürsu, Nilüfer Aydan, Pervin Par, Sami Ayanoğlu, Birsen Menekşeli

Hayat Var / My Only Sunshine (2008) is a coming-of-age drama that interrogates identity and belonging in a geopolitically extraordinary city like Istanbul that bridges the past and the future, the East and the West and the tradition and modernity. The Istanbulites are susceptible to chronic ailments, social and sexual identity issues and eternal loneliness. The film's main characters, a bedridden grandfather suffering from a pulmonary disease, a divorced father – a bi-sexual fisherman/smuggler who procures women to the anchored ships – and a girl on the threshold to adulthood, schematically represent the past, the present and the future. The male characters comply with the 'masculinity in crisis' motif prominent in post-1980-*coup d'état* films, while Hayat, her name, literally 'life' and life-giving in the film, asthmatic herself, is in charge of the oxygen tubes of the grandfather and protection of her father from the police and jilted boyfriends. She drifts through life with an infant-like murmur sucking her thumb often in a foetal position; the flapping of a bird accompanies her. Abused and exploited by the grown-ups to satisfy their sexual or emotional needs, bullied by classmates and derided by teachers in the typically middle-class environment of the school

Figure 57 Hayat Var / My Only Sunshine (Reha Erdem, 2008) (Courtesy of Reha Erdem)

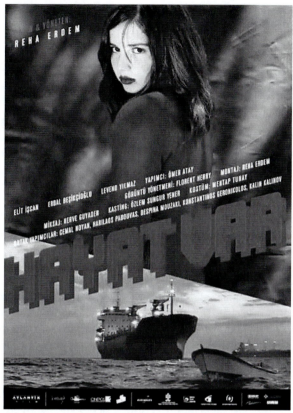

Figure 58 Hayat Var / My Only Sunshine (Reha Erdem, 2008) poster (Courtesy of Reha Erdem)

as the girl from a wooden shack without a 'classic' family, a kitten and a gyrating stuffed teddy bear that sings 'You Are My Sunshine' are her only companions. Her inimical mother slaps her when she starts her menstruation (womanhood equals shame), the local grocer rapes her when she turns 14 and the middle-aged neighbour Kamile with lesbian tendencies emotionally exploits her to alleviate her own loneliness. Silent Hayat develops her own survival mechanism, grabbing handfuls of chocolate bars from the grocery after each violation to buy popularity at school; dreaming in front of the television; stealing from her grandfather who sells the television set and kicking the turkey in the backyard just like another neglected child in Béla Tarr's *Sátántangó* (1994), who tortures a cat while her prostitute mother serves a customer.

Beyond a *bildungsroman* on the growing pains of one adolescent living in the extreme, *My Only Sunshine* presents a sombre picture of a city carrying the burden of its history, Istanbul as the interface of two cultures, not unlike **Derviş Zaim**'s ***Tabutta Rövaşata / Somersault in a Coffin*** (1996). Neither the Istanbul of tourists, the Bosphorus illuminated with cruise ships, nor the Istanbul of the inhabitants, includes those on the periphery. Hayat's home is a shack open to the foreboding waves; her *mahalle* (the neighbourhood), the 'smallest operative unity of the community in the Ottoman Empire…a compact *Gemeinschaft* with its boundaries protected by its own toughs and faithful dogs' (Mardin 1981: 214), has become uncanny with the local store owner as the molester but the city itself suffocates its young and old. In the last episode, Hayat asks the carpenter's apprentice if he is from Istanbul and when the answer is negative, she is happy for the first time.

From its **arabesque** music to the narrative, the film carries several motifs of **Yeşilçam melodramas**. In fact, **Yeşilçam** films are heard on the unseen television – a Cinderella story, *Rüyalar Gerçek Olsa / If Dreams Could Come True* (**Hulki Saner**, 1972) and a rape and reconciliation drama, *Fatma Gülün Suçu Ne? / What's the Crime of Fatma Gül?* (**Süreyya Duru**, 1986), both of which feature strong women protagonists. The image and sound editing with unexpected twists, the control of tension and the repetitions, flashbacks and flash-forwards that merge reality and imaginary, succeed in building a film that is as rebellious as the protagonist. Yet the film conforms to the traditions of **Yeşilçam** with the clichés of poverty, rape and prostitution and the contrived stereotypes – the local grocer as the rapist, the stepfather as the policeman, the father as the pimp, the neighbour as an alcoholic and lesbian and the young apprentice from the provinces, another outcast, as the true love. The representations of women are also very conventional. Hayat bears in silence the verbal abuse of boys at school, the sexual abuse of the local grocer, the burdens imposed on her by her father and grandfather, the restrictions of reaching adulthood (the righteous stepfather reprimands her for exposing her legs, the mother slaps her when she starts menstruating, she gives her a long dress). Her mother is labelled 'a whore' by the grandfather for deserting her father. A neighbour was raped when she was even younger than Hayat and she talks about it in a pragmatic tone. Apart from the caricaturized schoolteacher, all the other women are prostitutes, moulded from the male point of view. Erdem's choice of a female child to literally shut the door behind her grandfather to condemn him to death by refusing to replace the oxygen tank and run along the waves to the endless horizon in joyful revelry is significant in suggesting the role of the woman in liberating the future. Yet, one wonders why the manifestation of her transformation is the red lipstick, an allusion to prostitution.

My Only Sunshine, according to Erdem is 'an indictment of "loveless-ness" in modern society and an invitation to rebellion – to open the door and search for love, which is the only remedy when all systems fail' (Erdem 2008). Nonetheless, in the final sequence, the exhilarating rhythm of **Orhan Gencebay**'s *Dert Bende Derman Sende* (literally, 'I've got the pain, you've got the remedy'), which heightens the dramatic effect as the boat carrying the two rebellious youngsters accelerates towards the horizon, is gradually superseded by the sad melodies of the *saz*, a reminder, perhaps, of the illusory nature of happy ends.

Director, Screenwriter, Editor: **Reha Erdem**; Producer, Art Director: Ömer Atay; Production: Atlantik Film; Cinematographer: Florent Herry; Music: Orhan Gencebay; Sound: Herve Guyader; Cast: Elit İşcan, Erdal Beşikçioğlu, Levend Yılmaz, Banu Fotocan, Handan Karaadam

Hayatboyu / Lifelong (2013) begins with a couple past their prime making love with the woman on top (we feel him feeling her weight throughout the film). The camera follows her every move, inside the house or at the gallery where she exhibits her works. The first close-up of her husband appears after 40 minutes into the film and the first time we are given a chance to understand his thinking mechanism (the scene in the earthquake-devastated Van) is 20 minutes later. Ela, a contemporary artist, is at a deadlock with her work that does not sell (her daughter: 'Why don't you make something people can hang on their walls?') and her private life, including the infidelity of her husband, which exacerbates her self-consciousness about ageing. Shying away from the cameras in public, she is often shown examining her image in the mirror – including a scene of frontal nudity – or undressing with the mirror behind her, for the gaze of the audience. (Defne Halman's hold-no-barriers acting is very generous to present a woman aware of the passage of time.)

As in ***Köprüdekiler / Men on the Bridge*** (2009), certain motifs, whether religious – the occasional appearance of a mosque and minaret, the distant sound of *ezan*, the *Bayram* and a visit to a cemetery – or nationalistic – the picture of Kemal Atatürk in the grandmother's living room – do not blend with the narrative apart from adding local colour for the international audience. On the other hand, the house-hunting episode, when the agent addresses the husband while the customer is the wife, tells more about the customs of the country.

The parallel images of Ela's installation involving a terrifying rock to be placed on top of a glass ceiling as a trope for her precarious marriage and a chimney that falls on a car during an earthquake as a reminder of the unpredictable threat of death and destruction, do not create an effective correlation within the dramatic structure. The spiral staircase of the ultra-modern apartment is an appropriate trope for the vicious circle of the couple's life that delays the rupture for the sake of security and in that sense, the film has had its precedents in commercial as well as art cinema, including Michael Haneke's *Cache / Hidden* (2005) (high-income couple, successful career woman, dinners with friends, designer kitchens, alienation that accumulates with time). The main difference with Haneke's film is the nature of what is 'hidden', which brings an important political dimension to his film, whereas *Lifelong*'s attempts at going outside the high-tech home and facing reality (through the earthquake episodes) remain contrived. The artists and architects, the sophisticated galleries and women clad in *bohemian chic* outfits make a 'boutique film' that lacks deeper insight into the dilemmas of the characters although the photography of Emre Erkmen with its icy blue tones succeeds in creating a remarkable atmosphere of alienation that gnaws two people trapped in a confined space. At the 32nd International Istanbul Film Festival (2013), **Aslı Özge** received the Best Director award and Emre Erkmen, Best Director of Photography for *Lifelong*.

Director, Screenwriter: **Aslı Özge**; Producers: Nadir Öperli; Production: Augustus Film, Bulut Film, Kaliber Film; Cinematographer: Emre Erkmen; Editors: Natali Barrey, **Aslı Özge**; Sound: Pepijn Aben; Cast: Onur Dikmen, Gizem Akman, Hakan Çimenser, Dafne Halman

Hazal (1979) is a love story that takes place during Turkey's transition to modernity, explored through feudal lives in an insular Anatolian village. Betrothed to the son of the village head, who has disappeared, Hazal is forced to marry his 11-year-old brother Ömer. The story resembles *I Love You, Rosa* by Moshe Mizrai (1972), in which a widow marries the 11-year-old brother of her husband in nineteenth-century Palestine according to Jewish customs. Contrary to the sentimental solution in that film, *Hazal* ends in tragedy.

The film does not abstract the issues of women from other issues but rather links them with issues arising from feudalism and the social and economic disorders of the capitalist system. Hazal's tragedy arises from the custom of demanding money for the bride, which cannot be met by the construction worker Emin; her sister-in-law Feşo who cannot marry for the same reason, has an affair with the shaman, brought to produce virility in Ömer and commits suicide when discovered by Hazal and Ömer.

The relationship between Hazal and Ömer is nuanced. Under pressure from family and friends, Ömer tries to prove his manhood, but a tender friendship develops between the two and at the end, he closes his eyes to her escape, **Özgentürk**

Figure 59 Poster of *Hazal* (Ali Özgentürk, 1979) (Photo: Gönül Dönmez-Colin)

sending a message of hope for the future through Ömer gaining consciousness against oppression and backwardness, but sacrifices have to be made. As the dynamite explosions are heard on the road (metaphorically announcing the rupture of feudalism), the corpses of Hazal and Emin hang down from the horses that turn in a circle.

Hazal is important along with other films on the transition to modernity and the resistance of tradition as in *Köprü / The Bridge* (1975), made by **Şerif Gören**, another former assistant of **Yılmaz Güney**. The village is divided on the issue of the paved road, which will facilitate transportation and commerce, but at the same time bring the evils of progress with it. The scene when the villagers meet the state land surveyors is dramatic as they slowly identify the yellow spots in the distance as surveyors in uniform measuring the land. Despite the clear message of the film indicting feudalism and backwardness, in this scene **Özgentürk** opens a parenthesis about forced modernity from above (the policy of the Republican state) showing the state representatives actually dividing the village into parcels.

This debut feature of **Ali Özgentürk** is rich in magical realism starting with the frozen composition in the opening sequence alluding to Sergei Parajanov's *Sayat Nova / The Colour of Pomegranates* (1968), merging the aesthetic beauty of the wild colours of the countryside – the blue, the grey and the dominant gold – with the harsh realism. The appearance of the blind weavers in blue informing the audience of the flow of the narrative and dividing the film into episodes, recalls the chorus of the prophesizing witches in *Macbeth*, but it could also be considered as a Brechtian distantiation device. The **social realist** approach carries strong influences of **Yılmaz Güney**. The film was successful nationally and internationally, winning the Best New Director award at the San Sebastián International Film Festival, 1980 and the Golden Ducat, Ecumenical Jury and Audience awards at the Mannheim–Heidelberg International Film Festival, 1980, among others. It was shown at the Directors' Fortnight section of the Cannes Film Festival. It was sold to several countries, which was rare in that epoch for a Turkish film.

Director: **Ali Özgentürk**; Producer: **Abdurrahman Keskiner**; Production: Umut Film; Screenwriters: **Ali Özgentürk**, **Onat Kutlar** (based on *Kutsal Ceza / Sacred Punishment* by Necati Haksun); Cinematographer: Muzaffer Turan; Editor: Özdemir Arıtan; Music: **Zülfü Livaneli**, Arif Sağ; Cast: **Türkan Şoray**, Talat Bulut, Hüseyin Peyda, Harun Yeşilyurt, Meral Çetinkaya, Keriman Ulusoy, Gülen Ökten

Hazinses, Sami (b. Diyarbakır, 1925 – d. Istanbul, 2002) Actor, composer; RN: Samuel Agop Uluçyan. One of the unforgettable comedians of Turkish cinema, Sami Hazinses devoted 45 years to Turkish cinema, but hid his Armenian identity for fear of reprisals; his secret was discovered at his funeral when the procession had to be transferred from the mosque to the church. He started his film career in 1953, playing mostly in comedies and composing popular songs for films such as *Şöför Nebahat / Nebahat, the Driver* (**Metin Erksan**, 1959/60).

Heper, Alp Zeki (b. Istanbul, 1939 – d. Istanbul, 1984) Director, screenwriter, producer. One of the few Turkish film-makers who attempted experimental cinema,

Heper worked at the Swiss cinemateque in Lausanne and studied film at the IDHEC (Institut des Hautes Etudes Cinématographiques) in Paris. His first two short films (1963) received awards: *Bir Kadın / A Woman* won an IDHEC prize and *Şafak / Sunrise*, about the oppression of the woman in society, both an IDHEC and the Austrian Ministry of Culture award. On his return home, he worked as assistant to **Akad** in *Üç Tekerlekli Bisiklet / Tricycle* aka *The Three-Wheeled Bicycle* (1962), following which he established his film company. His first fiction film, *Soluk Gecenin Aşk Hikâyeleri / Love Stories of a Pale Night* (1966), a Freudian approach to sexual repression, carries the influence of Bunuel whom he met during his Paris years and the abstract and psychological effects of surrealism. More like a black-and-white slide show than a moving picture, the film presents, through the male gaze (of the actor), a woman's soul in three manifestations: incest (Marliese Schneiderhan), slave (Mine Cezzar) and prostitute (Ayfer Feray). Totally banned by the Film Commission Control as 'pornographic', the film created a wave among the artistic and intellectual circles with its rejection of conventional narrative and the taboos of a closed society (mother, sister and mistress amalgamated into one; fetishism of phallic symbols – statues, guns, shoes); the merging of illusion and reality and the integration of location (such as the love-making scene in front of the majestic Dolmabahçe Palace) with the city traffic in the background. It was defined as the first experimental film of Turkey. During an interview he gave, Heper stated that he wanted to juxtapose love, i.e. freedom, with terror and torture, hoping that love would annihilate oppression, but he was blamed for obscenity. His second film, *Dolmuş Şöförü / Collective Taxi Driver* (1967), a social satire, failed despite the presence of two stars, **Fatma Girik** and **İzzet Günay**. Trying to save his company from bankruptcy, he made *Eşkıya Halil* aka *Haydut / Bandit Halil* (1968) with a very popular star, **Cüneyt Arkın** in the lead. With its relative success, he made *Kara Battal'ın Acısı / The Pain of Kara Battal* in the same year, an attempt at the issue of East/West divide through the story of a Turkish worker repairing a Byzantine fort, unjustly executed for the murder of a Greek girl, which was his last film. He died of cancer in 1984 (Toker 1974: 87–95; Scognamillo 1990: 120).

Himmet Ağanın İzdivacı / The Marriage of Himmet Agha (1916–18), the first feature film, but not the first to reach audiences, focusing on love–marriage and social issues through the story of an old man forced to marry a young woman, is a free adaptation from Moliére's *Le Marriage Forcé / The Forced Marriage*. Shooting was suspended when most actors were recruited to serve in the War of the Dardanelles and completed in 1918 by **Fuat Uzkınay**, who replaced **Sigmund Weinberg**, a Romanian citizen of Polish Jewish origin, who was fired when war broke out between Romania and the Ottoman Empire, but according to the unpublished memoirs of film critic, Nurullah Tilgen, Reşat Rıdvan, a well-known man of theatre completed the film (Scognamillo 1987: 26).

Director: **Sigmund Weinberg**, **Fuat Uzkınay** (?), Reşat Rıdvan (?); Producer: Merkez Ordu Sinema Dairesi (Central Army Office of Cinema); Screenwriter: **Sigmund Weinberg**; Cinematographer: **Fuat Uzkınay**; Cast: Arşak Benliyan, Behzat Butak, **Ahmet Fehim**, İ. Galip Arcan, İsmail Zahit, Kemal Emin Bara, Lusi Arusyak, Rosali Benliyan

Historical dramas (see **war films**)

Hudutların Kanunu / The Law of the Borders (1966) is a remarkable classic of Turkish cinema and the first film to bring together **Lütfi Ö. Akad** and **Yılmaz Güney**. Declared by the critics as the most important film until its time, by **Akad** as 'people's cinema', it is narrated like a folk tale using the language of the ordinary people and focusing on their plight in a realistic manner, a novelty for the escapist Turkish cinema of the period. It is also a reflection on the peasant, worker and student movements that found expression in the aftermath of the 1960 *coup d'état*, and the issue of land reform that surfaced. The film's misadventures with the censorship board began with the rejection of the original script of **Yılmaz Güney** underscoring the relationship between the state and the individual, which was re-written by **Akad** shifting the focus to the socio-economic base of smuggling. Nonetheless, the Central Film Control Commission forbade its participation in foreign events despite invitations from the Berlin and Venice Film Festivals. *The Law of the Borders* remains one of the most censored films of Turkish cinema, shown one year after completion with changes in several scenes.

Some critics of the period consider *Law of the Borders* as part of a trilogy, along with *Kızılırmak-Karakoyun* (1967) and *Ana / The Mother* (1967), named the Anatolian trilogy. One of the staple motifs of **Akad**, the trapped man, is central to the narrative. Through the role of Hıdır, the performance of **Güney** shows the nuances of the human character; a toughened lone smuggler who can harbour profound paternal love, respect for women and reverence for education, a character that he further develops in *Ağıt / Elegy* (1971).

Shot in the style of a western, the narrative unfolds with the remains of Hıdır's brother brought to the village. A smuggler caught in the act, he wounded a lieutenant before dying. The new lieutenant representing the state warns Hıdır against illegal acts. They make a pact about giving up smuggling and returning to agriculture despite the barrenness of the land, in exchange for the establishment of a school, which is Hıdır's only hope for the future of his son. The landlord employs Hıdır and the other smugglers but thwarts their return to legal work by asking Hıdır to smuggle for him. Maddened by Hıdır's refusal, he sends his animals to the field to destroy the new crop, leaving no alternative for Hıdır but smuggling. The lieutenant is presented in a positive light in the film to please the censor board; nonetheless, the film underscores the futility of regulations concocted by officials ignorant of local circumstances. In this sense, the film is contemporary in exposing the plight of the peasants in border towns resorting to criminal activities in the absence of legal possibilities to earn a living.

The class hierarchy is clearly drawn in the film, extending to the presentations of space, such as the village, the fields, the market place, the police station, the mansion of the landlord and the cave where the smuggled goods are stored. While the school represents the hope for a democratic and classless society, the barren fields and the landlord Duran Ağa, who benefits from smuggling, represent feudalism. The lieutenant and the teacher, the idealist state employees, are the representatives of the aspired classless society of the new democracy and their attraction to each other is foreseeable. Hıdır, most probably a Kurd as are most protagonists of **Güney** (a number of Kurdish words are inconspicuously inserted into the dialogue), belongs to a class outside the state, as the representative of the poverty-stricken people suffering under the yoke of feudalism; hence his death at the border is significant. The 'border' in the title of the film, rather than referring to the actual border between Turkey and probably Syria (the other side which does not exist in the film) is a trope for the economic, social and political crisis in a transitional moment that is the harbinger of social breakdown and nation-state anarchy. The border also refers to the human borders/limitations, an important theme in the works of **Akad**. As foreshadowed in the opening sequences, Hıdır's efforts to reach beyond his limitations in a fight against pitiless feudalism, barren land and the indifferent state end in failure. On the other hand, **Akad** and **Güney**, who had researched in the area of Urfa, living with the local people to authenticate the existing script, succeed in surpassing the borders of **Yeşilçam** by creating an outstanding work that is as relevant today as it was almost half a century ago. The film was restored by Martin Scorsese's World Cinema Foundation with the initiative of the board member **Fatih Akın** at Cineteca di Bologna/L'Immagine Ritrovata Laboratory, from the single positive print that survived the 1980 *coup d'état* and shown at the Cannes Film Festival in 2011.

Director: **Lütfi Ö. Akad**; Screenwriter: **Akad, Yılmaz Güney**; Producer: Cahit Gürpınar; Production: Dadaş Film; Cinematographer: Ali Uğur; Editor: Ali Ün; Music: Nida Tüfekçi; Cast: **Yılmaz Güney**, Pervin Par, **Muharrem Gürses, Tuncel Kurtiz, Erol Taş**, Hikmet Olgun, Atilla Ergün, Osman Alyanak, Aydemir Akbaş, Atilla Ergün

Hun, Ediz (b. Istanbul, 1940) Actor. The last romantic hero of Turkish cinema, Ediz Hun started his acting career opposite two stars, **Hülya Koçyiğit** and **Türkan Şoray** in *Genç Kızlar / The Young Girls* (Nevzat Pesen, 1963). A matinée idol with his clean-cut innocent face, an affluent urban intellectual with his suave appearance (a rarity in **Yeşilçam** to depict the urban rich in a positive light), a naive and sensitive romantic designed for the popular **melodramas**, his image was distinct from the customary one-dimensional male images. He played in around 130 films and television series, except during the sex furore of the 1970s when he went to Norway to complete his university education in biology, returning in 1982. During the 1980s, he co-operated a printing press, lectured in ecology and played in television series. He was a member of parliament for Istanbul in 1999. Among his other well-known films are: *Son Kuşlar / The Last Birds* (Erdoğan Tokatlı, 1965); *Hıçkırık / Sob* (1965) and *Samanyolu / The Milkyway* (1967) by **Orhan Aksoy**; *Ankara Ekspresi / Ankara Express* (Muzaffer Aslan, 1970) and *Anadolu Kartalları / Eagles of Anatolia* (**Ömer Vargı**, 2011).

I

Irmak, Çağan (b. İzmir, 1970) Director, screenwriter, actor. Commercially the most successful director of social **melodramas**, Çağan Irmak graduated from the Radio and Television Department of the Aegean University, receiving prestigious awards with his short films. He worked as assistant to important film-makers and directed for television before scripting and directing his first feature, *Bana Şans Dile / Wish Me Luck* (2002), an action-thriller about misguided Turkish youth. He established his name with *Mustafa Hakkında Herşey / All About Mustafa* (2003), about a successful businessman who re-constructs his past after a car accident; *Babam ve Oğlum / My Father and Son* (2005), a very popular film about the post-trauma of the 1980 military intervention and *Ulak / The Messenger* (2007), a **fantasy** mystery about a fictitious religion. *Issız Adam / Alone* (2008) is a good example of 'masculinity in crisis' films that have gained prominence in the 2000s. The narrative pattern is somewhat similar to *Uzak / Distant* (**Nuri Bilge Ceylan**, 2002), focusing on a provincial man comfortably settled in the metropolis, who has lost his soul. His provincial mother, always forgiving just as in **Ceylan**'s film(s), reminds him, 'the city devours one, makes one forget being human'. He likes casual sex and he is violent (**Ceylan** as İsa in *İklimler / Climates*, 2006). He has built his life alone and is afraid of close ties. Whereas **Ceylan** is distinctive with his film language, **Irmak** is the audience favourite, with the dream worlds he creates similar to **Yeşilçam** – romantic boat trips, hand-in-hand walks in crowds and modern homes out of interior decoration magazines. The theme of maladaptation to the city that feeds nostalgia for the past – the vinyl LPs of the 1970s, second-hand books, 35mm cameras – also has its commercial appeal. *Karanlıktakiler / In Darkness* (2009) is about an old Istanbulite, as a metonymy for Istanbul, raped by a migrant Anatolian, producing a monster, a trope for the urban landscape of Istanbul. A comedy-drama, *Prensesin Uykusu / Sleeping Princess* (2010), about a librarian and a 10-year-old, and *Dedemin İnsanları / My Grandfather's People* (2011), a **melodrama** with the background of the population exchange between Turkey and Greece, are his other films to date. Irmak has also written and directed popular television series.

Işık, Ayhan (b. İzmir, 1929 – d. Istanbul, 1979) Actor, screenwriter, producer, singer, painter; RN: Ayhan Işıyan. One of the most popular actors, renamed by his fans *taçsız kıral* (the king without a crown), Ayhan Işık graduated from the Academy of Fine Arts in 1953. Winning a competition organized by a star magazine in 1952 diverted him from painting to cinema. His breakthrough came with **Kanun Namına / In the Name of Law** (**Akad,** 1952). In 1959, he went to Hollywood to try his luck and although he did not succeed as an actor, he learned valuable lessons of cinema. After his return, he appeared as the lead in numerous films, becoming very popular with the *Küçük Hanım / Little Miss* series (1960s–70s) as the *jeune premier* of the period acting opposite **Belgin Doruk**. With about 200 films to his credit, some of his most memorable roles are in **Otobüs Yolcuları / The Bus Passengers** (**Ertem Göreç,** 1961), **Acı Hayat / Bitter Life** (**Erksan,** 1962) and **Üç Tekerlekli Bisiklet / Tricycle** aka **The Three-Wheeled Bicycle** (**Akad, Ün,** 1962).

İ

İklimler / Climates (2006), foregrounding the disintegration of a relationship, is the last segment of what this author considers a tetralogy that could be called 'A Portrait of the Provincial Artist as an Urban Intellectual' along with *Kasaba / The Small Town* (1997), *Mayıs Sıkıntısı / Clouds of May* (1999) and *Uzak / Distant* (2002). From this point of view, *Climates* can be regarded as a prequel to *Distant* that features the ex-provincial, now urban photographer Mahmut, already divorced, having a clandestine liaison with a woman attached to someone else, corresponding to the Serap character in *Climates*, played by the same actor, Nazan Kesal. Ceylan's real-life mother plays the mother of the protagonist in both films. In *Climates*, the central motifs of homecoming and escape from home that were pivotal to the previous three films are merged into the possibility of a home, a sense of establishing roots and belonging to someone or somewhere.

During the vacation of the couple in the south, İsa (**Nuri Bilge Ceylan**), a college professor with an incomplete PhD thesis is immersed in his work taking pictures while his young partner Bahar (spring) (Ebru Ceylan) sheds silent

Figure 60 İklimler / Climates (Nuri Bilge Ceylan, 2006) (Courtesy of NBC Film and Zeynep Özbatur Atakan-Zeyno film/Yapımlab)

Figure 61 İklimler / Climates (Nuri Bilge Ceylan, 2006) (Courtesy of NBC Film and Zeynep Özbatur Atakan-Zeyno film/Yapımlab)

tears. **Ceylan**'s İsa is a Woody Allen style self-parody, portraying a clumsy man approaching middle age who stumbles in the opening scene. Considering women as extensions of himself, he is paternalistic toward Bahar, insisting she should be wearing a jacket when she is not cold; or trying to force his mistress to eat the peanut he dropped on the floor. His insecurity about his male identity is further revealed during conversations with his equally insecure colleague. Taking place in the office, the tennis court or the sauna and in the absence of women, these short bravura exchanges between two men are revealing about gender issues in Turkey. For the local critic Fatih Özgüven, the protagonist is settled in the city but not at ease with the 'climate' of the city. His behaviour during the Serap episode carries the obvious signs of a provincial man savouring a clandestine affair in the city and just like Mahmut's habit of spreading a towel on the bed before intercourse in **Distant** carries the 'smell' of the country. *Climates* continues the story of the male character who lives his climates between the city and the country (Özgüven 2006).

Both Mahmut of **Distant** and İsa of *Climates* prefer sex without attachments. İsa crosses the country to convince Bahar to return home with him, but when he wins her back (conqueror mentality), he is on the run again. Both men are deceitful, a staple motif in **Ceylan**'s films. After violent sex with his mistress, İsa visits his mother to have his trousers repaired, and pretends all is well with Bahar;

he lies to Bahar about not continuing that liaison during their break-up and he gives false hope to the taxi driver by taking his address to mail him his picture, then throwing the paper away. In short, İsa is the anti-hero that creates neither identification, nor empathy in the audience.

The presentation of Bahar is somewhat problematic from a feminist point of view. She is the ideal partner coveted by the traditional male: young and beautiful; silent and submissive; ready to die rather than live without him (she covers his eyes while he is driving the motorcycle and they both fall); a career woman willing to give up her job for the man she loves. Her dreams are significant. In the scene on the beach, just before İsa announces his intention to break the relationship, she dreams of İsa telling her he loves her, but then covering her with sand; in the final bedroom episode, after having spent the night together, which Bahar considers as a return to normal, she recounts her dream of flying over her mother's grave in an open and vulnerable manner, to be informed once again that the relationship is over.

The intensity of the disintegration of the relationship rendered with minimal dialogue is as masterful as in an Antonioni film. İsa and Bahar live in Istanbul, but we see them together only in the holiday resort, Kaş, in the summer and in the snow-covered Ağrı in winter. Their union takes place in anonymous hotel rooms. The differences of the couple, apart from the age gap, are revealed in scenes such as Bahar sitting in the balcony in full daylight while İsa remains indoors with his head placed inside a drawer for comfort. In fact, the neck problem of İsa and the film crew appearing at the end carry an intertextuality with Tsai Ming-liang's *The River* (1997), both films revealing the sadness of modern existence, particularly in traditional societies that experience the trauma of liminality.

Among the national and international awards the film received are the Cannes Film Festival, Fipresci Prize, 2006 and the International Istanbul Film Festival, Best Turkish Film and People's Choice, 2007.

Director, Screenwriter: **Nuri Bilge Ceylan**; Producers: **Zeynep Özbatur**, Fabienne Vonier, Cemal Noyan, **Nuri Bilge Ceylan**; Production: Pyramide, NBC Film and IMAJ; Cinematographer: **Gökhan Tiryaki**; Editors: **Nuri Bilge Ceylan**, Ayhan Ergürsel; Sound: Olivier Dô Hù, İsmail Karadaş, Thomas Robert; Cast: Ebru Ceylan, **Nuri Bilge Ceylan**, Nazan Kesal, Mehmet Eryılmaz, Arif Aşçı, Can Özbatur, Fatma Ceylan, Semra Yıldız, Abdullah Demirkubuz, Feridun Koç, Ceren Olcay, Zeker Saka

İlyadis, Kriton (b. Adapazarı, 1916 – d. Istanbul, 1980) Cinematographer. Perhaps the most long-standing cinematographer of Turkish cinema with over 100 films to his credit between 1944–77, including *Bir Millet Uyanıyor / A Nation is Awakening* (1966) and *İngiliz Kemal* (1968) of **Ertem Eğilmez**; *Lüküs Hayat / Luxurious Life* (1950), ***Kanun Namına / In The Name of The Law*** (1952), *Öldüren Şehir / The Murderous City* (1954) and *Katil / The Killer* (1953) of **Lütfi Ö. Akad**; *Kırık Plak / The Broken Record* (1959) and *Namus Uğruna / For Honour* (1960) of **Osman Seden**, Kriton İlyadis is a good example of the rarely remembered contribution of the ethnic minorities to the development of Turkish cinema, which has theoretically ignored them although he was praised by the distinguished directors he collaborated with for his innovative approach to the employment of light and shadow, the deep focus and exceptional framing and as 'a great observer who could capture universal truth with an Anatolian wisdom and render it with modesty in a simple unadorned form' (**Akad** 2004: 195).

İlyadis, Yorgo (b. Adapazarı, 1914 – d. Thessaloniki, 1974) Composer, actor, cinematographer, sound engineer. Older brother of **Kriton**, Yorgo Ilyadis trained as a sound engineer in Germany and worked on hundreds of local and imported films. Some of his memorable works are the films of **Lütfi Ö. Akad** that are among the classics today: *Kanun Namına / In The Name of The Law* (1952) and *Katil / The Killer* (1953) as sound engineer and *Vurun Kahpeye / Strike the Whore* (1949) and *Vesikalı Yarim / My Licensed Love* (1968) as sound editor. He also composed the music for several films.

İnanç, Çetin (b. Ankara, 1941) Director, screenwriter, producer. One of the pioneers of **fantasy films** in Turkey, internationally known for his *Star Wars* re-make, the pseudo-science-fiction, *Dünyayı Kurtaran Adam / The Man Who Saves the World* (1982) (discovered in the West in the 2000s, becoming a cult classic while being designated as one of the worst films ever made), Çetin İnanç worked as assistant to **Atıf Yılmaz** for seven years before shooting his first feature. In 1971, he broke records with a Turkish western, *Çeko*. In the aftermath of the 1971 *coup d'état*, during a period of severe political censorship, he churned out countless B-movies, from adaptations of popular cartoons, sex comedies to religious yarns ('Ramazan films', to be shown during the fasting month), focusing on **Cüneyt Arkın** action films (*Dört Yanım Cehennem / The Mummy*, 1982) in the 1980s and moving to television series in the 1990s. Notorious for shooting films in one to ten days, with minimum technical facilities but maximum innovative practicality and with 136 films to his credit, İnanç's style of film-making is revealed to the public in a book of his memoirs, *Jet Film-maker* (2013). A sequel was made to *The Man Who Saves the World* called *Dünyayı Kurtaran Adam'ın Oğlu / The Son of the Man Who Saves the World*, aka *Turks in Space*, also with **Cüneyt Arkın** in the lead (**Kartal Tibet**, 2006).

İnanır, Kadir (b. Ordu, 1949) Actor, director, screenwriter. One of the significant stars of Turkish cinema, who is said to have started the *école* Kadirism, Kadir İnanır studied journalism and public relations and starred in *photo-romans* before entering the film industry in 1968. In about a year, he achieved hero status, which he has maintained. *Selvi Boylum, Al Yazmalım / The Girl with the Red Scarf* (1977) and *Bir Yudum Sevgi / A Taste of Love* (1984) by **Atıf Yılmaz**; *Ah, Güzel Istanbul / Oh, Beautiful Istanbul* (1981), *Kırık Bir Aşk Hikayesi / A Broken Love Story* and *Amansız Yol / Desperate Road* (1985) by **Ömer Kavur**, *Yılanların Öcü / The Revenge of the Serpents* (1985) and *Katırcılar / The Muleteers* (1987) by **Şerif Gören** and *Dila Hanım / Mrs Dila* (1977) by **Orhan Aksoy**, are some of the films with his memorable performances. Among around 150 films in which he appeared, the ones opposite the *sultana* **Türkan Şoray** are some of the most popular. In 2013, he played in a Turkish/Russian co-production, *Elveda Katya / Good-bye Katia*, directed by Ahmet Sönmez. He also directed *Ah... Gardaşım / Oh... My Brother* (1991), a rather predictable story with local colour interspersed.

İpekçi, Handan (b. Ankara, 1956) Director, screenwriter, producer, editor. Internationally acclaimed for her second feature, *Büyük Adam, Küçük Aşk* aka *Hejar / Big Man, Small Love* (2001) about an unusual friendship between a retired Kemalist judge and a 5-year-old Kurdish orphan, Handan İpekçi is one of the major women film-makers of Turkey. She studied Radio-Television at the Communications Faculty of Gazi University, making her directorial debut with a documentary, *Kemençenin Türküsü / The Ballad of the Kemancha* (1993). She took a political stand with her first feature film, *Babam Askerde / Dad is in the Army* (1994), delving into the period of the 12 September 1980 *coup* through the stories of three children from different backgrounds with a common issue: a father in prison. An original experiment in manipulating spatio-temporality, *Saklı Yüzler / Hidden Faces* exposed the vicious circle of archaic customs although the film's endorsement of the recent exclusionary media discourse that attaches 'honour killings' to the Kurdish ethnic identity was unjustified. With *Çınar Ağacı / The Plane Tree*, she tried her hand at commercial cinema, focusing on a disintegrating family. The conservative approach to family echoing the ideology of the ruling AKP party – supporting the sacrosanctity of marriage despite male infidelity and physical abuse, presenting homosexuality as disease – brought heavy criticism on the film.

İpekçi, İhsan (b. Thessaloniki, 1901 – d. Istanbul, 1966) Producer, screenwriter, novelist. Coming from a silk merchant family in Thessaloniki, İhsan İpekçi graduated from the prestigious Galatasaray Lyceum in Istanbul. Impressed by the film scene in Berlin, he initiated the opening of the movie theatre, Elhamra (Ciné Alhambra) in 1923 and a year later, Melek Theatre with a capacity of 1,000 spectators (Emek Theatre today) and imported films. Melek was sold during the economic difficulties of the 1940s, but in 1954, Yeni Melek was established. The family operated another movie house, Alhambra, in İzmir. Luring **Muhsin Ertuğrul** from Kemal Film, they produced his *Ankara Postası / Ankara Express* (unofficial English title), which had unprecedented success, opening the doors to İpek Film to have a monopoly over productions until 1942. *İstanbul Sokaklarında / On the Streets of Istanbul* (1931), a co-production between Turkey/Egypt/Greece, with sound processed in Paris, was directed by **Muhsin Ertuğrul** for İpek Film, established by İhsan and his brother Kani İpekçi in 1928. Under the pen-name of İhsan Koza, he wrote novels and scripts. Some of the well-known films he produced are *Bir Millet Uyanıyor / A Nation is Awakening* (1932); ***Aysel, Bataklı Damın Kızı / The Girl From the Marshes*** aka ***Aysel, the Girl From the Swampy Roof*** (1935) by **Muhsin Ertuğrul** and *Yalnızlar Rıhtımı / The Quay of the Lonely Ones* (**Akad**, 1959).

J

Jîn (2013) is a forceful reminder of the destruction of the universe, human beings and nature by absurd manifestations of hate for the other and a strong message of peace, rendered with remarkable photography. Idyllic scenes of nature with animals living in harmony are often accentuated with still images, or the camera lingering on leaves trembling in the soft wind, the grasshopper, the turtle, the reindeer, the lizard, the birds becoming one with hundreds-of-years-old trees. The tranquillity is disturbed by passing planes, trucks, gunfire and explosions. Nature is a silent witness to centuries of crimes committed by human beings. An elegy is heard in the dark lamenting the absent mother, which introduces the young guerrilla (Deniz Hasgüler) preparing to leave the mountain. Her face is revealed in daylight. Wearing a red scarf, she climbs rocks and trees if necessary, communicating tenderly with animals, which juxtaposes with the gun on her back. The first dialogue is heard after almost 25 minutes into the film, when she asks a shepherd for bread after she comes down from the mountain. Changing into civilian clothes that she steals from a house, she is accosted by the same shepherd, then by the man at the bus stop who sells tickets, and barely escapes a rape attempt by using her guerrilla warfare skills, which is a reminder of her true identity to the viewer who is carried away by her sweet disposition toward the animals. Passing as Leyla, the girl whose clothes she has stolen, she refuses to speak Turkish at the headquarters when she is arrested without identity papers on a bus journey, only to be sexually harassed by the Kurdish interpreter. Released during an attack, she returns to the mountain where she tries to heal the leg of a wounded donkey, then a Turkish soldier. Facing the soldier brings her back to her reality and she changes into the guerrilla clothes, but tries to help the soldier nonetheless. The episode when the soldier calls his mother on his cell phone and then the guerrilla girl speaks to her mother as well is charged with emotion, a reminder of the absurdity of war; whether the guerrilla or the soldier, all are human with mothers worrying about them. When the soldier asks her name, she shouts in anger, 'My name is Jîn!' having realized the futility of assuming the Leyla character. The final episode is beautifully choreographed. She climbs on a tree to hide from the bombers; then a scream is heard and she is lying on a rock with blood on her foot. The bear she offered an apple and the donkey whose wound she cleaned are beside her, the reindeer she encountered

Figure 62 Jîn (Reha Erdem, 2013) (Courtesy of Reha Erdem)

Figure 63 Jîn (Reha Erdem, 2013) (Courtesy of Reha Erdem)

earlier joining them. There is a movement; she is alive. Then another blast, and the screen turns blank. The end-credits begin to roll.

Jîn means life in Kurdish and Jin means woman. The protagonist is disadvantaged as a Kurd and as a woman. Travelling in the forest with a red *pushi* (scarf), telling people she is visiting her sick grandmother, she resembles Little Red Riding Hood, the wolf replaced with real people. In fact, the film is like a fable, the image of Jîn sleeping under the full moon and surrounded by the animals in the final episode are like images from fairy tales although the plight of the Kurdish people is very real. Jîn tries to read the geography book she steals along with food and clothes: 'Where am I living?' is the sentence posed in the book, which is a question faced by Kurdish people, without land and without language. The music from violoncellist Hildur Guðnadóttir's album *Without Sinking* contributes to the impact of the film enormously, but the title of the piece accompanying the prologue, *Unveiled* is particularly significant for a film that tries to remind those who seem to have forgotten, the precious nature of all beings.

Director, Screenwriter, Editor, Sound Designer: **Reha Erdem**; Ömer Atay; Producers: **Reha Erdem**; Production: Atlantik Film, Mars Entertainment Group, Imaj, Bredok Filmproduction; Cinematographer: Florent Herry; Art Director: Ömer Atay; Music: Hildur Guðnadóttir; Cast: Deniz Hasgüler, Onur Ünsal, Yıldırım Şimşek, Şahin Pişkin

K

Kaç Para Kaç / A Run for Money (1999), perhaps the most commercial film of **Reha Erdem**, made after ten years in the advertisement sector, presents the dollar as the most crucial item in the lives of the urban middle class. The film begins with a dollar bill flying in the air, followed by a scene in a children's park where three kids find $100 in the sandbox. Two parents choose to rush to the bank to change the money; the third, a quiet family man, Selim, refuses to take his share of the loot, but when he finds a bag full of dollars, he cannot say no. Almost $500,000 is stolen from a bank by a trustworthy employee of 15 years, who forgets the bag in a taxi. Someone comments, 'The state steals from the citizen, what can the citizen do but follow suit and the lira is not good enough', which recalls Meryem's comments in **Zeki Demirkubuz**'s *Üçüncü Sayfa / The Third Page* (1999), 'Everyone has their back to the wall, what will they do, if not strike back?'

Figure 64 Kaç Para Kaç / A Run for Money (Reha Erdem, 1999) (Courtesy of Atlantik Film Reha Erdem)

Selim, whose name signifies 'honest, calm and serious', leads a monotonous life selling men's shirts in his family shop. The perma-press suit he wears to work defines his character, class and political stand as an introvert, middle-class conservative family man accustomed to his routine. His wife, his pensioner father and his daughter have demands, all associated with money. His favourite sentence is 'Do you think money is earned easily?' The newly acquired money gives him the power to make his family happy but it also begins to take control and replace human values. He lies, cheats and slanders, ending paranoid and alone.

The film is a parody of the depolarized Turkish life after the 1980 *coup d'état*. It reflects the repercussions of the 'dollarization' of the society during the transition to market economy under the policies of Turgut Özal (prime minister and president, 1983–93), who claimed that free trade would force businessmen to improve production, and the sight of fancy foreign goods would encourage the people to work harder. However, an economy that is indexed to the dollar, the high inflation rate and the degeneration of values are not unique to Turkey.

Erdem's depiction of the city, the monstrous modern buildings made in haste by and for the *nouveau riche* next to the hundreds-of-years-old fountains, exposes the ethos of the period. The message of the film is conveyed without moral judgement through Selim's psychological changes. His behavioural disorders are revealed step by step through his encounters with a flirtatious neighbour, a greedy street vendor, an art-swindler friend and a customer who offers to pay in several currencies, pointing to the flexibility of standards when crime, slander, swindle and commerce are entwined. The scene when he meets the man who tried to rob his shop and the bank teller whose embezzled money he appropriated is a masterfully crafted farce: he runs from the teller and the robber runs from him. They are all stuck in a small boat, a nifty trope for the country. In the meanwhile a passenger is yelling, 'Pickpocket!' Everyone is in the same boat!

Director, Screenwriter: **Reha Erdem**; Producer, Art Director: Ömer Atay; Production: Atlantik Film; Cinematography: Florent Herry, Jean-Louis Vialard; Editor: Nathalie LeGuay; Music: Dave Henley, Justin Langlands; Cast: Taner Birsel, Bennu Yıldırımlar, Zuhal Gencer Erkaya, Engin Alkan, Sermet Yeşil

Kader / Destiny (2006), built on a monologue by Bekir during a picnic in *Masumiyet / Innocence* (1997), intended to inform Yusuf (and the audience) about the background of the characters, is a prequel that does not shift the time frame to the past. Uğur (Vildan Atasever), Bekir (Ufuk Bayraktar) and Zagor, three culturally disadvantaged aimless youths, live on the periphery of Istanbul, where men spend the day gambling in the cafe, bullying the weaker and eventually getting involved in crime as victim or victimizer. Bekir's family is the kind of middle class with a false conscience in the Marxist sense. The son is expected to continue the small family business, marry a suitable girl and be gratuitous to god and his parents for daily blessings. Uğur's family is dependent on a young man of the neighbourhood, who provides their needs, sleeping with the mother, while the bedridden father is in the next room. Her brother works in the cafe and is constantly harassed sexually by the idle youth. Zagor's background is not

Figure 65 Kader / Destiny (Zeki Demirkubuz, 2006) (Courtesy of International Istanbul Film Festival)

revealed except that he is a dangerous criminal. Uğur, already the object of desire for the sex-starved males, builds her escape route through her love for Zagor. Bekir's life is changed irreversibly when Uğur walks into his shop one day and literally awakens him from his slumber. Meeting Uğur leads him to destruction, but she is not a *femme fatale*. Rather, she is the mover, who remains unmoved. She destroys the patriarchal order. With a paralyzed father and orders to take from no one, she makes her decisions, which do not correlate with the norms of society that have established everyone's roles regardless of individuality. Holding the picture of his fiancée, a bright smiling face wearing a headscarf, in one hand and the picture of Uğur, with life breathing through each contour in the other, it does not take long for Bekir to make a decision. In a society where the binaries are precise between Madonna and Magdalene, he is for Magdalene.

Bekir's infatuation with Uğur liberates him. From a sullen young man treading the way home every evening with a plastic bag in hand, sitting at a table prepared with care by a perfect home-maker and reprimanded by his parents when he fails to play his role, he transforms into a free man who can get on a bus to Kars 20 hours away, if he wishes. He prefers to choose to which family to carry the plastic bag, such as the family of Uğur in dire straights after Zagor kills their benefactor, Cemal. In fact, the last scene shows him forming a new family (man–woman–child, although he is neither the father nor the husband). Through the door that refuses to close behind Uğur, we see him looking at mother and child

Figure 66 Kader / Destiny (Zeki Demirkubuz, 2006) (Courtesy of International Istanbul Film Festival)

sharing an affectionate moment in the next room. If he will be destroyed, he will be responsible for it, and not destiny.

The framing of Demirkubuz to reflect the character's interior world – placing Bekir between the dark shadows of two flags but facing the open sea – is perhaps too obvious, but effective nonetheless. Using blackouts for chapters works when it is not arbitrary; the transitions, however, are often rough, rendering the flow of the narrative ambiguous, caused probably by the second editing to shorten the length. The constant presence of the television screen is nothing new for **Demirkubuz** cinema (or the cinema of his contemporaries) and the hotel lobbies where idle men stare at the screen while waiting is a motif that goes back to **Ömer Kavur** and his 'hotel films', the sub-**genre Kavur** developed with *Anayurt Oteli / Motherland Hotel* (1987). In *Destiny*, the scene from *Innocence*, Uğur screaming at Yusuf after he approaches her for sex is heard in the hotel lobby by Bekir, who has just had a similar confrontation with Uğur (a deconstructionist approach making the fictionality of fiction, or the artificiality of art apparent).

Intertextuality is what differentiates *Destiny* and other works of **Demirkubuz**, who references his own films, the films of others (often **Yeşilçam**) and literature, particularly Dostoevsky and the fragmented post-modern characters, who try to invent their own order in an order-less world. As a post-modern character, Bekir exemplifies multiple selves and his giving-up of fixed ego structures encapsulates the real attack on bourgeois society rather than the rebellious hero (Russell 1982: 56 in Fokkema 1991: 62).

Director, Screenwriter, Cinematographer, Editor, Producer: **Zeki Demirkubuz**; Production: Mavi Film, Inkas Film; Sound: İsmail Karadaş; Music: Edward Artemiev; Cast: Ufuk Bayraktar, Vildan Atasever, Engin Akyürek, Müge Ulusoy, Ozan Bilen, Settar Tanrıöğen, Erkan Can, Mustafa Uzunyılmaz, Güzin Alkan, Hikmet Demir, Gönül Çalgan

Kanun Namına / In the Name of the Law (1952), one of the classics of Turkish cinema, is based on a true story that happened in post-World War II Istanbul; a turner killed three people for jealousy, locked himself in his shop and after a skirmish with the police, committed suicide. In the film, the ending is changed to the surrender of the protagonist after pleas from his wife. Several local critics compared the film to *Le Jour se Léve / Daybreak* (1939), the fourth collaboration of Marcel Carné with screenwriter and poet, Jacques Prévert, an example of French poetic realism in film about a working-class man who kills to free his woman from the domination of another man. Others maintained that it was influenced by the Hollywood re-make, *The Long Night* (1947) by Anatole Litvak, starring Henri Fonda (Onaran 1994: 55). Despite its reliance on **melodrama** and the routine good/bad dichotomy, the film is a milestone in terms of the character portrayals, the location shooting, the shifting camera angles, the high-contrast and occasionally low-key lighting, deep shadows and oblique angles that bring a new sense of reality to the **Yeşilçam** style filmmaking. For the first time, the camera (the remarkable work of Enver Burçkin) is placed on the street successfully (**Faruk Kenç** had experimented with it in *Yılmaz Ali*, 1940) using eye-level shots. The chase scenes that carry the audience from one historical district to the other as the hero, Nazım (**Ayhan Işık**), jumps into trucks and barges or hides in trams, are superbly choreographed involving the city as an important part of the diegesis. The film is a pioneer in casting the majority of the actors without former training in theatre, hence ending the period of the influence of theatre on cinema, considered a handicap to its development. The inexperienced **Ayhan Işık** in the lead would eventually become an important star.

Nazım and Ayten (Gülistan Güzey) are a loving couple, whose happiness is endangered by evil elements – Ayten's sister Nezahat who is in love with Nazım and the suave playboy Halil, whose conspiracy will lead to tragedy. The film begins with the police giving five minutes to the criminal to surrender and book-ends with the same scene; the filmic duration of the five minutes constitutes 85 minutes with flashback sequences. The use of a wind-up duck to mark transitions is significant as tropes were rather rare for the period. Originally seen in Ayten's house before the start of the concert, it appears when Ayten accepts a ride with Halil (**Muzaffer Tema**) to Nazım's repair shop, then Nezahat (Neşe Yulaç) plays with it while suggesting to Halil to divide the couple and re-appears when Nazım returns home after having been seduced by Perihan (Pola Morelli).

The film is also significant as a social critique of the nascent capitalism and the decadence of the affluent followers of fashionable Western lifestyles, articulated with tango music. The familial surroundings are accompanied by classical Ottoman music, although the protagonists are at ease in both spaces.

Director: **Lütfi Ö. Akad**; Screenwriter: **Akad, Osman F. Seden**; Producer: **Osman F. Seden**, Şakir Seden; Production: Kemal Film; Cinematographer: Enver Burçkin; Sound: **Yorgo İlyadis**; Cast: **Ayhan Işık**, Gülistan Güzey, **Muzaffer Tema**, Neşe Yulaç, Pola Morelli, Settar Körmükçü, **Talât Artemel**, Muzazzez Alçay, **Nubar Terziyan**, Osman Alyanak, **Muhterem Nur**

Kaplanoğlu, Semih (b. İzmir, 1963) Director, screenwriter, producer, editor. Winner of the Golden Bear for *Bal / Honey* (2010) (the second for Turkey after **Metin Erksan**'s *Susuz Yaz / A Dry Summer*, 1963), Semih Kaplanoğlu graduated from the Cinema and Television Department of the Nine September University in İzmir with the 16mm, black-and-white short, *Mobapp – Meşru Olmayan Bir Aşkın Parçalanmış Portreleri / Mobapp –The Fragmented Portraits of an Illicit Love* (1984) about a public servant's love for a shop dummy, a film with the influences of German expressionism. He worked as camera assistant, prepared cinema programmes for television, wrote and directed television series, made commercials and wrote articles on plastic arts and film in various journals before his first feature *Herkes Kendi Evinde / Away From Home* (2001). The film explored the notions of identity and belonging through the desperate journeys of three characters, an elderly man returning home after half a century of absence, a youth who has decided to leave the country and a young woman searching for her identity away from home. His second film, *Meleğin Düşüşü / Angel's Fall* (2004), a story of incest, probed into the darkness of the soul when home became 'uncanny'. Kaplanoğlu created the *Yusuf Trilogy* inspired by the *Apu Trilogy* of Satrajit Ray with influences of Turkish poetry. All three films are about the mother–son relationship. The form recalls Andrei Tarkovsky's freely autobiographical *Zerkalo / Mirror* (1975), narrating the life of a character as a child, an adolescent and an adult in his forties. Also evoking *Mirror* are the free flow of oneiric images; the blending of memories and fantasies; the employment of the sounds of nature; characters appearing and disappearing like 'the girl in the bookshop'; leitmotifs such as the stuttering child (in both cases, the problem resolves at the end when the director's message becomes clearer), the burlesque fall of the doctor in *Mirror* and the stationmaster (mother's love interest) in *Milk* and mostly, the construction of a unique sense of time, the past and the present existing instantaneously and informing the future. Conceived in reverse chronological order, *Yumurta / Egg* (2007) foregrounds the return of the prodigal son (an urban poet running a bookstore) to his rural roots; *Süt / Milk* (2008) takes place in a provincial town and presents the same character as an adolescent loner in the process of cutting his ties with his mother, while *Bal / Honey* (2010) focuses on the childhood of the character living on the edge of the forest and the unexpected loss of his idolized father. Despite the difference of a certain number of years in between, which is subtly indicated through costumes and objects, each film maintains the present reality. In the absence of past/present dichotomy, time extends over a flat surface in a Bergsonian sense, past and present existing symbiotically on the same plane in a process of 'becoming'. 'The past co-exists with the present it has been' (Deleuze 2005: 80). Space gradually shifts from the city to the town and to the mysterious forest, bringing another dimension, which Kaplanoğlu defines as 'spiritual realism' and the trilogy aims at approaching metaphorically to the spirit of the world, to spirituality that is slowly diminishing and through nature, to reach unspoiled essence. Contrary to the tendency of the contemporary Turkish cinema (**Ceylan**) to link the provincial with ennui, Kaplanoğlu asserts that *ennui* is identified by the exterior gaze when the provincial is regarded with distance. In his films the province is like the uterus, the point of departure; for the one at the centre, it carries an element of nostalgia, connected with a sense of belonging. Home is the central motif; it appears in a different form in each film, culminating in the natal home of Yusuf.

Kaplanoğlu does not use non-diegetical music/sound. He prefers to establish a relationship with the different sounds of space and nature – sounds that pass unnoticed in daily life. Digital effects do not interest him. He would rather 'record' time, at times blurring screen time with real time. In *Angel's Fall*, the influence of Balthaus paintings is dominant. For the trilogy, Kaplanoğlu admits to have added the expressionists as well as Camille Pissarro and Gustave Courbet to expose the rapid change of the Anatolian rural landscape, which is the focus of *Milk*. Religious narratives are used to evoke concepts. Epilepsy (with resonances of Dostoevsky) is employed as a motif (or point of contact according to Kaplanoğlu) that marks critical points of transformation (Dönmez-Colin 2012, 154–7).

Kara Çarşaflı Gelin / The Bride in Black Chadoor aka ***The Dark Veiled Bride*** (1975), based on three stories of Bekir Yıldız, narrates in a semi-documentary style, problems in the south-east of Turkey – the blood feuds and smugglings, the feudal oppression of the landless and the patriarchal traditions that destroy the lives of women. Little Güllüşan is given to the family of the murder victim to protect her brother from the blood feud and she is treated badly by the victim's wife Zara. When the landlord who resists the land reforms kills Zara's older son Müslim, her younger son Vakkas confronts the landlord and Güllüşan kills the landlord while trying to protect her beloved Vakkas. In the patriarchal feudal system, when the issue is oppression of the landlord or the dictates of the customs, women are expected to self-sacrifice (***Bedrana***, 1974).

The script of Marxist intellectual **Vedat Türkali** underscores corruption at higher levels as responsible for the oppression of the less advantaged, with a message that as long as the rulers seek self-interests, exploitation will not be eliminated. While **porno films** had free reign, this film was censored three times, and was only released after a grant of clearance by the Supreme Court. During a period when the government was trying to thwart land reform projects, this was not a surprise.

Director: **Süreyya Duru**; Production: Murat Film; Screenwriter: **Vedat Türkali**; Cinematographer: Ali Uğur; Cast: Hakan Balamir, Semra Özdamar, **Aytaç Arman**, **Aliye Rona**, Hüseyin Peyda, Zülfikar Divani, İhsan Yüce, Rengin Arda

Karabey, Hüseyin (b. Istanbul, 1970) Director, screenwriter, producer, cinematographer, editor, activist. One of the leading members of the generation that has followed the **New Turkish Cinema** movement, with stories that rely on a political agenda, Kurdish film-maker Hüseyin Karabey graduated from the Film and Television Department of Marmara University. Before his accomplished feature film, ***Gitmek / My Marlon and Brando*** (2008), he directed short films and documentaries, mostly about human rights abuses, among which *Boran* (1999), a four-episode tragedy, is about three political activists, 'disappeared' during custody and their mothers, the title referring to wild pigeons that cannot be tamed.

When the Turkish government decided to 'improve' the jails according to Western standards, he made *Sessiz Ölüm / Silent Death* (2001) about the prison system, shot in five countries, including the US, and in 2012 returned to the same theme with eight other film-makers with *F Tipi Film / F-Type Film. Hiç Bir Karanlık Unutturamaz / No Darkness Will Make Us Forget* (2011), an animation film about the funeral of the Armenian journalist Hrant Dink with only the voice of his widow, was very powerful. He has also made a documentary about the German dancer, Pina Bausch, *Pina Bausch ile Bir Nefes / A Breath with Pina Bausch* (2005), shot during her visit to Istanbul. *Bir Hayatı Masal Gibi Anlatmak / Life is a Fable, a Narrative* (2012) is another documentary about a theatre personality who enters the character of Frieda Kahlo while impersonating her and her own life also follows a similar pattern. His second feature, *Sesime Gel / Come to My Voice* is in post-production.

Karanlık Sular / The Serpent's Tale (1994), the debut feature of multi-media artist, **Kutluğ Ataman** is the first Turkish film to be included in the archives of the Oscar Academy, the recipient of several awards and on the way to becoming a cult classic. Combining political allegory with escapist **fantasy**-horror, it is also an attempt to apply Western-style filmmaking to an Eastern narrative. The web of intrigue and mystery is woven through ancient catacombs and fortresses and extravagant villas to challenge the spectator to reflect on the current political themes of the Islamic world through the story of the first female calligrapher of

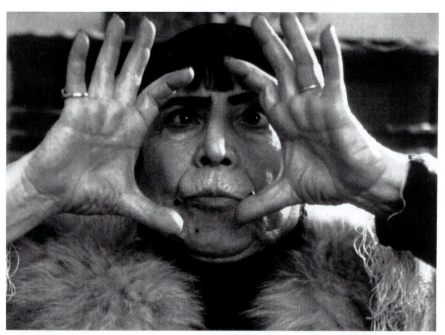

Figure 67 Karanlık Sular / The Serpent's Tale (Kutluğ Ataman, 1994) (Courtesy of Kutluğ Ataman)

Turkey whose futuristic novel was eaten by her servant. In the opening scenes, Arabic writing coalesces to form the image of a face, challenging the Islamic taboo of creating an image – especially the face and the eyes. A traditional heretic art form, Turkish Islamic calligraphy uses ornamental Arabic script decoratively to create a text, which could also be viewed as an image. (**Ataman** carries this motif further in his video installations.) The cast includes Semiha Berksoy, the opera diva who is the protagonist of **Ataman**'s 7 hours and 42 minutes long performance film, *Kutluğ Ataman's semiha b. Unplugged* (1997–98). The labyrinthine Istanbul with secret passages evokes the Orientalist gaze of Alain Robbe-Grillet (*L'immortelle / The Immortal*, 1963), among others, presenting the city as mystical but uncanny; the city underneath the city and under the waters of the Bosphorus evoke Orhan Pamuk's *Black Book* (1990). Some of the issues – lost manuscripts, secret religions, dungeon rituals, the vampire hero that dies after lifting his eyes to the minaret – are rather prosaic although **Ataman** tries to bring a new perspective to the clichés. The love story between a neurotic mother and her vampire son suggests a double entendre – the dark waters in the Turkish title, referring to the waters of the Bosphorus, could also be a trope for amniotic fluid. With collision of different worlds and cultures (East/West, living/dead, old/new) meeting, merging or consuming one another as the central motif, *The Serpent's Tale* is a contemporary Gothic film that underscores the liminal position of modern Turkey trying to balance the glories of the past with the demands of the present, just like the protagonist Lamia, caught between traditions and modernity. For **Ataman**, 'it's a film about Istanbul, and its disappearance' (Dönmez-Colin 2012: 136).

Director, Screenwriter, Producer: **Kutluğ Ataman**; Production: Temaşa Film; Cinematographer: Chris Squires; Editor: Annabel Ware; Sound Design: Blake Leyh; Cast: Gönen Bozbey, Metin Uygun, Daniel Chace, Semiha Berksoy, Eric Pio

Karanlıkta Uyananlar / Those Awakening in the Dark (1964), a film made in the **social realist** style with the collaboration of several left-wing artists, deals with the social consequences of a strike at a paint factory. The title refers to workers who wake up before dawn and metaphorizes their political awakening. The opening images of the misty skyline of Istanbul at dawn with the slums, the factory chimneys and the anonymous workers hurrying in a mechanical rhythm set the tone. The paint industry, which exploits both the workers and the financial resources of the state, is the main target and just as in **Ertem Göreç**'s earlier film ***Otobüs Yolcuları / The Bus Passengers*** (1961), 'Those who unite do not lose' is the message. Despite the dark tone, the strike action gives some relief and the parallel love stories of childhood friends from different classes – the welder and the rich man's son – with girls from their own class, add the romantic element. The film presents the artist as superficial, irresponsible and removed from the society and the reality of daily life, caricaturizing the character of the woman painter. Just as in several other **Yeşilçam** films, the poor neighbourhoods are depicted as friendly communities where people protect each other. The rich are isolated, alienated and alone.

Unlike *The Bus Passengers*, the characters in *Those Awakening in the Dark* are multifaceted. The protagonist, the son of the factory owner, is modest, but when he inherits the throne of power he follows the status quo, sacrificing the workers including his childhood friend, the welder. On the other hand, the brave welder who has achieved class awareness can easily become destructive and degenerate. At the end, the rich man returns to his agreeable old self and the welder sees his mistakes and joins the good ones although the advice of one of the older workers, 'Everyone is human according to where they live', resonates throughout the film.

The subject was a novelty for Turkish cinema, although not for real life. A year earlier, with the leadership of **Metin Erksan** and the support of **Göreç**, a devout unionist, the first Union of Film Workers (Sine-İş) was founded and soon after the set-workers went on strike. Although they were not able to achieve a contract, they sowed the seeds for action. Twelve years later, in 1975, after four months of negotiation, a contract was signed.

The film is the outcome of much research by the director and the scriptwriter about the logistics of the industry, the raw material used to make paint, where it was obtained, the cost, the state's relations with those who produced the paint and similar technical and bureaucratic aspects. For the intellectuals of the 1960s, the film was a source of pride. However, the blockades in front of cinema halls by sympathizers of the governing party, the struggles with **censorship** including the recall after the awards at the Golden Orange Film Festival in Antalya in 1965 (Best Script, Best Music, Best Third Film) were debilitating for the film-makers. It was finally released for distribution after the approval of the Ministry of the Interior.

Director, Editor: **Ertem Göreç**; Producer: **Lütfi Ö. Akad**, Beklan Algan; Production: Filmo Ltd.: Screenwriter: **Vedat Türkali**; Cinematographer: Turgut Ören, Mahmut Demir; Music: Nedim Otyam; Cast: **Fikret Hakan**, Beklan Algan, **Ayla Algan**, **Kenan Pars**

Karatma Geceleri / Blackout Nights (1990) is based on the eponymous autobiographical novel (1974) of Rıfat Ilgaz about a poet on the run from the police with charges of communism, accrued due to his poetry book *Sınıf / Class* (the actual title of Ilgaz's censored book) before the end of World War II. The film opens with still images of 1940s Istanbul in sepia accompanied by classical Turkish music of the period, which abruptly cuts to colour images of a doctor examining the back of the protagonist, Mustafa Ural (**Tarık Akan**), the poet wanted for publishing an objectionable book in a period of witch hunts for communists. His collaborators from the journal he publishes have already been arrested and tortured. He moves in the dark, trying to rely on friends, some of whom can be disloyal to protect their interests. State fascism is brewing in the dark, or blaring from the radio as Turkey's ally Germany is about to lose the war. The tight security measures including curfews and blackouts create a claustrophobic atmosphere where many are tortured in police custody without a trial. Ironically, the protagonist is arrested when the war is over.

The film exposes a country torn by poverty – low wages, a shortage of wood to burn, rationing of food, including bread. The 'national chief' (President İsmet İnönü) has decided to support Hitler. The war news is followed through newsreels

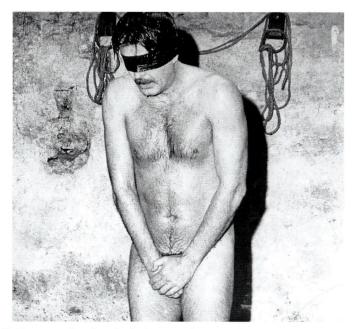

Figure 68 Karatma Geceleri / Blackout Nights (Yusuf Kurçenli, 1990) (Courtesy of International Istanbul Film Festival)

that precede feature films in the theatres while *ezan* is chanted in Turkish from the minarets (which lasted 18 years, 1932–50, returning to Arabic). The main trope, the blackout, refers to the severe censorship of artists and writers and their torture in custody, the bad lungs of the protagonist representing the sick atmosphere of the country. The image of him prostrate on the cold stone of the *hamam* (the Turkish bath) is like a premonition. The scene when he is blindfolded and stripped of his clothes for humiliation; his realization of the betrayal of his wife with his soldier friend, İlhan, in the last scene when he is unexpectedly brought to trial and sees her waiting, not for him, but for İlhan, who is charged with embezzlement, are strong moments of the film. The character of a German communist dissident who declares that ideology comes before nationalism and is happy when his country loses the war to put an end to Hitler's fascism, is well drawn.

Considered the *chef-d'oeuvre* of **Yusuf Kurçenli** and one of the boldest political films of Turkish cinema, *Blackout Nights* carries a film noir atmosphere with the long shots of night scenes under incessant rain showing men wearing long coats and fedora hats shadowing the fugitive. **Akan**'s measured acting creates an audience identification that draws parallels between the post-WWII and post-*coup-d'état* Turkey. The film received awards nationally and internationally.

Director, Screenwriter: **Yusuf Kurçenli**; Producer: Senar Turgut; Production: Senar Film; Cinematographer: Colin Maunier; Editor: İsmail Kalkan; Music: Cem İdiz; Cast: **Tarık Akan**, Nurseli İdiz; Bülent Bilgiç, Deniz Kurtoğlu, Gülsen Tuncer, Gökhan Mete, Erol Günaydın, **Menderes Samancılar**

Karılar Koğuşu / Women's Jail (1989), inspired by the letters of **Kemal Tahir** from jail to the outlawed communist poet Nazım Hikmet, takes place in a prison in the provincial town of Malatya in the oppressive atmosphere of the 1940s, when İsmet İnönü is the president. Writer Murat (**Kadir İnanır**) is imprisoned for 15 years for the objectionable books found in his house. In his cell, he reads Ziya Gökalp, a nationalist writer who advocated 'becoming Turkish, Muslim and modern' while a picture of Nazım Hikmet, with whom he is corresponding, hangs on the wall. As a man of conscience, he scribes for the illiterate women to help them contest their sentences instead of trying to find a solution to his situation and chats with the warden uneasy with the Hat Reform of Kemal Atatürk, the modernity imposed from above: 'I cannot remember the front and the back of this damned hat. Evidently, not something one is used to...' While the writer sits outside of his cell with the wardens, the women stay inside their quarter, the seductive prostitute Tözey (**Hülya Koçyiğit**) reading the coffee cups; they all listen to the same music.

With the reforms of the new republic, the status of the women has begun to change and a new employee is a woman, but **Refiğ** is harsh on her character. 'The government gave permission to women to work and I was saved', she declares, happy to stay away from her husband and six children. She wants to liberate herself from the clutches of a marriage to a poor and helpless man and have lovers, a typical stand of male film-makers who systematically equate women's liberation with sexual liberation. She is a bad woman, who spends her money on gold teeth instead of feeding her children and elopes with the warden to use his money. The benevolent writer does not want to help her to get her divorce. Family values must be preserved. Even a woman who poisoned her husband with her young lover gets better treatment, but she must die for justice to prevail. In a masterfully choreographed scene, she is pulled out of her bed half-naked in degradation, gagged to buffer her screams and dragged by men in front of the writer who observes but cannot interfere. The hangman does not have the heart to accomplish the deed; the warden pulls the rope over her head.

According to doyen critic Atilla Dorsay, to see from a film-maker like **Refiğ**, who always had faith in the institution and ideology of the state, a film that severely criticizes the state policy and its applications that send many writers, artists and workers to the dungeon, is remarkable (Dorsay 2004). The film won five awards at the 27th Antalya Golden Orange Film Festival including the Best Film and was successful at the box-office.

Director, Screenwriter: **Halit Refiğ**; Producer: **Türker İnanoğlu**; Production: Erler Film; Cinematographer: Çetin Gürtop; Music: Melih Kibar; Cast: **Kadir İnanır**, **Hülya Koçyiğit**, **Perihan Savaş**, Tuncer Necmioğlu, **Erol Taş**, Ayşegül Ünsal

Karpuz Kabuğundan Gemiler Yapmak / Boats Out of Watermelon Rinds (2004) is a nostalgic film about the film-maker's adolescence as a peasant boy engrossed with cinema. During the summer vacation, Recep (İsmail Hakkı Taslak) and Mehmet (Kadir Kaymaz) tread the dirt road to town each day to earn some money. Mehmet is apprenticed to a mean barber (**Ahmet Uluçay**) whereas Recep works for the mild-mannered watermelon vendor. The town seems emptied of its inhabitants,

Figure 69 Karpuz Kabuğundan Gemiler Yapmak / Boats Out of Watermelon Rinds (Ahmet Uluçay, 2004) (Courtesy of International Istanbul Film Festival)

or this is **Ahmet Uluçay**'s way of showing the stagnation of the province in 1960s Turkey, where the only escape for precocious boys whose imaginations travel far with the trains they regularly watch, is the movies. **Uluçay** once said he would commit suicide if he did not make movies. However, unlike most 'cinema on cinema' films, the boys are more interested in the workings of the procedure rather than the movie itself. They want to make a projector to move the images. Recep is often busy trying to imagine the frame with his hands. The scenes when they stare at a still image of the sea inside the barn and pretend they are lying on a beach or when Recep narrates a magnificent story, are signs of an auteur in the making. **Uluçay**'s alter ego appears as the 'fool', the epileptic Ömer (a mild reproach to his villagers for treating him like a fool all these years). The boys are constantly reminded by the girls and the local merchants that the town is not the village; they should go where they belong – the fields. 'We'll work like a dog and they'll take the pictures', resumes Recep when the photo shop owner sends them away. Even today, not many village boys become artists, painters or film-makers.

Boats Out of Watermelon Rinds carries the enthusiasm, honesty and naivety (in a positive sense) of an autodidact who tells a universal story using the local colour that is drawn through observations of his keen eye as an insider. It is as sharp as the picture of a watermelon Recep makes that his boss admits one cannot differentiate from the real.

The only feature of the director who passed away subsequently, the film received numerous national and international awards including the Jury Special Prize at the San Sebastian Film Festival and Montpellier Mediterranean Film Festival's Golden Antigone for Best Film.

Figure 70 Karpuz Kabuğundan Gemiler Yapmak / Boats Out of Watermelon Rinds (Ahmet Uluçay, 2004) (Courtesy of International Istanbul Film Festival)

Director, Screenwriter: **Ahmet Uluçay**; Producers: Serdar Tahiroğlu, Diloy Gülün; Production: İFR; Cinematographer: İlker Berke; Editor: **Mustafa Preshava**, Senad Preshava; Music: Ender Akay, Alper Tunga Demirel; Cast: İsmail Hakkı Taslak, Kadir Kaymaz, Gülayşe Erkoç, Aysel Yılmaz, Boncuk Yılmaz, Hasbiye Günay, **Ahmet Uluçay**

Kasaba / The Small Town (1997), the first film of what this author considers a tetralogy comprising *Mayıs Sıkıntısı / Clouds of May* (1999), *Uzak / Distant* (2002) and *İklimler / Climates* (2006) that could be called 'A Portrait of the Provincial Artist as an Urban Intellectual' questions identity and belonging through the childhood of **Ceylan** and his sister Emine, underscoring memory and temporality. Time and remembrance is essential to the film. Evoking Andrei Tarkovsky in *Zerkalo / The Mirror* (1973), Ceylan delves into the personal histories of his characters. The grandfather (Mehmet Emin Ceylan) reflects on the passage of time, reminiscing about his adventures abroad as a young soldier and prisoner. The grandmother (Fatma Ceylan) laments the loss of a prodigal son. The father, the educated man who has seen the world but returned home (the alter ego of Ceylan's father) pours his knowledge to the disinterested. The cynical nephew Saffet (Mehmet Emin Toprak), abandoned by his father, suffocates without prospects, playing the devil's advocate and little Ali's dreams are burdened by the guilt of his cruelty to a turtle. Within the actual time frame of the late 1990s, **Ceylan** sculpts three different levels of temporality – the grandfather's 'past', during the depression years of World War I; the father's 'past', the post-World War II Turkey, underdeveloped and poor, and the children's 'present', the 1970s. Real-life recollections and memories of **Ceylan**'s family, childhood dreams and fantasies merge with the actual present. Just as in the

Figure 71 Kasaba / The Small Town (Nuri Bilge Ceylan, 1997) (Courtesy of International Istanbul Film Festival)

Italian neo-realist movement and the French *nouvelle vague*, the image becomes *time-image*, the screen as 'the cerebral membrane where immediate and direct confrontations take place between the past and the future, the inside and the outside' (Deleuze 2005: 121). The fluidity of *thought-images* (*thought*-waves) circulates in the time-memory universe of Ceylan's mind.

Figure 72 Kasaba / The Small Town (Nuri Bilge Ceylan, 1997) (Courtesy of International Istanbul Film Festival)

Although the general structure is day succeeded by night, the narrative follows the four seasons that smoothly merge. Just like Tarkovsky, what interests Ceylan is not the specific sequences progressing in time, but the rhythm itself. Snow falling gently as observed through the classroom window flows into the images of the plum trees in the spring as the children wander in the fields and to summer by the time they reach the meeting ground of the family, then autumn, when they are back indoors, completing the cycle of seasons–life.

Based on the short story, *Cornfields*, written by **Ceylan**'s sister, Emine Ceylan, the film starts with the children playing in the snow, intercut with the shots of Saffet observing from the corner of the frame. The rural classroom sequences have an ethereal quality, 'pure recollection images', summoned from the depths of memory (Deleuze 2005: 51–2), but selectively. Intangible objects (a flying feather) and sounds – drops of water from wet socks hissing on the stove, a squeaking door, chirping birds and the familiar refrain of incomprehensible textbooks – revive the calm and compassion (where even a late arrival is not reprimanded) of the past before the loss of innocence. The idyllic outdoor scenes of spring echo the re-birth of nature with the plum trees offering their fruit albeit in a graveyard, the ancient tombs with Arabic inscriptions reminding one of the inescapable presence of death. The seemingly idyllic family gathering in the summer in the cornfields is marred by the memory of a dead son as well as other issues, from mundane – inflation, unemployment – to spiritual – the ways of an unjust god who would take the life of an innocent child – the loneliness of each member manifesting itself in silent tears. The indoor ending is sombre with thoughts of death and dying.

The question of belonging to a homeland and the possibility of return, which **Ceylan** develops further in *Mayıs Sıkıntısı / Clouds of May* (1999) and *Uzak / Distant* (2002), is introduced during the discussion. Saffet, the outsider, always positioned on the edge of the frame, is perhaps the young **Ceylan**, who wants to escape, 'I don't want to stay here for the rest of my life'. The rest of the dialogue is more like an interior monologue of coming to terms with the joys and pains of leaving home: 'Trees on the right, trees on the left'; 'Why do you speak so *distant*?'; 'One says, "my tree, my earth"'; 'What's the difference if you're buried under your own earth when you're dead? The earth is the same earth.' Motifs relating to home occur periodically in the film, such as the turtle that carries his home on his back, or the stork that flies away but comes back to the same spot.

Made with a budget of $15,000 using friends and family as actors, *The Small Town* received accolades at film festivals (including the Caligari Prize, Berlin 1998) with its remarkable photography (largely still camera shots) and stylized poetry.

Director, Producer, Screenwriter, Cinematographer: **Nuri Bilge Ceylan**; Production: NBC Film; Editors: Ayhan Ergürsel, **Nuri Bilge Ceylan**; Sound: Mustafa Bölükbaşı, Ergun Ünal; Cast: Mehmet Emin Toprak, Mehmet Emin Ceylan, Sercihan Alloğlu, Semra Yılmaz, Havva Sağlam, Cihat Bütün, Latif Altıntaş, Muzeffer Özdemir

Kaşık Düşmanı / Spoon Enemy aka *A Wedding Room* (1984), referring to an old adage in its title, which delegates women to the position of 'a mouth to feed', satirizes the helplessness of men when all the women of a village, except a half-wit, die in a gas explosion. A black **comedy**, the film marks **Bilge Olgaç**'s return to cinema after the 1970s crisis in **Yeşilçam**. Inspired by an actual event, it denounces the secondary position of women in the rural milieu despite their indispensible participation in the economy. A gas tube explodes during a wedding party with only women and children as guests and almost all are killed. The village men, accustomed to spend the day in the local café while the women work in the fields and in the house, are helpless in performing the simplest daily chores, most of which, such as fetching water from the fountain, are considered as feminine. Attempts at procuring wives from the next village fail since the bride money has risen with the high demand. **Olgaç** exposes the weakness of macho men and satirizes their masculinist mentality through crafty use of the male point of view in the narrative although the men in the film are so entrenched in their ways that one wonders if they learn a lesson from the experience.

As a politically engaged film-maker, **Olgaç** also draws attention to class differences and the gap between the urban and rural through secondary characters – a journalist and his wife – while drawing attention to the Orientalist gaze of the West, which is also exploitative. The German film crew stages a mock wedding between the groom who has lost his bride to the accident and one of their members for a documentary and drop the young man when their mission is accomplished.

At the 7th International Women's Film Festival in Créteil, France, *Spoon Enemy* won the Best Film and the French Journalists' Special Press Awards and Halil Ergün was chosen as the Best Actor by the audience.

Director, Screenwriter: **Bilge Olgaç**; Producer: Mehmet Ali Yılmaz; Cinematographer: Ümit Gülsoy; Music: Mutlu Torun; Cast: **Perihan Savaş**, Halil Ergün, **Aliye Rona**, Seden Kızıltunç, İsmet Ay

Katırcılar / The Muleteers (1987), a forerunner to Bahman Ghobadi's *Zamani baraye masti asbha / A Time For Drunken Horses* (2000), shows the harsh living conditions of the Kurds in border towns, forced into smuggling for a living. Working for the local merchants who will not acknowledge them in daylight, the smugglers are informed to the authorities and caught. On a three-day journey in a blizzard, three handcuffed men and four gendarmes try to reach the town for the trial, accompanied by Ayşegül, a woman journalist from Istanbul, sent to concoct a sensational story. She eventually foregoes her ambitions and serves as a catalyst to instigate the human qualities in both the soldiers with the guns and the smugglers with the handcuffs.

The film wagers the Kurdish smugglers, poor landless peasants forgotten by the state in a struggle to earn their bread, against the pretentious and corrupt bureaucrats and merchants. The images of the village men sitting in cafés where women are not admitted, except the outsider, and the caricaturization of small bureaucrats competing for the attention of a woman from the city, are critical of the machismo. The soldiers on duty, however, caught between orders and their conscience, are shown in a humanistic light. One is from Diyarbakır, most likely a Kurd, another is from Istanbul with 26 days to his release. In the shelter, they play yes/no game for a coca cola; look at the family pictures and pray side by side with the prisoners. What separates them is the uniform. Lost in the blizzard, they ask the prisoners for direction, who fake ignorance. Rüstem (**Kadir İnanır**) is told his handcuffs will be unlocked if he promises not to escape, but he is not a hypocrite. Worried about his sick daughter, he will escape to visit her.

Under the oppressive conditions of the period, the smugglers, played by Turkish actors, are not given Kurdish names, but their identity is obvious in the way they dress and the way they interact with the authorities. They are called 'the mountain people' by the soldiers, a derogatory term for the Kurds. Some of the dialogue during their interrogation is rather tongue in cheek: The commandant: 'Why do you carry a gun?' The smugglers: 'There are bandits, wolves, "the anarchists" (referring to the Kurdish guerrillas).' The commandant: 'Do you get involved in such things, anarchy–*manarchy*?' Of course, not!!

Using the blizzard as a trope for the condition of the country, the film sends a message of peace by stressing the possibility of human nature to overcome differences if given the chance, otherwise the oppressor and the oppressed are both doomed.

Director: **Şerif Gören**; Screenwriters: Hüseyin Kuzu and Eyüp Halit Türkyazıcı (based on a short story by Fırat Çelik); Producers: Kadir and Ferit Turgut; Production: Uzman Film; Cinematographer: Erdal Kahraman; Editor: Veli Akbaşlı; Cast: Halil Ergün, **Kadir İnanır**, Ayşegül Aldinç, Necmettin Çobanoğlu, Bülent Bilgiç

Kavur, Ömer (b. Ankara, 1944 – d. Istanbul, 2005) Director, producer, screenwriter. Considered the first *auteur* of modern Turkish cinema, the most distinct characteristic of Ömer Kavur's cinema is the journey. This journey may stretch over kilometres as in *Amansız Yol / Desperate Road* (1985); it may take place inside the individual as in ***Anayurt Oteli / Motherland Hotel*** (1987) or as in ***Gizli Yüz / The Secret Face*** (1991), the actual journey may serve as a trope – the pendulum and the clock becoming a leitmotiv in a mystical exploration of the spatio-temporal. The presence of clocks in civic buildings, clock towers in public squares as well as individual timepieces is a signature motif for Kavur, but also an emblem of the new era within the Turkish historical context. Most clock towers that appear in Kavur's films were erected at the end of the nineteenth century, shaping the development of modern Turkish culture and the process of Westernization, of which cinema was also a part. Kavur's characters are isolated and alone, which leads them to self-reckoning. He tries to understand society through the oppression it exercises on individuals.

Kavur studied in Paris at the IDHEC (Institut des Hautes Etudes Cinématographiques) and received his training working with Bryan Forbes and Alain Robbe-Grillet. While watching three to four films during the day at the French cinemateque, for three years he worked on the night shifts of Paris hotels to support his studies, an experience that inspired the 'hotel' motif in his films. On his return to Turkey, Kavur made several documentaries and about 200 commercials before his first feature, *Yatık Emine / Emine, the Leaning One* (1974), with which he contested the established clichés of the commercial **Yeşilçam** about women

Figure 73 Yusuf ile Kenan / Yusuf and Kenan (Ömer Kavur, 1979) (Courtesy of International Istanbul Film Festival)

and prostitution. *Yusuf ile Kenan / Yusuf and Kenan* (1979) drew attention to the social and economical malaise of unwanted children and the plight of desperate migrants in the merciless metropolis ('They keep coming... breeding anarchists'). The film was banned when the screening was attacked by fascist elements.

Entering the industry as a 'schooled' film-maker, rather than following the prevalent master–apprentice tradition and resisting the star system alienated Kavur. Yet, he succeeded independently, particularly during a period of transition from the **social realist** films inspired by **Yılmaz Güney**'s *Umut / The Hope* (1970) to a more personal *auteur* cinema (interrelating with the period of de-politicization following the 1980 *coup d'état*), which found its best idiom in his works. His intimate and self-reflexive films, although socially relevant and ideologically committed, have appealed to like-minded individuals rather than targeting mass audiences.

In *Motherland Hotel*, considered his *chef-d'œuvre*, a hotel manager's isolation takes psychopathological dimensions. *Gizli Yüz / The Secret Face* (1991) and *Akrebin Yolculuğu / Journey on the Clock-hand* (1997) follow the interior journey of the protagonist through an actual journey that extends to remote towns of Anatolia, carrying the same motif of provincial hotels that shelter but also threaten, an appropriate trope for 'motherland'. As the photographer of *The Secret Face* searches for letters to decipher in the faces, the repairman in *Journey on the Clock-hand* looks for clocks to repair to revive the time that has stopped. The obsessive love of Zebercet for the mysterious woman who arrives with 'the delayed Ankara train', the photographer's love for the elusive woman and the passion of the repairman for a married woman are manifestations of the hopelessness of love, but also the impossibility of communication, one of the fundamental themes of Kavur's work.

According to Kavur, the clock, 'which defines old time and new time, is the concept of change, its meaning imbedded in our anachronistic situation: Turkey is an Eastern country with deep-rooted traditions, which are constantly changing with the influence of the West; there is a point of clash, or harmony' (Tan 1991: 56). The character in search (a person, or the truth through that person) could be the alter ego of the film-maker. 'Cinema itself is a search…but the search is one of the primal forces of life…therefore the resemblance of the character in the film to the character behind the camera is normal and healthy' (Selçuk 1997: 14).

While the uncanny side of the metropolis is underscored in *Yusuf and Kenan, Ah, Güzel İstanbul / Oh, Beautiful Istanbul* (1981) and *Körebe / Blindfold* (1984), small town malaise is focal in *Kırık Bir Aşk Hikayesi / A Broken Love Story* (1982) recounting a doomed love affair, **Motherland Hotel** and **Journey on the Clock-hand**. *Amansız Yol / Desperate Road* (1985), a thriller with a social base, draws a panorama of the country from Istanbul to Mardin, not as a tool to embellish the narrative but as a commentary on the society. *Gece Yolculuğu / Night Journey* (1987), 'a critique of a system that defends wrong values and therefore fails' according to Kavur, 'is a very personal film that is not autobiographical'. *Buluşma / Meeting* is a short film that Kavur contributed to *Aşk Üzerine Söylenmemiş Herşey / Everything Untold about Love* (1996), a portmanteau project comprising five films by five directors.

Melekler Evi / The House of Angels (2000), which Kavur defined as a 'Turkish style *film noir*' and 'a Baroque story of black passion with a dose of violence' carries the photographer motif of *The Secret Face* and shares similarities with the earlier film in terms of its music, but the social malaise of drug trafficking is the major feature of the narrative, which brings the film closer to the thriller **genre** with political overtones.

Stressing the importance of the script, Kavur had a close relationship with literature. His films are collaborations with well-known authors and scriptwriters: *Emine, the Leaning One*, Refik Halit Karay; *Oh, Beautiful Istanbul* (1981) Füruzan; *A Broken Love Story* (1982) and *Göl / The Lake* (1982), Selim İleri; *Körebe / Blindfold* (1984) and *A Desperate Road* (1985), **Barış Pirhasan**; **Anayurt Oteli / Motherland Hotel** (1987), Yusuf Atılgan; *The Secret Face*, Orhan Pamuk; *Journey on the Clock-hand*, **Macit Koper**; *The House of Angels*, Feride Çiçekoğlu, although he always maintained control over the final product.

Karşılaşma / Encounter (2002), Kavur's last film, is a psychological drama about life, love and overlapping destinies woven around his signature motif of quest. The story, originally suggested by Orhan Pamuk for **The Secret Face**, is narrated by a chemotherapy patient.

The great film-maker who once said, 'Lack of communication is the most important chronic illness of our time' and reflected the sense of alienation, isolation and exclusion of man in all his work, died of lymph node cancer at the age of 61.

Kaygun, Şahin (b. Adana, 1951 – d. Istanbul, 1992) Director, screenwriter, producer, actor, art director, photographer, graphic designer. A remarkable photographer, responsible for the first Polaroid exhibition in Turkey and the founder of the advertising company, Art Film, Şahin Kaygun's first film was a period piece about the first Muslim Turkish woman to appear on stage, *Afife Jale* (1987) starring **Müjde Ar** in the title role. He directed, scripted and produced *Dolunay / Full Moon* (1987), an intimate film on the psychological problems of a woman artist. He was also the art director in ***Anayurt Oteli / Motherland Hotel*** (**Kavur**, 1987) and *Adı Vasfiye / Her Name is Vasfiye* (**Yılmaz**, 1985).

Kenç, Faruk (b. Bingazi, 1910 – d. Istanbul, 2000) Director, producer, screenwriter, cinematographer. The nephew of Enver Pasha, the founder of the Central Army Office of Cinema, Faruk Kenç is an important name of the transition period that terminated The Period of Theatre Man of **Muhsin Ertuğrul**. He was educated at the Bavarian State School of Photography. His *Dertli Pınar / The Troubled Spring* (1943) was the first fully dubbed film, ending the period of sound films that lasted between 1932–43. Kenç introduced new faces through competitions – **Belgin Doruk**, **Ayhan Işık**. One of the founders of the Producers of National Film Association, he made 26 black-and-white films, starting with *Taş Parçası / Piece of Stone* (1938), an adaptation from renowned author Reşat Nuri Güntekin, and stopping in 1964 after *Çöl Kanunu / The Law of the Desert* (unofficial English title). He is also the director of the first detective film of Turkey, *Yılmaz Ali* (1941). Most of his films are lost.

Kenter, Müşfik (Galip) (b. Istanbul, 1932 – d. Istanbul, 2012) Actor, dubbing artist. One of the best character actors of Turkish theatre and cinema, Müşfik Kenter started his career with the state theatre in 1955, moving on to private theatre in 1959 with his sister, **Yıldız Kenter** and working with **Muhsin Ertuğrul**. In 1962, with **Yıldız Kenter**, he established the Kent Players. His memorable roles on stage include in Anton Chekhov's *The Seagull*, Edward Albee's *Who's Afraid of Virgina Woolf?*, William Shakespeare's *Hamlet* and Bertolt Brecht's *Three Penny Opera*. His *Bir Garip Orhan Veli / A Strange Orhan Veli* was staged for over a quarter of a century. Among his distinguished roles in cinema are in *Murtaza* (**Tunç Başaran**, 1965), ***Sevmek Zamanı / A Time to Love*** (**Metin Erksan**, 1965), *Üç Arkadaş* (**Memduh Ün**, 1971), *Hayallerim Aşkım ve Sen* (**Atıf Yılmaz**, 1987) and *Piano, Piano Bacaksız* (**Tunç Başaran**, 1991). He also appeared in several television series and taught theatre.

Kenter, Yıldız (b. Istanbul, 1928) Actor; RN: Ayşe Yıldız. One of the best character actors of Turkish theatre and cinema, Yıldız Kenter studied acting in New York. She is the co-founder of Kent Players with her brother, **Müşfik Kenter**. Among her numerous awards is Best Actress at the Bastia Film Festival in Corsica for her part in **Halit Refig**'s film *Hanım / The Lady* (1988).

Keskiner, Abdurrahman (b. Osmaniye, Adana, 1941) Producer. Originally a farmer, Keskiner started his film career during the shooting of *Dağların Oğlu /*

The Son of the Mountains (**Yılmaz Atadeniz**, 1965) when he met **Yılmaz Güney**. Soon he became **Güney**'s manager, eventually co-founding **Güney Film** and producing *Seyyit Han* aka *Toprağın Gelini / Seyyit Han* aka *The Bride of the Earth* (**Güney**, 1968). After *Umut / The Hope* (**Güney**, 1970), he established the Umut Film Company (1971). In the 1970s when the video market began to flourish, he joined the **arabesque** trend, producing films with star singers such as İbrahim Tatlıses. The first producer (with **Kenan Ormanlar** and Mehmet Soyarslan) to open a stand at the Cannes Film Festival (1981), Keskiner made numerous B-films to support the films of his dreams (Evren 2012: 146). The winner of numerous national and international awards, among other noteworthy films of Keskiner are *Hazal* (**Ali Özgentürk**, 1979) and *Muhsin Bey / Mr Muhsin* (**Yavuz Turgul**, 1987).

Kıral, Erden (b. Gölcük, 1942) Director, screenwriter, producer, film critic. One of the most important representatives of what is known as the middle generation, Erden Kıral started his career in a political climate of turbulence and excelled in **social realist** films. A Silver Bear winner at the Berlin Film Festival, *Hakkaride Bir Mevsim / A Season in Hakkari* (1983) is his *chef-d'oeuvre*. Educated in ceramics at the Academy of Fine Arts in Istanbul, Kıral began as a film critic and worked as a stage hand on the sets of **Bilge Olgaç** and **Vedat Türkali**, was assistant director in *Çalıkuşu / The Wren* (**Osman F. Seden**, 1966) and directed numerous commercials. He made four short films (all lost) before his first feature, *Kanal / The Channel* (1978) on the struggles and failure of an idealist government official against the established feudalistic structure in the rural milieu. Both *The Channel* and *Bereketli Topraklar Üzerinde / On Fertile Lands* (1979) foreground class differences and the oppression of the underprivileged but oppression by the oppressed is a prominent theme in the latter. Marxist theory, the committed cinema of **Yılmaz Güney** (*Umut / The Hope*, 1970) and the Brazilian *Cinema Novo*, particularly Glauber Rocha, are the major influences of Kıral's earlier work. Along with *Hakkaride Bir Mevsim / A Season in Hakkari* (1982), about an urban exile in a remote Anatolian village, they are major prototypes of Third Cinema in terms of addressing power structures, the oppression of the less advantaged and the issues of identity and belonging in situations of exclusion, exile and economic migration.

Despite the international accolades *A Season in Hakkari* brought, it was banned in Turkey along with *On Fertile Lands*, compelling Kıral to self-imposed exile in Germany, where he pursued his career resolutely on the burning issues of his mother country. With *Ayna / The Mirror* (1984) and *Dilan* (1986), still on the rural milieu, his camera shifted to personal stories, entering the private life of peasants ignored by the ideology, especially the plight of women, condemned to wait silently behind closed doors. The claustrophobic atmosphere of these films took a visibly political turn in *Av Zamanı / Time for Hunting* (1988), on the psychological traumas of the 1980 *coup d'état* and the contagious nature of terror. *Mavi Sürgün / The Blue Exile* (1993), inspired by the autobiography of an exiled intellectual, marks Kıral's return to his motherland. *Avcı / The Hunter* (1997), on the relativity of truth (relying heavily on Kurosawa's *Rachômon*, 1950) through a *ménage à trois* imbued in local legends, is a film Kıral would rather erase from his filmography. *Yolda / On the Way* (2005) is based on personal experiences with the legendary **Yılmaz Güney** regarding *Yol / The Way* (**Şerif Gören**, 1982), which was originally trusted to Kıral when it was called *Bayram*, but abandoned by **Güney** due to conflicts between the two directors. The film continues the theme of exile while exploring diverse aspects of freedom and imprisonment, physical, spiritual and metaphorical; the alienation of the intellectual in an industrialized society and a long journey that runs parallel to an interior journey of settling of accounts with the heavy burden of memories. Whereas in *Hakkari*, the journey ends in a world that contrasts the world of the intellectual, but also mirrors his soul and the journey in *The Blue Exile* culminates in the writer/intellectual becoming one with nature, in *On the Way*, overshadowed by the 1980 *coup d'état*, the journey of the film-maker/intellectual is endless, as reflected in the scene when the protagonist and his guards drive in circles in the heavy fog trying to find the prison that would incarcerate one of the most important artists of Turkey – **Yılmaz Güney**.

Vicdan / Conscience (2008), an action **melodrama** with overtures to his earlier engagé films, underlining the dehumanizing aspect of factory work, surprised his followers with its fast tempo, the lavish use of digital effects and the commercialized eroticism. *Yük / Load* (2012) was an attempt to combine labour consciousness concerning miners with a classic *ménage à trois* – the driving force of most films of Kıral.

Erden Kıral'dan Haliç / The Golden Horn from Erden Kıral (2010), a visual feast focusing on the multicultural texture of the historical area, combining documentary images with a fictional story of a Greek ex-resident returning to the city, is Kıral's only documentary. It was commissioned for the programme of Istanbul as the European Capital of Culture. Kıral is also the director of a medium-length film, *Ay Hikayeleri / Tales of The Moon* adapted from Hans Christian Andersen's *Tales of the Moon* and Alphonse Daudet's *The Mirror*, which is part of *Aşk Üzerine Söylenmemiş Herşey / Everything Untold About Love* (1996) comprising five films by five directors.

Kırmızıgül, Mahsun (b. Diyarbakır or Bingöl, 1969) Director, screenwriter, actor, composer, singer, producer, businessman; RN: Abdullah Bazencir. A popular Kurdish singer of the **arabesque genre** (16 million albums in eight years), Mahsun Kırmızıgül's first film, a **melodrama** called *Beyaz Melek / The White Angel* (2007) was successful at the box-office. *Güneşi Gördüm / I Saw the Sun* (2009) about the expulsion of a Kurdish family from south-eastern Anatolia, was in second place in the top ten, selling 2.5 million tickets. The film follows the official point of view. Laden with several sensitive issues, from human trafficking and child marriage to male chauvinism, what works in the film is the issue of homophobia. The episode about the transvestite brother involves a smartly choreographed chase through the bars in the back streets and a very dramatic finale when he is naked on the Galata Bridge. *New York'ta Beş Minare / Five Minarets in New York* (2010) starts with Islamophobia in the West and ends with a story of blood-feud in Anatolia, transmitting a blatant message of peace and love. Playing the lead role in all his films, Kırmızıgül also makes television series.

Kızılırmak Karakoyun / Red River Black Sheep (1967) is based on an Anatolian legend, narrated by Nazım Hikmet and adapted to cinema originally by **Muhsin Ertuğrul**. The re-make by **Lütfi Ö. Akad** is one of the most successful collaborations between **Akad** and **Yılmaz Güney** (their second), which played a role in the directing career of **Güney**. Shephard Ali Haydar (**Güney**) is in love with Hatice, the daughter of the nomad head, which does not comply with customs. Before he can have her, Ali Haydar has to cross the river with his sheep that will be fed salt for three days and nights without any of them drinking water. The feat is accomplished, but the head gives his daughter to the son of the highland rancher. With the nomads to support him, Ali Haydar meets the wedding procession on the bridge, which collapses during the scuffle and the lovers are drowned. Considered by some critics of its time as a trilogy (Anatolian Trilogy) with *Ana / The Mother* (1967) and ***Hudutların Kanunu / The Law of the Borders*** (1966), the film exposes the injustices of the feudal system that destroys everyone involved, the bridge serving as a trope, but indirectly alludes to the political circumstances of the period. Another re-make was made in 1993 by **Şahin Gök**.

Director, Screenwriter: **Lütfi Ö. Akad**; Producer: Kadir Kesemen; Production: Dadaş Film; Cinematographer: Ali Uğur; Editor: Diamani Filmeridis; Music: Orhan Gencebay, Abdullah Nail Bayşu; Cast: **Yılmaz Güney**, Nilüfer Koçyiğit, Kadir Savun, Osman Alyanak, Tuncer Necmioğlu, Senih Orkan, Murat Tok, Haluk Orçun

Kızıltan, Özer (b. Istanbul, 1963) Known internationally for ***Takva / Takva – A Man's Fear of God*** (2006), his first film that interrogated organized religion, Özer Kızıltan studied law at Istanbul University before switching to cinema and graduating in 1994 from the Cinema and Television Department of Mimar Sinan University. *Takva* brought several national and international awards, including the Fipresci at the 57th Berlin Film Festival, whereas his second film, *Beni Unutma / Don't Forget Me* (2011), a love story in the style of the **Yeşilçam melodramas**, did not receive the same success. He mostly makes television series.

Koçak, Mevlut (b. Sıvas, 1944) Editor. With 40 years in the editing room and about 200 films to his credit, Mevlut Koçak is one of the most important names in Turkish cinema when the subject is editing. He started as a 15-year-old apprentice in 1971 with Erman Film and was soon promoted to the editing room. The editor of most of the films of **Ömer Kavur** and several of **Atıf Yılmaz**, he was instrumental in the inclusion of an award for editors at national film festivals.

Koçyiğit, Hülya (b. Istanbul, 1947) Actor. One of the top stars of **Yeşilçam**, **Hülya Koçyiğit** is memorable for her performances in *Susuz Yaz / A Dry Summer* (**Erksan**, 1963), the Migration Trilogy of **Akad** and *Derman / Remedy* (1983), *Firar / Escape* (1984) and *Kurbağalar / The Frogs* (1985) of **Şerif Gören**. In addition to numerous national awards, she was awarded the Best Actress at the

Amiens Film Festival in France for her role in *Bez Bebek / The Rag Doll* (**Engin Ayça**, 1988). In 1991, she was chosen as the state artist of the Republic. In a career that spans over five decades, she has acted in close to 180 feature films. Since the late 1980s, she has also been acting in television series.

Kolçak, Eşref (b. Erzurum, 1927) Actor. Starting his film career in 1947, Eşref Kolçak has performed in close to 200 films and television series, playing opposite most stars of Turkish cinema. Some of his memorable films are *Düşman Yolları Kesti / The Enemy Blocked the Roads* (unofficial English title) (1959) and *Namus Uğruna / For Chastity* (1960) of **Osman F. Seden**, and *Bir Şöförün Gizli Defteri / The Secret Book of A Taxi Driver* (unofficial English title) (**Atıf Yılmaz**, 1957).

Koper, Macit (b. Istanbul, 1944) Actor, screenwriter. Memorable for his role in *Anayurt Oteli / Motherland Hotel* (**Ömer Kavur**, 1987), Macit Koper started in theatre as an actor, dramaturge and director. His job at the Istanbul Municipal Theatre was terminated in 1980 by the military regime; he was allowed to return in 1989 after the legal procedures. He started screenwriting in 1963 and after *Rumuz Goncagül / Codename: Blossom* (**İrfan Tözüm**, 1987) worked consecutively for this director. He wrote the scripts and acted in several films of **Ömer Kavur** and other noteworthy film-makers, receiving awards as an actor and screenwriter.

Kosmos (2009) interrogates love/loveless-ness, institutionalized religion/shamanism, personal ownership/common property, societal constriction/freedom of spirit, borders/fluidity and rootless-ness/belonging. In the tradition of the **rural films** of **Yeşilçam**, it is structured around the village cafe – a male-dominant locale where conflicts arise or resolve and gossip is exchanged. Kosmos, the stranger from nowhere, wins the hearts of the inhabitants of a snow-covered border town with his alleged healing powers while robbing them of their worldly belongings. He breaks the masculinist codes by openly stating that he does not want to work; he wants love.

Kosmos is a character like Irimiás in *Satantango* (Béla Tarr, 1994) with messianic qualities. Just like Irimiás, a prophet, the devil, a charismatic conman, or all of these things, he arrives at a hopeless landscape. The town cafe is not much different from the dingy bar in Tarr's film. The film also carries intertextuality with the films of Andrei Tarkovsky, the abandoned interiors recalling *Stalker* (1979) and the free-floating extra-terrestrial imagery, *Solaris* (1972). The city of Kars (the locale of Orhan Pamuk's *Kar / Snow*, 2002) recognizable through wide-angle shots, possesses a timeless quality that befits the protagonist, who appears to be a timeless and space-less character. The film begins with Kosmos crying, which is the cry of the film according to **Reha Erdem**. Kosmos cries for the lack of faith – in God or in another human being. He tries to bring a third dimension to a border town, which can be achieved through spirituality, like a shaman sharing the pain of others by transference.

Border towns are particular as a physically marked perimeter encircling the nation-state and defining national identity in territorial terms while creating the

Figure 74 Kosmos (Reha Erdem, 2009) (Courtesy of Reha Erdem)

anomaly of ethnic identities that do not correspond to territorially based identities. The border is a zone of transition from well-known territory under the control of the state to little-known territory not under the control of the state. The unknown, on the other side, generates curiosity, promise, threat and fear. Borders can be sites of exchange, negotiation, subversion and violence. Metaphorically, Kosmos, as the unknown who comes from the other side, offers an alternative way, not only alternative healing, but perhaps an alternative language for communication as he develops with Neptun, the sister of the little boy he saves from drowning, which extends to the artistic choice of Erdem who plays with spatio-temporality and deconstructs reality, creating a different reality out of culturally specific elements. The continuous sounds of artillery fire signalling the military manoeuvres along

Figure 75 Kosmos (Reha Erdem, 2009) (Courtesy of Reha Erdem)

Figure 76 Kosmos (Reha Erdem, 2009) (Courtesy of Reha Erdem)

the border with Armenia (although place names are not mentioned); the rival politicians trying to gather support for and against the opening of the border and four brothers that don't share the same parents locked in a dispute about inheritance lead the viewer to larger philosophical questions suggesting a search for a cosmic overview of pantheistic oneness outweighing concerns about borders or inheritance. However, as Kosmos declares, 'For him who is joined to all that is living, there is hope', the camera shifts to the cows in the slaughterhouse. (**Erdem**'s concern for the destruction of nature by human folly is the central theme of his next film, *Jîn*, 2013.)

The film received several national and international awards, among which are the Best Film, Best Director, Best Cinematography and Special Jury award for Sound Design at the 46th Antalya Golden Orange Film Festival, 2009.

Director, Screenwriter, Editor: **Reha Erdem**; Producer: Ömer Atay; Production: Atlantik Film; Cinematography: Şenol Toz, Florent Herry; Cast: Sermet Yeşil, Türkü Turan, Hakan Altuntaş, Sabahat Doğanyılmaz, Korel Kubilay, Akın Anlı, Sencar Sağdıç

Köksal, Neriman (b. Istanbul, 1929 – d. Istanbul, 1999) Actor; RN: Hatice Kökçü. The first *vamp* of Turkish cinema, Neriman Köksal was known as 'fosforlu' (phosphorus) after her role in *Fosforlu Cevriye / Cevriye, the Phosphorus* (Aydın Arakon, 1959) as a macho woman, the image that gradually became very popular. She acted in almost 190 films, including television series.

Köprüdekiler / Men on the Bridge (2009) exposes social and political issues of Turkish society through parallel but not intersecting stories of people who daily cross the Bosphorus Bridge that joins the continents of Asia and Europe. The lack of proper education which leads the youth to unemployment and desperation, the terrorist activities that divide the nation, nationalism that arises parallel to these issues and the anachronism of religion are exposed without passing moral

Figure 77 Köprüdekiler / Men on the Bridge (Aslı Özge, 2009) (Courtesy of International Istanbul Film Festival)

Figure 78 Köprüdekiler / Men on the Bridge (Aslı Özge, 2009) (Courtesy of International Istanbul Film Festival)

judgement. All actors except the two policemen play themselves, which reinforces the docu-drama style of the film.

On the bridge, which represents modernity and progress with the high-rises in the background, Roma flower boys ply their trade in the pouring rain amidst dense traffic. They live in the slums and share their bread sitting on the floor. They can only stare at food samples in restaurant windows. They have no money to lose their virginity. With no education and no chance of employment, their destiny is to live on the streets, get high, laugh at their fate and sing rap, *Neyim*

Figure 79 Köprüdekiler / Men on the Bridge (Aslı Özge, 2009) (Courtesy of International Istanbul Film Festival)

Var ki Rap'tan Gayri / What do I have except Rap? Housing shortages for the less advantaged in a metropolis that expands regularly (**Metin Erksan**'s *Acı Hayat / Bitter Life*, the satirical **Kemal Sunal** comedies of the 1970s–80s) are foregrounded through the desperate hunt of the young couple, the minibus driver and his wife whose dreams are shaped by television programmes. Free-market consumerism has resulted in dissatisfied youth, who see more and want more. The conversations between the two young policemen, apart from sexist comments about women, reveal the attitude of ordinary citizens regarding the political atmosphere: they oppose the representation of the Kurds in parliament and blame the government for making concessions to Europe in the negotiations regarding joining the European Union.

The film holds a mirror to burning social issues without passing moral judgement; neither does it go deep into the roots of the issues it raises, which is an opportunity missed in a skilfully constructed film.

Director, Screenwriter: **Aslı Özge**; Producers: Fabian Massah, **Aslı Özge**; Production, Cinematographer: Emre Erkmen; Editors: Vessela Martschewski, Aylin Zoi Tinel, Christof Schertenleib; Sound: Florian Beck; Cast: Fikret Portakal, Murat Tokgöz, Umut İlker, Cemile İlker

Körmükçü, Hazım (b. Istanbul, 1898 – d. Istanbul, 1944) Actor, screenwriter, director; RN: Kazım Körmükçü. A theatre actor who could play several instruments and perform *Karagöz* shows (shadow play), Hazım Körmükçü entered cinema in 1932. He acted in most of the films of **Muhsin Ertuğrul**, including *İstanbul Sokaklarında / On the Streets of Istanbul* (1931) and *Aysel, Bataklı Damın Kızı / The Girl From the Marshes* aka *Aysel, the Girl From the Swampy Roof* (1935).

Kurçenli, Yusuf (b. Çayeli, Rize, 1947 – d. Istanbul, 2012) Director, screenwriter, producer. One of the less acknowledged members of the '68 generation of film-makers, Kurçenli studied journalism at Istanbul University and worked in television between 1973–80. His first feature, *Ve Recep ve Zehra ve Ayşe / And Recep and Zehra and Ayşe* (1984) was about the clash of the patriarchal tradition with the background of a carefree and modern vacation village. Never released theatrically, the film was shown directly on television, which was rare for the period. *Gramafon Avrat / Gramophone* (1987), based on a story by Sabahattin Ali about a private singer in the milieu of a provincial town on the brink of modernization, and *Karatma Geceleri / Blackout Nights* (1990), about a wanted poet's hide-and-seek with the police during World War II, brought him acclaim. With *Gramophone*, *Blackout Nights* and *Raziye* (1990) from Melih Cevdet Anday's novel, he gave some of the best literary adaptations to Turkish cinema, the choice of a certain generation of authors displaying his involvement in their political histories. *Çözülmeler / The Disintegration* (1994) and *Gönderilmemiş Mektuplar / Unsent Letters* (2003) were love stories. His last film, the semi-autobiographical *Yüreğine Sor / Ask Your Heart* (2010) was about religious discrimination in the nineteenth century against the Greek Orthodox population along the Black Sea, who were compelled to live anonymously. This was the first leg of a trilogy that he could not complete with his death in 2012. His other films are *Ölmez Ağacı / Immortal Tree* (unofficial English title) (1984) and *Merdoğlu Ömer Bey / Mr Ömer, the Son of the Brave* (unofficial English title) (1986). He also directed television series and a documentary on international trafficking of antiques, *Antika Talanı / Antique Pillage* (1997).

Kurdish cinema within Turkey has begun to distinguish itself following relaxation of language restrictions, the support of the Mesopotamian Cinema Collective, as part of the Mesopotamian Cultural Centre (MKM) in Istanbul, and the availability of the digital medium. A new generation of film-makers – **Hüseyin Karabey**, **Kazım Öz**, Müjde Arslan, **Miraz Bezar**, **Orhan Eskiköy**, **Zeynel Doğan** – has emerged, determined to tell their stories with powerful short films, documentaries and fiction works.

The East and the West, the well-known binary pair, refers not only to two reputedly unique civilizations (the Orient and the Occident), but also to the divisions between the country itself. The dichotomy between Turkey's East and West problematizes the semiotic unity of Turkey as a cultural sign, and consequently the identity of Turkey as a nation. Turkish cinema traditionally has used the east of the country, but particularly the ethnic minorities such as the Kurds and the geography of their homeland without giving a name, or language, but rather with an Orientalizing gaze. Until the 1990s, ethnic minorities, particularly the Kurds, were shown as Turks. They were the poor illiterate easterners from the mountains, identified with the black *shalvar* (loose pants), the *poshu* (the traditional scarf), lack of proper discourse in the official language and poverty. The oppressive conditions of their lives were attributed to centuries-old customs and traditions, and mainly to feudalism, but never to the lack of effective government policies.

(The ideological revival of feudalism in the 2000s is manifest in several primetime television series that show the Kurds as smugglers, terrorists or perpetrators of honour killings.) **Yılmaz Güney** showed both the Kurds and the Turks as human beings suffering under state oppression. The Kurdish identity of his characters was delivered through circumlocution due to heavy censorship, which regularly condemned several of his films for 'leftist' inclinations. *Seyyit Han* aka *Toprağın Gelini / Seyyit Han* aka *The Bride of the Earth* (1968) is considered as the first film to present Kurdish characters. *Umut / The Hope* (**Güney**, 1970) and *Endişe / The Anxiety* (**Şerif Gören**, 1974), written by **Güney**, are about the Kurdish people. *Sürü / The Herd* (**Zeki Ökten**, 1978), written by **Güney**, is about the plight of the Kurds, but if the Kurdish language were used, all those who took part in the film would have been punished by prison sentences according to **Güney**. *Yol / The Way* (**Şerif Gören**, 1982) takes place in Diyarbakır, Urfa and Siirt, areas heavily populated by Kurds, but Kurdish is not spoken, although the dubbing was done in Europe. **Güney** tried to create a Kurdish atmosphere by the use of music. Nonetheless, the film was banned for 17 years.

In the 1990s, a 'cinematic counter-telling' (Shohat 2003: 51) started (*Mem û Zin / Mem and Zin*, **Ümit Elçi**, 1991; *Siabend u Xece / Siyabend and Xece*, **Şahin Gök**, 1993), but such counter-narratives were limited due to governmental pressures and subtle forms of censorship. Building on the tradition of **Yılmaz Güney**, Nizammettin Ariç shot *Stranek Ji Bo Beko / Ein Lied Für Beko / A Song for Beko* (1993), about the struggles of the Kurdish people against the Turkish state, in the Kurdish language in Armenia and İbrahim Selman made *Silent Traveller* (1994) in Greece. *Tirej* (2002) by Halil Uysal was directed and acted by real-life guerrillas. Iraqi Ravin Asaf, who migrated to Germany in 1986, made *Sarı Günler / Yellow Days* (2002), co-produced with **Kadir Sözen** about a Kurdish village, where the tranquillity of life is disrupted by the arrival of a blond German soprano who studies Kurdish folk dances. The film was withdrawn from the International Istanbul Film Festival (2003).

Just like Palestinian cinema, Kurdish cinema has developed largely in exile by transnational film-makers: **Yüksel Yavuz**, **Yılmaz Arslan**, **Kadir Sözen**, **Ayşe Polat**, Güliz Sağlam, **Nuray Şahin**, Yusuf Yeşilçay, Kudret Güneş are some of the distinguished names.

Serious studies of the beginnings of Kurdish cinema within the borders of Turkey, Turkish films about the Kurds and the presentation of the Kurdish identity in Turkish cinema have been lacking. Müslüm Yücel's *Türk Sinemasında Kürtler / Kurds in Turkish Cinema* (2008) and *Kürt Sineması: Yurtsuzluk, Sınır ve Ölüm / Kurdish Cinema: Homelessness, Border and Death* (Müjde Arslan, 2009) are pioneer attempts that are available only in Turkish. The term 'Kurdish cinema' is open to discussion. What constitutes Kurdish cinema? The language, the subject, the approach, the ethnic origin of the director/producer, or all of these factors? **Handan İpekçi**'s *Büyük Adam, Küçük Aşk,* aka *Hejar / Big Man, Small Love* (2001), about the Kurds with Kurdish partially spoken, and **Yeşim Ustaoğlu**'s *Güneşe Yolculuk / Journey to the Sun* (1999), about ethnic 'othering' featuring two Kurdish actors in the lead, participated in several Kurdish film festivals abroad. For **Kazım Öz**, instead of the Kurdish cinema, one should speak of cinema that reflects the lives of the Kurds. Every film that is about the Kurds can be considered as Kurdish cinema, but everyone who is a Kurd, does cinema and shoots in the south-east does not necessarily do Kurdish cinema even if the subject is about the Kurds. **Mahsun Kırmızıgül**'s agenda is the box-office and not the Kurdish issue. A 'literature of the "other"' exists which uses the issues of the 'other' as commodity (Dönmez-Colin 2008: 103). For **Hüseyin Karabey**, 'Kurdish cinema' should be discussed through freedom. If one day everyone will be able to make 'the cinema of Turkey', there will not be a need to identify 'Kurdish cinema' (Aydemir 2013: 61).

The overall theme of the films of the new generation of Kurdish film-makers is identity and the language issue; the social and economic issues of the Kurdish people are secondary. The search for the homeland, crossing the borders and particularly the preservation of memory are central motifs in *Min Dit / Ben Gördüm / The Children of Diyarbakır* aka *Before Your Eyes* (**Miraz Bezar**, 2009); *Babamın Sesi / The Voice of My Father* (**Orhan Eskiköy, Zeynel Doğan**, 2012), *Ana Dilim Nerede? / Where is My Mother Tongue?* (Veli Kahraman, 2012) and *Ben Uçtum, Sen Kaldın / I Flew, You Stayed* (Müjde Arslan, 2012).

Films by Kurdish film-makers receive aid from the Ministry of Culture, just like other films from Turkey, but private funding is almost impossible and these films are not shown on television. Despite accolades at international film festivals, the chances of reaching the public, especially the Kurdish people, except in large cities, are very slim.

Kurtiz, Tuncel (b. İzmit, 1936 – d. Istanbul, 2013) Actor, screenwriter, director, producer; RN: Tuncel Tayanç. One of the doyen actors of contemporary Turkish cinema, Tuncel Kurtiz built a career as an international stage and screen actor working with noteworthy companies and film-makers in several European countries as well as Turkey. Some of his memorable roles in cinema are in *Bitmeyen Yol / Unending Road* (**Duygu Sağıroğlu**, 1967); *Umut / The Hope* (**Yılmaz Güney**, 1970); *Otobüs / The Bus* (**Tunç Okan**, 1976); *Sürü / The Herd* (**Zeki Ökten**, 1978); *Bereketli Topraklar Üzerinde / On Fertile Land* (**Erden Kıral**, 1979); *İnat Hikayeleri / Tales of Insurgence* (**Reis Çelik**, 2003) and *Auf der Anderen Seite / Yaşamın Kıyısında / The Edge of Heaven* (**Fatih Akın**, 2007). He also made a film, *Gül Hasan / Hasan, the Rose* (1979).

Kurtlar Vadisi Irak / Valley of the Wolves, Iraq (2006), the most expensive and the highest grossing Turkish movie of its time and the television series, *Kurtlar Vadisi / Valley of the Wolves*, combine the ideologies of nationalism, conservatism and Islamism. The pattern follows the 'historical fantasies' of **Yeşilçam** (*Malkoçoğlu, Tarkan*); violence is justified by the initial aggression of the enemy – massacre, torture, rape or insult to honour. Polat Alemdar and his men represent the nationalist conservative line and the Kerkuk Turkmenians, the Islamist. The film is based on a true story that is referred to as the 'Hood Event'. In 2003, a Turkish intelligence team on a mission to Iraq was arrested by the US forces in the

Kurdish town of Suleimanaie and kept in detention, handcuffed and hooded. One of them committed suicide to save his honour. When his farewell letter reaches Polat Alemdar, an elite Turkish intelligence officer, he goes to the area with a small group of men to retaliate. 'I will make hell of the life of the man who dares to put a sack over the head of a Turk!' vows Alemdar.

With its caricaturized binaries of good/evil, the film presents the US men in Iraq as corrupt sadistic Muslim-torturers who traffic in human kidneys. While Alemdar kills the Kurds to restore the honour of his country, the Americans kill civilians attending a wedding (the Mukaradeep wedding massacre). The film was a box-office success with 4,256,567 spectators and made $20 million at the box-office. It was the most viewed film of 2006 and the only Turkish film that ever attracted such a large number of spectators. It was also released in 14 foreign countries including Belgium, The Netherlands, Austria, the UK, Switzerland, Denmark, Russia, Australia and the US. In Germany alone 700,000 people saw it. However, Turkish critics thought the film was a mediocre imitation of some Hollywood movies that are made for political propaganda purposes and it exploited nationalistic sentiments. It was followed by two other box-office hits with similar ultra-nationalistic sentiments, *Valley of the Wolves: Gladio* (Sadullah Şentürk, 2008) and *Valley of the Wolves: Palestine* (Zübeyr Şaşmaz, 2011).

Director: **Serdar Akar**, Sadullah Sentürk; Producer: Raci Şaşmaz; Production: Pana Film; Screenwriter: Raci Şaşmaz, Bahadır Özdener; Editor: Kemalettin Osmanlı; Art Director: Yavuz Fazlıoğlu; Music: Gökhan Kırdar; Sound: Alan O'Duffy; Cast: Necati Şaşmaz, Abdilkarim Tahlil, Billy Zane, Ghassan Massoud, Gary Busey, Diego Serrano, Gürkan Uygun, Bergüzar Korel

Kutlar, Onat (b. Alanya, 1936 – d. Istanbul, 1995) Screenwriter, author, producer; RN: Mehmet Arif Onat Kutlar. One of the founders of the **cinematheque** and the International Istanbul Film Festival, Onat Kutlar left his studies in law to go to Paris (1961) where he studied philosophy. He was the recipient of the Chevalier de l'ordre des Arts et des Lettres from France (1994) and the Cultural Medal from Poland (1974). He died in a terrorist attack on a popular cafe of intellectuals. The Fipresci Prize at the Istanbul Film Festival is given in his name.

Kuyu / The Well (1968), **Metin Erksan**'s most controversial film and one of the classics of Turkish cinema, is a rural drama that focuses on a tragic relationship, founded on male obsession and female resistance. Based on a newspaper article and decorated with **Erksan**'s fantasies, it displays the defencelessness of a young village woman, oppressed but resolute, against the perverse determination of a man obsessed with her. The film opens with Osman (**Hayati Hamzaoğlu**) watching Fatma (Nil Göncü) bathing in the river (the classic narrative convention of **Yeşilçam melodramas** to forewarn the audience of imminent sexual violence). He steals her clothes and points a gun to her face, demanding that she be his wife. When she resists, he ties a rope around her waist and pulls her through the arid landscape. Neither several jail sentences nor her open defiance would make him change his mind. Dishonoured and outcast, Fatma kills Osman by throwing stones at him while he is washing his face in a well. In a dramatic finale, we see her head framed within the circle of the mouth of the well with light from behind, while he gropes in the dark, after which she has no choice but to kill herself.

Erksan presents the sexual impulse as a subliminal force. His protagonists are possessed by their obsessions in a psychopathological way. Fatma is literally tied to Osman with a rope and dragged for the large part of the film. The rope becomes a trope for man's sovereignty over woman, the paradisiacal landscape of arid mountains and gushing rivers alluding to the Garden of Eden and the eternal entanglement of the two sexes. The woman, who constantly tries to cut the rope, is freed only when the man dies but then she cannot stand living alone.

The film is irreproachable in terms of aesthetics. The minimalist narrative works in repetitions; the characters of the two protagonists, both loners in an indifferent world, are developed within the societal dynamics and with particular attention to human psychology; the cinematography and particularly the camera angles are skilfully executed. The scenes in the village market shot with a hidden camera are pure *cinema verité*. However, while several critics consider *The Well* an important representative of the cinema of resistance and argue that Erksan has foregrounded the oppression of women in a masculinist society with sensitivity, others condemn the graphic display of male brute power, denouncing the film as the sexual fantasies of a macho man, rendered voyeuristically by a male film-maker. **Erksan** claimed that the film took its inspiration from the message in *An-Nisa, sur'a IV – ayet* (verse) *19* of the Qur'an, which states that it is unlawful for men to possess women by force; they should consort with them in kindness because if they hate them, they hate a thing wherein Allah has placed much good.

The film received six awards at the Adana Golden Boll Film Festival (1969), including Best Film and Best Director.

Director, Screenwriter: **Metin Erksan**; Producer: Necip Sarıcıoğlu; Production: Ortak Film; Cinematographer: Ali Uğur, Mengü Yeğin; Music: Orhan Gencebay; Cast: **Hayati Hamzaoğlu**, Nil Göncü, Demir Karahan, **Aliye Rona**, Osman Alyanak, T. Fikret Uçar, Ahmet Kostarika, Reşit Çildam, Mustafa Dağhan, Abdurrahman Palay

L

Livaneli, Ömer Zülfü (b. Konya, 1946) Director, screenwriter, composer, singer, novelist, producer, politician, columnist. A multi-faceted personality, Zülfü Livaneli is known for his award-winning literary works, films and compositions, including films scores for ***Otobüs / The Bus*** (**Tunç Okan**, 1976) and ***Yol / The Way*** (**Şerif Gören**, 1982). He has directed four films: *Yer Demir, Gök Bakır / Earth of Iron, Sky of Copper* (1987); *Sis / The Fog* (1989); *Şahmaran: Bir İstanbul Masalı / Shahmaran: A Tale of Istanbul* (1993) and *Veda – Atatürk* (2010). He has received several national and international awards with the first three films. He is the co-founder of the Greece–Turkey Friendship Association with Mikis Theodorakis. His compositions have been performed by famous artists such as Joan Baez and Maria Farantouri. One of his award-winning novels, *Mutluluk / Bliss* (2007) was made into a film by Abdullah Oğuz. A well-known social democrat, he was elected to the Grand National Assembly as a deputy from Istanbul in 2002. He has been a good-will ambassador to UNESCO-Paris since 1996. In 2007, he published his memoirs, *Sevdalım Hayat / Beloved Life* (unofficial English translation).

Lola ve Bilidikid / Lola und Bilidikid / Lola and Bilidikid (1998), the second feature of **Kutluğ Ataman**, focuses on Turkish transvestites within the 'guest worker' community of Berlin, who are subject to social prejudices by their people in an environment where discrimination is already a threat. The film develops parallel themes of homophobia, the search for visibility in a foreign environment and the yearning for a sense of belonging. Osman, Lola and Murat, sons of a guest worker family, live in Kreutzberg in the Turkish ghetto. As the eldest, Osman assumes the patriarch's role after his father's death, repressing his natural instincts within the confines of his imposed identity and exercising power on the meeker. (The last episode reveals his earlier aggression against Lola, raping him and then throwing him out for 'not being a man'.) Lola is the star of a transvestite show, *Die Gastarbeiterinnen / The Female Guestworkers* and in love with Bilidikid, who loves him (her) back but cannot forego his machismo. Germany-born 16-year-old Murat, curious about gay life, finds the brotherly love denied at home in a transvestite named Lola, unaware that he is his brother. Violence erupts when family secrets come out of the closet. 'Murat's identity is doubly convoluted, for it is caught in the crosscurrents of an ethnic drama and a sexual orientation trauma.

Figure 80 Lola ve Bilidikid / Lola und Bilidikid / Lola and Bilidikid (Kutluğ Ataman, 1998) (Courtesy of Kutluğ Ataman)

The *mise en scène* and filming of tawdry public bathrooms, dingy apartments, and threatening streets at night are highly claustrophobic, as are the exploitative and explosive social relations of Turkish (and German) men, who, having come out of the ethnic enclave and the closet, must now contend with psychological hostility and physical violence from all sides' (Naficy 2001, 1999).

Ataman underscores the alienation of the individual in the industrialized atmosphere of Berlin. The night scenes in desolate parks that shelter men who try to forget their loneliness in the comfort of another warm body reflect the stark reality facing outcasts anywhere, and these images are not much different from the night scenes in ***The Bus***, when the Turks react to the unknown with trepidation but also curiosity. **Ataman**'s handling of the question of sexual identity, however, is very precise. Lola's lover, Bilidikid, thinks he is a man because he is the one who penetrates. He wants Lola to have an operation so that they can move to Turkey and live as man and wife. He yearns for an uncomplicated identity that would help him belong to a society without facing discrimination, but Lola fears that a 'normal life' will destroy his relationship with Bilidikid, who likes him for his 'otherness'.

Murat is introduced to the dark side of Berlin against the background of the statue of an angel, the redemption and hope in the film (Çiçek 2006). He explores his sexual inclination with a German school friend. To help Bilidikid avenge Lola's death, he lures the neo-Nazis into a deserted building wearing Lola's red wig, where 'two radical characters of both cultures, Bilidikid, who embodies the machismo of the Turkish male and the neo-Nazi leader, representing fascist ideology attack and kill each other. After the self-destruction of the extreme elements of both cultures, director **Ataman** places Murat and one of the neo-Nazi youth at a corner in the building, abandoned both physically and metaphorically. There, in a state of panic, beaten and bloodied, the two are stripped of their cultural differences, they become human, and they become the same' (Çiçek 2006).

Lola's murderer is not the neo-Nazis but his brother Osman. This revelation releases the mother from the role of the passive female veiled inside the house; she enters the public space leaving her scarf on the pavement. Unlike Turna in *40 Quadratmeter Deutschland / Forty Square Meters of Germany* (**Başer**, 1986), here is a woman capable of tearing the veil of false security imposed by traditions. Murat, representing the second generation, also rejects the patriarchy that has oppressed his identity. Powerless, Osman is left behind in the Turkish ghetto.

Director, Screenwriter: **Kutluğ Ataman**; Producer: **Zeynep Özbatur Atakan**, Martin Hagemann and James Schamus; Production: Boje Buck Produktion, Westdeutscher Rundfunk (WDR), Zero Film GmbH; Cinematographer: Chris Squires; Editor: Eva J. Lind; Music: Arpad Bondy; Cast: Gandi Mukli, Erdal Yıldız, Baki Davrak, Inge Keller, Celal Perk, Mesut Özdemir, Murat Yılmaz, Hakan Tandoğan

M

Masumiyet/Innocence (1997) is a **melodrama** of three unlikely characters thrown into a society that has lost its innocence. Yusuf (Güven Kıraç) is released from prison after serving a ten-year sentence. Unwilling to leave for lack of prospects outside, he resembles Franz Biberkopf (*Berlin Alexanderplatz*, Fassbinder, 1980) whose head spins when the prison doors close behind him. He has lost all his family during an earthquake, except his sister 'silenced' by his interference during her elopement and his murder of her lover. At a provincial hotel, he meets the self-styled prostitute Uğur (**Derya Alabora**) pursuing Zagor, her homicidal lover from one prison town to another; her infatuated pimp, Bekir (**Haluk Bilginer**) and her mute daughter from a short marriage, Çilem. Without better prospects and in desperate need to belong, Yusuf becomes part of their lives, growing a one-sided attachment to cynical Uğur and replacing Bekir after Bekir's suicide. In the key episode of the film, one of the rare scenes in the open air with full daylight, Bekir tells his story to Yusuf while Çilem, the innocent child, silent in her deaf-and-dumb world, except for her constantly interrogating gaze, blends with the tranquil landscape. (**Demirkubuz** built *Kader / Destiny*, 2006 on this episode.)

From the title of the film to the narrative, **Demirkubuz** questions the moral values of a masculinist society, underscoring their variability. Ironically, the oppressed housewife's 'honour' is her curse, while the streetwise sex-worker's 'fall' is her liberation. Yusuf's encounter with the recomposed family (Bekir is not Uğur's partner, Çilem is not his daughter) is crucial in his transformation from a man who kills for family honour to one willing to pimp for a prostitute and to recompose yet another family if she accepts. Although his moral judgements remain constant, he has acquired compassion.

Ironically, a film depicting an uncompromising woman, does not give her a real voice. As in the **Atıf Yılmaz**'s classic, *Adı Vasfiye / Her Name is Vasfiye* (1985), Uğur is present only under the male gaze, under the scrutiny of Bekir and Yusuf and her story is told by Bekir. The camera angles do not reveal her point of view of the two men. The two other female characters, Yusuf's sister and Uğur's daughter, are mute, victims of domestic violence although their muteness can also be considered a trope for resistance to patriarchy.

Shot in 19 days with a $90,000 budget, *Innocence* is constructed as a *road movie* but we may also define it as a *hotel movie*, a sub-**genre** that has had its precedents, particularly with **Ömer Kavur**'s *Anayurt Oteli / Motherland Hotel* (1987) and *Gizli Yüz / The Secret Face* (1991). In decrepit hotels inert characters incessantly watch **Yeşilçam melodramas** with crimes of passion, desperate men pimping the women they would rather wed, deaf-and-dumb little girls, improbable coincidences and love suicides – not unlike the plot of the film. Even **Demirkubuz** appears among the absorbed audience watching *C Blok / Block C* (1994). Adopting the recognizable themes of **Yeşilçam**, his familiar ground from years of assistantship, yet stripping them of the sensationalist elements, he underlines the significance of the approach – with distance and irony in his case – over narration.

Director, Screenwriter: **Zeki Demirkubuz**; Producer: **Zeki Demirkubuz** and Nihal G. Koldaş; Production: Mavi Filmcilik; Cinematographer: Ali Utku; Editor: **Mevlut Koçak**; Music: Cengiz Onural; Sound: Erkin Hadimoğlu; Production designer: Adnan Tezel; Cast: **Derya Alabora**, Haluk Bilginer, Güven Kıraç, Melis Tuna, Yalçın Çakmak

Mavi Sürgün / The Blue Exile (1993), the first film of **Erden Kıral** after his return from self-imposed exile in Germany, continues the theme of exile and state oppression of the thinker/intellectual, which he has explored in *Hakkari'de Bir Mevsim / A Season in Hakkari* (1983), returning to the theme in *Yolda / On the Way* (2005).

The film is based on the autobiography of a Turkish journalist and intellectual Cevat Şakir (1890–1973) exiled to Halicarnassus (today's Bodrum) for three years

Figure 81 Mavi Sürgün / The Blue Exile (Erden Kıral, 1993) (Courtesy of International Istanbul Film Festival)

by the Liberation Courts for publishing a story about deserters in the World War I who were shot without a trial. Parallel to a months-long train journey from Ankara to Bodrum, the film traces the psychological journey of an exile to his turbulent past that involves a crime of passion. In Bodrum, he tries to erase his past and cleanse his soul through identification with nature, becoming the Fisherman of Halicarnassus and marrying an illiterate local girl. The episode when he throws buckets of water at the walls of his house in a frenzy is the manifestation of his need to purge and a turning point in his life, a catharsis.

The film begins with a tableau of a whirling *dervish* – a circle, which becomes the main trope. During the train journey, the past of the protagonist haunts him: memories of his protective mother, his distant and cruel father, his Italian wife and the burden of patricide. The landscape framed by the window-pane changes from desert brown to warm green as he begins to face his predicaments. **Kıral** uses numerous stylistic flashbacks that merge recollections, dreams and associations. Blending of the actual images with the images of the interior world of the protagonist at times obscures the narrative although he successfully returns to the principal motif of the circle (of life and the universe).

The subject of the Liberation Courts, formed during the first years of the Turkish Republic (1923) and their repressive practices had been taboo until the 1990s. *Kurt Kanunu / The Law of the Wolf* (Ersin Korkmaz, 1992), based on a **Kemal Tahir** story, and *Kelebekler Sonsuza Uçar / Butterflies Fly to Eternity* (**Mesut Uçakan**), released the same year as *The Blue Exile*, have approached the subject but avoided dialogue. **Kıral**'s film focuses on the exile rather than the reasons behind the exile, which results in certain blackouts in the narrative of a visually captivating film.

Director: **Erden Kıral**; Producer, Cinematographer: **Kenan Ormanlar**; Production: Bayerischer Rundfunk, Kenmovie Filmcilik, Kentel Film, Stefi 2; Screenwriters: **Erden Kıral**, **Kenan Ormanlar**, Elly Scheller-Ormanlar; Editor: Karin Fischer; Music: Timur Selçuk; Sound: Simon Happ; Cast: Can Togay, Hanna Schygulla, Özay Fecht, Ayşe Romey, Tatiana Papamoshou, Halil Ergün

Mayıs Sıkıntısı / Clouds of May (1999), which literally means the boredom of May, is the second film of what this author considers a tetralogy also comprising *Kasaba / The Small Town* (1997), *Uzak / Distant* (2002) and *İklimler / Climates* (2006) that can be called 'A Portrait of the Provincial Artist as an Urban Intellectual'. Filmed in the same small town Yenice as *The Small Town*, where **Ceylan** spent his childhood, it underscores the feelings of obligation and guilt when shooting with non-professional actors in actual circumstances, particularly if they are family members. Muzaffer (Muzaffer Özdemir) is an independent film-maker (**Ceylan**'s persona) working on commercially unviable projects to the dismay of his provincial parents. His return home to use the family for his film project (*Kasaba / The Small Town*), and especially his selfish and insincere behaviour, disturbs their tranquillity. The father, Emir Bey (the director's father, Mehmet Emin Ceylan who played in *The Small Town*) is about to lose the land he has nourished to prospectors for lack of better foresight. Cousin Saffet (Mehmet

Figure 82 Mayıs Sıkıntısı / Clouds of May (Nuri Bilge Ceylan, 1999) (Courtesy of International Istanbul Film Festival)

Figure 83 Mayıs Sıkıntısı / Clouds of May (Nuri Bilge Ceylan, 1999) (Courtesy of International Istanbul Film Festival)

Emin Toprak) (also from **The Small Town**) is still suffocating in the claustrophobic atmosphere, having again failed the entrance examinations to the university. Relying on Muzaffer's assistance for a job in the city, he is disillusioned with his detachment when the shooting terminates (Saffet as Yusuf arrives at the door of Muzaffer/Mahmut in **Distant**). Little Ali is still dreaming of a musical clock but now he has learned about cheating as a survival skill. Mother Fatma is still the foundation of the family although father Emin is the more dramatic character with his intuitiveness and idiosyncrasies.

The opening sequences establish the tone of the film as cousin Saffet gazes at the small town framed by the window, feeling 'the pain and sting of absence from the centre' (Jameson 1991: 281) while the radio announces the skirmishes between the political parties. The same detachment (or wish for) would re-appear in the final scenes of **Bir Zamanlar Anadolu'da / Once Upon a Time in Anatolia** (2011) with the long pensive gaze of the doctor through the morgue window.

The classroom episode resembles **The Small Town**, exposing with humour the futility of the archaic system of education. When Muzaffer asks Ali what they teach him at school, he answers innocently: 'Nothing'. In **The Small Town**, small children recite 'How happy is the one who says I am a Turk' every morning and read paragraphs on how to be a good citizen, without understanding a word; little Mesut is asked to write on the board: 'Mesut loves Atatürk'. The nationalist indoctrination foregrounded in these two films is revisited in the gaze of Yusuf, the country cousin in **Distant** as he stares at nationalist youth waving flags. The episode of Muzaffer brooding on a swing at the children's park is significant. Ali appears in the next shot, but only from behind. Muzaffer thinks of his childhood, seeing himself in Ali (as he has mentioned to his mother earlier). Nostalgia for what is lost is the dilemma of an individual cut off from his roots, who knows there is no going back 'home'. The image of the turtle, which is repeated in both films, is significant in this context. Traditionally perceived as a nomad travelling with its home, the turtle is also the prisoner of its home. For a man privileged with the anonymity of the city, 'the family centred ethnocentrism' and 'normalcy and non-deviant everyday life' (Jameson 1991: 280) of the insular small town life, neither a town nor a village, but forever condemned to liminality, where family members support each other to the point of suffocation and everyone knows everyone else's story, is too confining. The sense of claustrophobia the small town creates is accentuated by the camera that dwells on minor details such as the itching feet of the mother. One seems to be condemned to wait in an obscure corner with real or imaginary illnesses until death arrives. But what is worse is the vanishing 'autonomy' of the small town. 'What was once a separate point on the map has become an imperceptible thickening in a continuum of identical products and standardized spaces from coast to coast' (Jameson 1991: 281). Ali's fascination with the lighter that plays *lambada* when you click it is a case in point (a wind-up toy appears in **Distant**). The devastation of nature as small towns advance towards modernity is dramatically staged in the episode when the father walks out of the set (like the little girl in Jafer Panahi's **meta-film**, *Badkonak-e sefid / The White Baloon*, 1995) and rushes on his bicycle to the woods that employees of the ministry of agriculture have marked for destruction.

After its world premiere at the 50th Berlin Film Festival's competition section, *Clouds of May* brought several national and international prestigious awards to **Ceylan** and was theatrically released in Europe, Latin America and South Korea, but did not do well commercially in Turkey.

Director, Screenwriter, Cinematographer, Producer: **Nuri Bilge Ceylan**; Production: NBC Film; Editor: Ayhan Ergürsel, **Nuri Bilge Ceylan**; Sound: İsmail Karadaş; Music: J. S. Bach, Handel, Schubert; Cast: Mehmet Emin Ceylan, Muzaffer Özdemir, Fatma Ceylan, Mehmet Emin Toprak, Muhammed Zimbaoğlu, Sadık İncesu

Meleğin Düşüşü / Angel's Fall (2004) is the first direct attempt at foregrounding incest in Turkish cinema, one of the several courageous works that have appeared in the early 2000s exposing sexual taboos, particularly regarding violence against women. The film opens with Zeynep climbing a hill slowly wearing layers of baggy clothes and heavy boots. She ties the spool of yellow thread in her hand to a wooden post and pulls it, but the string snaps. The distraught Zeynep descends, re-wraps the thread and begins to climb, but the thread breaks again. Back to the post in tears, she loops the thread around a few times and proceeds up the hill. As she walks off the frame, the screen turns black and then the title appears in bold yellow font. In the next scene, she is on the edge of a precipice above a picturesque landscape, timeless and elusive. In the last scene of the film, she stands naked (and light like a feather) in front of a high balcony, the cityscape below alive with the overpowering Galata tower in the distance and the waters of the Golden Horn almost beneath her feet; a flock of birds suggest hope. Between these two elevated spaces, darkness prevails – in the long corridors of the hotel where she cleans the rooms, in her father's work place where she brings the lunch daily, in the streets and in the homes – underscoring the psychic tensions of displacement. Important

Figure 84 Meleğin Düşüşü / Angel's Fall (Semih Kaplanoğlu, 2004) (Courtesy of Semih Kaplanoğlu)

events happen in darkness, such as the violation of Zeynep's body by her father, or the suicide of Funda, the unfaithful Selçuk's wife, in another part of town.

Home is uncanny for **Kaplaoğlu**'s characters. Zeynep's young admirer at the hotel offers a life together in his village, but Zeynep knows that the river runs only in one direction. Just like Uğur of *Innocence* and *Destiny*, she is too cautious to expect salvation from a man. Zeynep wishes to erase her troubles by changing her identity, but she is shamed when seen by her father wearing the red negligee of Selçuk's wife. Changing back to her usual oversized rags and to her prescribed identity, she prepares the dinner for her father who waits until the meal is served and then slaps her. Sexuality is a sin when it is visible. As Zeynep rushes out of the room, the camera stays with the father, giving a chance to the spectator to decipher his psyche.

The thread Zeynep unspools in the opening sequence is an allusion to a Turkish tradition performed before religious holidays. If the woman reaches the top without breaking the thread, then her wish will be granted. On numerous occasions, Zeynep plays with the spool, unwinding the thread and muttering prayers, an indication of her obsession with the eventual fulfilment of her wish. (The thread or rope is a central motif in other films of Kaplaoğlu as well, which he interprets as a wish for stability or belonging.)

Weight – arising from the feeling of guilt, helplessness and loneliness – is a strong trope in the film. Just as she pulls her estranged body up the slope in the opening scene, Zeynep hauls a dead woman's luggage up another slope. The luggage promises her a new identity, and with a twist of fate, it is instrumental in her release from the heaviest burden, her incestuous father.

Charged but silent, *Angel's Fall* commences without dialogue until 6 minutes and 18 seconds into the film and then only a single word is heard. The first dialogue is 7 minutes and 18 seconds after the film begins, in a style reminiscent of the films of the Taiwanese Tsai Ming Liang, one of the influences on Kaplanoğlu, for whom the silence in the film is a metaphor for the sufferings of incest victims. Living in shame and denial (the father and the daughter have tea discussing routine matters), they become strangers to their body (Dönmez-Colin 2008: 170–3).

Before Zeynep appears naked in front of the balcony, she drinks several glasses of water. Water is life. Will the 'angel' fall (to the earth) as the title suggests? Or fly high?

Director, Screenwriter: **Semih Kaplanoğlu**; Producers: **Semih Kaplanoğlu**, Panayiotis Payazoglu, Yorgos Lykiardopoulos, Lilette Botassi; Production: Kaplan Film; Cinematographer: Eyüp Boz; Editors: **Semih Kaplanoğlu**, Ayhan Ergürsel, Susan Hande Güneri; Cast: Tülin Özen, Budak Akalın, Musa Karagöz, Engin Doğan, Yeşim Ceren Bozoğlu, Özlem Turhal, Can Kolukısa

Melodrama, as an organizing modality, an aesthetic register or form that is fluid across a range of **genres** – tragedy, **comedy**, romance – and spatial geographies (Gledhill 2000), has been one of the most popular **genres** in Turkish cinema, particularly during the **Yeşilçam** years from the 1950s to the 1980s. Set in 'modern' homes with art-deco furnishings, among the wealthy, leisured upper class, similar to 'white telephone' films of 1930s Italy, the narratives were adapted from famous novels of world literature, Turkish popular novels, 'Turkified' from Hollywood films popular in Turkey or based on original scripts that used hyperbole to appeal to the fantasies of the spectators. Some film-makers who started with this **genre** were easily forgotten while others made their mark. In the hands of **Atıf Yılmaz**, **Fevzi Tuna** and **Ömer Kavur**, focusing on issues of women, melodramas gained a psychological dimension.

Muhsin Ertuğrul is credited for introducing **melodrama** to Turkish cinema with *Istanbul'da Bir Facia-i Aşk / A Love Tragedy in Istanbul* (1922) that recounts the misfortunes of men who fall prey to a smart seductress. With *Aysel, Bataklı Damın Kızı / The Girl From the Marshes* aka *Aysel, the Girl From the Swampy Roof* (1935), he applied the **genre** to the rural milieu in the story of a deceived and deserted young maiden and set the precedence for countless similar **rural** melodramas. The popular Anatolian personality, **Muharrem Gürses** played an important role in the establishment of the village melodrama. Usually adapted from his novels, the 'Gürses melodramas' juxtaposed the good/bad, rich/poor and pretty/ugly binaries through hyperbolic love stories that stressed the positive values.

Atıf Yılmaz entered the industry with a strong melodrama, *Kanlı Feryat / Bloody Scream* (1951), but within the **genre**, created some landmarks such as *Selvi Boylum, Al Yazmalım / The Girl With the Red Scarf* (1977). **Lütfi Ö. Akad** also used the **genre** with success in films such as *Yanlızlar Rıhtımı / The Quay of the Lonely Ones* (1959). Some of the other successful film-makers of the **genre** are Muzaffer Arslan (*Billur Köşk / Cristal Palace*, 1962; *Ankara Ekspress / Ankara Express*, 1971), **Orhan Aksoy** (*Hıçkırık / The Sob*, 1965; *Kezban*, 1968), Nejat Saydam (*Mahpus / The Prisoner*, 1973), Mehmet Dinler (*Sinekli Bakkal / The Grocery with Flies*, 1967), Ülkü Erakalın (*Beklenen Şarkı / The Awaited Song*, 1971), **Türker İnanoğlu** (*Kiralık Koca / The Hired Husband*, 1962), Temel Gürsu (*İzin / Leave*, 1975, based on a **Yılmaz Güney** script), **Safa Önal** (*İnleyen Nameler / Wailing Melodies*, 1969 with famous singer, Zeki Müren) and **Ertem Eğilmez** (*Boş Çerçeve / Empty Frame*, 1969) (Onaran 1994: 180).

The reason behind the success of the melodramas is audience identification. **Fatma Girik, Filiz Akın, Hülya Koçyiğit, Türkan Şoray** were the most popular woman stars and **Cüneyt Arkın, Ediz Hun, Kadir İnanır, Kartal Tibet, Tarık Akan**, the handsome heroes. The specialness of these stars was 'a hysterical mimesis' of being 'caught in the other's imaginary, an idealistic identification in relation to the other's body and desire. Their appeal was being different but at the same time, ordinary' (Campbell 2005: 195). To protect their image, the women refused compromising roles.

Christine Gledhill asserts that Hollywood transformed melodrama by negating the 'class opposition' of European melodrama (Gledhill 1992: 103–24). Since the struggle between the aristocracy and bourgeoisie was not the issue within the socio-political system of the American culture, class oppositions were transformed into rural/urban and rich/poor oppositions, which is the backbone of Turkish melodrama. **Yeşilçam** equated lower class/rural with the east/local culture and upper class/urban with the west/foreign culture. The 'othering' of the West was an important element although **Yeşilçam**'s position was rather ambivalent. The upper class, presented as the object of desire, was also shown as the source of moral corruption, displayed with American cars, blonde women in provocative dresses, cocktail parties, whisky and gambling. Rural/lower class women were chaste and loyal. They dressed modestly, respected their elders and never contradicted their men. Men were poor, but honest. Emotions were expressed at extremities using hyperbole through the dialogue as well as performance that was shown in close-up.

Yeşilçam was closer to Eastern melodrama that focuses on the family rather than Western melodrama that routinely originates from a conflict in the family and then concentrates on the individual. Linear narrative followed the classical 'boy meets girl' tradition of Hollywood and relied on the cause–effect principle. Destiny, rather than one's struggles was the determining factor in overcoming obstacles and reaching a goal. The dissolution of a family or the separation of a couple were the typical motives for the conflict, which was perpetuated by false accusations, misunderstandings, infidelity, revenge, honour or class differences. Seduction, a frequent motif of Arab (particularly Egyptian) as well as South Asian melodrama, was an integral part of most melodramas, what Thomas Elsaesser defines as 'the metaphorical interpretation of class conflict as sexual exploitation and rape' (Elsaesser 1985: 168). The deceived and deserted woman, 'fallen' but always honourable, was very popular although she never found happiness. As social evil, she had to be eliminated to protect the family/society. When a good man came along and tried to make an 'honest woman' out of a prostitute, the first manifestation of the change was the headscarf (in ***Vesikalı Yarim / My Licensed Love***, **Akad**, 1968, **Türkan Şoray** dons the scarf to be worthy of an honest man although her skirt remains above her knees).

Yeşilçam endorsed the state ideology in glorifying the army. The army was usually the cause of several misfortunes in the melodramas. The lovers could not unite because the girl was given to another man while her fiancé was serving his country; the beloved son did not return from the army or the virtuous wife became a fallen woman when left without male protection, but the army as an institution was never reproached. Deaths or separations were attributed to *kader* (destiny).

Melodramas continue to attract audiences. **Çağan Irmak**'s *Babam ve Oğlum / My Father and My Son* (2005), which exploits the terror of the 1980 *coup* to build a **melodrama** that exalts the family over ideology, was dismissed by the foreign guests at the Istanbul International Film Festival as a 'tear-jerker', but was seen by almost four million people and praised by some local critics. According to critic/archivist Agah Özgüç, 'the audience needed a film that could reflect the sensibilities of the 1960s **Yeşilçam** using modern technology' (Dönmez-Colin 2008: 214).

Meta-films (*matruşka films*) focus on the insider issues of the film industry, the psychology of the film teams or the difficulties of making films. Among the prominent examples is **Yavuz Özkan**'s *Film Bitti / The Film Ended* (1989) about a performer couple about to divorce, obliged to play lovers and the repercussions of their frustrations, caught between the poetic love story on the screen and the daily friction at home, on the director and his cast and crew. **Atıf Yılmaz**'s *Hayallerim, Aşkım ve Sen / My Dreams, My Love and You* (1987) critiques cinema and the star system while casting the top star, **Türkan Şoray** in the lead playing herself, a first for an actor in a self-reflexive role. **Yavuz Turgul**'s tragi-comic satire *Aşk Filmlerinin Unutulmaz Yönetmeni / The Unforgettable Director of Love Movies* (1992) foregrounds the demise of **Yeşilçam**, criticizing those who deride the industry as denying an important part of the cinema history. **Ömer Kavur**'s *Gece Yolculuğu / Night Journey* (1987) is about a film-maker in location search who takes a decision to stop making films dictated by others, and shoot what he wants. Oğuzhan Tercan's *Uzlaşma / The Consensus* (1992) based on the true story of the murder of journalist Abdi İpekçi, focuses on the actor Berhan Şimşek, who is asked to play the murderer Mehmet Ali Ağca (who also shot the Pope), but he has to look like him. **Nuri Bilge Ceylan**'s *Mayıs Sıkıntısı / Clouds of May* (1999) features a self-centred film-maker who exploits his family and Murat Şeker's *İki Süper Film Birden / Two Super Films* (2006) is a **comedy** about young cinema lovers through the story of a Machiavellian character who wants to make an experimental film without a script and without actors.

Mine (1982), a pioneer in exploration of the emotional and sexual needs of women in a society that negates love, was one of the most successful films of its period, coinciding with the belated arrival of the feminist movement. In the provincial town of Samsun, a cinema with 200-seat capacity was closed to men when 190 women arrived (Dönmez-Colin 2004: 145). With her role as Mine, **Türkan Şoray**, the top star of Turkish cinema liberated herself from her self-imposed taboos about kissing and going to bed on screen to create a flesh-and-blood character.

The opening shot establishes an idyllic town, serene with chirping birds and a calm sea. Married to the older uninspiring stationmaster before finishing high school, Mine depends on barbiturates to escape the pains of her unfulfilled hopes and desires while she waits for 'a new face with the arrival of each train'. Men fantasize about her. The town doctor laments, 'A light is lit at the station and we are like moths… The malaise of the town is Mrs Mine and it is contagious.' Restraining herself from ordinary activities like taking a walk, or having ice-cream in public to avoid derogatory remarks, she finds comfort in her friend, Perihan, the school-teacher and her urban intellectual brother, İlhan, who casts a critical eye but only from distance. His social awareness does not go beyond jeering remarks about the 'Dallas Café' inside the monumental Seljuk madrassa. For Perihan (voicing **Yılmaz**), he is 'just like many of our intellectuals' who escape responsibility. Mine's awakening, which has been developing through the books Perihan lends her, culminates in a confrontation with her husband when she tells him he never saw her as a human being: she has always been waist, hip, breast…for him and for the rest of the menfolk. When a group of intoxicated men attacks her, no one interferes. She defends herself with her husband's hunting gun, wounding two. Then she runs to İlhan and pleads with him to sleep with her. 'They all think I did anyway.' At the end, they leave the house like criminals, but with pride, their hands joined as they run the gauntlet. Although he had never declared love or promised her a future together, he is involved against his better judgement. In the morning, the town is back to normal, street cleaners, the train, but her window is empty.

According to some critics, this is the first time in Turkish cinema that a married woman commits adultery. It was also a small revolution to cast **Şoray**, the icon of chastity, as the adulteress although the repulsive qualities of her husband somewhat alleviated the transgression. **Yılmaz**'s critical eye on the urban individual, distant to the texture of the society en masse, is very precise. The ending proves that it is no longer possible to be a passive spectator to the misery of the other. However, several questions remain unanswered. Does Mine give herself to the man because she has evolved through the experience to an independent woman, or is her act only a rebellion against an unjust and hypocritical society? Why doesn't the man reflect on this aspect but accept her willingly? Does a woman need a man to be emancipated? Just like in *Bir Yudum Sevgi / A Taste of Love* (1984), **Yılmaz** seems to offer one solution to women imprisoned in unhappy marriages: try another man. Seeking liberation in individual struggle does not seem to be an alternative for 1980s Turkey.

Director: **Atıf Yılmaz (Batıbeki)**; Producer: **Atıf Yılmaz**, Sadık Deveci, **Ömer Kavur**; Production: Delta Film; Screenwriters: **Atıf Yılmaz**, Deniz Türkali, Necati Cumalı; Cinematographer: **Salih Dikişçi**; Music: Cahit Berkay; Cast: **Türkan Şoray**, Cihan Ünal, Hümeyra Akbay, Kerim Afşar, Belkıs Dilligil, Selçuk Uluergüven, Celile Toyon, Orhan Çağman

Muhsin Bey / Mr Muhsin (1987) is a tragi-comic social commentary on the economic and cultural transformation of Turkey during the post-*coup d'état* years of the 1980s and the free-market policies of President Turgut Özal (prime minister and president, 1983–93), similar to the Thatcher–Reagan policies. The story is told through the cultural clash between Mr Muhsin Kanadıkırık (broken wing), a middle-aged impresario played in remarkable style by **Şener Şen** and Ali Nazik (**Uğur Yücel**), an Anatolian youth from Urfa with a promising voice who betrays him by becoming a celebrated **arabesque** star and seducing his romantic love object, the widow Sevda. Unlike the romantic **comedies** and **melodramas** of **Yeşilçam** that use fantasies of social climbing to replace social analysis, or the engagé cinema that critiques the imposition of socio-economic circumstances as an important factor for a desire for social climbing, *Mr Muhsin* brings a cultural dimension to the issue in a period of transition when survival equals opportunism, intellectualism is shunned and money is the only valuable commodity. The **Yeşilçam** cliché of rags to riches through being discovered as a singer also receives a realistic treatment. The **arabesque** culture, associated with the liminality of the migrant Anatolians, who are neither able to preserve their culture nor adapt the culture of the western metropolises, has transformed the urban culture. Mr Muhsin, an Istanbul gentleman of principles with a passion for

Figure 85 Muhsin Bey / Mr Muhsin (Yavuz Turgul, 1987) (Courtesy of International Istanbul Film Festival)

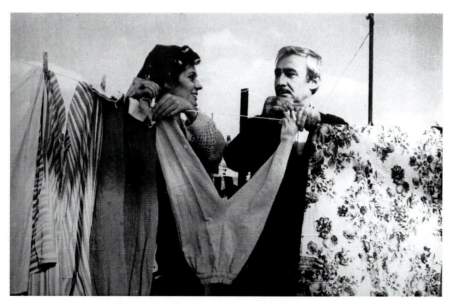

Figure 86 Muhsin Bey / Mr Muhsin (Yavuz Turgul, 1987) (Courtesy of International Istanbul Film Festival)

Turkish classical music, an impresario with the old values, tries to resist the influx of degenerate club bosses, television producers and recording company moguls, but he fails. On the other hand, Ali Nazik, who represents the new culture, quickly obtains success.

The characters are identified through the spaces they occupy in the film. The Beyoğlu district, with its back streets, music halls and singing contests, carries a certain nostalgia that is commensurate with the cinematic style of **Turgul**, laden with **Yeşilçam** clichés of friendship, love/betrayal and unforeseen events. Yet, he intermingles these elements with a search for an original narrative that balances the comic elements with the sentimental aspect, creating a memorable character and a remarkable film that is often included in lists of the ten best Turkish films of all time.

Director, Screenwriter: **Yavuz Turgul**; Producer: **Abdurrahman Keskiner**; Production: Umut Film; Cinematographer: Aytekin Çakmakçı; Music: Atilla Özdemiroğlu; Cast: **Şener Şen**, Sermin Hürmeriç, **Uğur Yücel**, Osman Cavcı, Erdoğan Sıcak, Erdinç Üstün

N

National cinema debate surfaced in the 1960s as a reaction to the **cinematheque** group that considered **Yeşilçam** escapist and exploitative, its plagiarism and cliché formulae incompatible with a national cinema that aims at international standards, excluding from their circle **Metin Erksan**, who had received the Golden Bear the previous year with his *Susuz Yaz / A Dry Summer* (1963), and other prominent film-makers: **Halit Refiğ**, **Lütfi Ö. Akad** and **Atıf Yılmaz**. Two concepts of national cinema, *ulusal* cinema and *milli* cinema, divided the film-makers further. Both words mean national except *milli* is Ottoman; some critics consider both trends Ottomanist and *milli* cinema essentially Islamist but unable to lay an open claim to religion due to Item 163 of the constitution that forbids using religion for such a purpose (Aydın 1997).

Ulusal cinema, a cinema with nationalist ambitions, emphasizing the behaviour of all Turkish people through a common history and a heritage of traditional, cultural and social life experiences, was initiated by **Halit Refiğ** who advocated **Yeşilçam**, supported by a large audience as the true national cinema; it was not possible to reach the Turkish people using the Western forms. Several film-makers, who found the **cinematheque** and its publication, *Yeni Sinema / New Cinema*, 'hostile' to Turkish cinema, signed to refuse to collaborate with them, proposing in return, *Asya Tipi Üretim Tarzı – ATÜT* (Asian Style of Production). **Refiğ** published his articles in *Ulusal Sinema Kavgası / National Cinema Dispute* (1971), underscoring the anti-imperialist role of cinema similar to what the theoreticians of Third Cinema promulgated and stressing the importance of promoting the cultural heritage. His *Gurbet Kuşları / The Birds of Nostalgia* aka *Migrating Birds* aka *Birds of Exile* (1964), *Haremde Dört Kadın / Four Women in the Harem* (1965) and *Bir Türk'e Gönül Verdim / I Fell in Love with a Turk* (1969) are examples of this stand. Starting in 1967, **Metin Erksan**, **Halit Refiğ**, **Memduh Ün** and **Atıf Yılmaz**, engaged in the *ulusal* cinema concept, published a journal called *Ulusal Sinema* (*National Cinema*), which had only three editions.

Milli cinema focused on the identity of the Turks within the Islam–Turk culture since leaving Central Asia and underlined the degeneration caused by Westernization (Onaran 1994). **Yücel Çakmaklı** (*Kızım Ayşe / My Daughter, Ayşe*, 1974) was the forerunner of the trend that focused on national stories built within the framework of commercial considerations, but always with a religious message. The aim was to regain the audience alienated by the cheap sex furore on one side and the militant politics on the other. For **Yılmaz Güney** for whom cinema had an active role in the class struggle, such movements were to be examined as counter-developments against the revolutionary democratic movement. For him, to be national was to be anti-imperialist. 'What is called "Islamic cinema" is only the manifestation of a reactionary attitude,' he claimed, 'In many corners of the world, Muslim people struggle for their liberation. Cinema that narrates the revolutionary struggles of the Muslim people is not Islamic cinema but revolutionary cinema. Instead of the geographical or religious angles, we must evaluate the problem from the angle of class' (**Güney** 1994a: 27–9).

New Turkish Cinema, not to be confused with the New Cinema movement that was started in 1970 with **Yılmaz Güney**'s *Umut / The Hope*, emerged in the late 1990s following a stagnant period when film production was negligible. The dominance of the *auteur* and the *mise en scène*, the self-reflexive counter-cinema practices, a deliberate distantiation to avoid audience identification, the subversion of the **genres**, the use of counterpoint and elliptic editing, the attention to camera work and the script (often written by the director) and the tendency to use non-professional actors, are the characteristics of the New Turkish Cinema that has distinguished itself with its search for new economic, aesthetic and thematic models in exploring national, global and personal identities in the modern world. The main themes are survival in the urban jungle, nostalgia for the rural home, alienation in a constantly changing society, the threat to physical and/or mental space/territory and the atmosphere of insecurity when the familiar becomes uncanny.

Derviş Zaim, **Zeki Demirkubuz**, **Yeşim Ustaoğlu** and **Nuri Bilge Ceylan** are the pioneers of this movement that also includes **Semih Kaplanoğlu**, **Tayfun Pirselimoğlu**, **Handan İpekçi**, **Barış Pirhasan** and **Reha Erdem** among others. However, the movement is not a *nouvelle vague* in the French sense; the conduit of each film-maker is unique despite thematic and artistic convergence points and certain parallels in the modes of production. **Zaim**, whose debut feature *Tabutta Rövaşata / Somersault in a Coffin* (1997) is considered a landmark for the emergence of this new period, calls his generation 'alluvionic film-makers'; they flow in the same direction, but the linkages take different forms. They work 'independently but also parallel to one another, similar to the sediments of alluvium that together form an alluvion. At times, they come together, and at times, spread apart, as do alluvia'. This analogy, he believes is accurate in defining the dynamics and diversity of the group, which pursues different styles and different forms of production, financing and distribution (**Zaim** 2008: 86).

Born in the 1960s, film school graduates or products of the traditional apprentice–master system, the film-makers of the New Turkish Cinema are familiar with the national cinematic tradition as well as the cinemas of the West, not only the theory and the aesthetics, but also the alternative modes of production and exhibition. The opening of several film schools, global advancements in technology and communications, financial initiatives that have become available

– European funds and government loans – and the relaxation of the censorship regulations could be cited as contributing factors for the new vitality, which is recognized in the West as well as in the home territory with numerous prestigious awards including the Grand Prix and Best Male Actor awards (shared by Mehmet Emin Toprak and Muzaffer Özdemir) at the Cannes Film Festival in 2003 for **Ceylan**'s *Uzak / Distant* (2002), a first for Turkish cinema since *Yol* (**Şerif Gören**) shared the Palme d'or with *Missing* of Costa Gavras in 1982 and the Golden Bear at the Berlin Film Festival for *Bal / Honey* of **Semih Kaplanoğlu**.

In the new millennium, a new generation has emerged with films directly focused on the social, economic and political issues of the country. Some of these film-makers are Kurdish and essentially foreground the issues of the Kurdish people in their films: **Hüseyin Karabey** (*Gitmek / My Marlon and Brando*, 2008), **Kazım Öz** (*Fotograf / The Photograph*, 2001; *Bahoz / Fırtına / The Storm*, 2008), **Orhan Eskiköy** and **Zeynel Doğan** (*Babamın Sesi / Dengê Bavê Min / The Voice of My Father*, 2012). Others, **Özcan Alper** (*Sonbahar / Autumn*, 2007; *Gelecek Uzun Sürer / The Future Lasts Forever*, 2011); **İnan Temelkuran** (*Bornova, Bornova*, 2009); **Emin Alper** (*Tepenin Ardı / Beyond the Hill*, 2012), focus on the issues of unemployment, the generation gap, the cultural degeneration, the question of citizenship, the freedom of expression, the state terrorism, the violence against women and the paranoia of the 'other'. 'Masculinity in crisis', which is an important theme in the films of **Ceylan** and his generation, is intensified in the younger generation's films. Liminal characters, between the East and the West, the urban and the rural, modernity and tradition, the imposed Turkish/Muslim/white/male identity and individuality are the anti-heroes of these films.

Nur, Muhterem (b. Monastir, Yugoslavia, 1932) Actor, singer, dancer; RN: Aysel Muhterem Kısa. Belonging to a refugee family, Muhterem Nur worked in factories for several years until she had a chance to enter cinema as an extra. A popular star of the 1950s–60s as the weeping willow, her breakthrough came with her role as the blind girl in **Memduh Ün**'s *Üç Arkadaş / Three Friends* (1958). Her career declined with the gradual demise of **melodramas** and she resorted to singing and dancing in second-class music halls for her living. The industry began to appreciate her contribution to Turkish cinema with an honour award from the International Istanbul Film Festival in 1998, the Lifetime Achievement Award from the Antalya Golden Orange Film Festival in 2003 and from the Bursa Silk Road Film Festival in 2008. She was married to the legendary **arabesque** singer Müslüm Gürses in 1986, who passed away in 2013.

O

Oğuz, Orhan (b. Kırklareli, 1948) Director, cinematographer, screenwriter. Starting as a camera assistant when he was only 16, Orhan Oğuz made short films and exhibited his photography before launching a career as a cinematographer in 1978. He received several awards as a cinematographer from the Antalya Golden Orange Film Festival: *Tomruk / Log* (**Şerif Gören**, 1982), *Amansız Yol / Desperate Road* (**Ömer Kavur**, 1985), *Dul Bir Kadın / A Widow* (**Atıf Yılmaz**, 1985) and *Fırtına Gönüller / Stormy Hearts* (Ümit Efekan, 1984). In 1987, he received the best cinematographer award of the Film Critics Association and made his directorial debut with *Herşeye Rağmen / Despite Everything*, for which he is also the cinematographer. The film received several national and international awards including the youth prize at the Cannes Film Festival. Following the rather insignificant *Üçüncü Göz / The Third Eye* (1989) and *İki Başlı Dev / Purgatory* (1991), *Dönersen Islık Çal / Whistle If You Come Back* (1993) drew attention with its focus on a current theme in the 1990s – social exclusion. The story of a friendship between a dwarf barman and a transvestite prostitute, the film is somewhat contrived but attention to details without voyeurism is noteworthy, so is the observation of a city experiencing gentrification. *Manisa Tarzanı / Tarzan of Manisa* (1994) and *Kara Kentin Çocukları / Losers of the Dark City* (1999) passed unnoticed whereas *Hayde Bre* (2010) failed on several grounds. One of the founders of the Eskişehir Anadolu University, Oğuz continues his career directing mostly television series.

Okan, Tunç (b. Istanbul, 1942) Director, actor, producer, screenwriter, editor; RN: Okan Külen. A dentist by profession, Tunç Okan has made few films but each one has made a mark in the history of Turkish cinema. He was chosen by the popular *Ses* magazine in 1965 for its cover, which led to main roles with the stars of the period in a dozen films. He stopped his acting career to study in Bern and in 1976, without any previous experience, he produced and directed the internationally acclaimed ***Otobüs / The Bus*** (1976), banned in Turkey for a long period. He received his doctorate from Bern University in 1980. He co-produced and directed *Cumartesi Cumartesi / Drole de Samedi / Saturday Saturday* (1985) in Neuchatel, Switzerland, adapted from Friedrich Dürrenmatt, with a distinguished French cast. Then he adapted Adalet Ağaoğlu's *Fikrimin İnce Gülü* to screen as

Fikrimin İnce Gülü / Sarı Mersedes / Mercedes Mon Amour (1992), a **comedy** about the misadventures of a Turkish worker who returns to his village with the Mercedes Benz he buys with his hard-earned money. The film garnered several awards at the Antalya Golden Orange Film Festival and was chosen as the best film of the year by the critics. *Umut Üzümleri / Grapes of Hope* (2012), adapted from a story by Fakir Baykurt, is about the conflict between the individual and the system that remains unchanged despite changes in production and living styles.

Okay, Yaman (b. Giresun, 1951 – d. Istanbul, 1993) Actor. Starting his acting career on stage, Yaman Okay entered **Yeşilçam** with *Sürü / The Herd* (**Zeki Ökten**, 1978). Some of his memorable roles were in *Bereketli Topraklar Üzerinde / On Fertile Land* (**Kıral**, 1979), *Yılanı Öldürseler / If They Could Kill the Snake* (**Şoray**, 1981), *Asiye Nasıl Kurtulur? / How Can Asiye Be Saved?* (**Atıf Yılmaz**, 1986), *40 Quadratmeter Deutschland / Forty Square Meters of Germany* (**Tevfik Başer**, 1986) and *Reise der Hoffnung / Journey of Hope* (Xavier Koller, 1990). Husband of actor and screenwriter Meral Okay, he died of pancreatic cancer when he was 42.

Olcay, Zuhal (b. Istanbul, 1957) Actor, singer. Starting her career in cinema in 1983, Zühal Olcay gave memorable roles in *Amansız Yol / Desperate Road* (1985), *Gece Yolculuğu / Night Journey* (1987) and *Gizli Yüz / The Secret Face* (1991) of **Ömer Kavur**, *Abschied vom Falschen Paradies / Farewell to False Paradise / Yanlış Cennete Elveda* (**Tevfik Başer**, 1988) and *Hiçbiryerde / Innowhereland* (**Tayfun Pirselimoğlu**, 2002). She is also a well-known singer.

Olgaç, Bilge (b. Kırklareli, 1940 – d. Istanbul, 1994) Director, screenwriter, producer. Considered as the only full-fledged woman film-maker of Turkish cinema with over 30 films to her credit, several of which she wrote, Bilge Olgaç started her film career in 1962 within **Yeşilçam** as an assistant to **Memduh Ün**. Her first film, *Üçünüzü de Mıhlarım / I'll Nail the Three of You* (1965) was a gangster yarn with **Yılmaz Güney**, the 'ugly king', who slaughtered everyone to restore the family honour. After several similar films with macho heroes, she drew attention with *Linç / Lynch* (1970), an indictment of the prison system, reputed to be the first Turkish film without a female character (except a girl that briefly appears in a dream). *Açlık / Hunger* (1974) was a critique of the land, the landlord and the predicaments of women in feudal societies. Disillusioned by the gangster yarns and porno fare that **Yeşilçam** began to manufacture during the politically repressive 1970s, Olgaç left the big screen after completing the controversial docu-fiction *Bir Gün Mutlaka / One Day For Sure* (unofficial English title) (1975), written by **Yılmaz Güney** about the political climate of the period. Working on television commercials for almost a decade, she returned with a powerful black **comedy**, *Kaşık Düşmanı / Spoon Enemy* aka *A Wedding Room* (1984) and continued her career within the traditions of **Yeşilçam** but with a focus on the plight of the underprivileged women in the rural milieu. *Gülüşan* (1986) exposed the suppressed sexual world of a man whose yearning for a son reaches fanatical proportions. *Üç Halka Yirmibeş / Three Rings Twenty-five* (1986) denounced patriarchal hypocrisy. *İpekçe / Silky* (1987), one of her most accomplished films, was about the tragedy of a beautiful woman who mysteriously arrives in a remote village and *Gömlek / The Shirt* (1988) was an indictment of the feudal system.

Despite awards at film festivals, her films did not have many distribution opportunities. The most important woman film-maker of Turkey died poor and alone when her modest apartment at the centre of Istanbul, heated by an old stove, caught fire; she was burned alive with the reels of her films.

Ormanlar, Kenan (b. Scopia, 1937) Cinematographer, screenwriter, producer. One of the most important cinematographers of Turkish cinema, Munich-based Kenan Ormanlar went to Germany in 1960 to study cinema. Later he continued his studies in Warsaw and Paris. The recipient of several awards, he is best remembered for his remarkable work in *Endişe / Anxiety* (Şerif Gören, 1974); *Zavallılar / The Poor* aka *The Suffering Ones* (Yılmaz Güney, Atıf Yılmaz, 1974); *At / The Horse* (Ali Özgentürk, 1982); *Hakkaride Bir Mevsim / A Season in Hakkari* (1983); *Ayna / The Mirror* (1984), *Av Zamanı / Time for Hunting* (1988) and *Mavi Sürgün / The Blue Exile* (1993) of **Erden Kıral**.

Otobüs / The Bus (1976) is one of the landmark films on migration and cross-border trafficking with its precise rendition of an acute problem and remarkable film language. Its international screening became an event. Although the film won several important awards, Turkish officials, expatriates and a large number of local critics considered it an exploitative disgrace. The government censored it for deriding the Turks (showing them eating bread and onions, disobeying the traffic rules etc.). It was shown on private television channels two decades later.

The exodus of Turkish workers to Germany began after a treaty was signed between the two countries in 1961, but those seeking employment were not supported by an organized government programme. Hundreds of naïve peasants were the victims of schemes that robbed them of their limited resources. *The Bus* is one such story. Several male peasants are packed in a decrepit bus for a journey to Germany where they are told they will have jobs. Through a foggy country landscape that blurs the vision and augments the disorientation and anxiety of the travellers, the bus follows a route pre-planned by a Hamburg mafia, worse swindlers than the Turkish driver who confiscates all the money and the passports and leaves the bus parked at the centre of the main square in Stockholm. The unsuspecting peasants pull the curtains and start waiting. Stepping out for their natural needs in the dark, they see a world that is nefariously different. A man and a woman copulate in a telephone booth and an addict asks for drugs in the toilet (a *clin d'oeil* to the West's stereotyping of all Eastern men as dealers). One of them loses his way and freezes to death, falling into an icy pool; the response of a passer-by is 'filthy foreign bum'. Another follows a gay man, mistaking his advances for friendship. A party scene, caricaturized to underscore the affluent decadence of the West, displays a playboy contest based on the cars the men drive, the image of which is printed on their bikini slips. Porno movies are watched as the orgy commences, but when the hungry peasant devours all the available food, he is thrown out for bad manners, to be killed for the colour of his skin and his dark moustache.

Most displacement films establish the protagonist's identity and its destabilizations through attempts at, and failures of, self-location valourizing the use of space/place. Film scholar Hamid Naficy points out, 'Exilic border spaces and border crossings are inscribed not only in fixed transitional sites, such as airports, seaports, tunnels, hotels, and motels, but also in mobile spaces such as vehicles and suitcases. Claustrophobia pervades the mise-en-scène, shot composition, and often the narratives of films that feature buses and trains as vehicles and symbols of displacement. And since these vehicles travel through countryside and wide-open spaces and between countries, there is always a dialectical relationship in the accented films between the inside closed spaces of the vehicles and the outside open spaces of nature and nation. Inexorably, vehicles provide not only empirical links to geographic places and social groupings but also metaphoric reworkings of notions of travelling, homing, and identity' (Naficy 2001: 257). Inside the bus is the village, where everyone knows each other. Outside are merciless strangers. Those who stay together are safer, the bus becomes a trope for the ghettos in the peripheries of the industrial centres such as the shantytowns around Istanbul where people transport their village customs and traditions. In **Gelin / The Bride** (**Akad**, 1973), the patriarch Hacı İlyas declares, 'inside the walls of this house is Yozgat, Istanbul is outside'.

Unlike other immigration films of the period, *The Bus* is not about integration; the Turks are lost in Stockholm as soon as they arrive (no papers, no vocabulary, no existence), before facing the customary adaptation and integration problems, rendering the assumed efficacy of the social system of Sweden irrelevant. At the end, the bus is confiscated and the peasants are arrested without having a chance to benefit from the 'affluence' of Swedish society (Bassan 1979: 186–7).

The Bus is about the impossibility of dialogue between two different cultures, a materialist society (capitalist or communist) and a typical third world society according to **Okan**. There is no dialogue in the film between the Turks and the Swedes. Without incriminating the developed countries, the film questions the viability of the globally emulated Western development model of consumer society, emulated as a solution for happiness. The driver is a trope for the *petite bourgeoisie* of the underdeveloped countries anxious to become Western at all costs but not able to find their place in the society they admire. The West is not only about money, sex and development, as the driver imagines (Thoraval and Hennebelle 1979: 187–8).

Despite the use of hyperbole and the stereotypical and caricaturized representations of both the Western and Eastern elements, particularly in the Stockholm episodes, the film is close to reality in terms of reflecting the first impressions of the pioneer Turkish workers with implications for the unresolved border issues today. The hypocrisy of the Western concept of charity (with distance and usually coinciding with Christmas) is smartly exposed through the images of the Salvation Army singing hymns for peace while foreign peasants starve to death at the centre of affluent Stockholm. The phantasmagorical ending of the towed bus exploding in mid-air is a very strong message to what came to be known in recent years as 'fortress Europe' (Dönmez-Colin 2008: 70–1).

Director, Screenwriter, Editor: **Tunç Okan** (stated as 'Bay Okan' in the end-credits); Producer: Arif Keskiner, **Tunç Okan**, Cengiz Ergun; Production: Pan Film; Cinematographer: Güneş Karabuda; Music: **Zülfü Livaneli**, Pierre Favre, Leon Françoli; Cast: **Tunç Okan, Tuncel Kurtiz**, Björn Gedda, Aras Ören, Nuri Sezer, Hasan Gül, Sümer İşgör

Otobüs Yolcuları / The Bus Passengers (1961), based on a script by Marxist intellectual **Vedat Türkali**, is one of the first examples of the **social realist** movement along with another **Göreç–Türkali** collaboration, *Karanlıkta Uyananlar / Those Awakening in the Dark* (1964), both made in the aftermath of the 1960 *coup d'état* that was relatively liberating for the left ideology. A love story interwoven with a true story of corruption in the construction business, the film was a box-office success, particularly due to its star cast. The protagonist Kemal (**Ayhan Işık**), a handsome intelligent young man whose education was interrupted for financial reasons, drives the municipal bus, loves literature and writes poetry. 'When I got worried, I read; the more I read, the more worried I got', he tells the university student Nevin (**Türkan Şoray**), his romantic interest, who is the modest daughter of a rich bad man. Kemal is the demarcation line between the good and the bad. A man with political consciousness, he does not hesitate to use brute force to fight injustices, believing the arena must not be left to inequality, exploitation or capitalism.

The binaries of rich/poor are clearly marked, particularly by territory as in **Yeşilçam** films. Ordinary citizens live in harmony in friendly neighbourhoods despite the occasional strife; the 'degenerate' rich are isolated and alone. Nevin is kind-hearted but his younger brother and his friends are depicted as Turkish James Deans, rebels without a cause with leather jackets and motorcycles. At the end, the good – the proletariat that live with their sweat – triumph over the bad rich that live in plenty but without meaning. Despite giving precedence to the message over artistic concerns, the weakness of similar **social realist** films, solidarity's indispensible role in the combat against the oppressor is an important issue raised in the film, which is also the message in **Yılmaz Güney**'s *Umut / The Hope* (1970).

In accordance with the norm of the period, the city is presented as an attractive space with historical and cultural identity. As Kemal's bus crosses over the bridges, panoramic images of Istanbul are revealed with the mosque of Sultan Suleiman the Magnificent dominating the view. The city's Western face is accentuated, showing the passengers throwing their tickets into public garbage cans when they leave the bus. But **Göreç**'s camera also dwells on the new settlements, testimony to the rapid expansion of the city through migration and the subject of shady construction deals and quick riches schemes. Utopia can soon turn to dystopia.

Director: **Ertem Göreç**; Producer: Nusret İkbal; Production: Be-Ya Film; Screenwriter: **Vedat Türkali**; Cinematographer: Turgut Ören; Music: Yalçın Tura; Folk songs: Ruhi Su; Cast: **Ayhan Işık, Türkan Şoray**, Senih Orkan, Salih Tozan, Suna Pekuysal, Ahmet Tarık Tekçe, Reha Yurdakul, Atıf Kaptan, Suphi Kaner, Avni Dilligil, Diclehan Baban

Ö

Ökten, Zeki (b. Istanbul, 1941 – d. Istanbul, 2009) Director, screenwriter, producer, editor. Renowned for the internationally acclaimed *Sürü / The Herd* (1978), Zeki Ökten entered **Yeşilçam** as third assistant to **Halit Refiğ** and spent a few years assisting other renowned film-makers, **Lütfi Ö. Akad**, **Medun Ün** and especially **Atıf Yılmaz**. Ökten made his first feature *Ölüm Pazarı / Death Market* in 1963, which drew some interest at the box-office, mostly due to its cast – Tanju Gürsu, **Erol Taş** and Altan Erbulak – but did not satisfy him. He returned to assistantship with **Yılmaz** for nine years and then shot *Kadın Yapar / Woman Does It* (1972), following it with 24 more films up to 1988, among which *Bir Demet Menekşe / A Bouquet of Violet* and *Askerin Dönüşü / The Return of the Soldier*, made the same year (1973) from scripts by the renowned writer Selim İleri, were promising. *Kapıcılar Kralı / The King of Doormen* (1976), *Çöpçüler Kralı / The King of Garbage Men* (1977), *Faize Hücum / The Rush On Interest* (1983) (scripted by **Fehmi Yaşar**) and *Yoksul / The Poor*, slapstick comedies with a social message, with **Kemal Sunal** in the lead, were successful nationally. *Sürü / The Herd* (1978) and *Düşman / The Enemy* (1979), both written by **Yılmaz Güney**, received numerous national and international awards, but Ökten's name was overshadowed by **Güney**. *Pehlivan / The Wrestler* (1984), a realistic portrait of a village boy's dreams and disillusions, and *Ses / The Voice* (1986), one of the first films to deal with the trauma of the 1980 *coup*, also written by **Yaşar**, garnered awards although *The Voice*, despite Ökten's good intentions, failed to present a deeper analysis, perhaps due to censorship. After *Düttürü Dünya / The Queer World* aka *Wacky World* (1988), another **Kemal Sunal** film that focused on the housing problems of the less advantaged from a tragi-comic angle, he withdrew from the industry except for a short film in 1995, *Hep Aynı / Always the Same*, about the generation gap. In 2000, he returned with *Güle Güle / Raindrop*, a **melodrama** about the reunion of ageing friends on the island where they were born, presenting human landscapes from daily life – a religious mechanic, a military officer, a provincial homemaker, an old bachelor who has never left the island and a romantic who dreams of joining his love in Cuba, each character representing a segment of Turkish society. The **Zeki Alasya–Metin Akpınar** duo who made people laugh for so many years made them cry in this film that was successful at the box-office and awarded as the Best Film at the 37th Golden

Orange Film Festival. *Gülüm / My Rose* (2003), on the generation gap and the erosion of values, was not very successful. *Çinliler Geliyor / The Chinese Are Coming* (2007), a gentle satire on globalization, modernism, real estate and the tourism boom and the domination of the Internet, was somewhat anachronistic in style for the film-going public of the 2000s.

Önal, Sefa (b. Istanbul, 1931) Screenwriter, director, producer. With almost 400 scripts that have been filmed, Sefa Önal has made it into the Guinness Book of World Records. He started directing in 1973 and has made about 40 films, the last one being *Hicran Sokağı / Street of Sadness* (unofficial English title) (2007). Among his remarkable contributions as screenwriter are ***Vesikalı Yarim / My Licensed Love*** (**Lütfi Ö. Akad**, 1968) and *Dönüş / Return* (1972) and *Bodrum Hakimi / The Judge of Bodrum* (1976) by **Türkan Şoray**.

Önder, Sırrı Süreyya (b. Adıyaman, 1962) Director, screenwriter, composer, actor, columnist, politician. Having spent seven years of his life as a political prisoner, Sırrı Süreyya Önder co-directed his first film *Beynelmilel / International* (2007) with Muharrem Gülmez on the darkest days of the 1980 *coup d'état*, which has left deep scars on the modern Turkish psyche. The film starts as a **comedy** about a romantic love story, but ends with unexpected political violence, a reference to the lives of ordinary apolitical citizens trusting in false security who are awakened one day with the stark reality. He is one of the directors of *F-Tipi / F-Type Film* (2012), about solitary confinement cells in prisons.

Figure 87 Beynelmilel / International (Muharrem Gülmez, Sırrı Süreyya Önder, 2007) (Courtesy of International Istanbul Film Festival)

Öz, Kazım (b. Tunceli (Dersim), 1973) Director, screenwriter, producer, cinematographer, editor. One of the pioneers of **Kurdish cinema** that drew attention in the early 2000s, Kazım Öz focuses on absence and loss in his films. He graduated in civil engineering from the Yıldız Technical University in Istanbul (1998) and did his masters in the Cinema and Television Department of Marmara University (2003). He was one of the young film-makers actively involved in the student movements of the 1990s who started to make short films within the Mesopotamia Cultural Centre (MKM). He acted on stage, co-directed documentaries and worked as assistant director to **Yeşim Ustaoğlu** in *Güneşe Yolculuk / Journey to the Sun* (1998). His 27-minute *Ax / Toprak / Land* (1999) was about an elderly Kurd who refuses to leave his village after it is evacuated by the military. His first feature *Fotograf / The Photograph* (2001) was made with the support of the Mesopotamian Cinema Collective, part of MKM. *Bahoz / Fırtına / The Storm* (2008), which takes place in and around the University of Istanbul, focalizes the student movements of the 1990s, but for Öz it could refer to any student movement (and not limited to Kurdish students) as little has changed. *Dur / Uzak / Far Away* (2005), a documentary on migration and its aftermath, is the outcome of a project that began in 1997, when he visited his natal village after a long absence and noticed an unbearable silence – no voices of children, no sign of life except a handful of silent old people – which prompted him to explore the stories of similar villages emptied of two generations, mainly through migration. The film traces his journey from Istanbul to his natal village and then to Köln, to where many of the younger villagers have emigrated. Through stylistic narrative devices such as the staged return gaze and the non-matching voice-over, Öz exposes the pain of loss and absence while attempting to bridge the spatio-temporal, generational and cultural gap experienced by the Kurdish people who do not have a homeland. *Son Mevsim: Şavaklar / Demsala Dawî: Şewaxan / The Last Season: Shawaks* (2009) about a year in the life of nomads is another documentary.

Özbatur Atakan, Zeynep (b. Istanbul, 1966) Producer. One of the most successful producers of the generation schooled in the profession, Zeynep Özbatur Atakan is the recipient of the European co-production prize – Prix **Eurimages** (2010). She has been working in film and commercial production since 1986. A graduate of the Department of Cinema and Television at Marmara University (1991), in 1994, she became one of the founding members of CO Productions, which produced numerous commercials. Then she founded her own production company, Zeyno Film, in 2007, which is also involved in training young professionals in the Turkish cinema industry. Her credits as producer include the award-winning *İklimler / Climates* (2006), *Üç Maymun / Three Monkeys* (2008) and *Bir Zamanlar Anadolu'da / Once Upon a Time in Anatolia* (2011), all directed by **Nuri Bilge Ceylan** and supported by **Eurimages**.

Özer, Muammer (b. Bilecik, 1945) Director, screenwriter, producer, actor, cinematographer, editor. Known for the award-winning, *Bir Avuç Cennet / A*

Figure 88 Kara Sevdalı Bulut / Cloud Madly in Love (Muammer Özer, 1989) (Courtesy of International Istanbul Film Festival)

Handful of Paradise (1985), a drama about an Anatolian couple's desperate efforts to have a home, even if it is an old bus, Muammer Özer's studies were interrupted at an early age because of poverty. He tried to make short films and advertisements during his military service. In 1970, he went to Germany and after working there for a period, he went to Finland to study film. Moving to Sweden in 1977, he initiated Kaleidoscope, the Foreign Film-makers' Association (1981), which showed films about immigrants made by immigrants. Eventually these events evolved into an International Immigrant Film Festival. Following his first feature, *Kardeş Kanı / Splittring* (1984), his *Kara Sevdalı Bulut / Cloud Madly in Love*, shot in Istanbul in 1987 was confiscated (negative and the print) by the police in 1988 following an alert from the film laboratories, a first for the police to confiscate a film before passing through the censors. Compared to *Midnight Express*, the film was cleared in 1989 after a long judicial procedure and protests in Turkey and abroad, but its screening was forbidden in Turkey due to the subject of torture, considered a threat against national security. The film is a strong polemic against institutionalized terror and torture through the story of a tortured woman who tries to create a new identity after prison. *A Handful of Paradise* garnered several national and international awards. *Hollywood Kaçakları / Hollywood Runaways* (1997), a nostalgic film with autobiographical elements, focused on idle boys in a poor neighbourhood, who decide to go to Hollywood to realize their dreams.

Özge, Aslı (b. Istanbul, 1975) Director, screenwriter, editor, producer. A graduate of the Marmara University's Cinema and Television Department in 1999, Aslı

Özge won several awards with her short film, *Büyük Harf C / Capital C*. Moving to Berlin to continue her studies, she co-founded the production company EEE and made her first feature *Ein Bisschen April / Biraz Nisan / A Little Bit of April*, an improvisational film, in 2003. ***Köprüdekiler / On the Bridge*** (2009), about urban underdogs, shot in documentary style with mostly non-professionals, was invited to numerous film festivals after premiering at the Locarno and Toronto Film Festivals and won awards. ***Hayatboyu / Lifelong*** (2013), presenting the other end of the spectrum, an affluent artist couple's confrontation of the complexities of love, life and relationship, premiered at the Berlin Film Festival and garnered her the Best Director award at the 32nd International Istanbul Film Festival, 2013. House-searching with all its implications, whether in Germany or in Turkey, whether up-market or down the scale, is a strong motif in her fiction, with all the implications of the power play and the psychological tension of an existential situation.

Özgentürk, Ali (Habip) (b. Adana, 1945) Director, producer, editor. Internationally acclaimed with his first film, ***Hazal*** (1979) and the second, ***At / The Horse*** (1982), Ali Özgentürk has tried a new form and new film language with each film, sustaining his belief in cinema without compromise. He spent his earlier years working in the cotton fields and factories and during high school participated in a student theatre company. While studying philosophy and sociology at the University of Istanbul, he founded 'Street Theatre'. He entered the industry in 1974 as camera assistant and then assistant to **Yılmaz Güney** and **Atıf Yılmaz**, among others. He was the co-screenwriter in ***Endişe / The Anxiety*** (**Şerif Gören**, 1974), the assistant director in ***Sürü / The Herd*** aka ***The Flock*** (**Zeki Ökten**, 1978) and the screenwriter in ***Selvi Boylum, Al Yazmalım / The Girl with the Red Scarf*** (**Atıf Yılmaz**, 1977). His first short film, *Ferhat* (1974) was awarded internationally. In the **social realist** tradition of **Yılmaz Güney**, *Hazal* focused on the feudal customs that resist modernization; ***The Horse*** foregrounded the migration issue in the claustrophobic atmosphere of the post-*coup d'état* metropolis. With *Bekçi / The Guard* (1985), about an apolitical Balkan immigrant, moulded by the state ideology, whose sense of duty abstracts him from his environment, Özgentürk began to search for a personal idiom, amalgamating fantastic elements into the narrative, which he had already tried with ***Hazal***, with the chorus of old weavers and in ***The Horse*** with the 'mad woman'. *Su da Yanar / Water Also Burns* (1987), an intimate essay on the dilemmas of a film-maker in a personal and political impasse, was banned by the Istanbul prefecture for trying 'to expose the life and ideas of a communist poet in exile, Nazım Hikmet, indicted for treason' and Özgentürk was brought to trial. The charges were dropped after demonstrations in Istanbul and a strong international petition, but the film remained banned. *Çıplak / Nude* (1993) underscored with humour the gap between art and the common man, provoking the traditionally gendered concepts of nudity and shame in conflict with modernism in liminal societies. *Mektup / The Letter* (1997) interrogated the leftist political tradition in Turkey through the story of an immigrant to the US who becomes alienated from his roots and his search for identity while searching for his father. *Balalayka* (2000), foregrounding cross-border prostitution from the ex-Soviet Union, was a road movie with humour, which gathered characters with different backgrounds and agendas under the roof of a bus. *Kalbin Zamanı / The Time of the Heart* (2004), a romantic **crime** story involving the love of three men for one woman spanning over three time periods, featured the historic Pera Palas Hotel, carrying an intertextuality with Agatha Christie, Alfred Hitchcock, Mata Hari and Pierre Loti, who were once its esteemed guests. The film was book-ended with a parallel animation, *Alfred and Agatha*, designed by Özgentürk. Other films of Özgentürk are *Yengeç Oyunu / Crab Game* (2009), *Görünmeyen / The Invisible* (2011) and *Beni Sev / Love Me* (2011).

Özgentürk, Işıl (b. Gaziantep, 1948) Director, screenwriter, columnist, author. The screenwriter of award-winning *At / The Horse* (**Özgentürk**, 1982) among others, Işıl Özgentürk directed her feature film, *Seni Seviyorum Rosa / I Love You Rosa* in 1992, produced by her husband at the time, **Ali Özgentürk**, which received the Jury Special Prize of the International Istanbul Film Festival. She gives screenwriting workshops and master-classes as well as continuing as a columnist at the *Cumhuriyet* daily newspaper.

Özkan, Yavuz (b. Yozgat, 1942) Director, screenwriter, producer, actor, art director. Starting as a stage actor and director, making short films and writing scripts in the 1970s, Yavuz Özkan made his debut feature, *Yarış / The Race* in 1977 and followed it with *Maden / Mine* (1978) and *Demiryol / Railroad* (1979) that established him as a political film-maker. After a sojourn in Paris for eight years, he returned home and began to make dramas about relationships: *Yağmur Kaçakları / Fugitives of Rain* (1988), *Umud Yarına Kaldı / Hope is Delayed Until Tomorrow* (1989), *Film Bitti / The Film is Over* (1989), *Büyük Yanlızlık / The Great Solitude* (1990), *Ateş Üstünde Yürümek / Walking On Fire* (1991), *İki Kadın / Two Women* (1992), *Bir Sonbahar Hikayesi / An Autumn Story* (1993), *Yengeç Sepeti / Lobster Pot* (1994), *Bir Kadının Anatomisi / Anatomy of a Woman* (1995), *Bir Erkeğin Anatomisi / Anatomy of a Man* (1997) and *Hayal Kurma Oyunları / Dreaming Games* (2004) are all intense family dramas of bourgeois lives. *Two Women* was controversial in depicting a lesbian relationship between a prostitute and the wife of the politician who rapes her. He has been instrumental in the training of the new generation of film-makers, such as **Pelin Esmer**.

Özön, Nijat (b. Istanbul, 1927 – d. Ankara, 2010) Film historian and translator. One of the pioneer historians of cinema, who published the first cinema encyclopaedia (*Ansiklopedik Sinema Sözlüğü*, 1958) and the first serious film journal (*Sinema*, 1956), Nijat Özön is a graduate in Turkology and library science from the Ankara University (1952). He has contributed immensely to the recording of the history of Turkish cinema. He is the author of several books on the subject, which are not translated into other languages. Some of these are *Türk Sineması Tarihi 1896– 1960* (3rd edn 2013); *Sinema, Televizyon, Video Bilgisayarlı Sinema Sözlüğü* (2000); *Karagözden Sinemaya Türk Sineması ve Sorunları: Tarih, Sanat, Estetik,*

Endüstri, Ekonomi, vol I and *Eleştirme ve Eleştiri Yazıları: Sinema ve Toplum, Denetleme, Sinema ve TV,* vol II (1995) and *Sinema El Kitabı* (1964). He also translated the works of André Bazin and Sergei Eisenstein into Turkish.

Özpetek, Ferzan (b. Istanbul, 1959) Director, screenwriter. A transnational film-maker who made his name with his first film, *Il bagno Turco-Hamam / Hamam / The Turkish Bath* (1997) and the subsequent *Harem Suaré* (1999), Ferzan Özpetek went to Rome in 1978 to study film history, art and costume. He worked as assistant director to Maurizio Ponzi, Massimo Troisi, Ricky Tognazzi and Marco Risi. A western hero's search for himself in an exotic land found its voice in *The Turkish Bath,* a co-production between Turkey, Italy and Spain about gay love that springs in the traditional steam bath between a successful young Italian with marital problems and the handsome son of the custodian of the *hamam. Harem Suaré* was a Turkish, Italian, French co-production, again with exotic elements of forbidden love between the emperor's favourite concubine and the palace eunuch. Both films premiered at the Cannes Film Festival and received distribution in about 20 countries in addition to several festival awards. His other films, *Fate Ignoranti / The Ignorant Fairies* (2001), *La Finestra di Fronte / Facing Windows* (2003), *Cuore Sacro / Sacred Heart* (2005), *Saturno Contro / Saturn in Opposition* (2007), *Un Giorgo Perfetto / A Perfect Day* (2008), *Mine Vaganti / Loose Cannons* (2010) and *Magnifica Presenza / Magnificent Presence* (2011) are generally Italian family dramas, successful at the box-office and recognized at international film festivals.

P

Pandora'nın Kutusu / Pandora's Box (2008) explores modernism and the feeling of entrapment in tradition, while questioning memory and belonging – issues Turkish society has not yet reconciled. Using an elliptic style, the film focuses on the mother Nusret (Tsilla Chelton) with Alzheimer's disease, her three estranged children and her grandson, although the true central character is Istanbul and its citizens (as a metonym for Turkey) who have lost their equilibrium in a struggle to escape the clutches of tradition and face modernity. The older daughter, Nesrin (**Derya Alabora**), chooses conventional marriage whereas the younger, Güzin, 'the intellectual career woman' pursues free love. Feeling caged, neither is happy having lost the power to resist. Their younger brother, the non-conformist Mehmet, maintains his equilibrium and certain innocence. Murat, the grandson, ignored while the two previous generations settle accounts, is seeking another way and naively finding it in his grandmother.

Ustaoğlu's camera privileges landscape over action and space is almost another character demanding screen time. The verticality of the skyscrapers and the horizontality of the livid waters of the Bosphorus on a cold and pitiless morning, the mind-boggling traffic of the metropolis, the concrete overpasses and the claustrophobic dark corners, all confirm the relationship of the individual to the architecture. The narrow corridors between the vertical skyscrapers that threaten to crush the individual do not provide breathing space, a feeling captured effectively on the face of the mother when she looks out of the window in Nesrin's apartment. Güzin's apartment is in the gentrified area of the city, whereas Mehmet squats in a transitional area occupied by gypsies and Kurdish immigrants, in the process of being gentrified. Heidegger argues that, in practical terms, dwelling involves the *primal* oneness of the earth and sky, divinities and mortals. Mortals are in the *fourfold* (in saving the earth, in receiving the sky, in awaiting the divinities and in initiating mortals) by dwelling (Heidegger 1971: 148). In this sense, dwelling 'becomes itself the fundamental human activity, in the light of which both place and space find their first clarification. The built environment is crucial in supporting and reflecting a person and group's way of being-in-the-world as a certain embodied grasp of the world, a particular way of taking up the body and the world, a specific orientation disclosing certain aspects of a worldly horizon' (Jager 1983: 154). The world in which we find ourselves completes us in

Figure 89 Pandora'nın Kutusu / Pandora's Box (Yeşim Ustaoğlu, 2008) (Courtesy of Yeşim Ustaoğlu)

Figure 90 Pandora'nın Kutusu / Pandora's Box (Yeşim Ustaoğlu, 2008) (Courtesy of Yeşim Ustaoğlu)

what we are, and therefore the specific nature of the built environment becomes crucial. In other words, people are immersed in their world, and this immersion is qualitative, subtle – in many ways, overwhelming (Seamon 1998: 2). 'People choose their space' as **Ustaoğlu** claims, 'Becoming *kitsch* during the process of building a consumerist society, erecting prison walls around us by allowing the issue of security to enter our lives, losing our values while embracing alien lifestyles (the "gated community" where Nesrin lives) naturally lead to problems in relationships…Even for a young man like Murat who is struggling for individual space, the only refuge is the harbour' (Dönmez-Colin 2012: 233).

Dissatisfaction with urban existence is the overriding theme of most Turkish films of the 2000s. However, women film-makers seem to be more analytical and confrontational. Unlike her male counterparts who usually mystify the countryside in one-dimensional voyages, in *Pandora's Box*, **Ustaoğlu** uses the countryside as a conduit for characters from different generations to confront their predicaments.

The grey tone of the opening scene of the film and the contrast between the giant cruise ships and the anachronistic fishermen's boats present a landscape closer to Ara Güler's magnificent black-and-white photographs of the Galata Bridge darkened by the black steam from the ferries than the postcards for tourists. The Topkapı Palace, the mosques, all manifestations of Turkish history are hidden behind the fog. As if to challenge their timeless horizontality, a concrete post appears in the foreground as the day breaks. The juxtaposition of open and closed spaces and the change of light are crucial. The scenes in the corridors, the elevator, the under-passes, in darkness, and between the heavy traffic are recurrent. When they look for their mother in dark corners, she appears in open spaces. The colours become warmer as the film progresses. Contrary to the first morning scene that frames Murat sleeping on the concrete in the grey harbour, in another morning scene, he is framed in close-up with his grandmother. The men catching fish on the bridge, the Golden Horn, and criss-crossing ferries transmit energy. Children, unlike those that torture cats in the back streets, play happily in the Luna Park. In the village, Murat returns to his childhood, sliding on his uncle's sleigh. He shares the bread and the blanket with his grandmother. When she starts her determined journey toward the mountain, he does not interfere. What initially begins as a road movie transforms into an inner voyage that affects all characters.

Although **Ustaoğlu** dislikes to be identified as a 'woman' film-maker, to form affinities with the women characters in *Pandora's Box* is easier. Men are constantly on the run – the father, the son and finally the grandson. The only character who stays is Nesrin's husband, scorned by his son for passivity. **Ustaoğlu** underlines that she creates her characters with cognizance as well as intuition, 'to escape or hide in the lap of their mothers or wives is the weakness of men'. She feels closer to Mehmet 'with an eye for seeing, which the others lack. An unadulterated trust exists in his soul'. The young Murat belongs to a generation that worries **Ustaoğlu** the most, the children of over-protective middle-class parents, unprepared for life in the servile tradition of a military society, without consideration for individuality. When a mugger threatens to cut his throat with a knife, Murat feels the blood run through his veins and at that moment he matures (Dönmez-Colin 2012: 237).

Director: **Yeşim Ustaoğlu**; Producer: **Yeşim Ustaoğlu**, Serkan Çakarer, Behrooz Hashemian, Setareh Farsi; Production: Ustaoğlu Film, Silk Road Production, Le Petites Lumières, The Match Factory, Stromboli Pictures, ZDF/ARTE Production; Screenwriter: **Yeşim Ustaoğlu**, Sema Kaygusuz; Cinematographer: Jacques Besse; Editor: Franck Natkache; Music: Jean-Pierre Mas; Sound: Bernd von Bassewitz; Art Director: Elif Taşcıoğlu, Serdar Yılmaz; Cast: Tsilla Chelton, **Derya Alabora**, Onur Ünsal, Övül Avkıran, Osman Snant, Tayfun Bademsoy, Nazmi Kırık

Pars, Kenan (b. Istanbul, 1920 – d. Istanbul, 2008) Actor, director, screenwriter, producer; RN: Kirkor Cezveciyan. Although he never hid his Armenian identity, very few people knew the real name of the man who captured **Yeşilçam** with his European appearance and played the bad man in countless films. He started acting with **Lütfi Ö. Akad**'s *Öldüren Şehir / The Murderous City* (1954). In 1961, he formed his company Mask Film and directed six films. When he stopped receiving offers, he opened a kiosk near his house and sold lottery tickets.

Pençe / The Claw (1917), based on a play by the renowned author Mehmet Rauf and made during the Ottoman Empire, is the first complete feature film of Turkish cinema along with *Casus / The Spy* (1917). Controversy remains as to which was made first. The first 'fallen women' of Turkish cinema were the two protagonists of this silent black-and-white film that praises free love against marriage, comparing the second to the claw grabbing the heart. Leman, with an unappeasable appetite for men, has a liaison with Pertev, and Feride, an adulteress, with his friend Vasfi. The stern criticism of the film by **Muhsin Ertuğrul** in the *Temaşa* journal is considered as the first film criticism. Unfortunately, the film is lost.

Director, Screenwriter: **Sedat Simavi**; Producer: Müdafaa-i Milliye Cemiyeti (The Association for National Defence); Cinematographer: **Yorgo İlyadis**; Cast: Bedia Muvahhit, Elisa Binemeciyan, Nurettin Şevkati, Raşit Rıza Samako

Pirhasan, Barış (b. Istanbul, 1951) Director, screenwriter, poet, translator. A graduate in English Language and Literature from the Bosphorus University, the son of **Vedat Türkali**, Barış Pirhasan wrote poetry, translated books (Lewis Carroll and Constantin Cavafy), worked as assistant director to **Ömer Kavur** and **Atıf Yılmaz** and scripted some of their films before making his first feature, *Küçük Balıklar Üzerine Bir Masal / A Fable on Little Fish* (1990). Between 1989–92, he studied directing at the National Film and Television School in the UK. His second feature, the transnational *Usta Beni Öldürsene / Sawdust Tales* (1997), a timeless parable on survival through the story of a circus troupe, which he scripted, won several national awards. His third feature, *O da Beni Seviyor / Summer Love* (2001) brought the Alawi culture to screen through a teenage love story. *Adem'in Trenleri / Adam and the Devil* (2007) foregrounded a man of religion, whose stereotypical identity in the first half is contested in the second, sending a message to the viewer about pre-judgements regarding human character.

Pirselimoğlu, Tayfun (b. Trabzon, 1959) Director, screenwriter, producer, art director, author. A truly independent film-maker who follows his convictions

Figure 91 Rıza (Tayfun Pirselimoğlu, 2007) (Courtesy of Tayfun Pirselimoğlu)

about cinema without compromise, Tayfun Pirselimoğlu studied at the Middle East Technical University in Ankara, switching to painting and gravure at the Hochschüle für Angewandte Kunst (Academy of Applied Fine Arts) in Vienna and holding exhibitions in various European cities. He received recognition with two shorts, *Dayım / My* Uncle (1999) and *Sukut Altındır / Silence is Gold* (2002). *Hiçbiryerde / Innowhereland* (2001), about the search of a mother for

Figure 92 Pus / Haze (Tayfun Pirselimoğlu, 2009) (Courtesy of Tayfun Pirselimoğlu)

Figure 93 Saç / Hair (Tayfun Pirselimoğlu, 2010) (Courtesy of Tayfun Pirselimoğlu)

her disappeared son, is his first feature. The 'Conscience and Death' trilogy, comprising *Rıza* (2007), *Pus / Haze* (2009), and *Saç/ Hair* (2010) is about lonely people who escape from the confining conditions of the provinces to be devoured in the cold and indifferent metropolis, living either in fantasies of escape, having clandestine love affairs, or vicariously entering the lives of the others in front of the television set, until one day everything gets out of hand.

Pirselimoğlu is also the author of three novels and books of short stories.

Polat, Ayşe (b. Malatya, 1970) Director, screenwriter. Arriving in Germany as an 8-year-old, Kurdish film-maker Ayşe Polat studied German philosophy and cultural sciences in Berlin and Bremen and made 8mm shorts and videos. Starting with her first feature *Auslandstournee / Tour Abroad* (1999), a *bildungsroman* and a road movie, Polat began to explore the meaning of home, homeland and identity for the displaced and the trauma of absence and loss. The film foregrounds the father–daughter relationship between a drag queen and the orphaned child of his ex-colleague, on a quest for the little girl's estranged mother, which takes them to Turkey. The film ends with the pair taking a taxi back to the airport after the rejection of the girl by her mother, a metaphor for the rejection of the 'other' in the natal country. Her second film, *En Garde*, which won several awards including the Silver Leopard for Best Film and Best Actress at the International Locarno Film Festival (2004) and the German Film Critics Award for Best Fiction Film, is about the friendship between two girls, 16-year-old Alice with an extreme sense of hearing and Berivan, an illegal Kurdish girl waiting for the verdict of the immigration authorities, in a Catholic educational institute. What binds them together is their love of fencing. She followed it with *Luks Glück / Luk's Luck* (2010). *Die Erbin / The Heiress* (2013) is about a writer who goes from Germany to her deceased father's natal village in Turkey to write a novel about him, whose voice is guiding her through the past and the present.

Porno films furore started in 1974 with the sex **comedy**, *Beş Tavuk, Bir Horoz / Five Chickens, One Cock* by Oksal Pekmezoğlu, narrating the adventures of peasant Kazım (Sermet Serdengeçti, the first sex star with a background in theatre) diagnosed as oversexed, who has affairs with five sex-starved high society women before his forced marriage to a girl he assaults. Several well-known actors – Nebahat Çehre, Fatma Belgen, Mine Mutlu, Seyyal Taner, Senar Seven, Münir Özkul, Feridun Çölgeçen, **Zeki Alasya** – played in the film, adapted from Italian Marco Vicario's *Homo Eroticus / Man of the Year* (1971) about a Sicilian peasant (Lando Buzzanca) with three testicles and his escapades with wealthy Northern women. The film followed the **Yeşilçam** tradition of the binaries of rich/poor and the eventual triumph (albeit through his sexual prowess) of the anti-hero, similar to **Kemal Sunal** comedies.

Developing into a sub-**genre** of 'sex and adventure comedies', these films originally interspersed sex scenes throughout a **comedy** film, but by the end of the 1970s, two-thirds of the general output was sex films, shot in 16mm with local 'hard-core' or cuts from foreign films inserted (an estimate of 130 by 1979). Many European sex films were imported and cheaply Turkified. The 1980 military intervention terminated the furore although porno cinemas have remained, showing double and triple bills, and VCR markets flourished, both at home and among the diaspora through workers before the establishment of Internet viewing. Involving nudity and obscenity, it is questionable that these films could be considered 'hard-core' by present standards.

Presheva, Mustafa (b. Kosovska Mitrovica (present day Kosova), 1961) Editor, actor. Mustafa Presheva moved to Istanbul in 1992 during the war in the former Yugoslavia. He received the Best Editor award at the Antalya Golden Orange Film Festival with *Tabutta Rövaşata / Somersault in a Coffin* (1996) and *Filler ve Çimen* (2000), both by **Derviş Zaim** and with *Vicdan / Conscience* (**Erden Kıral**, 2008).

Pütün, Yılmaz Güney (b. Adana, 1937 – d. Paris, 1984) Actor, producer, screenwriter, director. Turkey's internationally most celebrated film-maker, the hero of millions of fans, a legend who is said to have directed films from jail, 'Yılmaz Güney' as he is internationally known, was born to Kurdish parents who migrated from the east to Adana. Speaking only Turkish in an atmosphere of ethnic oppression exercised by the state policies of Turkification, he became aware of his origins when he visited his father's native village for the first time as a 16-year-old and his mother's village two decades later. The latter and the maternal tribe of Jibran are fictionalized in *Sürü / The Herd* (**Zeki Ökten**, 1978).

Güney was introduced to cinema when he was 13, watching action films in the open-air theatres of poor neighbourhoods. He carried reels from one theatre to the other on his bicycle during summer vacations and made contacts with the local representatives of major film companies, while publishing short stories in literary journals. He interrupted his studies in law in Ankara to switch to the Faculty of Economy at Istanbul University to be closer to the world of cinema and entered **Yeşilçam** as a set worker and extra, having his first chance as an actor, scriptwriter and assistant director in **Atıf Yılmaz**'s *Bu Vatanın Çocukları / The Children of this Nation* (1958). He was jailed in 1961 for communist propaganda and afterwards exiled to Konya, which aborted his university education. His commercial career began in 1963, scripting heroic **melodramas** and starring in more than 20 films in a year. He broke the prevalent good-looking hero image (the blond, blue-eyed **Göksel Arsoy**) and with his dark skin, large nose and thin silhouette created his own myth. Nick-named 'the ugly king', he was 'the people's choice', a hero to identify for the poor and oppressed. In **Akad**'s *Hudutların Kanunu / The Law of the Borders* (1966), which he co-wrote with **Akad**, he departed from the traditional hyperbolic performances of **Yeşilçam**, transmitting the human side of a toughened smuggler, a character he developed further in *Ağıt / Elegy* (1971).

He directed his first film, *At, Avrat, Silah / Horse, Woman, Gun* in 1966 and formed his company Güney Filmcilik / Güney Film in 1968, continuing in the style that made him popular with *Bir Çirkin Adam / An Ugly Man* (1969). The epic *Seyyit Han* aka *Toprağın Gelini / Seyyit Han* aka *The Bride of the Earth* (1968) condemned the self-destructive mentality of patriarchy that determined the fate of the rural woman; *Aç Kurtlar / Hungry Wolves* (1969), defined by local critics as an 'epic of banditry', was shot during his military service in the east. The atmosphere of the **social realist** movement that emerged in the 1960s advocating a different cinema than the state-sanctioned escapist **melodramas**, **war films** and insignificant adaptations, prepared the ground for *Umut / The Hope* (1970), a turning point in Turkish cinema. The film brought a new dimension to the ideological analysis of the transitional man.

Güney's 'ugly king' period, considered 'commercial trash' by the middle-class intelligentsia, also focused on the common man's struggles to exist in an unjust world, hence their immense success with the masses. His anti-hero (often inspired by his own life and played by him) was forced to violence or illegal means by circumstances, but he lost because individual revolt/salvation only led to a dead-end. With *The Hope*, Güney entered into dialogue with his audience through a pathetic protagonist whose tragic end was inevitable because he tried to find solutions to his problems by individual means and not by collective action. Destiny was not the reason behind poverty and desperation as generally assumed.

The trilogy *Ağıt / Elegy*, *Acı / Pain* and *Umutsuzlar / The Hopeless Ones* and also *Baba / The Father* were all made in 1971. For the first time in Turkish cinema, the issues of landless peasants resorting to smuggling or flocking to the cities as migrant workers gained visibility.

Arkadaş / The Friend (1974), the last film Güney directed in Turkey, had a strong impact with its indictment of the ex-revolutionaries transforming into apathetic bourgeois. While shooting *Endişe / Anxiety* (1974), he was arrested with the charge of having killed judge Sefa Mutlu during an argument. **Şerif Gören**, one of his assistants, finished the film. The next time he was able to go behind the camera was in 1983 in Paris when he shot *Duvar / Le Mur / The Wall* about a children's prison, his last film, which returned to the key chronotope of his 'narratives of siege' (Naficy 2001: 191).

Children are integral to Güney's cinema. In *The Hope, The Father*, and *Yol* (Şerif Gören, 1982), although in the background, they are an essential part of the diegesis. *The Wall* (1983) is their story. In *Arkadaş / The Friend* (1974), the bourgeois children on the beach are juxtaposed with the rural children playing in the water of the fountain. The most important characteristic of Güney's cinema is its humanism. He tells human stories, mostly inspired by his life. Cabbar of *The Hope* is his father. The blood feuds motif in his films connects with a childhood trauma when his father was shot in front of his eyes, although he did not die.

Güney's reputation in the West is built around two very important films which he did not direct, but scripted while in prison and instructed his assistants to direct: *The Herd* by **Zeki Ökten** and *Yol / The Way* (1982) by **Şerif Gören**. Both film-makers were influenced by Güney's cinema and ready for changes despite several productive years they had spent within the confines of **Yeşilçam**.

Güney's name appeared in more than 100 films, many of which disappeared into the vaults of censorship boards or were left to disintegrate except for about 12 that he sent abroad before his escape from prison, re-appearing in France to receive the Golden Palm at the Cannes Film Festival of 1982 for *Yol*, sharing it with *The Missing* of Costa Gavras. The following year his citizenship was revoked, his films were recalled and his name erased from film history. In 1984, he died in Paris from stomach cancer. The audiences in Turkey were able to see *Yol* on 12 February 1999, 17 years after its Cannes success (Dönmez-Colin 2008: 116–129).

Adana-Paris by Ahmet Soner is a documentary on Güney through testimonials of 42 friends, family, colleagues and cellmates.

Q

Queer cinema is new for Turkey where the One Nation–One Language–One Religion official policy of the state has been extended to the issue of sexual identity, with cinema endorsing One Sexuality – heterosexuality – and designating the family as the ideal medium to practise it. The reticence to discuss alternative sexual choices, gay and lesbian identities, is not only peculiar to countries like Turkey, where Muslim tradition has silenced society into conformism, encouraging hypocrisy and double-standards, alienating individuals. Such issues have been problematic both in mainstream Hollywood movies and in independent productions since the beginning. Even today, most Hollywood films treat gays, lesbians or transsexuals in a superficial manner as motifs in heterosexual films, usually comedies. Alternative sexual identities and the freedom of sexual orientation have gradually become visible in alternative culture, which has had its repercussions in cinema, but film-makers still exercise auto-censorship and evade issues that would create controversy and endanger wide distribution. Critic/archivist Agah Özgüç cites *Ver Elini Istanbul / Istanbul Give me Your Hand* (1962) by Aydın Arakon, written by the celebrated poet/author/columnist Atilla İlhan as the first attempt at lesbian relations. 'Two women tried to kiss each other with trepidation, but the rationale behind the kiss was obscure and the scene was cut by the censors' (Dönmez-Colin 2008: 156). **Atıf Yılmaz**, with one eye on the artistic concerns and the other on the box-office, was a pioneer with *İki Gemi Yanyana / Two Ships Side by Side* (1963) showing two women kissing on the lips. **Halit Refiğ**'s *Haremde Dört Kadın / Four Women in the Harem* (1965), a period film that insinuated lesbian relationships between the concubines of a pasha was criticized severely. From 1974 to 1980, lesbianism was exploited in 'sex comedies'.

Serious films began to appear only in the 1990s. **Atıf Yılmaz**'s *Dul Bir Kadın / A Widow* (1985) was the most discussed film of the year, showing the erotic fantasies of two women who found comfort in each other. His *Düş Gezginleri / Walking After Midnight* (1992), considered the first realistic lesbian film, showed two women making love. **Yılmaz** claimed that his focus was the distribution of power in society and not the lesbian relationship and drew the criticism of feminist groups on the premise that he was reducing woman-to-woman relations to an exercise of power. **Ömer Kavur** addressed homosexuality in *Yusuf ile Kenan / Yusuf and Kenan* (1979) and *Anayurt Oteli / Motherland Hotel* (1986); in the former, brothers rape a boy (a common occurrence in the villages) and hang him, and in the latter, a 17-year-old boy cruises at night although unlike the novel where the sexual nature of the meeting between him and the protagonist is very clear, in the film, the relationship is ambiguous. *Denize Hançer Düştü / Balcony* (**Mustafa Altıoklar**, 1992) is about two women sexually attracted to each other while rehearsing Jean Genet's *Balcony* on stage.

In *İntikam Meleği* aka *Kadın Hamlet / The Angel of Vengeance* aka *Woman Hamlet* (1976), **Metin Erksan** portrayed Hamlet as an androgynous female cross-dresser in a man's white suit and a red tie, like a modern dandy, smoking cigars while her attractive long black hair was blowing in the wind, whereas Ophelia was a young effeminate painter. Along with *Köçek / Dancing Boy* (Nejat Saydam, 1975), *Beddua / Curse* (**Osman Seden**, 1980), *Dönersen Islık Çal / Whistle If You Return* (**Orhan Oğuz**, 1993), *Woman Hamlet* is considered as one of the four important films that show characters with sexual identities outside the societal norms. In *Dancing Boy*, **Müjde Ar** appears as a man but plays with the two sexual identities. In *Curse*, Bülent Ersoy (who has had a sex change operation in real life) plays a singer whose sexual identity is problematic for him and for others. In *Whistle If You Return*, Fikret Kuşkan plays a transvestite.

Lesbian stories possess intrinsic commercial value, appealing to the fantasies of men, but homosexuality is taboo in androcentric societies. Turkish cinema typecasts homosexuals as marginal characters, whose parodying of feminine traits are intended to produce humour. They often come from the bourgeois class and work as hairdressers, fashion designers or make-up artists. In general, homosexuality is used as an expression of decadence in society and the loss of moral values (Suner 1990: 47).

Kutluğ Ataman, a multi-disciplinary artist and an activist for gay rights, explores the fragility of personal identity through characters who have become dislocated from conventional categories and are compelled to re-invent themselves, be they a transvestite Turkish belly-dancer at the heart of Berlin (***Lola und Bilidikid / Lola and Bilidikid***, 1997), a transsexual activist who wears a wig when the police cut her hair for prostituting (*Peruk Takan Kadınlar / Women Who Wear Wigs*, 1999), or an androgynous young rebel from the outskirts of Istanbul (*2 Genç Kız / 2 Girls*, 2005). Italy-based **Ferzan Özpetek**'s *Il bagno Turco-Hamam / Hamam / The Turkish Bath* (1997) allows its protagonist to explore his sexual identity without 'othering' him with established definitions of gender. *Teslimiyet / Other Angels* (Emre Yalgın, 2010) is a realistic depiction of the transgender community in Istanbul. The award-winning *Zenne Dancer* (Mehmet Binay and Caner Alper, 2011) is probably the first bona fide queer film. Based on the true story of a young man murdered by his father when he came out, the film deals with cultural and legal issues affecting gay men through the story of three characters: a flamboyant dancer, a gay provincial man and a German photo-journalist.

Noteworthy is a German documentary, *Çürük / The Pink Report* (2011) by Ulrike Böhnisch, about Turkish gay men's exemption from the military, which includes a humiliating procedure of psychological tests, anal examinations (which is discontinued) and photographical proof of gay sex (which has now changed to a photo with make-up).

Pembe Hayat KuirFest was held for the first time in 2011.

R

Refiğ, Halit (b. İzmir, 1934 – d. Istanbul, 2009) Director, screenwriter and producer. One of the most important film-makers of Turkish cinema, **Halit Refiğ**'s work reflects the dichotomies of a country straddling tradition and modernity and the East and the West. He studied engineering at the Robert College in Istanbul, before his military service in Korea, Japan and Ceylon (Sri Lanka of today). While abroad, he made amateur 8mm documentaries. On his return, he wrote film criticism before entering the industry as assistant to **Atıf Yılmaz** and **Memduh Ün** and as a screenwriter. His first film, *Yasak Aşk / Forbidden Love* (1961) was made into a television series in 1974 by the state television TRT as *Aşk-ı Memnu / Forbidden Love*.

Cognizant of Western movements with his knowledge of English and French, Refiğ could discern the local specificities of film-making in Turkey, prioritizing audience expectations. Turkish cinema was neither an established enterprise like in the US nor funded by the state like in the USSR. Hard work was required to meet the demands of the audience. For a deeper understanding of the realities of his country, he tried to enrich his limited resources with the novels of **Kemal Tahir**, combining this knowledge with German expressionistic framing, dialectical intellectual editing and a focus on the east/west and urban/rural divide. Women's predicaments during social and political change, whether in the *harem* of a decaying empire during the struggles for independence; as peasants in the village; as a foreign bride trying to assimilate to Turkish culture or as an urban lady or an underprivileged migrant in the metropolis, became key motifs in his films.

At the end of the 1960s, Refiğ began to advocate **Yeşilçam** as the true national cinema with its popularity with the audiences, who were alienated by the Western forms. A polemic started with the **cinematheque** and its publication, *New Cinema* that shunned most Turkish productions in favour of European cinema. Refiğ and his circle proposed, what they called *Asya Tipi Üretim Tarzı – ATÜT* (Asian style of production).

Şehirdeki Yabancı / A Stranger in Town (1962) is included as one of the ten best films of the **social realist** movement. *Şafak Bekçileri / Guardians of Dawn* (1963) made with the collaboration of the Air Force and the 114th fleet, underscores the progressive and reactionary conflicts in the country and the role of the army in the 27 May 1960 *coup d'état* through a thorny love story between a landowner's daughter and an air force officer. *Gurbet Kuşları / The Birds of Nostalgia* aka *Migrating Birds* aka *Birds of Exile* (1964) is considered as the first serious study of migration from the rural to the urban. Although migration started a decade earlier and migrant characters have always been part of modern Turkish cinema, the social realities of migration had been overlooked, hence the success of the film nationally and internationally. *Haremde Dört Kadın / Four Women in a Harem* (1965) was a failure at the box-office, but gained classic status decades later. *Bir Türk'e Gönül Verdim / I Gave My Heart to a Turk* (1969), about the love between a Turkish man and a foreign woman, was a commercial success.

From the 1970s onwards, Refiğ also directed for television. *Yorgun Savaşçı / Tired Warrior* (1979), based on a **Kemal Tahir** novel, commissioned by the state television TRT, was burned by the junta responsible for the 1980 *coup* for defaming Atatürk and the War of Independence. Despite this traumatic experience, Refiğ continued to work, receiving critical praise with *Teyzem / My Aunt* (1986), *Hanım / Madame* (1988) and *Karılar Koğuşu / Women's Ward* (1989). His last feature was *Köpekler Adası / Island of Dogs* (1997).

His book, *Ulusal Sinema Kavgası* (1971) is about the issues of Turkish cinema between 1965–70 focusing on the rupture in the mid-1960s between film critics, writers and other intellectuals with a Western vision and others who promoted local products.

Halit Refiğ Sineması Üzerine Düşünceler / Halit Refiğ, Thoughts on His Cinema (2009) is an important bio-documentary made by veteran cinematographer Çetin Tunca.

Religion has not been an effective active agent in Turkish cinema, which has been historically secular. **Yeşilçam** followed the culturally endorsed behaviour regarding religion to appease the traditional values of the conservative family. A singer abandoning her career for an honourable marriage would enter the mosque to ask Allah for forgiveness (*Meryem ve Oğulları / Meryem and Her Sons*, **Osman Seden**, 1977), or a repentant prostitute would don the headscarf (*Vesikalı Yarim / My Licensed Love*, **Akad**, 1968). The depiction of characters representing religion was stereotypical. The *hodja* was caricaturized as a fat old charlatan with a long beard exploiting naive believers for personal interest. *Aynaroz Kadısı / The Cadi (Islamic Judge) of Athos* (**Muhsin Ertuğrul**, 1938), adapted from a stage play by Musâhipzâde Celâl (1927) and severely censored for its erotic scenes, is perhaps the first example of a religious man as a corrupt philanderer. The films focusing on the National Struggle for Independence (*Milli Mücadele*) were not favourable towards religion. *Vurun Kahpeye / Strike the Whore* (**Akad**, 1949) presents a fanatical local *imam* instrumental in the lynching of a young schoolteacher. In its third version, in 1973, **Halit Refiğ** changed the ending, arguing he focused on the intellectual evolution of the author, Halide Edip Adıvar, who after 1926 embraced Islamic values. When the teacher's fiancée arrives and opens her clutched fist, instead of the medallion, he finds the Qur'an, but Hadji Fettah is still the instigator of the lynching. In *Teyzem / My Aunt* (**Refiğ**, 1986), the stepfather who the protagonist claims has sexually abused her, contributing to her insanity, is seen with a skullcap preparing for daily prayers. Mosques regularly appear although performing the actual *namaz* or showing a preaching session was unusual for **Yeşilçam**. The heroine wearing a short skirt, heavy make-up, false lashes and a scarf that hardly covered her hair would enter the mosque and pray out loud while standing. Islamizing the clichés of Hollywood, babies were abandoned in the courtyards of mosques.

In the 1960s, hastily made 'prophet films' depicting the lives of the prophets were popular, particularly in some parts of Anatolia. In a period of political turmoil and the free-reign of exploitative films, cinema with an Islamic agenda was advocated by **Yücel Çakmaklı** as *milli* cinema as opposed to *ulusal* cinema (see **national cinema**). His *Birleşen Yollar / Crossing Roads* aka *Merging Paths* (1970), a commercial success mostly due to its star, **Türkan Şoray**, became the prototype for Islamic films that exploited the formula of a love interest between an innocent traditional person and a degenerate 'modern' one for religious propaganda, the modern person eventually discovering the true path although sometimes it was too late for a happy ending. The clash of the good and the old with the bad and the new served as a vehicle to expose the theme of the suffering of Muslims under an unjust and non-Islamic system (Kandiyoti and Saktanber 2002: 262). A contemporary version could be *Büşra* (Alper Çağlar, 2009), the naïve love story between the university graduate daughter of a rich and conservative family who wears the headscarf and a liberal journalist.

In the early 1990s with the unprecedented success of *Minyeli Abdullah / Abdullah of Minye* (**Çakmaklı**, 1989), Islamists began to use cinema as a platform. In a symposium organized by the Islamic Research Fund, a decision was taken to 'Islamize' the newspapers, cinema, television and theatre, and called on the industrialists who had been building mosques to invest in arts. It was declared: 'with art began the alienation of our people, with art it will be ended' (Şen, 1990). **Mesut Uçakan** comments that the term *beyaz sinema* (white cinema) was coined when certain film-makers 'were alienated by the *milli* cinema movement'; the superficiality and verbosity of the term did not produce effective results and the term was interpreted differently by different people. On the other hand, they could not coin a new term to describe the new movement, which they derided to call 'Islamist cinema' or 'Islamic cinema'. Journalist Abdurrahman Şen is responsible for coining 'white cinema'. 'What we imply with all these terms fundamentally is the devotion to Islam' (Tosun 1992: 76–8). Adherents claimed that since the foundations of the Turkish Republic, with few exceptions, cinema has served negative aims instead of directing society, particularly the youth, to positive channels. Masses lacking the necessary education have been influenced by the negative images on screen and have become alien to their beliefs and cultures. Mainstream cinema presented women as a commodity or sex objects; its outlook was similar to that of *cahiliyye*, the pre-Islamic Arabia. (The Qur'an states that during *cahiliyye* women were the lowest elements of society, even below animals.) **Mesut Uçakan**'s very popular *Yalnız Değilsiniz / You Are Not Alone* (1990) and its sequels focused on young women embracing Islam and the banning of the headscarf in universities.

Binary oppositions, the trademark of **Yeşilçam**, are the basis of these films, the predominant one, tradition versus modernity, coded through dwellings – ligneous

Figure 94 Yalnız Değilsiniz / You Are Not Alone (Mesut Uçakan, 1990) (author's archive)

houses in friendly neighbourhoods versus luxurious villas with swimming pools or impersonal apartment blocks; through manner of living – praying, demonstrations of family values versus western music, alcohol and drug abuse, gambling, free sex, night-life; and through the bodies of women – head-scarves, modest clothing versus mini-skirts and bikinis, excessive make-up and bouffant hair-styles. The religious enlightenment of the divided self is carried through young females, which corresponds to the gendered aspect of the polemic on religious identity in real life, conducted particularly through the headscarf issue.

Originally, such films oriented towards reclaiming the Muslim self, perceived as having been robbed of its authenticity and heritage, attracted a large audience. However, the lack of aesthetic quality was a drawback for the establishment of Islamist cinema as a **genre**. The melodramatic and sentimental content, the soap-opera style, the stereotypical characters and the propagandistic and didactic approach could not maintain the interest of the young that constitute the majority of the audience. The trend was also criticized by its own sector, one of the weekly Islamist magazines declaring *Minyeli Abdullah*, not worthy enough to be called a work of cinema and another leading Islamist magazine denouncing this new culture as 'Islamist arabesque'. Gradually, the newspapers, journals, television stations and websites owned or subsidized by rich Islamist industrialists/businessmen, inside and outside Turkey, have replaced 'white cinema' to carry on the combat to re-image the Islamist political identity. Nonetheless, **Mesut Uçakan**, **İsmail Güneş** and a number of others continue to make films although neither *Anne ya da Leyla* of **Uçakan**, nor *İmam / The Imam* (2005) of **Güneş** was popular. **Güneş** has begun to make films subduing religious messages, but focalizing on violence in society.

Religion has gained visibility in the 2000s, as the main theme, as a principal motif, or as detail to embellish the narrative, which could be related to the increased visibility of religious life since the victories of the AKP, the Islamist Justice and Development Party, but also to the need for assertion of Muslim identity in the post-9/11 world. *Takva / Takva – A Man's Fear of God* (Özer Kızıltan, 2006) underlines the clash between spirituality and modern living; *Adem'in Trenleri / Adam and the Devil* (**Pirhasan**, 2007) focuses on an unworldly *hodja* with a benevolent nature; *Beş Vakit / Times and Winds* (**Erdem**, 2006) is structured around religious motifs, the Turkish title referring to *namaz*, the sessions of prayer performed five times a day and the *ezan*, chanted from the minaret, calling the devout to prayer. For local critics, the religious characters both in *Takva – A Man's Fear of God* and *Adam and the Devil* are built on Catholic stereotypes, rather than authentic Muslim clerics and in *Times and Winds*, the morning *ezan* is chanted after the rise of the sun, a fallacy for Islamic tradition. Pointing to similar discrepancies in **Erdem**'s *A ay / Oh, Moon* (1989) and *Kaç Para Kaç / Run for Money* (1999), critics conclude that **Erdem**'s approach to daily prayers is rather subjective. *Girdap / Whirlpool* (Talip Karamahmutoğlu, 2008), based on a true story and inspired by several suicide bombing events by Al-Qaeda as well as the PKK (the outlawed Kurdish Workers' Party), traces the development of a provincial youth to a devoted Muslim through his roommates entering into a political communalist circle, alienating himself from his family and friends, becoming a fundamentalist full of hate and eventually, a suicide bomber. Just like *Takva*, the film divided opinion as to whether it criticized or condoned religion.

The Islamic religion has been exploited in experiments in horror films in the 2000s (see **fantasy films**). Religious authorities claim that such films quote the Qur'an out of context and in a manner harmful to the sensibilities of the viewers, which they claim could create fear of religion.

Destiny, fate and submission are essential elements in the films of **Zeki Demirkubuz**, which are not nurtured by religion itself, but rather by a religious essence. **Semih Kaplanoğlu**, whose *Yusuf Trilogy* is laden with religious imagery, argues that in recent films religion is presented mostly from an Orientalist point of view, or these films are the products of a certain curiosity about religion.

Rona, Aliye (b. Daraa in Syria, 1921 – d. Istanbul, 1996) Actor. Typecast as the Anatolian woman in numerous noteworthy films from *Yılanların Öcü / Revenge of the Serpents* (**Metin Erksan**, 1962) to *Bitmeyen Yol / Unending Road* (**Duygu Sağıroğlu**, 1965), Aliye Rona entered cinema in 1947 acting in about 200 films. She was the sister of the popular theatre actor, Avni Dilligil. Her death in a retirement home where the elderly were said to be abandoned and physically abused, was another sad example of the indifference of the state to its artists.

Rural films (see **village films**)

Rural melodramas (see **village films**)

S

Sabancı, Kudret (b. İzmir, 1966) Director, screenwriter. Known for his collaboration with **Serdar Akar** as founder of Yeni Sinemacılar / New Film-makers Film Company, Kudret Sabancı studied cinema and television and made several award-winning shorts, video clips, documentaries and advertisement films. He directed *Laleli'de Bir Azize / A Madonna in Laleli* (1998), an action film from a script by **Akar**, shot simultaneously with **Akar**'s *Gemide / On Board* (Romanian Ela Manea played the female lead in both films). An 'on land' version of '*On Board*', the film breaks linear time with jump-cuts to the future in the first part and to the past in the second. The camera angles and the penetrating music of **Uğur Yücel** as the leitmotif for each character contribute to the atmosphere of tension. He is one of the directors of *Anlat İstanbul / Istanbul Tales* (2005) along with **Ümit Ünal**, Selim Demirdelen, Yücel Yolcu and Ömür Atay. He also shot the multi-million dollar re-make, *Karaoğlan* (2012) (see **adaptations**), in which Turkic states unite against the Mongols to prevent the invasion of Anatolia and the murder of Çise Hatun, the betrothed of a Turkic statesmen. He continues to direct television series.

Sabuncu, Başar (b. Istanbul, 1943) Director, screenwriter, cinematographer, actor. Best known for *Zengin Mutfağı / Kitchen of the Rich* (1988), Başar Sabuncu started as a playwright and theatre director. After the *coup d'état* of 12 March 1971, he stayed in Paris for two years. On this return, he joined the Istanbul Municipal Theatre, staging several plays of Nazım Hikmet, the communist poet who died in exile in Moscow. Following the 12 September 1980 *coup*, he was made redundant and prosecuted for signing the petition of the intellectuals. He returned to his job after eight years and a long court procedure. His career in cinema began in 1978 writing social comedies for other directors. He scripted and directed his first film *Çıplak Vatandaş / The Naked Citizen* (1985), which was a success, after which he wrote the scripts of all of his films: *Kupa Kızı / Queen of Hearts* (1986), based on Joseph Kessel's novel and a variation on *Belle de jour* (Louis Buñuel, 1967); *Asılacak Kadın / A Woman to be Hanged* (1987); the complex and personal *Kaçamak / Impromptu* (1988); *Zengin Mutfağı / Kitchen of the Rich* (1988) and *Yolcu / A Boat Anchored in the Desert* (1993), adapted from a Nazım Hikmet play.

Sabuncu focuses on the individual dramas of lives condemned to vicious circles as a trope for larger disorders of society, which is particularly evident in ***Kitchen of the Rich*** and *Yolcu / A Boat Anchored in the Desert*. The latter, reminiscent of Rainer Fassbinder's *Bolwieser / The Stationmaster's Wife*, foregrounds three characters – a one-eyed station master, his unsatisfied young wife and a crippled switchman – cut off from the world by the incessant snowstorms during the War of Independence. The arrival of a mysterious young soldier hastens the rupture.

Homages were organized to Sabuncu's name at the British Film Institute in London (1988), the French cinémathèque in Paris (1991) and the Montpellier Mediterranean Film Festival (1992).

Saç / Hair (2010) is the last segment of the 'Conscience and Death' trilogy that includes *Rıza* (2007) and *Pus / Haze* (2009), focusing on the alienation of provincial characters who live in the periphery, the city of Istanbul appearing as another character. Starting from the premise of the significance of hair in the Islamic tradition which gives rise to social and political issues, the film shows how a strand of hair can bind or separate people. The three principle characters are somehow related to hair: one sells it, the other buys it and the third is sensitive about it. They complement each other through hair, the wig shop serving as a microcosm for the issues of society. The feeling of loneliness is accentuated in the film through stylistic choices: long static shots, the absence of music and the reliance on either silence or deafening street noise to increase the mood. The protagonist Hamdi (Ayberk Pekcan), who operates the wig shop, is in total solitude. He needs the woman who sells her hair, Meryem (Nazan Kesal), but he cannot touch her. He connects with life through the glass window. He stares at a prostitute on the street waiting for customers, but he cannot go near her. The same scene is repeated in the beginning, the middle and the end to accentuate the vicious circle of the character.

The contrasts are significant; the most prominent, life and death as the main trope in all three films that have a murder as a base. Rıza commits murder when his truck is broken; the man in *Haze* wants to kill his wife and in *Hair*, Hamdi, a

Figure 95 Saç / Hair (Tayfun Pirselimoğlu, 2010) (Courtesy of Tayfun Pirselimoğlu)

Figure 96 Saç / Hair (Tayfun Pirselimoğlu, 2010) (Courtesy of Tayfun Pirselimoğlu)

passive man, kills the husband of a woman he wants to possess. They all include the rituals of washing of the corpse, the funeral rites and spaces resembling a mausoleum (such as the *hamam*). In *Hair*, a man who will soon die chain-smokes while dreaming of going to Brazil with the woman he desires; a caretaker talks to his mistress on the phone while washing a corpse in the morgue and asks her if he should buy *rakı* (Turkish national drink) for their evening escapade. A dog lying in the middle of the road, presumed dead, is breathing. In three key episodes, Hamdi is seen lying in a horizontal position on the cold cement. Reality and illusion is another obvious contrast. At the end of the film, we return to the wig shop; Hamdi is still in front of the window staring at the billboard that shows the advertisement for Brazil and the husband he has killed is back home, alive. What looks unreal is real, just as in real life. Bombarded by the media incessantly, death has become matter of fact, creating indifference to the tragedy of the others. The motif of perpetual watching – Hamdi watches the traffic and the advertising boards, Meryem watches the television – emphasizes the passivity of the characters, apoliticized and de-sensitivitized.

Contrasting the two faces of the city where modernity and tradition try to survive side by side, **Pirselimoğlu** emphasizes the vital issues of the metropolis – the migration and the traumas of the newcomers, the continuous modernization process – underscoring the cultural complexity of a city that is unique as the meeting point of the East and the West. At a shopping centre with a foreign name, ready-made food is eaten from styrofoam containers while Meryem, an Anatolian woman wearing a t-shirt with .com written on the back sweeps the garbage; in the

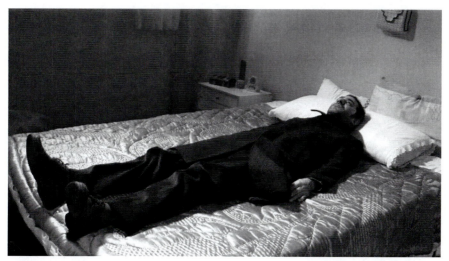

Figure 97 Saç / Hair (Tayfun Pirselimoğlu, 2010) (Courtesy of Tayfun Pirselimoğlu)

traditional men's café, tea is served in a small glass according to custom. Food is consumed in big shopping malls as well as in filthy *lahmacun* (Middle Eastern pizza) stands. The despair of the citizens who are not able to attune to the fast development of Istanbul is on all faces.

Istanbul has always been part of Turkish cinema, but since the 1990s, it has been presented as an uncanny space. In *Hair*, even the historical *hamam* (the Turkish bath) is a cold empty space – like a mausoleum – offering no relief, unlike the exotic *hamams* of some other films. For a foreigner, or someone who has visited the city as a tourist, Istanbul is hardly recognizable in the film, part of which is shot in the Golden City where shantytowns mushroom at an incredible speed. On the other hand, luxurious apartment blocks or gated communities constantly expand, pushing the shantytowns further. *Haze* shows a certain sector getting richer while the rest get poorer. 'The city is like an animal fattening itself by eating the small ones; Anatolians keep coming to be swallowed by this animal. People are afraid, alienated. Human relations are severed. The silence is related to the lack of communication' (Dönmez-Colin 2012: 213).

Director, Screenwriter: **Tayfun Pirselimoğlu**; Producer: Veysel İpek, Nikos Moustakas, **Tayfun Pirselimoğlu**; Cinematographer: Ercan Özkan; Editor: Erdinç Özyurt; Cast: Ayberk Pekcan, Nazan Kesal, Rıza Akın

Sağıroğlu, Duygu (b. Trabzon, 1932) Director, screenwriter, editor, art director. Considered as one of the most important film-makers of the period 1960–67, named the 'Golden Period' by some critics, Duygu Sağıroğlu started his career as a stage designer. He entered cinema in 1959 as assistant director to **Atıf Yılmaz** and worked in numerous films as assistant director, art director or designer. His first feature *Bitmeyen Yol / The Road Without End* (1966), merging poetic realism with social concerns while using a universal language, is one of the best migration films made in the first half of the 1960s. It was censured for two years. He continued along the same line with *Ben Öldükçe Yaşarım / I Live as Long as I Die* (1965), starring **Yılmaz Güney**, and *Namus / Honour* (1972), after which he surrendered to the pressures of censorship and the temptation of **Yeşilçam** for survival, directing costume dramas, B-movies, adventure yarns, never recapturing the success of his first film.

Salman, İlyas (b. Malatya, 1949) Actor, director, author, screenwriter, musician, activist. **İlyas Salman** started acting at the Istanbul Municipal Theatre. His first role in cinema was in *Baskın / Raid* (**Atıf Yılmaz**, 1978). Generally typecast as a peasant, he drew attention with **Sinan Çetin**'s *Çiçek Abbas / Abbas in Flower* (1981) and *Çirkinler de Sever / The Ugly Also Love* (1982). He gave a memorable performance in the **comedy** *Fikrimin İnce Gülü / Sarı Mersedes / Mercedes Mon Amour* (**Okan**, 1992) as a guest worker returning home from Germany with a Mercedes he has bought with his sweat. After a long silence, he returned with *Lal Gece / The Night of Silence* (**Reis Çelik**, 2012) in which he plays a middle-aged ex-prisoner about to be wed to a teenager. He is also the director of two feature films.

Samancılar, Menderes (b. Adana, 1954) Actor, poet, politician. Starting with *photo-romans*, Menderes Samancılar had his first role in cinema in **Yılmaz Duru**'s *İnce Memed Vuruldu / İnce Memed is Shot* (1975). He has played in countless films and television series. ***Karartma Geceleri / Blackout Nights*** (**Yusuf Kurçenli**, 1990), *Dönersen Islık Çal / Whistle If You Come Back* (**Orhan Oğuz**, 1993) and ***Gözetleme Kulesi / The Watch Tower*** (**Pelin Esmer**, 2012) are some of the landmarks. He also played in Claude Lelouch's *Hasards ou Coïncidences / Chance or Coincidence* (1998).

Saner, Hulki (b. Istanbul, 1925 – d. Istanbul, 2005) Director, screenwriter, producer, composer, musician. A graduate in chemistry, Hulki Saner continued his studies in the US while gaining experience in the field of his real interest: music. On his return to Turkey, he entered the municipal conservatory and graduated. He sang in the Istanbul Opera and composed music. In 1956, he started to compose film music and by 1958, he was directing and producing films (*Sevmek Günah mı? / Is it Sin to Love?*; unofficial English title). As one of the most productive film-makers with over 200 films to his credit, he made mostly **comedies**, becoming very popular with the *Turist Ömer / Ömer, the Tourist* series (1964–73) starring **Sadri Alışık**, but artistically, his films could not rise above the average escapist entertainment fare. He also distributed films through his company, Saner Film.

Savaş, Perihan (b. Istanbul, 1955) Actor; RN: Şerife Perihan. Starting a stage career as a 5-year-old at the Istanbul Municipal Theatre, Perihan Savaş took part in numerous plays before entering cinema in 1971. Her first lead role was with *Korkusuz Beşler / The Brave Five* (Yücel Uçanoğlu, 1972), which was followed by several insignificant films. Her breakthrough came with *Bedrana* (**Süreyya**

Duru, 1974). After a period of cheap **melodramas** as a duo with the **arabesque** stars of the period, her collaboration with **Bilge Olgaç** in *Kaşık Düşmanı / Spoon Enemy* aka *A Wedding Room* (1984) and *İpekçe / Silky* (1987) brought her memorable roles, followed by *Karılar Koğuşu / Women's Jail* (**Halit Refiğ**, 1989), in which she played a convict on death row for poisoning her husband. Despite appearing in over 120 films, in an industry dominated by men, Perihan Savaş was exploited by the producers and harassed by the paparazzi, which often led to disappointments. In 2012, she was the recipient of the Honorary Award of the Adana Golden Boll Film Festival.

Sayar, Leyla (b. Istanbul, 1939) Actor, dancer. After studying at the Ankara State Theatre for a period, Leyla Sayar started her cinema career in 1958, appearing in numerous roles, mostly B-movies, except a few by well-known names, such as *Şafak Bekçileri / Guardians of Dawn* (**Halit Refiğ**, 1963) and *Suçlular Aramızda / Criminals Among Us* (**Metin Erksan**, 1964). In the latter, she plays the devious mistress of a scheming rich man, who double-crosses him and exposes his evil actions. Queen of eroticism in the 1960s, perhaps the most famous vamp of Turkish cinema, she evoked fetishism and catered to sado-masochistic fantasies with her erotic accessories. In *Şehrazat-Dişi Örümcek / Scheherazade – The Female Spider* (1964), she was the praying mantis who cruised bars and killed men after a night of sex until she found true love. She stopped acting in 1972 for a career in cabaret dancing, but was not successful. She embraced religion in 1976 and led an ascetic life, breaking her isolation in 2011.

Scognamillo, Giovanni (b. Istanbul, 1929) Film critic and historian, author, actor. Coming from a film background, his father the owner of Star Film that imported foreign films and operated the Elhamra theatre, Giovanni Scognamillo is a Levantine of Italian origin. After graduating from Italian high school, he began to write film criticism for foreign journals and continued this activity with Turkish publications. He has been writing books on cinema, science fiction, **fantasy**, horror and occultism for six decades. A documentary was made about him: *Beyoğlu'nda Bir Levanten: Giovanni Scognamillo / A Levantine in Beyoğlu: Giovanni Scognamillo* (Ebubekir Çetinkaya, 2006).

Seden, Osman Fahir (b. Istanbul, 1924 – d. Istanbul, 1998) Director, screenwriter, producer. Along with **Atıf Yılmaz, Lütfi Ö. Akad, Metin Erksan, Memduh Ün** and **Halit Refiğ**, Osman Fahir Seden is considered as one of the most important film-makers of the *The Period of Cinema Men* that followed the Transition Period (1945–50). He was born in Istanbul in 1924 to the family that founded Turkey's first private production company and studio, Kemal Film in 1922. Seden studied law, worked in the family company as a translator of the dialogues of foreign films and travelled to the US in 1949 to sign contracts with the majors for importing their films. By 1951, he assumed the responsibility of Kemal Film, producing and writing scripts (*İstanbul Kan Ağlarken / As Istanbul Was Bleeding*, Kani Kıpçak, 1951). When **Lütfi Ö. Akad** joined Kemal Film in 1952, their five-year collaboration resulted in one of the classics of Turkish cinema, **Kanun Namına / In the Name of Law**. He wrote *İngiliz Kemal Lavrens'e Karşı / English Kemal against Lawrence*, which was brought to screen by **Akad** (1952). He started directing with *Kanlarıyla Ödediler / They Paid With Their Blood* (1955), which carries the influences of **Akad** mixed with American gangster **melodramas**. He continued with formulaic urban dramas, displaying a move toward a less affective narrative with *Düşman Yolları Kesti / The Enemy Blocked the Roads* (1959) and *Namus Uğruna / In the Name of Honour* (1960). He tried every **genre** to keep Kemal Film alive including **Kemal Sunal** comedies, **Türkan Şoray** dramas and **arabesque melodramas**, made in haste, although he would have preferred personal films like *Çalıkuşu / The Wren* (1966), a period piece adapted from renowned author Reşat Nuri Güntekin's novel. Having established his own company, Seden Film in 1974, he made his last film *Suçlu / The Guilty*, his 133rd in 1989. In the 1990s, he switched to television series and continued to be very productive until his death in 1998 (Özgüç 2001: 165–6). He also played small roles in the films he directed. The initiation of the star system is attributed to Seden.

Selvi Boylum, Al Yazmalım / The Girl with the Red Scarf (1977) is considered as the best love story of **Yeşilçam** cinema and listed among the ten best Turkish films of all time. Young peasant girl Asya (**Türkan Şoray**) and truck driver İlyas (**Kadır İnanır**) fall madly in love at first sight and elope. They are married with a religious ceremony (customary in the rural milieu although not considered legal) and have a son, Samet. The third character, Cemşit (Ahmet Mekin), inadvertently causes the disintegration of the union by asking İlyas to tow a stranded minibus with his truck, which costs him his job. Transferred to a repair workshop and separated from his red truck, which is almost an extension of himself (he talks to it), he begins to drink. His old girlfriend Dilek uses this opportunity to win him back. Abandoned with her baby, by a twist of fate, Asya is sheltered by Cemşit, a responsible and dependable man, unlike the flighty İlyas. Eventually they marry. Several years later, by another twist of fate, İlyas has an accident near their house while drunk and Cemşit brings him inside. İlyas wants to claim his family and Asya still loves him, but she needs to re-evaluate the meaning of love and the definition of father, husband and lover. When little Samet runs to Cemşit, calling him 'father', the decision is made for her.

Whereas the text of Aitmatov foregrounds the stories of the two men, **Yılmaz** focuses on the woman. The film begins with a close-up shot of Asya and ends the same way. Asya is presented as an independent woman with choices. She decides to elope with the man she loves rather than marry someone she has never seen. She takes the initiative to speak to İlyas's boss on his behalf (only to be slapped by İlyas for making him lose face) and she leaves the home where she is not happy. To prepare the audience for Asya's choice in the finale, **Yılmaz** made certain insertions regarding her life with Cemşit. She is legally married; she has discarded her peasant clothes and she has a job, working in a *kilim* co-operative.

Dialogues are reduced to a minimum in the film; the narrative flows through the interior voices/monologues, the three principal actors synchronizing with jests

Figure 98 Selvi Boylum, Al Yazmalım / The Girl with the Red Scarf (Atıf Yılmaz, 1977)
(Courtesy of International Istanbul Film Festival)

Figure 99 Selvi Boylum, Al Yazmalım / The Girl with the Red Scarf (Atıf Yılmaz, 1977)
(Courtesy of International Istanbul Film Festival)

Figure 100 Selvi Boylum, Al Yazmalım / The Girl with the Red Scarf (Atıf Yılmaz, 1977)
(Courtesy of International Istanbul Film Festival)

and mimics while facing the audience, a novelty for Turkish cinema, which was
Atıf Yılmaz's way of preserving the lyrical text while emphasizing visuality. This
is particularly effective in the sequence when Asya and İlyas meet and the camera
circles around the two characters. Married to Cemşit, Asya reflects: 'What was
love? An overflowing stream, leaves trembling in the autumn wind, raindrops that
hit the window and disperse, a fluttering heart? At the end, the overflowing river
settles down, the leaves dry and fall, the rain ends and the sun appears. What was
love? Is it the warm, friendly human hand that protects, is it human labour? Love
was goodness, love was labour.'

The winner of several awards, the film was restored in 2010 by Çiçek Film,
Groupama Gan Foundation for Cinema and the Technicolour Foundation for
Cinema Heritage with the support of the Ministry of Culture and Tourism and
shown at the 29th Istanbul Film Festival, 2010.

Director, Producer: **Atıf Yılmaz**; Production: **Yeşilçam** Film; Screenwriter: **Ali Özgentürk**
(based on Chingiz Aitmatov's story, *Kızıl Cooluk Calcalım*); Cinematographer: Çetin
Tunca; Music: Cahit Berkay; Cast: **Türkan Şoray**, **Kadir İnanır**, Ahmet Mekin, Nurhan
Nur, Hülya Tuğlu

Serengil, Öztürk (b. Artvin, 1930 – d. Istanbul, 1999) Actor, producer. One of the most popular **comedy** actors of **Yeşilçam**, typecast as 'Adanalı Tayfur' (Tayfur from Adana), **Öztürk Serengil** started on stage in 1953, switching to cinema with *Üçüncü Kat Cinayeti / Murder On the Third Floor* (unofficial English title) (**Orhan Elmas**, 1954). He acted the 'bad man' in numerous films before choosing **comedy**. He played in close to 300 films and participated in television shows, his coinage of slang words that were readily adapted by his followers creating controversy.

Seyyit Han aka *Toprağın Gelini / Seyyit Han* aka *The Bride of the Earth* (1968), considered as the first film to present Kurdish characters, foregrounds the silence that ruins women's lives in feudal societies regulated by merciless behavioural codes. Although it was shot in the town of Yenice in Adana where **Güney** was born, the name of the woman is Keje, a Kurdish name. Seyyit Han's struggles against the local landlord can be decoded as the struggle of the oppressed against the oppressor and a parallel can be drawn to the plight of the Kurds in Turkey, but this aspect is so subtle that even the censors could not decipher it. (They only objected to the name Keje.)

Just like, *Ağıt / The Elegy* (1971), *Seyyit Han* also toys with the western **genre** that heroicizes the outlaw. Seyyit Han (**Yılmaz Güney** with a Clint Eastwood aura) is a brave loner in love with Keje (Nebahat Çehre), but before he can have her, he has to subjugate all his enemies. Keje's brother does not want his sister to become a widow. Assumed dead after an absence of seven years that includes long jail sentences, he returns to claim his bride just when she is about to wed the village headman, Hamdi Bey. Keje is ready to elope with him but when her brother reminds her that the honour of the family is in her hands, she sends him away. As the men dance and shoot in the air, Hamdi Bey makes a sinister plan to mend his hurt pride. Keje is buried in the ground except for her head, which is covered with a basket supporting a daisy at the centre. Seyyit is challenged to a marksmanship contest. He falls into the trap and kills the woman he loves. His gun, the symbol of his manhood, destroys his love. Keje has accepted to be buried alive to save the family honour. Just like many Anatolian women, her fate is decided by men – her brother, her husband or the village head.

Director, Screenwriter: **Yılmaz Güney**; Producer: **Abdurrahman Keskiner**, Yılmaz Güney, Yaşar Tunalı; Production: Güney Film; Cinematographer: Gani Turanlı; Music: Nedim Otyam; Cast: **Yılmaz Güney**, Nebahat Çehre, **Hayati Hamzaoğlu**, Nihat Ziyalan, Danyal Topatan, Neda Aksoy, Çetin Başaran

Sevmek Zamanı / A Time to Love (1965) merges the Western idea of *mimesis* with the Eastern philosophy of Sufism, foregrounding the East/West dichotomy through a doomed love story. House painter, Halil (**Müşfik Kenter**) falls in love with the picture of a young bourgeois woman while working in her family's vacation house on one of the affluent Prince Islands near Istanbul. One day Meral catches him staring at her portrait and tries to convince him to love her instead of the image. On the surface, he is afraid of rejection and loss, considering their

Figure 101 Sevmek Zamanı / A Time to Love (Metin Erksan, 1965) (Courtesy of International Istanbul Film Festival)

social differences. They 'belong to different worlds' (a standard **Yeşilçam** cliché). An educated rich woman, she comes to the island in the summer for vacation and he, in winter, for work. He is an Eastern man who listens to classical Turkish music (*ud*); in her world, it is either Bach's *Toccata and Fugue* or disco. He lives in the woods, she in luxurious apartments. He can be fulfilled by falling in love with her image (which is common in Middle Eastern folklore, including the *Arabian Nights*); she reads Ovid's *The Art of Love* and dreams of tangible love. His boss and confidant Mustafa is like a dervish; her confidants Mine and Oya are from her petite bourgeois life. Commensurate with the **Yeşilçam** stereotypes, Meral's father is a typical businessman who protects his interests and her fiancé Başar (the name associates with success) is rich and virile. (Başar has had its antecedents in *Acı Hayat / Bitter Life* and *Suçlular Aramızda / The Culprit Are Among Us*, played by **Ekrem Bora**). Halil and Meral are the two faces of Istanbul, during a period of transition to modernity, which is embraced by the upper classes but not digested; hence, their degenerate behaviour. To stress the contrasts, **Erksan** intersperses images of mosques and shrines, juxtaposing them with modern buildings.

Space is foreboding and uncanny in the film. The island, exuding a vacation mood in the summer as the spectator imagines, is dark and deserted, more befitting Halil's disposition as an introvert immersed in the melancholy familiar to Istanbulites (Orhan Pamuk's *hüzün*). The second space is a shooting polygon, linked to the degenerate character of Başar and his friends, who beat Halil when he tries to see Meral. The third space is Halil's hut inside the forest (a trope for the darkness in his soul). The last episodes take place on the lake inside the forest, on a boat – a floating space, a place without a place, that exists by itself, that is closed in on itself and at the same time is given over to the infinity of the sea – the great reserve of the imagination, heterotopia par excellence (Foucault 1984: 49).

Erksan carries the East/West dichotomy to his filming style as well. He merges **Yeşilçam** clichés including the crime of passion (Halil and Meral are killed by Başer) with modern Western narrative. At the same time, he interrogates photography and reality. The photograph itself is 'both a pseudo-presence and a token of absence. Like a wood fire in a room, photographs…are incitements to reverie. The sense of the unattainable that can be evoked by photographs feeds directly into the erotic feelings of those for whom desirability is enhanced by distance', which Sontag calls 'attempts to contact or lay claim to another reality'. Furthermore, Halil's relationship with Meral's picture involves a third party, the photographer, who, through the act of photographing, participated in her 'mortality, vulnerability, mutability. Precisely by slicing out this moment and freezing it, all photographs testify to time's relentless melt' (Sontag 1977: 15–16). When Halil learns about Meral's marriage, he dresses a dummy with a wedding gown and goes to the lake on a rowboat with her portrait. Meral escapes from the wedding ceremony to reach Halil and throws the dummy into the water to bring her reality to Halil's fantasy world.

The film is also noteworthy in terms of gendered identities. Halil and Başer are like yin–yang, Halil possessing the feminine qualities of spirituality and sensitivity and Başer the masculine and the physical aspect. One offers platonic love, the other, sexual. The character of Meral is a reflection of the imagery of a male film-maker of an androcentric society. Her position – rich and educated – is acquired without effort (her father is wealthy). She is conditioned to exist for men and her choice is determined by which man she can make happier. Her feeling of guilt forces her to respond to the man who loves her passionately. She accepts unconditionally the platonic love that creates a false feeling of security without considering her physical needs. Along the same lines, the wedding gown Halil carries to the boat also confirms to the traditional values (or audience expectations) as the symbol of union between man and woman.

Although it could not attract distributors when it was made, interest grew after television screenings; the film gradually gained cult status and a DVD was released in 2007.

Director, Screenwriter, Producer: **Metin Erksan**; Production: Troya Film; Cinematographer: Mengü Yeğin; Sound: **Yorgo İlyadis**; Music: Metin Bükey; Cast: **Müşfik Kenter**, Sema Özcan, Süleyman Tekcan, Oya Bulaner, Abdullah Demiryan, Kemal Ergüvenç, Ayban Erkmen, Fadil Garan, Osman Karahan, Mehmet Omar, Adnan Uygur

Sezer, Şerif (b. Mudanya, 1943) Actor. Renowned for her remarkable roles in *Yol / The Way* (Şerif Gören, 1982); *Hakkaride Bir Mevsim / A Season in Hakkari* (Erden Kıral, 1982) and *Camdan Kalp / A Heart of Glass* (Fehmi Yaşar, 1990), Şerif Sezer has been acting on stage, in cinema and on television for almost four decades. Generally type-cast as the woman from the East, she is the recipient of numerous national awards.

Sezin, Sezer (b. Istanbul, 1929) Actor, producer; RN: Mesrure Sezer. First appearing on stage when she was only 11, Sezer Sezin switched to cinema in 1944, playing insignificant roles. Her breakthrough came with *Damga / The Stigma* (1948) (started by Seyfi Havaeri and completed by **Lütfi Ö. Akad**), but she became a star with *Vurun Kahpeye / Kahpeye / Strike the Whore* (**Akad**, 1949), and played in the films of several other upcoming film-makers – **Atıf Yılmaz, Memduh Ün**. In 1956, she co-founded Exportfilm and produced three films. The character of a tough masculine woman that **Metin Erksan** cast her in with *Şöför Nebahat / The Driver Nebahat* (1960) stayed with her for a while, particularly with the sequels in 1964 and 1965. She always played strong women characters, but she is particularly memorable for her role in *Üç Tekerlekli Bisiklet / Tricycle* aka *The Three-Wheeled Bicycle* (**Akad, Ün**, 1962). She also participated in two French productions partially shot in Istanbul: *Tintin et le mystère de la Toison d'Or / Tintin and the Golden Fleece* (Jean-Jacques Vierne, 1961) and *L'immortelle* (Alain Robbe-Grillet, 1963). In 1967, she stopped cinema and concentrated on theatre until the mid-1970s, returning 40 years later as a guest performer in **Safa Önal**'s *Hicran Sokağı / Street of Sadness* (unofficial English title) (2007).

Simavi, Sedat (Süleyman) (b. Istanbul, 1896 – d. Istanbul, 1953) Director, screenwriter, journalist, author, caricaturist. The founder of one of the oldest national newspapers of Turkey, *Hürriyet*, and a number of magazines including the well-known weekly *Yedigün*, Sedat Simavi is the director of *Pençe / The Claw* and *Casus / The Spy* (1917), both of which are considered as the first complete films of Turkish cinema.

Social realist movement in Turkish cinema was triggered by the military *coup* of May 1960, which overthrew the Democrat Party regime (1950–60) of prime minister Adnan Menderes and introduced the progressive Constitution of 1961. The social and political atmosphere was ripe for political activism and for cinema to concentrate on the pressing issues of an underdeveloped country where class differences, inequality and corruption were widespread. The burgeoning of film magazines (*Yeni Sinema, Sine-Film, Sinema 65*), the establishment of film clubs and the founding of the **cinematheque** (1965) created a favourable atmosphere for young engagé film-makers such as **Metin Erksan, Duygu Sağıroğlu** and **Ertem Göreç** to seek a national film language and a personal style. According to film scholar Aslı Daldal, Turkish social realism, 'lacking the social unification of the anti-Fascist war and the rich literary tradition of Italy was less based on solid social and artistic grounds than the Italian social realism; in cinema it almost "naively" reflected the artistic and political objectives of a "new intelligentsia", trying to harmonize its traditional Ottoman heritage with the universal proclivity of neo-Kemalism' (Daldal 2003: 40).

   The social realist movement produced remarkable films such as *Gecelerin Ötesi / Beyond the Nights* (1960), *Yılanların Öcü / The Revenge of the Serpents* (1962) and *Susuz Yaz / A Dry Summer* (1963) by **Metin Erksan**; *Şehirdeki*

Yabancı / The Stranger in the City (1963), **Gurbet Kuşları / The Birds of Nostalgia** aka **Migrating Birds** aka **Birds of Exile** (1964) and **Haremde Dört Kadın / Four Women in the Harem** (1965) by **Halit Refiğ**; **Otobüs Yolcuları / The Bus Passengers** (1961) and **Karanlıkta Uyananlar / Awakening in the Dark** (1964) by **Ertem Göreç** and *Bitmeyen Yol / The Road Without End* (1965) by **Duygu Sağıroğlu**. These films were not sufficient to transform the established infrastructure of commercial cinema, but the movement prepared the ground for the committed films of **Yılmaz Güney** by introducing the concept that cinema was not only a vehicle for entertainment but also an art that could transmit individual or societal messages.

Although the movement was a short experiment during the middle-class rule between 1960–65, it reflected the search for identity in a period of rapid transition from traditionalism to modernism. Committed film-makers were united with a strong anti-bourgeois and anti-capitalist agenda. They also tried to find a new film language by experimenting with depth of field, multiple camera angles and location shooting. Filmic allegories of underdevelopment, from the point of view of aesthetics, these films show a commitment to Glauber Rocha's Fanonian (Frantz Fanon, *The Wretched of the Earth*, 1961) inspired manifesto, 'An Aesthetic of Hunger' or 'An Aesthetic of Violence' (Rocha 1965: 13–14), combining slow, reflexive rhythms with adamant harsh images and sound although they were made by an educated, middle-class, radical elite and sporadically transmitted a paternalistic vision of the masses. Just as in the films of the *Cinema Novo* movement, salvation came from the city and was not generated by the community. The movement remained eclectic. A mixture of modernist cultural avant-gardism and Marxism was displayed in different ways by different film-makers. Due to financial restraints, a populist tendency had to be employed (to the chagrin of the intellectuals) to entertain the masses while educating them. Severe political campaigns against the movement and personal and ideological differences between the film-makers and some critics of the left resulted in the underestimation of the movement, which could have flourished. *Those Awakening in the Dark* had a long struggle with censorship. The newly founded freedom was relative. The Constitution Court revived the censorship regulations established in 1939 in the wake of WWII, arguing they were not anti-constitutional. During this period, which **Yılmaz Güney** would later define as the McCarthy years, a small detail, a dialogue, the colour of a garment or even a name could easily receive the stamp of 'separatist aims' or 'threat to national wholeness and togetherness' and result in the rejection of a script.

Soğuk / Cold (2013), inspired by Anton Chekhov's *Tri Sestry / Three Sisters*, marks the return of **Uğur Yücel** to serious cinema. The names Olya, Masha and Irina, the dissatisfaction with the life at home and the dreams of Moscow as a place to return are Chekhov but the rest is contemporary and local. Three Russian sisters come to the border town of Kars, in the northeast of Turkey (controlled by Russia between 1878–1917 and Armenia 1918–20 and the setting of Orhan Pamuk's *Kar / Snow*, 2002) to earn money through prostitution, a common

Figure 102 Soğuk / Cold (Uğur Yücel, 2013) (Courtesy of International Istanbul Film Festival)

phenomenon after the fall of the Soviet Union. Cross-border prostitution has had its negative repercussions on the already oppressive lives of women under the yoke of the patriarchy, which **Yücel** denounces vehemently, determined to speak for the subaltern. The film does not pass judgement on the prostitutes, neither does it romanticize their act by finding humanistic motivations (taking care of a child back home, as in *Sonbahar / Autumn*, **Özcan Alper**, 2008). One of the sisters states that there is more money in prostitution than in working in a factory. They are the peons of the new world order. The nightclub (called *pavyon* in Turkish) where prostitutes ply their trade is pivotal to **Yeşilçam** and open to filmic exploitation (seductive song and dance numbers forced into the diegesis), which **Yücel** avoids. The film respects the prostitute and avoids nudity and sex, discretion that can only be found perhaps in the films of **Demirkubuz**. On the other hand, Turkish characters are reduced to stereotypes: all men are brutes and all women are victims. The protagonist, Balabey (Cenk Medet Alibeyoğlu, a non-professional), at times resembling Ahmet Uğurlu as Mahsun in *Tabutta Rövaşata / Somersault in a Coffin* (**Zaim**, 1997) clutching his pet rooster, and at times Harry Dean Stanton in *Paris, Texas* (Wim Wenders, 1984) walking between the rails in mysterious determination, is so kind-hearted as to pray for the salvation of a prostitute before making love to her, but selfishly engrossed in black passion, abandoning his pregnant wife at childbirth does not bother his conscience, neither does committing fratricide for revenge. His brother is a trigger-happy boor, compensating his impotence with his gun.

The film draws attention to archaic traditions, the feudal system that curbs individualism, societal pressures about forming a family when one is not ready, sexual hunger and lack of sex education resulting in unhappy marriages based on duty rather than love: 'You'll do what a woman does. I'll do what a man does', the newly married man cautions his miserable wife. Kars is shown mostly in the dark, buried in snow, isolated, insular and backward. The film ends with taciturn Balabey leaving four corpses behind and entering a tunnel; **Yücel** is offering no hope that things will change one day.

Director, Screenwriter: **Uğur Yücel**, Producer: Erol Avcı; Production: TMC; Cinematographer: A. Emre Tanyıldız; Editor: Ulaş Cihan Şimşek, Mark Marnikovich; Art Director: Gülay Doğan; Cast: Cenk Medet Alibeyoğlu, A. Rıfat Şungar, Valeria Skorokhodova, Yulia Vanyukova, Yulia Erenler, Şebnem Bozoklu, Ezgi Mola, Rıza Sönmez

Sonbahar / Autumn (2007) is a film about collective memory, the irremediable scars of recent political history, lost generations, lost ideals and lost traditions. Yusuf (Onur Saylak) – alluding to Prophet Yusuf thrown into a well – was thrown into jail in 1997 for his ideals as a 22-year-old university student. He experienced the hunger strikes of 2000 against the conditions of solitary confinement, which were terminated by bloody interventions, euphemized by the state as 'Back to Life Operations'. Released for health reasons ten years later, he returns to his village on the Black Sea. His father is dead; his girlfriend is married and his dog does not recognize him. His old and sickly mother is barely surviving where only the children and the elderly have remained, the young having departed for the cities, to work or to study. He frequents the tavern with his old friend Mikail (Serkan Keskin), who has abandoned his ideals and settled into the family business of

Figure 103 Sonbahar / Autumn (Özcan Alper, 2007) (Courtesy of Özcan Alper)

Figure 104 Sonbahar / Autumn (Özcan Alper, 2007) (Courtesy of Özcan Alper)

carpentry. Meeting Eka (Megi Koboladze), a beautiful Georgian prostitute who supports her mother and child, is like a ray of sunshine but a love story between a man who has risked his life for socialism and a woman for whom socialism is a nightmare is doomed from the start.

Özcan Alper belongs to the generation that started university in the 1990s and the film is also significant in terms of its focus on the resuscitation of the left after the apoliticized decade following the 1980 *coup*. He documents the struggles of Yusuf to come to terms with the personal trauma surrounding the part he played in the student movement. By presenting this loss of experience, he turns the audience into witnesses, thus transforming a personal loss of experience into a collective experience of loss that was caused by the military interventions of three decades, followed by curbing of political activities.

The first feature of **Alper**, shot mostly in the Hemshin language, *Autumn* is a search for supressed identity for the director, a Hamshentsi or Hemshinli (descendant of the Armenians from Hemshin who converted to Islam in the seventeenth century), through the voices and the songs of the land and the moods of the sea that change from calm waters to turbulent waves as autumn slowly blends into winter. Hemshin culture is documented with anthropological details – the grave in the garden, the desire to go to the plateau and the traditional bagpipe, *tulum*. The film's intertextuality with literature, particularly Chekhov (*Uncle Vanya* as a key motif, the melancholy that is accompanied by a desperate sense of hope) is connected with the influence of Russian authors on **Alper**, but also springs from the proximity of Hopa to the former USSR (18 km from the present Georgia). Not only does the area possess a multicultural texture of ethnic identities that do not necessarily correspond to territorially based identities, but also the border itself is a strong metaphor for multiple identities if we see culture as a process involving negotiating differences of all kinds with the flow of people, ideas and goods across national borders (Ewing 1998: 267). At the same time, the concept of 'borderland' as a way of thinking about identity through the process of metaphorical extension – psychological, sexual or spiritual – which is present when different cultures, classes or sexual orientations meet each other (Anzaldúa 1987: preface), is foregrounded in the film, particularly through the linguistic borders.

A winner of numerous national and international awards, the film received strong support from the workers' groups and the unions, and reached 150,000 viewers; it is estimated to have sold hundreds of pirated DVDs.

Director, Screenwriter: **Özcan Alper**; Producer: F. Serkan Acar, **Kadir Sözen**; Production: Kuzey Film; Cinematographer: Feza Çaldıran; Editor: Thomas Balkenhol; Art Director: Canan Çayır; Sound: Mohammed Mokhtari; Cast: Onur Saylak, Megi Koboladze, Serkan Keskin, Raife Yenigül, Nino Lejava, Sibel Öz, Cihan Camkerten, Serhan Kirpir, Yaşar Güven

Sonku, Cahide (b. Sana/Yemen, 1916 – d. Istanbul, 1981) Actor, director, producer, screenwriter; RN: Cahide Serap. Starting her stage career as a 16-year-old, Sonku launched her film career with *Söz Bir, Allah Bir / One Word, One God* (1933). With *Aysel, Bataklı Damın Kızı / The Girl From the Marshes* aka *Aysel, the Girl From the Swampy Roof* (1934), she captured the audience and soon became the first star of Turkish cinema, adopted by the republican intellectuals as the Turkish Greta Garbo, her blonde features and aloof disposition identifying her with the West. She appeared as the *femme fatale* in numerous roles. In 1950, she established her company, the destruction of which in 1963 during a fire triggered her downfall.

Sorak, Ömer Faruk (b. Ankara, 1964) Director, producer, screenwriter. Co-director of *Vizontele* (2001) with **Yılmaz Erdoğan**, **Ömer Faruk Sorak** is the director of box-office hits such as *G.O.R.A.* (2004), *Sınav / Exam* (2006), *Yahşi Batı* (2010) and *Aşk Tesadüfleri Sever / Love Loves Coincidences* (2011) and numerous clips for popular singers.

Soygazi, Hale (b. Istanbul, 1950) Actor. Miss Europe in 1972, Hale Soygazi worked as a model and appeared in several movies before drawing attention with *Maden / Mine* (**Yavuz Özkan**, 1978), which brought her the Best Actress award at the Antalya Golden Orange Film Festival, 1978. After a break, she returned with the lead role in *Bir Yudum Sevgi / A Taste of Love* aka *A Sip of Love* (**Atıf**

Figure 105 Hale Soygazi in *Bir Yudum Sevgi / A Taste of Love* aka *A Sip of Love* (Atıf Yılmaz, 1984) (Courtesy of International Istanbul Film Festival)

Yılmaz, 1984), winning the same award. Some of her significant roles are in *Bir Avuç Cennet / A Handful of Paradise* (**Muammer Özer**, 1985); *Kadının Adı Yok / Woman Has No Name* (1987), *Bekle Dedim Gölgeye / I've Asked the Shadow to Wait* (**Yılmaz**, 1990) and *Cazibe Hanımın Gündüz Düşleri / Reveries of Mrs Cazibe* (**İrfan Tözüm**, 1992). She continues her acting career with television series.

Söylemez, Belmin (b. Istanbul, 1966) Director, copywriter, editor, producer. Belmin Söylemez graduated from the Queen's College in London in 1984. She made music videos and promotion films. Her short films and documentaries were shown at international festivals and have won awards. She has exhibited her photography in Istanbul. *Şimdiki Zaman / Present Tense* (2012), her first feature, focuses on a young unemployed woman who applies for a fortune-telling job in a café, pretending she has the experience. Connecting with different women through the sessions, she tries to face her problems as a divorcée, estranged from her family, soon to be homeless. The film has received national and international acclaim.

Sözen, Kadir (b. Gaziantep, 1964) Director, screenwriter, producer. Settling in Germany at an early age with his family, Kadir Sözen graduated in economics in Cologne. He established Hasret Film in 1991. Documentaries he made for German television companies brought him awards. His first feature, *Soğuk Geceler / Kalte Nächte / Cold Nights* (1995), a German production, was about street children busking from town to town with an old alcoholic named Mahmud, who exploited them. *Winterblume / Kış Çiçekleri / Winter Flowers* (1996), a notable example of 'accented cinema' (Naficy, 2001), reminiscent of **Tunç Okan**'s *Otobüs / The Bus* (1974), was about the drastic measures employed by an illegal immigrant expelled from Germany to re-join his family (he played the father). He was the producer and screenwriter of *Takiye: Allah Yolunda / Takiye: On the Way to God* (Ben Verbong, 2010) about the Islamist holdings in Europe with actual victims taking part as actors. His films have received several awards.

Suçlular Aramızda / Criminals Among Us (1964), a film with a social message, foregrounds the malaise of quick-riches schemes in a society that creates degenerate characters that determine the fate of the disadvantaged. It begins with the well-choreographed silhouettes of two men in the dark, reminiscent of the traditional theatre, shadow play, accompanied by jazz music; two desperate characters are to steal a priceless necklace from the mansion of a prominent businessman. Cut to a banquet where Halis Bey (Atıf Kaptan), a shrewd Anatolian (supporting the Laz accent of the Black Sea) who has become rich through illegal use of subventions to developing countries, boasts about his achievements while the equally distasteful guests gossip about the dubious source of his wealth. When the necklace he gave to his daughter-in-law, Demet (**Belgin Doruk**), as a wedding present is stolen, he gives a *coup d'oeil* to the spectator of his fault-proof cunning. The emeralds are false. His son Mümtaz (**Ekrem Bora**), a rival to his father in dishonesty, agrees to pay the thieves to avoid scandal but the father is worried about being considered a fool. The necklace changes hands several times and appears in unexpected places while one murder and several attempts at other murders carry the narrative with twists and turns until the bad man receives his punishment (in his own hands) and the good are united.

Similar to other **Yeşilçam** films, the binaries of rich and poor are established through dwellings – the rich in a *yalı* on the Bosphorus, the poor in the slums. What distinguishes **Erksan**'s work is the attention to detail, which creates memorable images such as the corpse of the main thief Yusuf carried to the cemetery on a one-horse carriage, or the visit of Demet to the slums wearing a fancy hat and looking like a caricature. Dialogues are meticulously scripted to reflect class differences and social climbing. Halis Bey, criticized by his son for his gauche mannerism, comments: 'You're noble. The sons of the likes of me are always noble.' The son is in the habit of defeating his opponents in a word game each time he is confronted with his wrong doings, which renders the culturally less advantaged helpless. The economic power of the rich protects them from the state, police, law and justice. Their life-styles reflect their degenerate characters. Halil (Tamer Yiğit), Yusuf's unfortunate partner in crime, gives his last liras to Yusuf's widow, whereas the association for aiding the poor where Demet and other bourgeois women collect funds resembles a social club.

The audience is prepared for the emotional attachment that develops between Halil and Demet slowly, according to their rhythm and through the subtle images of the famous cinematographer of the period, Mengü Yeğin, such as showing the two shadows appearing together on the water. Demet walking along the sea and Halil sitting on a rock with his hand covering his face suggests a non-diegetic conversation has taken place and he has told her the truth about her husband. When the husband and wife face each other in the woods, discussing divorce, the circular movement of the camera (a recurring motif of **Erksan**'s films) in such a tight space exudes the tension felt by the characters, but also gives the impression that the scene is choreographed for theatre.

One of **Erksan**'s signature motifs is the surreal element, which appears in several instances such as a half-naked black man in the house of the mistress, catching the rhythm of the music. In the boardroom, Mümtaz reveals a skull under the globe and asks his secretary to climb on the table and stand with her legs open under the globe, and then he begins to kiss her legs. The masked ball for charity where the guests are expected to wear whale's costume and the skilfully choreographed fight scenes are memorable. The music is mostly jazz, with an occasional Adamo thrown in (a popular song in Turkey at the time). Before Mümtaz throws himself over board, he tells the guests (and the audience) that he is a product of his society. The evil is punished and the good triumph: Demet and Halil are holding hands in the motorboat, but between two policemen. Justice must prevail.

Director, Screenwriter: **Metin Erksan**; Producers: Özdemir Birsel, Nüzhet Birsel, Saltuk Kaplangı; Production: Birsel Film; Cinematography: Mengu Yeğin; Music: Fecri Ebcioğlu; Cast: **Belgin Doruk**, **Ekrem Bora**, Tamer Yiğit, **Leyla Sayar**, **Erol Taş**, Atıf Kaptan, Hakkı Haktan

Sunal, (Ali) Kemal (b. Istanbul, 1944 – d. Istanbul, 2000) Actor, screenwriter, producer. One of the most popular **comedy** actors of Turkish cinema, who starred in numerous commercials, Kemal Sunal began as a stage actor, moving on to screen with *Hababam Sınıfı / The Rascal Class* aka *The Chaos Class* aka *Outrageous Class* (1975). He was often typecast as a poor, honest, somewhat naive, not particularly attractive but kind-hearted man, who 'got the girl' at the end. Light-hearted on the surface, his films focused on social and political issues such as housing shortages for the less advantaged or corruption. Sunal completed his studies that were interrupted during the 1980 *coup d'état*, graduating from the Communications Faculty of Marmara University, writing a thesis on the reception of the Kemal Sunal Comedies of the 1970s–80s, interrogating the ideological oppression of the state on art, which was later published as a book. His films have been shown regularly on television since the 1990s.

Susuz Yaz / A Dry Summer (1963), which foregrounds the problem of a woman without male protection in the rural milieu through a man's obsession to possess water that passes through his land, opened the path of Turkish cinema to the world, receiving the Golden Bear at the Berlin Film Festival in 1964. With *A Dry Summer*, **Erksan** continues the theme of obsessive ownership that he had explored in *Yılanların Öcü / Revenge of the Serpents* (1962), focusing on the ownership of water. In the first part of the film, the peasant Osman (**Erol Taş**) refuses to share the water with his neighbours because the source is on his property. When they kill his dog, he retaliates by killing one of them. His newlywed younger brother Hasan (Ulvi Doğan) assumes the crime and is imprisoned for eight years.

Figure 106 Susuz Yaz / A Dry Summer (Metin Erksan, 1963) (Courtesy of International Istanbul Film Festival)

In the second part, living under the same roof with his brother's young wife Bahar (**Hülya Koçyiğit**), arouses Osman's voyeuristic fantasies. He is seen caressing the legs of a cow and sucking its udders in front of her and making love to his pillow. Inventing a story about Hasan's death, he convinces lonely Bahar to live with him. When Hasan is released with the amnesty, he cleanses his honour by killing his brother in a graphically violent scene, releases the water and reclaims his wife, but now another jail sentence awaits him and Bahar will be unprotected again.

The film is a strict adaptation of a short story by the acclaimed author Necati Cumalı, who was considered populist by some critics of the time, his point of view lacking social consciousness for the plight of the oppressed, focusing only on men–women relationships. Spatio-temporal reality is vague in the film; a roadside indicates proximity to İzmir on the Aegean. The amnesty that frees Hasan takes place in 1951 in Cumalı's story, following the 1950 victory of the populist Democrat Party (ousted by the military in 1960). Questioning the validity of calling the film **social realist**, these critics commented that **Erksan**'s was actually 'bourgeois realism' showing the conflict among small landowners but avoiding more crucial issues, such as the advent of capitalism, the landlord/landless peasant conflicts and the plight of agricultural workers. The water problem was solved indirectly through the honour killing. **Erksan**'s approach to the village society was from a metaphysical perspective with a focus on the conflict between the good and the bad, a typical **Yeşilçam** cliché. The sadomasochistic Osman, looking appalling, deprives the villagers of the water, kills for greed and lusts after his sister-in-law, whereas his good-looking brother assumes a murder he does not commit, forgives his unfaithful wife and releases the water. The audience is relieved when he finally kills Osman after a long graphic scuffle in the water (Coş 1975).

Director: **Metin Erksan**; Producer: Metin **Erksan**, Ulvi Doğan; Production: Hitit Film; Screenwriter: **Metin Erksan**, Kemal İnci, İsmet Soydan based on a story by Necati Cumali; Cinematographer: Ali Uğur; Editor and Sound Engineer: Turgut İnangiray; Music: Manos Hatzidakis, Ahmet Yamacı; Cast: **Erol Taş**, **Hülya Koçyiğit**, Ulvi Doğan, Ercan Yazgan, Hakkı Haktan

Sürer, Nur (b. Bursa, 1954) Actor, activist; RN: Şennur Sürer. Known for her performances in engagé films, particularly for her role as a political prisoner in **Tunç Başaran**'s *Uçurtmayı Vurmasınlar / Don't Let Them Shoot the Kite* (1989), Nur Sürer has played in over 40 films and television series. Some of her significant performances are in **Erden Kıral**'s *Bereketli Topraklar Üzerinde / On Fertile Lands* (1979); *Ayna / Der Spiegel / The Mirror* (1984); *Reise der Hoffnung / Journey of Hope* (Xavier Koller, 1990), winner of Best Foreign Film at the Oscars; *Derman / Remedy* (1984); *Yılanların Öcü / Revenge of the Serpents* (**Şerif Gören**, 1985) and *Yara / Seelenschmerz / The Wound* (**Yılmaz Arslan**, 1998). She twice received the Best Actress award of the Antalya Golden Orange Film Festival: in 1989 with *The Kite* and in 2002 with *Sır Çocukları* (Ümit Cin Güven, Aydın Sayman).

Sürü / The Herd (1978) is a realistic portrayal of Turkey in transition to capitalism. The film problematizes the disintegration of a nomadic Kurdish tribe and its patriarchal structure with the changes in the economic structure of the country. Berivan (Melike Demirağ), from the Halilan tribe, is given in marriage to Şivan (**Tarık Akan**), the eldest son of Hamo (**Tuncel Kurtiz**), the patriarch of the Veysikan tribe, to end the blood feud. The couple love each other but Hamo blames Berivan for draining their heritage with her miscarriages. He reprimands Şivan for surrendering to a woman. After the loss of her third child, Berivan becomes mute. Şivan's hopes of a better life in the city and a cure for Berivan's illness collapse when the sheep they are to sell in Ankara perish on the train journey, inhaling the fumes of DDT sprayed on the wagons earlier. The asphyxiation of the sheep metaphorizes the suffocation that engulfs the country.

The film is spatially divided into three parts, all of which foreground the uncanny nature of temporality and liminality: the encampment; the train to the capital Ankara and the capital itself. In the encampment, a temporary shelter, the tribe continue their traditional life-style in the open air; women and children attend daily chores, while the patriarch Hamo watches. Nomadic life is documented almost ethnographically. Scenes of women preparing the men for a long journey possess ritualistic qualities. The camera moves from one silent face to another, the eyes reflecting the pain of homelessness.

The tranquillity of the atmosphere has an eerie quality. Conflict is confined to claustrophobic indoor spaces, inside the tents or close to them, where the weaker are abused and humiliated. Hamo beats Şivan for protecting his wife, Şivan beats Berivan to mend his pride; one woman is almost choked for mentioning Berivan's sickness; another is brutalized for making sexual advances to her husband.

Figure 107 Sürü / The Herd (Zeki Ökten, 1978) (Courtesy of International Istanbul Film Festival)

Berivan's image sitting beside Hamo in the packed train compartment transmits her wish for invisibility. The arid landscape and the faces of the people at the stations reflect the oppression and suffering. A handcuffed bard holding a *saz* (traditional string instrument) accompanied by two gendarmes sings a ballad from the War of Independence, 'The bandit cannot rule the world'. Asked what his crime was, he responds 'To sing songs'. (The song is sung by **Zülfü Livaneli**, who also suffered under the military dictatorships.) As the train moves, we see graffiti on the walls outside: 'Down with the Landowners!'

During the long march through the wide boulevards of the capital, the camera pans from the desperate tribe to the conspicuous Turkish flags, the statues of Atatürk, the giant **Yeşilçam** posters, Atatürk's modern mausoleum, the high-rises, the slums and the pedestrians in modern clothes staring in amazement at the men in black *shalvar* trying to move the flock through the dense traffic, with Şivan carrying Berivan on his back. When the two Turkeys come face to face, there is confusion and chaos. Şivan remembers a song he had learned in the army: 'Ankara, Ankara, the beautiful Ankara, everyone with bad luck wants to see you', unaware that Ankara, the capital, the metonym for the state, has no solution to his problems. Just then, someone carrying a pack of bulletins is shot with a bullet from a speeding car, an allusion to the murders of leftist intellectuals.

A countryman shelters Şivan and Berivan inside a construction site, in an unfinished room open to the elements, a false shelter, like the capital. The young son has already acquired political consciousness, but the man believes that the rich in the city are not like the landlords back home, 'You give your bribe and get the job done. It is easier here.' The son reminds him that he has no money for a home, for the doctor or for the education of his son, while millions of liras are owned by three or four persons. 'Where does it go, the work of the millions? The rich of here is the same as the landowners over there.' The father proposes to go to the music hall to listen to **arabesque** music, the 'opium of the masses' according to **Güney**.

Berivan dies inside the construction site, a space that promises future comfort and security. The landscape of Ankara, with its sacred and secular elements, is indifferent to Şivan's misery; he is arrested for attacking a callous man who thinks the death of a woman is extraneous. Berivan's corpse is dragged from the construction site by her countryman bewildered by the thought of losing his job – a powerful exposé of the alienation and degeneration of a simple rural man in the urban environment. Abandoned by his young son, Hamo is lost in the crowd. Turkish flags, statues of Ataturk, bank signs, Pepsi cola signs, cars, the signs of development and modernity pass in front of his (and our) eyes as hundreds of idle people, obviously without a job, flow with the traffic. Capitalism has arrived, but with a price tag.

The political message of the film is merged with social criticism. The backwardness and ignorance of one social or ethnic stratum reverberates through the rest of society. The youngest son sells the ancient tablets he discovers in a cave to an itinerant vendor without recognizing their value as cultural heritage and the vendor sells them to traffickers in antiques (alluding to the pilfering of the national treasures when Turkey did not claim its heritage). He gives the money to a lame prostitute for pathetic sex on the train among the sheep (the social malaise of the sex trade). The legs of several sheep break because the driver pulls the brakes abruptly to teach the tribe a lesson for not bribing him properly (corruption).

Women as metaphor for the oppressed, a common trope globally, is crucial to **Güney**'s cinema. Placed in liminal spaces, women are at a double advantage to men, although feudal oppression destroys men and women alike. When the loss of identity is not a conscious one (as in the case of ethnic minorities in Turkey) its power is more destructive. People affected by deep melancholia lose their voice; they are no longer able to speak for themselves as their main argument is against themselves. Berivan's silence is a metonym for oppressed people without a voice, the poor, the women, but particularly the Kurds, silenced, physically and metaphorically, not able to speak their own language, although this message is very subtle in the film to circumvent state censorship (Dönmez-Colin 2008: 133).

Scripted by **Yılmaz Güney** while in prison and directed by **Zeki Ökten**, the tragic story of the disintegration of a tribal family (and their customs and traditions) received international acclaim, garnering several awards, including the Golden Leopard at the Locarno Film Festival. In 1981, the Antalya Golden Orange Film festival administration refused to accept the film for competition because the Turkish citizenship of Melike Demirağ was revoked for her role as the wife of Şivan, played by **Tarık Akan**, already blacklisted. In 2011, Golden Orange rectified the situation by honouring the film with several awards.

Director: **Zeki Ökten**; Producer, Screenwriter: **Yılmaz Güney**; Production: Güney Film; Cinematographer: İzzet Akay; Editor: Özdemir Arıtan; Art Director: Rauf Ozangil, Sabri Aslankara; Music: **Zülfü Livaneli**; Cast: **Tarık Akan**, Melike Demirağ, **Tuncel Kurtiz**, Şenel Gökkaya, Meral Niron, Erol Demiröz, **Yaman Okay**

Süt / Milk (2008), the second film of the *Yusuf Trilogy* that begins with *Yumurta / Egg* (2007) and ends with *Bal / Honey* (2010), problematizes Turkey's transition to modernity through the routine life of an adolescent in a provincial town. Seventeen-year-old Yusuf, who lives alone with his mother, is seriously occupied with poetry. His role models that decorate the walls of his bedroom are the Western poets who have suffered the pains of modernism: Baudelaire from the countryside, who began to write poetry at a young age and felt the agony of change and Rimbaud who had problems with his mother.

Although the film maintains ties with the present and avoids settling on its presumed date, the 1980s, selective details evoke the epoch, such as the door-to-door delivery of milk slowly becoming archaic. Patriarchal praxis continues despite the development of modern cities even in remote corners. The collision between the traditional Muslim mores and the demands of the young, and especially the women are felt intensely in the family. Yusuf's mother discovers her femininity as the boy matures. Observed from the man's point of view (son's), this becomes an issue.

As an epileptic (sickness as a trope for the sensitive nature of Yusuf, his artistic nature, his otherness) young man, unable to pass the entry exams to university, refused by the army when other boys are leaving with send-off ceremonies,

Figure 108 Süt / Milk (Semih Kaplanoğlu, 2008) (Courtesy of Semih Kaplanoğlu)

Figure 109 Süt / Milk (Semih Kaplanoğlu, 2008) (Courtesy of Semih Kaplanoğlu)

rituals, gunfire and rowdiness, Yusuf's transition to manhood in a masochistic society is already problematic. The affair of his mother – considered untouchable and sacred – with the train station chief in the countryside where honour killings are common, tests his conscience. He follows the man hunting. Perhaps he will grab a stone and kill him, but with a twist of fate, a carp appears and distracts him.

The motive of the snake, considered ominous in the culture, is introduced early in the film as a contrast to milk that conjures purity and chasteness. In the opening scene, a woman hangs upside down while the villagers try to entice the snake out of her body with boiled milk. When Yusuf discovers her mother's affair, the black shadow of the serpent falls on her bed (a shadow on their house or his mother's honour, a contamination, or a manifestation of Yusuf's own repressed feelings and desires, although **Kaplanoğlu** denies such connotations), he does not show the 'manhood' to kill it, despite his mother's terror of snakes. He is hurt and angry.

In the final episode, the lights on the foreheads of the miners are turned on the spectators for six minutes, evoking the oeuvre of Tsai Ming Liang, an important influence on **Kaplanoğlu**. While shooting the mine scene, **Kaplanoğlu** decided to end the film with a round object similar to the cup in which the milk was boiled in the first episode – 'a white image, as if it were our own light. The second reason was to say we are not in darkness. (Hence, the prologue and the epilogue are outside the narrative.) During this period, people may reflect on the film. For this kind of cinema, it means making the audience revive the film before sending them away abruptly, and this could be a good thing' (Dönmez-Colin 2012: 153).

Director: **Semih Kaplanoğlu**; Producers: **Semih Kaplanoğlu**, Guillaume de Seille, Bettina Borekmper, Johannes Rexin; Production: Kaplan Film, Arizona Film, Heimat Film; Screenwriters: **Semih Kaplanoğlu**, Orçin Köksal; Cinematographer: Özgür Eken; Editor: François Quiquere; Cast: Melih Selçuk, Başak Köklükaya, Şerif Erol, Rıza Akın, Saadet Işıl Aksoy

Ş

Şahin, Nuray (b. Tunceli, 1974) Director, screenwriter, actor. A film-maker of Kurdish origin, Nuray Şahin studied at the DFFB (Deutsche Film-und-Fernsehakademie Berlin) and made three shorts and two documentaries before her feature film *Folge der Feder / Tüyü Takip Et!* aka *Helin'in Hayalleri / Follow the Feather* (2004), the story of a young woman from a small town with an Alevi population who are tied to their beliefs in nature, music, dances of trance and dreams. Promising her father on his death-bed to find her mother and sister in Germany, she embarks on a long journey following a white feather which leads her to them and eventually to the man of her dreams. Shot in German with songs in Zazaki, spoken in the area, the film won the Audience Award at the Mannheim–Heidelberg Film Festival, 2004.

Şahin, Osman (b. Mersin, 1940) Screenwriter, author. The screenwriter for over 20 noteworthy films, Osman Şahin started as a physical education teacher in high-schools, was forced into retirement by the 1980 junta, sent into exile and later imprisoned for 18 months for a novel review he had written. He is the recipient of several prestigious awards, among which are the Sait Faik Abasıyanık (1994), Ömer Seyfettin (1992) and Yunus Nadi (1998 and 2003) prizes, given in the name of three distinguished writers. Some of his well-known scripts are for *İpekçe / Silky* (**Bilge Olgaç**, 1987), *Kan / Blood* (1985) and *Kurbağalar / The Frogs* (1985) by **Şerif Gören**.

Şamdereli, Yasemin (b. Dortmund, Germany, 1973) A third-generation immigrant from Turkey, Yasemin Şamdereli's first film *Almanya – willkommen in Deutschland / Almanya – Welcome to Germany* is a **comedy** based on her grandparent's experiences as 'guest-workers' in Germany. A quote from Max Frish that sets the tone of the film also summarizes the guest-worker phenomenon: 'We called for workers; people came.' In the 1960s when Turkey was a closed society, the peasants, examined by German doctors like cattle in a market (reminiscent of a scene in **Güney**'s *Baba / The Father*, 1971), head for Germany, their utopia and dystopia, where men will take longer than women to adapt. The mis(conceptions) of the two cultures about each other, rendered with humour, are very precise in the film, but after the death of the grandfather (as a trope for the wish to return), the film becomes melodramatic, schematic, predictable and moralistic. It also reinforces the assimilation policy of the German State. The characters are the kind of Turks the Germans would like: well integrated, not religious and without any problems with the Germans.

Şan, Cemal (b. Tunceli, 1966) Director, screenwriter, producer, actor, cartoonist. One of the founders of Yeni Sinemacılar (New Film-makers), Cemal Şan worked as assistant director to **Tunç Başaran** (*Uçurtmayı Vurmasınlar / Don't Let Them Shoot the Kite*, 1989). He was the screenwriter and assistant in *Dönersen Islık Çal / Whistle If You Return* (**Orhan Oğuz**) and *Işıklar Sönmesin / Let There be Light* (**Reis Çelik**). His first film, *Ali* (1996), was about a young man who finds salvation in refusing to talk and walk because he cannot tolerate the chaos and the physical and psychological annihilations around him. He made a love trilogy comprised of *Zeyneb'in Sekiz Günü / Eight Days of Zeynep* (2007), about the heart, *Dilber'in Sekiz Günü / Eight Days of Dilber* (2008), about the soul, and *Ali'nin Sekiz Günü / Eight Days of Ali* (2008), about the mind. *Dilber* was successful in breaking the clichés of **village films** with a strong peasant girl who does not become a fallen woman when her lover deserts her but grabs an axe and arrives at the door of the father of the boy asking why she was not chosen as a suitable bride. Instead of letting herself be locked in a barn as an 'honour killing' victim, she declares in front of the villagers that she will marry the first man who comes along the dirt road, who happens to be the lame janitor of the school. *Acı / Pain* (2009), remarkably shot in a mountain village, was publicized as a political film although it lacked serious political context.

Şekeroğlu, Sami (b. Elazığ, 1937) Archivist, academician. Founding Klüp Sinema 7 (Club Cinema 7) in 1962 and organizing several film activities when he was still a student at the State Academy of Fine Arts, Sami Şekeroğlu convinced noteworthy film-makers – **Metin Erksan, Halit Refiğ, Memduh Ün, Atıf Yılmaz** – to donate their films to found the Turkish Film Archive (1967). It became the State Fine Arts Film Archive within two years, a member of FIAF (Federation of International Film Achieves) in 1967 and an authorized and permanent member in 1973. In 1970, Şekeroğlu became the director and in 1974, he started the first cinema education in Turkey based on research he conducted in New York, Chicago and Hollywood. It became the Cinema and Television Institute by 1975. He has worked in several positions from lecturing, research to administrative duties. In 1985, he made an experimental film, *Toprak Adamları / The People of the Land* (unofficial English title), which received the Cinema Award of the Ministry of Culture.

Şen, Şener (b. Adana, 1941) Actor; RN: Ali Haydar Şen. The son of the popular actor Ali Şen (1918–89), Şener Şen started on stage in 1958. His breakthrough in cinema came with the popular *Hababam Sınıfı / The Rascal Class* aka *The Chaos Class* aka *Outrageous Class* films of the 1970s as Body Ekrem, a physical education teacher, becoming a memorable duo with **Kemal Sunal**. He acted in numerous films with **Sunal** and **İlyas Salman**, typecast as a wheeler-dealer swindler peasant, until he broke the mould playing the lead in *Namuslu / The Honest* (**Ertem Eğilmez**, 1984), a satire on the value of money in society, which broke records and gave Şen a new personality, an honest and naive man in an imbalanced world experiencing the pains of transition from tradition to modernity. *Züğürt Ağa / The Broke Landlord* (**Nesli Çölgeçen**, 1985); *Arabesk / Arabesque* (**Ertem Eğilmez**, 1988) and *Çıplak Vatandaş / The Naked Citizen* (1985) and *Zengin Mutfağı / Kitchen of the Rich* (1988) of **Başar Sabuncu** distinguished him as a popular **comedy** actor. The fetish actor of **Yavuz Turgul**, he performed an anachronic bandit in *Eşkıya / The Bandit* (1996), drawing more than two and a half million spectators to the cinemas. The speciality of his acting craft is the manner in which he employs the heritage of Turkish performance arts – improvisation, shadow play, *meddah* (storyteller) – rather than adapting Western principals of acting.

Şoray, Türkan (b. Istanbul, 1945) Actor, director, screenwriter. The legendary star of Turkish cinema, Türkan Şoray started her acting career in 1960 at a very young age, captivating the new urban audience – the migrant workers from Anatolia – with her big brown eyes, wet lips and round figure and 'oppressed sexual woman' image. Unlike the blonde **Cahide Sonku** of earlier years whose European appearance and mysterious sensuality appealed to the urban educated middle class, Şoray was claimed as the typical Turkish woman and crowned as the *sultana* (a term once used to refer to the wives of Ottoman sultans) of

Figure 110 Türkan Şoray in *Vesikalı Yarim / My Licensed Love* (Lütfi Ö. Akad, 1968) (Courtesy of International Istanbul Film Festival)

Turkish cinema. Initially, she accepted the roles stars would reject – kissing or showing bare legs, but once her popularity was established, she created the myth of the icon beyond reach, establishing the famous Türkan Şoray rules. She could remain a virgin even when she worked as a prostitute and she always remained faithful to her first love. The audience found the 'apotheosis, our elevation from mundane to the celestial' (Marsden, Nachbar and Groff Jr 1982: 65). Şoray was ideal for 'fetishistic scopophilia' (Mulvey 1975). Close-ups of her face, her wet lips and dreamy eyes were accentuated to arouse the males on the screen but also the spectator. Furthermore, she was the 'deal girl' according to theorist Seçil Büker; she left men in peace and they loved her forever – although in some rare instances, they did leave her. 'When her husband's life is threatened, she shoots the would-be killers and goes to jail, but while she is there, he remarries. At first she thinks of shooting him, but then relents – she knows how to forgive, and will not kill for revenge. So alongside the other images we have that of the forgiving, magnanimous soul' (Büker 2002: 164). Women identified with Şoray until the 1980s opening to free-market economy, the entry of women into the workforce and the belated arrival of feminism, all of which made the weeping willows and false moralities obsolete, and a new star was born, **Müjde Ar**, a tangible woman of the times. Şoray had to change. *Mine* (**Yılmaz**, 1982) in which she played the titular hero, an adulteress, was a small revolution.

In the hands of expert directors, Şoray gave memorable roles. *Vesikalı Yarim / My Licensed Love* (**Lütfi Ö. Akad**, 1968) and *Selvi Boylum, Al Yazmalım / The Girl with the Red Scarf* (**Atıf Yılmaz**, 1977) are classics. She is one of the rare actors capable of parodying her own screen image in *Hayallerim, Aşkım ve Sen / My Dreams, My Love and You* (**Yılmaz**, 1987). *Otobüs Yolcuları / The Bus Passengers* (**Göreç**, 1961), *Acı Hayat / Bitter Life* (**Erksan**, 1962) and *Hazal* (**Ali Özgentürk**, 1979) are some of the films with her unforgettable performances.

Şoray directed four films between 1972–81, starring in the lead. Her first film *Dönüş / Return* (1972), scripted by **Sefa Önal** as were her next two films, from a story by Şoray, focuses on a peasant woman deserted by her 'guest worker' husband in Germany, who defends herself against the advances and aggressions of the *agha* and other sex-starved village men who retaliate by stoning her house. When her husband and his German lover die in a car accident, she adopts their child. The film focalizes women's predicaments in patriarchal societies and the alienation of the 'guest workers' although the second aspect was rather undermined by pressure from the producers who insisted on highlighting Şoray's role for the box-office. **Şerif Gören** was her assistant and editor in the film, which created a sceptical attitude to the actual authorship, in male-dominated **Yeşilçam** that refused to support a star becoming a film-maker. The film won awards internationally and did well on the diaspora market in Germany. Her second film, *Azap / Pain* (1973), the least successful of the four, was an ordinary **melodrama**. In *Bodrum Hakimi / The Judge of Bodrum* (1976), Şoray played a conscientious career woman in conflict with the most powerful and influential man of the area. According to film critic Dorsay, the film uses with mastery one of the most effective themes of cinema, impossible love. The *mise en scène*, the clever use of the locale and locals, the subtle juxtaposition of the town bureaucrats and the flighty tourists, the seamless editing, the effective cinematography, the background music and the acting, particularly Şoray's powerful rendition of the judge, bring a certain realism to a story that carries the classical elements of *photo-roman* literature. However, this is a film of 'missed opportunities'. The depiction of the local *agha* as a philanthropist is already a more realistic rendition than the 'cruel master' cliché of **Yeşilçam**. The 50 plus *agha* from the East sent into exile after the 1960 *coup d'état* were welcomed with open arms on their return. The issue of the lake ownership recalls a political scandal of the period. Yet, such elements with a potential to key social statements are used as vehicles to build the love story and abandoned thereafter – a lapse that could be attributed to the dominant censorship regulations of the epoch (Dorsay 1989: 251–3). *Yılanı Öldürseler / If They Could Kill the Snake* (1981), based on a story by Yaşar Kemal (scripted by Şoray, Kemal and **Işıl Özgentürk**), drew attention with the successful use of non-diegetic sound to create the atmosphere of a legend, flashbacks, fade-outs and super-imposition of voices.

Performing in more than 200 films, since the 1990s, **Şoray** has been spending more time participating in television series and presenting her programme *Sinema Benim Aşkım / Cinema is My Love*. She was chosen as good-will ambassador to UNESCO in 2010. She collected her memoirs in *Sinemam ve Ben / My Cinema and Me* (2012).

T

Tabutta Rövaşata / Somersault in a Coffin (1997) is a landmark for the emergence of **New Turkish Cinema**. **Derviş Zaim** shot his debut feature in 24 days, although the project had existed for eight years. The budget was negligible; the actors, except two, were non-professionals. However, the film won several national and international awards and did well at the box-office. Its originality lies in the way it alternates neo-realism, science fiction and **fantasy**. The story, the dialogues, the decor and the acting are very simple. The narrative is compact. The actors are credible. The understated *Sufi* overtones of the background music build the mood effectively. Its minimalist approach is an important departure from the hyperbolic **Yeşilçam** tradition.

Trying to do a 'no budget' film was worse than trying to do a somersault in a coffin, according to **Derviş Zaim**, who thought of the underground project while studying in London. He wanted to tell the story of a homeless vagrant he once knew, a thief who washed the cars he stole before returning them. Distinguished theatre performer Ahmet Uğurlu volunteered for the lead; **Tuncel Kurtiz** of international fame accepted the supporting role and the fishermen's haunts along the Bosphorus served as decor for Turkey's first *guerrilla* style film, representing 'the aesthetics of lack' (Durgun 1996: 12).

Mahsun (Ahmet Uğurlu) (his name ironically meaning strong and firm in Ottoman Turkish) wavers between stealing cars (a false shelter) and the police station (an uncanny shelter); both are claustrophobic spaces. Watching a television crew shooting a film in front of the Rumelihisarı fortress, built by Sultan Mehmet II during the siege of Constantinople, he learns that before the siege, the Sultan brought peacocks, considered a symbol of prosperity and abundance by the Ottomans, from Iran to the fortress, but they disappeared after his death. President Süleyman Demirel, having received 50 peacocks as a gift from the Iranian president, has decided to donate these to the fortress as part of a new policy to revamp historical landmarks. However, the new facelift of the city in the global race for tourism does not include displaced souls like him. Rejected at the gate of the fortress, he jumps over the fence in the dark to reach the peacock that for him represents unattainable love and beauty. In his exclusion, the peacock is his only connection to the world. He confides in the bird, telling him all his troubles and when he is hungry, he decides to eat it.

Mahsun's 'transgression' is watched on television in the teahouse (heard but not seen by the viewer). In a high-angle shot emphasizing their vulnerability, the characters gaze at us in amazement. The announcer repeats the declaration of Mahsun at the police station, 'I am unemployed, I am hungry, if they did not catch me, I would have eaten the peacock.' Then she adds, 'If you want to know the details of the story, stay with us. We'll be back after the commercials' (Suner 2006: 245). Television has penetrated into the lives of the ordinary citizens, particularly in the 1990s with the spread of private channels, making private public and widening the distance between human dramas and human feelings, sensationalizing trauma by what Kaplan calls 'empty empathy' (Kaplan 2005: 22), the nonchalant and monotonous repetition of crimes and terror, global, national or individual.

Istanbul, the minarets, the bridges, the hilltops and especially the shores of the Bosphorus are an integral part of Turkish cinema, the Bosphorus as the dream venue for countless films. **Zaim** shows the Bosphorus that the cruise boats do not see. In a decrepit cafe, a heroin addict who prostitutes to support her habit, a couple of desperate fishermen and the wretched Mahsun who owes for 600 glasses of tea are the only regulars; the 'rags to riches' policy of President Turgut Özal (1989–93) has widened the gap between the poor and the rich. Shots of the suspension bridge that crosses the two continents, the symbol of modernity for many Turks, are juxtaposed with the images of destitute men surviving on a piece of bread. For those who do not belong, the cold and cruel Bosphorus, on the shores of which a man can freeze to death (fisherman Sarı), is a bitter reminder of their exclusion.

The original title of the film uses a soccer term, *rövaşat*, meaning bicycle kick, which is replaced by 'somersault' in the English title. Both are unlikely to be performed in tight spaces. The film is about pushing borders. Mahsun and the others around him try to build equilibrium in their lives – a home, a shelter, someone to love – under impossible conditions, but also reject this equilibrium, which makes them dramatic characters. *Tabutta Rövaşata* displays remarkable maturity for a debut film. Surrealistic episodes, such as the fishing boat crushing against the Tower of Leander in a 'fantastic' crescendo, do not undermine its humanistic and realistic qualities.

The film received several national and international awards, among which are the Audience award and Jury Special Prize at the 15th Torino International Festival of Young Cinema, 1997; 19th Montpellier Mediterranean Film Festival Critics award and Golden Antigone special mention, 1997; Thessaloniki Film Festival, Best Actor (Ahmet Uğurlu) and Silver Alexander, 1997 and 16th International Istanbul Film Festival, Fipresci (Federation of International Film Critics), Best Film and Special Jury Prize of the Jury.

Director, Screenwriter: **Derviş Zaim**; Producers: **Ezel Akay**, **Derviş Zaim**; Production: IFR; Cinematographer: Mustafa Kuşçu; Editor: **Mustafa Presheva**; Music: Baba Zula-Yansımalar, Bab-ı Esrar; Sound Designer: Ender Akay; Sound Editors: Selim Kocabaşı, Ufuk Çoban; Art Director: Aslı Kurnaz; Cast: Ahmet Uğurlu, **Tuncel Kurtiz**, Ayşen Aydemir, Şerif Erol, Fuat Onan, Ahmet Çadırcı, Mahmut Benek, Nadı Güler, Figen Evren, Barış Çelikoğlu

Tahir, Kemal (b. Istanbul, 1910 – d. Istanbul, 1973) Screenwriter, novelist. A writer known for his left politics, Kemal Tahir served 12 years of a 15-year prison sentence. However, his book, *Devlet Ana / Mother State* received a strong reaction from the left. Tahir believed that the structure of the West adapted by the Republic did not work. In the West, the church and the social classes could exist without the state but in Turkey, without the state, the society would dismantle. He also thought that Marxist ideology needed to be transformed before applying to Turkish realities. In the 1960s, he wrote screenplays for **Atıf Yılmaz** under the pseudonym of Murat Aşkın. Some of his novels adapted to screen are *Haremde Dört Kadın / Four Women in a Harem* (**Halit Refiğ**, 1965), *Karılar Koğuşu / Women's Ward* (1989) and *Yorgun Savaşçı / Tired Warrior* (1979). The last, focusing on the period between the fall of the Ottoman Empire and the birth of modern Turkey, was burned by the junta.

Takva / Takva – A Man's Fear of God (2006), a controversial film about spirituality and materialism, focuses on the Islamic orders which were banned by Kemal Atatürk but resurfaced in the last few years and questions the feasibility of *takva*, the basic concept of Islamic teaching that commands the fear of God and the avoidance of sin, in a capitalist system.

The film begins with the İsra *sur'a* verse 81 of Qur'an, 'The constant truth has arrived, the false and precarious were destroyed. The false and precarious are doomed to be destroyed sooner or later' and ends with a quotation from the *Apocalypse sur'a* of the exiled communist poet Nazım Hikmet, 'There have been many signs. The time is ripe. *Haram* has become *helal, helal haram.* We

Figure 111 Takva / Takva – A Man's Fear of God (Özer Kızıltan, 2006) (Courtesy of International Istanbul Film Festival)

are racing by ourselves, my rose. Either we will take life to the dead stars, or death will descent on our world'; two versions of the apocalypse, one from the religious and one from the communist point of view, although the latter is not further developed in the film.

Muharrem (Erkan Can), the son of an émigré Albanian family, lives alone in a wooden house left by his parents in the old section of town. His private space is organized within the parental tradition and the dictates of *takva* and his life, within the routine of home, work and sect. His insular existence of asceticism and devotion changes drastically when an entrepreneur sheik (Meray Ülgen), who trusts his utmost devotion, appoints him to look after the worldly matters of the *dergâh* (the dervish lodge) to collect rent from the tenants, which Muharrem embraces as a 'divine' mission. But this mission, which results in his leaving the traditional space, results in changes in his mode of living (moving to the *dergâh*), his status (from a disciple to a private aide to the sheik) and his exterior appearance (wearing the dervish robe during rituals and modern stylish clothes while working outside for the sheik). He begins to use all the amenities of modern living – an expensive watch, a mobile phone and a luxurious car with a driver. When he interacts with the 'other', the false security of his existence shaped by the parental home and the sect crumbles. He becomes an individual questioning the value of money when he witnesses the consumerist society and the inequalities in living standards – extravagant shopping malls and slums – which are contradictory to his religious convictions, as also are the sharing of the public space with women and the open displays of temptation – women's underwear in shop windows. Answers are not to be found in the sect, which has its rationale behind the seemingly contradictory actions (a reference to the capitalist neo-liberal policy of the ruling Islamist Justice and Development Party – AKP). Finding himself in a limbo affects his equilibrium and changes his character from a modest and subservient man to an aggressive hypocrite. In his dreams, he is disturbed by the temptations of money, women, alcohol and sex, which often follow the *zikr* (or *dhikr*, the Islamic repeating of the 99 names of Allah) rituals to accentuate the contradictions that torment him. Unable to adapt to his new circumstances, he becomes catatonic, imprisoned in his own body. At his sick bed, we see the daughter of the sheik, the fetish of his wet dreams, with henna on her palms, a sign of recent marriage. Perhaps she is married to Muharrem as the sheik suggested once, although this offer was rejected by Muharrem.

Sexuality and religion are not topics easily discussed in Turkish society and cinema; in that sense, the film is a daring attempt in approaching taboo subjects. However, while criticizing capitalist Islam and presenting false religion as opportunistic, the film fails to interrogate religion itself and its relation to politics and economy, particularly in the atmosphere of modern Turkish society in the new millennium.

Takva received numerous national and international awards, among which are the Swarovski Cultural Award, Toronto 2006 and eight awards at the Antalya Golden Orange Film Festival 2006, including Best Actor (Erkan Can).

Director: **Özer Kızıltan**; Producer: Sevil Demirci, Önder Çakar, **Fatih Akın**, Klaus Maeck, Andreas Thiel; Production: Yeni Sinemacılar, Córazon International; Screenwriter: Önder Çakar: Cinematographer: Soykut Turan; Editor: Andrew Bird; Music: Gökçe Akçelik; Cast: Erkan Can, Güven Kıraç, Meray Ülgen, Duygu Şen, Settar Tanrıöğen, Öznür Kula, Erman Saban, Engin Günaydın, Hakan Gürsoytrak

Taş, Erol (b. Erzurum, 1926 – d. Istanbul, 1998) Actor. Memorable for his remarkable performances in *Yılanların Öcü / Revenge of the Serpents* (1962) and the Golden Bear winner *Susuz Yaz / A Dry Summer* (1964) of **Metin Erksan**; *Şehirdeki Yabancı / Stranger in the City* (**Halit Refiğ**, 1962) and *Hudutların Kanunu / The Law of the Borders* (**Akad**, 1967), Erol Taş entered cinema by chance when noticed by **Akad** while he was trying the protect the film crew from the neighbourhood thugs during a shooting. He acted mostly the bad man in over 300 films.

Taşdiken, Atalay (b. Beyşehir, Konya, 1964) Director, screenwriter, producer. Graduating from the Selçuk University in Konya in teacher training in physics, Atalay Taşdiken gained experience by working in the advertising sector for several years. In 1993, he made a television feature, *Beş Numaralı Kamp / Camp Number Five*, a co-production between Turkey, Russia and Uzbekistan. *Mommo / Mommo – The Bogeyman* (2009), the story of two children orphaned by the death of their mother and abandoned by their father, is his first feature for theatrical release. Reminiscent of the post-Islamist revolution Iranian films that narrate the struggles of rural children among irresponsible adults (Majid Majidi), always with a humanist message, the film has won a number of national and international awards.

Tatil Kitabı / Summer Book (2008) focuses on a dysfunctional provincial family, mostly through the point of view of Ali, a boy of around 10, whose summer vacation determines the time-frame, with occasional shifts to the other characters. The thrust of the film is patriarchy, perpetuated over generations through conformism, resulting in characters moulded into the same uniform model, who fail to become individuals. In the opening scene, a wide-angle shot of children in uniform slowly changes into a close-up of the distraught face of Ali, the child protagonist and the closing sequence returns to Ali in uniform again among his classmates. As the camera moves away, leaving him inside that frame, the chances of him breaking the vicious circle appear rather slim.

Lemon merchant Mustafa is authoritarian with his two sons, insisting that the elder, Veysel, stay in the military school despite the young man's protests and forcing Ali to sell chewing-gum during the summer holiday, ignoring the embarrassment of a sensitive child. He is critical of his younger brother Hasan (Taner Birsel), who left home to study, terminated his studies to marry, then returned home divorced, to work at his father's shop. Mustafa's relations with his wife Güler are strained and she is suspicious of his having an affair. During a business trip, he suffers from a brain haemorrhage and eventually dies, before

Figure 112 Tatil Kitabı / Summer Book (Seyfi Teoman, 2008) (Courtesy of Bulut Film Yamaç Okur and Nadir Öperli)

which he informs Ali about money left in his pick-up truck. Hasan tries to learn the truth about the mistress and the money, following clues in the agenda of Mustafa, but if he solves the mystery the audience is not privy to it, except what he reports to Mustafa's wife: there is no mistress and no money. He is probably lying, but practically everyone is deceitful in the film, including Ali, who tells his father in a coma that he sold all the chewing-gum in the box. He is somewhat modelled after another Ali in **Nuri Bilge Ceylan**'s *Mayıs Sıkıntısı / Clouds of May* (1999) who learns cheating for survival at an early age, lying about the eggs he is supposed to carry without breaking. What is significant is the ending of the film, when Hasan sits in his deceased brother's chair and begins to act like him. While earlier he had supported Veysel's dreams of following his education in a civil university, now he advises him to go back to the military school.

Summer Book can be decoded as the story of one man through different stages of his life. It is representative of the 'return to the provincial roots' films that made their mark in the 2000s, particularly foregrounding 'masculinity in crisis'. Taking place in the Mediterranean town of Silifke, it is a return for **Seyfi Teoman**, who revives some of his childhood memories through the film. Hasan, the uncle who returns to the village, is a failure in the eyes of his brother; Veysel, who dreams of the big city, returns temporarily. To remain, to leave and to return is central to the film, although the privilege of choice seems to be confined only to the male characters. Women are conspicuously absent, apart from Güler, a typical homemaker whose sorrow is expressed in silent tears.

Carrying a minimalist atmosphere with minimal dialogue (the first word uttered is almost 7 minutes into the film) and without any music, the film draws the audience into the narrative built on moments of intersection between the characters with a magic realism that creates empathy through small details. A nervous Veysel puffs on his first cigarette with the trepidation of being caught by his father; little Ali surrenders his 'summer book' to a bully and sells the chewing-gum repeatedly to his mother, Güler while she buys it with affection; Güler pays a visit to a magician/sorcerer to prepare an amulet and attaches it under the mattress of her dying husband. The characters are in constant motion, walking or driving without going anywhere; the mood is created through the choice of locations, which are often repeated to accentuate the mundane existence of the inhabitants of small cities.

The film received numerous national and international awards including Best Turkish Film and Fipresci (Federation of International Film Critics) at the 27th Istanbul International Film Festival, 2008 and Bronze Zenith, Montreal World Film Festival, 2008.

Director, Screenwriter: **Seyfi Teoman**; Producer: Yamaç Okur, Nadir Öperli; Production: Bulut Film; Cinematographer: Arnau Valls Colomer; Editor: Çiçek Kahraman; Art Director: Nadide Argun; Cast: Taner Birsel, Tayfun Günay, Harun Özüağ, Ayten Tökün, Osman İnan, Rıza Akın, Zafer İnan

Taylan, Durul (b. 1969) Director. After studying engineering at the Istanbul Technical University, Durul Taylan directed several television series with his brother **Yağmur Taylan** before they made their first feature, *Okul / School* (2004), a horror/**comedy** film about teenagers made with teenagers, which reached

Figure 113 Vavien / Two-way Switch (Durul and Yağmur Taylan, 2009) (Courtesy of International Istanbul Film Festival)

over three million spectators. Their second feature *Küçük Kıyamet / The Little Apocalypse* (2006), a horror film, and *Vavien / Two-way Switch* (2009), a dark **comedy**, won several national awards. Their **comedy** series for television *Yabancı Damat / The Foreign Groom*, 106 episodes of the story of a mixed marriage, shot in Greece and Turkey, was very successful in the Balkan countries. They are also the directors of *Muhteşem Yüzyıl / The Magnificent Century*, a historical soap opera that has been criticized by the Islamist government of Tayyip Erdoğan for stressing the activities of Suleiman the Magnificent in the harem, rather than glorifying his feats on the battlefields. Running for several seasons, the series have been sold to several European, Middle Eastern and Central Asian countries.

Taylan, Yağmur (b. 1966) Director. A specialist in psychiatry, Yağmur Taylan joined his brother **Durul Taylan** and made a number of box-office hits (see **Durul Taylan**).

Tema, Muzaffer (b. Istanbul, 1919 – d. İzmir, 2011) Actor, producer, screenwriter. One of the most distinguished actors of **Yeşilçam**, Muzaffer Tema graduated from the Istanbul Municipal Conservatory and worked in the Ankara State Conservatory and the Presidential Philharmonic Orchestra, starting his film career with *Çığlık / Scream* (Aydın Arakon, 1949). He became very popular with *Dudaktan Kalbe / From the Lips to the Heart* (Şadan Kamil, 1951), which established him as the romantic male lead. ***Kanun Namına / In the Name of Law*** (1952) and *İngiliz Kemal Lavrens'e Karşı / English Kemal against Lawrence* (**Akad**, 1952) are particularly memorable. He spent 25 years in the US and acted in a number of foreign productions, among which are *A Certain Smile* (Jean Negulesco, 1958) and *12 to the Moon* (David Bradley, 1960). After establishing Tema Film in 1960, he produced four films and directed one. His resemblance to Alan Ladd shaped his taste for clothes and his mannerisms. He severed his ties with **Yeşilçam** during the porno furore of the 1970s.

Temelkuran, İnan (b. İzmir, 1976) Director, screenwriter, producer, editor, actor. One of the most promising representatives of the socio-politically engaged generation of film-makers that have emerged in the late 2000s, Temelkuran graduated from the Law Faculty of Ankara University before studying film in Madrid on a Spanish government scholarship, where he made an award-winning short documentary. He returned to Turkey in 2005 to work on *Made in Europe* (2007). Focusing on mundane conversations about women, manhood, brotherhood, betrayal and humiliation among three separate groups of illegal Turkish immigrants in three European cities (Madrid, Paris, Berlin), the film exposes the schizophrenic world of the uprooted in *cinéma vérité* style. Occupying European space without being considered part of it and wavering between two distinct and often contradictory identities, the destinies of these men evoke Turkey's liminal position in terms of its desire to be part of the European Union. ***Bornova, Bornova*** (2009), which garnered the top five awards at the 46th Antalya Golden Orange Film Festival, questions given and acquired identities in conflict with the demands of capitalist societies. Baring the masculinist world of men through male characters or masculinized females with his two features, Temelkuran focused on a 16-year-old provincial girl who becomes a wrestling champion in *Siirt'in Sırrı / Know My Name* (2012), a documentary he made with his wife Kristen Stevens. Unlike Özlem in **Bornova, Bornova** who survives in the world of men by becoming one of them, Evin excels in a sport appropriated by men by her perseverance without compromising her feminine nature, even when she becomes the provider for her large family, which she accomplishes with modesty and sensitivity.

Teoman, Seyfi (b. Kayseri, 1977 – d. Istanbul, 2012) Director, screenwriter, producer. An important representative of the generation of film-makers that have emerged following **Nuri Bilge Ceylan**, **Derviş Zaim** et al., and the recipient of several national and international awards, Seyfi Teoman directed one short film, *Apartman / The Apartment* (2004), on lack of communication, starring **Emin Alper**, and two features, **Tatil Kitabı / Summer Book** (2008) and **Bizim Büyük Çaresizliğimiz / Our Grand Despair** (2011), before being killed in a motorcycle accident. After studying economics at the Bosphorus University in Istanbul, he attended the prestigious Polish National Film School in Lodz. He was one of the producers of *Tepenin Ardı / Beyond the Hill* (**Emin Alper**, 2012). At the time of his death, he was working on his third feature with a working title, *Evliya / The Saint*. An award for debut Turkish films was established in his name in 2013 by the International Istanbul Film Festival, to be sponsored for five years by the popular actor/director **Cem Yılmaz**.

Tepenin Ardı / Beyond the Hill (2012), the debut film of an academician, drew attention when it returned with two prizes from the Berlin Film Festival – Best First Feature Special Mention Berlinale and Caligari Film Prize – Berlinale Forum. A family drama set in rural Anatolia, the film foregrounds three generations of men whose worlds involve guns, war and cruelty to animals (the crab and the dog) and women. Male bondage and the consequences of the lack of it in a gendered society that produces male perpetrators who are also victims (to be or not to be a man, being the crucial issue) while allocating females the role of the silent observer and the server (physically, emotionally and sexually) and 'otherness as a threat' constitute the core of the conflict.

City folks, Nusret (Reha Özcan) and his sons, war veteran Zafer (Berk Hakman) and the adolescent Caner visit Nusret's father Faik (Tamer Levent), a retired forester, obsessed with the presence of the *yörük* on the plateau – the nomadic shepherds of Anatolia seen mostly in the Taurus Mountains region. Along with Mehmet (Mehmet Özgür), his helper, and Sulu, his son, six men flex their muscles never accepting responsibility for their actions, profanity establishing the machismo from the start. The only females are Mehmet's wife Meryem, a woman of sound judgement confined to her house, and her precocious daughter; both observe from a distance. Occasionally resembling a thriller, the narrative proceeds almost like a parable. The script successfully builds a metaphor for

Figure 114 Tepenin Ardı / Beyond the Hill (Emin Alper, 2012) (Courtesy of Emin Alper)

the perennial fear of 'enemy inside, enemy outside', which Turkey exploits for its defence mechanism, refusing to face its dark history – Armenian genocide, massacre of the Kurds in Dersim, Alevis in Sıvas and the on-going civil war in the south-east – always looking for evil somewhere else. The invisible foe is the *yörük*, here as a trope for the Kurds and all the rest that are 'othered'. At the same time, in the microcosm, the family is investigated. People raised under authority are subservient to authority without question and when they are in a position of authority, they expect the same subservience.

The presence of a rifle as the key element steers the film's narrative. The war is defined through Zafer (ironically meaning victory), who suffers from

Figure 115 Tepenin Ardı / Beyond the Hill (Emin Alper, 2012) (Courtesy of Emin Alper)

hallucinations after his military service; he is the sacrifice along with the herd. The landscape reminiscent of westerns, with the rock walls of a canyon closing in and restricting movement, increases the mood of claustrophobia and reflects the dark souls of the characters who would blame the other rather than admit to crime. Key actions take place off-camera. Important issues are never discussed. Point-of-view shots allow the spectator to enter the psychology of the characters in a Chekhovian intertextuality that also references **Nuri Bilge Ceylan**'s work. The drum march at the end of the film is significant in accentuating human folly.

Director, Screenwriter: **Emin Alper**; Producers: **Emin Alper, Seyfi Teoman**, Enis Köstepen; Production: Bulut Film, Alper Film, Two Thirty Five; Cinematographer: George Chiper-Lillemark; Editor: Özcan Vardar; Art Director: İsmail Durmaz; Music: Volkan Akmehmet, İnanç Şanver; Cast: Tamer Levent, Reha Özcan, Mehmet Özgür, Berk Hakman, Furkan Berk Kıran, Banu Fotocan, Sercan Gümüş, Şevval Kuş

Terziyan, Nubar (b. Istanbul, 1909 – d. Istanbul, 1994) Actor; RN: Nubar Alyanak. Nick-named 'baba' (father), Nubar Terziyan was an important character actor of the Turkish cinema with his lovable 'uncle' image in over 400 films.

Teyzem / My Aunt (1986), a nephew's recollections of his aunt, is based on an autobiographical script by **Ümit Ünal**. During a period of military subjugation, 6-year-old Umur arrives in Istanbul with his family, for his father to hide at his maternal grandmother's house during the martial law. The house is a trope for the country, the second husband of the grandmother reigning terror. In reference to thousands who left the country during the dark years of military interventions, the characters have already escaped (Umur's mother Azade by marriage), or are dreaming about escaping. Üftade (**Müjde Ar**) is waiting for her boyfriend Erhan to rescue her and the son Niyazi, who plays in a band, is planning to go to Germany. Üftade uses Umur to meet Erhan, often leaving him alone, but innocent Umur thinks they are playing hide and seek, even when he is lost in the bazaar. Losing all hope of marrying flighty Erhan, Üftade marries her friend Şenay's (**Serra Yılmaz**) brother (**Uğur Yücel**), a man who is extremely attached to his mother, but unable to endure the abuses of her husband and his mother, returns home pregnant. When she claims to have been molested as a teenager by her stepfather, who appears to her in her nightmares metaphorically as an army officer (objected to by the censorship board), a grocer and a devout Muslim, she is sent to an asylum. Released as cured, she returns home and early one morning, throws herself in front of a passing truck, imagining the lights of the truck as the divine illumination that brings Erhan to her in her hallucinations. Everyone is relieved. Her brother, who embraced religion while in Germany and found a job as a guard at the Topkapı Palace, throws his guard hat in the garbage and runs away with his bride and the stepfather is happy to erase her from memory.

The film presents four women characters: Üftade, her mother, her sister Azade and her husband's sister. All the women are home bound. The mother is not given a voice in the film; she is aware of the sexual assaults of her husband on Üftade but keeps silent, which opens a gap between the mother and daughter that widens after

Üftade's divorce, considered a threat to the institution of marriage. Respectably married Azade is the only woman with a voice, but despite rebelling against the patriarchy by leaving home, she has confirmed the status quo by marrying. The six men, the stepfather of Üftade, a religious hypocrite; the idealist husband of Azade who compromises his family; the irresponsible Erhan; the boneless Niyazi; Üftade's impotent husband and the opportunist contractor, are all non-functional characters. Umur, representing the future, is the only one with insight who can understand Üftade.

The story is told by the nephew, Umur (**Ümit Ünal**) who returns to the family home as a young man and it is based on the notes of his aunt, which he hid when they were burning all her possessions. The child figure in the film is double-voiced; his limited view of the world is framed by adult knowingness and retrospective understanding (Lury 2010: 109).

The film is ahead of its time for exposing incest in the family and hypocrisies in society. The new city planning (or the lack of it) with the new economy, the destruction of the old houses to be replaced by monstrous apartment buildings, is carefully interwoven to the plot. Episodes of comic relief, such as the escape of Üftade from the sexual harassment attempt of the contractor thanks to the chiming clock that announces prayer time by the chanting of the *ezan*, are tongue-in-cheek humour that steer the film away from an ordinary family **melodrama**.

Director: **Halit Refiğ**; Producer: Fedai Öztürk; Production: Burç Film; Screenwriter: **Ümit Ünal**; Cinematography: Ertunç Şenkay; Art Director: Betül İncedayı; Music: Atilla Özdemiroğlu; Cast: **Müjde Ar**, Yaşar Alptekin, Mehmet Akan, Tomris Oğuzalp, Necati Bilgiç, Ayşe Demirel, **Uğur Yücel**, **Serra Yılmaz**

Tibet, Kartal (b. Ankara, 1939) Actor, director, screenwriter, producer. A graduate of Ankara State Conservatory, Kartal Tibet acted on stage for several years before starting his film career with *Karaoğlan* (Suat Yalaz, 1965) and continuing with the Tarkan adventure series while appearing in romantic roles. He started directing with *Tosun Paşa / Tosun Pasha* (1976) and made several comedies with **Kemal Sunal**. *Zübük* (1980), scripted by **Atıf Yılmaz**, brought a different dimension to the popular social-climbing comedies through a character who turns the corner by illegal and corrupt deals and becomes an outrageous politician. While criticizing the society, which creates opportunists who believe the means justify the ends, the film sent a message to viewers that to rid the society of such evil was only possible by holding a mirror to ourselves. *Şalvar Davası / The Case of Baggy Pants* (1983), starring **Müjde Ar** as the city-wise ex-villager who creates solidarity among women in rebelling against the patriarchy by withholding sex from their husbands, was a successful **comedy**. *Dünyayı Kurtaran Adam'ın Oğlu / The Son of the Man Who Saves the World* aka *Turks in Space* (2006), his last film for commercial release, was one of the most discussed films of the year. Reproved by the critics, it was viewed by 439,000 spectators. The film is a re-make of **Çetin İnanç**'s *Dünyayı Kurtaran Adam / The Man Who Saves the World* aka *Turkish Star Wars* (1982), notorious for its bootlegged scenes from *Star Wars IV: A New Hope* and the *Star Trek* series, among others. Tibet continues his career making television series.

Tiryaki, Gökhan (b. Istanbul, 1972) Cinematographer. A recipient of several Best Cinematographer awards with **Nuri Bilge Ceylan**'s films, Gökhan Tiryaki started in 1991 as a cameraman for the Turkish State Television, TRT. Since 1996, he has worked with distinguished film-makers, **Ceylan, Çağan Irmak, Reis Çelik**, the **Taylan** brothers and **Yılmaz Erdoğan**. With *Bir Zamanlar Anadolu'da / Once Upon a Time in Anatolia* (**Nuri Bilge Ceylan**) he received the Best Cinematographer award at the Durban International Film Festival, Dubai International Film Festival, ASPA (Asia Pacific Screen Award UNESCO) and the award of the **Yeşilçam Film Academy**.

Tözüm, Irfan (b. Erzurum, 1951) Director. Entering cinema during his high-school years as assistant director to **Duygu Sağıroğlu**, İrfan Tözüm spent several years as a journalist, directed commercials and *photo-romans*. He made his first film, *Çağdaş Bir Köle / A Contemporary Slave* in 1986. *Rumuz Goncagül / Codename: Blossom* (1988), *Cazibe Hanımın Gündüz Düşleri / Daylight Reveries of Mrs Cazibe* 1992), *Kız Kulesi Aşıkları / Hera Leandros* (1994) and *Mum Kokulu Kadınlar / Wax-scented Women* (1996) are some of his films that foreground passion (particularly the woman's) in a closed society.

Tuna, Feyzi (b. Balıkesir, 1939) Director, actor. One of the most innovative film-makers of what is referred to as *The Period of Cinema Men*, Feyzi Tuna worked as assistant to important film-makers, making his first film, the **melodrama**, *Aşka Susayanlar / Thirsty For Love* in 1964. He achieved success with *Yasak Sokaklar / Forbidden Streets* (1965) with a strong film language. Until the 1970s, he was known for his Turkification of foreign films. Then he began to explore local culture, adapting literary works such as *Kuyucaklı Yusuf / Yusuf from Kuyucak* (1985) from Sabahattin Ali, one of the most important Turkish authors, which brought him accolades, particularly for the way it dealt with the binaries of small town/big city through a love story. He also made the third version of the legendary folk tragedy, *Ezo* (1973), following the 1956 and 1968 versions by **Orhan Elmas**, after which he focused on urban stories. He has made 25 fiction films, a number of documentaries and about 90 television series. *Feyzi Tuna Sinemasında Toplumsal Eleştiri / Social Commentary in Feyzi Tuna's Cinema* (2009) is a documentary on the director made by Çetin Tunca, who contributed half a century of his life as a cinematographer to **Yeşilçam** cinema.

Turgul, Yavuz (b. Istanbul, 1946) Director, screenwriter. The director of two landmark films, *Muhsin Bey / Mr Muhsin* (1987), considered as one of the ten best films of Turkish cinema, and *Eşkıya / The Bandit* (1996), which returned spectators to the cinemas in the 1990s after a crisis of over two decades, Yavuz Turgul originally studied journalism and worked for *Ses / Voice* magazine. In 1976, he joined **Ertem Eğilmez** and Arzu Film as a scriptwriter in a period when popular **melodramas** were declining, **social realist** films were drawing attention and **arabesque** and soft porno were gaining popularity. He tried an alternative for the audience with **comedies** with basic features of **melodrama**. His scripts, mostly

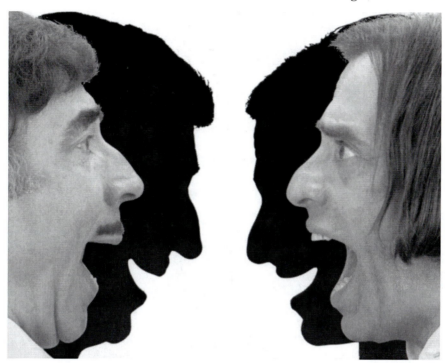

Figure 116 Gölge Oyunu / Shadow Play (Yavuz Turgul, 1993) (Courtesy of International Istanbul Film Festival)

about the tribulations of the eastern men in the metropolis with a sympathetic approach to the anti-hero (*Çiçek Abbas / Abbas in Flower*, **Sinan Çetin**, 1982 and *Züğürt Ağa / The Agha*, **Nesli Çölgeçen**, 1986), received accolades. His first feature, *Fahriye Abla / Sister Fahriye* (1984), established his signature themes – the metamorphosis and return, modernity versus tradition, East versus West, old versus new, the individual versus society and the archetypal binaries. The last was a staple of Arzu Film that has its origins in the traditional Turkish spectacles, such as *Karagöz*, which Turgul exploited to create realistic characters. Social change is determined by economic conditions and migration is an important agent, but Turgul considers the cultural dimension of change as the outcome of economic change. The character of Mr Muhsin in *Muhsin Bey / Mr Muhsin*, a satire on the prevailing **arabesque** culture of the 1980s, which established Şener Şen as his fetish actor, is a good example.

Male bondage as in *The Bandit* focuses on the new modes of solidarity and rivalry that have developed between men in the aftermath of the collapse of the patriarchal structure. The older man (sometimes with a shady past) is often the remnant of a disappearing culture – in *The Agha*, the rural hierarchy; in *Gölge Oyunu / Shadow Play* (1993), a certain **genre** of **comedy**; in *Mr Muhsin*, classical Turkish music; in *The Bandit*, the tradition of the armed rebel against injustices and in *The Hunting Season*, an anachronistic naïve police chief. The characters complement each other as light and darkness, or as female and male: the sage older man and the young passionate troublemaker (Muhsin Bey and Ali Nazik in *Mr Muhsin*; Mahmut and Abidin, the two stand-up comics in *Shadow Play*; Baran and Cumali in *The Bandit;* the idealist Nazım from the provinces and the flighty Halil in *Gönül Yarası / Lovelorn*, 2004 and Ferman and İdris in *Av Mevsimi / The Hunting Season*, 2010). But they never unite: in *Mr Muhsin*, Ali Nazik betrays his friend; in *Lovelorn* and *Hunting Season*, the troublemaker dies; in *The Bandit,* they both die; in *Shadow Play*, they remain side by side, unchanged and perhaps they are the most passive characters of Turgul, unaware of the impossibility of continuing as they are. In **Aşk** *Filmlerinin Unutulmaz Yönetmeni / The Unforgettable Director of Love Movies* (1992), a lament on the declining film industry, Haşmet Asılkan embodies the two contrasting characters within his own personality.

The female prototypes in his films are the virgin and the prostitute/free woman, the former generally asexual, powerless or mute and the latter sexual, passionate and dangerous (Müzeyyen Hanım in *Mr Muhsin*; the deaf-mute Kumru in *Shadow Play*; the mute Keje in *The Bandit;* the mute Melek in *Lovelorn* are examples of the virginal woman, whereas Emel in *The Bandit*, Dünya in *Lovelorn* and Asiye in *The Hunting Season* are a threat to men with their sexuality). Sexual relations between the sage man and the pure woman are not possible. Muhsin Bey's attempts are doomed. Baran never sleeps with Keje; in *Shadow Play*, Mahmut sleeps with the woman but she disappears afterwards bringing doubt to her existence. The sage man is impotent in a society where power is in the hands of the corrupt and shady.

Mr Muhsin, The Bandit and *Lovelorn* are particularly relevant in successfully reflecting the transformation of Istanbul within 30 years and *Shadow Play* is noteworthy for the new film language Turgul tries within the narrative clichés of **Yeşilçam**, using *fasıl heyeti* – musicians performing Turkish classical songs – as a chorus like a Brechtian distantiation device.

Türkali, Vedat (b. Samsun, 1919) Director, screenwriter; RN: Abdülkadir Pirhasan. A graduate of the Turkish Language and Literature section of the University of Istanbul, in the 1950s, the Marxist intellectual Vedat Türkali served seven years of a 9-year prison sentence for political activism. He is the screenwriter of award-winning classic films such as *Otobüs Yolcuları / The Bus Passengers* (1961) and *Karanlıkta Uyananlar / Those Awakening in the Dark* (1964) by **Ertem Göreç**; *Üç Tekerlekli Bisiklet / Tricycle* aka *The Three-Wheeled Bicycle* (**Lütfi Ömer Akad** and **Memduh Ün**, 1962) and *Bedrana* (1974) and *Kara Çarşaflı Gelin / The Bride in Black Chadoor* (1975) by **Süreyya Duru**. He directed three films based on his own scripts and published several books of poetry, scripts, novels and essays. He is the father of film-maker **Barış Pirhasan** and singer/actor/screenwriter Deniz Türkali.

U

Uçakan, Mesut (b. Kırıkkale, 1953) Director, screenwriter, producer. A staunch advocate of Islamist cinema, Mesut Uçakan studied journalism, worked as a film critic, assistant and screenwriter, making his first feature, *Lanet / The Curse* in 1978. Uçakan's *Yalnız Değilsiniz / You Are Not Alone* (1990), about the banning of the headscarf in the universities, appeared in a period when Islamist political parties were gaining ground. It became a box-office success with its appeal to young women experiencing a crisis of identity with its focus on the tribulations of a girl who chooses a devout lifestyle. Serpil, wearing a mini-skirt and riding a bicycle, feels alienated from her family due to their decadent lifestyle and embraces Islam with the support of her grandmother. When she changes into a long overcoat and a headscarf, her parents check her into a clinic for possible psychological disorders. The sequel begins with her release from the clinic and underscores the banning of the headscarf in the universities. *Kelebekler Sonsuza Uçar / Butterflies Fly to Eternity* (1993), a strong indictment of the Kemalist doctrines, challenges the official history of the Turkish Republic through the story of a learned man, Atıf Hodja, hanged for his beliefs – for his opposition to the Hat Reform of Kemal Atatürk – by the Liberation Courts that were established after the founding of the Turkish Republic. Uçakan aims to exonerate Atıf Hodja and set a precedent for similar cases, which he claims have remained taboo. Among his other films, all with a religious message, are *Anne ya da Leyla / Mother or Leyla* (2005) and *Anka Kuşu / The Pheonix* (2006), a number of documentaries and television series.

He is the author of *Türk Sinemasında İdeology / Ideology in Turkish Cinema* and the editor of a six-issue journal, *Mutlak Fikir Estetiği ve Sinema / Absolute Aesthetics of Idea and Cinema* (1977).

Uçurtmayı Vurmasınlar / Don't Let Them Shoot the Kite (1989) takes place in 1984 (post-1980 *coup*) inside a woman's prison. Four-year-old Barış, spending his childhood inside the prison walls with his mother incarcerated for narcotics, builds a strong relationship with a political prisoner, İnci (**Nur Sürer**), who teaches him about life outside. When he sees a kite flying, he thinks it is a bird. İnci promises to fly a kite together when they are free but she is released earlier than him. Barış believes that she will return as a kite. When a kite appears in the sky, his enthusiasm creates excitement among the prisoners and the guards shoot the kite.

Presented from the point of view of Barış, the film uses Barış (his name meaning peace) as a metonym for larger suffering. His narrative function is to code adult anxieties, fantasies and fears rather than act or represent his own interests and desires. As André Bazin points out, a sign of complicity is expected of children and when they show feelings associated with adults, the audience becomes very emotional. 'We are thus seeking to contemplate ourselves in them: ourselves plus the innocence, awkwardness and naiveté we lost. This kind of cinema moves us, but aren't we in fact just feeling sorry for ourselves?' (Bazin 1997: 121).

Rather than the individual stories of the prisoners, the film foregrounds the interaction between women confined to a closed space and the juxtaposition of the political prisoners' ward with the ordinary crimes ward creates a salient background. The message of hope, which at times borders between optimism and naivety, touches the spectators, regardless of cultural and historical background, hence its success with international audiences.

The film received the Best Turkish Film award of the 8th International Istanbul Film Festival, 1989 and several other national and international awards.

Director: **Tunç Başaran**; Producers: **Tunç Başaran**, Jale Onanç, Cengiz Ergün; Production: Odak Film, Magnum Film; Screenwriter: Feride Çiçekoğlu, **Tunç Başaran**; Cinematographer: Erdal Kahraman; Music: Özkan Turgay; Art Director: Jale Onanç; Cast: **Nur Sürer**, Ozan Bilen, Füsun Demirel, Hale Akınlıç, Yasemin Alkaya

Uluçay, Ahmet (b. Kütahya, 1954 – d. Istanbul, 2009) Director, screenwriter, producer. With only an elementary school education, Uluçay was introduced to cinema through a travelling projectionist, inventing his own machine as a teenager and showing film clips found in the town theatre's garbage to local peasants in an old stable. His first short film, *Optik Düşler / Optic Dreams* (1992) was made with an old Betamax he purchased from a worker returning from Germany. After its success, he made other shorts, *Koltuk Değneklerinden Kanat Yapmak / Wings Out of Crutches* (1993); *Minyatür Kosmos'ta Rüya / Dream in a Miniature Cosmos* (1995); *İnci Deniz Dibinde / The Pearl is in the Bottom of the Sea*; *Çerçöp Sahile Vurmuş / The Trash is on the Seashore* (1996) and *Şeytan Kovma / Exorcise* (2000), which were shown at national and international film festivals and won awards. All use animation, carry fantastic elements and evoke the traditional shadow play, *Karagöz*. **Karpuz Kabuğundan Gemiler Yapmak / Boats Out Of Watermelon Rinds** (2004) is an autobiographical *bildungsroman* about two village teenagers obsessed with cinema. With gently woven humour, the film divulges the pains of being gifted, talented and imaginative in the stifling environment of a village where ordinariness is asserted by excluding the other. His second film, *Bozkırda Deniz Kabuğu / Seashell in the Steppe* (2009), about the love of a shepherd boy for a girl he sees in a passing train, was left unfinished when he died of a brain tumour.

Umut / The Hope (1970), an authentic portrayal of Turkey in transition to market economy, is a turning point for Turkish cinema as the first truly realist film of the country and the best Turkish film up to the year it was made. The movement of

Figure 117 Umut / The Hope (Yılmaz Güney, 1970) (Courtesy of International Istanbul Film Festival)

social realism, which produced remarkable films, may not have been forceful enough to transform the established infrastructure, but it paved the way for **Güney**'s engagé films by introducing the concept that cinema was not only a vehicle for entertainment but also an art form that could transmit individual or societal messages. With *Hope*, **Güney** defied the established nomenclature of the dominant **Yeşilçam**, the studio and the star system, the formulaic narratives and cliché constructions designed for the box-office and using natural décor and non-professional actors focused on an anti-hero leading an un-heroic life.

In an age of mechanization and under threat from the newly-arrived taxi system, Cabbar, a quiet family man, struggles to support his wife, his ageing mother and his five children with two drained horses and a shabby phaeton, a trope for the ailing economy. In debt to everyone, his only hope is the lottery, failing which he goes on a treasure hunt. When all hope deserts him, he goes mad.

The theme of the futility of seeking solutions to poverty and oppression in sources outside oneself is introduced with the lottery ticket and developed in the second half of the film with the treasure hunt. Following the establishing shots of phaeton drivers and food vendors waiting in front of the train station, the camera draws attention to publicity boards. A bank sign under which Cabbar relieves himself, the advertisement for *Güney Sanayi* (the industry of the south) and the Coca-Cola logos decorating the kiosk where he buys a newspaper to check the lottery results, all represent Westernization, economic development and progress. A second theme is foreshadowed when Cabbar is the only driver without a customer: the Cabbars of this world are to remain hopeless and alone. The third theme, alienation and the absence of trust fed by the urban environment, is presented when the last passengers, a large migrant family arriving to benefit from the new economy, refuse Cabbar's fare for fear of being cheated by city people.

Cabbar's financial impasse is revealed through a discussion with his wife. He quit his cotton-picking job to escape exploitation and be his own boss. Refusing to return to the fields despite his wife's implorations, he has no resource but the lottery ticket. Solidarity with his class to organize resistance against exploitation and injustice does not occur to him; he only wants to save himself. While the other drivers take collective action, he chases empty dreams.

The theme of alienation and degeneration is re-visited at the market where Cabbar is slighted for unpaid loans, although the arrival of the taxi system affects the small repair shops as well. At home, Cabbar's children fight over a slice of watermelon from the garbage. When a private car hits and kills his horse, the owner blames Cabbar for negligence. At the police station, the accused bourgeois 'forgives' the victim, the proletariat Cabbar, who is thrown out. In desperation, Cabbar sells his gun – a symbol of hope for the oppressed to claim justice in **Güney** films – but is robbed of the money, an incident that extends the alienation theme. Joining Hasan to rob an American sergeant, he receives a beating.

The second part commences with the visit to the *hodja*, reputed to have supernatural powers. The journey of Cabbar, his friend Hassan and the *hodja* along the riverbank displays poor children bathing in dirty water. A scene that evokes the traditional shadow play, *karagöz*, accentuating the dark silhouettes of men and donkeys between the black earth and a cloudy sky is a premonition for the ill-fated expedition. (The allusion to shadow play is repeated in the prayer scene, when the shadows of their hands form a mystical circle.) When they find the tree Cabbar's daughter is supposed to have seen in the water, they dig for one month under the scorching sun, but do not find the treasure. Cabbar becomes mad, whirling with his eyes blindfolded as twigs of the dried-out tree drift in the wind, leaving his fate open-ended.

The Hope is unlike the revolutionary cinema of the West or the Third Cinema movement in South America, although comparisons were made to Brazilian Glauber Rocha and the 'cinema of agitation'. **Güney** exposes the contradictions of the society with precision, moulding a fantastic level into the realistic elements, which could be defined as magic realism, one of the points of conjunction of post-modernism and post-colonialism, as witnessed, for instance, in the work of Salman Rushdie, who considers illusion itself as reality, acknowledging but also questioning the hypnotic magic of cinema (Hutcheon 1995: 130–5). In a magic realist text, the realistic makes its voice heard through the fantastic and magic realist texts, preoccupied with images of borders and centres, work towards destabilizing their fixity (Slemon 1988: 9–24). **Güney** works within the borders of the cinematic screen, exploring the effect of the delicate fantasy at play within the perceptions of reality, formed by both Hollywood and the familiar **Yeşilçam**. The

first part of the film shares similarities with Vittorio de Sica's *Ladri di Biciclette /
Bicycle Thieves* (1948): the loss of the object that is the livelihood of the
protagonist is at the centre of the narrative in both films – the bicycle for Antonio
and the horse for Cabbar; the victim turns into a perpetrator in conflict with his
true ideals – Antonio becomes a thief in desperation and Cabbar tries to rob a
man; both protagonists consult someone with reputed psychic powers – a fortune-
teller in *Bicycle Thieves* and the *hodja* in *The Hope* – both of whom represent
the new commodified spirituality; both men are disillusioned by condescending
policemen, who do not serve the poor; both men are somewhat naive and less able
than their wives in dealing with daily life and both men are driven by motives
of self-interest and oblivious to others (although De Sica's approach is rather
sentimental, whereas **Güney** is critical of Cabbar).

The second part of the film was compared to John Houston's *The Treasure of
the Sierra Madre* (1948) although similarities are only on the surface. *The Hope*
exposes the corrupt order. 'The man whose feet are firmly on the ground does not
build hope on false dreams', as **Güney** claims, but he does not offer a solution.
He shows the enigmatic coexistence of the traditional and the modern, feudal
practices and bourgeois styles, socio-political awareness and lack of it, the way
his earlier films married individual bravura and socialist values in a discourse that
combined Western dramaturgy with documentary realism. In drawing attention to
the 'other', the film challenges the hegemonic forces, but the most modern theme
is the alienation of the individual in a segmented society where everyone focuses
on individual needs (Dönmez-Colin 2007: 48–9).

The Hope was chosen as the Best Film at the Adana Golden Boll Film Festival
and subsequently banned for propagating class differences in a country where
officially there are no classes – showing the torn clothes of the phaeton driver as
a symbol of poverty; giving the impression that the rich owner of the car would
not be tried for hitting the horse and showing discrimination for the poor when
Cabbar hunts for a job; alluding to American imperialism by presenting a soldier
from the military base in Adana; degrading religion (the morning prayer scene is
shown while the sun is rising) and provoking workers to resist authority. It was
later smuggled out of the country and screened at the Cannes Film Festival.

Director, Screenwriter: **Yılmaz Güney**; Producers: **Yılmaz Güney, Abdurrahman
Keskiner**; Production: Güney Film; Cinematographer: Kaya Ererez; Editor: Celal Köse;
Sound: Necip Sarıcıoğlu; Music: Arif Erkin; Cast: **Yılmaz Güney**, Gülsen Alnıaçık,
Tuncel Kurtiz, Kürşat Alnıaçık, Osman Alyanak, Enver Dönmez

Ustaoğlu, Yeşim (b. Sarıkamış, 1960) Director, screenwriter, producer. The most
prominent woman film-maker of contemporary Turkish cinema and one of the
key members of the vitality experienced in the 1990s that has been identified
as the **New Turkish Cinema**, Yeşim Ustaoğlu originally studied architecture,
receiving her master's degree in restoration from the Yıldız University of Istanbul.
She wrote articles for film and art magazines while working on her short films,
Bir Anı Yakalamak / To Catch a Moment (1984), *Magnafantagna* (1987), *Duet /
Duet* (1990) and *Otel / Hotel* (1992), the last winning the Grand Prix at the 14th

Montpellier Festival of Mediterranean Films in France. Born in the year of the first *coup d'état* and belonging to the generation referred to as '78, a generation that reached adulthood amidst the turmoil of two consecutive military interventions, Ustaoğlu's first feature, *İz / Traces* (1994), a psychological thriller about a police officer tormented by feelings of guilt arising from loss of integrity, set the tone of her political stance in cinema. Her second feature *Güneşe Yolculuk / Journey to the Sun* (1999), on ethnic strife and the othering of minorities, received several national and international awards. Her third, *Bulutları Beklerken / Waiting for the Clouds* (2004), challenged collective memory by excavating the 'forgotten' crimes against the Greek population of Anatolia. (During the shooting, she also made a documentary about the sufferings of the women of the Black Sea region, *Sırtlarındaki Hayat / Life on their Shoulders*.) *Pandora'nın Kutusu / Pandora's Box* (2008), which received the Golden Conch at the San Sebastian Film Festival, interrogated the present social and economic situation through three generations of a disjointed middle-class family, the Alzheimer patient protagonist serving as a metaphor for the amnesia surrounding the traumas of history. With *Araf / Somewhere in Between* (2012), Ustaoğlu focused on the dead-end lives of the underprivileged youth from the provinces and the plight of women in a society that limits their choices.

One of the recurring motifs in her films is water. In *Journey to the Sun*, each character is connected to water. The downpour that incessantly hits the windshield in the earlier part of *Pandora's Box* is repeated in *Somewhere in Between*, oppressively foggy images dominating the landscape in both. Her characters are determined by their spatio-temporality. The relationship of the individual to the architectural environment is manifest in the sharp angles of the dark and foreboding hotel rooms and corridors (*Hotel* and *Traces*), the labyrinthine alleys (*Journey to the Sun*), the verticality of the skyscrapers contrasting with the horizontality of endless highways, the enclosing under-passes, the modern gated communities that lock in the residents (*Pandora's Box*) and the monotony of the horizontality (*Somewhere in Between*). Her depiction of modern architecture is very different from the approach of some of the popular film-makers such as **Çağan Irmak** for whom modern architecture represents modernity and success – money and women – offering a dream world. For Ustaoğlu, modern architecture, as modernity itself, is badly adapted in Turkey; it is against human nature, the nature of the Turkish people and their traditions, and it creates isolation and alienation from the roots.

Each film of Ustaoğlu involves a loss that leads to a metamorphosis; a voyage culminates in self-discovery (except for *Somewhere in Between* where the desired voyage never happens and the protagonist is left with her loss without a proper catharsis). Identity issues are pivotal to all her films; the transition, as a private person and as a citizen, from adolescence to adulthood, breaking the ties with father/authority and attaining freedom by becoming an individual in a community-oriented society is the essential theme.

Despite international acclaim, her films receive mixed reactions in Turkey. Poor performers at the box-office, they are often shunned by national juries and critics for catering to the West – choosing controversial subjects presumed to be systematically favoured for funds by European organizations such as **Eurimage** – and targeting foreign festival audiences.

Uzak / Distant (2002), considered by **Nuri Bilge Ceylan** as his most autobiographical work, is the third segment of what this author considers a tetralogy with *Kasaba / The Small Town* (1997), *Mayıs Sıkıntısı / Clouds of May* (1999) and *İklimler / Climates* (2006) that could together be called, 'A Portrait of the Provincial Artist as an Urban Intellectual'. The film continues the central theme of home, identity and belonging established in the previous films. The protagonist Mahmut (Muzaffer Özdemir) is distant to the women in his life, his ex-wife, his mistress, his mother and his sister. He is distant to his country cousin, a reminder of the roots he had severed while trying to build a new identity. He is distant to his work, having succumbed to material gain rather than pursuing artistic dreams. He is distant to commitment, once coercing his wife to have an abortion. He is also distant to his immediate environment. In a spacious apartment, the bed is in the living room, where he sleeps in a sleeping bag like a transient traveller.

Distant starts with an early morning country landscape covered in snow. A tiny figure approaches the camera. A bus stops in the distance. Cut to a woman taking off her stockings, a man watching with a weary sigh. The image is blurred, facilitating its obliteration from memory when shame settles in. In the next shot, he is cleaning the spot on the bed rather annoyingly.

Through the persona of Mahmut, **Ceylan** reflects on the predicaments of an artist of his generation and a person with provincial ties. The transformation of the intellectual after the 1980 *coup d'état* in the apolitical atmosphere of the Turgut

Figure 118 Uzak / Distant (Nuri Bilge Ceylan, 2002) (Courtesy of International Istanbul Film Festival)

Figure 119 Uzak / Distant (Nuri Bilge Ceylan, 2002) (Courtesy of International Istanbul Film Festival)

Özal years (prime minister and president, 1983–93), parallel to the global social and economic changes and the increased hegemony of the neo-liberalist point of view, have distanced several engagé artists from their ideals. Mahmut, once an ambitious photographer making commercials for a ceramics firm, has parallels in the film industry as well with the once-idealist film-makers working on banal television series. *Distant* could be considered as the first film to foreground critically the neo-liberal lifestyles of the 'new intellectual'.

The introduction of Yusuf (Mehmet Emin Toprak), the country cousin, to the narrative is through another rural man, the doorkeeper, the 'outsider-within', the migrant/peasant incorporated into middle-class domestic spheres with the creation of middle-class housing as a response to the expansion of the urban middle classes, creating a powerful common physical and symbolic space for encounters between urban and rural classes (Özyeğin 2002: 47). Responsible for ensuring the sanctity of the dwelling and privy to the secrets of the inhabitants, but always positioned on the threshold, the Anatolian man watches Mahmut's mistress with a deprecatory gaze that also suggests a city-acquired resilience to behaviour contrary to his family-centred morals. His exchange with the middle-aged gay tenant with a young lover is accommodating, but he literally closes the door on the country cousin. The provincial 'other' is not welcome, not even by other provincials. Yusuf confirms the prejudices: he harasses women; does not flush the toilet; smokes cheap cigarettes; leaves his smelly shoes around; prefers the pop singer Sezen Aksu to Bach and sit-coms to Tarkovsky. Earning money is his only aim, and worst of all he brings the claustrophobic proximity of the small-town living with him (like the turtle in the two previous films that carries its home on its back) to the isolating but liberating anonymity of urban life that the city cousin Mahmut has chosen.

The relationship between Mahmut and Yusuf reflects the tension between the urban and the rural in Turkish society. Yusuf goes to cafes where strangers share tables; Mahmut acts like a stranger when he meets his mistress in a cafe. While Mahmut is 'distant', Yusuf is 'distanced'. The provincials are permitted to exist in the metropolis as long as they are invisible like the doorkeeper families confined to dingy basements if they have to live in proximity or isolated in squatter settlements. Mahmut pushes Yusuf to the back room at the end of a long corridor (his suppressed provincial past – with a traditional bed on the floor). Yusuf leaves the lights on and Mahmut switches them off just like the doors that Mahmut keeps closing as if to protect his home territory and chosen identity by leaving the 'other' outside, not realizing that by locking the other out, one also locks oneself in. In this sense, the trope of the mouse trapped in the kitchen is applicable to both characters, although the method of each for eliminating the animal is quite different.

Despite their differences, Mahmut and Yusuf are in essence the same character. The unidentified tiny dot in the distance in the opening episode, which gradually takes the shape of Yusuf, could be an allusion to Mahmut (or Mahmut's recollection of the event) who once left in the same manner, alone one early morning, without the customary good-bye rituals of family. During the absence of Mahmut, Yusuf leaves his designated corner and occupies Mahmut's living space, his desk and his armchair, littering the place with his cigarette butts. On Mahmut's return, during an encounter between the two in the corridor, positioned in the thresholds of two doors (the in-between space), Yusuf looks like a boy holding the wind-up soldier he bought for his nephew. While the camera is on Mahmut, reprimanding Yusuf, Yusuf's image is repeatedly reflected behind Mahmut through the mirror, but the image is blurred, merging the two characters and perhaps reflecting Mahmut's youth in Yusuf's image.

The closing episode is significant in this sense when Mahmut, the disillusioned urban artist/intellectual sitting on a bench fronting the Anatolian coast, decides to smoke the cheap cigarettes of his cousin that he had rejected earlier. Perhaps he is now prepared to face his suppressed 'other', although Yusuf is already gone from his life.

Distant won the Grand Prix and the Best Male Actor awards (shared between Mehmet Emin Toprak and Muzaffer Özdemir) at the Cannes Film Festival (2003). A few months earlier, Toprak died in a traffic accident.

Director, Producer, Screenwriter and Cinematographer: **Nuri Bilge Ceylan**; Production: NBC Film; Editor: Ayhan Ergürsel, **Nuri Bilge Ceylan**; Music: Mozart; Cast: Muzaffer Özdemir, Mehmet Emin Toprak, Zühal Gencer Erkaya, Nazan Kırılmış, Ebru Ceylan, Feridun Koç, Fatma Ceylan

Uzak İhtimal / Wrong Rosary (2009) is the story of three people with different backgrounds whose lives intersect in Istanbul: Musa (Nadir Sarıbacak), a provincial *müezzin*, recently appointed to a mosque in the cosmopolitan Galata district; his neighbour Klara (Görkem Yeltan), an orphaned young woman of Italian origin under the custody of the church and training to become a nun; and Yakup Demir (Ersan Ünsal), an aristocrat who trades in old books. Musa mixing his prayer

Figure 120 Uzak İhtimal / Wrong Rosary (Coşkun, Mahmut Fazıl, 2008) (Courtesy of International Istanbul Film Festival)

beads with Clara's which carries a cross is the event that justifies the English title, whereas the original title means 'distant possibility'. Although the film carries a message of tolerance between Christianity and Islam, it also suggests the practical impossibility of closing the distance despite best intentions. The appearance of Yakup Demir, Clara's real father, is somewhat unexpected and does not contribute much to the narrative except to accentuate the theme of existential alienation and lack of communication in an urban environment.

With long shots, minimal dialogue and smooth editing, the film builds a serene atmosphere with a nostalgic view of an area of Istanbul that was once the centre of multicultural life. Its weaknesses are the idolization of the two characters to the point of abstracting them from their environment; the tendency to follow the safe middle road and the use of a cliché of 1990s Islamist films in presenting a love story involving a dark, not very handsome Muslim devotee and a blonde, pretty woman outside his religion. Unlike in the Islamist films of that epoch, however, here Clara is the one to decide the direction the relationship will take, which is not in the direction of Musa.

The film shared the Tiger Award at the Rotterdam International Film Festival with *Be Calm and Count to Seven* (Ramtin Lavafipour, Iran, 2009) and *Breathless* (Yang Ik June, South Korea, 2009) and subsequently received several other national and international awards. However, it could reach barely over 30,000 viewers during the 17 weeks it was screened in Turkey.

Director: **Mahmut Fazıl Coşkun**; Producers: Tülin Çetinkol Soyarslan, İsmail Kılıçarslan, Tarık Tufan, **Mahmut Fazıl Coşkun**; Production: Hokusfocus Film; Screenwriters: Tarık Tufan, Görkem Yeltan, Bektaş Topaloğlu; Cinematographer: Refik Çakar; Editor: Çiçek Kahraman; Music: Rahman Altın; Sound: Murat Çelikkol; Art Director: Selda Çiçek; Cast: Nadir Sarıbacak, Görkem Yeltan, Ersan Uysal, Burçin Şenkal, Murat Ergün

Uzkınay, Fuat (b. Üsküdar/Istanbul, 1888 – d. Istanbul, 1956) Director, producer, cinematographer. The director of the documentary that is officially designated as the first national film, *Aya Stefanos'taki Rus Abidesinin Yıkılışı / The Demolition of the Russian Monument at St Stephan* (1914), Fuat Uzkınay studied physics and chemistry. He met **Sigmund Weinberg** during a projection while working at the Istanbul Sultanisi (high school) as a bureaucrat, which inspired him to open a cinema hall with Kemal and Şakir Seden (1914). Shortly after, he was taken into the army. The demolition of a monument erected by the Russian army to mark their victory in the 1876–7 war with Turkey was one of the propaganda events organized by the Committee of Union and Progress to gain favourable public opinion. It was intended to be filmed by a firm from Vienna, Sacha-Messter Gesellschaft, but due to nationalist feelings a Turk had to be appointed for the task, and the reserve officer Uzkınay with no experience in shooting a film was chosen. However, there is no evidence that this film was actually made. When **Weinberg** was dismissed from his position as the director of the newly founded (1915) Merkez Ordu Sinema Dairesi/MOSD (Central Army Office of Cinema), Uzkınay replaced him. According to **Nijat Özön**, he completed *Leblebici Horhor Ağa / Horhor Agha, The Chickpea Seller* (1916) and ***Himmet Ağa'nın İzdivacı / The Marriage of Himmet Agha*** (1916–18) started by **Weinberg** (Özön 1970: 14–16). According to Nurullah Tilgen, he was only the cinematographer and ***The Marriage of Himmet Agha*** was completed by Reşat Rıdvan (Scognamillo 1990: 26).

After a training trip to Germany in 1917, he became an active film-maker of the silent era as a cinematographer and documentarian. Following the defeat of the allies of the Ottoman Empire in WWI, MOSD was transferred to the Müdafaa-i Milliye Cemiyeti (Association for National Defence) and Uzkınay was appointed as its head. With the transfer of the association to the military academy in 1924, he was appointed as the head of the Laboratory for the Film-making Centre of the Army Command Headquarters until his retirement in 1953 (Özön 1970: 38). He is the producer and cinematographer of the *Bican Efendi* series, *Binnaz* and *Mürebbiye* and the cinematographer of *Boğaziçi Esrarı* aka *Nur Baba / The Mystery of the Bosphorus* (**Muhsin Ertuğrul**, 1922) (Özön 1970: 36–8).

Ü

Üç Maymun / Three Monkeys (2008), deviating from the self-reflexive films of **Nuri Bilge Ceylan**, focusing on the individual, foregrounds guilt, complicity and oblivion through a family situation. A crime committed by an outsider is transferred to the family and a crime committed by the family is transferred to an outsider. Covering the truth and partaking in complicity and oblivion preserve the unity of the family, a metonym for the state, with a reference to the collective amnesia about the crimes in history, the ghosts of which may appear as the figure carved on an illuminated rock in **Ceylan**'s next film, *Bir Zamanlar Anadolu'da / Once Upon a Time in Anatolia* (2011). The title refers to the proverbial monkeys who see/hear/speak no evil, which has a positive connotation as a proverb in Japanese and Buddhist traditions, but a negative one in the Western world. In the Japanese tradition, there may be a fourth monkey, 'do no evil', which may be referring to the dead son. The camera is also in complicity with the characters: it does not see the accident, the corpse, the intimacy of Servet and Hacer, the prison life of Eyüp and the murder of Servet. Crime and punishment is central to the *film noir* style of the film, but just like Béla Tarr in *The Man from London* (2007) the way **Ceylan** deconstructs the sub-**genre** and reconstructs something different can qualify *Three Monkeys* as an anti-thriller.

Elliptic in style, the film begins with an anonymous corpse that is hardly visible and ends with an identified corpse that is invisible. (*Once Upon a Time* begins with the search for an evasive corpse and ends with a real corpse on the morgue table.) An ominous thunderstorm is heard with the appearance of the title on the screen, a premonition of the murky nature of the narrative. The plot is reminiscent of *Baba / The Father* (**Yılmaz Güney**, 1971). An employee in dire straits assumes the crime of his boss for a large amount of money and goes to jail. During his incarceration, his wife is seduced by the culprit and his son frequents bad company. On his release, he is not killed by his son as in the previous film, but obliged to cover the son's crime, who kills the real culprit, or does he?

The first image is that of an exhausted driver in close-up but soon the camera moves outside to track the circles of the car's backlights until they become dots and disappear in a fade-out. Whose is the gaze? Later in the film, when the boy understands that his mother is locked in her bedroom with her lover, he puts his eye to the keyhole; what we see is not the interior of the room, but his eye in

Figure 121 Üç Maymun / Three Monkeys (Nuri Bilge Ceylan, 2008) (Courtesy of NBC Film and Zeynep Özbatur Atakan-Zeyno film/Yapımlab)

close-up inside the frame of the keyhole. The camera is on the watcher and not on the watched. During the final encounter between Servet, the boss (Ercan Kesal) and Hacer (Hatice Aslan) before Servet's murder, Hacer goes down on her knees and cries, 'You're my destiny'. The camera observes the scene from a distance, from the viewpoint of someone watching, perhaps the murderer. Is it the cheated husband Eyüp (Yavuz Bingöl) or the son İsmail (Ahmet Rıfat Şungar)?

From the narrative that involves love, passion, betrayal, infidelity, a suspicious husband and crime (without suspense) and the dialogues to the use of pathetic fallacy – the thunder and lightning – the film proceeds like a typical **Yeşilçam**

Figure 122 Üç Maymun / Three Monkeys (Nuri Bilge Ceylan, 2008) (Courtesy of NBC Film and Zeynep Özbatur Atakan-Zeyno film/Yapımlab)

Figure 123 Üç Maymun / Three Monkeys (Nuri Bilge Ceylan, 2008) (Courtesy of NBC Film and Zeynep Özbatur Atakan-Zeyno film/Yapımlab)

melodrama, similar to what the mother and son watch on television every night. The difference is the existential issue of the characters, who have no one but themselves to blame. The contrast and desaturation of the colours, the concentration particularly on the red (as a manifestation of Hacer's newly released sexuality); the mouth-level shots; the awkward silences and the avoidance of eye contact, accentuate the aloneness of the characters. The industrial dystopia, the miserable railroad tracks, the station, the old train, the house soon to be demolished, the busy thoroughfare and the ships in the sea (a reference to a half-sunk ship in the snow in *Uzak / Distant*, 2002, observed by Yusuf) draw a picture of a waste land. The sense of imprisonment, a Dostoyevskian motif that re-occurs in the films of the **New Turkish Cinema** film-makers, is accentuated during the prison visits, when both the father and the son are shown behind bars. The feeling of guilt is there before the film begins, with a drowned child, who appears only to those who suffer from it.

Sound is creatively used in the film. The earlier car scene that starts the sparks of attraction between Servet and Hacer is shot with an original exploitation of the voice-over; we hear the voice of Servet who is not in the frame, or his lips are not moving. When the son returns home unexpectedly and the mother is receiving her lover, the couple cannot hear him open the door because of a passing train. Chanting from the minarets, *ezan*, is heard when someone is lying (Hacer denying the affair) or debating with their conscience (Eyüp about forgiving her). It is also heard when İsmail slaps his mother as if to reprimand her.

Sons are shown as ambivalent to the affairs of their mothers in contemporary Turkish cinema. In *Three Monkeys*, the son first notices the phone calls. He comes home unexpectedly, hears his mother laughing and puts his eye to the keyhole. Devastated by what he has seen, his eye catches the kitchen knife as in *Süt / Milk* (**Semih Kaplanoğlu**, 2007), Yusuf hiding behind the lover of his mother near the lake and contemplating killing the man with a heavy stone. Yusuf is distracted by a fish and chooses to compete for his mother's love by offering it to her, but İsmail slaps his mother.

The cell-phone, an insignificant gadget, becomes significant in the film. That is how Hacer's affair with her husband's boss begins and that is how it is exposed. When it rings in the office of the boss, the lyrics of rejected love foreshadow the affair. Later, her family suspects her because of the phone calls. The **arabesque** melody of the ring is a reference to another gadget in *Mayıs Sıkıntısı / Clouds of May* (1999), the *lambada* music of the lighter, which is also referenced in *Once Upon a Time in Anatolia*, with the ring of the cell-phone of the commissar, the theme song from *Love Story*.

Although the focus is a woman, the cause of all trouble, who will not even admit guilt, foreshadowing *Once Upon a Time in Anatolia*, another crime story with a murder committed because of an adulterous woman, it is a fallacy to take this as misogyny on the part of the director, as assumed by several critics. The obsession of Hacer with the rather unattractive Servet, who seems to treat her like an object, is an enigma on the surface, but as **Ceylan** has explained during his press conferences, the feeling of powerlessness, which is in everyone, attracts her to what she sees as a symbol of power. Her circumstances both at home and at work confirm this contention. In fact, **Ceylan** claims that, more than a reference to the politics of the country, the film is a commentary on class differences.

Director: **Nuri Bilge Ceylan**; Producer: **Zeynep Özbatur**; Production: Zeyno Film; Screenwriters: **Nuri Bilge Ceylan**, Ebru Ceylan, Ercan Kesal; Cinematographer: **Gökhan Tiryaki**; Editors: Ayhan Ergürsel, Bora Gökşingöl, **Nuri Bilge Ceylan**; Cast: Yavuz Bingöl, Hatice Aslan, Ahmet Rıfat Şungar, Ercan Kesal, Cafer Köse, Gürkan Aydın

Üç Tekerlekli Bisiklet / Tricycle aka *The Three-Wheeled Bicycle* (1962) is a love story about a lonely woman with a small child and the man she hides in her house, who is chased and trapped, one of the staple motifs of **Lütfi Ö. Akad**'s cinema. The film is shot like a theatre piece, the camera rarely leaving the young mother's house with the attic, the bedroom and the living area, except for a number of occasions when she goes to the village. **Sezer Sezin**'s measured acting as Hacer transmits the suppressed sexuality of a woman who has to defend herself against the local machismo. The scenes when she crosses the village streets under the lustful gaze of the idle men at the cafe are particularly remarkable. **Akad**, who customarily shied away from erotic scenes, shows **Ayhan Işık** (Ali, the outlaw) and **Sezin** involved in passionate embraces in a number of episodes. A tricycle serves as a trope for the recomposed family – the young mother, the outlaw who becomes her lover and the little boy who thinks he is his real father. Bought by the outlaw who becomes a surrogate father involuntarily, the bicycle receives a symbolic kick when the real father arrives.

Director: **Lütfi Ö. Akad**, **Memduh Ün**; Producer: Nusret İkbal; Production: Be-Ya Film; Screenwriter: Hüsamettin Gönenli (**Vedat Türkali**) based on Orhan Kemal's book; Cinematographer: Çetin Gürtop and Mustafa Yılmaz; Editor: **Memduh Ün**; Decor: **Akad**; Cast: **Ayhan Işık**, **Sezer Sezin**, Küçük Kenan, Nuri Genç, Saadettin Erbil, Reha Yurdakul, Osman Alyanak

Figure 124 Üçüncü Sayfa / The Third Page (Zeki Demirkubuz, 2000) (Courtesy of International Istanbul Film Festival)

Üçüncü Sayfa / The Third Page (2000) is a strong commentary on the unstable social structure and the fragile economy of late-1990s Turkey, shot in *film noir* style with a *femme fatale* and a man with good intentions who falls into her trap while trying to help her. İsa (Ruhi Sarı) lives in a run-down basement flat in the back streets of downtown Istanbul, acting in small roles in television series. One day, he is beaten as the suspect for the disappearance of $50 from a small mafia operation. Unable to cope with the blows of life, he contemplates suicide, but instead kills his landlord who comes to collect the overdue rent.

The film is dedicated 'to the defeated, forgotten', those whose stories are hidden on the third page of newspapers. The characters are excluded and oppressed by a society that prefers them to be invisible, confining them to dark corners; even public spaces like a children's park are available only in the dark. The opening sequences in the office of a mafia thug draw attention to the portrait of Tansu Çiller, the prime minister of the period whose dubious dealings in the acquisition of her fortune are yet to be investigated. In a farcical scene that mirrors the dollarization of Turkish society, the bullies that come to collect the missing money from İsa ask for dollars, not Turkish lira. Meryem (Başak Köklükaya), the young village woman who tries to help İsa, is not yet versed in the language of the new economy: 'How much is $50 in Turkish money?' 'Buying rate or selling rate?' Cell phones and calculators come out, the boss is consulted and the daily exchange rate is confirmed. The event takes place on the threshold, a favourite trope for **Demirkubuz**.

Unhappily married Meryem, the mother of two children, is extracted from her roots and confined to a basement apartment, surviving in a male-dominant society. Her sole connection to the outside world is the television screen. The soap operas she watches incessantly mould her identity. There seems to be tender love developing between the two less privileged individuals, but Meryem turns out to be the mistress of the landlord although she is happy the brute is dead. In fact, she was present when the killing took place. Now she wants İsa to kill her husband. Subject to violence and harassment by her alcoholic husband and by the dubious landlord, she trusts no one. 'Everyone has his back to the wall, what will he do if not strike back' is her motto that echoes the atmosphere in the country.

Interviews with ordinary citizens on the street who represent three different age groups are cut into the narrative as if to link the surface **melodrama** with something more tangible. An old man declares he has no dreams; a middle-aged man thinks dreams are a waste of time, but a 21-year-old wants to share his ideas with people like '**Yılmaz Güney**, who was also 21 when he came to Istanbul. Sultan Mehmet conquered Istanbul at the same age.'

The Third Page is also about the media, which plays an important role in Turkish daily life. Numerous private television channels broadcast a wide range of programmes, from soap operas to local **arabesque**. İsa earns his living playing in small roles in television series; the walls of his bachelor pad are decorated with posters of his heroes (**Cüneyt Arkın** in *Dört Yanım Cehennem / The Mummy*, **Çetin İnanç**, 1982); Meryem's actions and reactions are shaped according to the soap operas. Often it is not evident whether she is able to see the difference between real life and make believe. After the murder, she goes home to watch television.

The economical style of **Demirkubuz** places all key events outside the frame almost like a Greek tragedy. The narrative unfolds through the seen and the unseen. A fight is heard in the next room; a woman screams; the protagonist grabs a knife and listens, but the fight, which would have more cinematic possibilities, is not shown. The camera takes a deliberate distance.

The film's closed form (dingy basement, small spaces, dark corridors) intensifies the feeling of claustrophobia and entrapment that connects with one of the staple tropes of **Demirkubuz**, the prison. The only outdoor scene is in a children's park, which looks uncanny in the dark, with the conspicuous absence of the sounds of children, painfully reminding the protagonists of the loss of innocence. Meryem's movement towards more open spaces (a large apartment on an upper floor) leads her to a false paradise similar to what she envies on the television screen. Her peasant scarf gone, she prides herself with a bouffant hair-do. She has arrived. She represents the new citizen, the end justifies the means.

Dostoyevskian themes of crime and punishment, responsibility and conscience, central to the work of **Demirkubuz**, are interwoven into the plot with unexpected twists and turns which carry the story skilfully to the end.

Director, Screenwriter, Producer: **Zeki Demirkubuz**; Production: Mavi Filmcilik; Cinematographer: Ali Utku; Editor: Nevzat Dişiaçık; Sound: Cafer Cebetaş, Zafir Saka; Cast: Ruhi Sarı, Başak Köklükaya, Cengiz Sezici, Serdar Orçin, Emrah Elçiboğa, Naci Taşdöven

Figure 125 Üç Arkadaş / Three Friends (Memduh Ün, 1958) (Courtesy of International Istanbul Film Festival)

Ün, Memduh (b. Istanbul, 1920) Director, screenwriter, producer, actor, editor. One of the most important film-makers of the 1960s, master of **Halit Refiğ** and **Tunç Başaran**, a film-maker for over half a century, Ün studied medicine, played professional soccer and worked as a clerk before launching a film career as an actor in *Damga / The Stigma* (Seyfi Havaeri / **Akad**, 1948). In 1951, he co-founded Yakut Film with Dr Arşavir Alyanak and directed his debut feature, *Yetim Yavrular / The Orphans* (1955), which he also scripted, playing the lead. He repeated the success formula of this film with several other dark village **melodramas**. *Üç Arkadaş / Three Friends* (1958), the story of a blind girl (**Muhterem Nur**) and three kind-hearted men (**Fikret Hakan**, Salih Tozan and Semih Sezerli) was considered the best Turkish film until its time and the best film of its director, although the script is somewhat irrational and naïve and the poverty of the lumpen-proletariat characters rather romanticized. (In 2011, the film was restored by the Mimar Sinan Fine Arts University Centre for Cinema and TV, with the assistance of Groupama Gan Cinema Foundation, France.) He followed the success of *Three Friends* with similar works foregrounding solidarity among ordinary people (*Ayşecik / Little Ayşe, Mahallenin Sevgilisi / The Favourite of the Neighbourhood* and *Kırık Çanaklar / Broken Pots* all made in 1960 and a re-make of *Three Friends* in colour in 1971). Founding Uğur Film in 1960, he concentrated on adventure yarns (the first Turkish James Bond film, *Altın Çocuk / The Golden Boy*, 1966) and detective stories, while continuing 'ordinary people **melodramas**' and making comedies to attract the box-office. *Ağaçlar Ayakta Ölür / Trees Die Upright* (1964), focusing on old age, and *Büyük Yemin / The Great Oath* (1969), denouncing the tradition of blood feud and the secondary status of women (scripted by **Duygu Sağıroğlu**), drew attention with their film language and technical mastery. In the 1970s, he contributed to **Fatma**

Figure 126 Zıkkımın Kökü / Bullshit (Memduh Ün, 1992) (Courtesy of International Istanbul Film Festival)

Girik's rise to stardom (*Ağrı Dağı Efsanesi / The Legend of Mt Ararat*, 1975). In the 1980s, he shot several films with **Kemal Sunal**, *Garip / The Poor One* (1986), about a poor football fan's fight for the custody of a girl he adopts by chance, being one of the most popular. *Bütün Kapılar Kapalıydı / All Doors Were Closed* (1990), an ex-activist's maladaptation to the societal changes in post-1980 *coup* Turkey after her release from prison, received national and international accolades. *Gün Ortasında Karanlık / Darkness at Midday* (1991), about a handicapped child and his mother, was a novelty in terms of the subject. Ün's last two films, carrying nostalgic biographical elements relating to the rural past, are nostalgic **meta-films** that focus on cinephilia (the protagonists', the director's and the audience's). The very successful *Zıkkımın Kökü / Bullshit* (1992), based on a biographical story of renowned Turkish author Muzaffer İzgü, foregrounds a poor boy with a *laterna magica*, whereas *Sinema Bir Mucizedir / Cinema is Like a Miracle*, completed by **Tunç Başaran** during Ün's illness (2005) and reminiscent of *Cinema Paradiso* (Giuseppe Tornatore, 1988) is an adaptation from another renowned Turkish author, Ülkü Tamer's *Allaben Öyküleri / Allaben Stories.* Some of the other noteworthy films of Ün are *Akasyalar Açarken /*

336   Ünal, Ümit

Figure 127 Zıkkımın Kökü / Bullshit (Memduh Ün, 1992) (Courtesy of International Istanbul Film Festival)

When the Acacias are in Bloom (1962), *Namusum İçin / For My Honour* (1965), *İnsanlar Yaşadıkça / As Long As They Live* (1969) and *Kanlı Nigar / Bloody Nigar* (1981). He is the co-director of *Üç Tekerlekli Bisiklet / Tricycle* aka *The Three-Wheeled Bicycle* (1962) with **Lütfü Ö. Akad**.

   Memduh Ün, Küçük İnsanların Büyük Dünyası / Memduh Ün, Big World of Small People (2009) is a documentary on the master by Çetin Tunca, who spent half a century in **Yeşilçam** as a cameraman. He has been shooting bio-documentaries on the masters of Turkish cinema to compensate for the deficiencies in the Turkish archives.

Ünal, Ümit (b. Tire, 1965) Director, screenwriter, producer, actor. A distinguished screenwriter who has also become a distinguished director, Ümit Ünal graduated from the Cinema and Television Department of the Faculty of Fine Arts, Nine September University in İzmir in 1985. After a period of assistantship, he started writing scripts, among which *Teyzem / My Aunt* (**Halit Refiğ**, 1986), *Hayallerim, Aşkım ve Sen / My Dreams, My Love and You* (**Atıf Yılmaz**, 1987) and *Berlin in Berlin* (**Sinan Çetin**, 1993) are the most memorable. Before making his first feature, *9* (2002), he published two novels and a collection of short stories and worked in the advertising sector. A no-budget film focusing on police interrogations about the murder of a foreign girl in a lower class neighbourhood of Istanbul, the first entirely digital Turkish film, *9* exposed the fascistic tendencies of the society, the vanishing of neighbourhood culture and its replacement with fear. Shot in a single space (the depot of a film company) in four days using only one frame, the film prioritizes the story, the dialogue and the characters; movement was created by fast editing. Ünal scripted and directed a section of *Anlat İstanbul / Istanbul*

Tales (2004), with **Kudret Sabancı**, Selim Demirdelen, Yücel Yolcu and Ömür Atay, following five fairy-tale characters whose paths cross in the fairy-tale city, Istanbul, which has become uncanny. *Ara / Ara* (2007), *Gölgesizler / Shadowless* (2008), *Kaptan Reza / Captain Reza*, the horror/ thriller *Ses / The Voice* (2010) and *Nar / Pomegranate* (2011), a **fantasy** film with tension, are his other films.

Ünlü, Onur (b. İzmit, 1973) Director, producer, screenwriter, poet. A graduate of Anadolu University in communications, Onur Ünlü received his masters degree from Marmara University. He made his first feature film *Polis / Police* in 2006 and followed it with *Çocuk / The Child* (2007), *Güneşin Oğlu / The Son of the Sun* (2008) and *Beş Şehir / Five Cities* (2009). *Celal Tan ve Ailesinin Aşırı Acıklı Hikayesi / The Extremely Tragic Story of Celal Tan and His Family* (2011) garnered him the Best Film and Best Screenplay awards at the Adana Golden Boll Film Festival, 2011. He received the Best Film, Best Screenplay and Fipresci (Federation of International Film Critics) awards at the 32nd International Istanbul Film Festival with *Sen Aydınlatırsın Geceyi / Thou Gild'st the Even* (2013), a black-and-white film about ordinary Anatolians with extraordinary abilities. The film starts with a quotation from Euripides, 'Man is created from anxiety'. Cemal, who can see through walls, Yasemin, who can move objects with her fingers and Defne, who can freeze time, still suffer from the pains of being human despite their supernatural abilities and despite living in a town with two suns and three full moons.

Focusing on the themes of death, vulnerability and crime, Ünlü mixes **fantasy** and tragi-comedy with black **comedy** in a personal idiosyncratic style to show the absurdity of life and the destitution of the modern man in a Beckettian sense. He also works in television series.

Figure 128 Sen Aydınlatırsın Geceyi / Thou Gild'st the Even (Onur Ünlü, 2013) (Courtesy of International Istanbul Film Festival)

V

Vargı, Ömer (b. Istanbul, 1953) Director, screenwriter, producer, editor. Choosing cinema as a career after studying physics, Ömer Vargı had his first film experience as first assistant in **Şerif Gören**'s *Endişe / Anxiety* (1974). He directed hundreds of commercials, becoming a partner in Filma-Cass in 1982 and producing **Gören**'s *Güneşin Tutulduğu Gün / The Day of the Eclipse of the Sun* (1983), co-producing *Amerikalı / The American* (**Gören**, 1993) and the box-office hit *Eşkıya / The Bandit* (**Yavuz Turgul**, 1996) among others. His directorial debut, *Herşey Çok Güzel Olacak / Everything's Gonna Be Great* (1998) was about modern losers in the metropolis caught between expectations and reality. *İnşaat / Under Construction* (2003) was a **comedy** about two construction workers in the slums who dream of going to Italy to work illegally. When the owner of the construction site, who is also the driver for a mafia boss, starts bringing corpses to the site, they are in a lucrative business as gravediggers. *Kabadayı / For Love and Honour* (2007) and *Anadolu Kartalları / The Anatolian Eagles* (2011) are his other films.

Vesikalı Yarim / My Licensed Love (1968), a cult classic, is a desperate love story between a downtown prostitute (licensed to practice her trade) and a married greengrocer from the outskirts. The film was inspired by a short story of Sait Faik (*Menekşeli Vadi / Valley of Violets*) and a poem of Orhan Veli called *Tahattur / Remembering*: Seni Nasıl Unuturum Vesikalı Yarim / Alnımdaki bıçak yarası senin yüzünden / Tabakam senin yadigarın / İki elin kanda olsa gel diyor telgırafın (How could I forget you my licensed love / The knife wound on my forehead is because of you / My cigarette case is a gift from you / Your telegram says come no matter what).

The film juxtaposes two different spaces: Sabiha's (**Türkan Şoray**) world is centred around Beyoğlu, a fantasy of desire for men with its night-life and women of pleasure; Halil's (**İzzet Günay**) world is in the outskirts, where life is shaped by customs and traditions and duty to religion and to family is pivotal to existence. The differences of the lovers come to the surface early in the film when Halil arrives at the nightclub with a fruit basket from his orchards as a present for Sabiha who mocks him. However, identities are not constant and the duality exists in everyone; love can transform a hardened prostitute into a pure human being with feelings and blind an obedient son and responsible husband to the point of

Figure 129 Vesikalı Yarim / My Licensed Love (Lütfi Ö. Akad, 1968) (Courtesy of International Istanbul Film Festival)

hurting his family. Love for a prostitute, as the title indicates, carries a duality itself, which suggests the impossibility of the union. Halil is struck by a fantasy – a mysterious beautiful woman whose perfume, make-up and control over situations and over men (all of which are facades that he cannot discern) mesmerise him. She shows her 'motherly' side the first night, allowing him to sleep in her place until the bridge is open, the bridge connecting the traditional old town with the Westernized Beyoğlu, metaphorically instrumental for the bourgeoning of their love. When they live together, she irons his shirts like a wife and he reprimands her for going out without his permission, walking around aimlessly and answering back when he talks to her (for breaking the essential taboos). How long would the fantasy last? It is significant that when he stabs Sabiha and she tells the police she stabbed herself, Halil says 'now she really destroyed me'. What is destroyed is his fantasy, when she transforms into the protective mother/wife. It is time for him to return home.

My Licensed Love is distinguished among the **melodramas** of **Yeşilçam** with its composite script, poetic dialogues, measured directing and acting that are almost minimalist and the departure from the **melodrama** conventions in presenting the impossibility of love arising, not from forces outside the characters – fate, chance, misunderstandings, bad characters, family pressures – but from the protagonists themselves. Also significant is how **Akad** treats his characters; neither the prostitute nor the man who abandons his family is subject to moral judgements or demeaning shots. Both are reborn through their love but to expect the lovers to exist abstracted from the others is utopic. The film ends neither in tragedy nor in a happy end. Halil returns to his mundane life (his wife asks him

Figure 130 Vesikalı Yarim / My Licensed Love (Lütfi Ö. Akad, 1968) (Courtesy of International Istanbul Film Festival)

if he is hungry as if he only left in the morning) and Sabiha to exist among men indifferent to her plight as the closing sequence of her walking among men as if she is invisible implies. They should have met long ago, as Sabiha reminds Halil, a classic line from the film.

Safa Önal's nuanced dialogues reflect the vulnerability of the characters that prevent confrontation, which could also have led to solutions. Sabiha cannot ask Halil if he is married: 'What if he says "yes"?' or 'What if it is not true and he gets angry?' When Halil's father meets Sabiha, he can only say, 'How's Halil?' which wounds her more than any outpouring of anger.

The film carries the *hüzün* of Orhan Pamuk that is the outcome of the liminal status of Turkey between two cultures and the conflict between European and Islamic values that have created confusion and loss of identity (*Kara Kitap / The Black Book* references it in the episode of look-alike prostitutes). The two faces of the city, which is traditionally represented as female and often as a prostitute in both literature and cinema, are symbolized through the duality of Sabiha's character, which can also be read as a metaphor for the modern urban woman who moves freely (or would like to) in what is customarily allocated to men – the public space. The courage of the film is holding the camera on Saliha in the last sequence and letting the audience identify with a woman who steps out of the space controlled by men, without permission, and becomes one with the city, which makes *My Licensed Love* a film of 'transgression' (Çiçekoğlu 2007: 117, 124).

My Licensed Love was restored after 45 years through the sponsorship of the Groupama Gan Foundation at Mimar Sinan Fine Arts University's Centre for Television and Cinema and shown at the 32nd Istanbul International Film Festival, 2013.

Director: **Lütfi Ö. Akad**; Producer: Şeref Gür; Production: Şeref Film; Screenwriter: **Sefa Önal**; Cinematographer: Ali Uğur; Sound: **Yorgo İlyadis**; Music: Metin Bükey; Cast: **İzzet Günay**; **Türkan Şoray**; Ayfer Feray; Semih Sezerli; Aydemir Balkan

Village films (rural films, rural melodramas) as a sub-**genre** of **melodrama** were initiated by **Muhsin Ertuğrul** with *Aysel, Bataklı Damın Kızı / The Girl From the Marshes* aka *Aysel, the Girl From the Swampy Roof* (1935) although the film was shot near Istanbul, like many other village films, made by urban middle-class casts and crew. Some village films were adapted from theatre, others from literature. In the 1950s, village stories found a valid medium in literature with Mahmut Makal's *Bizim Köy / Our Village* (1950), a village boy's account of his life, and other works by talented authors such as Yaşar Kemal, Orhan Kemal and Necati Cumalı. However, cinematic versions were generally contrived and condescending. Makal would lament in *Our Village*, 'Where are our artists? … What masterpieces might be born of this sweat that runs in torrents? Those who still think of the Turkish village in terms of "The shepherd plays upon his pipe, how romantic is his life", do not know this country' (Makal 1954: 270). **Lütfi Ö. Akad**'s *Beyaz Mendil / White Handkerchief* (1955), based on a Yaşar Kemal story, is the first noteworthy film in this **genre**, which approaches the socio-cultural aspect of rural life realistically. The principal actor, **Fikret Hakan**, lived for a year with the local people of the Black Sea village chosen for the film to prepare his role, which was rare for **Yeşilçam**. The background music was also authentic.

Following the 27 May 1960 *coup d'état*, **rural films** gained a veristic dimension inspired by the upsurge of realistic novels of the soil. **Metin Erksan**'s *Susuz Yaz / A Dry Summer* (1963) exposing one man's obsession to possess the water and his brother's wife and **Yılmaz Güney**'s *Seyyit Han Toprağın Gelini / Seyyit Han The Bride of the Earth* (1968), exposing the tragedy awaiting the rural woman who sacrifices her happiness for the honour of her family, were very successful.

Atıf Yılmaz (Batıbeki) combined **comedy** with local legends and folklore to thwart censorship in depicting village reality. The state was lenient to 'village literature' but very harsh to its equivalent in cinema, as is the case in countries with a low literacy rate. **Yılmaz** made some of the most memorable films of Turkish cinema, often using parables and allegory, the only means of political expression in repressive regimes (as was evidenced in the cinemas of the former Iron Curtain countries during the USSR period).

Traditionally, village films had their own patterns and stock characters. The old defended the customs and traditions, and belief in God and were rarely involved in action (*İsyancılar / The Rebels*, Abdurrahman Palay, 1966). The middle-aged remained passive. The youth was naïve, honest, and hard-working, accepting his fate, just like the older generation, but when threatened he could grab his gun and turn into a hero like a typical western cowboy. He often fought against nature – hunger, draught, sickness, flood – and bad people. Woman suffered more. Her tribulations began at adolescence and ended at death. If she was beautiful (and she was always beautiful in films, with heavy make-up), she attracted men. When her man did not return from the war, or from Germany, she became prey to bad characters. The one who was between the young and old and carried the characteristics of both was the 'fool', identified as 'retarded' or 'deranged'. Shabbily dressed and often lame, but with strong human qualities, he brought comic relief to **melodramas**. He protected and aided the lovers, played *saz* (traditional string instrument) and sang folk songs. With his particular cunning, he could expose the dark dealings of the bad ones (*Beyaz Mendil / The White Handkerchief*, **Akad**, 1955). The bad could easily be identified through their mannerisms, language and clothing; they were the cowards who depended on guns, power and money to rob, rape, and slaughter. They often acted in groups. Sometimes, the line was very thin between the good and the bad. The village boy could become a bandit when he had no alternative. Certain village films (***Hudutların Kanunu / The Law of the Borders***, **Akad**, 1966; *Ağıt / Elegy*, **Güney**, 1971) presented positive out-laws. Among the secondary characters were the 'outsiders', usually from the city; the males deceived and deserted innocent maidens and the females destroyed families by seducing the husbands. The 'foreigners' from the West (*Bir Türk'e Gönül Verdim / I Gave My Heart to a Turk*, **Halit Refiğ**, 1969) could adapt to village life and stay, whereas those who arrived with their ideals (doctors, lawyers, teachers) were not very successful. The village was presented only through its functional spaces, the main road to show arrivals – workers returning from Germany, bandits, bad guys of the landlord – or departures – eloping lovers. Winding alleys were for clandestine rendezvous. The final action scene used these alleys, gardens and rooftops. The village square was where wedding processions passed, bloody confrontations took place and the hero died. The village café was the heart of the village, where the news or gossip was heard and verbal challenges were made. The village was surrounded by fields, streams, forests and mountains, each of which had a function in the narrative. The seemingly peaceful village life was always threatened by blood feuds, property conflicts, rapes, exploitation and inequalities that were ready to explode and they did explode (Scognamillo 1973b: 34–9).

In the 2000s–10s, cinema has turned the camera once again on the village by urban film-makers, often of provincial origin, who seem to feel nostalgic about pure open spaces and severed roots, identified with the mother in several films. In *Sonbahar / Autumn* (**Özcan Alper**, 2008) the protagonist, released from jail, returns home to spend his last days with his mother. In *Yumurta / Egg* (**Semih Kaplanoğlu**, 2007), Yusuf returns to his natal village for the funeral of his mother. *Pandora'nın Kutusu / Pandora's Box* (**Yeşim Ustaoğlu**, 2008) is also about the return to rural roots in search of values lost in the city although **Ustaoğlu's** perspective is more confrontational. *Vizontele* (**Yılmaz Erdoğan, Ömer Faruk Sorak**, 2001) is a modern village **comedy** that includes even the fool, Deli Emin (crazy Emin), the inventor who does what the others cannot do.

Vizontele (2001), based on the childhood memories of **Yılmaz Erdoğan**, is a film about the link between mimetic representation tools – radio, cinema and television – and the societal milieu. It focuses on the arrival of television in Hakkari in 1974, five years after the official transmittance, a time that corresponds to the start of the military operation in Cyprus. The officials from the capital Ankara bring the television set but do not explain how it is used. They leave the responsibility to the mayor, who considers it his duty to find a solution to beat his political opponent, the operator of the cinema hall. The town already has a megaphone and the telephone, but the latter alienates them rather than bringing them together, as shown in the amusing scene when the mayor tries to speak with his son in the army but is speechless. The radio is repaired, but no one listens to it except Deli Emin's (crazy Emin) (**Yılmaz Erdoğan**) dead mother; Emin runs to the graveyard each time her favourite song is on, but the song usually ends before he arrives. At the end, he connects the graveyard with cables and instals a megaphone. Cinema is part of social life but unlike the urban custom of sitting in chairs in a theatre, it is watched from balconies and treetops while eating, lying down or chatting. As people are not knowledgeable about the television, the owner of the cinema hall induces the *imam* to speak against it. When it finally works, ironically, the family see the image of their dead son on the screen, which prompts the mother to bury the television set because if the dead are not buried properly, they appear as ghosts.

With its popular cast and memorable scenes that create a tragi-comic atmosphere, the film received three awards at the Antalya Golden Orange Film Festival and broke box-office records with 3.5 million spectators. A sequel was made by **Erdoğan** alone, *Vizontele Tuuba* (2004), foregrounding the atmosphere of anarchy in the summer of 1980 just before the 12 September 1980 *coup* when the right and left factions with unclear agendas were divided within themselves.

Directors: **Yılmaz Erdoğan**, **Ömer Faruk Sorak**; Producer: **Yılmaz Erdoğan**, Necati Akpınar, Beşiktaş Kültür Merkezi; Screenwriter: **Yılmaz Erdoğan**; Cinematography: **Ömer Faruk Sorak**; Music: Kardeş Türküler; Cast: **Yılmaz Erdoğan**, **Cem Yılmaz**, Tolga Çevik, Erkan Can, Cezmi Baskın, Şafak Sezer, Demet Akbağ, Yeşim Salkım

Vurun Kahpeye / Strike the Whore (1949), the first film of **Lütfi Ö. Akad**, adapted from Halide Edip Adıvar's novel, is one of the early examples of serious Turkish cinema during a period of transition from the monopoly of the theatre to a search for cinematic language. It is also the first film on the war of independence since **Muhsin Ertuğrul**'s *Bir Millet Uyanıyor / A Nation is Awakening* (1932). *Strike the Whore* is noteworthy for foregrounding a positive woman protagonist, a progressive teacher in a small Anatolian village, who struggles against backwardness and religious fundamentalism. Aliye (**Sezer Sezin**) represents the idealist-enlightened woman of the Kemalist generation, patriotic but also feminine, ready to die for her country and for the man she loves. The idealist woman teacher is not new to Turkish cinema, but here the values of the republic are consecrated through her body, as evidenced in her speech while taking her oath: 'Your earth is my earth, your home is my home; I will be the mother and the guiding light

Figure 131 Vurun Kahpeye / Strike the Whore (Lütfi Ö. Akad, 1949) (Courtesy of International Istanbul Film Festival)

Figure 132 Vurun Kahpeye / Strike the Whore (Lütfi Ö. Akad, 1949) (Courtesy of International Istanbul Film Festival)

for this place and for your children. I will fear nothing'. Unfortunately, she falls victim to the conspiracies of the fanatic local *imam*, who provokes the villagers to lynch her for treason. The public square, which traditionally reflects the culture, values and beliefs of the society as a place of gathering becomes the locus of social hysteria and Aliye's life is sacrificed for the new values she represents.

The film was never officially censored, but Islamist extremists stopped the projection in many areas of Anatolia. With the aid of Fondation Groupama Gan, *Strike the Whore* was restored and shown during the 29th Istanbul Film Festival, 2010.

Director: **Lütfi Ö. Akad**; Producer: Hürrem Erman, Hasan Erman; Production: Erman Film; Screenwriter: **Akad**, Selahattin Küçük (based on a novel by Halide Edip Adıvar); Cinematographer: Lâzar Yazıcıoğlu; Editor: **Akad**, Ömer Sermet; Sound: **Yorgo İlyadis**; Music: Sadi Işılay; Cast: **Sezer Sezin**, Kemal Tanrıöver, Settar Körmükçü, Arşavir Alyanak, Mahmure Handan, Vedat Örfi Bengü, Temel Karamahmut, Nurdoğan Öztürk

W

War films and historical action films were popular when the family was the principal spectator. *Bir Millet Uyanıyor / A Nation is Awakening* (**Muhsin Ertuğrul**, 1932) was the prototype of War of Independence films. When Turkey as a NATO ally sent troops to Korea, a number of Korean War films were made (*Kore'de Türk Kahramanları / Turkish Heroes in Korea*, Seyfi Havaeri, 1951), the popularity of which encouraged the producers to invest in the **genre**, covering diverse periods from the Ottoman era to the War of Independence. Cyprus films were also established in this period, but intensified after the invasion of the island in 1974 in the atmosphere of exalted nationalist fervour (*Önce Vatan / First the Homeland* (unofficial English translation), **Duygu Sağıroğlu**, 1974).

Historical action films with fantastic elements, which presented superheroes in the style of cartoon characters, casting the same actors in similar roles to facilitate audience identification, were popular in the 1960s–70s. Prominent film-makers, **Memduh Ün, Yılmaz Duru, Çetin İnanç, Yılmaz Atadeniz, Cüneyt Arkın, Yücel Çakmaklı, Metin Erksan** and **Halit Refiğ** contributed to the trend (Onaran 1994: 180). Malkoçoğlu (a sixteenth-century war hero), Kara Murat (a loyal fighter in the court of Sultan Mehmet, the Conqueror) and Battal Gazi (veteran Battal, a legendary folk hero of the eighth century, reputed to have led the Arab forces in their attempt to conquer Constantinople) were all played by **Cüneyt Arkın**. Tarkan (created in 1967 and not placed in a particular period) and Karaoğlan were played by **Kartal Tibet** (Maktav 2006: 71–83). These heroes fought unknown enemies with fascistic chauvinism; violence was justified by the initial aggression of the enemy – massacre, torture, rape or insult to honour. The three ideologies, nationalism, conservatism and Islamism have been at the core of these films, with the contemporary version, the controversial *Kurtlar Vadisi / Valley of the Wolves* television series, the film, ***Kurtlar Vadisi Irak / Valley of the Wolves, Iraq*** (**Serdar Akar**, 2005) and its sequels, following the same formula.

Levent Şekerci's *Nefes: Vatan Sağolsun / The Breath* (2009), dealing with the civil war with the Kurdish guerrillas from the point of view of the soldiers trapped by the rebels, took third place with 2.4 million ticket sales at the box-office and received positive reviews from the local press. Three films on the Battle of Gallipoli made within a year were disappointments: *Çanakkale Çocukları / The Children of Gallipoli* (**Sinan Çetin**, 2012), *Çanakkale 1915 / Gallipoli 1915*

(Yeşim Sezgin, 2013) and *Çanakkale Yolun Sonu / End of the Road* (**Serdar Akar**, Kemal Uzun, Ahmet Kahraman, 2013).

Weinberg, Sigmund (b. 1868 – d. ?) Director, screenwriter, cinematographer, photographer, merchant. The pioneer of cinema (and gramophone) in Turkey, who projected films in the Palace of the Sultan and in schools, opened the first cinema hall in continuous operation, made short films, tried his hand at features and was involved in theatre, Sigmund Weinberg has become a myth as little is known about his past and his life after he was expelled from the country as a Polish Jew of Romanian nationality during the war between Romania and the Ottoman Empire (Scognamillo 1990: 19).

As the local agent of the French company, Pathé Brothers, Sigmund Weinberg opened the first movie theatre in 1908 in the Pera district (Beyoğlu) and called it Cinema-Théatre Pathé Fréres. He was appointed as the head of the Merkez Ordu Sinema Dairesi/MOSD (Central Army Office of Cinema), founded in 1915. In 1916, with the equipment of the army, he began to shoot the fiction film, *Leblebici Horhor Ağa / Horhor Agha, The Chickpea Seller* adapted from Armenian Dikran Chuhaciyan's operatta staged in 1875, but stopped when one of the leading actors died. The shooting of his first feature film, ***Himmet Ağanın İzdivacı / The Marriage of Himmet Agha*** (1916), was also suspended when most actors were recruited to serve in the War of Dardanelles and completed in 1918 by Reşat Rıdvan with **Fuat Uzkınay** as cinematographer according to Nurullah Tilgen (Scognamillo 1990: 26) and with **Uzkınay** as director according to historian **Nijat Özön** (Özön 1970: 14–16).

Y

Yaşar, Fehmi (b. Kahramanmaraş, 1954) Director, screenwriter, producer, actor. Fehmi Yaşar worked with notable film-makers such as **Yılmaz Güney**, **Zeki Ökten** and **Şerif Gören** as assistant and screenwriter before making his first and only feature, *Camdan Kalp / A Heart of Glass* (1990), the drama of an urban intellectual whose efforts to enter the psyche of the easterners is his tragedy. Disappointed when the film was not successful at the box-office despite awards at film festivals, he gave up cinema to open *Hayal Kahvesi / Dream Cafe* that became the favourite locale of the film community, which he expanded to a chain of cafes around Istanbul. The films he wrote the screenplay for are *Faize Hücum / The Rush On Interest* (1983), *Pehlivan / The Wrestler* (1984) and *Ses / Voice* (1986) by **Zeki Ökten**, *Bir Yudum Sevgi / A Taste Of Love* aka *A Sip of Love* (1984) by **Atıf Yılmaz** and his own, *A Heart of Glass*.

Yavuz, Yüksel (b. Karakocan/Elazığ, 1964) Director, screenwriter. A transnational film-maker of Kurdish origin, Yüksel Yavuz joined his parents in Germany when he was 16. In Hamburg, he studied economics and politics, then cinema. His documentary, *Mein Vater, der Gastarbeiter / Yabancı İşçi Babam / My Father, the Guest-worker* (1994) was chosen as the Best Film at the International Documentary Film Festival in Munich. His first feature, *Aprilkinder / Nisan Çocukları / April Children* (1998) is a portrait of a Kurdish family struggling between the old and new worlds with their three children, all conceived during the father's summer holidays in Turkey. *Kleine Freiheit / Küçük Özgürlük / A Little Bit of Freedom* (2003), a small-budget film about an inter-ethnic relationship – the friendship between a Kurd and an African – is set in Hamburg's immigrant district of Altona, capturing the reality of young illegal immigrants with a visual style that conveys an authentic sense of instability, loss and solitude. The three languages spoken in *A Little Bit of Freedom* – Turkish, German and Kurdish – accentuate the issue of multiple identities, while the film raises questions regarding the meaning of home. *Close-up: Kurdistan* (2007) is a documentary.

Yazı Tura / Toss Up (2004) is a film about men whose identities are in conflict with their society. The subject of traumatized war veterans is not a novelty for Hollywood, but *Toss Up* is exceptional for Turkey for lifting the shroud of nationalism and showing the stark reality of a civil war without heroes.

Figure 133 Yazı Tura / Toss Up (Uğur Yücel, 2004) (Courtesy of International Istanbul Film Festival)

In 1999, Rıdvan the Devil (Olgun Şimşek), a soccer player from Central Anatolia, returns from the war against the Kurdish guerrillas with one leg missing; in the same explosion, Cevher the Ghost (Kenan İmirzalıoğlu) from Istanbul has become deaf in one ear. Both are bitter and angry in their failure to find their place in a masculinist society exposed in the film through all-male cafés and bars, collective alcohol and drug abuses, the presence of knives, switch-blades and guns and the equation of power with sexual prowess. In a world of the survival of the fittest, cripples, even war veterans, are considered a nuisance.

The issues of masculine identity in a patriarchal society oppressed by societal pressures is perpetuated through generations. Cevher's father deserted Tsula, the Greek woman he loved, and their son Teo with pressure from his friends during the Cyprus war. The earthquake, which kills the uncle, wounds the father and destroys the cafe, is the breaking point. Saving his father is like a catharsis for Cevher, who is now faced with another dilemma, a gay Greek half-brother who arrives from Greece with his mother. Despite his revulsion, Cevher kills two men to protect his brother; the only human act he performs is murder. When arrested, he says 'I am a war veteran. I fought for you. I have medals.' No one cares.

The film is shot on digital video (DV) in *cinema verité* style that objectively records the two veteran's lives with jump-cuts from past to present and from Göreme to Istanbul. The images of the peasants travelling with chickens on buses, women gazing inconspicuously at Rıdvan returning home as a cripple and Rıdvan sensing their pity, his mother's attempt at taking his arm and his agitation, the humiliation shared by mother and son as she baths him like a child and the macho Cevher's terror when bullied by those he cannot bully, are powerful. **Yücel** somehow loses momentum in the second half when the historical animosity between Greece and Turkey is unexpectedly introduced to the narrative ('This is my house,' Teo claims, 'these are my toys'), which was already explosive with the Kurdish issue. The issue of gay identity is also questionable as a contributing factor to the narrative development.

The film garnered 11 awards at the 41st Antalya Golden Orange Film Festival, including the Best Film and several other awards from Istanbul, Ankara and Adana Film Festivals and the Fipresci (Federation of International Film Critics) prize at the Mannheim–Heidelberg Film Festival in Germany, reaching around 260,000 viewers in Turkey.

Director, Screenwriter: **Uğur Yücel**; Producers: Hakkı Göçeoğlu, **Uğur Yücel**, Defne Kayalar, Haris Padouvas; Production: Mahayanafilm, Cinegram; Cinematographer: Barış Özbiçer, Emre Tanyıldız, Tayfun Çetindağ, Roy Kurtluyan; Editor: Valdis Oskarsdottir; Music: Erkan Oğur; Cast: Olgun Şimşek, Kenan İmirzalıoğlu, Bahri Beyat, Eli Mango, Engin Günaydin, Teoman Kumbaracıbaşıoğlu, Erkan Can

Yazgı / Fate (2001), the first film in **Zeki Demirkubuz**'s 'Tales About Darkness' trilogy is loosely based on Albert Camus's novel, *L'Étranger / The Stranger* (1942), with a fairly altered story although the intertextuality with Dostoyevsky is a common underlying element in both works. The Dostoyevskyan notion of freedom and the consciousness of freedom as sources of suffering that may cease at the cost of human suffering, is integral to the work of Camus, which is in the spirit of debate and dialogue with Dostoyevsky, challenging Dostoyevsky with the possibility of a new positive absurd hero and humanist politics of freedom and justice. The protagonist Musa is a clerk in a custom's office who is neither happy nor unhappy. Just like Camus's Meursault, he lives in a state of anomie, unable to show any emotion even at his mother's sudden death. He is even relieved. He marries the office secretary when she asks him and ignores her affair with the boss. Struggling to find meaning where there is no meaning is absurd. He is a stranger confronted with the absurdity of his life, but society reacts by imposing meanings on the stranger. If one does not play the game, one is condemned, as Camus noted in the preface of the 1955 edition of his book; refusing to lie complicates life.

Demirkubuz sets his film within the socio-political realities of Turkey. Musa is an archetype of the average citizen, apoliticized in the aftermath of several military interventions. He lives between home and work without questioning the reasons behind the way things are. When his neighbour (fashioned after Raymond in Camus's novel) asks him to write a letter to lure his girlfriend to his home with the idea of 'teaching her a lesson', he agrees to avoid confrontation without reflecting on the consequences of the action on the woman; he even lies on behalf of the neighbour. Arrested for someone else's crime, Musa does not defend himself. Why fight injustice when one has no confidence in the justice system? Violence and misery have become routine with the invasion of the private space by the television screens. While Musa watches the screen without emotion, **Demirkubuz**'s camera shifts to the window and the poor searching for food in the garbage appear as a blurred image, which is not noticed by Musa.

The film is shot in a minimalist fashion with very little movement of the camera. It starts with Musa opening the door to his apartment and turning on the light and ends with him shutting the door and the lights going out. The door is an essential trope in the films of **Demirkubuz** as well as **Nuri Bilge Ceylan**. It appears as an object that exists in connection with what is inside and what is outside. It may forbid the street, or it may forbid the room in a system of traditions and prohibitions. In the long final episode, before his release from prison, Musa is obliged to endure an unofficial interrogation by the head warden, which connects with the opening scene of *Innocence / Masumiyet* (1997), but also alludes to the 'Grand Inquisitor' chapter in *The Brothers Karamazov* of Dostoyevsky. The door of the office refuses to close despite several attempts by the warden. Does it represent his wish to 'normalize' the Musas of the world to act like everyone else, to believe in God (or keep it a secret, if otherwise), express sorrow at funerals and happiness when exonerated for crimes they did not commit? Or Musa's desire to escape to his absurd world, which he equates with freedom?

Director, Producer, Screenwriter, Editor: **Zeki Demirkubuz**; Production: Mavi Film; Cinematographer: Ali Utku; Cast: Serdar Orçin, Zeynep Tokuş, Engin Günaydın, Demir Karahan

Yeşilçam, the cinematic style popular from the 1950s to the end of the 1970s, is one of the few styles that have been so much subject of critical derision (perhaps another one is Bollywood). Until the change of the scholarly tide in the 2000s, **Yeşilçam** was dismissed by films scholars, critics and intelligentsia as escapist, kitsch and artificial. Popular cinema is once again dominant in Turkey, providing a useful site for the negotiation of cultural meaning and values and inviting the vast mass of moviegoers to participate in the on-going conversation of cultural modernities. Born in a period of political populism during the Democrat Party (DP) reign (1950–60) and the establishment of the rural Anatolian capital endorsing its own culture, Yeşilçam, as in the model of Bollywood explored by film scholar Wimal Dissanayake, is best understood within the boundaries of cultural modernity. The socio-economic discourse – urbanization, industrialization, massification, expansion of transport, proliferation of technology and the emergence of consumer culture; the cognitive discourse on instrumental rationality to understand society; political dimensions of modernity and most importantly the discourse of experientiality and participation in modernity foregrounding issues of new perspectives demanded by the evolving contexts of living and sensory experience, are essential in understanding popular cinema, which reflects the ways in which movie-goers become both objects and subjects of the process of cultural modernization (Dissanayake 2003: 202). With the emergence of the *nouveau riche* class (usually of provincial roots) that followed the move to capitalism, going to the cinema lost its prestige as a social event for the elite class like other Western cultural activities – theatre or opera – where one arrived in long gowns and with specially printed tickets. The new spectator (caricaturized in **Yeşilçam** movies as snoring at the operas) transported their traditional identity and expected from cinema what they were accustomed to receive from the bards, the troubadours and the storytellers of yesterday. The increased internal migration and the profitable market in Anatolia urged the industry to consider the masses rather than an elite audience when choosing the scripts. For the producers, cinema was not a tool for art and culture but a means of entertainment with the aim of financial profit. In the absence of a model to meet the growing audience demand, time to reflect or the capital to invest, the industry was moulded according to the wishes of the spectator, who wanted the values of the accustomed folk culture to be preserved with its common heroes and common values that could apply to everyone all the time. The balance/imbalance/return-to-balance sequence of the narrative was cathartic. The producers did not question history, society or politics and the directors and actors followed during a period when the repercussions of the international Cold War reached Turkey, and curbing of different expressions or tendencies, individual or collective, was the norm.

From the beginning, **Yeşilçam** directly or obliquely addressed the concept of community. Nationalism, in general, is fed on imagined communitarian ideals. The interconnection between notions of secularism, nationalism, and community can be transferred to commercially oriented cinemas such as Yeşilçam, be they patriotic, nationalist, satirical or parodic. The glorification of the past that was manifest in the *Karaoğlan* films of the 1960s is repeated with *Fetih 1453 / The Conquest 1453* (Faruk Aksoy, 2012) as an outcome of the essentialities and angsts of modernity. Although popular cinema cannot be equated with cultural nationalism, scholar Wimal Dissanayake maintains that cinema, 'which is a metonym of modernity, has played a crucial role in the recrudescence of cultural nationalism' (Dissanayake 2003: 222).

Yeşilçam generally ignored the ethnic mosaic of the country in favour of the official state policy of assimilation and Turkification. Until the 1990s, the Kurd was the ignorant dark man from the mountain, devoted to his master. The presentation of non-Muslims carried an 'inferential' racism, their accents or mannerisms often intended as a mild joke. They were rarely given a name; the women were called 'Madame' and were often hired as instructors of Western manners, or as seamstresses. Or they operated brothels or guest-houses. Greek characters were usually old men (often fishermen) that the family would adopt as 'uncle', or spinsters for some obscure reason. The Jewish characters were connected with small commerce. This stereotypical stand was not completely fabricated. In real life, many Armenian women of limited means were hired as governesses, many families did have an old Greek/Armenian neighbour their children called 'uncle' (such as Agor Amca in *Bir Kırık Bir Bebek / A Broken Doll*, **Nisan Akman**, 1987) and many Jewish men were shopkeepers. The only non-Muslims that the Muslim population in general had some contact with were these 'assimilated' ones. The non-Muslims existed only when they were like us.

Yeşilçam endorsed the state ideology in glorifying the army. The soldiers in their uniforms were handsome and romantic, although their soldier identity superseded their romantic identity. If an honourable Turkish man (a soldier, a civil policeman) fell in love with a subversive element (a spy, a Kurdish rebel), he never sacrificed his duty for love. Instead, the women changed identities, embracing Muslim/Turkish identity. The Turkish man was the saviour. He could even marry these women – after Turkifying them – as they were not bad, but rather victims of bad fate.

Yeşilçam supported the rural culture and oral traditions. It had anonymous characteristics and a system of hierarchy that did not allow for diverse opinions or expressions. In a convenient manner to avoid taking a stand, it was abstracted from the realities of daily life by hiding behind narratives where space, time, characters and the narrative were not topical (Ayça 2000: 6–8).

One of the representational strategies of Yeşilçam, which can be connected with the traditional Turkish aesthetic forms, is the frontality of the performer vis-à-vis the spectator, which in the earlier open theatres indicated a specific relationship between the viewer and the actor, a sign that they both existed – as actor and audience. The diegetic inserts of the song sequences were calculated to appeal to the masses and carried certain erotic nuances that could escape the censors, but had other significances similar to dance sequences in popular Hindi films, which 'introduce interesting ambivalences of feeling and thought...in the unfolding of the narrative the lead woman character may be portrayed as submissive, traditional, innocent, and coy while her dance sequences allow her a greater freedom and to celebrate her body and acquire a sense of agency...In popular films, female characters are often delineated as stereotypes, earning the opprobrium of critics. However, in the dance performances the initial contradictions, the self-divided nature of stereotypes are foregrounded, generating both assurance and anxiety. Two areas of particular interest in dance sequences are the parameters of performative space and the complicated relationship between the performer and the spectator' (Dissanayake 2003: 220).

A typical **Yeşilçam** movie would set the binaries as 'here' and 'there'. 'Here' was the deracinated young man, poor but honest, the economic migrant to the city. He lived in the outskirts with people like himself, in 'the remembered village in a new guise' reviving 'the old community ties in new forms' (Nandy 1998: 6). 'There' was downtown Beyoğlu, the cradle of evil, where people were degenerate and values slippery. The young man earned his living working from dawn to dusk; in Beyoğlu life began after dark. The biggest threat to a man's integrity was the woman. The **Lütfü Ö. Akad** classic, *Vesikalı Yarim / My Licensed Love* (1968) is the most successful rendition of this formula.

Split identity was very common, which somehow betrayed Yeşilçam's conception of national identity that echoed the official ideology of One State–One Nation–One History–One Religion. In a 1970s movie, **Hülya Koçyiğit**, one of the coveted stars of the period, is cast as triplets: a femme-fatale, a retarded woman and a *lumpen*, plus the shrill voice of a deserted wife on the phone. Mistaken identity, not indigenous to Turkey, was a fascination. A poor Anatolian boy would fall in love with a rich city girl thinking she is the maid – a necessary device to prove the lower class hero is not a fortune-chaser. She would renounce her privileged social status for love, but not before the preparation of the audience with a mutually hostile stereotyping between the educated urban bourgeois and the agrarian peasant or proletariat.

Yeşilçam reflected human relations in the same manner as they were conducted in the socio-economic structure of Turkey. The dependence on foreign elements rather than national resources and the lack of a firm stand resulted in an impasse at the micro level for cinema and the macro level for the country. The government changes, the military interventions, the changes in laws and regulations affected the cinema sector, which failed to become an industry, staying in the hands of the middleman and the importers. The producers were exploited by the distributors; the theatre owners had to resort to the star system for survival. Since the producers did not re-invest in the industry, capital was not accumulated (Vedat Türkali 2001). The arrival of television (1968), the gradual multiplication of free channels, the video furore, the political climate in the country and the dilapidated condition of the cinema halls, could all be cited as factors that aided the decline of **Yeşilçam** that in its heyday was producing almost 300 films annually. With its decline at the end of the 1970s, the industry returned to a situation similar to the one experienced at the beginning. Foreign films, this time American, took over, Hollywood hegemony leaving little room for a national cinema to develop. Many film companies tried soft-porno and kung-fu films to regain the audience, but alienated the family and the women, who had constituted the largest part.

Perhaps a certain naiveté reflecting the spirit of the epoch when ideals still existed is the nostalgic attraction of **Yeşilçam** after decades.

Yılmaz, Atıf (see **Batıbeki**)

Yılmaz, Cem (b. Istanbul, 1973) Director, screenwriter, producer, actor. Starting as a cartoonist, in 1995, Cem Yılmaz began to run stand-up **comedy** shows at cultural centres. He starred in *Herşey Çok Güzel Olacak / Everything's Gonna Be Great* (**Ömer Vargı**, 1998), *Vizontele* (**Yılmaz Erdoğan**, **Ömer Faruk Sorak**,

Figure 134 Hokkabaz / The Magician (Cem Yılmaz, Ali Taner Baltacı 2006) (Courtesy of International Istanbul Film Festival)

2001) and *G.O.R.A* (**Sorak**, 2004), which he also scripted. Scripting his first film *Hokkabaz / The Magician* (2006), co-directing it with Ali Taner Baltacı and acting in it, he attracted more than one million viewers. A *road movie*, which was the third on the list of the 'most watched films' in 2006, having earned $9.3 million at the box-office, the film was also praised by local critics.

Yılmaz, Güney (see **Pütün**)

Yılmaz, Serra (b. Istanbul, 1954) Actor. A transnational actor of stage and cinema, Serra Yılmaz is at ease with Italian **melodramas** or Turkish fantastic tales; there is hardly a **Ferzan Özpetek** film without her appearing in a big or small role in it. Among her other noteworthy appearances at home are *9* (2002), *Ses / Voice* (2010) and *Nar / Pomegranate* (2011) of **Ümit Ünal**.

Yol / The Way (1982), written by **Yılmaz Güney** in prison, shot by **Şerif Gören** according to **Güney**'s instructions and edited in Paris, underscores state oppression where the society has become a panopticon (Foucault 1995: 216). The oppression of the military regime and the embedded feudalism that control and rule the lives of all citizens are exposed through the parallel stories of five prisoners on leave, underscoring the double disadvantage of the underprivileged and ethnic minorities such as the Kurdish people.

The film begins with a group of men receiving mail at a half-open prison on an island, a microcosm for the society outside. Permissions for temporary leave have been frozen after the military *coup* of 1980, but there has been some hope recently. The list of those allowed to visit their families during the approaching religious holiday is posted and it creates a different kind of anxiety for the chosen. The naïve Yusuf from Antep, who entered the prison as an adolescent, is taking his canary along as a present to his wife; his countryman Mevlüt knows that she is dead, but one cannot give bad news in prison. Mehmet Salih (Halil Ergün), a driver by profession, is morally responsible for the death of his brother-in-law during an aborted armed robbery. The bachelor Ömer, an introvert young Kurd from a smugglers' village on the Syrian border, is dreaming of his horse and the pastures of his village and does not plan to return to the prison. The pensive Seyit Ali (**Tarık Akan**), another Kurd, is on a voyage of pain and hatred to punish his unfaithful wife Ziné (**Şerif Sezer**) to cleanse the family honour.

Yusuf, held at a checkpoint and returned to prison for lack of necessary papers never learns of the death of his wife; Mevlüt is trapped inside archaic feudal customs; Ömer's idyllic village is surrounded by the gendarmes; Memet Salih is rejected when he confesses his cowardice to his wife's family. Seyit Ali is in a dilemma of love, pity, hatred, revenge and duty as understood from his conversation with Memet Salih on the train. Through almost impenetrable snow, he reaches the village. Instead of killing his wife, he devises a crueller plan: to leave her to the elements of nature for god to accomplish the deed. Although his conscience overrides at the end, it is too late. With her thin clothes and weak body that had not seen the light for eight months, she is already frozen in the blizzard in front of her son.

Figure 135 Yol / The Way (Şerif Gören, 1982) (Courtesy of International Istanbul Film Festival)

Yol is thematically multi-layered. State oppression, particularly during the military dictatorship, is underlined subtly with whispered dialogues of torture and silently observed episodes at the checkpoints and on the town streets that display the pictures of Kenan Evren, the general responsible for the *coup* (who has been compared to Pinochet), placed next to that of Kemal Atatürk, the founder of the Turkish Republic. The poverty, which increases as you go further east, is documented unsparingly with the view of the slums of Diyarbakır, an essentially Kurdish city, where the children who sell *simit* (Turkish pretzel) fight to have a turn on a rental bike (a reference to ***Umut / The Hope*, Güney**, 1970) and puff cigarette butts even as young as six or seven. Little boys who should be at school sing a few songs on the buses for a piece of bread. The poverty in the countryside is ten-fold. 'Smuggling is over now', says one man who does not know how else to earn a living, 'and if you are a Kurd, you are finished.'

Women and honour is a strong theme in *Yol*; the rural woman is born a slave and dies a slave. Ziné's 'crime' is not clear; whether she could not resist temptation and has become a 'fallen woman' during her husband's incarceration is not revealed in the film. Her sister-in-law shows pity but will not accept the gold chain Ziné offers because it is *haram* (religiously forbidden as opposed to *halal*), probably acquired for selling her body. Conditioned by men to accept the patriarchal rule, she tells Ziné her life is in the hands of her husband. Ziné has no choice. Her father warns Seyit Ali: 'For eight months, she is tied with a chain like a dog. For eight months, she did not see the light. It is *haram* for her. For eight months, not a drop of water touched her body. That is what she deserves. ... Şeytan (Satan)! She thinks she will evoke your pity. Don't let your heart soften, don't let your hand tremble; wipe this mud off our face; don't you ever pity her' (Dönmez-Colin 2004: 48).

Mevlut's adventures are the moments of comic relief in the otherwise deeply tragic film. His reaction to the constant chaperoning of his courtship with his fiancée by two female relatives in black *chadors* pushes him to a *meyhane* (a male bar) and a brothel, where, ironically, the prostitute's room number corresponds to his cell number. On the wall, beside the rules and regulations, the price, the caution to use a condom, is written, 'God's word is the deed', a common Muslim expression.

Mehmet and his wife, escaping the vengeful family with their children, board the train but they are shamed by the crowd when caught making love in the washroom. 'Immoral microbes! Infidels!' shout the men ready to lynch them. While in police custody, they are killed in front of their children by her youngest brother. Ömer is obliged to marry his brother's widow and father his children; the dreams of his beloved horse and a young girl he noticed on the way are shattered. No one asks the opinion of the women.

Yet, *Yol* is not a film without hope. Unlike traditional **rural melodramas** that structure the narrative around the highest-ranking male of the family, usually the father, **Güney** exposes the disintegration of the system. As the father in ***Sürü / The Herd*** (**Zeki Ökten**, 1978) is a raging bull helpless against the societal changes that gradually weaken the patriarchy, Ziné's father, who endorses her death sentence, is a blind old man with one foot in the grave. Seyit Ali's remorse after his wife's death is the melting of the ice; Ömer's decision to combat oppression is already advancement and the courage displayed by Memed Salih to admit truth despite losses is significant. The film does not have the schematic progressive elements in the classic sense, but there is a sign of forward change, which is the result of the changes within the characters, the 'individual inner conflict' between the old and the new and the positive and negative that makes a society evolve (Rothik 1994: 291).

The first Turkish film, according to **Güney**, which uses Kurdish songs and dialogue, *Yol* was banned in Turkey for 17 years after sharing the Golden Palm at the Cannes Film Festival with *Missing* of Costa Gavras. The audiences in Turkey saw *Yol* on 12 February 1999 with the subtitle *Kurdistan* that accompanies the shot of Ömer kissing his homeland when he descends from the bus, erased.

Director: **Şerif Gören**; Producer, Screenwriter: **Yılmaz Güney**; Production: Cactus Film/ Güney Filmcilik; Cinematographer: Erdoğan Engin; Editors: Yılmaz Güney/Elizabeth Waelchli; Music: Sebastian Argol, Kendal; Cast: **Tarık Akan**, **Şerif Sezer**, Halil Ergün, Necmettin Çobanoğlu, Hikmet Celik, Tuncay Akça

Yumurta / Egg (2007) is the first film of the *Yusuf Trilogy* that progresses in reverse chronological order while maintaining the present reality, time and space interacting and fusing in a Bakhtinian sense, time becoming almost visible for contemplation while space is charged and responsive to the movements of time (Bakhtin 1981: 84). The protagonist is an urban poet, severed from his provincial past – personified in the film by his mother and her house. He returns to his natal town for the funeral of his mother and through a young woman who aids him in

Figure 136 Yumurta / Egg (Semih Kaplanoğlu, 2007) (Courtesy of Semih Kaplanoğlu)

his voyage to his self, he learns to face his dilemmas. The egg of the title, which breaks in his hand in a dream earlier, which the little boy, his childhood persona, fails to find, is offered to him by the young woman in the final episode, after he has reconciled with his old friends, his town and his mother in their terms by executing the sacrifice ritual.

The opening shots are that of an elderly woman wearing a headscarf approaching with determined steps; she stops and looks, right and left, the scenery is emptied of her presence, then she appears again walking towards some cypress trees (connected with graveyards in the Muslim tradition). Then the path is emptied of her image again. The next episode is inside a second-hand bookshop, a disorganized space that includes a makeshift bed. A weary male drinks wine. He does not answer the telephone when it rings. A woman's disturbed voice asks him to call home, but before he could do so, a provocative young woman enters the shop (Tülin Özen of *Meleğin Düşüşü / Angel's Fall*, 2004) with a bottle of wine (the camera lingering in close-up on her cleavage) and exchanges it with a cookbook when her charms fail to arouse the man who is distracted by the telephone message. The sounds of a closing shutter, ignition keys, the roaring of

Figure 137 Yumurta / Egg (Semih Kaplanoğlu, 2007) (Courtesy of Semih Kaplanoğlu)

an engine are heard as the titles pass on a black screen and the next image is a metaphoric long tunnel with *ezan* (the call to prayer) chanted softly as if leading him to his destination. By daybreak, he is at a marketplace and following the mellifluous prayers he joins the mourners, the funeral and the graveyard, where the path in the opening scene becomes visible again.

Returning home, Yusuf (Nejat İşler) hears the clattering of china in the kitchen and his eyes catch the white neck of a young woman he has never seen before. Ayla (Saadet Aksoy), a distant cousin, was his mother's companion for several years and she seems to have appointed herself to take care of Yusuf, offering tea at regular intervals, preparing a clean towel and toothbrush for him and trying relentlessly to keep him in town until he comes to terms with his feelings of loss and guilt and receives atonement. If the woman in the bookshop represents temptation (the devil, *shaytan* in Islam) – the low-cut black dress above her knees, the wine bottle – associated with Istanbul, gendered as a prostitute in the **Yeşilçam** tradition, the provincial Ayla is the angel of redemption, or his guardian angel (his *hafaza*). In fact, the film is imbued in religious motifs: the repeated chanting of *ezan*, the funeral rites shown in ethnographic details, the shrine, the ritual of the sacrifice of a ram, again filmed in minute detail, and the smearing of the ram's blood on Yusuf's forehead as his eyes are focused on Ayla, who watches like an angel from a higher position above, and the name of Yusuf as the Islamic version of Prophet Joseph, who was thrown into a well by his brother; in his dreams Yusuf tries to climb out of the well, but does not succeed.

Yusuf's mother created a different image of him, perhaps for her survival in the closed atmosphere of the rural milieu. She gave his poetry book to his friends on his behalf and offered a scarf to Ayla for the religious holiday *Bayram*, which surprises Yusuf. Everyone knows him, but he hardly remembers anyone, including the man he used to help build wells. 'The Well' is a poem in his book, but the inspirations that fed his creativity are forgotten. With the aid of Ayla, he finds a certain peace in the town that moves in its own rhythm. The lawyer is gone to İzmir and will be back the next day, the herd is gone grazing. Even when the windshield wipers of his car are broken and he can guess that the electrician who is an admirer of Ayla is the culprit, he is not angry. They take the trip with Ayla to a shrine, passing through his once favorite place, Gölcük with a beautiful lake, old aunts who mistake them for a couple and a wedding party that he watches with curiosity, Ayla observing him from a distance. He leaves Ayla at the door of the house before driving back to Istanbul; she is still worried because despite performing the ritual of the sacrifice, his atonement has not yet been accomplished. Stopping beside the road in exhaustion, Yusuf enters green fields with the soothing bells of the herd in the distance. In the dark, a shepherd's dog jumps on him and he falls. When he comes to himself they face each other for a while and he begins to cry; his catharsis has come. In the next episode, he is back at his mother's home, having breakfast with appetite, his guardian angel pouring him tea with a mischievous smile on her face.

The film received numerous national and international awards including the Golden Tulip for Best Film and the People's award at the 27th International Istanbul Film Festival and the Best Film and five other awards at the 44th Antalya Golden Orange Film Festival.

Director, Producer: **Semih Kaplanoğlu**; Production: Kaplanfilm, Arizona Film, Heimat Film; Screenwriters: **Semih Kaplanoğlu**, Orçun Köksal; Cinematographer: Özgür Eken; Editors: Ayhan Ergürsel, Suzan Hande Güneri, **Semih Kaplanoğlu**; Art Director: Naz Erayda; Sound: Giorgos Mikrogiannakis; Cast: Nejat İşler, Saadet Aksoy, Ufuk Bayraktar, Tülin Özen, Gülçin Santırcıoğlu, Kaan Karabacak, Zehra Kaplanoğlu

Yüce, Seren (b. Istanbul, 1975) Director, screenwriter, producer. A graduate of Bilkent University in Ankara in archaeology, **Seren Yüce** worked on television series and as first assistant to **Özer Kızıltan** in *Takva / Takva – A Man's Fear of God* (2006); **Fatih Akın** in *Auf der Anderen Seite / Yaşamın Kıyısında / The Edge of Heaven* (2007) and **Yeşim Ustaoğlu** in *Pandora'nın Kutusu / Pandora's Box* (2008). With his first feature, *Çoğunluk / Majority* (2010), he won the Lion of the Future – Luigi de Laurentiis award at the Venice Film Festival.

Yücel, Uğur (b. Istanbul, 1957) Actor, director, screenwriter, producer, composer, editor. One of the most popular actors in Turkey, Yücel studied at the Istanbul conservatory and worked with prominent theatre companies before making his directorial debut with a short silent, which he accompanied with percussion instruments. He received acclaim for his roles in *Muhsin Bey / Mr Muhsin* (1987) and *Eskiya / The Bandit* (1996) of **Yavuz Turgul**. He composed the music of *Gemide / On Board* (**Serdar Akar**, 1998) and *Laleli'de Bir Azize / A Madonna in Laleli* (**Kudret Sabancı**, 1998). His directorial debut *Yazı Tura / Toss-Up* (2004), despite several national and international awards, was not successful at the box-office. He tried a more commercial approach with *Hayatımın Kadınısın / You're the Woman of My Life* (2006), a **melodrama** starring **Türkan Şoray**, which went unnoticed. *Ejder Kapanı / Dragon Trap* (2010), about a serial killer modelled on violent Hollywood productions, particularly David Fincher's *Seven*, despite its weak dramatic structure, was number two at the box-office for two weeks due to the popularity of the performers – Yücel and the superstar Kenan İmirzalıoğlu. Yücel made a return to serious cinema with ***Soğuk / Cold***, which premiered at the Berlin Film Festival, 2013.

Z

Zaim(oğlu), Derviş (b. Limasol, Cyprus, 1964) Director, screenwriter, producer. Internationally recognized as one of the forerunners of **New Turkish Cinema** with his 'no budget' debut, *Tabutta Rövaşata / Somersault in a Coffin* (1997), Zaim graduated in economics from Bosphorus University and received his Master's degree in Cultural Studies from Warwick University (UK). He has built his film career on issues of aesthetic confrontations with the past and collective memory as a means of interpreting the present. The overriding theme is conscience. *Filler ve Çimen / Elephants and Grass* (2001) and *Çamur / Mud* (2003) approach two highly political issues, respectively, the criminal organization within the state, identified as 'deep state', and the trauma of the partition of the island of Cyprus on its inhabitants, incidents that were easily erased from the collective memory. Along with Zaim's 2004 documentary, *Paralel Yolculuklar / Parallel Trips*, part of a joint project with the Greek Cypriot Panicos Chrysanthou, *Mud* was the first

Figure 138 Çamur / Mud (Derviş Zaim, 2003) (Courtesy of Derviş Zaim)

to foreground the trauma of the Cypriots victimized as pawns in a political match, the issue of ethnic identity, the paranoia ethos and the personal ethics. Zaim later produced Chrysanthou's feature *Akamas* (2006) about a love affair between a Turkish and a Greek Cypriot and returned to the traumas of the partition in 2010 with *Gölgeler ve Suretler / Shadows and Faces* that focuses on the events leading to the partition.

Zaim has used the traditional art forms of Turkey in content and form to reflect on spatio-temporality in a tetralogy. ***Cenneti Beklerken / Waiting for Heaven*** (2006) is an allegorical period piece on the relationship of the artist with the state that uses the miniature art of the East and the Renaissance art of the West to conceptualize the probable interface between the two forms, which could enrich both. *Nokta / Dot* (2008) on calligraphy, experiments with *ihcam* (writing of calligraphy in one stroke), merging past and present, and hence constructing time and space as an interconnected whole. *Shadows and Faces* (2010) uses shadow play to bring past, present and future simultaneously on screen to reflect on the darker side of human beings (also referring to the shadows which have fallen on the faces of once-friendly neighbours). ***Elephants and Grass*** had already focused on another form of art, water marbling, a form dependent on chance and coincidence (a metaphor for the lives of the characters), although marbling was not at the centre of the narrative. *Devir / Cycle* (2012), shot in documentary style with non-professionals, explores the world of shepherds caught between tradition and modernity. His eighth film is *Balık / Fish* (2013), on the relationship between human beings and nature. Zaim is also the author of an award-winning novel, *Ares Harikalar Diyarında / Ares in Wonderland* (1992).

Figure 139 Nokta / Dot (Derviş Zaim, 2008) (Courtesy of Derviş Zaim)

Figure 140 Zavallılar / The Poor aka *The Suffering Ones* (Yılmaz Güney, Atıf Yılmaz, 1974) (Courtesy of International Istanbul Film Festival)

Zavallılar / The Poor aka ***The Suffering Ones*** (1974) presents prison, a regular trope for entrapment in **Yılmaz Güney**'s films, as a refuge for the poor, unemployed and desperate when the world outside is crueller. The protagonists, Abuzer (**Yılmaz Güney**), Arap (Güven Şengil) and Hacı (Yıldırım Önal) are homeless marginals excluded by society, who beg to remain inside at least until the spring. The film draws on several elements from the usual **Yeşilçam melodramas** – child crime, love for a fallen woman, prison relations – without resorting to **melodrama**. As the audience is informed of the events that led to the men's sentencing, a subtle criticism of the anomalies of a society that gives men no choice but crime emerges. Arap's situation is an indictment of the lack of social security that leads to exploitation of labour; he reacted against the injustice of being used as a guard without pay during a construction with a false promise of a place to open a teahouse once it is completed. Hacı's drama is a strong critique of the capitalist order that contributes to the social malaise of merchandizing women; the prostitute he dreamed of sharing his life double-crossed him. Abuzer's story exposes the consequences of the society's indifference to unprotected minors; as a child, he witnessed his mother murder a man to whom her husband sold her; left on his own, he was pushed to crime. Although the film exposes the inequalities and injustices in society with precision, just like the other socially and politically motivated **Güney** films, it does not preach a solution; it prepares the ground for the audience to find their own answers, which **Güney** claimed was his understanding of revolutionary cinema (Dönmez-Colin 2008: 127).

Güney was imprisoned for hiding anarchist students soon after he started the film in 1972, directing one-third; it was completed three years later with the same actors, by **Atıf Yılmaz**.

Directors, Screenwriters: **Yılmaz Güney**, **Atıf Yılmaz**; Producer: **Yılmaz Güney**; Production: Güney Film; Cinematographer: **Kenan Ormanlar**, Gani Turanlı; Music: Şanar Yurdatapan, Atilla Özdemiroğlu; Cast: **Yılmaz Güney**, Yıldırım Önal, Güven Sengil, Nuran Aksoy, Birtane Güngör, Seden Kızıltunç, Mehmet Şahiner, Hülya Şengül, Kamran Usluer

Zengin Mutfağı / The Kitchen of the Rich (1988), which is based on Vasfı Öngören's titular theatre piece, is a social and political satire that uses Brechtian aesthetics to expose a society caught between military dictatorship and political militarism. The sounds of aircraft, police sirens and barking dogs in the opening scene, heard from the confines of a basement kitchen, is an exordium to two decades of Turkish history: the turbulent 1970s, the time of the narrative (12 March 1971 '*coup* by memorandum') and the actual time of the film that saw another military take-over (12 September 1980). Protest from the ultra-fascist elements to the staging of the play in 2013 is evidence of the contemporaneity of the work.

Organized as a theatre piece, the film takes place in a single space, a rich man's kitchen (the country) where five characters representing different factions of society live their dilemmas. The servile cook, Lütfü Usta (**Şener Şen**), believes in the magnanimity of his master, who rules from above (the state), but is never seen. Lütfü Usta is happy with the drastic measures of the junta that establish (false) security as the strikers and the students who demonstrate are agitators needing a good lesson. Nonetheless, he cannot be unaffected by the events around him although he never leaves the premises. He begins to ask the question, 'Who am I serving?' and shows reaction by poisoning the aggressive dog, soon realizing this is not a solution as dogs can be perpetually replaced. The wolf dog is a trope for the Grey Wolves, the paramilitary movement of the extreme right, prominent in the early 1970s against the left and the unions, and the security forces of the fascist state in general. The cook's young helper thinks only of her university student boyfriend Selim and marriage as a way out of the kitchen. Selim is a gentle boy studying Turkology who does not hesitate to inform on his friend for financial gains, a good candidate to be sent to a camp by the master to be brainwashed into a fascist. The master's driver follows orders to keep his job, but he will also be awakened from the slumber of his false security. His worker brother is involved in union activism (referring to the mass strikes of 15–16 June 1970, a very important event in Turkish unionism history). Lütfü Usta narrates the story in flashback, dialoguing directly with the audience. His transformation from an obedient servant to a citizen with political conscience is particularly noteworthy although the film is open ended. When everyone is gone and the cook is ready to leave, he addresses the audience with a question: is it harder to leave or to serve the kitchen; then he remembers the activist Ahmet's words, 'we need you here', referring to many who left the country after 1971, including **Sabuncu** who had a period of sojourn in Paris.

Director, Screenwriter: **Başar Sabuncu**; Producer: **Türker İnanoğlu**, Nahit Ataman; Production: Arzu Film, Erler Film; Cinematographer: Erdal Kahraman; Sound: Gökhan Şıracı; Cast: **Şener Şen**, Nilüfer Açıkalın, Gökhan Mete, Oktay Korunan, Osman Görgen

Züğürt Ağa / The Broke Landlord (1985) is a black **comedy** on the tribulations of a village landlord with fading authority who follows the promises of the popular culture and migrates to the city but fails to adapt to the new order. The film is a pioneer for focusing on an *agha* (landlord) rather than a landless peasant in reflecting the tribulations of the Anatolian migrant during the transition to market economy after the 1980 *coup* and the liberal policies of the Turgut Özal (prime minister, 1983–89; president, 1989–93) civil government when consumerism became the fantasy of the masses. Written by **Yavuz Turgul**, the film is considered as part of a trilogy that includes *Muhsin Bey / Mr Muhsin* (1987) and *Aşk Filmlerinin Unutulmaz Yönetmeni / The Unforgettable Director of Love Movies* (1992) directed by **Yavuz Turgul**, **Şener Şen** acting in all three. The first part of the film foregrounds the collapse of the old order. The village is called 'Haraptar' meaning 'ruinous', which will also be the name of the grocery store of the agha in the city. The second part is about migration to the city and the problem of adaptation. The agha cannot adjust to the changing times because for him it is better to pray for rain in the village than to wait for customers in his city store. The scene where he tries to sell tomatoes in rich neighbourhoods is particularly remarkable as high **comedy**. Finally, his boots, highlighted as symbol of his authority and riches in the rural first part, are sold for food in the city.

Contrary to the **Yeşilçam** cliché of the oppressive and exploitative agha, the film presents a more realistic depiction of a character with his virtues and vices, parodying the institution and exposing its demise with the development of the capitalist system.

Director: **Nesli Çölgeçen**; Producer: Kadri Yurdatap; Production: Mine Film; Screenwriter: **Yavuz Turgul**; Cinematographer: Selçuk Taylaner; Editor: **Mevlut Koçak**; Music: Atilla Özdemiroğlu; Cast: **Şener Şen**, Erdal Özyağcılar, Nilgün Nazlı, Füsun Demirel, Atilla Yiğit, Can Kolukısa, Bahri Selin

Select bibliography

Agee, James and Evans, Walker (1939) *Let Us Now Praise Famous Men,* Boston: Houghton Mifflin.

Akad, Lütfi Ö. (2004) *Işıkla Karanlık Arasında,* Istanbul: Kültür Yayınları. (All technical details about Akad's films, including dates are presented as stated in this book.)

Akın, Gülten (1983) '*At* filminin Ozanca Görünümü', in *At* by Ali Özgentürk, Istanbul: Say Kitap Pazarlama.

Akşit, Onur (2011) 'Turkish Cinema and Science Fiction', in *International Golden Boll Congress on Cinema,* Adana: 18th International Golden Boll Film Festival.

Althusser, Louis Pierre (1992) *The Future Lasts Forever,* R. Veasey (trans.), New York: New York Press.

Anonymous (1966) '*Sevmek Zamanı* Neyi Anlatır veya Sinema Üzerine Düşünme', in *Görüntü Dergisi,* (Nov), 2, 15 quoted by Cihan Altınay in 'Türk Sinemasında Metin Erksan Gerçeği' in *Beyazperde*, Ankara: (May 1990), 7, 12.

Anonymous (1993–2013) Catalogues of International Istanbul Film Festival, Istanbul: IKSV.

Anonymous (2005) *Mithat Alam Film Merkezi Söyleşi, Panel ve Sunum Yıllığı*, Istanbul: *Mithat Alam Film Merkezi*, Online. Available HTTP: http://www.mafm.boun.edu.tr/files/178_Goksel_Arsoy.pdf (accessed 1 June 2012).

Anonymous (2006) 'In production: *Auf der anderen Seite des Lebens',* in *German Film Quarterly,* 3, 32.

Anonymous (2011) Siyaset Bilimi, Ezel Akay Etkinliği – Q&A after the screening of *Killing the Shadow.* Istanbul: SBF Online. Available HTTP: http://www.youtube.com/watch?v=7_dogSFm (accessed 15 March 2012).

Anzaldúa, Gloria E. (1987) *Borderlands / La Frontera: The New Mestiza,* San Francisco: Aunt Lte Books.

Anzaldúa, Gloria E. (2010) 'Cultural Tyranny', in *Literary Theory: An Anthology,* J. Rivkin, M. Ryan (eds), 2nd edn, New Jersey: Wiley-Blackwell.

Armes, Roy (1987) *Third World Film-making and the West,* Berkeley, Los Angeles, and London: University of California Press.

Ayça, Engin (2000) 'Yeşilçam'ın Masal Büyüsü', in *Cumhuriyet Dergi* (8 Oct), Istanbul, 6–8.

Aydemir, Gökşen (2013) 'Bir Gün Hepimiz Türkiye Sineması Yapacağız' in *Film Arası: Türkiye'de Kürt Sineması,* (Interview with Hüseyin Karabey), Istanbul, 3, 60–61.

Aydın, Mukadder Çakır (1997) '1960'lar Türkiye'sinde Sinemadaki Akımlar', in *24 Kare*, XXI (Oct–Dec).

Aytaş, M., Tüysüz, D., Ulutaş, S. (2011) 'Rising of Crime Genre in Turkish Cinema' *International Golden Boll Congress on Cinema,* Adana: 18th International Golden Boll Film Festival.

Bakhtin, Mikhail (1981) *The Dialogic Imagination: Four Essays* (trans. of *Voprosy literatury i estetiki*)*,* Michael Holquist (ed.), Caryl Emerson and Michael Holquist (trans.), Austin and London: University of Texas Press, 84–258.

Bassan, Raphael (1979) 'Bay Okan: LE BUS', in *CinémAction: Cinemas de l'Emigration,* Guy Hennebelle (ed.) 8, (Summer), 186–187.

Bate, Jonathan (2000) *The Song of the Earth,* London: Harvard University Press, 64.

Bazin, André (1997) 'Germany Year Zero', in *Bazin at Work: Major Essay and Reviews from the Forties and Fifties,* Bert Cardullo (ed.), London and New York: Routledge, 121–124.

Belge, M., Günçıkan, B. (2006) *Linç Kültürünün Tarihsel Kökeni: Milliyetçilik,* Istanbul: Agora, p. 109.

Berry, Chris (2006) 'Zeki Demirkubuz: by the Light of the Dark' in *kader: Zeki Demirkubuz.* S. Ruken Öztürk (ed.), Ankara: Dost, Ankara Sinema Derneği.

Bozarslan, Hamid (2001) 'Human Rights and the Kurdish Issue in Turkey: 1984–1999', in *Human Rights Review* 3:1, 45–54.

Bourdieu, Pierre (2001) *Masculine Domination,* R. Nice (trans.), Cambridge: Polity Press.

Brown, Wendy (2006) *Regulating Aversion: Tolerance in the Age of Identity and Empire,* Princeton: Princeton University Press.

Burns, Rob (2006) 'Turkish-German Cinema: from Cultural Resistance to Transnational Cinema?' in *German Cinema Since Unification,* David Clarke (ed), London and New York: Continuum.

Butler, J. (1993) *Bodies That Matter,* London and New York: Routledge.

Büker, Seçil (2002) 'The Film Does Not End with an Ecstatic Kiss', in *Fragments of Culture: The Everyday of Modern Turkey,* Deniz Kandiyoti and Ayşe Saktanber (eds), London and New York: I.B. Tauris.

Campbell, Jan (2005) *Film and Cinema Spectatorship: Melodrama and Mimesis,* Cambridge: Polity Press.

Campbell, Russell (2006) *Marked Women: Prostitutes and Prostitution in the Cinema,* Madison: University of Wisconsin Press.

Caruth, Cathy (ed.) (1995) *Trauma: Explorations in Memory.* Baltimore: Johns Hopkins University Press.

Caruth, Cathy (2006): 'Literature and the Enactment of Memory', in: *Trauma and Visuality in Modernity,* Saltzman, L. and Rosenberg, E. (eds.), Hanover: Dartmouth College Press/University of New England Press, 189–221.

Cavafy, C. P. (1992) *Collected Poems,* Edmund Keeley and Phillip Sherrard (trans.), George Savidis (ed.), New Jersey: Princeton University Press.

Chandler, Daniel (1994): *Semiotics for Beginners,* Online. Available HTTP: http://www.aber.ac.uk/media/Documents/S4B/semiotic.html (accessed 4 June 2012)

Coş, Nezih (1975) 'Hangi Toplumsal Gerçekçilik – *Susuz Yaz?* in *Yedinci Sanat,* 24, 1:6.

Coş, Nezih and Ayça, Engin (1975a) 'Yılmaz Güney'le Konuşma (2)', in *Yedinci Sanat,* 19, 1:10, 3–17.

Coş, Nezih and Ayça, Engin (1975b) 'İnceleme: Pamuk Tarlalarının Durumu ve ENDİŞE Üstüne', in *Yedinci Sanat,* 21, 1:02.

Çetin, M., Uzkınay, M. (2003) 'İlk Türk Sinemacımız: Fuat Uzkınay', *Biyografi Analiz,* 6/3, 1, 4–7.

Çiçek, Filiz (2006) 'Film Reviews: *Lola and Bilidikid*', *Scope, IV* (February) Nottingham.

Çiçekoğlu, Feride (2007) *Vesikalı Şehir*, Istanbul: Metis.

Daldal, Aslı (2003) *Art, Politics and Society: Social Realism in Italian and Turkish Cinemas*, Istanbul: Iris Press.

Deleuze, Gilles (2005) *Cinema 2: The Time Image*, London: Continuum International Publishing Group.

Dennison, Stephanie and Song, Hwee Lim (2006) (eds) *Remapping World Cinema: Identity, Culture and Politics in Film*, London: Wallflower Press.

Derida, Jacques (1981) *Positions*, Chicago: Chicago University Press.

Dissanayake, Wimal (1988) 'Cultural Identity and Asian Cinema: An Introduction' *Cinema and Cultural Identity: Reflections on Films from Japan, India and China*, Wimal Dissanayake (ed.), New York/London: University Press of America.

Dissanayake, Wimal (2003) 'Rethinking Indian Popular Cinema: Towards new frames of understanding', in *Rethinking Third Cinema*, Anthony R. Guneratne and Wimal Dissanayake (eds.), New York and London: Routledge.

Dorsay, Atilla (1965) 'Özgürlüğün Sınırlarını Sansür Kısıtlıyor', in *Sinema*, 1:1, Online. Available HTTP: http://www.iletisim.bahcesehir.edu.tr/arsiv/docs/428.pdf (accessed 2 March 2012).

Dorsay, Atilla (1989) *Sinemamızın Umut Yılları: 1970–80 Arası Türk Sinemasına Bakışlar*, İstanbul: İnkılap Kitabevi.

Dorsay, Atilla (1995) *12 Eylül Yılları ve Sinemamız: 160 Filmle 1980–90 Arası Türk Sinemasına Bakışlar*, Istanbul: İnkilap Kitabevi.

Dorsay, Atilla (2004) *Sinemamızda Çöküş ve Rönesans Yılları: Türk Sineması 1990–2004*, İstanbul: Remzi Kitabevi.

Dönmez-Colin, Gönül (2004) *Women, Islam and Cinema*, London: Reaktion Books.

Dönmez-Colin, Gönül (2006) *Cinemas of the Other: A Personal Journey with Film-makers from the Middle East and Central Asia*, 1st ed, Bristol: Intellect Ltd.

Dönmez-Colin, Gönül (2007) 'Umut / The Hope', in *The Cinema of North Africa and the Middle East*, Gönül Dönmez-Colin (ed.), London and New York: Wallflower Press, pp. 41–49.

Dönmez-Colin, Gönül (2008) *Turkish Cinema: Identity, Distance and Belonging*, London: Reaktion Books.

Dönmez-Colin, Gönül (2012) *Cinemas of the Other: A Personal Journey with Film-makers from the Middle East and Central Asia: Iran and Turkey*, 2nd edn, Bristol: Intellect.

Durgun, Duygu (1996) 'Gerilla tarzı film üretimiyle 'yoksulluğun estetiği' [interview], in *Cumhuriyet Gazetesi* (Dec), 12.

Eleftheriotis, D., Needham, G. (2006) *Asian Cinemas: A Reader and Guide*, Honolulu: University of Hawai'i Press.

Ellis, John (1982) 'The Literary Adaptation – an Introduction', in *Screen*, 23/1, 4.

Elsaesser, Thomas (1985) 'Tales of Sound and Fury' in *Movies and Methods*, Bill Nichols (ed), vol.II, Berkeley and Los Angeles: California UP, pp 166–189.

Elsaesser, Thomas (2005) 'Double occupancy and small adjustments: Space, place and policy in the New European Cinema since the 1990s', in *European Cinema: Face to Face with Hollywood*, Amsterdam: Amsterdam University Press, 108–130.

Erdem, Reha (2008) *My Only Sunshine*, press kit, Istanbul: Atlantik Film.

Erdoğan Nezih '*Vizontele*: Türk Sinemasinda Modernleşmenin Temsili', Online. Available HTTP: http://www.neziherdogan.net/articles/vizontele.html (accessed 31 December 2012).

Erdoğan Nezih (1998) 'Narratives of Resistance: National Identity and Ambivalence in the Turkish Melodrama Between 1965 and 1975', *Screen* 39:3, 259–271.

Erdoğan Nezih (2003) 'Powerless Signs: Hybridity and the Logic of Excess of Turkish Trash', in *Mapping the Margins: Identity Politics and Media*, Ross K. and Derman, D. (eds), New Jersey: Hampton Press, 163–176.

Erdoğan Nezih (2004) 'The Making of Our America: Hollywood in a Turkish Context', in *Hollywood Abroad: Audiences and Cultural Exchange*, Malvyn Stokes and Richard Maltby (eds.), London: bfi, 121–132.

Erdoğan Nezih and Dilek Kaya, D. (2002) 'Institutional Intervention in the Distribution and Exhibition of Hollywood Films in Turkey', *Historical Journal of Film, Radio and Television*, 22: 1, p. 47.

Evren, Burçak (1990) *Türk Sinemasında Yeni Konumlar,* Istanbul: Broy Yayınları.

Evren, Burçak (1993) *Başlangıcından Günümüze Türkçe Sinema Dergileri*, Istanbul: Korsan Yayın.

Evren, Burçak (1995) *Sigmund Weinberg, Türkiye'ye Sinemayı Getiren Adam,* İstanbul: Milliyet Yayınları.

Evren, Burçak (2012) *apo gardaş: Abdurrahman Keskiner,* Adana: Altın Koza.

Ewing, Katherine Pratt (1998) 'Crossing Borders and Transgressing Boundaries: Metaphors for Negotiating Multiple Identities', in *Ethos, Journal of the Society for Psychological Anthropology,* 26: 2 (June) 262–267.

Eyüboğlu, Selim (2001) 'Bir Memleket Metaforu Olarak Kadın', in *Türk Film Araştırmalarında Yeni Yönelimler–1*, Derman, Deniz (ed.), Istanbul: Bağlam, 37–45.

Ezra, Elizabeth and Rowden, Terry (2006) 'General Introduction: What is Transnational Cinema?' in *Transnational Cinema: The Film Reader*, Elizabeth Ezra and Terry Rowden (eds), London and New York: Routledge.

Ferguson, Harvie (1997) 'Me and My Shadow: On the Accumulation of Body Images in Western Society', Parts 1&2', *Body and Society* (Sept) 3/31, 1–31.

Fiske, John (1987) *Television Culture: Popular Pleasures and Politics*, London: Methuen.

Fokkema, Aleid (1991) *Postmodern Characters; A Study of Characterization in British and American Postmodern Fiction,* Postmodern Studies, 4, Amsterdam/Atlanta: Rodopi.

Foucault, Michel (1995) *Discipline and Punish: The Birth of Prison,* New York: Vintage Books, 195–210.

Foucault, Michel (1984) *Dits et écrits* 'Des espaces autres', in *Architecture, Mouvement, Continuité*, 5, (Oct) 46–49.

Fraser, Nancy (1990) 'Re-thinking the Public Sphere: A Contribution to the Critique of Actually Existing Democracy', in *Social Text*, Durham: Duke University Press, 25, 56–80.

Freud, Sigmund (1922) *Beyond the Pleasure Principle* (trans. from the second German edition, C.J.M. Hubback), London, Vienna: International Psycho-Analytical.

Freud, Sigmund (1930) *Civilization and Its Discontents – Complete Psychological Works of Sigmund Freud, Volume XXI (1927–1931)*, Strachey, J. (trans.) New York: Norton, 1961.

Freud, Sigmund (2010) *Beyond the Pleasure Principle*, Published on the Internet, London: Bartleby. Online. Available HTTP: www.bartleby.com/276/ (accessed 15 March 2012).

Gledhill, Christine (1992) 'Speculations into the relationship between soap opera and melodrama', in *Quarterly Review of Film and Video* 14, 1–2, 103–124.

Gledhill, Christine (2000) 'Rethinking Genre', in *Reinventing Film Studies,* Gledhill, C. and Williams, L. (eds) London, Arnold and New York: Oxford University Press.

Göle, Nilüfer 'Europe: A Common Dream?', Online. Available HTTP: www.ourworld. compuserve.come/home pages/usazerb/123.htm (accessed 2 Jan 2012).

Grant, Catherine (2002) 'Recognizing *Billy Budd* in *Beau Travail:* epistemology and hermeneutics of an auteurist "free" adaptation', in *Screen,* 43:1, (Spring), 57–73.

Griffiths, Robin (ed.) (2008) *Queer Cinema in Europe,* Bristol: Intellect Books.

Güçhan, Gülseren (1992) *Toplumsal Değişme ve Türk Sineması,* Ankara: Imge.

Güney, Yılmaz (1982) Written for the release of *Düşman / The Enemy* in Germany and published as a manifesto, (June) 208–212 and in 1985, *Siyasal Yazılar:* Yılmaz Güney III, Berlin: Mayıs Yayınları.

Güney, Yılmaz (1994a) *Sürü,* Istanbul: Yılmaz Güney Kültür Sanat Vakfı.

Güney, Yılmaz (1994b) *Yol,* Istanbul: Yılmaz Güney Kültür Sanat Vakfı.

Gürata, Ahmet (2006) 'Translating Modernity: Remakes in Turkish Cinema' in *Asian Cinemas: A Reader and Guide,* Eleftheriotis, D., Needham, G. (eds), Honolulu: University of Hawai'i Press, 242–254.

Habermas, Jurgen (1989) *The Structural Transformation of the Public Sphere: An Enquiry into a Category of Bourgeois Society,* Cambridge: MIT.

Hall, Stuart (1996) 'Introduction: Who needs identity?', in *Questions of Cultural Identity,* S. Hall and P. du Gay (eds), London: Sage Publications, pp. 1–17.

Hammond, M., Humphrey, D., Randell, K. and Thomas, P. (July 2003) 'The Trauma Debate Continued', *Screen,* 44/2.

Heidegger, M. (1962) *Being and Time.* John Macquarrie and Edward Robinson (trans.), Oxford: Blackwell.

Heidegger, M. (1971) *Poetry, Language, Thought.* Albert Hofstadter (trans.), New York: Harper & Row.

Hutcheon, Linda (1995) 'Circling the Downspout of Empire: Post-colonialism and Postmodernism' (1989) in *The Postcolonial Studies Reader,* Ashcroft Bill et al. (ed.) London and New York: Routledge.

Jager, Bernd (1983) 'Theorizing and the Elaboration of Place: Inquiry into Galileo and Freud', in A. Giorgi, A. Barton, and C. Maes, (eds), *Duquesne Studies in Phenomenological Psychology,* 4. Pittsburgh: Duquesne University Press, 154–155.

Jameson, Fredric (1991) *Postmodernism, or, the Cultural Logic of Late Capitalism,* Durham: Duke University Press.

Johnson, Robert A. (1989) *He: Understanding Masculine Psychology*; Perennial Library Series, Revised edition, Harper Perennial, Berkeley: Mills House.

Kandiyoti, D., Saktanber, A. (ed) (2002) *Fragments of Culture: Everyday Life in Modern Turkey,* London and New York: I.B. Tauris.

Kaplan, E. Ann (1983) *Women and Film: Both Sides of the Camera,* London and New York: Routledge.

Kaplan, E. Ann (1989) 'Problematizing Cross-Cultural Analysis: The Case of Women in the Recent Chinese Cinema,' in *Wide Angle* 11: 2: 40–50.

Kaplan, E. Ann (2005) *Trauma Culture: The Politics of Terror and Loss in Media and Literature.* New Brunswick, NJ: Rutgers University Press.

Karakaya, Serdar (2011) 'Improvement in Quantity and Decline in Quality in Comedy Films of Turkish Cinema in Recent Years (2000–2010)', in *International Golden Boll Congress on Cinema,* 2011, 18th International Golden Boll Film Festival.

Koç, Ayşegül (2004) 'Vagina Dentata'lar, Femme Fatale'lar: *C Blok, Masumiyet, Üçüncü Sayfa* ve *İtiraf'ta Kadının Temsili*', in *Türk Film Araştırmalarında Yeni Yönelimler* IV: Türk Sineması Hayali Vatanımız. Esra Özcan, (ed.), Istanbul: Bağlam Yayınları.

Kristeva, Julia (1980) *Desire in Language: A Semiotic Approach to Literature and Art,* Leon S. Roudiez (ed.), T. Gora, A. Jardine, L.S. Roudiez (trans.), New York: Columbia University Press.

Laclau, E. (1990) *New Reflections on the Revolution of our Time.* London: Verso.

Lewis, Reina (1996) *Gendering Orientalism: Race, Femininity and Representation,* London and New York: Routledge.

Lury, Karen (2010) *The Child in Film: Tears, Fears and Fairy Tales*, New Brunswick, New Jersey: Rutgers University Press.

Makal, Mahmut (1954) *Our Village,* Sir Wyndham Deedes (trans.), in *New World Writing,* New York.

Maktav, Hilmi (2006) 'Vatan Millet Cinema', in *Birikim,* 207 (July).

Malik, Sarita (1996) 'Beyond "the cinema of duty"? The pleasures of hybridity: Black British film of the 1980s and 1990s', in Andrew Higson (ed.), *Dissolving Views: Key Writings on British Cinema*, London: Cassell, pp. 202–215.

Mardin, Şerif (1981) 'Religion and Secularism in Turkey', in *Atatürk: Founder of a Modern State,* A. Kazancıgil and E. Özbudun (eds), London: C. Hurst.

Marks, Laura U (2000) *The Skin of the Film: Intercultural Cinema, Embodiment, and the Senses,* Durham and London: Duke University Press.

Marsden, Michael T., Nachbar, John G., Groff Jr., Sam L. (ed.) (1982) *Movies as Artifacts: Cultural Criticism of Popular Film,* Ann Arbor: Nelson-Hall.

Mulvey, Laura (1975) 'Visual Pleasures and Narrative Cinema', *Screen,* V/3 (Autumn).

Naficy, Hamid (ed.) (1999) *Home, Exile, Homeland: Film, Media, and the Politics of Place.* New York and London: Routledge.

Naficy, Hamid (2001) *The Accented Cinema; Exilic and Diasporic Filmmaking,* Princeton and Oxford: Princeton University Press.

Nandy, Ashis (1998) 'Introduction: Indian Popular Cinema as a Slum's Eye View of Politics' in *The Secret Politics of Our Desires: Innocence, Culpability and Indian Popular Cinema*, Ashis Nandy (ed.), Delhi: Oxford University Press.

Oğuz, Orhan (2011) 'Yusuf Atılgan'ın Hikayelerinde Köy, *Turkish Studies International Periodical For the Languages, Literature and History of Turkish or Turkic,* 6/3 (Summer) 1097–1115.

Onaran, Âlim Şerif (1994) *Türk Sineması I*, Ankara: Kitle.

Ostrowska, D., Roberts, G. (eds.) (2007) *European Cinema in the TV Age,* Edinburgh: Edinburgh University Press.

Özgüç, Agah (1994a) 'Film Karelerinde Yaşayan Eski İstanbul', in *Cumhuriyet Dergi,* 414 (27 Feb).

Özgüç, Agah (1994b) *Türk Film Yönetmenleri Sözlüğü*, Afa Yayıncılık, Istanbul.

Özgüç, Agah (2001) 'Ustalara Saygı: Osman Fahir Seden', in the catalogue of 20th International Istanbul Film Festival, Ali Sönmez (ed.), 165–166.

Özgüç, Agah (2003) *Türk Film Yönetmenleri Sözlüğü*, Istanbul: Agora.

Özgüven, Fatih (2006) 'Hava serin, iklim aynı', in *Radikal,* Online. Available HTTP http://www.radikal.com.tr/haber.php?haberno=202686 (accessed 15 April 2011).

Özön, Nijat (1962) *Türk Sinema Tarihi,* Istanbul: Artist Reklam Ortaklığı.

Özön, Nijat (1968) *Türk Sineması Kronolojisi: 1895–1966,* Istanbul: Bilgi.

Özön, Nijat (1970) *Fuat Uzkınay,* Istanbul: Sinematek Yayınları, Online. Available HTTP http://www.mustafacetin.org/tr/fuat-uzkinaynijat-ozonsinematek-yayist1970-2 (accessed 23 March 2013).

Özön, Nijat (1995) *Karagözden Sinemaya: Türk Sineması ve Sorunları,* I&II, Istanbul: Kitle.

Öztürk, Serhat (1990) 'Metin Erksan'la Söyleşi', in *Beyazperde* (May) 7, supplement, Ankara, 2.

Özyeğin, Gül (2002) 'The Doorkeeper, the Maid and the Tenant', in *Fragments of Culture: The Everyday of Modern Turkey,* Deniz Kandiyoti and Ayşe Saktanber (eds), London and New York: I.B. Tauris, 43–72.

Piven, Jerry S. (2004) *Death and Delusion: A Freudian Analysis of Mortal Terror,* Greenwich: Information Age Publishing (IAP).

Radstone, S. (ed.) (2001) 'Trauma and Screen Studies: Special Debate', *Screen*, 42/ 2.

Rheingold, Joseph C. (1967) *The Mother, Anxiety, and Death: The Catastrophic Death Complex*, London: Churchill.

Rocha, Glauber (1965) 'The Aesthetics of Hunger' Burnes Hollyman and Randal Johnson (trans.) Online. Available HTTP https://www.amherst.edu/media/view/38122/original/ ROCHA_Aesth_Hunger.pdf (accessed 4 Aug 2012).

Rothik, Jurgen (1994) 'Interview with Yılmaz Güney in 1983 for the Spanish State Television' in *Yol*, Yılmaz Güney, Istanbul: Yılmaz Güney Vakfı, 13–15.

Russell, Charles (1982) 'Subversion and legitimation: the avant-garde in postmodern culture', in *Chicago Review* 33, 2:54–59.

Said, Edward W. (1994) *Culture and Imperialism,* New York: Vintage Books.

Saktanber, Ayşe (2002) *Living Islam: Women, Religion and the Politicization of Culture in Turkey,* London and New York: I.B. Tauris.

Scognamillo, Giovanni (1973a) 'Türk Sinemasında Yabancı Uyarlamalar-1', *Yedinci Sanat* 9,1:11, 61–73. Online. Available HTTP: http://www.iletisim.bahcesehir.edu.tr/arsiv/ sorgu_goster.php?yazar=Giovanni%20Scognamillo (accessed 5 October 2011).

Scognamillo, Giovanni (1973b) 'İnceleme: Türk Sinemasinda Köy Filmleri (2)', *Yedinci Sanat,* 5, 1:7, 34–39'. http://www.iletisim.bahcesehir.edu.tr/arsiv/sorgu_goster. php?yazar=Giovanni%20Scognamillo (accessed 5 October 2011).

Scognamillo, Giovanni (1987) *Türk Sinema Tarihi: 1896-1986* (1st ed), Istanbul: Metis.

Scognamillo, Giovanni (1990) *Türk Sinema Tarihi: 1896–1986* (2nd ed), Istanbul: Metis.

Seamon, David (1998) 'Concretizing Heidegger's Notion of Dwelling: The Contributions of Thomas Thiis-Evensen and Christopher Alexander' http://www.tu-cottbus.de/ theoriederarchitektur/wolke/eng/Subjects/982/Seamon/seamon_t.html (accessed 5 December 2011).

Selçuk, Aslı (1997) 'Hikayemi sinemayla anlatıyorum', interview in *Cumhuriyet*, 3:5.

Sheen, Erica (2000) 'Introduction', in Robert Giddings and Erica Sheen (eds) *The Classic Novel: From Page to Screen,* Manchester: Manchester University Press.

Shohat, Ella (2003) 'Post-Third-Worldist culture: Gender, nation, and the cinema' in *Rethinking Third Cinema,* Antony R. Guneratne and Wimal Dissanayake (eds), New York and London: Routledge.

Slemon, Stephen (1988) 'Magic Realism as Post-Colonial Discourse', *Canadian Literature* CXVI, 24.

Sontag, Susan (1977) *On Photography*, London: Penguin Books.

Suner, Asuman (1990) 'Sinemada Bir Karşı Söylem Olarak Eşcinsellik', *Beyaz Perde,* VII (May), 47–48.

Suner, Asuman (2006) *Hayalet Ev: Yeni Türk Sinemasında Aidiyet, Kimlik ve Bellek,* Istanbul: Metis, 245.

Süalp, Zeynep Tül Akbal (2009) 'Usual Suspects and Unusual Up-comings in Current Turkish Cinema', Panel discussion held during the Istanbul International Film Festival, April 2009, recorded and transcribed by Gönül Dönmez-Colin.

Şen, Abdurrahman (1990) *Kültür, Sanat ve Edebiyat Üzerine Politik Yazılar,* Istanbul: Cemre.

Şensöz, Ali Deniz (2013) 'Turkish Film Industry 2012 Report' in *Meetings on the Bridge: Film Project Development Workshop,* 32nd Istanbul Film Festival, Istanbul, 2013, 18–20.

Tan, Pervin (1991) 'Ömer Kavur'la Gizli Yüz Üzerine: Söyleşi', in *Antrakt.*

Thiis-Evensen, T. (1987) *Archetypes in Architecture*, Oslo: Norwegian University Press, 251.

Thoraval, Y., Hennebelle, G. (1979) 'La "folle équipée" de clandestins turc en Suéde, racontée par Bay Okan: *LE BUS*', *CinémAction: Cinemas de l'Emigration,* Guy Hennebelle (ed.) 8, (Summer), 187–190.

Toker, Okan (1974) 'Deneysel Sinema ve Alp Zeki Heper' *Yeni Ortam Gazetesi,* Istanbul, 13/2, 87–95. Online. Available HTTP: http://e-dergi.atauni.edu.tr/index.php/gsfd/article/viewFile/3072/2964 (accessed 10 March 2012).

Tosun, Necip (1992) *Mesut Uçakan'*la Sinema Söyleşileri', Istanbul: Nehir Yayınları, 76–78.

Tremain, Shelley (ed.) (2005) *Foucault and the Government of Disability,* Ann Arbor: University of Michigan Press.

Turner, Graeme (2008) *Film as a Social Practice IV,* London and New York: Routledge.

Türk, İbrahim (2001) *Halit Refiğ: Düşlerden Düşüncelere Söyleşiler,* Istanbul: Kabalcı.

Türkali, Vedat (2001) *Tüm Yazıları Konuşmaları,* Istanbul: Gendaş Kültür.

Willemen, Paul (1995) 'The National', in *Fields of Vision: Essays in Film Studies, Visual Anthropology, and Photography*, Leslie Devereaux and Roger Hillman (eds), Berkeley and Los Angeles: University of California Press, 29.

Yılmaz, Atıf (1991) 'Hayallerim, Aşkım ve Sen', in *Hürriyet Gazetesi*, 2 April, 2.

Yoshimoto, Mitsuhiro (2006) 'The Difficulty of Being Radical: The Discipline of Film Studies and the Post-Colonial World Order' in *Asian Cinemas: A Reader and Guide*, Dimitris Eleftheriotis and Gary Needham (eds), Honolulu: University of Hawai'i Press.

Zaim, Derviş (2008) 'Your Focus is Your Truth: Turkish Cinema, "Alluvionic" Filmmakers and International Acceptance', in M. Christensen and N. Erdoğan, (eds) *Shifting Landscapes: Media and Film in European Context,* Newcastle: Cambridge Scholars Publishing, 2008, 86–108.

Modern Middle East Authoritarianism

Roots, Ramifications, and Crisis

Edited by Noureddine Jebnoun, Mehrdad Kia, Mimi Kirk

While the Arab uprisings have overturned the idea of Arab "exceptionalism," or the acceptance of authoritarianism, better analysis of authoritarianism's resilience in pre- and post-uprising scenarios is still needed. *Modern Middle East Authoritarianism: Roots, Ramifications, and Crisis* undertakes this task by addressing not only the mechanisms that allowed Middle Eastern regimes to survive and adapt for decades, but also the obstacles that certain countries face in their current transition to democracy.

This volume analyzes the role of ruling elites, Islamists, and others, as well as variables such as bureaucracy, patronage, the strength of security apparatuses, and ideological legitimacy to ascertain regimes' life expectancies and these factors' post-uprisings repercussions. Discussing not only the paradigms through which the region has been analyzed, but also providing in-depth case studies of Tunisia, Egypt, Libya, Algeria, Saudi Arabia, Iraq, and Iran, the authors arrive at critical conclusions about dictatorship and possibilities for its transformation.

Employing diverse research methods, including interviews, participant observation, and theoretical discussions of authoritarianism and political transition, this book is essential reading for scholars of Middle East Studies, Islamic Studies and those with an interest in the governance and politics of the Middle East.

July 2013 | 272 Pages | HB: 978-0-415-84500-7
http://www.routledge.com/books/details/9780415845007/

Available from all good bookshops

An Atlas of Middle Eastern Affairs

2nd Edition

By Ewan W. Anderson, Liam D. Anderson

Illustrated by Ian Cool

This revised and updated version of *An Atlas of Middle Eastern Affairs* provides accessible, concisely written entries on the most important current issues in the Middle East, combining maps with their geopolitical background. Offering a clear context for analysis of key concerns, it includes background topics, the position of the Middle East in the world and profiles of the constituent countries.

Features include:

- Clearly and thematically organised sections covering the continuing importance of the Middle East, the background, fundamental concerns, the states and the crucial issues related to the area.
- Original maps integrated into the text, placing international issues and conflicts in their geographical contexts.
- Case studies and detailed analysis of each country, complete with relevant statistics and key facts.

A comprehensive further reading section, enabling students to cover the topic in more depth.Updated to include recent developments such as the "Arab Spring," this book is a valuable introduction to undergraduate students of political science and Middle East studies and is designed as a primary teaching aid for courses related to the Middle East in the areas of politics, history, geography, economics and military studies. This book is also an outstanding reference source for libraries and anyone interested in these fields.

Aug 2013 | 336 Pages | HB: 978-0-415-68095-0 PB: 978-0-415-680967
http://www.routledge.com/books/details/9780415680967/

Available from all good bookshops

The International Relations of the Contemporary Middle East

Subordination and Beyond

Edited by **Tareq Y. Ismael, Glenn E. Perry**

The Middle East, a few decades ago, was seen to be an autonomous subsystem of the global international political system. More recently, the region has been subordinated to the hegemony of a singular superpower, the US, bolstered by an alliance with Israel and a network of Arab client states.

The subordination of the contemporary Middle East has resulted in large part from the disappearance of countervailing forces, for example, global bipolarity, that for a while allowed the Arab world in particular to exercise a modicum of flexibility in shaping its international relations. The aspirations of the indigenous population of the Middle East have been stifled by the dynamics of the unequal global power relationships, and domestic politics of the countries of the region are regularly subordinated to the prerogatives of international markets and the strategic competition of the great powers.

Employing the concept of imperialism, defined as a pattern of alliances between a center (rulers) in the Center (developed) country and a center (client regime) in the Periphery (underdeveloped country) - as an overall framework to analyse the subordination of the region, this book is essential reading for students and scholars of the Middle East, International Relations, and Politics in general.

Aug 2013 | 304 Pages | PB: 978-0-415-66135-5 | HB- 978-0-415-66134-8
http://www.routledge.com/books/details/9780415661355/

Available from all good bookshops